GW00992529

Beginning Windows NT Programming

Julian Templeman

Wrox Press Ltd.

Beginning Windows NT Programming

© 1998 Wrox Press

First Published   September 1998

Published by Wrox Press Ltd, 30 Lincoln Road, Olton, Birmingham B27 6PA , UK.
Printed in USA

ISBN 1-861000-17-0

Trademark Acknowledgements

Wrox has endeavoured to provide trademark information about all the companies and products mentioned in this book by the appropriate use of capitals. However, Wrox cannot guarantee the accuracy of this information.

Credits

Author
Julian Templeman

Contributing Authors
Neil Matthew
Rick Stones
Gavin Smyth

Managing Editor
John Franklin

Editors
Victoria Hudgson
Chris Hindley
Adrian Young
Timothy Briggs
Ian Nutt

Technical Reviewers
Michael Barry
Neil Matthew
Christophe Nasarre
Marc Simkin
Rick Stones
Byron Vargas

Cover/Design/Layout
Andrew Guillaume

Index
Andrew Criddle

About the Author

Julian lives in London with his wife Jane, three children, two cats, a dog, three PCs, a Mac, a PDP-11 and an aging Mercedes. He and Jane run Templeman Consulting Limited, which provides training and consultancy in C++, Windows programming, MFC, COM and ActiveX in the UK and beyond.

In such spare time as he has, he writes articles and reviews for programming journals, and contributes as an author and technical reviewer for Wrox Press. He's also a keen musician, and can often be found playing guitar, mandolin, Dobro and bass (although not simultaneously).

Julian first set fingers to keyboard (or more accurately keypunch) while learning Fortran as part of a B.Sc. in Geology at Imperial College in London, in the late 1970's. He never became a geologist, recognizing at an early stage that computers were far more fun than rocks, involving a lot more staying indoors, a lot less mud and camping, and a lot more toys to play with. During a postgraduate course at the Natural History Museum in London, he strayed into programming and has never left.

Since then he's had a number of programming jobs, most of which have been in science or engineering, and which have involved computer graphics in some way.

Julian can be contacted at `julian@groucho.demon.co.uk`

Acknowledgements

As always, many people have been involved in the development of a book such as this.

I still remember the now-defunct Windows Tech Journal with fondness, and will always be grateful to J.D, Cecelia Hagen and Kevin Weeks for giving me an entry into writing and encouraging my initial efforts.

Many thanks go to the team at Wrox, who have done such a good job of taking my ramblings and turning it into something that others may (may!) want to read. John Franklin did his usual excellent job of managing the proceedings and (even more importantly) got the cheques signed. Victoria Hudgson, Chris Hindley, Adrian Young, Ian Nutt and Tim Briggs undertook the unenviable task of editing my prose, and didn't let me get away with very much. Thanks also go to the technical reviewers for doing such an important job so carefully. All errors which may remain in the text are, of course, my responsibility and not theirs.

Finally, my thanks must go to my family, who once again have put up with the disruption which a project like this brings to family life, and who have been willing to let me escape to Wales in order to get on with writing in peace. My love and thanks to all of you.

Beginning
Windows NT
Programming

Chapter 5: Interfacing with the System 131

Introduction

This book is about learning to program with Windows NT, but not the part that most Windows books cover. To most people, 'Windows' is simply the graphical interface that they see on the computer screen, but there is a lot more to it than that, as you're about to find out.

In the case of Windows NT, behind the interface lies an operating system of considerable complexity and power. There are many books which will teach you how to program Windows GUI applications using C++ or Visual Basic, telling you how to create windows and dialog boxes, handle messages and so on, but comparatively few which tell you how to interact with the operating system underneath. This book seeks to present how NT works, and to teach the reader to exploit the advantages that it has over Windows 95/98. This book supplements other titles that deal with the core GUI programming for 32-bit Windows, by helping you to unleash the power of an industrial strength operating system in your programs.

So what we're concentrating on here is the non-GUI system services that Win32 provides for our use. Among other topics, we'll examine:

- The architecture of Windows NT
- Use of DLLs
- NT's structured error handling mechanism
- Programming multithreaded processes
- NT security
- NT services
- Interprocess communication

Note that a great deal of the material in this book is also applicable to Windows 95 and Windows 98, because they are also 32-bit Windows operating systems which use the Win32 API.

> An *API (Application Programming Interface)* is a collection of programming functions used to support a particular set of functionality. Thus the Win32 API is the collection of functions you use to write Win32 programs. You'll also see 'API' used as a colloquial term for a function from the collection, so that people sometimes talk about 'the *RegCreateKey()* API function' or even just 'the *RegCreateKey()* API'.

Where a feature isn't also supported by Windows 95 and 98, it will be clearly pointed out in the text.

This book is based on version 4.0 of NT, which was released in 1996. Superceding version 3.51, most of the changes are in the user interface, with the addition of the Windows 95-style shell and some other features from 95, such as Internet access and better laptop support. There are changes in the architecture of the operating system, designed to improve performance, but from the point of view of the features we'll be discussing in this book, there is little difference between NT 3.51 and NT 4.0.

Who's This Book For?

This book is for those who want to learn about the nuts and bolts of programming Windows NT using the Win32 API. You may be a systems programmer on another platform who now wants to understand the Microsoft environment, but the only requirement is that you are a competent C++ programmer.

This book isn't suitable if you're new to programming or don't already know C++. If that describes you then check out *Ivor Horton's Beginning C++*, which provides a comprehensive coverage the ANSI standard C++ language.

What You Need to Use This Book

To use this book, you need Visual C++ (version 5.0 or 6.0) installed on Windows NT 4.0 (Workstation or Server), with service pack 3. NT4.0 requires at least a 486 DX4 with 32 MB of memory.

For Visual C++, you'll need quite a lot of hard disk space — a typical installation is 270 MB. You can do a minimal installation which takes up around 70 MB, but this will mean longer compile times as the CD-ROM will be utilized more often.

Conventions Used

We use a number of different styles of text and layout in the book to help differentiate between the different kinds of information. Here are examples of the styles we use and an explanation of what they mean:

> *These boxes hold important, not-to-be forgotten, mission critical details which are directly relevant to the surrounding text.*

Background information, asides and references appear in text like this.

- ▶ **Important Words** are in a bold type font.
- ▶ Words that appear on the screen, such as menu options, are in a similar font to the one used on screen, for example, the File menu.
- ▶ Keys that you press on the keyboard, like *Ctrl* and *Enter*, are in italics.

▶ All filenames are in this style: **CriticalSection.cpp**.

▶ Function names look like this: **CreateFile()**.

▶ Code which is new, important or relevant to the current discussion, will be presented like this:

```
int main()
{
    cout << "Beginning Windows NT Programming";
}
```

▶ Code you've seen before, or which has little to do with the matter at hand, looks like this:

```
int main()
{
    cout << "Beginning Windows NT Programming";
}
```

API function prototypes appear in a box like this:

```
LONG RegFlushKey(HKEY hk);
```

Tell Us What You Think

We have tried to make this book as accurate and enjoyable for you as possible, but what really matters is what the book actually does for you. Please let us know your views, whether positive or negative, either by returning the reply card in the back of the book or by contacting us at Wrox Press, using either of the following methods:

E-mail:	feedback@wrox.com
Internet:	http://www.wrox.com/

Source Code and Keeping Up-to-date

We try to keep the prices of our books reasonable, and so to replace an accompanying disk, we make the source code for the book available on our web site:

http://www.wrox.com/

The code is also available via FTP:

ftp://ftp.wrox.com
ftp://ftp.wrox.co.uk

If you don't have access to the Internet, then we can provide a disk for a nominal fee to cover postage and packing.

Errata & Updates

We've made every effort to make sure there are no errors in the text or the code. However, to err is human and as such we recognize the need to keep you informed of any mistakes as they're spotted and amended.

While you're visiting our web site, please make use of our *Errata* page that's dedicated to fixing any small errors in the book or, offering new ways around a problem and its solution. Errata sheets are available for all our books — please download them, or take part in the continuous improvement of our tutorials and upload a 'fix' or pointer.

For those without access to the net, call us on **1-800 USE WROX** and we'll gladly send errata sheets to you. Alternatively, send a letter to:

Wrox Press Inc.,   Wrox Press Ltd,
1512 North Fremont,   30, Lincoln Road,
Suite 103   Olton,
Chicago,   Birmingham,
Illinois 60622   B27 6PA
USA   UK

Windows NT Under The Hood

Let's start by taking a brief tour through Windows NT. We'll examine the design criteria that led to the development of NT, and we'll also look at some of the differences between NT and Windows 95. For most of this chapter, we'll be focusing on the major points of the NT architecture, and getting a feel for how it works. There is not a lot of code here, as the idea is to provide points of reference that will guide us through the chapters to come.

Design Criteria

Windows NT was written to fulfil a number of design criteria, which we'll list briefly here, before discussing them in more detail later on in this chapter and throughout the rest of the book.

Firstly, there is **security**, where NT meets the US Department of Defense level C2 security classification. Exactly what this means, we'll see later. Security is fully explained in Chapter 8.

Next is **portability**, that is, source level portablility rather than binary level. Windows 3.x and 95 are firmly tied to the Intel family of processors. Windows NT, on the other hand, has been designed to be portable by isolating all hardware-specific elements in a **Hardware Abstraction Layer** (HAL). Thus, porting NT to a new architecture is a case of writing new HAL code, and it should not be necessary to touch the rest of the operating system. Although the majority of NT systems run on Intel processors, NT has been ported to run on DEC Alpha.

Scalability means that an NT system can take advantage of multiple processors, if they are available.

NT implements a mature and robust form of **multiprocessing**. It has full **pre-emptive multitasking** of processes and introduces the idea of threads, otherwise known as 'lightweight processes' — these are discussed in more detail in Chapter 6. Pre-emptive multitasking means that the operating system is in control rather than the individual processes (as was the case with Windows 3.x). Having the processes in control might seem more democratic, but it does nothing to improve system performance.

Robustness is provided by applications running in their own address spaces, not having direct access to the hardware, and only contacting the kernel indirectly using APIs. This means that it is hard for applications to interfere with one another or with the kernel, and makes NT far more stable, and far less prone to GPFs (General Protection Faults) than Windows 3.x or even 95.

NT is modular in design and is **extensible**, so that new functionality can easily be added to all levels of the operating system. It is possible to add new drivers and even whole file systems, without having to reinstall the entire system.

Distributed processing means that networking is built into the operating system itself, and programs can communicate using facilities such as Named Pipes, Remote Procedure Calls (RPC) and Sockets. We'll be looking at these IPC (InterProcess Communication) mechanisms in Chapter 11.

Internationalization — in order to make it a truly international operating system, NT supports full **localization**, and also has built-in support for the **Unicode** character set. NT's native character set is Unicode — see Chapter 5, where these topics are discussed further.

Differences Between NT and Windows 95/98

Windows 95 and Windows NT are both 32-bit operating systems that can be programmed using the Win32 API. What, then, are the major differences between NT and 95?

Windows 95 has not been designed to be portable, and is optimized for Intel processors. Also, it has not been designed to be a server, although this is a marketing limitation, rather than a technical one. Microsoft decided that NT should be the proper operating system for network servers, so they made Windows 95 unable to act as a server, although it can function in peer-to-peer networks.

Despite being 32-bit and having a new interface, Windows 95 is actually closer to Windows 3.1 than NT. There was quite a fuss during the Windows 95 beta program, when Andrew Schulman (originator of the *Undocumented* series of books) took a close look at what was actually going on inside this 'brand new' operating system, and published *Unauthorized Windows 95* as a result. He discovered that 95 contains a lot of original 16-bit code, with 32-bit layers on top, so that we have the 16-bit `GDI.EXE` and `GDI32.DLL`, the 16-bit `KRNL386.EXE` and `KERNEL32.DLL`, and so on. That isn't too surprising, because Windows 95 is supposed to be compatible to a large extent with Windows 3.x, and the best way to ensure compatibility is to use the same code. Where it does matter is that the old 16-bit code is not designed to work in a multitasking system, and this impacts on Windows 95's multitasking performance. Windows 95 is only truly pre-emptive in its multitasking if it is running pure 32-bit code, which is almost never the case.

Windows 95 doesn't support any of the NT security, so you're limited to what DOS gives you, or what can be provided by third-party add-ons. It also has no real concept of 'users' or logging on, and can't run services. It also has very limited support for Unicode and COM.

You'll find that Windows 95 isn't as stable as NT, because although processes are isolated from one another, they can still get at parts of low memory that are used by the system. This leads to the rather strange situation that it is harder for applications to interfere with each other than it is for them to crash the system. For this reason, Windows NT is still the preferred operating system for most developers.

Windows 95 doesn't use NTFS, and is limited to the old FAT filing system, although Windows 95 OSR2 and Win98 can use FAT32, which offers some improvements.

As you can see from this list, there are quite a lot of areas in which Windows 95 differs from NT, some of which are quite significant.

Overall Organisation

Now that we've got some background on Windows NT, let's take a look at its architecture. We'll start at the highest level, by looking at the overall organization of the operating system itself.

Before describing how NT is structured, we'll take a few minutes to discuss typical ways in which operating systems are designed. There are numerous ways to organize the code in operating systems, from the simple to the sophisticated. We'll be looking at three of them:

- **Monolithic,**
- **Layered**
- **Client-Server**

Operating System Architectures

All operating system architectures, apart from the most rudimentary, have some means of separating the user code from the operating system code, supported by hardware memory management. This protects the system from the havoc that user programs might try to wreak upon it, inadvertently or otherwise. In Windows NT terminology we talk about user programs operating in **user mode**, and the system executing in **kernel mode**. This is illustrated in the diagram below:

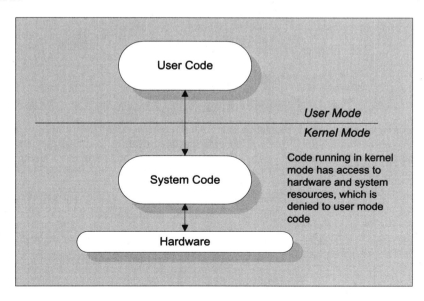

The above diagram demonstrates how the system code has access to the hardware and other resources, which are denied to code running in user mode. This is a very good thing as far as a multi-user or multitasking operating system is concerned, because we might well have more than one task trying to access a resource at a time.

As we'll see, this division between kernel and user mode code isn't quite as clear cut in NT as it is with some other systems, but it provides a useful basis on which to start the discussion.

The simplest approach to operating system design is to have a **monolithic** system, composed of a lot of functions running in kernel mode, which simply call one another as necessary.

Although this type of system requires less in the way of design than others, there are drawbacks in some monolithic systems. Two major ones which spring to mind are **robustness** (if one part crashes, so does the rest) and **extendability** (it may be difficult to add or replace parts of the system).

Layered operating systems improve matters by separating functionality into modules which then operate in layers, with higher-level layers calling lower-level ones as required. This is shown in the diagram below:

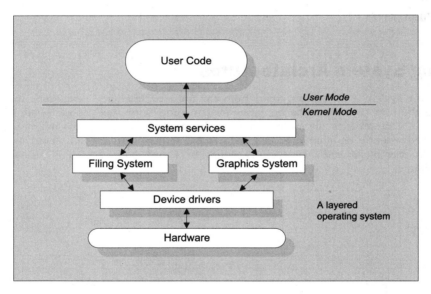

One advantage of this system model is that layers only need to know about contacting those immediately above and below them. This permits the building and testing of the system from the ground up, implementing low-level modules first, and the reverse — using stub code for yet-to-be-designed hardware and developing support services first.

The third type of organisation follows a **client-server** model. Operating system services are implemented as server processes running in user mode, as shown here:

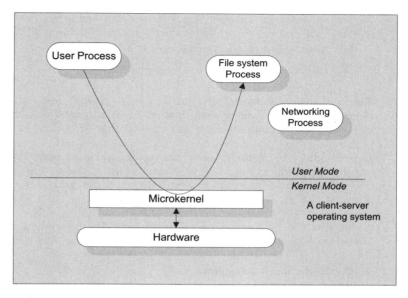

A client-server operating system

The user and system processes both run in user mode, with the system processes acting as servers to the user process clients. All communication between the two is done by passing calls through the **microkernel**, which acts as a broker between clients and servers. How much of the operating system is implemented in the microkernel, and how much is in user-mode processes, varies from system to system.

This architecture has certain advantages, in that it is possible to make the system more robust, so that you can restart a single component if it fails. It is also possible to run system processes on different processors in a multiprocessor system.

The Windows NT Architecture

Windows NT combines two of these models, being partly client-server and partly layered. The overall architecture is summarized in the following diagram:

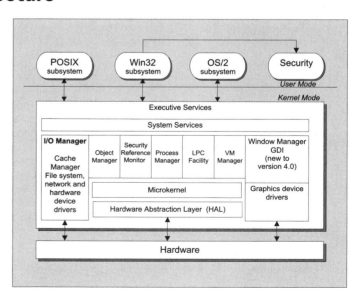

We can see from the diagram that Windows NT comprises two parts:

> A set of subsystems which run in user mode
> The **Executive**, which runs in kernel mode

The Executive is an operating system in its own right, and only lacks a user interface of its own to be fully functional. It is comprised of a series of modules, and operates in a layered manner, with higher-level modules using lower level ones to perform specific tasks.

These modules are usually called 'managers', and work something like objects in an object-oriented program, in that they are independent of one another, and cooperate using a carefully selected set of interfaces. Since they're designed this way, it is possible to replace a module, provided that its interface remains the same.

As we saw for client-server operating systems, NT has certain modules of system code which execute as separate processes in user mode. These are called **subsystems**, and there are two types:

> **Environment subsystems**
> **Integral subsystems**.

NT is very unusual among operating systems, in that it allows you to run programs from several other operating systems as well as native NT programs. This is achieved through the environment subsystems, which provide operating environments that emulate other operating systems.

The environment subsystems supplied with NT currently comprise:

> **Win32** and **WOW** (Windows On Win32), which can also run 16-bit Windows and DOS programs
> **OS/2**, which runs OS/2 version 1.x character-mode applications
> **POSIX**, which runs Unix text-mode applications which conform to the POSIX standard (POSIX.1)

These subsystems provide all that is needed to run a native Win32, OS/2 or POSIX application, so those applications have no idea that they aren't running under their native operating system.

The Win32 subsystem also includes a 'console API' that we'll see more about in Chapter 10, which is used to provide text-mode I/O in windows, and supports functionality similar to that provided by the 'curses' library under Unix. OS/2, POSIX and DOS programs use the Win32 console API facility for doing their text-mode I/O.

Integral subsystems are those which provide important operating system services, the most important being the security subsystem (Chapter 8), which is responsible for implementing the security policy on a local machine. Components of NT networking are also implemented as integral subsystems, in particular, the workstation and server services, which implement the local and remote ends of a network connection.

The modular architecture allows for new subsystems to be added as required. Since subsystems are user-mode programs (like all user applications), they cannot directly access hardware or other system resources. This adds to the robustness of NT, in that it is possible for a client application, or even a subsystem, to crash, without affecting the core of the operating system. Life is, however, imperfect and NT, like all other systems, does occasionally throw a GPF (otherwise known as a 'Blue Screen of Death'). However, NT's architecture does reduce the risk of such a catastrophic breakdown.

By using these subsystems, NT behaves in a client-server manner, with the subsystems as servers and the individual applications as clients.

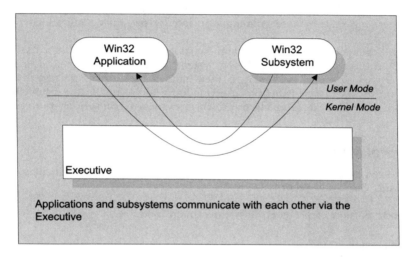

Applications and subsystems communicate with each other via the Executive

As you can see from the diagram, applications talk to the subsystem via the Executive. Communication between applications and subsystems uses **Local Procedure Calls** (**LPCs**).

LPCs are the way in which user mode communicates with kernel mode. Applications and subsystems can act as servers by providing their own APIs which programs can call. When such a call is made, from a second application or server, an LPC message is sent to the first application, via the Executive, which implements the API routine, sending the result back as another LPC. Thus the two user-mode applications do not communicate with each other, only through the LPC facility in the Executive.

Kernel Mode Versus User Mode

Let's look a little more closely at the differences between kernel mode and user mode, and see what this means to Windows NT programs.

Applications run in user mode, while operating system functions run in kernel mode (which is also variously known as **supervisor mode**, **protected mode** or **ring 0**).

Kernel mode is privileged, in that code in this mode can access all memory and hardware, including memory belonging to user-mode processes. User mode applications, on the other hand, cannot access memory belonging to:

▶ Any other user-mode process

▶ Any kernel process

▶ The system hardware

Contrast this with the situation in Windows 95, where even though an application can't access another application's address space, all applications still have access to parts of system memory, leaving the operating system more vulnerable to interference than applications.

User-mode applications call operating system functions in the kernel. When this happens, the processor traps the thread and the operating system takes ownership of it. The system call is executed in kernel mode, and ownership is then handed back to the process in user mode. This means that the thread must switch from user mode to kernel mode to execute the system code, and then back again. This **kernel-mode transition** is expensive, consuming processor time and memory.

What's In Kernel Mode

We've already seen what runs in user mode, namely the various environment subsystems, such as POSIX, Win32, OS/2 and security.

The kernel mode portion of NT comprises three main modules:

▶ The **Microkernel**

▶ The **Hardware Abstraction Layer** (HAL)

▶ **Executive Services**, which comprises System services and the managers, such as the I/O Manager, Object Manager and so forth

We'll look at each of these in more detail shortly.

One of the main structural differences between NT version 3.51 and version 4.0 is that some functionality which was implemented as part of the Win32 subsystem has been moved into the kernel. In particular, the window manager, graphics interface and graphics device drivers have moved from the Win32 subsystem into the kernel. Why was this done?

The Win32 environment subsystem provided the graphics, window and message services which are also needed by the other subsystems, so to avoid duplication it acted as a sort of 'graphics server' in NT 3.5x. This proved to be a bottleneck, so NT version 4.0 has moved these functions into the kernel, where they'll be available to everyone. This alteration does mean that NT is now more vulnerable to failure in the USER and GDI systems, and so is designed to shut down if they fail. In previous versions if they crashed you'd be left with a machine which was still running but which had no GUI, just a blue screen, which was of little practical use!

The Microkernel

The microkernel is the very heart of Windows NT, and it implements the most fundamental processes. Because of its importance, it is immune to normal memory and thread management processes, so it never gets pre-empted or swapped out.

NT implements what is termed a 'modified microkernel' architecture. In pure microkernel systems, only the very minimum number of processes run in kernel mode, preferably just those which perform hardware manipulation and message passing. This tends to be inefficient, however, as there is a lot of kernel/user mode switching going on, so NT has placed quite a lot of functionality in the kernel, making for a more efficient system.

We, as users of the system, never see the microkernel itself, but it is still useful to know a little about what position it occupies in the system.

The NT microkernel is responsible for various tasks, including:

- Keeping the processor(s) busy and efficient
- Scheduling threads, interrupts and exceptions — it handles threads by allowing those with higher priority to execute at the expense of lower-priority ones
- Synchronizing activity between the processors on multiprocessor machines
- Initiating system recovery after a power failure and managing shutdown
- Handling synchronization of the NT Executive Services, such as I/O Manager and Process Manager

The kernel also manages **microkernel objects**, the 'fundamental particles' used to operate the system. These can be divided into two groups:

- Dispatcher objects, which control the synchronization of system objects — these include mutexes, events, threads and timers
- Control objects, which control the operation of the microkernel — these include asynchronous procedure calls, interrupts, I/O and process objects

Microkernel objects are never seen by user mode code, but are manipulated by the modules that make up the Executive Services.

The HAL

The **Hardware Abstraction Layer**, or **HAL**, is at the lowest level in NT. It comprises a library of hardware-specific routines that sits between the hardware and the rest of the operating system. The HAL provides standard entry points for access by higher-level functions, hence the word 'abstraction' in the name.

NT has been designed to be portable, so that getting NT to run on a new system should mainly involve writing a new HAL library for the target hardware, and recompiling everything for the target processor. In fact, there may be many different HALs available, which enable NT to run on different architectures, or different configurations of the same architecture (for instance, single and multi-processor versions).

Device drivers will, of necessity, contain device dependent code, but they'll avoid processor and platform dependencies as much as possible by using HAL routines.

The Executive Services

Lastly, we come to the top layer — the **Executive Services**, which provide a set of common services that can be used by all components of the operating system.

At the very top we have a thin top layer called **system services**, which provides the interface between the kernel and the user-mode subsystems. Beneath this, we have the various components that make up the Executive Services:

- Graphics Device Interface (GDI)
- Graphics Device Drivers
- I/O Manager
- Object Manager
- Process Manager
- Local Procedure Call Facility
- Security Reference Monitor
- Virtual Memory Manager
- Window Manager

These all work together to perform tasks, so that when, for example, we want to start an application, the Process Manager calls the Object Manager to create a process and thread objects.

Executive Objects

The modules in the Executive are sometimes called 'object services', in that they all work with 'executive objects', which are data structures belonging to and managed by the Executive Services. They are abstract data types used to represent system resources, and representing them in this way has several benefits, which we'll mention after we list the object types.

All resources which can be shared between processes in NT are implemented as objects, which can be referred to by a handle. Here's a list of some of the most common object types, together with a description, and a note of which module in the Executive is responsible for creating them:

Object	Created By	Description
Process	Process Manager	An application plus the resources it needs
Thread	Process Manager	The basic unit of scheduling within the system
Section	Memory Manager	A region of shared memory
File	I/O Manager	An open file or I/O device
Port	LPC Facility	A destination for messages passed between processes

Object	Created By	Description
Access token	Security system	Security information about a process
Event	Executive support services	A notification that something has happened
Semaphore	Executive support services	A way to limit the number of threads using a resource
Mutant*	Executive support services	A way to enforce mutual exclusion
Timer	Executive support services	A way of counting time
Symbolic Link	Object Manager	A way of indirectly referring to an object
Registry Key	Configuration Manager	A key to an entry in the registry

We saw above that resources which *can be shared between processes* are represented as executive objects. Resources and data structures which are only used internally by the Executive, however, are not provided as objects, because there is no need.

In fact, representing resources as objects is useful because it means that we can:

▶ Provide humanly readable names for resources

▶ Ensure data integrity

▶ Share resources among processes

▶ Control access to resources

For example, when we represent resources as objects which we access via a handle, we can use the NT security mechanism to provide access control to a registry key in the same way as to a file.

Data integrity can be assured by implementing data structures as objects, each of which can only be manipulated by API calls. The internal structure of the resource is hidden, and the functions used to manipulate the resource can ensure its proper use.

In order to prevent any one process from hogging system resources, each has a quota that limits the number of object handles it can have open.

These objects are accessible to applications running in the various environment subsystems, although how they are presented will vary from subsystem to subsystem. For instance, Win32 provides processes, threads, events and other Win32 objects which are directly based upon their respective executive objects. The POSIX subsystem, on the other hand, has no notion of 'objects' at all, and so it presents the executive objects in terms of POSIX processes, pipes and other Unix resource types.

* If you know anything about Win32 synchronization objects, rest assured that this isn't a misspelling for 'mutex'... it really is 'mutant'.

Object Handles

NT (like Unix) has based its object handling on a file handling metaphor:

- You need to open an object before you can use it, and you can either open an existing object, or create a new one
- When you open it, you must specify the access you require (in other words, what you want to do to the object)
- When you open an object, you are given a handle, which is used in all subsequent operations on the object — when you've finished with the object, you close the handle
- If two processes get handles to the same object, then they share access to the object

Object handles are very important in NT programming, and we'll come across a large number of them as we progress through the book.

Object Manager

The Object Manager is the module that is responsible for creating, managing and deleting the executive objects we have just discussed.

When a process creates an object as a result of executing a Win32 API call, the Win32 subsystem requests the Object Manager to create the object, which it does by performing the following steps:

- Allocates memory for the object
- Gives the object a security descriptor, which says who is allowed to do what to the object
- Stores the object name in an object directory structure
- Provides an object handle and returns it to the user-mode process

Let's comment briefly on one of these steps — security. As we've said, security is very important to NT, and it is therefore important to be able to control access to the large number objects in the system. For this reason, the Object Manager always attaches security information to the object, in the form of a security descriptor, so that access to it can be controlled right from the start. We'll see a lot more about this in Chapter 8.

The Object Manager manages objects in the following ways:

- It keeps a count of handles to objects, so that it knows when it is safe to delete them — it won't delete anything while the user still has a handle open on it
- Each time a thread wants to use a handle, the Object Manager checks whether the thread is allowed to do what it wants — this applies regardless of the type of the underlying resource
- It monitors resource usage, not allowing threads to open too many handles at once

I/O Manager

As its name implies, the I/O Manager is responsible for managing all I/O for the system. A large part of its task is managing communication between drivers, whether they be file system, hardware or network drivers. It does its work asynchronously, so that the processor pre-empts a thread which needs data, while the I/O manager is getting the data.

NT uses a layered driver structure. While the lowest levels talk directly to the hardware, higher levels (such as file systems) talk to the lower ones. For example, if we request something from a file system driver, it will, in turn, talk to a hardware disk driver, or a network driver for network mapped drives. Part of the I/O Manager's job is to help this communication.

The NT I/O system is packet driven, so that requests are passed between components as **I/O Request Packets** (IRPs), structures which govern how the request is processed at each stage. The job of the I/O Manager is to create the IRPs, pass them to the drivers for processing, and free them when they have been processed. The drivers accept IRPs and perform the required operation, before passing them back to the Manager, or forwarding them on to another driver for further processing.

This hierarchical driver structure helps in other ways as well — the higher the level of the driver, the more portable it is likely to be. In the case of top-level drivers, like file systems, no changes should be necessary when porting from one architecture to another.

The I/O Manager treats everything like a device driver, even file systems, and it provides a uniform interface so that many drivers can communicate with each other. Since file systems are treated the same as other device drivers, there is no reason why file system drivers cannot be installed and removed. This leads to the idea of an 'installable file system'. If at some time in the future, NT needs to support some other type of file system, it will be possible to install the ability to handle the new system as easily as installing support for a new printer.

Some operations which are common to many drivers are included within the I/O Manager. Writers of new drivers now face a simpler task than would have been the case previously.

NT also supports **asynchronous I/O** (also called 'overlapped' I/O in Win32) in addition to the more common synchronous variety. We're all familiar with synchronous I/O where you issue a read or write request, and then wait for the function to return when the I/O has been completed.

Asynchronous I/O gives the possibility of greater efficiency, because the I/O request is queued and the called function returns immediately, leaving you able to continue processing. This is discussed in more detail in Chapter 7. If you're reading data, you can use synchronization methods to find out when the operation has completed, before using the data which has been retrieved for you.

Process Manager

The Process Manager creates and destroys processes, and is responsible for managing process and thread objects. It provides a standard set of services in environment subsystems for using processes and threads. Applications can use whatever calls they're accustomed to, such as `CreateProcess()` under Win32, or `fork()` under POSIX.

Local Procedure Call Facility

Applications call the environment subsystems to provide them with services. Communication between them is done using the LPC mechanism, which is similar to the RPC (Remote Procedure Call — see chapter 11 on IPC), but optimized for two processes on the same machine. Applications don't see this mechanism — it is as if a function has been called directly, and not via an intermediate mechanism.

Security

We know that NT is a secure operating system, designed so that no one can use system resources to which they're not entitled.

NT Security is built around a system of **access tokens** and **security descriptors**. Every process has an access token, which identifies it and the groups to which it belongs. Every object has a security descriptor, which contains lists of who is allowed (or denied) access to the object. When a process wants to use an object, the security system compares its access token with the object's security descriptor, and makes a decision on whether to allow access or not.

Since all objects and processes have such security information, it is easy to ensure that access is only granted to the right processes.

> *For compatibility reasons, NT incorporates the FAT (File Allocation Table) file system.*
> *Because FAT files have no security features apart from the DOS read-only flag, it is not*
> *possible to secure files and directories on a FAT system.*

The security system also provides for auditing access to objects, so that you can obtain a complete record of all accesses to objects, if necessary.

Most of the security system runs as an integral subsystem, but part of it, the **Security Reference Monitor**, resides in the kernel. This module works with the Object Manager, processing requests from the Object Manager for security information about objects. NT security is discussed in detail in Chapter 8.

Registry

The system registry, most commonly just called the registry, is central to the way in which NT operates. It is a hierarchical database, which contains information about the configuration of NT itself, of the hardware, and of applications.

The registry database has six top level keys, called **hives**, which are named as follows:

- HKEY_LOCAL_MACHINE
- HKEY_CURRENT_CONFIG
- HKEY_USERS
- HKEY_CURRENT_USER
- HKEY_CLASSES_ROOT
- HKEY_DYN_DATA

HKEY_LOCAL_MACHINE holds software and hardware configuration information for the machine. **HKEY_CURRENT_CONFIG** is a pointer to the local machine's current configuration settings. **HKEY_USERS** contains settings for all users registered on the system, while **HKEY_CURRENT_USER** is a pointer to the settings for the currently logged-in user. **HKEY_CLASSES_ROOT** becomes very important if you want to work with COM or OLE, and is a shortcut to entries under **HKEY_LOCAL_MACHINE\SOFTWARE\Classes**. **HKEY_DYN_DATA**, included in the registry through being inherited from Windows 95, cannot be opened in NT 4.0.

Entries are arranged under these hives as a hierarchy, which can be viewed and edited using the regedit tool:

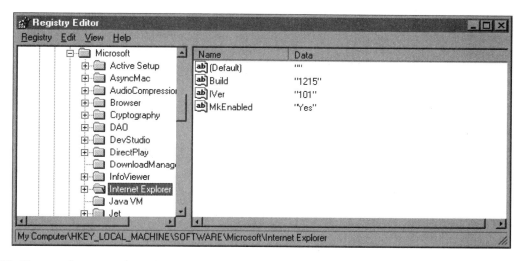

Win32 provides a number of API calls for manipulating registry entries. All entries within the registry can have NT security applied to them, so it is possible to guard against non-privileged users changing the system configuration.

It is recommended that you use registry entries rather than the old Win16 idea of **.ini** files for storing application-specific data. We will be discussing the features, and dangers, of the registry in full in Chapter 3.

Important Topics

The sections which follow highlight some of the most important aspects of NT's architecture, and introduce topics that we'll be going on to examine in more detail throughout the book.

Processes and Threads

A **process** is an application or a modular part of an application. Windows NT regards a process as a set of objects and threads running in an address space, together with any resources needed. This means that a process ties together executable code, data, an address space, system resources and at least one thread.

Process objects are created by the Object Manager, and they have a set of attributes, as follows:

- **Process ID**, which uniquely identifies the process
- **Access token**, which contains the security settings for the process
- **Quota Limit**, which sets how many object handles the process can have open at once
- **Exit Status**, which holds the status when the process exits
- **Execution Time**, which holds the total execution time for all the threads in the process

A **thread** is the basic unit of scheduling in the system — it is threads that are scheduled, not applications or processes. A thread has a set of registers, a kernel stack, a user stack in the process space, and a thread environment block. This is called the thread's context, and is stored when execution switches from one thread to another. This, along with other topics related to threads and processes, will be discussed in more detail in Chapter 6, but we'll introduce some of these concepts here.

Objects and memory allocated by a thread belong to its process, not the thread. This means that memory (and hence variables) can be shared between threads in a process.

Since it is threads that are scheduled and not processes, it is common in NT to write multithreaded programs rather than use multiple single-threaded programs. The reason for this is that, under NT, switching execution between threads is more efficient than switching between processes, and since all threads belonging to a process share the same address space, sharing of data is simpler than it is between processes. However, there are a couple of drawbacks to using threads — they are more difficult to program than processes, and are more prone to error.

NT implements pre-emptive multitasking, in which each thread is given a timeslice in which to execute. When it uses up its slice, or if it blocks for some reason (such as pending I/O), the operating system saves the thread's context, loads the context of the next thread in the queue, and executes it. This form of multitasking behaves much better, and more predictably, than the cooperative multitasking found in Win16.

All threads have a priority which governs how they're scheduled. It is possible to raise or lower the priority of a thread, but you need to be careful because this can affect the operation of other processes, and in extreme cases even lock up the system.

It is important that threads can communicate with one another in order to synchronize their operation. It is also vital that data which is shared by more than one thread be guarded so that only one thread can access it at a time.

NT provides some executive objects that implement thread synchronization, such as events, semaphores, timers and mutants. The environment subsystems provide their own mechanisms for using these objects, and we'll see in Chapter 6 how Win32 implements thread synchronization.

To summarize:

- A process is an application or a modular part of an application
- A thread is the basic unit of scheduling in the system
- A module is a block of executable code loaded into memory
- A task is a module in memory plus the resources it needs in order to operate

Memory Management

Each user-mode process under NT has a notional 4GB address space, and can't access any other. Processes view their memory as one, flat 4GB chunk, laid out like this:

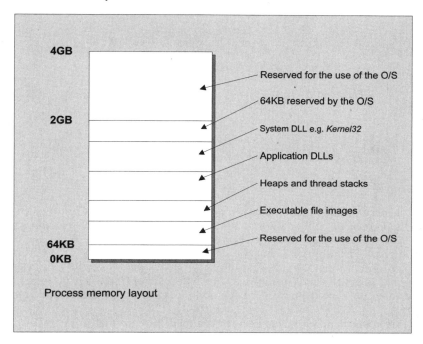

The top 2GB is reserved for system use, with the bottom 2GB left for the process. This address space gets mapped onto the actual memory available on the hardware, and when the amount allocated exceeds the available physical memory, a paging file (`pagefile.sys`) is used to save what there isn't room for in real memory.

> *It is the MIPS R4000 that mandates 2GB of system space. Intel processors could get away with less, but it has been left at 2GB to help portability.*

Memory-Mapped Files

Memory-mapped files (covered in Chapter 7) are an interesting and vital part of NT's memory management scheme. NT allows a file on disk to be treated as part of a process's address space, the process allocating such space for a file, and then using it as if it were a large array in memory.

A file that a process wishes to map may be extremely large, so it may not all actually be in memory at once. The parts which are in memory are called **views** of the file, as shown in the diagram below.

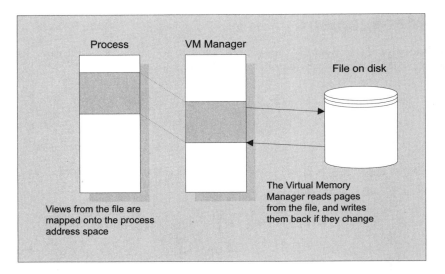

Views from the file are
mapped onto the process
address space

The Virtual Memory
Manager reads pages
from the file, and writes
them back if they change

The **Virtual Memory Manager** (VMM) is responsible for reading **pages** (into which Win32 virtual memory is divided) of data from the file, and mapping them onto the process address space. If the process then writes a page into the memory, the VMM will write that page back to disk. In this way, it appears to the process that the entire file is in memory.

Memory mapped files are also a useful way to share memory between processes, since the VMM can map the same piece of memory onto the address spaces of two different processes.

Applications are often handled using memory-mapped files, so that if an instance is already running, NT creates a new view of the executable file. In this way, several processes can be running the same application. The **NT Redirector** can make this work over a network, mapping views of files on the server so that they appear to be in the local address space, and managing the network connection. This is illustrated in the diagram below:

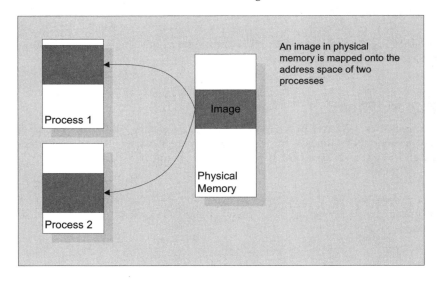

An image in physical
memory is mapped onto the
address space of two
processes

Views of an executable can also be provided by mapping, so that a process only has in memory those parts of an executable which it needs:

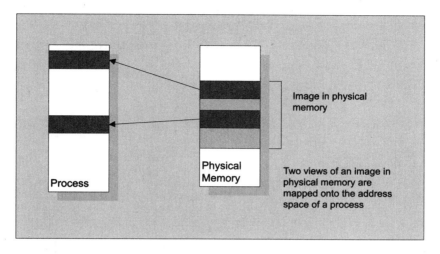

Virtual Memory

The idea of **virtual memory** — that is, extending the amount of physical memory available by using disk space — is not new. (In fact, it was first implemented in 1959 on the Atlas computer at Manchester University.) VM systems allow processes to use more memory than is physically present on the machine, by swapping some of the contents to disk, or other storage system, when the memory gets full. The file that holds the swapped memory is commonly called a **paging file** (or page file), and the default page file lives in the root of the NT system drive as **pagefile.sys**. If you have more than one drive, you can create page files on these other drives as well.

NT's virtual memory mechanism was designed to address various requirements. It needs to:

▶ Be portable to different architectures

▶ Work with the subsystems

▶ Work with multiple processors

Memory is moved between physical memory and the page file in 4kB or 8kB pages, depending on the processor. When a page is in real memory, it is said to be *valid*, and when it is in the page file it is *invalid*. If you try to access an address which is on an invalid page, a page fault results, and the VMM has to bring the page back into memory, possibly swapping a currently valid page onto disk in order to make room for it.

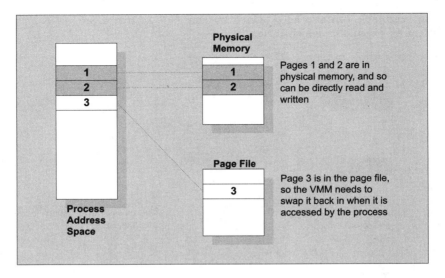

Each process has a 'working set' of pages, which varies between a minimum and a maximum size. The minimum working set is what the process needs to have loaded in order to run, and it can load extra pages in up to its maximum. To help with load balancing, if the VMM sees that the process isn't causing many page faults, then it may reduce the working set. Conversely, if the process is generating a lot of page faults, its working set may be increased.

The VM mechanism uses a FIFO (first in first out) policy to determine which pages to discard in order to make room for new ones, so that those which have been in memory the longest will get paged out. The alternative — discarding those which have been used least frequently — would require too much overhead.

Moving pages between physical memory and the page file uses a significant amount of processor time. It is the main reason why it is a good idea to put as much real memory in an NT machine as you can afford, because that will cut paging to the minimum.

Allocating and Committing Memory

Allocating memory is a two-stage process:

- A block of addresses is reserved for future use
- When it is needed, that memory is committed, and the VMM allocates page file space

Why two stages? A thread can reserve a block which it thinks it might need. This is a quick and inexpensive process. Later, when it actually needs the memory, it commits some of it, and can then use the pages. This is a far more expensive process. No thread running in the process's address space has access to the block, once reserved, and only the thread that reserved the block can go on to commit it and use it. Thus, allocating memory in this way guarantees that a thread gets its own block of memory when it requires it.

Page Flags

Memory pages are protected by a set of flags, as follows:

- Read-only
- Read/write
- Execute-only
- Guarded
- No-access
- Copy-on-write

The first two are pretty obvious, allowing read-only and read/write access to a page. If the hardware allows, 'execute-only' means that a thread cannot read or write the page, but can start executing at an address within the page. Intel processors don't support this, so this mode of operation is equivalent to read-only.

Guarded pages are designed to help verify the integrity of stacks and other data structures. You can place a guarded page either side of a data structure. If anything tries to write off the end of the structure, a write occurs to a guarded page. This generates an exception and the caller gets a message.

No-access pages can't be accessed in any way, and are used (for example) where a virtual page has been allocated but not committed.

Copy-on-write Pages

The last one, copy-on-write, is worth special mention. It is used as a means to be efficient when two processes are sharing a piece of memory.

If both processes want read/write access to the memory, then copy-on-write means that both share exactly the same data until one writes to it. When that happens, the VMM makes a copy of the page, which can only be accessed by the thread that is doing the writing. This is an example of **lazy evaluation**, where the VMM doesn't perform a potentially expensive operation until it absolutely has to.

Copy-on-write protection is also used with code pages, especially when debugging. When you set a breakpoint, a breakpoint instruction must be added to the code, which changes the contents of the page. The VMM then makes a private copy of that page for the thread which set the breakpoint.

Memory is discussed in more detail in Chapter 7.

Multiprocessing

NT is built to run on systems which have more than one processor. Multiprocessor systems have great potential for true multitasking, but bring their own special brand of headache.

There are two basic types of multiprocessor system — **symmetric** and **asymmetric**.

In asymmetric multiprocessing (ASMP), the operating system runs on one processor, and all the user jobs run on the other processor (or processors). These types of system, are relatively easy to create, and can be useful where, say, one processor has a coprocessor or access to more memory. They tend not to be very portable because they depend fairly heavily on hardware details, but it is relatively easy to modify an existing single-processing operating system to work as an ASMP system.

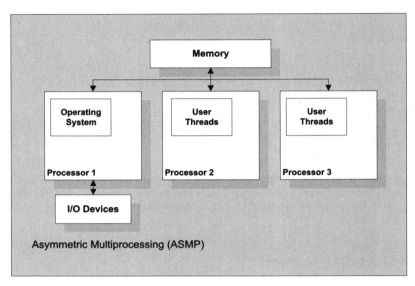

Asymmetric Multiprocessing (ASMP)

Symmetric multiprocessing (SMP) allows the operating system and user threads to run on any, or all, of the processors available. This tends to be a better overall design because:

▶ It enables the operating system itself to engage in multiprocessing (and the operating system is a significant user of processor time)

▶ It gives improved opportunities for load balancing

▶ It leads to more robustness, because the operating system can switch to another processor if one fails

▶ Hardware for SMP systems tends to be more uniform, so there is a greater possibility of writing a portable multiprocessing operating system

However, they are more difficult to write, and usually need to be constructed from the ground upwards.

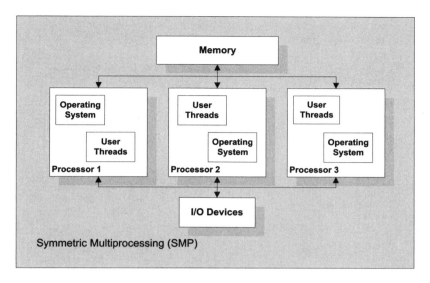

Symmetric Multiprocessing (SMP)

Windows NT is one of several full SMP operating systems (including Solaris and Linux), so the OS code can run on any, or all, of the processors in the system. Programs which use multiple threads can also run on any processor.

16-Bit Windows and DOS Programs

Although NT is a different operating system from the Windows 3.x/95/98 family, it still has to fit into a world which still wants to use existing DOS and 16-bit Windows programs. To this end, a considerable amount of effort has been put into ensuring that NT can run many well-behaved Win3.x and MS DOS programs. It obviously isn't possible to ensure that every such program can be run using NT, because some Win3.x and MS DOS programs rely upon direct hardware and memory access, in a way that cannot be tolerated by a system such as NT.

MS DOS and 16-bit Windows programs can be run in an environment subsystem called a **Virtual DOS Machine**, or VDM. Unlike other environment subsystems, there can be more than one VDM running at a time.

A VDM is a process that emulates a complete MS DOS environment within which MS DOS and Win3.x applications can run. By emulating a complete computer, DOS applications can apparently issue BIOS calls, receive interrupts, appear to directly access certain hardware devices, and so on. The DOS environment uses the source code and drivers from MS DOS 5.0. It supports direct memory access, which is safe because it is running in its own address space, but doesn't allow direct access to disks, since this is risky.

The Win16 subsystem VDM is sometimes known as **WOW** (Windows On Win32). It is essentially a multithreading VDM, each of whose threads represents a 16-bit application.

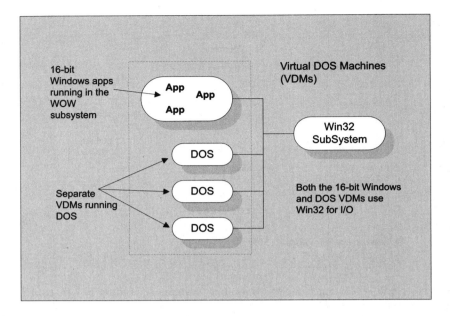

By default, all 16-bit Windows applications run together in a single VDM. This means that they all share the same address space, are cooperatively multitasked against one another, and hence behave in the same way that they would if they were running on a 'real' Win3.x machine. On NT version 4.0, we can create more than one Win16 subsystem, so that we can effectively give 16-bit applications their own address spaces. This means that it is possible to arrange for 16-bit applications to be pre-emptively multitasked against one another.

The DOS and Win3.x subsystems use the Win32 API and sometimes native NT services. The Win3.x VDM translates I/O calls to 32-bit and uses the Win32 subsystem, while DOS programs transparently use a Win32 console to perform text I/O.

File Systems

We've already seen that file systems are treated as device drivers by the I/O Manager, and can be installed and removed as easily as any other driver. The file system drivers are layered on top of the actual hardware drivers, as shown in the diagram below:

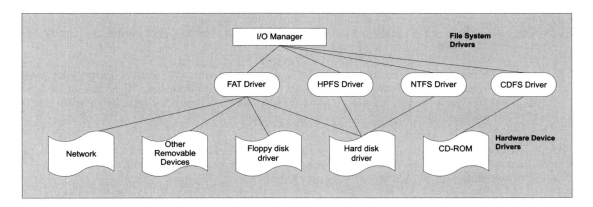

NT version 4.0 supports three filing systems:

▶ The **FAT** system, which is inherited from DOS

▶ The **NTFS** system, which is native to NT

▶ The **CDFS** system

Earlier versions of NT also supported the HPFS filing system, which was used to support the OS/2 subsystem.

Let's take a brief look at the capabilities and limitations of these:

The **FAT** (**File Allocation Table**) system is supported because of the need to run DOS and Win16 programs. The disk is divided into clusters, and a 'file allocation table' is a linked list showing which clusters belong to which files.

FAT was originally designed when disks were much smaller than today, so it is limited in the size of disk it can efficiently support — up to around 1GB in practice. It can be used on even larger disks, up to 2GB, but is very inefficient in its use of disk space.

The FAT system is inefficient for large disks, because the cluster size goes up the bigger the disk gets. The reason for this is to keep down the number of entries in the FAT, and it means that on a small disk a cluster might be 4kB, while on a large disk it might be 16kB or more. Obviously, storing small files of less than the cluster size is going to lead to wasted space, and is one reason why many big disks were partitioned into smaller logical disks. Other problems arise due to FAT storing filenames in a linear list — navigation time increases markedly with increasing disk size.

There is also a problem with the fragmentation of the FAT. Parts of one file are stored in many places across the surface of the disk, leading to poor access times. This occurs as a result of heavy disk use, and leads to inefficiency in storing large files.

The FAT system also uses the old DOS 8.3 file naming system, with limited support for long filenames; Windows 95 added something called **VFAT** which allows long filenames to be used with the FAT system. It too has no support for any security, apart from setting a 'read-only' bit in the file attributes.

> *Windows 95 Release 2 introduced a modification of the FAT system called FAT32, which overcame some of the limitations of the FAT system, and improved the use of long filenames. NT 3.51 and NT4.0 do not support the FAT32 filing system.*

We'll mention the HPFS system in passing, even though it isn't supported by NT 4.0. The High-Performance File System was released in 1990 for use with OS/2, and was supported by earlier versions of NT in order to support the OS/2 subsystem.

HPFS was designed to overcome many of the deficiencies of FAT. For instance, it provided much faster access to files, because it used a B-tree for storing filenames rather than the linear list used by the FAT system. It was designed to be efficient with large volumes, and could handle single volumes of up to 2GB in size more efficiently.

HPFS also introduced several features that have persisted into NT:

▶ Support for long filenames, allowing up to 254 characters in a name

▶ **Hot-fixing**, which automatically detects and avoids bad sectors on the disk, without the application being aware

▶ **Disk caching**, holding the most recently used items in a cache in case they're accessed again

▶ **Lazy writing**, which caches small writes until there is a larger amount to write

Although HPFS was an improvement on FAT, it still had limitations. The use of 512kB sectors meant that volumes were limited to 2GB each, and all the control information was still at the start of the disk — the whole disk would be lost if that was damaged.

The NT File System (NTFS) extends what FAT and HPFS offered, taking the best from them both and adding new features of its own. Here are a few of the highlights — we'll be investigating them in more detail in Chapter 7.

NTFS aims to be a more secure filing system, and it does this in two ways. Firstly, the control information which says where each file is on the disk can be mirrored to somewhere else on the disk, so that even if you completely lose one set, you can still use the disk. Secondly, NTFS implements file-system recovery — it keeps a record of transactions against the file system, so when doing a `CHKDSK`, it is possible to roll-back to the point where transactions were last committed to the drive in order to regain consistency in the file system.

NTFS has the ability to handle very large volumes (up to 2^{64} bytes, which is a lot!). It also supports the NT security system for files, making it possible to control very precisely who has access. Program files can also be marked as execute-only, which makes it very difficult for a virus to infect them. It also has Unicode support for filenames, and POSIX environment support, including links.

Note that Microsoft used to maintain that NT never needed defragmenting. It turned out that this wasn't the case, so NT 4.0 has API functions to support defragmenting. If you find that your NT system is running slowly and doing a lot of extra disk access, it may be worth looking at one of the defragmenters available on the market.

Internationalization

Earlier operating systems have been very English-language (and often US-culture) oriented, and it has been quite difficult to provide true support for other cultures and languages. NT has been designed from the start to be a truly international operating system, and it supports internationalization through two mechanisms — localization (based on the concept of locales) and Unicode (see Chapter 5).

A locale represents a distinct cultural or national identity, and combines a language, currency, and ways of writing numbers and dates, among other things. Thus 'British English' and 'US English' are different locales, as are 'French-speaking Canadian' and 'English-speaking Canadian'.

A default locale will be set when NT is installed, and users can change language and formatting options through the Control Panel. The Win32 subsystem provides some National Language Support (NLS) API functions, which provide correct date/time and currency formatting, string comparison routines and locale handling.

Unicode

Unicode is an industry standard character set which provides an alternative to the traditional ASCII set. Although it has been the mainstay of computers over many years, ASCII is very limited when used for languages outside US English, as there are very many essential symbols for which there is no room in the 8-bit, 256-character ASCII character set. The problem is even more acute when you start to consider languages such as Chinese and Japanese, where the numbers of symbols in the language may run into hundreds, if not thousands.

Unicode employs 16 bits per character, and so can represent 2^{16} (65536) characters. This gives more than enough room for all languages in common use today, as well as leaving space for mathematical, scientific and other useful symbols. The bottom eight bits correspond to the ASCII character set, so that it is quite simple to convert between ASCII and Unicode.

Unicode is the native character set of NT, and is also used extensively by OLE and COM. We'll see more about Unicode in Chapter 5.

Structured Exception Handling

If you're a C++ programmer you'll be used to the idea of catching program errors using exceptions. NT provides a parallel mechanism for handling system-level errors, which is called **Structured Exception Handling**, but which can be used from languages other than C++. Structured exception handling is extensively covered in Chapter 4.

Programs may encounter errors which are picked up by the system, either in hardware or software. Examples of these might be an attempt to divide by zero, or to access an invalid address. When one of these errors occurs, an exception is generated for which you can install a handler. Execution stops when the exception occurs, and the operating system goes looking for a handler. If it finds one, then the handler gets to process the exception, and if the error can be fixed, then life can carry on. If no handler is found, a default action is taken, which usually results in the termination of the program.

As we'll see in Chapter 4, NT structured exceptions look very much like C++ exceptions, and the two can be integrated.

The Future

NT 5.0, is a major upgrade of NT, and incorporates far more changes than the 3.51-to-4.0 transition. On the hardware front, there is the addition of the **Universal Serial Bus** (USB), full Plug-and-Play and **Power Management**, while the addition of **Instrumentation Services** makes it possible for hardware vendors to let their components notify the operating system of status information. For example, a disk drive is able to notify the system when it finds an unacceptably high number of bad sectors.

There is quite an upgrade to the filing system, too. The old restrictions imposed by drive letters has gone (hooray!), and it is also possible to get the system to manage disk space, automatically backing up unused files onto removable media when a threshold value is reached.

Many of the new features, some of which have already been released as add-ons for NT 4.0, are designed to make it easier to manage large networks:

▶ The **Active Directory**, which provides a centralized method for finding out about and accessing files, printers and other resources, even if they reside on other servers

▶ The **Microsoft Management Console** (MMC), a tool which allows administrators to control all users, services, applications and resources from a central point

▶ **Zero-Administration**, which provides completely centralized administration of workstations

NT 5.0 also supports clustering (previously only available with Windows NT 4.0, Enterprise Edition), although only with two machines, and provides graceful fail-over support if one of the paired machines fails.

The security system has been upgraded, with the addition of both public-key (RSA) and private-key (Kerberos-based) encryption methods. These are supported by an 'encrypted file system', so that file encryption is supported at the operating system level.

The system services in NT 5.0 also form the basis of the new Windows **DNA** (Distributed InterNet Applications Architecture), which aims to unite traditional networks and the Internet with a single unifying architecture, and which will free developers from many of the traditional chores associated with programming distributed applications.

Programming APIs

The environment subsystems all have their own programming APIs, which are used to write applications. The Win32 subsystem uses the Win32 API, the POSIX subsystem uses a POSIX API, and so on, and the subsystems convert these, where necessary, into NT calls. This book is an introduction to using the Win32 API to write user-mode programs, and doesn't touch on any of the others.

You may also hear mention of a mysterious and powerful **NT Native API**. The reason that this is mysterious is that it is a system-level API, not used by those who are writing user-mode code, and as such, is poorly documented. All the programs we'll write throughout the course of this book run under the control of the Win32 subsystem. However this subsystem isn't loaded until fairly late on in the NT startup process, after you get the blue screen and the 'dots' which indicate that **CHKDSK** is running. The Native API is used to write applications which run outside a subsystem, typically before any subsystem is loaded. As such, it is rather a specialized topic, and we won't mention it again.

Conclusions

We've had a brief tour of the architecture of Windows NT, and what we've seen is a sophisticated multitasking operating system, which is secure, portable and able to deal with the demands of modern computing.

In the chapters which follow, we'll investigate the essentials of NT in more detail, and see how to program them.

Dynamic Link Libraries

If you're a C++ programmer you'll be familiar with static libraries, but if you're new to Windows, you might not have come across DLLs (Dynamic Link Libraries) before.

We're going to start this chapter by looking at what DLLs are, and at some of the advantages and disadvantages they present. We'll go on to see how they work in more detail, in particular at what goes during the compile and link phase, as well as at how DLLs are loaded and unloaded at run time. We'll also examine how you go about implementing a region of memory in a DLL that can be shared across processes.

All the new ideas and concepts that we'll meet along the way will be demonstrated clearly in coded examples.

What Is A DLL?

A DLL is a particular type of executable file that can contain functions, data or resources, which will be used by other executables. As the name implies, a DLL can be loaded and unloaded dynamically, as required, and it is possible for one instance of a DLL to be shared by multiple applications.

When you use a static library, the linker copies code from the library to your executable. When you use a DLL, the code already exists in an executable form, and all that is needed is for the application to link to the DLL at run-time, and call the compiled object code in the DLL. No code from the DLL is incorporated into the executable module of the calling application.

If you don't already know, you might be surprised to learn that DLLs occupy a very important place in the Win32 programming world. The three main modules which provide the core functionality of NT are all DLLs:

- GDI32.DLL, which controls graphics functions, including printing
- USER32.DLL, which deals with hardware control, window creation, messaging and communications
- KERNEL32.DLL, which handles memory management, multitasking and resources

This means that every time you call a Windows API function, it results in a DLL function being called.

Types Of DLL

There are several types of DLL — object code DLLs, resource DLLs, device driver DLLs and so on. The programming components which are now becoming increasingly popular, such as **ActiveX controls**, are packaged as DLLs, despite not having a `.dll` extension.

Some functions have to be in DLLs, and cannot be provided in standard `.exe` files. For example, device drivers have to be DLLs, and some API calls, such as `SetWindowsHook()`, require callback functions that can only be called from within a DLL.

Resource DLLs are used to share resource data, and may be used to package resources such as fonts, icons, bitmaps or strings. All these will contain at least one code segment, with the exception of font DLLs, which do not need one.

Advantages And Disadvantages Of Using DLLs

Writing code as separate dlls presents us with several advantages, but as with everything, there is also a downside. Let's look at some of the plus points first.

Advantages

Run-time loading and unloading means that Windows applications that use DLLs facilitate efficient use of memory. If an application's code is divided up between DLLs, it only needs to load those which are necessary for the task in hand, for example, calculation or final report generation. In the past, DOS programs did this sort of thing using overlays, but the use of DLLs in Windows programs makes it much simpler.

The *modularity* brought by DLLs can make it a lot easier to develop code as a series of modules which can be independently developed, tested and maintained. Provided that the interface to the DLL — the list of functions which can be called by clients — remains constant, both DLL and client can be independently tested and developed.

Having an application divided into more than one part leads to *ease of updating*, because it is possible to update a single DLL, rather than having to update the whole application.

DLLs can be used by more than one client at a time, so we end up with truly *shared code*. If a printer driver is implemented as a DLL, then all clients use the same driver, and only one copy of the code needs to be loaded into memory.

DLLs can also be *programming language independent*. Provided that the functions made available by a DLL do not use language specific argument types, such as C++ objects, the DLL can be called from any language that supports their use. This makes DLLs a good way of packaging up legacy code, such as old Fortran calculation code, in a way which can be used by applications written in languages like Visual Basic or C++.

It may sound as though DLLs are a thoroughly good thing from the point of view of the Windows programmer, and indeed they are, but there is a downside to using them which you need to be aware of. Let's take a look at some of these now.

Disadvantages

The first, fairly obvious downside is that applications now come in several parts, so it is possible to lose bits of applications. This isn't something which happens very often, but it is a possibility.

Splitting an application into parts means an increase in complexity. Consequently care needs to be taken to maintain compatibility between the parts.

It is quite possible to end up with multiple copies of the same DLL on a machine, especially when you're considering the more common, redistributable DLLs that many people distribute with programs. Some applications keep DLLs in their own directory, while others put them in the Windows system directory, and if several applications all install the same DLL, you can end up with several copies.

The biggest problem, however, is *versioning*. One of the major weaknesses with the DLL concept is that it relies upon path and file names. The information in an `.exe` file simply says that function `A()` can be found in DLL `'xyz.dll'`.

When this DLL needs to be loaded at run-time, Windows looks in a standard list of places (which includes the current directory, the Windows system directories, and all the directories on the path) for the named file. When it finds a file with the right name, it tries to use that one, and I'm sure that you can foresee some of the problems that might occur. Firstly, the DLL file may have been renamed, and since the search is based on filename, it won't be found. Secondly, a different version of the same DLL might be found in a directory earlier in the search path, and it might not contain the function. Thirdly (and least likely), the search might encounter another (completely different) DLL with the same name, and try to use that! This dependence of DLLs on path and file names can make supporting applications a nightmare, as their misbehavior may be dependent on the client's machine setup.

So, as you can see, DLLs are very useful and flexible, but not always trouble free.

> *Incidentally, Microsoft's Component Object Model has been developed in order to provide all the advantages of DLLs, but without the disadvantages. Packaging code as COM objects is well outside the scope of this book, but it is worth considering if you want to provide packaged functionality for use by a number of COM-aware clients.*

How DLLs Work

Having looked at what DLLs are and where they are useful, let's go on to examine how they work when writing programs.

The Compile/Link Phase

When you want to use a function in a DLL, you need to provide some sort of reference to it, so that the linker will know how to handle external references to the function in the code. These references are usually provided by an **import library**. This is a binary file which lists the functions exported from a DLL.

> *By default, none of the functions or classes defined within the DLL are available to clients. In order to make them 'visible', they must be **exported** when the DLL is built. These exported functions and classes provide the interface to the DLL. Programs using the DLL then **import** functions and classes from the DLL.*

An import library provides the same service to the linker that a header file does to the compiler — it provides just enough detail to enable the tool to process references to functions in the class or DLL, knowing that the actual 'linking' to the code will occur sometime in the future.

You use an import library just like you'd use a static library, so when you want to use a DLL in a program, you add its import library to the list of libraries which will be searched by the linker. In Visual C++, this means that you add it to the list of object and library modules specified on the Link tab of the Project | Settings... dialog.

When the linker finds an external reference, it searches object and static library files to see if it can resolve it. If it can, it links static code into the executable. If it can't, it searches the import libraries it knows about, and if it finds a reference, it places a **relocation record** into the executable. A relocation record is a piece of data which gives the name of the function and the DLL in which it occurs. At run time, Windows uses the relocation record to access the correct DLL, loading it into memory if necessary.

Loading And Unloading

When a process wants to use a DLL, the first step is to load it into memory, if it is not already there. When loading a DLL under Windows NT, the system looks in a series of directories, as follows:

▶ The directory from which the application loaded
▶ The current directory
▶ The Windows System32 directory
▶ The Windows System directory
▶ The Windows directory
▶ Directories listed in the **PATH** variable

The DLL is then mapped onto the address space of the calling process, as shown in the diagram below. This is essential since DLLs have to share the address space of the calling process. This mapping mechanism makes it appear to the caller that it is the only user of the library.

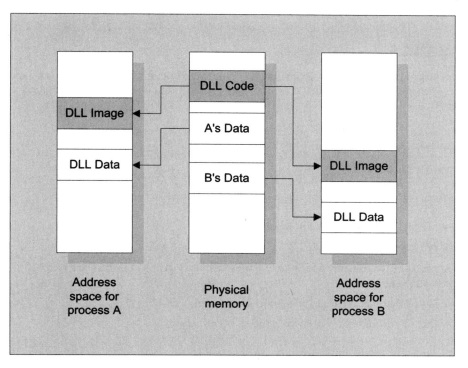

32-bit DLLs don't share their global data. Each process is given its own copy of the DLL's global and static variables through file mapping (discussed in Chapter 7).

This has two consequences:

- Eliminates problems arising due to multiple clients overwriting global data, as exist in the 16-bit world
- Global data is not shared between clients (unless it is specified as **shared**, as we shall see later in this chapter)

Unlike 16-bit DLLs, 32-bit DLLs don't have their own stack, but rather use the stack of the calling process.

The last step in the loading sequence is to increment the reference count for the DLL kept by the operating system. Since the DLL may be used by more than one client, it is necessary for the operating system to know when the library is no longer required.

When a process has finished using the DLL, the reference count is automatically decremented. When the count reaches zero the system knows that the DLL is no longer being used by any processes and can therefore be unloaded.

Using DLLs

We've covered a little bit of the theory behind DLLs. Now let's move on to see how to create and use them in practice.

Creating DLLs

In the same way that a C++ program has the **main()** function as an entry point (and UI Windows programs have **WinMain()**), the main entry point to a DLL is a function called **DllMain()**:

```
BOOL WINAPI DllMain (
    HINSTANCE hInstDll,      // handle to DLL module
    DWORD dwReason,          // reason for calling the function
    LPVOID pReserved);       // reserved
```

This function will be called when the following conditions occur:

- A process calls the DLL for the first time
- A process releases a DLL
- A process dynamically loads or unloads a library using **LoadLibrary()** or **FreeLibrary()**
- A new thread is created by a process using the DLL
- A thread belonging to a client process terminates

Note that you don't have to include an entry point function, since if you don't, the linker will generate a default version for you which does nothing and always returns **TRUE**. You will only need to provide this function if you need to do some special processing when one of the conditions listed above occurs.

Here's the outline of a typical DLL entry-point function:

```
BOOL WINAPI DllMain(HINSTANCE hInstDll, DWORD dwReason, LPVOID pReserved)
{
   BOOL bResult = FALSE;

   switch(dwReason)
   {
   case DLL_PROCESS_ATTACH:
      bResult = TRUE;
      break;
   case DLL_PROCESS_DETACH:
      bResult = TRUE;
      break;
   case DLL_THREAD_ATTACH:
      bResult = TRUE;
      break;
   case DLL_THREAD_DETACH:
      bResult = TRUE;
      break;
   }
```

```
        return bResult;
  }
```

The first argument of the function is the handle of the DLL, and is actually its base address. The **HINSTANCE** of a DLL is the same as its **HMODULE**, so you can use **HINSTANCE** in functions which require a module handle.

The second argument to this function tells you why the function has been called. It may take one of the following values:

DLL_PROCESS_ATTACH
DLL_PROCESS_DETACH
DLL_THREAD_ATTACH
DLL_THREAD_DETACH

The first of these, **DLL_PROCESS_ATTACH**, means that the DLL is attaching to the address space of the current process, either as a result of process startup, or as a result of a call to **LoadLibrary()**. The third parameter of **DllMain()** will be **NULL** if the library is being loaded dynamically, and non-**NULL** if it is being loaded at process startup. If you return **FALSE**, the loading fails and the process does not start.

The second, **DLL_PROCESS_DETACH**, means that the DLL is detaching from the process address space, either because of process shutdown, or because of a call to **FreeLibrary()**. The third parameter will be **NULL** if the DLL is being unloaded via **FreeLibrary()**, and non-**NULL** otherwise. Note that you don't get individual calls to **DllMain()** for each thread already running in the process — there is just one call for the process, and that should be used to clean up after individual threads. Note that this event is never received if the process is killed by a call to **TerminateProcess()**.

DLL_THREAD_ATTACH is called when the current process creates a new thread, and the call is made in the context of the new thread. The DLL can use this call to set up **Thread Local Storage** for the new thread. (Thread Local Storage is explained in Chapter 6) Note that this call is only made for threads created after the DLL has attached to the process, so if the DLL is loaded dynamically, existing threads do not get this function called for them.

Finally, **DLL_THREAD_DETACH** is called when a thread belonging to the calling process exits cleanly, which means without using **TerminateThread()**. The DLL can use this to clean up resources allocated to the thread. Note that this function can be called for a thread, even if **DLL_THREAD_ATTACH** wasn't called. This may well be the case if the thread existed before the DLL was attached to the process.

C++ And DLLs

At the beginning of this chapter, we saw that one of the advantages of DLLs is that if we don't use language-specific features, they can be used by a variety of clients. Sometimes, though, we may want to produce a DLL which is language specific, and it is often very useful to make a C++ DLL that exports members of C++ classes. We'll see how to do this in the next section.

Exporting Symbols

As we noted earler, nothing is visible outside the DLL by default — you need to export symbols in order to make them usable.

We can export symbols from a DLL using two methods. The older (and non-compiler specific) method uses linker definition files, while Visual C++ has built-in keywords which make the job easier. We'll see how both of these methods work in a moment.

All the DLL code we generate in this book will use the second method.

Using A Linker Module Definition File

The older method involves creating a **linker module definition file**, usually known as a `.def` file. This file can be used to provide quite a lot of extra information to the linker, but in this case we'll confine ourselves to considering how it is used with DLLs.

Here's what a typical simple definition file might look like. At its most basic, it consists of a **LIBRARY** section, which defines the name of the DLL, and an **EXPORTS** section, which lists the names of all objects exported from this library:

```
LIBRARY   "fred"
EXPORTS
          func1
          func2
```

This tells the linker that the DLL is called `fred.dll`, and that it exports two functions, called `func1()` and `func2()`. These two functions can now be called by clients, while all others within the DLL remain private.

Exporting By Ordinal Number

As well as exporting symbols by name from a DLL, it is possible to assign each a number, and export these ordinal values in the linker definition file, like this:

```
LIBRARY   "fred"
EXPORTS
          func1 @1
          func2 @2
```

Each symbol in the **EXPORTS** section is followed by an ordinal of the form '**@nn**', where **nn** denotes one or more decimal digits. These values must start at **1**, and must be consecutive. Note that if you don't give ordinals for all the exported names, you can get strange behaviour, with functions not being assigned to the ordinal you expect.

Exporting by ordinal number is now rather frowned upon, because of the risk of applications not running on other Win32 platforms.

If ordinals are present, the linker will generate the DLL and import library so that they use the ordinal number rather than the full symbol name. Using ordinals in a DLL can have several advantages:

▶ It saves space in the DLL if there are a lot of exported symbols

▶ It makes searching for symbols quicker than using symbol names

▶ It can make a DLL more secure, since it is more difficult to discover what a DLL is doing if it doesn't contain exported names

It does, however, leave you open to versioning problems, because you must be very careful not to change the order or position of the exported functions.

Exporting C++ Class Members

There's one complication when exporting C++ classes and class members. The linker definition file requires us to give exact names, so we have to find the full C++ names for the classes and functions we intend to export. C++ (unlike C) compilers generate symbols which include information about class membership, function arguments, return types and so on. The symbols generated are not really intended for human reading. They are messy and hence are often known as 'mangled names'.

You can get the names from the linker map file, where they'll appear in the 'Publics by Value' section. Here's a small sample from an actual map file, showing the sort of mangled names which are generated:

```
    Address          Publics by Value            Rva+Base    Lib:Object0001:00000000
 ??0Drive@Toolkit@@QAE@D@Z 10001000 f drive.obj0001:0000021a
 ?numDrives@DriveCollection@Toolkit@@SAFXZ 1000121a f drive.obj
 0001:00000281       ?hasDrive@DriveCollection@Toolkit@@SA_ND@Z 10001281 f drive.obj
 0001:000002b9       ?EnumDrives@DriveCollection@Toolkit@@QAEPBVDrive@2@XZ 100012b9 f
 drive.obj
 0001:00000420       ?getCurrentDir@FileSys@Toolkit@@SAXXZ 10001420 f drive.obj
 0001:00000430       ?setCurrentDir@FileSys@Toolkit@@SAXXZ 10001430 f drive.obj
 0001:00000440       ?getWindowsDir@FileSys@Toolkit@@SAXXZ 10001440 f drive.obj
 0001:00000450       ?getSystemDir@FileSys@Toolkit@@SAXXZ 10001450 f drive.obj
 0001:00000460       ??4FileSys@Toolkit@@QAEAAV01@ABV01@@Z 10001460 f drive.obj
```

So, if we wanted to export the **getSystemDir()** function which belongs to class **FileSys** in namespace **MyNamespace**, we'd have to specify the following line in the **EXPORTS** section of the linker definition file:

```
?getSystemDir@FileSys@MyNamespace@@SAXXZ
```

If you're going to want to call this function from a language other than C++, you may want to consider providing a C wrapper function, whose only job is to call the C++ function. You can then export the C function rather than the C++ function it wraps.

Using __declspec With Visual C++

A newer (and much more convenient) way to handle symbols in DLLs is by using the Visual C++ **__declspec** keyword to define DLL exports and imports.

__declspec is a Microsoft-specific keyword which is used to provide extra information to Visual C++. There are nine specifiers which can be used with __declspec, of which two are applicable to DLLs:

▶ dllexport, which declares a function, class or global data variable as being exported from a DLL

▶ dllimport, which declares a function, class or global data variable as being imported from a DLL

Supposing we have a function which we'd like to export from the DLL, so it can be called by clients:

```
void func()
{
    // do something here
}
```

This will be declared in a header file as:

```
void func();
```

We can make the function exportable by declaring it with the dllexport attribute:

```
void __declspec(dllexport) func();
```

And that's all we need to do. The linker will take care of the rest of the job, and will automatically generate an import library for you when the DLL is linked.

In the client, we want to use the function from the DLL. We do this by declaring a prototype with the dllimport attribute:

```
void __declspec(dllimport) func();
```

The linker recognizes this as an imported function, and will search the import libraries in order to resolve the reference.

Using The Preprocessor

The prototypes used when importing and exporting functions are very similar, and it is possible to use the preprocessor to allow you to use the same header file in both the DLL and its clients. The following code extract shows you how this is done:

```
#ifdef IN_DLL
#define DLL_DECL __declspec(dllexport)
#else
#define DLL_DECL __declspec(dllimport)
#endif
```

Place this at the top of the header file, and edit your function prototypes and class definitions to use the preprocessor symbol:

```
void DLL_DECL func();
class DLL_DECL fred { … };
```

When you include the header in DLL code, make sure that **IN_DLL** is defined, so that functions and classes are declared as exports. Clients won't define **IN_DLL**, so the relevant functions and classes will be declared as imports.

Try It Out — Creating A Simple DLL

We'll illustrate what we've been discussing so far by creating a simple DLL using Visual C++. Start by creating a new **Win32 Dynamic-Link Library** project, which will set up the compiler and linker flags correctly for building a DLL. I've called the project **testdll**, which will mean the resulting DLL will be called **testdll.dll**.

In this simple example, we're just going to add one function which prints a string, but even this minimal functionality will be enough to demonstrate how to build and use DLLs. Create a C++ header file, **testdll.h**, which we'll use to declare the DLL's exported function, so that it can be used in both the DLL and clients. Here's the code:

```
// testdll.h

#ifdef IN_DLL
#define DLL_DECL __declspec(dllexport)
#else
#define DLL_DECL __declspec(dllimport)
#endif

void DLL_DECL printString();
```

We're using the preprocessor technique we described above, so that the prototype will be usable within both the DLL and client code, depending on whether **IN_DLL** has been defined.

The function itself is defined in the DLL source code file:

```
// testdll.cpp

#include <windows.h>
#include <iostream>

using namespace std;

// Define IN_DLL so we make the function exportable
#define IN_DLL
#include "testdll.h"

void DLL_DECL printString()
{
  cout << "This is in the DLL" << endl;
}
```

That's the entire code for the DLL. We haven't provided a `DllMain()` function, so the compiler will do the necessary for us. Once we've built the project, we can look at the DLL to check that it has been built correctly, and there are two convenient ways to do this under NT. Firstly, if you have Visual C++ installed, you can use the dumpbin command line tool to list information about the DLL. This is what it looks like on my machine

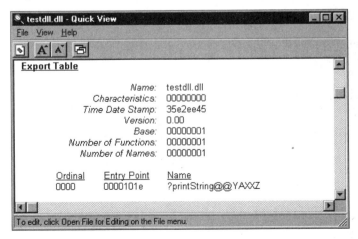

This shows us that the DLL exports one C++ style mangled name. A useful alternative to dumpbin is the QuickView program supplied with Windows 95 and NT, which gives you the ability to view many types of programs. If you run QuickView on the DLL, you get similar information to that provided by dumpbin:

Supposing we decide that having a C++ mangled name isn't a good idea, because we'd like to use it from a C program. We can include a **#pragma** which tells the linker to add another, alternative name for the entry point:

```
#include <windows.h>
#include <iostream>

using namespace std;

// Define IN_DLL so we make the function exportable
#define IN_DLL
#include "testdll.h"

#pragma comment(linker, "/export:printString=?printString@@YAXXZ")

void DLL_DECL printString()
{
  cout << "This is in the DLL" << endl;
}
```

The **#pragma** passes the **/export** option to the linker, telling it to add **printString** as an alias for the C++ mangled name. If you run the DLL through dumpbin, you'll see the alias:

```
        1 ordinal base
        2 number of functions
        2 number of names

  ordinal hint RVA        name
        1    0 0000101E ?printString@@YAXXZ
        2    1 0000101E printString
```

Using the **#pragma** adds another name, and can be awkward because you have to find the C++ mangled name in order to write the command. If you just wanted to export the alias instead of the C++ name, you can do it by using a linker definition file. Remove the **#pragma** line, then create a file **testdll.def** containing the following code:

```
LIBRARY "testdll"
EXPORTS
    printString
```

When the linker sees the export name **printString**, it recognizes that it is the unmangled name of the function and uses it instead of the mangled name, so you only end up with one symbol in the DLL.

> *Note that this will still work with a C++ client, because when the client program is linked, the linker arranges for the correct program to be called.*

Try It Out — Using The DLL

Now that we have a DLL, we'll go on to use it from a client program. Create a console application **DllTest**, and add a source file to it, which contains the following source code:

```
// DllTest.cpp

#include <windows.h>
#include <iostream>

using namespace std;

#include "testdll.h"

int main()
{
   cout << "In main" << endl;

   printString();

   cout << "Back in main" << endl;
   return 0;
}
```

Before building the project, you'll need to do the following:

1 Copy the header file, **testdll.h**, which is needed for the function prototype, into the project directory, or add the path to the **#include** directive above.

2 Add the import library, **testdll.lib**, to the list of libraries searched by the linker, which you do by adding it to the list of modules in the **Object/library modules** edit control on the 'Link' tab of the **Project | Settings...** dialog.

3 Copy **testdll.lib** to the project directory — it is needed so the linker can resolve the reference to the function

4 Finally, move the DLL itself, **testdll.dll**, into the project directory.

We include the header file in the code, but because we haven't defined **IN_DLL**, the function is declared as **__declspec(dllimport)**, which is just what we want.

Once you've done this, you can build and execute the project. It should execute correctly no matter which of the options you've used to export the function from the DLL. If you try running the code, this is what you should see:

Loading DLLs

There are two ways to load a DLL into memory — **implicit** and **explicit**.

Implicit Loading

Implicit loading (or 'load-time dynamic linking') means that the DLL is loaded into memory along with the client program. In order for this to work, you need to have linked with an import library, and the correct DLL needs to be present on the search path.

Implicit loading of a DLL only allocates the virtual memory required. The code isn't actually loaded from disk until it is needed, so there isn't a memory overhead in using implicit loading.

Explicit Loading

Explicit loading (also called 'run-time dynamic linking') means loading DLLs on demand at run-time, using the `LoadLibrary()` API call.

As you might expect, a client loading a DLL in this way doesn't need to be linked with an import library. If the DLL is already loaded, the call to `LoadLibrary()` simply increments the reference count. If it isn't loaded, the DLL will be loaded into memory, the reference count set to one, and its `DllMain()` function called with `dwReason` set to `DLL_PROCESS_ATTACH`.

Try It Out — Dynamically Loading The DLL

Let's see how to use `LoadLibrary()` to load a DLL and execute a function, by writing a program which will dynamically load our test DLL.

Here's the code, which you should put into a new console project:

```
// ExplicitLoad.cpp

#include <windows.h>
#include <iostream>
using namespace std;

int main()
{
    // Create a function prototype for the DLL function we want to call
    typedef void (*funcPtr)();
```

```
    // Load the library
    HINSTANCE hLib = LoadLibrary("TestDll");
    if (hLib == 0)
    {
        cout << "LoadLibrary failed (" << GetLastError() << ")" << endl;
      return -1;
    }

    // Get the address of the function
    funcPtr pFunc = reinterpret_cast<funcPtr>(GetProcAddress(hLib, "printString"));
    if (pFunc == NULL)
    {
        cout << "GetProcAddress failed (" << GetLastError() << ")" << endl;
      return -1;
    }

    // Execute the function
    pFunc();

    // Free the library
    FreeLibrary(hLib);

    return 0;
}
```

A call to **LoadLibrary()** is used to load the DLL into memory, if it isn't already there. If you don't give a file extension, **.dll** will be assumed. If successful, the function returns a handle to the DLL, otherwise it returns zero.

The **GetProcAddress()** function is used to obtain a pointer to a function exported by the DLL. The name must be given exactly as it was exported, and if the call is successful, a function pointer will be returned. If you want to use a function which has been exported by ordinal number, use the **MAKEINTRESOURCE()** macro, like this:

```
    // Get the function with ordinal 1
    funcPtr pFunc = reinterpret_cast<funcPtr>GetProcAddress(hLib, MAKEINTRESOURCE(1));
```

If you're looking for a C++ function which doesn't have an alias, you'll need to use the mangled name, like this:

```
    funcPtr pFunc = reinterpret_cast<funcPtr>GetProcAddress(hLib,
    "?printString@@YAXXZ");
```

The function pointer returned to you can be used to execute the function; the pointer returned has the type **FARPROC**, and needs to be cast appropriately before use. If the call wasn't successful, you'll get a **NULL** pointer returned. Note the use of a **typedef** to make the declaration of the return type and the pointer cast simpler.

Once you have the pointer, you can use it to execute the function, and when you've finished with the library you should call **FreeLibrary()**, passing it the handle to the DLL. Calling **FreeLibrary()** will cause the reference count to be decremented, and the library will be unloaded if the count reaches zero. If you try running the program, you should see an output like the following:

Remember that you'll need to copy the DLL into your project directory.

This is typically the way in which things like device drivers work. Every printer driver has to implement a set of standard functions, so that an application can load a driver DLL, look for the standard functions and execute them.

Using Shared Memory With DLLs

Earlier in the chapter, we saw how under Windows NT, DLLs no longer have a single copy of global and static data, so it isn't possible to use that as a means to share memory among processes which load the same DLL.

In fact, it is possible to share memory between the processes using a DLL, if you use another feature of the linker definition file.

The **SECTIONS** keyword is used to set up memory sections within the executable being linked. A section is a piece of address space which is named, and which may have attributes assigned to it. Once you've created one or more sections, you can tell the linker which variables should be stored in which section.

The standard sections you'll find in an executable or DLL are shown in the table below:

Section	Contents
`.bss`	Uninitialized data
`.CRT`	Read-only C Runtime data
`.data`	Initialized data
`.debug`	Debug data
`.edata`	Exported names table
`.idata`	Imported names table
`.rdata`	Read-only runtime data
`.reloc`	Fixup table information
`.rsrc`	Resource data
`.text`	Application or DLL code
`.tls`	Thread local storage
`.xdata`	Exception handling data

In this case, we want to create a memory section which has the **SHARED** attribute. There is only one copy of each shared section, to which all clients have equal access. Here's how you'd set up a shared section in the linker definition file:

```
LIBRARY  "fred"

SECTIONS
        .share   READ WRITE SHARED
EXPORTS
        func1
        func2
```

We've set up a single shared section called '.share'. By convention, names of sections start with a period, but apart from that they can be anything you like.

You dictate which data items are to be stored in the shared section using the **data_seg** compiler **#pragma**, like this:

```
#pragma data_seg(".share")
int nSharedVal = 0;
#pragma data_seg()
```

The **nSharedVal** variable is stored in the shared segment, so that when this code is used in a DLL, every client will share the variable.

> *Note that you need to provide an initial value for the variable. If you don't, the variable will be placed in the default* **.bss** *section*

Try It Out — Using Shared Memory in DLLs

In order to show how shared memory is used in practice, we'll modify our simple DLL that we created at the start of this chapter so that it maintains a count of how many processes are attached to it. Every time the DLL is loaded by a process, the DLL will increment a counter. This has to be shared in order for it to be accessible across processes.

First, we want to add a function which will return the counter value to the client program, so add its prototype to the header file:

```
// TestDll2.h

#ifdef IN_DLL
#define DLL_DECL __declspec(dllexport)
#else
#define DLL_DECL __declspec(dllimport)
#endif

void DLL_DECL printString();
long DLL_DECL getCount();
```

The DLL source file needs several changes, including the addition of a **DllMain()** function:

```cpp
// TestDll2.cpp

#include <windows.h>
#include <iostream>

using namespace std;

// Define IN_DLL so we make the functions exportable
#define IN_DLL
#include "testdll2.h"

#pragma comment(linker, "/section:.share,RWS")

#pragma data_seg(".share")
long lCount = 0;
#pragma data_seg()

BOOL WINAPI DllMain(HINSTANCE hInst, DWORD dwReason, LPVOID pImp)
{
    switch(dwReason)
    {
    case DLL_PROCESS_ATTACH:
        InterlockedIncrement(&lCount);
        break;
    case DLL_PROCESS_DETACH:
        InterlockedDecrement(&lCount);
        break;
    case DLL_THREAD_ATTACH:
        break;
    case DLL_THREAD_DETACH:
        break;
    }

    return TRUE;
}

long DLL_DECL getCount()
{
    return lCount;
}

void DLL_DECL printString()
{
    cout << "This is in the DLL" << endl;
}
```

The first **#pragma** call tells the linker that the section called '**.share**' is going to have RWS (read, write and share) attributes. If you don't do this and specify the 'S' attribute, the section will be created but won't be shared. This allows you to set up the shared section without using the linker definition file.

The pair of **#pragma data_seg()** calls tell the linker that the initialized variable **lCount** is to be stored in section **.share**.

We now provide our own `DllMain()` function, so that we can adjust the counter when the DLL is attached to, or detached from, a process. Note that we're using the `InterlockedIncrement()` and `InterlockedDecrement()` functions to handle the counter, which give us protection against thread context switches occurring at an inappropriate time. See Chapter 6 for more information on these functions and their use. The last thing we add is an exported function, which will pass the value of the counter back to the client.

Rebuild the DLL and then examine it with `dumpbin  /exports`. You'll see the new section given in the list of segments at the end:

```
Summary
      8000  .data
      1000  .idata
      4000  .rdata
      3000  .reloc
      1000  .share
     28000  .text
```

We can then modify the client code to print out the DLL's counter:

```cpp
// DllTest2.cpp

#include <windows.h>
#include <iostream>

using namespace std;

#include "testdll2.h"

int main()
{
    cout << "In main" << endl;

    printString();

    cout << "DLL process counter is " << getCount() << endl;

    cout << "Back in main" << endl;

    // Pause the process...
    char c;
    cin >> c;

    return 0;
}
```

The changes we have made here are very straightforward. We have added a line to output the count maintained in shared memory of the DLL, and a line to pause the program. Because it pauses before exiting, you can run multiple copies in separate console windows, and verify that the counter is incremented as you would expect:

Creating A Resource-Only DLL

A DLL can be used simply to hold resources, such as bitmaps, icons, strings and even fonts. Packaging them in a DLL provides a simple way to share resources between applications. It is also useful when you need different national language versions of the same application, such as American and British English, German, French and so on.

To create a resource-only DLL, start by creating a non-MFC DLL project in AppWizard. Then create a new resource script file, save it as a **.rc** file, and add it to the DLL project, using the Project | Add To Project | Files... menu item. You can then add resources to the project in the normal way, using Visual C++'s resource and dialog editors.

Create a C++ source file, add it to the project, and define a minimal DLL initialization function:

```
#include <windows.h>

extern "C"
BOOL WINAPI DllMain( HINSTANCE hInstance, DWORD dwReason, LPVOID )
{
    return TRUE;
}
```

We include this function because all resource-only DLLs (except font DLLs) need to have at least one code segment. Including a dummy **DllMain()** function is a simple way to provide it. You can now build the DLL, which will contain the resources you wish to share.

> *Note that if you don't supply a **DllMain()** function, Visual C++ will provide a dummy one for you. Other compilers may require you to provide it.*

A client which wants to use the DLL needs to load it dynamically using **LoadLibrary()**, and then use the API functions which deal with finding and loading resources, such as **LoadResource()**, **LoadBitmap()** and **LoadIcon()**.

Summary

Dynamic link libraries are one of the fundamental units of application structure in Windows, and we've seen in this chapter how they work and how to build and use them. DLLs provide a powerful mechanism for making applications modular, and for providing parts of applications as language-independent components, which if necessary can be loaded at run-time. The modularity provided by DLLs has many advantages, but can also lead to problems due to the way in which DLLs are named and located.

Working With The Registry

The **system registry** (usually known simply as 'the registry') is a database which holds all the hardware, software and user configurations for a Windows NT system. Knowing what the registry is and how to manipulate it is becoming increasingly important in Win32 programming.

> *Both Windows NT and 95 use the registry in much the same way. There are, however, some differences between them in the way that some functions operate, and these have been marked out in boxes similar to this.*

Before You Start

It is extremely important to ensure that the registry is properly backed up, because if anything happens to it, your machine can be rendered useless. There are several ways to back up the registry:

▶ If you've got a tape backup device on your machine, the Windows NT backup utility (**ntbackup.exe**) will backup the registry.

▶ The Emergency Repair Disk holds a copy of part of the registry, but you need to regenerate it whenever you've added or removed hardware or software. This disk can be created when you install Windows NT, and can also be regenerated by running the Repair Disk utility (**rdisk.exe**).

▶ The registry editor (**regedit.exe**) can be used to save and restore parts (or even the whole) of the registry.

What Does The Registry Contain?

The registry contains all the hardware, software and user settings for the machine, including:

▶ Application configuration data, which used (in the old 16-bit Windows days) to be stored in application INI files

▶ Hardware configuration data

▶ Device driver configuration data

▶ Network protocols and adapter card settings

▶ Standard system INI file settings, such as those stored in **win.ini** and **autoexec.bat**.

▶ Dynamic information about system performance — although not strictly stored in the registry files, it is viewed via the same interface

Here are a few specific examples:

▶ The registry stores file extension associations, RPC name server information and security information

▶ All OLE and ActiveX information is held there

▶ It stores user profile data, settings for each user account on the machine

▶ It supports networks, can keep user profiles centrally and download the information when a user logs on — administrators can also access registries on remote machines

Registry support across networks is one of the essential things needed to make distributed application technologies, such as Remote Data Objects and DCOM, work easily and effectively.

What Uses The Registry?

Many user and system programs depend upon the registry for their correct operation. For instance, setup programs add information for new hardware and software to the registry, and can query the registry to see what components are already installed.

Administrative tools use the registry to control security and access, and it is also heavily used to control the system hardware. The NT Hardware Recognizer (**ntdetect.exe**) places a list of the hardware it finds into the registry at startup, while device drivers load and store configuration data using the registry. The NT kernel places its version information into the registry at startup, and finds out which device drivers to load, based on the information the Recognizer has provided.

Registry Architecture

On both Windows NT and Windows 95, the registry is a hierarchical database (and before you start wondering, it is a proprietary database, so you cannot manipulate it from outside).

Internally, the registry is structured rather like a file system. There, you have directories which can contain files or other directories:

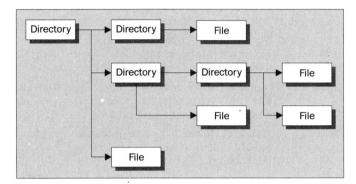

The registry has an equivalent structure of **keys**, which can contain **values** or other **subkeys**:

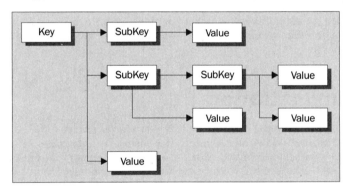

> *Note that a key doesn't have to have a subkey or value associated with it, in the same way that a directory doesn't have to contain subdirectories or files. Quite often the simple presence or absence of the key can be used as a flag.*

Continuing the analogy, it is common to refer to keys using a path-like syntax, with the key levels being separated by backslashes, e.g.

```
\Software\Microsoft\DevStudio\AddIns
```

At the top level of the registry we have six root keys, known as **hives**. If keys and values are analogous to directories and files, then hives can be thought of as analogous to logical drives.

Under Windows NT, the registry has six hives, as shown in the table below:

Hive Name	Content
HKEY_LOCAL_MACHINE	Holds hardware configurations, software information and network protocols for the machine on which this registry file lives.
HKEY_USERS	Holds security and settings information for all user accounts, including application-specific information. Because of security, you'll only be able to see information for your own account, and the default settings.
HKEY_CURRENT_USER	Holds the information for the currently logged in user. This is a link to the appropriate user entry in **HKEY_USERS**.
HKEY_CURRENT_CONFIG	A link to the current hardware configuration entry in **HKEY_LOCAL_MACHINE\Config**. This key only appears if there are multiple hardware configurations.
HKEY_CLASSES_ROOT	A shortcut to **HKEY_LOCAL_MACHINE\SOFTWARE\Classes**, this holds all file association, shell interface and COM/ActiveX information.
HKEY_DYN_DATA	Stores hardware data for each component of the system, and performance data for the system as a whole.

The **HKEY_CURRENT_USER** holds information for the logged-in user, so it makes it easy to retrieve or set data for the current user. You don't have to trawl through the **HKEY_USERS** hive looking for information.

Registry Administration

This section briefly discusses the ways in which you can administer the registry manually. Although we're concerned with programming, it is useful to introduce these topics here since you will often find yourself needing to inspect or edit the registry in the course of software development — **COM** and **ActiveX** make extensive use of the registry.

> *A word to the wise — if you need to modify the registry, do as much as you can using safe methods, such as the Control Panel applets and System Admin Tools! Editing the registry by hand can be a risky business if you're not completely sure of what you're doing, especially since the Microsoft registry editors do not possess an 'undo' function. It is quite possible to leave yourself with an unusable machine as a result of careless editing.*

Editing The Registry By Hand

Windows gives you two tools which you can use for editing the registry:

- `regedit.exe` is the newer of the two editors, and was introduced for Win95
- `regedt32.exe` is an older version, still available on NT 4.0

We'll confine ourselves to using the first of these, which is from now on referred to as 'RegEdit'. This gives you the ability to:

▶ Browse the registry hives

▶ Search for keys and values

▶ Add, delete, edit and rename keys and values

▶ Save registry trees out to disk, and read them back

If you start up the editor, usually by using the Run... command from the Start menu, you'll get a display like this, showing the six hives for the local machine:

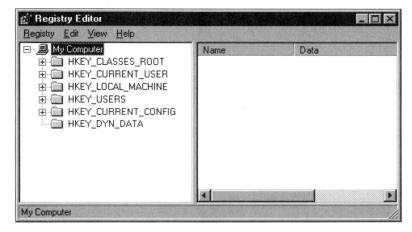

The screen layout looks rather like Explorer, and it works in much the same way, with the status bar at the bottom showing the 'path' to the currently selected key. Click on a hive or key name to expand the tree. The expanded tree will be shown in the left pane, and any values associated with the current key in the right pane, like this:

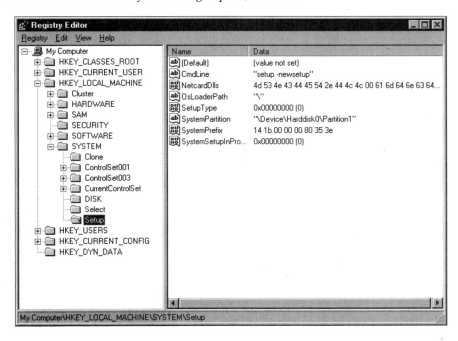

65

The screenshot above shows the eight values associated with the key `My Computer\HKEY_LOCAL_MACHINE\SYSTEM\Setup`. The icon next to each of the value names shows the type of data this value holds: in this case four character strings and four hexadecimal integers.

Editing Entries

To edit an entry, double-click on its name to bring up an editing dialog:

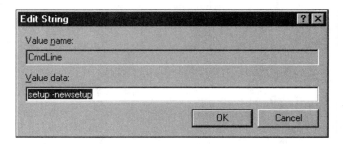

You can now enter the new data and press OK to save it.

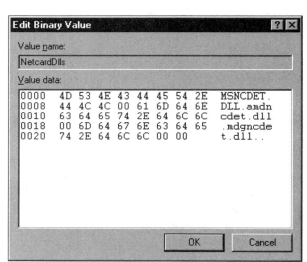

Note that the dialog reflects the type of data represented by the value, so that if you're editing binary data, you will get a different editing dialog:

Editing like this is easy, but also very risky, because there's no undo in the editor — all changes that you make are 'live', and are written to the database as they are made.

Adding, Deleting and Renaming Entries

The Edit menu will let you add, delete and rename values and subkeys. New subkeys and values can be added to the currently selected item in the tree. RegEdit is rather limited, in that it will only let you add string, binary or DWORD values. If you're manipulating the registry from a program, there are quite a few more data types you can use.

Subkeys and values can be deleted using the delete key, and renamed using Edit | Rename. You might not get a confirmation dialog box when deleting, so be careful not to make a mistake.

Registry Scripts

The Export Registry File... and Import Registry File... entries on the Registry menu give you the ability to save a branch of the registry hierarchy out to a disk file, and also to read one of these files and incorporate its information back into the registry. RegEdit also allows you to import and export registry files from the command line.

As an example, suppose we choose the **My Computer\HKEY_LOCAL_MACHINE\SYSTEM\Setup** key which was shown above. Use the menu item to save the branch to a file:

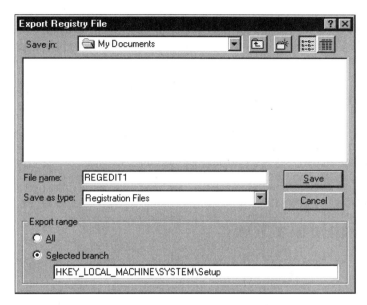

You can use the radio buttons to control whether you dump the entire registry tree, or only the selected branch. The data will be saved in a file of type **.reg**, in the format shown below:

```
REGEDIT4

[HKEY_LOCAL_MACHINE\SYSTEM\Setup]
"SetupType"=dword:00000000
"CmdLine"="setup -newsetup"
"SystemSetupInProgress"=dword:00000000
"SystemPrefix"=hex:14,1b,00,00,00,80,35,3e
"SystemPartition"="\\Device\\Harddisk0\\Partition1"
"OsLoaderPath"="\\"
"NetcardDlls"=hex(7):4d,53,4e,43,44,45,54,2e,44,4c,4c,00,61,6d,64,6e,63,64,65,\
  74,2e,64,6c,6c,00,6d,64,67,6e,63,64,65,74,2e,64,6c,6c,00,00
```

Registry files have some similarities to old-style Windows INI files, with keys in square brackets being followed by a list of value names and data. When a **.reg** file is imported, it creates or updates keys and values from the information supplied. Once again, changes cannot be undone. Note that double-clicking on a **.reg** file imports it.

Cleaning Out The Registry

Applications store their data in the registry, and nowadays it is considered polite for an application to remove its registry entries when it is uninstalled. You'll find that most applications should come with an **uninstall routine**, which will remove all traces of the application and clean up the registry, but there are times when you may need to go in and clean things up yourself. Over time, your registry will fill up with all sorts of information about applications, ActiveX controls and other items which are no longer present on the system.

It is possible to edit things by hand, but you risk (at best) missing something, or (at worst) removing something you shouldn't. A helper is available in the form of the `RegClean.exe` program, available from the Microsoft web site. RegClean will examine the registry, find all the entries relating to software which is no longer installed, and delete them for you. There were a few horror stories associated with older versions, but the latest one creates a registry script of all the changes it has made, so if it turns out that a mistake has been made, you can use the script to restore the registry to its original condition.

> *If you have access to the Microsoft Developer Network (MSDN), there is an alternative utility available called RegMaid, which comes complete with C++ source code. Also, Matt Pietrek presented a tool called CleanReg in the September 1996 edition of Microsoft Systems Journal.*

Registry Manipulation

Let's move on to see how we can manipulate the registry from within a program, using Win32 API functions.

There are quite a number of registry functions, but unless you're writing a registry browser or editor, you would typically want to carry out only the following simple operations:

- Browse, search for and read keys and values
- Create new keys and values
- Edit keys and values

In the following sections, we'll find out how to do these tasks, and also see how the housekeeping can be made a lot simpler by writing a C++ class to do a lot of the work for us.

Opening The Registry

You don't need to open or load the registry on the local machine, but if you want to access registry information on another machine (and have the security access to do so), you can use `RegConnectRegistry()`:

```
LONG  RegConnectRegistry(
    LPTSTR  pMachine,            // name of  machine
    HKEY  hKey,                  // key  to  open
    PHKEY  hResultKey);          // key  handle
```

If the first parameter is **NULL**, then the function accesses the registry on the local machine. The second parameter specifies the top-level key, that is the hive, to be opened. This parameter can only currently be either **HKEY_LOCAL_MACHINE** or **HKEY_USERS**, and any other value will cause the call to fail. The third parameter holds the **HKEY** returned from the function, which is used to access the remote registry.

Creating A Class For Registry Operations

In a normal program, there are relatively few occasions when we would want to access the registry. However, whenever such action is required, there is quite a lot of housekeeping to do, such as keeping track of keys and closing them when they are no longer needed. Since the registry is a hierarchical structure, we often want to walk this structure in some way, either looking for a particular key or value, or enumerating a series of keys and subkeys.

Our **Registry** class will not only bind together the registry API calls and do some housekeeping for us, but will also hold state information, so that we can easily move around the registry without having to keep track of where we are.

We will take a few shortcuts, in that we will assume we're working on the local registry, and we won't concern ourselves with security at all, but if these are important to you, they will be easy to add.

The Registry Class

Here is the full definition of the class, which should be typed into a header file called **registry.h**. We'll briefly run through the structure, and then discuss each member in more detail as we cover the relevant API functions:

```
//registry.h

#ifndef REGISTRY_H
#define REGISTRY_H

// Size of string buffers used in the class
#define REG_BUFF_SIZE 255

class Registry
{
    HKEY hkHive;      // hive we're using
    HKEY hkKey;       // current key

    TCHAR fullKeyName[REG_BUFF_SIZE+1];    // full path to key
    TCHAR className[REG_BUFF_SIZE+1];      // class name for key
    LPTSTR pKeyName;                       // buffer used in enumerating keys
    LPTSTR pValueName;                     // buffer used in enumerating values

    int nKeyIndex;      // subkey enumeration index
    int nValIndex;      // value enumeration index

    // QueryInfo data
    DWORD numSubkeys;
    DWORD maxSubkeyLength;
    DWORD maxClassLength;
    DWORD numValues;
    DWORD maxValueNameLength;
```

```
      DWORD maxValueDataLength;
      DWORD SDLength;
      FILETIME lastWriteTime;

      void setHiveName();
      bool checkHiveName(LPCTSTR t, HKEY* pHive);
      bool queryInfo();

  public:
      Registry();
      ~Registry();

      // Return the string representing the path to the current key
      LPCTSTR getKeyPath() { return fullKeyName; }

      // Open a hive
      bool openHive(HKEY hk=HKEY_LOCAL_MACHINE);

      // Open a subkey relative to the current one
      bool openKeyRel(LPCTSTR pKey);

      // Open a key from an absolute path
      bool openKeyAbs(LPCTSTR pKey);

      // Move back up a level
      bool upOneLevel();

      // Create or open a subkey relative to the current one
      bool createKeyRel(LPCTSTR pKey, LPCTSTR pClass=NULL);

      // Create or open a key from an absolute path
      bool createKeyAbs(LPCTSTR pKey, LPTSTR pClass=NULL);

      // Enumerate subkeys
      LPCTSTR enumKeys(bool bReset=false);

      // Enumerate values
      LPCTSTR enumValues(LPDWORD pdwType, LPBYTE pData=NULL, LPDWORD pSize=NULL,
         bool bReset=false);

      // Get values
      bool getBinaryValue(LPCTSTR pName, LPBYTE pData, LPDWORD pSize);
      bool getDWordValue(LPCTSTR pName, LPDWORD pData);
      bool getStringValue(LPCTSTR pName, LPTSTR pData, LPDWORD pSize);

      // Set values
      bool setBinaryValue(LPCTSTR pName, LPBYTE pData, DWORD dwSize);
      bool setDWordValue(LPCTSTR pName, DWORD dwData);
      bool setStringValue(LPCTSTR pName, LPTSTR pData, DWORD dwSize);

      // Delete keys and values
      bool deleteKey(LPCTSTR pName);
      bool deleteValue(LPCTSTR pName);

      // Get info on current key
      DWORD numberOfSubkeys() { return numSubkeys; }
      DWORD numberOfValues() { return numValues; }
      LPCTSTR getClassName() { return className; }
```

```
      // Saving and restoring keys
      bool saveKey(LPCTSTR pFile, HKEY hk = NULL);
      bool loadKey(LPCTSTR pSubkey, LPCTSTR pFile, HKEY hk);
};

#endif
```

First, let's see what data members we have. The class contains two **HKEY** data members, which identify the current hive and the currently open key. When a **Registry** object is created, these will be set to **NULL** in the constructor. The three strings are used to hold the full path to the current key (e.g. **HKEY_CLASSES_ROOT\Software**), the class name for the current key and a buffer for use when enumerating subkeys and values.

The two integers which follow are used to keep track of where we are when enumerating subkeys and values, and these are followed by a set of variables which hold the values returned by the **RegQueryInfoKey()** function.

The constructor for the class simply initializes data members. If you've downloaded the source code for this example, you can find this, together with the rest of the implementation of this class, in **registry.cpp**:

```
Registry::Registry()
{
   hkKey = NULL;
   hkHive = NULL;
   nKeyIndex = 0;
   nValIndex = 0;
   pKeyName = NULL;
   pValueName = NULL;
}
```

Now let's look at the member functions, starting with the three private ones. The **setHiveName()** function is used to copy the name of the current hive into the **fullKeyName** buffer:

```
void Registry::setHiveName()
{
   if (hkHive == HKEY_LOCAL_MACHINE)
     _tcscpy(fullKeyName, _T("HKEY_LOCAL_MACHINE"));
   else if (hkHive == HKEY_USERS)
     _tcscpy(fullKeyName, _T("HKEY_USERS"));
   else if (hkHive == HKEY_CURRENT_USER)
     _tcscpy(fullKeyName, _T("HKEY_CURRENT_USER"));
   else if (hkHive == HKEY_CLASSES_ROOT)
     _tcscpy(fullKeyName, _T("HKEY_CLASSES_ROOT"));
   else if (hkHive == HKEY_CURRENT_CONFIG)
     _tcscpy(fullKeyName, _T("HKEY_CURRENT_CONFIG"));
}
```

*Note the use of the portable character functions and macros. By including **<tchar.h>** and using **_tcscpy()** and **_T()**, we ensure that the code can be compiled to use either ANSI or Unicode. See Chapter 5 for more details of the ANSI and Unicode character sets.*

checkHiveName() does the reverse, checking a string to see if it represents one of the top-level hives, and if so, returning the appropriate key:

```
bool Registry::checkHiveName(LPCTSTR t, HKEY* pHive)
{
    bool bOK = true;
    *pHive = NULL;

    if (!_tcscmp(t, "HKEY_CLASSES_ROOT"))
        *pHive = HKEY_CLASSES_ROOT;
    else if (!_tcscmp(t, "HKEY_LOCAL_MACHINE"))
        *pHive = HKEY_LOCAL_MACHINE;
    else if (!_tcscmp(t, "HKEY_USERS"))
        *pHive = HKEY_USERS;
    else if (!_tcscmp(t, "HKEY_CURRENT_USER"))
        *pHive = HKEY_CURRENT_USER;
    else if (!_tcscmp(t, "HKEY_CURRENT_CONFIG"))
        *pHive = HKEY_CURRENT_CONFIG;
    else
        bOK = false;

    return bOK;
}
```

The third function, queryInfo(), is used to retrieve information about the currently open key, and we'll discuss this next.

Querying Key Data

You can find out information about a key using the RegQueryInfoKey() function:

```
LONG  RegQueryInfoKey(
    HKEY  hKey,               // key under which the new one is to be
                             // created
    LPTSTR  pClass,           // class name
    LPDWORD  pSize,           // class name buffer size
    LPDWORD  dwReserved,      //
    LPDWORD  dwNumKeys,       // number of subkeys
    LPDWORD  dwMaxSubkeyLen,  // length of longest subkey
    LPDWORD  dwMaxClsLen,     // length of longest class name
    LPDWORD  dwNumValues,     // number of values
    LPDWORD  dwMaxValLen,     // length of longest value name
    LPDWORD  dwMaxDataLen,    // length of longest value data buffer
    LPDWORD  dwSecDescLen,    // length of security descriptor information
    PFILETIME  pLastWrite);   // time of last write
```

This data is especially useful when you want to know the class name for the key, and how many subkeys and values it has. The length fields can help you allocate buffers of the right size when retrieving information from the key.

We'll add some of this information to our Registry class, as it will be useful to us when we come to enumerate over subkeys and values. The class declaration already includes data members for most of the values returned from the function:

```
// QueryInfo data
DWORD numSubkeys;
DWORD maxSubkeyLength;.
DWORD maxClassLength;
DWORD numValues;
DWORD maxValueNameLength;
DWORD maxValueDataLength;
DWORD SDLength;
FILETIME lastWriteTime;
```

The private member function **queryInfo()** maintains these members, and we call it every time we open a new key:

```
bool Registry::queryInfo()
{
    TCHAR tc[REG_BUFF_SIZE+1];
    DWORD bufsize = sizeof tc;

    LONG err = RegQueryInfoKey(hkKey, tc, &bufsize,
                static_cast<LPDWORD>(NULL), &numSubkeys, &maxSubkeyLength,
                &maxClassLength, &numValues,
                &maxValueNameLength, &maxValueDataLength,
                &SDLength, &lastWriteTime);

    if (err == ERROR_SUCCESS)
    {
        _tcscpy(className, tc);    // save class name away
        SetLastError(ERROR_SUCCESS);
        return true;
    }
    else
    {
        SetLastError(err);
        return false;
    }
}
```

Some of these values will be useful to users of the class, so we provide some inline member functions to return them:

```
// Get info on current key
DWORD numberOfSubkeys() { return numSubkeys; }
DWORD numberOfValues() { return numValues; }
LPCTSTR getClassName() { return className; }
```

Creating A Key

Let's have a look now at how to create registry keys. As we saw earlier, a registry key can have zero or more associated values and/or subkeys. A key without a value can be used as a flag.

Where To Save Information

You can save stuff anywhere in the registry that you like, but there are some guidelines. Application information is normally stored in the **HKEY_LOCAL_MACHINE** hive under the **Software** key. It is common to create subkeys of the form:

```
HKEY_LOCAL_MACHINE\Software\<Organisation>\<Package>\<Version>\...
```

Examples might include:

```
HKEY_LOCAL_MACHINE\Software\Microsoft\DevStudio\5.0\
HKEY_LOCAL_MACHINE\Software\Stingray Software\Visual Case\1.0\
```

Below this level, subkeys will be entirely application specific. Note that key names can contain spaces.

Information specific to a particular user, such as application layout preferences, should be stored under **HKEY_CURRENT_USER**. This will ensure that the right set of user-specific application settings will be loaded. Good examples of the sort of thing stored here are the settings a user has made using the Control Panel. There are, for instance, a whole lot of values which are associated with the **Colors** key:

```
HKEY_CURRENT_USER\Control Panel\Colors\ButtonFace
HKEY_CURRENT_USER\Control Panel\Colors\ButtonText
HKEY_CURRENT_USER\Control Panel\Colors\Hilight
```

If you look using the registry editor, you'll see that all the values are strings. On my machine, ButtonFace has the value "131 153 177", ButtonText has the value "0 0 0" and Hilight is "0 128 128". When they're used, the strings will be parsed to retrieve the red, green and blue values.

Using RegCreateKeyEx()

The **RegCreateKeyEx()** function is used to create a new key, or open an existing one. It should be used in preference to the older (and simpler) **RegCreateKey()** function, which is now only provided for backward compatibility with Windows 3.1. **RegCreateKeyEx()** is a fairly complex function, as you'll see from its prototype:

```
LONG  RegCreateKeyEx(
    HKEY hKey,                          // key under which the new one is to
                                        // be created
    LPCTSTR pSubkey,                    // name of new key
    DWORD  dwReserved,                  // reserved - use zero
    LPTSTR pClass,                      // name of the class of the key
    DWORD  dwFlags,                     // creation flags
    REGSAM sam,                         // security access for the key
    LPSECURITY_ATTRIBUTES pAttrib,      // security attributes
    PHKEY  pResult,                     // hkey of new subkey
    LPDWORD pDisp);                     // disposition
```

The return value from the function will be **ERROR_SUCCESS** if the call worked.

The first parameter is the handle for the key under which you want to create or open a subkey. This parameter is often an **HKEY** representing one of the hives, such as **HKEY_CLASSES_ROOT**.

The second parameter is the name of the subkey you want to create. What if you want to create a key under **HKEY_LOCAL_MACHINE\Software**? Well, you've got two options.

The more long-winded of the two is to specify the **HKEY** as **HKEY_LOCAL_MACHINE** and the subkey to be "**Software**" to get the key of **HKEY_LOCAL_MACHINE\Software**. You can then use this key in another call to **RegCreateKeyEx()** to create the new key.

It is simpler to do it all in one, giving **HKEY_LOCAL_MACHINE** as the **HKEY**, and "**Software\MyKey**" as they new key, since the routine is intelligent enough to parse the name and figure out which parts of the tree already exist.

The third parameter is unused, and must be **NULL**. Parameter four is the **class name** for the key, which identifies the type of registry key. It can be used if you want to group registry keys into types for some reason. This parameter can be a pointer to any string you like, or **NULL**, and is not often used. This value doesn't show up in registry editors like RegEdit, but can be retrieved using **RegQueryInfoKey()**.

Argument five is a flag which says how the key will be opened or created:

Option Flag	Description
REG_OPTION_BACKUP_RESTORE	(NT only) The access value is ignored, and the key is opened with sufficient access to allow it to be backed up or restored. This flag will be ignored when running under Windows 95.
REG_OPTION_NON_VOLATILE	The key data is saved on disk so it won't be lost on system restart.
REG_OPTION_VOLATILE	The key data is held in memory, so may be lost on restart.

The first value is probably one we won't use very often. It is there to allow programs that need to save and restore the registry to open existing keys with sufficient permission to be able to back them up, without needing to involve themselves with security. This is safe, because backing up the data making up a registry key is rather different from wanting to use the key.

You can create new keys with **REG_OPTION_VOLATILE** if you want them to be lost when the machine is switched off, or **REG_OPTION_NON_VOLATILE** if you want them to be saved to disk.

> **Note that** REG_OPTION_VOLATILE **is ignored by Windows 95, which creates a non-volatile key and does not signal an error. Windows 95 also ignores** REG_OPTION_BACKUP_RESTORE

The sixth and seventh parameters are to do with the security settings of the key, and we'll look at them shortly.

The eighth parameter is what we're ultimately interested in — the **HKEY** of the subkey that has been either created or opened. Lastly, we have the disposition argument, which is a pointer to a **DWORD**. This is set by the function to tell you whether the subkey was created (**REG_CREATED_NEW_KEY**) or whether a new one was opened (**REG_OPENED_EXISTING_KEY**).

Key Security (Windows NT only)

One big difference between storing data in INI files and in the registry is that registry entries can have full NT security access applied to them, which will control who can edit or even read them. (Note that NT security is discussed in more detail in Chapter 8.)

When using `RegCreateKeyEx()`, the sixth and seventh parameters control the key's security. The sixth parameter, of type `REGSAM`, is a security access parameter which can take combinations of the following values:

Security Flag	Description
KEY_ALL_ACCESS	Combination of KEY_QUERY_VALUE, KEY_CREATE_SUB_KEY, KEY_CREATE_LINK, KEY_ENUMERATE_SUB_KEYS, KEY_NOTIFY and KEY_SET_VALUE
KEY_CREATE_LINK	Allow creation of symbolic links to other subkeys
KEY_CREATE_SUB_KEY	Allow creation of subkeys
KEY_ENUMERATE_SUB_KEYS	Allow enumeration of subkeys
KEY_EXECUTE	Allows the key to be read
KEY_NOTIFY	Enables change notification (NT only)
KEY_QUERY_VALUE	Allows subkey values to be queried
KEY_READ	Combination of KEY_QUERY_VALUE, KEY_ENUMERATE_SUB_KEYS and KEY_NOTIFY
KEY_SET_VALUE	Allow subkey values to be written
KEY_WRITE	Combination of KEY_CREATE_SUB_KEY and KEY_SET_VALUE

Unless you have some special need to restrict access, you will tend to use **KEY_ALL_ACCESS** for this parameter.

The seventh is a normal NT security attributes structure, which is discussed in more detail in Chapter 8. This value can be specified as **NULL** if you want to have default security access.

Opening Existing Keys

`RegCreateKeyEx()` can be used to open an existing key, but if you just want to test for the existence of a key, you may not want to use it, since it will helpfully create the key for you if it doesn't already exist. Instead, you can use `RegOpenKeyEx()`, which will open an existing key, and so can be used as a test for the existence of a key.

```
LONG  RegOpenKeyEx(
      HKEY hKey,              // key under which the new one is to be
                             // created
      LPCTSTR pSubkey,       // name of new key
      DWORD dwReserved,      // reserved - use zero
      REGSAM sam,            // security access for the key
      PHKEY pResult);        // hkey of new subkey
```

Closing Keys

Once you've finished with a key, you should call `RegCloseKey()`, which closes the handle of a key, freeing up any resources which may have been used.

```
LONG  RegCloseKey(HKEY  hk);
```

The function returns `ERROR_SUCCESS` if it worked.

Note that closing a key doesn't necessarily result in data immediately being written to disk. Key data *is* normally written whenever a key is closed and before shutdown, but the buffering used means that some changes may not be written at once. If you want to ensure that changes are written immediately, you need to call `RegFlushKey()`:

```
LONG  RegFlushKey(HKEY  hk);
```

Note that this is quite an expensive operation and uses system resources. It should only be used when you absolutely have to be sure that registry data is written to the disk at once.

Adding Key Creation And Opening Methods

Since our `Registry` class is going to keep track of the current key, we'll provide two ways to open and create keys. The two relative functions, `createKeyRel()` and `openKeyRel()`, take a subkey name which is relative to the current key, thus making it easy to navigate through the registry. We'll also provide a `upOneLevel()` function, which moves you one level back up through the hierarchy.

The absolute functions, `createKeyAbs()` and `openKeyAbs()`, take names which must be a full registry path. They close the current key and open or create a new one. Obviously, the first element of the name must be one of the top-level hives.

We don't need a key closing function in the class, as that will be done automatically when required. The first place we need to do it is in the class destructor:

```
Registry::~Registry()
{
    // Close registry keys
    if (hkKey != NULL)
        RegCloseKey(hkKey);
    if (hkHive != NULL)
        RegCloseKey(hkHive);

    // Delete enumeration buffers if any have been assigned
    delete pKeyName;
    delete pValueName;
}
```

The openKeyRel() Function

The first function we'll implement is the one to open an existing key that is a subkey of the one we currently have open:

```
bool Registry::openKeyRel(LPCTSTR pSubKey)
{
    // Open a subkey relative to the current one
    // If we haven't got a key open, we can't open a subkey!
    if (hkKey == NULL)
    {
        SetLastError(ERROR_INVALID_PARAMETER);
        return false;
    }

    HKEY newKey;
    LONG err = RegOpenKeyEx(hkKey, pSubKey, NULL, KEY_ALL_ACCESS, &newKey);
    SetLastError(err);

    if (err == ERROR_SUCCESS)
    {
        // Close the old key and save the new one
        RegCloseKey(hkKey);
        hkKey = newKey;

        // Amend the path string
        _tcscat(fullKeyName, _T("\\"));
        _tcscat(fullKeyName, pSubKey);

        // Get key info
        queryInfo();
    }
    return err == ERROR_SUCCESS;
}
```

The function is, as you'd expect, basically a wrapper around the `RegOpenKeyEx()` function. The first thing it does is to check that we have a key open. If we don't, we cannot open a subkey relative to it! Note how we're returning errors here. The method adopted in this class is similar to that used by most Win32 API functions, in that we use a `bool` flag to show success or failure, and then set the Win32 error code using the `SetLastError()` API call.

We try to open the specified subkey. If successful, we then save the `HKEY` as the new current key (after closing the old one). We set the `fullKeyName` string to reflect the full path to the new key, and call `queryInfo()` to get information about the new key. If the open failed, we return the error code from `RegOpenKeyEx()`.

The createKeyRel() Function

The routine to create a key as a subkey of an existing one is very similar, the obvious difference being that we're calling `RegCreateKeyEx()` instead of `RegOpenKeyEx()`. The function can also take a second parameter, which is the class name for the new key:

```
bool Registry::createKeyRel(LPCTSTR pSubKey, LPCTSTR pClass)
{
    // Create or open a key relative to the current one
    // If we haven't got a key open, we can't open a subkey!
```

```
      if (hkKey == NULL)
      {
         SetLastError(ERROR_INVALID_PARAMETER);
         return false;
      }

      HKEY newKey;
      DWORD dwDisp;
      LONG err = RegCreateKeyEx(hkKey, pSubKey, NULL,
         const_cast<LPTSTR>(pClass),
         REG_OPTION_NON_VOLATILE,        // non-volatile
         KEY_ALL_ACCESS, NULL,           // all access, no security
         &newKey,
         &dwDisp);                       // disposition

      SetLastError(err);

      if (err == ERROR_SUCCESS)
      {
         // Close the old key and save the new one
         RegCloseKey(hkKey);
         hkKey = newKey;

         // Amend the path string
         _tcscat(fullKeyName, _T("\\"));
         _tcscat(fullKeyName, pSubKey);

         // Get key info
         queryInfo();
      }

      return err == ERROR_SUCCESS;
   }
```

The operation of this function is exactly the same as that of **openKeyRel()**, with the only difference being the call to **RegKeyCreateEx()**. We're assuming a reasonable default set of parameters, requesting all access, and not setting any security. We get the disposition value back from the call, but we can ignore it.

The upOneLevel() Function

We can use the two functions we've just written to move down the hierarchy. Here's one which will allow us to move back up a level:

```
bool Registry::upOneLevel()
{
   // Find the string between the hive and parent key
   LPTSTR pFirst = _tcschr(fullKeyName, '\\');
   LPTSTR pLast = _tcsrchr(fullKeyName, '\\');
   if (!pFirst || !pLast)
   {
      return false;
   }

   // If they're the same, then there's only one slash, so the parent
   // is the hive
```

```
        if (pFirst == pLast)
        {
            openHive(hkHive);
        }
        else
        {
            TCHAR t[REG_BUFF_SIZE+1];

            // Point to character after the first '\', and copy to buffer
            pFirst += 1;
            _tcscpy(t, pFirst);

            // Set the last '\' to null to terminate the path
            pLast = _tcsrchr(t, '\\');
            *pLast = '\0';

            // Close the old key
            HKEY newKey;
            LONG err = RegOpenKeyEx(hkHive, t, NULL, KEY_ALL_ACCESS, &newKey);
            SetLastError(err);

            if (err == ERROR_SUCCESS)
            {
                // Close the old key and save the new one
                RegCloseKey(hkKey);
                hkKey = newKey;

                // Amend the path string
                setHiveName();
                _tcscat(fullKeyName, _T("\\"));
                _tcscat(fullKeyName, t);

                // Get key info
                queryInfo();
                return true;
            }
            else
                return false;
        }
        return true;
}
```

There are various ways we could implement this. As usual, I've gone for a simple method, which involves parsing the pathname in order to find the parent level, and then opening this as a subkey of the current hive. We look for the first and last backslashes in the path string. If there aren't any, then we cannot back up, so we return.

If the pointers to the backslashes are the same, then we must only have two components to the path, in which case the parent is the current hive. We can open the hive as the current key using the **openHive()** function:

```
bool Registry::openHive(HKEY hk)
{
    HKEY newKey;
    long err = RegOpenKeyEx(hk, NULL, NULL, NULL, &newKey);
    SetLastError(err);
```

80

```
    if (err == ERROR_SUCCESS)
    {
        // Close anything already open
        if (hkKey != NULL)
            RegCloseKey(hkKey);
        if (hkHive != NULL)
            RegCloseKey(hkHive);

        // Save the new keys
        hkHive = hk;
        hkKey = newKey;

        // Put the hive name into the path string, and get key information
        setHiveName();
        queryInfo();
    }

    return err == ERROR_SUCCESS;
}
```

Back in the calling function, if we do have more than one backslash, then we need to extract the substring between the first and last backslashes, as this is the path to the parent key. We declare a temporary buffer, and copy the path to it, starting with the character after the first slash. We also set the last slash to a null, thus ending the string. All that is left to do is to use this new string to open the parent key, and then do the housekeeping to save the key details and amend the path.

The openKeyAbs() Function

The next function we'll implement opens an existing key given a full path. I've taken the decision that we can't open a top-level hive from this function, so that the path has to contain at least one backslash:

```
bool Registry::openKeyAbs(LPCTSTR pSubKey)
{
    // Open a key, given the full path
    // We need to crack the hive off the front, and check it first
    TCHAR t[REG_BUFF_SIZE+1];

    // Check the string passed in isn't too long
    if (_tcslen(pSubKey) > REG_BUFF_SIZE)
    {
        SetLastError(ERROR_INVALID_PARAMETER);
        return false;
    }

    _tcscpy(t, pSubKey);

    LPTSTR pFirst = _tcschr(t, '\\');
    if (!pFirst)
    {
        SetLastError(ERROR_INVALID_PARAMETER);
        return false;
    }

    *pFirst = '\0';
```

```
    // Check the hive name and save as the current hive if OK
    HKEY hive;

    if (!checkHiveName(t, &hive))
    {
        SetLastError(ERROR_INVALID_PARAMETER);
        return false;
    }
    else
        hkHive = hive;

    // Point to the character after the null as the subkey
    LPTSTR pSub = pFirst+1;

    HKEY newKey;
    LONG err = ::RegOpenKeyEx(hive, pSub, NULL, KEY_ALL_ACCESS, &newKey);
    SetLastError(err);

    if (err == ERROR_SUCCESS)
    {
        // Close the old key and save the new one
        RegCloseKey(hkKey);
        hkKey = newKey;

        // Amend the path string
        _tcscpy(fullKeyName, pSubKey);

        // Get key info
        queryInfo();
    }

    return err == ERROR_SUCCESS;
}
```

We copy the string into a temporary buffer, and then look for the first backslash, which we turn into a **NULL**. This segments the string into a hive part, and a subkey part. We pass the first part to **checkHiveName()**, and return if this fails. If it succeeds, we save the hive away. We can then open the key, and update the saved key and path variables.

The createKeyAbs() Function

The final function creates a new key from a path, and the logic is very similar to that of the other functions we've just shown:

```
bool Registry::createKeyAbs(LPCTSTR pSubKey, LPTSTR pClass)
{
    // Create or open a key from an absolute path
    // Open a key, given the full path
    // We need to crack the hive off the front, and check it first
    int nKeyLen = _tcslen(pSubKey);
    LPTSTR t = new TCHAR[nKeyLen + 1];
```

```cpp
   // Check the string passed in isn't too long
   if (_tcslen(pSubKey) > REG_BUFF_SIZE)
   {
      SetLastError(ERROR_INVALID_PARAMETER);
      return false;
   }

   _tcscpy(t, pSubKey);

   LPTSTR pFirst = _tcschr(t, '\\');
   if (!pFirst)
   {
      SetLastError(ERROR_INVALID_PARAMETER);
      return false;
   }

   *pFirst = '\0';

   // Check the hive name and save as the current hive if OK
   HKEY hive;

   if (!checkHiveName(t, &hive))
   {
      SetLastError(ERROR_INVALID_PARAMETER);
      return false;
   }
   else
      hkHive = hive;

   // Point to the character after the null as the subkey
   LPTSTR pSub = pFirst+1;

   HKEY newKey;
   DWORD dwDisp;
   LONG err = RegCreateKeyEx(hive, pSub, NULL, pClass,
      REG_OPTION_NON_VOLATILE,          // non-volatile
      KEY_ALL_ACCESS, NULL,             // all access, no security
      &newKey,
      &dwDisp);                         // disposition
   SetLastError(err);

   if (err == ERROR_SUCCESS)
   {
      // Close the old key and save the new one
      RegCloseKey(hkKey);
      hkKey = newKey;

      // Amend the path string
      _tcscpy(fullKeyName, pSubKey);

      // Get key info
      queryInfo();
   }

   return err == ERROR_SUCCESS;
}
```

Here's a short program to test out the functions we've provided so far. We'll create a key 'Wrox' under HKEY_CURRENT_USER\Software, and then create two subkeys called 'NTProg' and 'Index':

```cpp
//regtest.cpp

#include <windows.h>
#include <iostream>
using namespace std;

#include "registry.h"

int main()
{
   Registry r;

   // Create an absolute key
   if (!r.createKeyAbs("HKEY_CURRENT_USER\\Software\\Wrox"))
   {
      cout << "createKeyAbs failed (" << GetLastError() <<")" << endl;
      return -1;
   }
   else
      cout << "'Wrox' key created" << endl;

   // Create a relative subkey
   if (!r.createKeyRel("NTProg"))
   {
      cout << "createKeyRel failed (" << GetLastError() <<")" << endl;
      return -1;
   }
   else
      cout << "'NTProg' key created" << endl;

   // See where we are
   cout << "Current path: " << r.getKeyPath() << endl;

   // Move up one...
   if (!r.upOneLevel())
   {
      cout << "upOneLevel failed (" << GetLastError() <<")" << endl;
      return -1;
   }

   // See where we are
   cout << "Current path: " << r.getKeyPath() << endl;

   // Create another key under 'Wrox'
   if (!r.createKeyRel("Index"))
   {
      cout << "createKeyRel failed (" << GetLastError() <<")" << endl;
      return -1;
   }
   else
      cout << "'Index' key created" << endl;
```

```
    // See where we are
    cout << "Current path: " << r.getKeyPath() << endl;

    return 0;
}
```

After creating a **Registry** object, we use **createKeyAbs()** to create the new 'Wrox' key, and then use **createKeyRel()** to add the 'NTProg' key beneath it. When we've done this, we print out the current registry path to check that we are where we think we ought to be! Using **upOneLevel()** takes us back up to the 'Wrox' level, where another call to **createKeyRel()** adds the 'Index' key. When the program is run, you get output like this:

Checking the registry entries in regedit confirms that the new keys have been edited correctly:

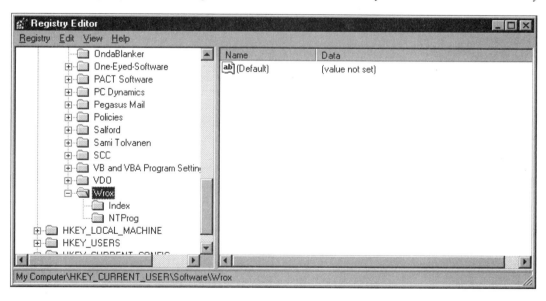

Working With Key Values

We've seen how to work with keys themselves; now, let's go on to examine how we can manipulate the values associated with keys, using the **RegQueryValueEx()** and **RegSetValueEx()** functions.

Registry Data Types

Before we actually look at these functions, we need to know the data types that can be used to create registry values. The two registry editors will between them allow you five types:

Value Type	Description
REG_BINARY	Binary data
REG_DWORD	A 32-bit value
REG_EXPAND_SZ	An environment variable reference, such as **%include%** (Regedt32 only)
REG_MULTI_SZ	An array of null-terminated strings (Regedt32 only)
REG_SZ	A null-terminated string

Note that string values can contain spaces, and such values don't have to be enclosed in quotes.

The **RegSetValueEx()** API function lets you create a further five types from within programs:

Value Type	Description
REG_DWORD_LITTLE_ENDIAN	Same as **REG_DWORD**
REG_DWORD_BIG_ENDIAN	A 32-bit value with the most-significant byte first
REG_LINK	A Unicode symbolic link
REG_NONE	Undefined
REG_RESOURCE_LIST	A resource list for a device driver

Querying And Setting Value Data

RegQueryValueEx() is used to retrieve the data and data type for a value associated with a given key:

```
LONG  RegQueryValueEx(
    HKEY  hKey,              // key under which the new one is to be
                            // created
    LPTSTR  pValue,          // name of value
    DWORD  dwReserved,       // reserved - use zero
    LPDWORD  pType,          // value type
    LPBYTE  pData,           // address of data buffer
    LPDWORD  pSize);         // size of data buffer
```

The value type returned will be one of the ten types we just listed. Listed below are a few points to note about the data buffer:

▶ The data is passed back as an array of bytes, so you'll need to convert it before you store or otherwise use it.

▶ The buffer size is given as a pointer to a **DWORD** variable. When the function returns, this variable holds the number of bytes copied into the buffer.

▶ If the buffer isn't large enough, **ERROR_MORE_DATA** is returned, and the size of buffer required is passed back in **pSize**.

▶ If you don't want the data, you can pass **NULL** for the last two parameters.

Values are set using the **RegSetValueEx()** function, which bears a certain resemblance to **RegQueryValueEx()**:

```
LONG  RegSetValueEx(
      HKEY hKey,              // key under which value is to be created
      LPCTSTR pValue,         // name of value
      DWORD dwReserved,       // reserved - use zero
      DWORD dwType,           // value type
      const BYTE* pData,      // address of data buffer
      DWORD dwSize);          // size of data buffer
```

If the value name is a null pointer, the data is added to the key itself, rather than to a named value. Note that value data is only limited by available memory, although for efficiency, the online documentation recommends that large amounts of data (greater than 2048 bytes) should be stored as files, and their names stored in the registry. In addition, items such as icons, bitmaps and fonts should be stored as files, rather than directly in the registry.

The fact that we have to pass data around as plain bytes plus a type means that getting and setting value data is very well suited to being represented by a series of C++ member functions. We'll implement the three most common types here. The relevant section from the class definition is shown below:

```
// Get values
bool getBinaryValue(LPCTSTR pName, LPBYTE pData, LPDWORD pSize);
bool getDWordValue(LPCTSTR pName, LPDWORD pData);
bool getStringValue(LPCTSTR pName, LPTSTR pData, LPDWORD pSize);

// Set values
bool setBinaryValue(LPCTSTR pName, LPBYTE pData, DWORD dwSize);
bool setDWordValue(LPCTSTR pName, DWORD dwData);
bool setStringValue(LPCTSTR pName, LPCTSTR pData, DWORD dwSize);
```

As usual with C++ class design, we have a trade-off between how much we hide the internals and do the housekeeping ourselves, and how much we make the client do. In this case we'll take a middle path, requiring the client to provide buffers for the data, but handling the conversion ourselves.

The **get...()** functions are pretty simple. Note that we don't bother with the value type, as we know what sort of data we should be retrieving. If you're implementing full error checking, you could check that the data is of the required sort:

```
bool Registry::getBinaryValue(LPCTSTR pName, LPBYTE pData, LPDWORD pSize)
{
   LONG err = RegQueryValueEx(hkKey, const_cast<LPTSTR<(pName), NULL, NULL,
      pData, pSize);
   SetLastError(err);
   return (err == ERROR_SUCCESS);
}
```

```
bool Registry::getDWordValue(LPCTSTR pName, LPDWORD pData)
{
   DWORD dwSize = sizeof(DWORD);
   LONG err = RegQueryValueEx(hkKey, const_cast<LPTSTR>(pName), NULL, NULL,
      reinterpret_cast<LPBYTE>(pData), &dwSize);
   SetLastError(err);
   return (err == ERROR_SUCCESS);
}

bool Registry::getStringValue(LPCTSTR pName, LPTSTR pData, LPDWORD pSize)
{
   LONG err = RegQueryValueEx(hkKey, const_cast<LPTSTR>(pName), NULL, NULL,
      reinterpret_cast<LPBYTE>(pData), pSize);
   SetLastError(err);
   return (err == ERROR_SUCCESS);
}
```

The **set...**() functions are similar, providing the data type and cast as necessary:

```
bool Registry::setDWordValue(LPCTSTR pName, DWORD dwData)
{
   LONG err = RegSetValueEx(hkKey, const_cast<LPTSTR>(pName), NULL, REG_DWORD,
      reinterpret_cast<const LPBYTE>(&dwData), sizeof(DWORD));
   SetLastError(err);
   return (err == ERROR_SUCCESS);
}

bool Registry::setStringValue(LPTSTR pName, LPCTSTR pData, DWORD dwSize)
{
   LONG err = RegSetValueEx(hkKey, const_cast<LPTSTR>(pName), NULL, REG_SZ,
      reinterpret_cast<LPBYTE>(pData), dwSize);
   SetLastError(err);
   return (err == ERROR_SUCCESS);
}

bool Registry::setBinaryValue(LPCTSTR pName, LPBYTE pData, DWORD dwSize)
{
   LONG err = RegSetValueEx(hkKey, pName, NULL, REG_BINARY, pData, dwSize);
   SetLastError(err);
   return (err == ERROR_SUCCESS);
}
```

Try It Out — Creating Key Values

We can now modify the test program to store values under the keys we create, like this:

```
//regtest2.cpp

#include <windows.h>
#include <iostream>
#include <tchar.h>
using namespace std;

#include "registry.h"
```

```
int main()
{
   Registry r;

   // Create an absolute key
   if (!r.createKeyAbs("HKEY_CURRENT_USER\\Software\\Wrox"))
   {
      cout << "createKeyAbs failed (" << GetLastError() <<")" << endl;
      return -1;
   }
   else
      cout << "'Wrox' key created" << endl;

   // Create a relative subkey
   if (!r.createKeyRel("NTProg"))
   {
      cout << "createKeyRel failed (" << GetLastError() <<")" << endl;
      return -1;
   }
   else
      cout << "'NTProg' key created" << endl;

   // See where we are
   cout << "Current path: " << r.getKeyPath() << endl;

   // Add a string value to the 'NTProg' key
   LPTSTR str = "Beginning NT Programming";
   if (!r.setStringValue("Title", str, _tcslen(str)+1))
   {
      cout << "setStringValue failed (" << GetLastError() <<")" << endl;
      return -1;
   }
   else
      cout << "'Title' value created" << endl;

   // Add a DWORD value to the 'NTProg' key
   if (!r.setDWordValue("FirstPage", 1))
   {
      cout << "setDWordValue failed (" << GetLastError() <<")" << endl;
      return -1;
   }
   else
      cout << "'FirstPage' value created" << endl;

   // Move up one...
   if (!r.upOneLevel())
   {
      cout << "upOneLevel failed (" << GetLastError() <<")" << endl;
      return -1;
   }

   // See where we are
   cout << "Current path: " << r.getKeyPath() << endl;

   // Create another key under 'Wrox'
   if (!r.createKeyRel("Index"))
   {
      cout << "createKeyRel failed (" << GetLastError() <<")" << endl;
```

```
            return -1;
        }
        else
            cout << "'Index' key created" << endl;

        // See where we are
        cout << "Current path: " << r.getKeyPath() << endl;

        return 0;
    }
```

We've used the **setStringValue()** and **setDWordValue()** functions to add a string and a numeric value under the 'NTProg' key. Note that the length given for the string value has to include the terminating null.

On running the program, the screen output will look like this:

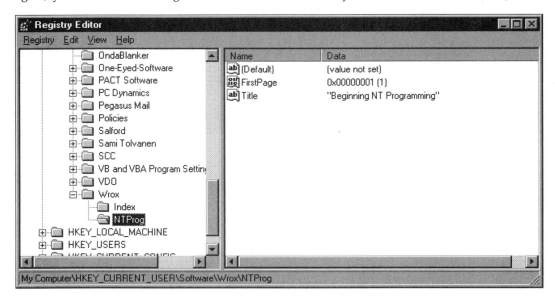

We can then check the new entries in RegEdit. (If you're running the program from scratch again, you'll have to use RegEdit to remove the 'Wrox' key so that it can be recreated.)

Retrieving Multiple Values

If you need to retrieve more than one value for a key, it is inefficient to use multiple calls to `RegQueryValueEx()`, so an API function, `RegQueryMultipleValues()`, has been provided for this purpose.

```
LONG  RegQueryMultipleValues(
      HKEY   hKey,            // key  to  query
      PVALENT  val_list,      // array  of  value  entry  structures
      DWORD  dwNum,           // number  of  items  in  array
      LPTSTR  pBuff,          // address  of  buffer  for  value  information
      LPDWORD  pSize);        // size  of  buffer
```

The function takes an array of **VALENT** structures:

```
typedef struct value_ent {
    LPTSTR ve_valuename;      // name of value to retrieve
    DWORD ve_valuelen;        // size of the data pointed to by ve_valueptr
    DWORD ve_valueptr;        // pointer to the data
    DWORD ve_type};           // value type, e.g. REG_SZ
```

In order to use the function, you declare an array of **VALENT** structures, and fill in the value name for each one. You also need to provide a buffer big enough to hold all the value data that will be returned. When the function executes, it finds each value and copies its data to the buffer, storing a pointer and length in the **VALENT** structures.

> *Note that the total amount of data returned by this function cannot exceed the system-imposed limit of one megabyte, in order to prevent excessive data transfer. If you exceed this limit, you'll get **ERROR_TRANSFER_TOO_LONG** returned by the function.*

Deleting Values

The `RegDeleteValue()` function will delete a value associated with a key:

```
LONG  RegDeleteValue(
      HKEY   hkey,            // handle  of  key
      LPCTSTR  pValue);       // name  of  value  to  delete
```

We can provide a simple member function to do this for us:

```
bool Registry::deleteValue(LPCTSTR pName)
{
    // Delete a value associated with a key
    LONG err = RegDeleteValue(hkKey, pName);

    SetLastError(err);
    return (err == ERROR_SUCCESS);
}
```

Enumerating Keys And Values

We've seen that `RegQueryInfoKey()` will tell us, among other things, how many subkeys and values are associated with a key, but how do you find out what they are? Two API functions are provided to help you.

The first, `RegEnumKeyEx()`, walks through the subkeys of a given key:

```
LONG  RegEnumKeyEx(
      HKEY hkey,                  // handle  of  key
      DWORD dwIndex,              // index  of  key  to  enumerate
      LPTSTR pName                // name  of  subkey
      LPDWORD pSize,              // size  of  buffer
      LPDWORD pReserved,          // reserved
      LPTSTR pClass,              // class  name
      LPDWORD pSize2,             // size  of  class  name  buffer
      PFILETIME pLastWrite);      // last  write  time
```

Given a zero-based index, this function will return you the name, class name and last write time of a subkey. If you don't want the class name, you can pass **NULL** for parameters six and seven. As usual, the number of characters written to each buffer are returned in the size parameters.

> *For this to work, the key must have been opened with **KEY_ENUMERATE_SUB_KEYS** access; this is included in the **KEY_ALL_ACCESS** access specifier, which we use to open keys in the Registry class.*

The name is a bit of a misnomer, as it doesn't enumerate the keys — you do! You initially call the function with an index of zero, and keep incrementing it until the function returns **ERROR_NO_MORE_ITEMS**. We can do much better by wrapping this in a member function, which itself keeps track of the next key to be returned, like this:

```
LPCTSTR Registry::enumKeys (bool bReset)
{
   // Enumerate all the subkeys for the current key, returning a
   // pointer to the name string. Return null when no more.

   if (bReset)
      nKeyIndex = 0;

   // Query the current key to find the maximum subkey size
   queryInfo();

   // Allocate a buffer to hold largest subkey name
   delete pKeyName;

   pKeyName = new TCHAR[maxSubkeyLength+1];
   DWORD bufsize = maxSubkeyLength+1;
   FILETIME lastWriteTime;

   // get the subkey info... don't worry about class name or file time
   LONG err = RegEnumKeyEx(hkKey, nKeyIndex++,
      pKeyName, &bufsize, NULL, NULL, NULL, &lastWriteTime);
   SetLastError(err);
```

```
      if (err == ERROR_SUCCESS)
         return pKeyName;
      else
         return NULL;
   }
```

The function uses an internal counter, **nKeyIndex**, to remember where it is. If you call the function with a **bool** value of **true**, it will reset this counter so you start again from the beginning. This simple version just returns the key name, so we don't retrieve the class name, and discard the last write time. The client just keeps on calling **enumKeys()**, and the function returns **NULL** when there aren't any more keys to retrieve.

The second API function, **RegEnumValue()**, does the same job for the values associated with a key:

```
   LONG  RegEnumValue(
         HKEY hkey,                   // handle of key
         DWORD dwIndex,               // index of key to enumerate
         LPTSTR pValName              // name of value
         LPDWORD pSize,               // size of buffer
         LPDWORD pReserved,           // reserved
         LPDWORD pType,               // value type
         LPBYTE pData,                // data buffer
         LPDWORD pDataSize);          // size of data buffer
```

As before, an index is used to specify which value you want, and the function will return **ERROR_NO_MORE_ITEMS** when you've run out. You can ignore the value type and data by passing **NULL** for the last three parameters.

*This function requires the key to have been opened with **KEY_QUERY_VALUE** permission; this is included in the **KEY_ALL_ACCESS** security which we use in the Registry class.*

Once again, we can provide a member function which will keep track of which values have been retrieved:

```
   LPCTSTR Registry::enumValues(LPDWORD pdwType, LPBYTE pData,
                                LPDWORD pSize, bool bReset)
   {
      // Enumerate all the values for the current key, returning a
      // pointer to the name string. Return null when no more.
      // We'll let the caller set up the buffer for the data, since
      // they presumably have some idea of what is there!

      if (bReset)
         nValIndex = 0;

   // Query the current key to find the maximum value size
      queryInfo();

      // Allocate a buffer to hold largest value name
      delete pValueName;

      pValueName = new TCHAR[maxValueNameLength +1];
```

93

```
        // get the value info...
        DWORD bufsize = maxValueNameLength+1;
        LONG err = RegEnumValue(hkKey, nValIndex++,
            pValueName, &bufsize, NULL, pdwType, pData, pSize);
        SetLastError(err);

        if (err == ERROR_SUCCESS)
            return pValueName;
        else
            return NULL;
    }
```

We'll get the caller to provide a data buffer, and we'll return them the type so that they know what to do with it.

Try It Out — Enumerating Keys and Values

Here's some example code which enumerates the keys and values that we've added to the registry:

```
//regtest3.cpp

#include <windows.h>
#include <iostream>
#include <tchar.h>
using namespace std;

#include "registry.h"

int main()
{
    Registry r;

    // Enumerate keys under 'Wrox' - first open the key
    if (!r.openKeyAbs("HKEY_CURRENT_USER\\Software\\Wrox"))
    {
        cout << "openKeyAbs failed (" << GetLastError() <<")" << endl;
        return -1;
    }
    else
        cout << "'Wrox' key opened, here are the subkeys:" << endl;

    // Now do the enumeration
    LPCTSTR pKey = NULL;
    while (1)
    {
        pKey = r.enumKeys();
        if (pKey == NULL) break;
            cout << pKey << endl;
    }

    // Now open the 'NTProg' subkey and enumerate its values
    if (!r.openKeyRel("NTProg"))
    {
        cout << "openKeyRel failed (" << GetLastError() <<")" << endl;
```

```
            return -1;
    }
    else
        cout << "'NTProg' key opened, here are the values:" << endl;

    LPCTSTR pVal = NULL;
    DWORD dwType;

    union UData
    {
        BYTE data[256];
        DWORD dwData[64];
    };

    UData u;
    DWORD dwSize = 256;

    while (1)
    {
        pVal = r.enumValues(&dwType, u.data, &dwSize);
        if (pVal == NULL)
            break;
            cout << pVal << " ";
        switch(dwType)
        {
        case REG_DWORD:
            cout << "is type REG_DWORD, ";
            cout << "value is '" << u.dwData[0] << "'";
            break;
        case REG_SZ:
            cout << "is type REG_SZ, ";
            cout << "value is '" << reinterpret_cast<LPTSTR>(u.data) << "'";
            break;
        default:
            cout << "<unknown>";
        }

        cout << endl;
    }

    return 0;
}
```

We first open the 'Wrox' key using **openKeyAbs()**, and check that it has worked. The loop calls **enumKeys()** and displays the string returned until the function returns a **NULL**.

The next step is to open the 'NTProg' subkey using **openKeyRel()**, and enumerate its values. The **RegEnumValue()** API call uses an array of bytes to return values, which we will need to convert to the right type before we can use them. When retrieving a string, we can simply cast the byte array to an **LPTSTR**, but **DWORD** values pose more of a problem. The solution we have adopted here is to make the byte array part of a union, so that we can treat the first four bytes as a **DWORD** when required.

The code loops around retrieving value names and data, until a **NULL** is returned for the name. When the data has been retrieved, we check the type, convert the data appropriately, and print it. Since we know what we're retrieving in this case, we haven't handled any types except **DWORD** and string.

```
"D:\TEMP\test\Debug\test.exe"
'Wrox' key opened, here are the subkeys:
Index
NTProg
'NTProg' key opened, here are the values:
Title is type REG_SZ, value is 'Beginning NT Programming'
FirstPage is type REG_DWORD, value is '1'
Press any key to continue_
```

Deleting Keys

The `RegDeleteKey()` function is used to delete keys:

```
LONG  RegDeleteKey(
    HKEY  hkey,                 // open key
    LPCTSTR  pName);            // name of subkey to delete
```

> *Note that this function works differently under Windows 95 and NT. In Windows NT, this function won't delete a key if it has subkeys, but in Windows 95 it will delete a key and all its subkeys.*

As we did for values, we can provide a member function to handle this:

```
bool Registry::deleteKey(LPCTSTR pName)
{
    // Delete a key and all its values
    // NOTE: on Win95 this will delete a key and all its subkeys.
    // On WinNT it will only delete a key without subkeys
    LONG err = RegDeleteKey(hkKey, pName);

    SetLastError(err);
    return err == ERROR_SUCCESS;
}
```

Saving And Restoring Key Data

`RegSaveKey()` will write the contents of a non-volatile key to a disk file:

```
LONG  RegSaveKey(
    HKEY  hk,                          // key to save
    LPCTSTR  pFile,                    // path for file to write to
    LPSECURITY_ATTRIBUTES  pSec);      // file security attributes
```

The key can be any open key, or one of the top-level hive **HKEY**s, such as **HKEY_CLASSES_ROOT**. If the key refers to a key on a remote machine, the file path is relative to the remote machine.

> *If using the FAT file system, you mustn't give a file extension or you will not be able to read the file using the RegLoadKey() or RegRestoreKey() functions.*

This is one of the registry API functions which behaves rather differently under Windows 95 and NT:

> ▶ If the file already exists, the return code is **ERROR_ALREADY_EXISTS** under NT, and **ERROR_REGISTRY_IO_FAILED** under Windows 95.

> ▶ If you don't give a path for the file, under NT it will be created in the current directory of the calling process, or in the System32 directory if it is a remote key. Under Win95, local and remote keys will be created in the Windows directory.

> ▶ The file will have the archive attribute set under NT, and the archive, hidden, system and read-only attributes under Win95.

> ▶ Under NT, the calling process must have **SE_BACKUP_NAME** privilege.

> ▶ The security attribute is ignored under Win95.

Although this function allows you to do the same sort of thing that RegEdit does with its import and export functions, there are actually major differences. When you save a key using **RegSaveKey()**, you don't save the entire path information — what you save is simply the information for the current key and its subkeys, with no idea of where in the tree it came from. In addition, the information will be written to the file as binary data, and not as a RegEdit-type script. If you want to write data in an ANSI format, like RegEdit, you'll have to implement the functionality yourself.

The data files produced by **RegSaveKey()** can be read using **RegLoadKey()**:

```
LONG  RegLoadKey(
      HKEY  hk,                    // key  under  which  to  restore
      LPCTSTR  pSubkey,            // name  of  new  key
      LPCTSTR  pFile);             // file  to  read
```

This will create a new subkey under the **HKEY** given, reading its data from the specified file.

The **RegRestoreKey()** function does a similar job, but in this case it will overwrite existing key values, and so can be used to restore a key to its original state:

```
LONG  RegRestoreKey(
      HKEY  hk,                    // key  where  restore  starts
      LPCTSTR  pFile               // file  to  read
      DWORD  dwFlags);             // option  flag
```

You pass this function a key and a filename, and it uses the data in the file to overwrite the key and all its subkeys. The only valid flag value is **REG_WHOLE_HIVE_VOLATILE**, which creates an entire hive in memory, so that it won't be permanently stored in the registry. If this is specified, the **HKEY** given must be **HKEY_USERS** or **HKEY_LOCAL_MACHINE**. You need to have the **SE_RESTORE_NAME** privilege in order to use this function.

You need to be careful when using this function, because the contents of the file will overwrite the existing structure under the key you specify, no matter what the name of the top-level key in the file might be. So if you accidentally give a file and key which don't match, you can end up with corrupted data being written to the registry.

> *The RegRestoreKey() function isn't available in Windows 95*

Adding Save And Load Functions To The Registry Class

Adding wrapper functions for the key saving and loading functions is easy enough, but it is slightly complicated by the need to ensure that the process has the correct rights. In order to simplify things, we'll use a helper function, `AdjustPrivilege()`, which we will develop and discuss further in Chapter 8 on security. You can see a full listing of the code there.

Let's deal with saving first. The function takes as arguments a filename, and an optional **HKEY**. If this is given, it specifies the key to save. If it isn't given, the current key is used. We use `AdjustPrivilege()` to set the **SE_BACKUP_NAME** privilege before saving, and exit if it can't be set:

```
bool Registry::saveKey(LPCTSTR pFile, HKEY hk)
{
   // Save a key to a file. If no key is specified, the current one
   // is saved

   if (!pFile)
   {
      SetLastError(ERROR_INVALID_PARAMETER);
      return false;
   }

   HKEY hkSave = (hk == NULL) ? hkKey : hk;

   // Adjust the privilege so we'll be able to save
   if (!AdjustPrivilege(SE_BACKUP_NAME, TRUE))
   {
      SetLastError(ERROR_PRIVILEGE_NOT_HELD);
      return false;
   }

   // This version ignores security. Do the save, then adjust the privilege back
   LONG err = RegSaveKey(hkSave, pFile, NULL);
   SetLastError(err);

   AdjustPrivilege(SE_BACKUP_NAME, FALSE);

   return err == ERROR_SUCCESS;
}
```

> *This example code assumes that the caller doesn't already have **SE_BACKUP_NAME** privilege. If they do, then the second call to **AdjustPrivilege()** will remove it, which probably isn't what you want to happen. The same caveat applies to the **loadKey()** function presented next. See the section 'Checking Privileges' in the Security chapter for information on how to check whether a client already has backup privilege.*

Loading is similar, except that we give the name for the new subkey which will be created. Once again, if a key isn't given, the current one is used:

```
bool Registry::loadKey(LPCTSTR pSubkey, LPCTSTR pFile, HKEY hk)
{
   // Load key data from a file. If hk is null, it will be created
   // under the current key

   if (!pFile || !pSubkey)
   {
      SetLastError(ERROR_INVALID_PARAMETER);
      return false;
   }

   HKEY hkLoad = (hk == NULL) ? hkKey : hk;

   // Adjust the privilege so we'll be able to load
   if (!AdjustPrivilege(SE_RESTORE_NAME, TRUE))
   {
      SetLastError(ERROR_PRIVILEGE_NOT_HELD);
      return false;
   }

   // This version ignores security. Do the load, then adjust the privilege back
   LONG err = RegLoadKey(hkLoad, pSubkey, pFile);
   SetLastError(err);

   AdjustPrivilege(SE_RESTORE_NAME, FALSE);

   return err == ERROR_SUCCESS;
}
```

Try It Out — Saving Registry Keys

Here's an example showing how we can save a key to a file:

```
//regtest4.cpp

#include <windows.h>
#include <iostream>
#include <tchar.h>
using namespace std;

#include "registry.h"

int main()
{
   Registry r;

   // Save 'Wrox' key - first open the key
   if (!r.openKeyAbs("HKEY_CURRENT_USER\\Software\\Wrox"))
   {
      cout << "openKeyAbs failed (" << GetLastError() <<")" << endl;
      return -1;
   }
   else
      cout << endl << "'Wrox' key reopened, saving..." << endl;
```

```
    if (r.saveKey("c:\\temp\\wrox"))
    {
        cout << "saveKey failed (" << GetLastError() <<")" << endl;
        return -1;
    }
    else
        cout << "'Wrox' key saved" << endl;

    return 0;
}
```

If you try building and running this code, you should see the following output:

Note that you'll need to be logged on to NT with Administrator privileges in order to run this code successfully.

Initialization Files

Finally, lets take a brief look at how the registry compares with the way system and application information was stored under earlier versions of Windows. Why is this of interest? Well, although applications you write should use the registry, you may well come across applications written for Windows 3.1, in which case they'll tend to use other mechanisms for storing their data. There are also a number of programs written for 32-bit Windows, which still use INI files rather than the registry.

Older, 16-bit versions of Windows didn't have the registry for storing information. Instead, ASCII data files, called **INI files** after their file extension, were used. Windows itself used two such files, **win.ini** and **system.ini**, intended to hold application and hardware/system information respectively. Applications sometimes added their data to **win.ini**, or created their own private INI file.

Windows NT supports the **autoexec.bat**, **config.sys** and INI files in order to be compatible with programs coming from DOS and Windows 3.x environments, although some programs written for 32-bit Windows still use INI files rather than the registry.

Microsoft now recommend that the registry is used to store application information rather than INI files, despite the fact that the MFC class library still uses INI files by default!

INI files had a structure rather similar to that of the files RegEdit produces when asked to export a key:

```
[section name]
key=value
```

Section names are enclosed in square brackets, and are followed by a list of key/value pairs. Here's a small section from an actual INI file on my machine:

```
[Recent File List]
File1=C:\TMP\ABC\PACIFIC.ABC
File2=C:\TMP\ABC\JIG1.ABC
File3=C:\TMP\ABC\HUCKLE.ABC
File4=C:\TMP\ABC\IRISH1.ABC

[Settings]
WinPos=0,1,-1,-1,-1,-1,22,22,600,454
SaveWindows=0

[Registered]
Name=
Company=
Number=
```

You write data to INI files using Win32 API functions, which are now only provided for backward compatibility:

▶ **WriteProfileString()** writes a single key/value pair to a named section in the **win.ini** file

▶ **WriteProfileSection()** replaces a complete section in the **win.ini** file

▶ **WritePrivateProfileString()** writes a single key/value pair to a named section in a private INI file

▶ **WritePrivateProfileSection()** replaces a complete section in a named INI file

Data is retrieved from INI files using an analogous set of functions:

▶ **GetProfileString()** gets the value associated with a key in a given section of **win.ini**

▶ **GetPrivateProfileString()** gets the value associated with a key in a given section of a private INI file

Although there are advantages to using plain-text INI files, in practice there are several severe problems associated with their use:

▶ They could be scattered anywhere over the disk, and there was no central organisation. Among other things, this made it very difficult to backup essential system and application data, as you weren't sure where all the data was.

▶ They were user-editable, with all the problems that implies.

▶ They were text-only, so it wasn't possible to store binary data.

▶ There was no notion of security applied to INI file entries.

However, sorting out a messed up INI file can be much easier than doing the same with a messed up registry, as many people have found to their cost!

Windows NT And INI Files

Although NT will support the use of INI files, it is possible to redirect the operation of the `Write/Get...()` functions, so that they use the registry rather than INI files. This means that older applications can be updated to use the registry without requiring any modification, as the redirection is done by the system. Note that no functions are provided to set this up — you'll have to do it yourself, using the information provided in the help system under the entries for the `WriteProfileString()` and `WritePrivateProfileString()` functions.

Mappings between INI files and registry keys are defined in the registry, under the `HKEY_LOCAL_MACHINE\Software\Microsoft\Windows NT\CurrentVersion\IniFileMapping` key. When an entry is made under this key, such as `...\IniFileMapping\MyProg.ini`, the Win32 Profile functions will write information which would have gone in this file to the registry. The keys and values below this key will then hold the sections and values from the INI file, or tell you where in the registry they are to be found.

On reading, if the data doesn't exist in the registry, the function will attempt to read it from the actual INI file instead.

Conclusions

In this chapter, we've seen what the Windows registry is, how it works and why it is important, and I hope that you now have a healthy respect for the registry, and some idea of the chaos that can result if it gets corrupted! It is very useful to have a centralized place where all system and application data can be stored, but not quite so useful that it can be edited (and possibly corrupted) quite so easily.

The Win32 API provides a full set of functions for manipulating the registry. We can work on both local and remote registries, if security allows, the latter feature being of particular interest to systems administrators.

Using the registry API functions requires quite a lot of housekeeping, and providing a C++ class to wrap the most common operations enables us to simplify a lot of what we need to do on a regular basis.

Error Handling In Windows NT

In this chapter, we are going to be looking at the comprehensive set of built-in error handling mechanisms provided by Win32. Use of the system error information and exception handling mechanisms gives us precise control over system error events. In particular, we'll be looking at:

▶ How to get hold of system error codes, and how to format and display the text corresponding to these codes.

▶ The Win32 Structured Exception Handling (SEH) mechanism — we'll see what this is, how it differs from C++ exception handling, and when to use one or the other.

▶ How to handle exceptions using filter functions, nested exceptions and how we go about raising exceptions.

▶ How to integrate the use of SEH with C++ exception handling so that we can manage SEH exceptions using C++ classes.

Everything discussed in this chapter is applicable to Windows 95 and Windows NT.

Getting System Error Information

It is inevitable that sometimes a system function is going to fail, and that you are going to need to find out what went wrong. Win32 has introduced a simple mechanism by which most of its API functions report errors. Every thread has a location within its Local Storage area where a Win32 function can store an error code. By looking at the contents of this location, you can retrieve the last error code that was set. Since there is only a single location, it will get overwritten by the next API function which executes, so you have to be careful to examine the error code (if you're interested) as soon as the function has executed.

> *Note that this is more properly thought of as a status code rather than an error code, because a value of zero means 'no error'.*

The Win32 API provides a function, `GetLastError()`, which allows you to retrieve this error code:

```
DWORD GetLastError();
```

The value returned by this function is a number, which corresponds to one of the system error codes listed in the online help, and defined in the `winerror.h` header file. As would be expected from an operating environment as complex as Win32, there are several hundred possible error codes. Just to give you a flavor, a small (and entirely arbitrary) selection of these codes is given in the table below:

Error Code	Name	Meaning
0	ERROR_SUCCESS	Nothing wrong!
2	ERROR_FILE_NOT_FOUND	The system cannot find the file specified
5	ERROR_ACCESS_DENIED	Access is denied
39	ERROR_HANDLE_DISK_FULL	The disk is full
111	ERROR_BUFFER_OVERFLOW	The filename is too long
487	ERROR_INVALID_ADDRESS	Attempt to access invalid address
1015	ERROR_REGISTRY_CORRUPT	The registry is corrupted
1151	ERROR_APP_WRONG_OS	The specified program is not a Windows or MSDOS program
1400	ERROR_INVALID_WINDOW_HANDLE	The window handle is invalid

Displaying Error Message Text

If you have an error code, how do you go about finding out the text that goes with it to explain its meaning? Well, if you're looking manually, you've got two options:

- Look in the online help
- Use the Error Lookup program supplied with Visual C++ (available from the Tools menu), which will display the text for any error number entered

To display the error message from within a program, you need to use the rather complex `FormatMessage()` function, which is used to build a message string from a message definition and optional inserts. Let's take a look at the function prototype:

```
DWORD FormatMessage(
    DWORD dwFlags,        // source and processing options
    LPCVOID lpSource,     // message source
    DWORD dwMsgID,        // requested message ID
    DWORD dwLangID,       // language identifier for requested message
    LPTSTR lpBuffer,      // pointer to message buffer
    DWORD nSize,          // size of message buffer
    va_list* pArgs);      // pointer to array of message inserts
```

*We won't go through all the possible arguments to this function in detail — if you want to
see how to use **FormatMessage()** in all its glory, consult the online documentation!*

This function allows you to specify a message definition which includes markers of the form
"%1", "%2" and so on (for instance, "Failed to open file %1), and also specify a list of
items, such as strings or integers, which can be plugged into the definition to create a formatted
message.

Although **FormatMessage()** is a general-purpose function, its attraction for us lies in the fact
that it can be used to retrieve and format the error text corresponding to system error codes.
This use of the function is illustrated in the following example:

```
DWORD dwLastErr = GetLastError();

if(dwLastErr != ERROR_SUCCESS)
{
    LPVOID lpMsgBuf;

    DWORD dwRet = FormatMessage(
        FORMAT_MESSAGE_ALLOCATE_BUFFER | FORMAT_MESSAGE_FROM_SYSTEM,
        NULL,
        dwLastErr,
        MAKELANGID(LANG_NEUTRAL, SUBLANG_DEFAULT), // Default language
        reinterpret_cast<LPTSTR>(&lpMsgBuf),
        0,
        NULL
    );

    // Display the string.
    MessageBox(NULL, reinterpret_cast<LPTSTR>(lpMsgBuf),
            "GetLastError", MB_OK|MB_ICONINFORMATION);

    // Free the buffer.
    LocalFree(lpMsgBuf);
}
```

In the above code, we use a combination of two flags as the first parameter:

- FORMAT_MESSAGE_ALLOCATE_BUFFER

- FORMAT_MESSAGE_FROM_SYSTEM

The first of these flags specifies that the function is to create a buffer to hold the error message,
which we will free via a call to **LocalFree()** when we've finished with it. In order to get at
the message buffer, we pass a **void*** pointer the **LocalFree()** function, which it will use to
return the buffer to us. We use the second flag, **FORMAT_MESSAGE_FROM_SYSTEM**, to tell the
function that we're formatting up a system error message, so that the function will search the
system error tables.

The second parameter is **NULL** because we're not supplying the message definition — it's coming
from the system tables. The third parameter is the message ID, which we'd obtained via a call
to **GetLastError()** at the start of the code example. The fourth parameter tells the function to
use the default language, and the fifth is the address of the **void*** pointer used to point to the

filled buffer. In this example, we've used the flag **FORMAT_MESSAGE_ALLOCATE_BUFFER**, so in this case, the sixth parameter is the *minimum* size of the buffer. If you're supplying your own buffer, then it represents the maximum size of the buffer, as you'd expect. The final parameter is **NULL**, as we're not interested in supplying any inserts.

*Note that if **FormatMessage()** fails, it return a system error code itself, so you can try using it again to see what went wrong with the previous call. This may not work, however, if the problem lay in your usage of the function.*

Try It Out — Creating A Message Display Function

We've just seen how to use the **FormatMessage()** function to display a system error message. We're going to do something similar here, but this time we'll use it as part of a routine for handling system errors. Here's the prototype:

```
void displayError(long lErr = -1);
```

Note that although error codes are **DWORD**s, we're using a **long** for the parameter. Because system error codes are always positive, we've chosen to use −1 as the default value. Remember that **DWORD**s are **unsigned longs**, though, so it isn't good practice to use them to try to pass negative numbers. Here's the code:

```
void displayError(long lErr)
{
    DWORD dwErr;
    if (lErr < 0)
        dwErr = GetLastError();
    else
        dwErr = (DWORD)lErr;

    LPVOID pb;

    DWORD dwRet = FormatMessage(
        FORMAT_MESSAGE_ALLOCATE_BUFFER | FORMAT_MESSAGE_FROM_SYSTEM,
        NULL,
        dwErr,
        MAKELANGID(LANG_NEUTRAL, SUBLANG_DEFAULT), // Default language
        reinterpret_cast<LPTSTR>(&pb),
        0,
        NULL);

    if (dwRet == 0)
        throw "Couldn't format error message";

    TCHAR title[80];
    wsprintf(title,"Error %d", dwErr);

    cerr << "Error " << err << ": " << reinterpret_cast<LPTSTR>(pb) << endl;

    LocalFree(pb);
    SetLastError(ERROR_SUCCESS);
}
```

The code is very similar to the example presented above, and there are only a few points to note. If no argument is given (or the argument is negative), then the last system error is displayed, using a call to the **GetLastError()** function. If a positive argument is given, however, it is taken as the number of the error to display. We then pass the error code to **FormatMessage()**. If the format command fails, we give up and throw an exception, otherwise we display the error number together with the error string. We've done this here by using **cerr**, but you could easily get the function to display a message box instead, using the line:

```
MessageBox(NULL, reinterpret_cast<LPTSTR>(pb), title, MB_OK | MB_ICONINFORMATION);
```

Finally, we clear the error by setting it to **ERROR_SUCCESS**, using a call to the Win32 API function **SetLastError()** (which we'll look at next).

If you want to see this function in action, you can try it out with the following test program:

```cpp
// DisplayError.cpp

#include <windows.h>
#include <iostream>

using namespace std;

void displayError(long lErr = -1)
{
    // Code for DiplayError() here
}

int main()
{
    // Declare dummy file name of non-existent file
    LPCTSTR myFile = "Dummy.dat";

    // Call CreateFile() to deliberately generate error
    HANDLE hFile;
    cout << "Calling CreateFile():" << endl;
    hFile = CreateFile(myFile,
              GENERIC_WRITE,
              0,
              NULL,
              OPEN_EXISTING,
              FILE_ATTRIBUTE_NORMAL,
              NULL);

    // Function returns INVALID_HANDLE_VALUE on failue
    if (hFile = INVALID_HANDLE_VALUE)
        displayError();
    else
        cout << "CreateFile() successful!" << endl;

    return 0;
}
```

Don't worry too much about the **CreateFile()** function at the moment — we'll be seeing a lot more of this in Chapter 7. All you need to know for now is that the **OPEN_EXISTING** parameter we have passed in means that the function is (unsurprisingly) looking to open a file that already exists. If we pass in the name of a non-existent file, we will therefore generate an error, which we can then format and display with our `displayError()` function. If you build and run this code, then you should see the following output:

```
"D:\BegNT\ch04Code\DisplayError\Debug\DisplayError.exe"
Calling CreateFile():
Error 2: The system cannot find the file specified.

Press any key to continue
```

Signalling Errors

The `SetLastError()` function will (not surprisingly) set the last error code for the calling thread. This means that you can use it to signal errors in your own programs, which can be retrieved with `GetLastError()` — provided, of course, that no other errors have occurred in the meantime!

```
void SetLastError(DWORD dwCode);
```

You can also, of course, use a call to `SetLastError()` to reset a code that the system stored once you've handled it. This can be useful because, whenever you get an actual error code back from `GetLastError()` (as opposed to `ERROR_SUCCESS`), you want to be sure that it hasn't already been handled. Resetting the error code to `ERROR_SUCCESS` will enable you to do this.

Try It Out — Formatting Your Own Errors

If you want to pass error codes around using `SetLastError()`, you'll need to provide an error text string, so that clients can use `FormatMessage()` to retrieve and print a suitable message.

In the next example, we're going to see how to use `FormatMessage()` to construct a string from a message definition and a couple of inserts:

```cpp
// FormatMessage.cpp

#include <windows.h>
#include <iostream>

using namespace std;

int main()
{
    // Here's the message definition string, with the '%1' and '%2' marking
    // the inserts
    TCHAR szMessage[] = "Unable to %1 file: %2";

    // And the filename
    TCHAR szFile[] = "fred.dat";

    // We'll fill in the operation later
    TCHAR szOperation[6];
    PVOID lpMsgBuf = 0;
```

```
    // Make up insert block. The final zero element marks the end of the
    // block, so we don't have to give a size
    LPTSTR pInserts[3];
    pInserts[0] = szOperation;
    pInserts[1] = szFile;
    pInserts[2] = 0;

    // Customise the message, depending on whether we're opening or saving
    lstrcpy(szOperation, "save");

    // Format up the message
    DWORD dwRet = FormatMessage(
        FORMAT_MESSAGE_ALLOCATE_BUFFER |        // system to allocate buffer
        FORMAT_MESSAGE_FROM_STRING |            // format from string provided
        FORMAT_MESSAGE_ARGUMENT_ARRAY,          // use insert array
        szMessage,                              // message definition
        0, 0,
        reinterpret_cast<LPTSTR>(&lpMsgBuf),    // buffer returned by call
        70,                                     // max. buffer size needed
        pInserts);                              // inserts array

    // Display the string.
    cout << reinterpret_cast<LPTSTR>(lpMsgBuf) << endl;

    // Free the buffer.
    LocalFree(lpMsgBuf);

    return 0;
}
```

If you load up this code in Visual C++, and build and run the example, you should see the following output:

What Is Structured Exception Handling?

Structured Exception Handling, usually known as **SEH**, is a mechanism provided by the Win32 API to handle system-level errors. Although it is similar in concept to C++'s built-in exception handling, the way in which you use it is rather different.

Both use similar mechanisms, and it is possible to integrate them (as we'll see later), but they're designed to report on different problems.

111

How Does SEH Differ From The C++ Exception Mechanism?

SEH is a mechanism which the operating system uses for reporting low-level problems such as memory access violations, stack overflows, divides by zero and so on. C++ exceptions, on the other hand, are part of the C++ language, and are designed to report on problems in application code.

So if Windows NT wants to signal that something is wrong at the system level, it may well use SEH to do it, and you'll need to use the SEH mechanism to handle those errors.
For exceptions in application code running under NT, you're better off using C++ exceptions wherever possible, for a couple of reasons. Firstly, they're more portable than SEH, and secondly, they're designed to work with objects. Having said that, however, knowing how to use SEH is still useful, and sometimes necessary, so that is what we'll be focussing on in this section.

Using SEH

The next few sections will be dealing with how you go about using SEH. This discussion assumes that you understand the basics of C++ exceptions, especially when we compare the two mechanisms, and look at how to integrate them so that you can use standard C++ syntax to handle SEH exceptions.

The __try And __except Blocks

SEH uses the same principle as exceptions do in C++ — the code which you want to test for exceptions is enclosed in a try block, which is followed by a handler block to deal with the exception condition. In SEH, the try block is implemented using the **__try** keyword, and the handler with **__except**:

```
__try {
    // do something
}
__except(filter_expression) {
    // handle expression
}
```

Note that __try and __except are Microsoft-specific. If you're using a C++ compiler other than Visual C++, SEH may be handled in a different way.

Here's where we see the first difference between SEH and C++ exception handling. In C++, the `catch` block is passed the object associated with the exception, and is designed to catch one sort of exception. This means that we may well end up with a chain of more than one `catch` block, if we need to watch out for more than one type of exception.

The **__except** block, on the other hand, takes a filter expression, which must resolve down to one of three integer values (-1,0,1). This value tells the exception mechanism how you intend to handle the exceptions that occur within the **__try** block.

The following table shows the three possible values, together with the symbolic constants which are often used to represent them:

Filter Code	Numeric Value	Meaning
EXCEPTION_EXECUTE_HANDLER	1	The __except block will handle the exception.
EXCEPTION_CONTINUE_EXECUTION	-1	The __except block will handle the exception and execution will continue with the instruction after the one which generated the exception.
EXCEPTION_CONTINUE_SEARCH	0	We're not going to handle this exception, so try to find another exception handler on the stack.

Note that, because we can only associate a single handler with a __try block, this value applies to all exceptions arising in the __try.

> *You need to be very careful when returning EXCEPTION_CONTINUE_EXECUTION, to ensure that it really is possible to continue execution after the exception has occurred. It is quite possible to end up in an endless chain of exceptions if you use this value in the wrong place!*

Try It Out — Using SEH In A Simple Example

Let's try this out in a simple example to see how this mechanism is used:

```cpp
// SimpleSEH.cpp

#include <windows.h>
#include <iostream>

using namespace std;

int main()
{
   int i = 3;
   int j;

   __try
   {
      j = i/0;
   }
   __except(EXCEPTION_EXECUTE_HANDLER)
   {
      cout << "Exception caught!" << endl;
   }

   return 0;
}
```

In this very crude test we are forcing a divide by zero, which causes an exception, and that gets caught by the __except block. Note that you'll get a compiler warning about the divide by zero when you build the program. When you run the program, you should see the following output:

At this point, two questions have probably occurred to you:

▶ How do I find out which type of exception has occurred?

▶ How do I decide whether to handle it or not?

Getting The Exception Code

We can find out what has happened using the GetExceptionCode() API function:

```
DWORD GetExceptionCode();
```

The value returned by this function is an integer which matches one of the following codes:

Exception Code	Meaning
EXCEPTION_ACCESS_VIOLATION	Cannot access the address specified
EXCEPTION_BREAKPOINT	Breakpoint hit
EXCEPTION_DATATYPE_MISALIGNMENT	Tried to read data not on the proper word boundary
EXCEPTION_SINGLE_STEP	One instruction executed in single-step mode
EXCEPTION_ARRAY_BOUNDS_EXCEEDED	Array-bounds exceeded (if supported by the hardware)
EXCEPTION_FLT_DENORMAL_OPERAND	Floating point value too small
EXCEPTION_FLT_DIVIDE_BY_ZERO	Divide by zero
EXCEPTION_FLT_INEXACT_RESULT	Value cannot be exactly represented
EXCEPTION_FLT_INVALID_OPERATION	Other floating point exception
EXCEPTION_FLT_OVERFLOW	Floating point overflow
EXCEPTION_FLT_STACK_CHECK	Stack over- or underflow during floating point operation
EXCEPTION_FLT_UNDERFLOW	Floating point underflow
EXCEPTION_INT_DIVIDE_BY_ZERO	Integer divide by zero

Exception Code	Meaning
`EXCEPTION_INT_OVERFLOW`	Integer overflow
`EXCEPTION_PRIV_INSTRUCTION`	Privileged instruction executed in user mode
`STATUS_NONCONTINUABLE_EXCEPTION`	The thread tried to continue, but the exception cannot be continued

Try It Out — Using The Exception Code

Let's try modifying the previous example (`SimpleSEH.cpp`) so that this time we catch the right type of exception — we're looking for a divide by zero exception. This time we'll call the file `ExceptionCode.cpp`:

```cpp
// ExceptionCode.cpp

#include <windows.h>
#include <iostream>

using namespace std;

int main()
{
   int i = 3;
   int j;

   __try
   {
      j = i/0;
   }
   __except(EXCEPTION_EXECUTE_HANDLER)
   {
      if (GetExceptionCode() == EXCEPTION_INT_DIVIDE_BY_ZERO)
         cout << "Divide by zero!" << endl;
      else
         cout << "Exception caught!" << endl;
   }

   return 0;
}
```

If we are only interested in divide by zero errors, we can further modify the handler like this:

```cpp
   __except(GetExceptionCode() == EXCEPTION_INT_DIVIDE_BY_ZERO)
   {
      cout << "Divide by zero!" << endl;
   }
```

The expression will return 1 (which is the value of **EXCEPTION_EXECUTE_HANDLER**) when the comparison succeeds, meaning the handler will get called, and 0 (which is the value of **EXCEPTION_CONTINUE_SEARCH**) if it doesn't, meaning the handler will be bypassed.

Again, you will see a compiler warning about the divide by zero when you build the project. When you run it, you should see the following output:

Filter Functions

The above example showed one method we can use to select a particular type of exception. This works fine while we were just looking for divide by zero errors, but suppose we want to handle several exceptions in the same handler? This could get very cumbersome. The most common way to get round this is to use a function as the **filter** expression. Any function will do, as long as it returns one of the three integer values:

1   (EXCEPTION_EXECUTE_HANDLER)

-1   (EXCEPTION_CONTINUE_EXCEPTION)

0   (EXCEPTION_CONTINUE_SEARCH)

Try It Out — Using A Filter Function

Here's our example again, but this time we'll modify to use a filter function that only traps divide by zero errors:

```cpp
// FilterException.cpp

#include <windows.h>
#include <iostream>

using namespace std;

int MyFilter(int nCode)
{
    int nRetCode = EXCEPTION_CONTINUE_SEARCH;

    switch(nCode)
    {
    case EXCEPTION_INT_DIVIDE_BY_ZERO:
    case EXCEPTION_FLT_DIVIDE_BY_ZERO:
        nRetCode = EXCEPTION_EXECUTE_HANDLER;
        break;
    }

    return nRetCode;
}

int main()
{
    int i = 3;
    int j;
```

```
   __try
   {
      j = i/0;
   }
   __except(MyFilter(GetExceptionCode()))
   {
      cout << "Divide by zero!" << endl;
   }

   return 0;
}
```

Here, we've implemented a simple filter function, **MyFilter()**, which simply returns the appropriate filter code to tell the except block to handle the exception — if it is a divide by zero error, we'll tell the **__except** block to handle it, otherwise we return **EXCEPTION_CONTINUE_SEARCH**.

If you try running this example, you should see the same output as the previous example.

Getting More Information

We know how to get hold of the error code for an exception, but what if we want to find out more information about it? We might want to find out the address of where the exception occurred, for example. Well, when you're in a filter function, it is possible to get more information about the current exception by calling the **GetExceptionInformation()** function:

```
LPEXCEPTION_POINTERS GetExceptionInformation();
```

> *Note that you can only call this function from within the filter function or expression, and not from within the handler itself.*

GetExceptionInformation() returns a pointer to an **EXCEPTION_POINTERS** structure, which in turn contains pointers to two other structures:

▶ An **EXCEPTION_RECORD** structure — this contains details of the current exception.

▶ A **CONTEXT** structure — this contains processor-specific register data.

The **CONTEXT** structure isn't used very often. It is highly machine dependent, and is only really useful in those cases when you need to know exactly what was in a particular register at the time an exception occurred.

The **EXCEPTION_RECORD** structure contains a number of fields, as shown below:

```
typedef struct _EXCEPTION_RECORD
{
   DWORD ExceptionCode;
   DWORD ExceptionFlags;
   struct _EXCEPTION_RECORD *ExceptionRecord;
   PVOID ExceptionAddress;
   DWORD NumberParameters;
   DWORD ExceptionInformation[EXCEPTION_MAXIMUM_PARAMETERS];
} EXCEPTION_RECORD;
```

And here is what the various fields mean:

▶ **ExceptionCode** is the same numeric code returned by **GetExceptionCode()**, which we saw earlier.

▶ **ExceptionFlags** can either be **EXCEPTION_CONTINUABLE** or **EXCEPTION_NONCONTINUABLE**.

▶ When processing nested exceptions, the **ExceptionRecord** pointer is used to point to the next in the chain of exception records.

▶ **ExceptionAddress** is the address where the exception occurred.

▶ **NumberParameters** defines the number of entries in the **ExceptionInformation** array.

▶ The **ExceptionInformation** array is designed to associate parameters with particular exceptions, but is currently only used in one case — for an **EXCEPTION_ACCESS_VIOLATION**, where the first element says whether a read or write caused the problem (0 indicating a read and 1 a write).

Nesting Exceptions

It is also possible to nest exception blocks, and, by using **EXCEPTION_CONTINUE_SEARCH**, you can pass the exception to an outer block.

Try It Out — Using Nested Exceptions

Let's see how this works by trying it out in an example. We'll just modify our existing code once again:

```cpp
// NestedException.cpp

#include <windows.h>
#include <iostream>

using namespace std;

int MyFilter(int nCode)
{
   int nRetCode = EXCEPTION_CONTINUE_SEARCH;

   switch(nCode)
    {
   case EXCEPTION_INT_DIVIDE_BY_ZERO:
      nRetCode = EXCEPTION_EXECUTE_HANDLER;
      break;

   case EXCEPTION_FLT_DIVIDE_BY_ZERO:
      nRetCode = EXCEPTION_EXECUTE_HANDLER;
      break;
    }

   return nRetCode;
}
```

```
int main()
{
    int i = 3;
    int j = 0;
    int k;

    __try
    {
        __try
        {
            k = i/j;
        }
        __except(GetExceptionCode() == EXCEPTION_ACCESS_VIOLATION)
        {
            cout << "Shouldn't get handled here" << endl;
        }

    }
    __except(MyFilter(GetExceptionCode()))
    {
        cout << "Divide by zero caught!" << endl;
    }

    return 0;
}
```

The inner **__except** block is only wanting to catch access violation exceptions, so the arithmetic exception gets passed to the outer block for processing. If you build and run the code this time, you should see the output:

The __finally Block

SEH provides one facility which C++ exceptions lack, and that is the ability to provide a **termination handler**, which will be called even if an exception does not occur. Why might you want to do this? Say we have a section of code protected by a critical section. We know that we have to enter and leave the critical section at the appropriate points, like this:

```
CRITICAL_SECTION cs;

...

EnterCriticalSection(&cs);

// Do what we have to do...

LeaveCriticalSection(&cs);
```

Supposing there's a chance of an exception occuring when we've acquired the critical section. If it terminates the thread, the section will remain locked and no-one else will be able to access it. We can handle the situation like this:

```
__try
{
   EnterCriticalSection(&cs);

   // Do what we need to do

}
__finally
{
   LeaveCriticalSection(&cs);
}
```

Now the critical section will be released whether an exception occurs or not. (See Chapter 6 for more on critical sections.)

> Note that you have to handle the exception in order for __finally blocks to get called. Unhandled exceptions will cause program termination, so you may need to be careful if you've placed critical code in your __finally blocks. You may be able to use an **unhandled exception filter** to get around this if it is a problem (see below).

Any code which you place in a `__finally` block will get called regardless, and you can use the `AbnormalTermination()` function to tell you whether you got there normally, or as a result of an exception. It does this by returning you **FALSE** in the former case and **TRUE** in the latter.

```
BOOL AbnormalTermination(VOID)
```

Since the `__finally` block will always get called, it doesn't have a filter expression.

Try It Out — Using A __finally Block

Let's see how this works in an example:

```
// FinallyBlock.cpp

#include <windows.h>
#include <iostream>

using namespace std;

int main()
{
   int i = 3;
   int j;

   __try
   {
      j = i/0;
   }
```

```
   __finally
   {
      if (AbnormalTermination())
         cout << "Error exit" << endl;
      else
         cout << "Normal exit" << endl;
   }

   return 0;
}
```

Note that **__finally** is an alternative to using **__except**, not an addition. You cannot chain a **__finally** block onto the end of an **__except** handler, and you'll get compiler errors if you try.

If you try the example above, you'll see that you now get a system error message, because we no longer handle the exception:

Once you dismiss the message box, though, you should see the handler text appear as the application cleans up:

Raising Exceptions

There's also an SEH analog of the C++ **throw** statement. Usually, if you've got to handle software exceptions, it'll be best to do so using C++'s built-in method, but we'll include the SEH version for completeness.

The **RaiseException()** function lets you raise an exception for the calling thread:

```
VOID RaiseException(DWORD dwCode,      // exception code
   DWORD dwFlags,                      // exception flags
   DWORD dwArgCount,                   // number of arguments
   const DWORD* pdwArgs);              // pointer to argument list
```

As you might expect, **dwCode** is the code for the exception you want to raise, and **dwFlags** determines how it will be handled. A value of zero for this argument means processing can continue after this exception, whilst **EXCEPTION_NONCONTINUABLE** means that processing cannot be continued.

> *Note that Windows clears bit 28 of whatever value you specify for the exception code, so that 0xffffffff will become 0xefffffff. This is done so that user-generated exceptions can always be differentiated from system-generated ones.*

You can include arguments which will be passed to the filter expression in the handler by specifying the number of arguments in **dwArgCount**, and giving a pointer to their start (**pdwArgs**). If the argument pointer is **NULL**, then the count is ignored.

Using An Unhandled Exception Filter

If an exception occurs which is not handled by a local handler, then a default exception handler for the thread is called. This is a system-provided routine, and it results in the well-known "Unhandled Exception" message being displayed. Using the **SetUnhandledExceptionFilter()** function, it is possible to install your own handler to deal with uncaught exceptions, so that you can take over processing all the exceptions generated by your thread, including ones which aren't caught by other handlers. Doing this can help your application handle unexpected exceptions gracefully, rather than crashing.

```
LPTOP_LEVEL_EXCEPTION_FILTER
    SetUnhandledExceptionFilter(LPTOP_LEVEL_EXCEPTION_FILTER lpTopLevel);
```

The argument is the address of the filter (handler function) to be installed, and the return value is the address of the previous filter, so that you can restore it later. If you call the function with an argument of **0**, then the default system handler is installed.

The handler function needs to have the following prototype:

```
LONG ExceptionProc(LPEXCEPTION_POINTERS lpPtrs);
```

As you might expect, the handler has to return one of the three standard values:

- **EXCEPTION_EXECUTE_HANDLER**
- **EXCEPTION_CONTINUE_EXCEPTION**
- **EXCEPTION_CONTINUE_SEARCH**

The **UnhandledExceptionFilter()** function passes an exception to the debugger if a process is being debugged, or it displays the Application Error message box and causes the Unhandled Exception handler to execute.

Try It Out — An Unhandled Exception Filter

Let's see how all this works in a practical example. It is very simple to set up such a handler, as shown in the following code:

```cpp
// UnhandledExceptionFilter.cpp

#include <windows.h>
#include <iostream>
```

```
using namespace std;

// Define our own exception value. This can be whatever we like, because
// the system ensures that our values won't clash with system values
const DWORD EX1 = 0x1;

// Set up the filter procedure
LONG UHFilter(LPEXCEPTION_POINTERS pe)
{
   cout << "In custom handler" << endl;

   if (pe->ExceptionRecord->ExceptionCode == EX1)
   {
      cout << "Handling EX1 error at " << hex
           << pe->ExceptionRecord->ExceptionAddress << dec << endl;

      return EXCEPTION_EXECUTE_HANDLER;
   }

   return EXCEPTION_CONTINUE_SEARCH;
}

int main()
{
   SetUnhandledExceptionFilter((LPTOP_LEVEL_EXCEPTION_FILTER)UHFilter);

   // Raise our exception
   RaiseException(EX1, 0, 0, NULL);

   return 0;
}
```

We start by defining a custom exception with a value of 1. The filter function checks the error code, extracting it from the **EXCEPTION_POINTERS** argument. If we are processing one of our custom errors, the handler prints out the address at which the exception occurred, and then returns **EXCEPTION_EXECUTE_HANDLER** to say that we want to handle it. If it isn't what we're looking for, it returns **EXCEPTION_CONTINUE_SEARCH** to send the system off to look for another handler.

First time through, don't install the filter function before raising the exception (just comment out the call to **SetUnhandledExceptionFilter()**). When you run the program, you'll see the Application Error message box, telling you that an unknown software exception has occurred, like the one that we saw earlier.

You'll see that our exception number is reported, along with the address at which it occurred. If you now install the filter function, you'll just get the message written to standard output, without the message box, and you will see that the address printed matches the one reported by the system. The output should look something like this (although obviously the address shown will be different on your machine):

If we actually want to process the error ourselves, we can use the
UnhandledExceptionFilter() function to control execution of an **__except** block:

```cpp
// UnhandledExceptionFilter_2.cpp

#include <windows.h>
#include <iostream>

using namespace std;

// Define our own exception value
#define EX1 0x1

// Set up the filter procedure
LONG UHFilter(EXCEPTION_POINTERS* pe)
{
    cout << "In custom handler" << endl;

    if (pe->ExceptionRecord->ExceptionCode == EX1)
    {
        cout << "Handling EX1 error at " << hex
             << pe->ExceptionRecord->ExceptionAddress << dec << endl;
        return EXCEPTION_EXECUTE_HANDLER;
    }

    return EXCEPTION_CONTINUE_SEARCH;
}

int main()
{
    SetUnhandledExceptionFilter((LPTOP_LEVEL_EXCEPTION_FILTER)UHFilter);

    __try
    {
        // Raise our exception
        RaiseException(EX1, 0, 0, NULL);
    }
    __except(UnhandledExceptionFilter(GetExceptionInformation()))
    {
        cout << "Caught our exception in main" << endl;
    }

    return 0;
}
```

If you run this version, you'll see:

Using SEH And C++ Exceptions

As you'll probably appreciate by now, the SEH and C++ exception handling mechanisms are designed to solve different problems. If we're into sweeping generalizations, we can say that SEH is there for catching system level errors, while C++ exception handling is for use by programmers writing application code.

We can have problems if we don't use both mechanisms, because:

> SEH does not guarantee that object destructors will get called.
> Not handling SEH exceptions makes your application less robust.

It is, however, possible for the two to work together, with only a little work required on your part. Win32 provides the **_set_se_translator()** function as part of the runtime library, which enables an SEH exception to be handled by a C++ class. The idea is that you create C++ classes for SEH exception types you wish to handle, and a translator function is called whenever an SEH exception occurs. You use the translator function to look at the SEH error which has occurred, and throw a C++ exception of the appropriate type.

Here is the prototype for **_set_se_translator()**:

```
_se_translator_function _set_se_translator(_se_translator_function func);
```

The function takes an argument of type **_se_translator_function**, which is the address of the new translator function, and returns a pointer to the existing function, so that it can be restored if necessary. As usual, an argument of zero results in the default system handler being reinstalled.

_se_translator_function is a **typedef** for a function pointer:

```
typedef void (*_se_translator_function)(unsigned int, struct EXCEPTION_POINTERS*);
```

We can see from this that a translator function must not return a value, and must take an **unsigned int** and a pointer to an **EXCEPTION_POINTERS** structure as arguments.

Try It Out — Using A Translator Function

Let's see how all this works by looking at a simple example, showing how such a translator function can be implemented:

```
// Translator.cpp

#include <windows.h>#include <iostream>
// include error handling routine header
#include <eh.h>

using namespace std;

void GenError();
void TransFunc( unsigned int, EXCEPTION_POINTERS* );
```

```
// Class which is mapped onto all SEH errors
class SysArithEx
{
   unsigned int nCode;
public:
   SysArithEx() : nCode(0) {}
   SysArithEx(unsigned int n) : nCode(n) {}
   ~SysArithEx() {}

   unsigned int Code() { return nCode; }
   LPTSTR Msg();
};

LPTSTR SysArithEx::Msg()
{
   switch(nCode)
   {
   case EXCEPTION_INT_DIVIDE_BY_ZERO:
      return "Integer divide by zero";

   case EXCEPTION_INT_OVERFLOW:
      return "Integer overflow";

   case EXCEPTION_FLT_DIVIDE_BY_ZERO:
      return "Floating point divide by zero";

   default:
      return "Unknown exception";
   }
}

void TransFunc(unsigned int u, EXCEPTION_POINTERS* pExp)
{
   cout << "In trans_func" << endl;
   throw SysArithEx(u);
}

void GenError()
{
   // Function which will cause an SEH divide by zero error
   __try
   {
      int x, y=0;
      x = 5 / y;
   }
   __finally
   {
      cout << "In finally" << endl;
   }
}

int main()
{
   try
   {
      // Install the translator function
      _set_se_translator(TransFunc);
```

```
      // Call a function which will cause an SEH error
      GenError();
   }
   catch(SysArithEx e)
   {
      cout << "Caught an arithmetic exception, code " << hex << e.Code() << dec
         << endl;
      cout << "Error was '" << e.Msg() << "'" << endl;
   }

   return 0;
}
```

We start by defining a class called **SysArithEx**, whose job is to catch certain arithmetic exceptions, such as divide by zero. All **SysArithEx** does is to store the exception code as an integer, **nCode**, and provide two functions:

▶ **Code()** for returning the error code

▶ **Msg()** for returning a text string describing the error

The translator function, **TransFunc()**, simply throws a C++ exception, tagging it with a **SysArithEx** object. It also outputs a statement, so that we can see where we are in the code. Note that the translator function gets passed the exception code and an **EXCEPTION_POINTERS** object, so that it has all available data with which to decide what to do.

In **main()**, we install the translator function by calling **_set_se_translator()**, and then call our **GenError()** function. This simply causes a divide by zero SEH exception to be generated. This exception is passed to the translator, which in turn throws a C++ exception. The **SysArithEx** object is caught, and then queried for the error code and description string.

If you build and run this example, you should see the following output:

```
"D:\BegNT\ch04Code\Translator\Debug\Translator.exe"
In trans_func
In finally
Caught an arithmetic exception, code c0000094
Error was 'Integer divide by zero'
Press any key to continue
```

Attracting The User's Attention

It it sometimes a good idea to attract the user's attention in some way when an error has occurred — we might want to do this by making an audible or visible signal. Before we leave our discussion of error handling, let's cover a few functions which can be useful when we want to make the user aware of an error.

One way of acomplishing this is to use the `Beep()` function. This will sound a tone of a given frequency for a given period:

```
BOOL Beep(DWORD freq, DWORD dwMilliSecs);
```

The return value is **TRUE**, if the call succeeded.

If you want slightly more sophisticated sound handling, two other functions are available in the basic Win32 API:

```
BOOL MessageBeep(UINT uType)

BOOL PlaySound(LPCSTR pszSound, HMODULE hMod, DWORD dwFlags);
```

The first of these, `MessageBeep()`, lets you play one of five pre-defined sounds, identified by passing in one of the following symbolic constants as the argument:

- **MB_ICONEXCLAMATION**
- **MB_ICONASTERISK**
- **MB_ICONHAND**
- **MB_ICONQUESTION**
- **MB_OK**

This function will play whatever sounds are currently associated with these values, which the user can change via the Control Panel.

The `PlaySound()` function will play a `.wav` sound file, either from disk or stored as a resource. The first parameter, `pzSound`, determines the sound to play. Depending on the setting of the flags in the third argument, the name may be interpreted as a system event, a filename or a resource ID. If the first parameter is zero, any currently playing waveform is stopped.

If loading from a resource, then the second parameter is the handle to the module which contains the resource. If not loading from a resource, then this parameter must be **NULL**.

The final parameter specifies the flags which affect how the sound is loaded and played. There are a number of possible values, as shown in the table below:

Flag	Meaning
SND_APPLICATION	The sound is played using an application-specific association.
SND_ALIAS	**pszSound** represents a system event specified in the registry or **win.ini** file.
SND_ALIAS_ID	**pszSound** is a predefined sound identifier.
SND_ASYNC	Plays the sound asynchronously. **PlaySound()** returns at once, and in order to stop the sound, it must be called again with a **NULL pszSound** parameter.
SND_FILENAME	Plays the sound from a file.

Flag	Meaning
SND_LOOP	Plays the sound repeatedly until **PlaySound()** is called again with a **NULL** parameter.
SND_MEMORY	Plays a sound from memory, the **pszSound** parameter points to the image in memory.
SND_NODEFAULT	Doesn't use a default sound — if the requested sound cannot be found, **PlaySound()** silently returns.
SND_NOSTOP	The function will immediately return if the resource needed to play the sound is already occupied. If this flag isn't specified, **PlaySound()** will try to stop the current sound in order to play the new one.
SND_NOWAIT	If the sound driver is busy, return immediately.
SND_PURGE	Stop playing sounds for the calling task. If **pszSound** is not **NULL**, just stop playing that sound. If it is **NULL**, stop playing all sounds
SND_RESOURCE	Plays a sound stored in a module's resources. The **hMod** parameter must be used to specify the module.
SND_SYNC	The function will not return until the sound has finished playing.

You may want to get the user's attention from a window which doesn't currently have the focus. In this case, just beeping is potentially confusing, because the user might not know where the beep has come from. The **FlashWindow()** function can be useful in this kind of situation. as it will momentarily flash the border of a window, thus allowing the user to see where the beep has come from.

```
BOOL FlashWindow(HWND hWnd, BOOL status);
```

The status flag determines whether the window border will be flashed alone, or whether the title bar will also appear to be enabled.

Summary

We have seen in this chapter that Win32 provides a rich set of error handling mechanisms. The system saves the code for the last error in a thread's local storage, and we've learned how we can retrieve this error code using the **GetLastError()** function, and how we can further retrieve and format the associated error message using the **FormatMessage()** function.

If we want to use this mechanism to signal our own error codes, we can use **SetLastError()**, and provide an error message string which the client can format using **FormatMessage()**.

Structured Error Handling provides a standard way of handling system errors. We've seen how to use the **__try**, **__except** and **__finally** constructs to provide exception handlers, and how to raise our own exceptions, and put our own unhandled exception handler in place. We've also seen how to integrate the SEH and C++ exception mechanisms using a translator function, so that we can, if we wish, use C++ to handle all exceptions which might occur in our code.

Finally, we saw some interesting ways of attracting the user's attention when something has gone wrong.

Interfacing with the System

The Win32 API provides us with a large number of relatively simple functions that can be used to get and manipulate system information. As these functions are largely unrelated, and do not fall easily into any of the other categories covered in this book, we will try to impose some sort of structure onto them, and cover them in groups. So in this chapter we'll be looking at functions that allow us to obtain information on:

- The system hardware
- Parameters relating to the disk and file system
- Accessing and setting the system time
- The current process
- The locale
- Logging off and shutting down

> *With the exception of logging-off and shutting down (which is NT-specific), everything is this chapter is applicable to both Windows 95 and NT. Where one or two flags are NT or 95-specific, the fact is noted in the text.*

System Hardware Information

There are two functions, `GetSystemInfo()` and `GetKeyboardType()`, that enable you to get information about the hardware on which your program is running.

GetSystemInfo()

First off, here is the API function defininion for `GetSystemInfo()`:

```
VOID GetSystemInfo(LPSYSTEM_INFO pInfo);
```

`GetSystemInfo()` returns a pointer to a structure called **SYSTEM_INFO**, defined in **<winbase.h>**, that contains various items of hardware-related information. This is what **SYSTEM_INFO** looks like:

```
typedef struct _SYSTEM_INFO {
    union {
        DWORD dwOemId;
            // Obsolete field...do not use

        struct {
            WORD wProcessorArchitecture;
            WORD wReserved;
        };
    };
    DWORD dwPageSize;
    LPVOID lpMinimumApplicationAddress;
    LPVOID lpMaximumApplicationAddress;
    DWORD dwActiveProcessorMask;
    DWORD dwNumberOfProcessors;
    DWORD dwProcessorType;
    DWORD dwAllocationGranularity;
    WORD wProcessorLevel;
    WORD wProcessorRevision;
} SYSTEM_INFO, *LPSYSTEM_INFO;
```

Many of these fields are rather esoteric, and it is unlikely that you will ever need to use them unless you get down to some serious hardware manipulation. Let's briefly cover some of the **SYSTEM_INFO** members.

The **wProcessorArchitecture** member of the union tells you which processor architecture you're running on. Obviously, for Windows 95 programs there can only be one value — **PROCESSOR_ARCHITECTURE_INTEL**. If you're running under NT, then there are four other possibilities too:

▶ **PROCESSOR_ARCHITECTURE_MIPS** — for MIPS architecture

▶ **PROCESSOR_ARCHITECTURE_ALPHA** — for DEC Alpha

▶ **PROCESSOR_ARCHITECTURE_PPC** — for PowerPC

▶ **PROCESSOR_ARCHITECTURE_UNKNOWN** — for anything else

Note that NT for MIPS and PowerPC are no longer supported by Microsoft.

The **wProcessorLevel** and **wProcessorRevision** fields are only used under NT, and denote the processor type and revision level. The meaning of each is dependent on the architecture. For Intel processors, the processor level takes one of the following values:

WProcessorLevel Value	Meaning
3	Intel 80386
4	Intel 80486
5	Intel Pentium

The processor revision is a value of the form *xyz*, where *xx* is 0xFF, *y* - *0xA* is the model number, and *z* is the stepping identifier.

For Windows 95 systems, **dwProcessorType** tells you the type of processor installed, and is one of the following:

▶ **PROCESSOR_INTEL_386**

▶ **PROCESSOR_INTEL_486**

▶ **PROCESSOR_INTEL_PENTIUM**

Windows NT adds the options **PROCESSOR_MIPS_R4000** and **PROCESSOR_ALPHA_21064**, although the documentation points out that this field is only provided for compatibility with Windows 95 and earlier versions of NT, and that NT programs should use the **wProcessorArchitecture**, **wProcessorLevel** and **wProcessorRevision** members.

The **dwNumberOfProcessors** member tells you the number of processors in the machine.

GetKeyboardType()

GetKeyboardType() is used to determine the type of keyboard present on the machine:

```
int GetKeyboardType(int nFlag);
```

The parameter value given for the flag determines the information that is to be retrieved:

Parameter Value	Effect
0	Returns the keyboard type
1	Returns the keyboard subtype
2	Returns the number of function keys on the keyboard

The return value is an integer. For *keyboard type*, the return values are interpreted as follows:

Type	Meaning
1	83-key IBM PC/XT or compatible
2	102-key Olivetti 'ICO' keyboard
3	84-key IBM PC/AT or compatible
4	101 or 102-key IBM enhanced keyboard
5	Nokia 1050 or similar
6	Nokia 9140 or similar
7	Japanese keyboard

The *keyboard subtype* is a manufacturer-dependent value. If you request the number of function keys, you'll get a value returned as follows:

Value	Number of Function Keys
1	10
2	12 (sometimes 18)
3	10
4	12
5	10
6	24
7	Specified by manufacturer

Version Information

The function **GetVersionEx()** returns operating system version information in an **OSVERSIONINFO** structure:

```
BOOL  GetVersionEx(LPOSVERSIONINFO  pVer);
```

> *This routine supersedes the older* GetVersion() *function, and it is recommended that* GetVersionEx() *should be used in all new software.*

The **OSVERSIONINFO** structure returned includes major and minor version and build numbers:

```
typedef struct _OSVERSIONINFO
{
   DWORD dwOSVersionInfoSize;
   DWORD dwMajorVersion;
   DWORD dwMinorVersion;
   DWORD dwBuildNumber;
   DWORD dwPlatformID;
   TCHAR szCSDVersion[128];
} OSVERSIONINFO;
```

The major and minor version numbers are fairly obvious. For example, Windows NT 3.51 has a major version number of '3' and minor version number of '51'. (Note that Windows 95 comes out with a major version of '3' and minor version of '95'!) The **dwPlatformID** parameter indicates the platform ID, and takes one of the following three values:

▶ **VER_PLATFORM_WIN32s**, for Win32s running under Windows 3.1

▶ **VER_PLATFORM_WIN32_WINDOWS**, for Windows 95

▶ **VER_PLATFORM_WIN32_NT**, for Windows NT

The final parameter, **szCSDVersion[]**, is a string containing arbitrary extra information about the operating system.

Note that, before the `OSVERSIONINFO` structure is used, its size must be set in its first parameter. This is how to set the size of the structure:

```
OSVERSIONINFO osv;

osv.dwOSVersionInfoSize = sizeof(OSVERSIONINFO);
GetVersionEx(&osv);
```

The SystemInfo Class

We can usefully create a 'system information' class which will allow us to get at the most useful information in the `SYSTEM_INFO` and `OSVERSIONINFO` blocks in a friendly fashion. Here is the header file, `sysinfo.h`:

```
// sysinfo.h

#ifndef SYSINFO_H
#define SYSINFO_H

class SystemInfo
{
    SYSTEM_INFO si;        // system information block
    OSVERSIONINFO os;      // OS information block

public:
    SystemInfo();

    // Processor and architecture information
    bool is386() const;
    bool is486() const;
    bool isPentium() const;

    bool isIntel() const
        { return si.wProcessorArchitecture == PROCESSOR_ARCHITECTURE_INTEL; }

    bool isMIPS() const { return si.wProcessorArchitecture ==
                                    PROCESSOR_ARCHITECTURE_MIPS; }

    bool isAlpha() const { return si.wProcessorArchitecture ==
                                    PROCESSOR_ARCHITECTURE_ALPHA; }

    bool isPowerPC() const { return si.wProcessorArchitecture ==
                                    PROCESSOR_ARCHITECTURE_PPC; }

    bool isUnknownArchitecture() const { return si.wProcessorArchitecture ==
                                    PROCESSOR_ARCHITECTURE_UNKNOWN; }

    WORD getArchitecture() const { return si.wProcessorArchitecture; }

    DWORD numProcessors() const { return si.dwNumberOfProcessors; }

    // Operating system information
    bool isWin95() const { return os.dwPlatformId == VER_PLATFORM_WIN32_WINDOWS; }
    bool isWinNT() const { return os.dwPlatformId == VER_PLATFORM_WIN32_NT; }
    bool isWin32s() const { return os.dwPlatformId == VER_PLATFORM_WIN32s; }
```

```
   // Operating system version information
   DWORD majorVersion() { return os.dwMajorVersion; }
   DWORD minorVersion() { return os.dwMinorVersion; }};

#endif
```

The class is really just a wrapper around a couple of structures, so we have two private data members, a **SYSTEM_INFO** and an **OSVERSIONINFO**, and various member functions which give us simple access to its fields. This means that a lot of the member functions are inline, and that there is comparatively little to go into the implementation file.

Here is the **sysinfo.cpp** file. You'll see that the main purpose of the constructor is to set up the structures, and to complain if it can't!

```
// sysinfo.cpp

#include <windows.h>
#include "sysinfo.h"

SystemInfo::SystemInfo()
{
   // Fill the information structures
   GetSystemInfo(&si);

   // GetVersionEx can return FALSE, so throw if it does
   os.dwOSVersionInfoSize = sizeof(OSVERSIONINFO);
   if (!GetVersionEx(&os))
      throw "SystemInfo: can't get OSVERSIONINFO";
}
```

The only functions that need special coding are those which return the processor type, since the fields used depend on the operating system. This is where it is useful to have the **OSVERSIONINFO** available in the same class. So **sysinfo.cpp** continues as follows:

```
// These use different fields depending on whether you're running on 95 or NT
bool SystemInfo::is386() const
{
   if (isWinNT())
      return si.wProcessorLevel == 3;
   else
      return si.dwProcessorType == PROCESSOR_INTEL_386;
}

bool SystemInfo::is486() const
{
   if (isWinNT())
      return si.wProcessorLevel == 4;
   else
      return si.dwProcessorType == PROCESSOR_INTEL_486;
}

bool SystemInfo::isPentium() const
{
   if (isWinNT())
      return si.wProcessorLevel == 5;
```

```
        else
            return si.dwProcessorType == PROCESSOR_INTEL_PENTIUM;
    }
```

Here is a test program which shows this class in use:

```cpp
// sysinfotest.cpp

#include <windows.h>
#include <iostream>

using namespace std;

#include "sysinfo.h"

int main()
{
    SystemInfo si;

    if (si.isIntel())
        cout << "Architecture is Intel" << endl;
    else
        cout << "Architecture is non-Intel" << endl;

    if (si.is386())
        cout << "Processor is a 386" << endl;
    else if (si.is486())
        cout << "Processor is a 486" << endl;
    else if (si.isPentium())
        cout << "Processor is a Pentium" << endl;
    else
        cout << "Processor is unknown" << endl;

    if (si.isWin95())
        cout << "Running on Win95" << endl;
    else if (si.isWinNT())
        cout << "Running on NT" << endl;
    else if (si.isWin32s())
        cout << "Running on Win32s" << endl;

    return 0;
}
```

On my machine, I get the following output:

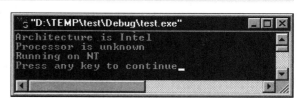

Disk Information

The next group of functions allows you to retrieve and set various parameters relating to the disk and file system.

Directory Information

There are three functions available, that allow you to get the paths to useful directories:

```
DWORD  GetCurrentDirectory(DWORD dwBuffSize,  LPTSTR  pBuff);
UINT  GetSystemDirectory(LPTSTR pBuff,  UINT  dwBuffSize);
UINT  GetWindowsDirectory(LPTSTR pBuff,  UINT  dwBuffSize);
```

In each of these functions, there are two parameters required: a buffer and a size. Since a Win32 path can be at most **MAX_PATH** characters in length, it is sensible to use a buffer of size **MAX_PATH+1** to prevent the possibility of overflow. The return value indicates the number of characters that are stored in the buffer, and will be set to zero if the function fails.

Another function, **SetCurrentDirectory()**, can be used to change the current directory:

```
BOOL  SetCurrentDirectory(LPCTSTR  pBuff);
```

The parameter, a string, specifies a directory path. This can be an absolute path, or relative to the current directory. The return value indicates whether or not the function succeeded in changing the directory.

Drive Information

There are various functions available that help us to find out about the drives available on the machine.

Determining the Exisiting Drives

We can use the function **GetLogicalDrives()** to find out which drives exist:

```
DWORD  GetLogicalDrives();
```

The return value has a bit set for each drive which exists on the system. So, bit 0 is drive A, bit 1 is drive B, and so on. A return value of zero means that the call failed.

Getting Descriptions of the Exisiting Drives

The function **GetLogicalDriveStrings()** does a similar job to **GetLogicalDrives()**, filling a buffer with text strings which describe the drives available on the system:

```
DWORD  GetLogicalDriveStrings(DWORD  dwBuffSize,  LPTSTR  pBuff);
```

If the function succeeds, then the return value will be the number of characters written to the buffer. If it fails, the return value will be zero. Each string within the buffer is followed by a null character, with a final extra null that terminates the list, for example:

```
C:\<null>D:\<null>E:\<null><null>
```

Getting the Drive Type

Once you know which drives are available, we can find out what type of device each drive represents. To do this, we use the function `GetDriveType()`:

```
UINT GetDriveType(LPCTSTR lpRoot);
```

Given a string containing the name of the root of a drive (e.g. `C:\`), the `GetDriveType()` routine will return one of the following return codes:

Return Code	Meaning
DRIVE_UNKNOWN	The type could not be determined
DRIVE_NO_ROOT_DIR	The root directory given does not exist
DRIVE_CDROM	The drive is a CD-ROM drive
DRIVE_FIXED	The disk cannot be removed from the drive
DRIVE_RAMDISK	The drive is a RAM disk
DRIVE_REMOTE	The drive is a remote drive
DRIVE_REMOVABLE	The disk can be removed from the drive

Try It Out — Getting Information about Logical Drives

The following program, `driveinfo.cpp`, shows how these functions can be used to enumerate the drives present on a machine:

```cpp
// driveinfo.cpp

#include <windows.h>
#include <iostream>

using namespace std;

int main()
{
   char sDrv[5];
   // Get the drive bit-set
   DWORD dwDrives = GetLogicalDrives();
   if (dwDrives == 0)
   {
      cout << "GetLogicalDrives failed!" << endl;
      exit(1);
   }

   // iterate over all the possible drives
   for (short n=0; n<32; n++)
   {
      // Do a logical & to see if the bit is set
      if (dwDrives & (1 << n))
      {
```

```
                // Make up a name of the form 'A:'
                wsprintf(sDrv,"%c:", ('A'+n));
                cout << "Have drive " << sDrv;
                // Append '\\' to make the root directory string
                strcat(sDrv,"\\");

                // Get the drive type and print it out
                UINT uType = GetDriveType(sDrv);
                switch(uType)
                {
                case DRIVE_UNKNOWN:
                    cout << " (error getting drive type)" << endl;
                    break;
                case DRIVE_NO_ROOT_DIR:
                    cout << " (root directory given was invalid)" << endl;
                    break;
                case DRIVE_CDROM:
                    cout << " - CDROM" << endl;
                    break;
                case DRIVE_FIXED:
                    cout << " - Fixed disk" << endl;
                    break;
                case DRIVE_RAMDISK:
                    cout << " - RAM disk" << endl;
                    break;
                case DRIVE_REMOTE:
                    cout << " - Remote" << endl;
                    break;
                case DRIVE_REMOVABLE:
                    cout << " - Removable" << endl;
                    break;
                }
            }
        }

    return 0;
}
```

On my machine the program gives the following output:

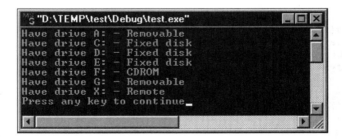

Getting Volume Information about a Drive

Moving on, we can use `GetVolumeInformation()` to tell us about a particular volume, and `SetVolumeLabel()` to change its label.

`GetVolumeInformation()` returns us a whole lot of information about the volume file system for a given drive:

```
BOOL  GetVolumeInformation(
      LPCTSTR  pRoot,                  // Root  of  volume  to  be  examined
      LPTSTR   pVolName,               // Volume  name
      DWORD    dwNameSize,             // Length  of  volume  name
      LPDWORD  pdwVolID,               // Volume  serial  number
      LPDWORD  pdwMaxCompLen,          // Maximum  component  length
      LPDWORD  pdwFileSysFlags,        // File  system  attributes
      LPTSTR   pFileSys,               // Filing  system  name
      DWORD    swFileSysNameSize);     // Length  of  name
```

Try It Out — Getting Volume Information

We can adapt the example program `driveinfo.cpp`, that we used above, so that it also uses the function `GetVolumeInformation()` to display some more information about each drive. Here's the full code for the new program, `driveinfo2.cpp`, with the amendments shown in the shaded boxes:

```cpp
// driveinfo2.cpp

#include <windows.h>
#include <iostream>

using namespace std;

int main()
{
    char sDrv[5];
    // Get the drive bit-set
    DWORD dwDrives = GetLogicalDrives();
    if (dwDrives == 0)
    {
        cout << "GetLogicalDrives failed!" << endl;
        exit(1);
    }

    // iterate over all the possible drives
    for (short n=0; n<32; n++)
    {
        // Do a logical & to see if the bit is set
        if (dwDrives & (1 << n))
        {
            // Make up a name of the form 'A:'
            wsprintf(sDrv,"%c:", ('A'+n));
            cout << "Have drive " << sDrv;
            // Append '\\' to make the root directory string
            strcat(sDrv,"\\");
```

```
                    // Get the drive type and print it out
                    UINT uType = GetDriveType(sDrv);
                    switch(uType)
                    {
                    case DRIVE_UNKNOWN:
                        cout << " (error getting drive type)" << endl;
                        break;
                    case DRIVE_NO_ROOT_DIR:
                        cout << " (root directory given was invalid)" << endl;
                        break;
                    case DRIVE_CDROM:
                        cout << " - CDROM" << endl;
                        break;
                    case DRIVE_FIXED:
                        cout << " - Fixed disk" << endl;
                        break;
                    case DRIVE_RAMDISK:
                        cout << " - RAM disk" << endl;
                        break;
                    case DRIVE_REMOTE:
                        cout << " - Remote" << endl;
                        break;
                    case DRIVE_REMOVABLE:
                        cout << " - Removable" << endl;
                        break;
                    }

                    // If we couldn't get the drive type, no point in getting volume
                    // information
                    if (uType == 0 || uType == 1)
                        exit(1);

                    TCHAR sVolName[32];
                    TCHAR sFSName[255];
                    DWORD dwVolID;
                    DWORD dwMaxLen;
                    DWORD dwFSAtt;

                    if (GetVolumeInformation(sDrv, sVolName, 31, &dwVolID,
                        &dwMaxLen, &dwFSAtt, sFSName, 254))
                    {
                        cout << ", vol=" << sVolName << ", FileSys=" << sFSName << endl;
                    }
                    else
                        cout << " (Couldn't get volume info)" << endl;
                }
            }

        return 0;
    }
```

We get the volume information for each volume in turn, and print out the volume name and the file system name. Here's what is displayed on my machine when I ran this program:

```
MS "D:\TEMP\test\Debug\test.exe"                    _ □ ×
Have drive A: - Removable
<Couldn't get volume info>
Have drive C: - Fixed disk
 vol=, FileSys=FAT
Have drive D: - Fixed disk
 vol=, FileSys=NTFS
Have drive E: - Fixed disk
 vol=, FileSys=FAT
Have drive F: - CDROM
 vol=DN600ENU2, FileSys=CDFS
Have drive G: - Removable
<Couldn't get volume info>
Have drive X: - Remote
<Couldn't get volume info>
Press any key to continue
```

Assigning a Label to a Drive

In the example above, Drives D: and E: don't have a volume label. However, we can assign labels to the drives by using the `SetVolumeLabel()` function:

```
BOOL  SetVolumeLabel(LPCTSTR  pRoot,  LPCTSTR  pVolName);
```

As before, the first parameter specifies the root directory of a volume. The second parameter is the new volume label. If this is NULL, then the function removes the volume label.

Free Disk Space on a Volume

Finally, the `GetDiskFreeSpace()` and `GetDiskFreeSpaceEx()` functions tell us about the free disk space on a volume.

> *There is, unfortunately, no matching **SetFreeDiskSpace()** function.*

The first of these, `GetDiskFreeSpace()`, reports the disk space in terms of clusters and sectors, so you have to do the arithmetic to extract the actual sizes:

```
BOOL  GetDiskFreeSpace(
    LPCTSTR  pRoot,                     // Root  directory  string
    LPDWORD  pdwSectorsPerCluster,      // Sectors  per  cluster
    LPDWORD  pdwBytesPerSector,         // Bytes  per  sector
    LPDWORD  pdwFreeClusters,           // Free  clusters
    LPDWORD  pdwClusters);              // Total  number  of  clusters
```

The number of bytes free will be:

```
BytesPerSector * SectorsPerCluster * FreeClusters
```

The total number of bytes will be:

```
BytesPerSector * SectorsPerCluster * Clusters
```

The `GetDiskFreeSpaceEx()` function returns the information in a more useful manner:

```
BOOL GetDiskFreeSpaceEx(
    LPCTSTR pDirName,                    // Directory name string
    PULARGE_INTEGER pBytesFreeToCaller,  // Bytes available to this caller
    PULARGE_INTEGER pTotalBytes,         // Total bytes
    PULARGE_INTEGER pTotalFreeBytes);    // Total free bytes
```

Note that we get returned the total number of free bytes, and the amount available to this caller. If the operating system implements any sort of quota system for disk space, the amount available to the user may be less than the total.

Try It Out — Getting Volume Information

We can modify our example program `driveinfo2.cpp` again, this time to return disk space information. Here's the full code:

```cpp
// driveinfo3.cpp

#include <windows.h>
#include <cstdio>
#include <iostream>

using namespace std;

int main()
{
    char sDrv[5];

    // Get the drive bit-set
    DWORD dwDrives = GetLogicalDrives();
    if (dwDrives == 0)
    {
        cout << "GetLogicalDrives failed!" << endl;
        exit(1);
    }

    // iterate over all the possible drives
    for (short n=0; n<32; n++)
    {
        // Do a logical & to see if the bit is set
        if (dwDrives & (1 << n))

        {
            // Make up a name of the form 'A:'
            wsprintf(sDrv,"%c:", ('A'+n));
            cout << "Have drive " << sDrv;

            // Append '\\' to make the root directory string
            strcat(sDrv,"\\");

            // Get the drive type and print it out
            UINT uType = GetDriveType(sDrv);
            switch(uType)
            {
```

```
        case DRIVE_UNKNOWN:
            cout << " (error getting drive type)" << endl;
            break;
        case DRIVE_NO_ROOT_DIR:
            cout << " (root directory given was invalid)" << endl;
            break;
        case DRIVE_CDROM:
            cout << " - CDROM" << endl;
            break;
        case DRIVE_FIXED:
            cout << " - Fixed disk" << endl;
            break;
        case DRIVE_RAMDISK:
            cout << " - RAM disk" << endl;
            break;
        case DRIVE_REMOTE:
            cout << " - Remote" << endl;
            break;
        case DRIVE_REMOVABLE:
            cout << " - Removable" << endl;
            break;
        }

        // If we couldn't get the drive type, no point in getting volume
        // information
        if (uType == 0 || uType == 1)
            exit(1);

        TCHAR sVolName[32];
        TCHAR sFSName[255];
        DWORD dwVolID;
        DWORD dwMaxLen;
        DWORD dwFSAtt;

        BOOL bVolInfo = GetVolumeInformation(sDrv, sVolName, 31, &dwVolID,
            &dwMaxLen, &dwFSAtt, sFSName, 254);

        if (bVolInfo)
            cout << ", vol=" << sVolName << ", FileSys=" << sFSName << endl;
        else
            cout << " (Couldn't get volume info)" << endl;

        ULARGE_INTEGER uAvailUser;
        ULARGE_INTEGER uTotal;
        ULARGE_INTEGER uFree;

        if (bVolInfo && GetDiskFreeSpaceEx(sDrv, &uAvailUser, &uTotal, &uFree))
            printf("  AvailUser=%I64u, Total=%I64u, Free=%I64u\n",
                uAvailUser.QuadPart, uTotal.QuadPart, uFree.QuadPart);
        else
            cout << "  (Couldn't get space info)" << endl;

    }
  }

  return 0;
}
```

Notice how we retrieve the values from variables of type **ULARGE_INTEGER**. A **ULARGE_INTEGER** is a structure designed to hold unsigned 64-bit integers. This can be a problem on machines which don't support 64-bit integer, so it provides a union of the 64-bit value (called **QuadPart**) and two **DWORD**s called **HighPart** and **LowPart**, like this:

```
typedef union _ULARGE_INTEGER
{
   struct
   {
      DWORD LowPart;           // low 32-bits
      DWORD HighPart;          // high 32-bits
   };

   DWORDLONG QuadPart;         // entire 64-bits
} ULARGE_INTEGER;
```

So all we need to do is to access the requisite member of the union. You can find out whether your compiler supports 64-bit integers by checking the value of the **_INTEGRAL_MAX_BITS** preprocessor symbol. For Visual C++ running on NT, it is 64, so we can use **QuadPart** to store large integers.

> *We have one problem with output — the C++ Standard Library isn't too happy with printing 64-bit integers, so we have to resort to* **printf()**, *using the* **'I64'** *flag to print a 64-bit unsigned quantity.*

Here's the sort of output you should see when you run the program:

```
"D:\TEMP\test\Debug\test.exe"
Have drive A: - Removable, (Couldn't get volume info)
   (Couldn't get space info)
Have drive C: - Fixed disk, vol=, FileSys=FAT
   AvailUser=349143040, Total=2146467840, Free=349143040
Have drive D: - Fixed disk, vol=, FileSys=NTFS
   AvailUser=456008704, Total=1636797952, Free=456008704
Have drive E: - Fixed disk, vol=, FileSys=FAT
   AvailUser=525860864, Total=526106624, Free=525860864
Have drive F: - CDROM, vol=DN600ENU2, FileSys=CDFS
   AvailUser=0, Total=570886144, Free=0
Have drive G: - Removable, (Couldn't get volume info)
   (Couldn't get space info)
Have drive X: - Remote, (Couldn't get volume info)
   (Couldn't get space info)
Press any key to continue_
```

As we would expect, 'available per user' and 'total free' amounts are the same, since we have no quota system in operation, and the CD drive has no free space at all.

Adding Logical Drive Classes

The drive information that we investigated in the previous section is an ideal candidate for encapsulation into two new classes:

`DriveCollection` represents the collection of logical drives present on the machine
`Drive` represents a single logical drive

Since they're both closely related and will often be used together, we can implement them in a single pair of files, `DriveCollection.cpp` and `Drive.cpp`.

> *As usual, the features implemented in these classes form a useful (but by no means complete) working set. You're welcome to tailor them further for your own needs.*

Let's look at the definition of the classes before going on to implement them.

The DriveCollection Class

With the `DriveCollection` class, we have the capability to do the following:

- Inquire how many logical drives are supported
- Inquire whether a particular drive letter is assigned
- Enumerate through all the drives in order of drive letter, including or omitting removable and network drives

The enumeration returns a pointer to a `Drive` variable — one per call, until it runs out of drives, when it returns `NULL`. There are various ways in which we could implement enumeration. In this case, we have a function called `EnumDrives()`, that creates the `Drive` variable on-the-fly, and returns it. The `Drive` variable is then held as a data member of the class. This is simple to program, but it does mean that you have to rely on the user not to delete the pointer himself.

Here is the definition of the `DriveCollection` class:

```
// DriveCollection.h

#ifndef DRIVECOLLECTION_H
#define DRIVECOLLECTION_H

class Drive;

// A DriveCollection represents the set of drives available on
// the machine.

class DriveCollection
{
public:
    enum TCollType {
        all = 0x00,
        noRemovable = 0x01,
        noNetwork = 0x02
    };
```

```
private:
   short nDrv;              // drive counter
   Drive* pd;               // pointer to current drive object
   TCollType collType;      // enumeration control flag

public:

   DriveCollection(TCollType t = DriveCollection::all) :
      nDrv(0), pd(0), collType(t) {};
   ~DriveCollection();

   static short numDrives();
   static bool hasDrive(TCHAR cDrive);

   void Reset() { nDrv = 0; };
   const Drive* EnumDrives();
   };

#endif
```

The three data members hold, respectively, a counter so that **EnumDrives()** can tell where it has got to, the pointer to the **Drive** variable returned by **EnumDrives()**, and a flag which controls which drives are enumerated. The enumeration flag values are held in the **TCollType** enumeration.

The member function **numDrives()** is a static member, which returns the number of logical drives. The member function **hasDrive()** is also a static, and will tell you whether a given drive letter is assigned. **Reset()** can be used to reset the enumeration back to the start, and **EnumDrives()** does the enumeration.

The Drive Class Definition

The **Drive** class represents a single logical drive, and contains the following information:

- The drive type
- The total disk space, free space, and free space available to the user
- The volume name
- The file system name

The **Drive** class is used mainly for querying drive properties, but it is also possible to use it to set the volume name.

This class is slightly larger than **DriveCollection**, as shown by its definition:

```
// Drive.h

#ifndef DRIVE_H
#define DRIVE_H

// Drive represents a logical disk drive
class Drive
{
   TCHAR letter;
```

```
        TCHAR sRoot[5];
        UINT uType;
        TCHAR sVolName[32];
        TCHAR sFileSysName[255];

        ULARGE_INTEGER uAvailUser;
        ULARGE_INTEGER uTotal;
        ULARGE_INTEGER uFree;
        bool bHasSpaceInfo;
        bool bHasVolInfo;

    public:
        Drive(TCHAR driveLetter);

        enum {MAX_DRIVES = 32};

        TCHAR driveLetter() const { return letter; }

        // Drive type
        bool isCDDrive() const { return uType == DRIVE_CDROM; }
        bool isFixedDrive() const { return uType == DRIVE_FIXED; }
        bool isRemovableDrive() const { return uType == DRIVE_REMOVABLE; }
        bool isRemoteDrive() const { return uType == DRIVE_REMOTE; }
        bool isRamDisk() const { return uType == DRIVE_RAMDISK; }
        UINT driveType() const { return uType; }

        // Space Info
        ULARGE_INTEGER totalDiskSpace() const { return uTotal; }
        ULARGE_INTEGER freeDiskSpace() const { return uFree; }
        ULARGE_INTEGER spaceAvailableToUser() const { return uAvailUser; }

        // Misc
        LPCTSTR volumeName() const { return sVolName; }
        LPCTSTR fileSystemName() const { return sFileSysName; }
        bool setVolumeLabel();

        bool hasSpaceInfo() const { return bHasSpaceInfo; }
        bool hasVolInfo() const { return bHasVolInfo; }
    };

    #endif
```

Despite its size, the class is pretty simple. Data members hold the return values from the various system calls, and inline functions are provided to report on them.

Implementing The DriveCollection Class

The `DriveCollection` class has three non-inline functions. The first, **numDrives()**, is a static function which reports the number of logical drives available:

```
// DriveCollection.cpp

#include <windows.h>
#include <tchar.h>
#include "DriveCollection.h"
#include "Drive.h"
```

```
DriveCollection::~DriveCollection()
{
   if (pd)
      delete pd;
}

short DriveCollection::numDrives()
{
   // Static function to return the number of logical drives
   short nDrives = 0;

   DWORD dwDrives = GetLogicalDrives();

   if (dwDrives == 0)
      return 0;

   for (short n=0; n<Drive::MAX_DRIVES; n++)
   {
      if (dwDrives & (1 << n))
         nDrives++;
   }

   return nDrives;
}
```

The second static function, **hasDrive()**, can be used to query for the presence of a particular logical drive:

```
bool DriveCollection::hasDrive(TCHAR driveLetter)
{
   // static function to tell us whether a particular drive letter
   // is supported

   // Check whether the drive exists
   DWORD dwDrives = GetLogicalDrives();

   if (dwDrives == 0)
      return false;

   if (dwDrives & (1 << (driveLetter - _T('A'))))
      return true;
   else
      return false;
}
```

The third function, **EnumDrives()**, is the most complex. Successive calls to **EnumDrive()** will return a pointer to a **Drive** object, representing each logical drive in turn. When there are no more drives, the function returns **NULL**:

```
const Drive* DriveCollection::EnumDrives()
{
   // Return drive objects representing the logical drives
   // available to the system
   DWORD dwDrives = GetLogicalDrives();

   if (dwDrives == 0 || nDrv >= Drive::MAX_DRIVES)
      return NULL;
```

```
    for (short n=nDrv; n<Drive::MAX_DRIVES; n++)
    {
       if (dwDrives & (1 << n))
       {
          // Save drive number for next iteration
          nDrv = n+1;

          // Create a drive object
          if (pd) delete pd;
          pd = new Drive(_T('A')+n);

          // Check against any flags which are set
          if ((collType & DriveCollection::noRemovable) && pd->isRemovableDrive())
             continue;

          if ((collType & DriveCollection::noNetwork) && pd->isRemoteDrive())
             continue;

          // If OK, return the drive object
          return pd;
       }
    }

    return NULL;
}
```

The function keeps track of the drives as it enumerates them, and checks whether either of the flags `DriveCollection::noRemovable` or `DriveCollection::noNetwork` was specified.

Here's a *code fragment* to show how you might use this function. We'll see it in use in a full program when we've implemented all the classes:

```
DriveCollection dc;

const Drive* pd = NULL;

// Loop till there are no more drives
for (;;)
{
   try
   {
      pd = dc.EnumDrives();
   }
   catch(const char* ps)
   {
      cout << "Error: " << ps << endl;
      break;
   }

   // Break out when there are no more drives
   if (!pd) break;

   cout << "Got drive '" << pd->driveLetter() << "'" << endl;
}
```

Implementing The Drive Class

The only non-inline function in the `Drive` class is the constructor, which makes the necessary system calls to fill in the data members:

```cpp
// Drive.cpp

#include <windows.h>
#include "Drive.h"

Drive::Drive(TCHAR driveLetter)
{
    // Check whether the drive exists, and throw if it doesn't
    DWORD dwDrives = GetLogicalDrives();

    if (dwDrives == 0)
        throw "Drive: GetLogicalDrives failed";

    letter = driveLetter;

    short nDrv = driveLetter - 'A';
    if (dwDrives & (1 << nDrv))
    {
        // Create a root string
        wsprintf(sRoot, "%c:\\", driveLetter);

        // Get type
        uType = GetDriveType(sRoot);
        if (uType == 0)
        {
            TCHAR sErr[256];
            wsprintf(sErr, "Drive: error getting drive type (%s)", sRoot);
            throw sErr;
        }
        else if (uType == 1)
        {
            TCHAR sErr[256];
            wsprintf(sErr, "Drive: root directory given was invalid (%s)", sRoot);
            throw sErr;
        }

        // Get volume information... if this is a removable drive which is empty,
        // these calls won't work. set the flags to reflect this.
        DWORD dwVolID, dwMaxLen, dwFSAtt;

        if (GetVolumeInformation(sRoot, sVolName, 31, &dwVolID,
            &dwMaxLen, &dwFSAtt, sFileSysName, 254))
            bHasVolInfo = true;
        else
            bHasVolInfo = false;

        // And disk space info
        UINT uOldMode = SetErrorMode(SEM_FAILCRITICALERRORS);

        if (GetDiskFreeSpaceEx(sRoot, &uAvailUser, &uTotal, &uFree))
            bHasSpaceInfo = true;
        else
            bHasSpaceInfo = false;
```

```
        SetErrorMode(uOldMode);
    }
    else
        throw "Drive: drive letter not found";
}
```

The code is pretty straightforward. Given a drive letter, the function checks that such a logical drive exists. If it does, it gets the drive type and saves it away, and then gets the volume and space information. If anything doesn't work, an exception is thrown. Note that removable drives might not have media in them at the time the call is made, in which case the volume information and disk space calls will fail. I've chosen a straight-forward way to handle this, which simply involves setting a flag to say whether or not these pieces of information are available.

Note the call to **SetErrorMode()**. If it isn't there and you're working with a removable drive that doesn't have a disk in it, you'll get a system error message box displayed. Setting the error mode as shown will suppress this so that the application can deal with the 'error' without the user having to intervene, which is obviously what we want here.

Try It Out - Using the DriveCollection Class

Here's our previous example rewritten to use the **Drive** and **DriveCollection** classes rather than the plain API calls:

```
// getdrive.cpp

#include <windows.h>
#include <iostream>
#include <cstdio>
using namespace std;

#include "Drive.h"
#include "DriveCollection.h"

int main()
{
    cout << "Found " << DriveCollection::numDrives() << " drives" << endl;
    cout << "We " << (DriveCollection::hasDrive('B') ? "have " : "haven't ") <<
        "got drive B:" << endl;
    cout << "We " << (DriveCollection::hasDrive('C') ? "have " : "haven't ") <<
        "got drive C:" << endl;
    cout << endl;

    DriveCollection dc;
    //DriveCollection dc(DriveCollection::noRemovable);
    //dc.Reset();

    const Drive* pd = NULL;

    do
    {
        try
        {
            pd = dc.EnumDrives();
        }
```

```
            catch(const char* ps)
            {
               cout << "Error: " << ps << endl;
            }

            if (pd)
            {
               cout << "Got drive '" << pd->driveLetter() << "'";
               //if (pd->isRemovableDrive())
               //   cout << " (removable)";

            switch(pd->driveType())
            {
            case DRIVE_UNKNOWN:
               cout << " (error getting drive type)" << endl;
               break;
            case DRIVE_NO_ROOT_DIR:
               cout << " (root directory given was invalid)" << endl;
               break;
            case DRIVE_CDROM:
               cout << " - CDROM";
               break;
            case DRIVE_FIXED:
               cout << " - Fixed disk";
               break;
            case DRIVE_RAMDISK:
               cout << " - RAM disk";
               break;
            case DRIVE_REMOTE:
               cout << " - Remote";
               break;
            case DRIVE_REMOVABLE:
               cout << " - Removable";
               break;
            }

            if (pd->hasVolInfo())
               cout << ", vol=" << pd->volumeName() << ", FileSys="
                    << pd->fileSystemName();

            cout << endl;

            if (pd->hasVolInfo() && pd->hasSpaceInfo())
               printf("  AvailUser=%I64u, Total=%I64u, Free=%I64u\n",
                  pd->spaceAvailableToUser().QuadPart, pd->totalDiskSpace().QuadPart,
                  pd->freeDiskSpace().QuadPart);

            }

      } while (pd);

   return 0;
}
```

The only real difference is in the few lines added at the start, which print the total number of drives, and check for two specific ones. When I ran the program, I got output like this:

```
"D:\TEMP\test\Debug\test.exe"                                    _ □ ✕
Found 7 drives
We haven't got drive B:
We have got drive C:

Got drive 'A' - Removable
Got drive 'C' - Fixed disk, vol=, FileSys=FAT
  AvailUser=349143040, Total=2146467840, Free=349143040
Got drive 'D' - Fixed disk, vol=, FileSys=NTFS
  AvailUser=455909376, Total=1636797952, Free=455909376
Got drive 'E' - Fixed disk, vol=, FileSys=FAT
  AvailUser=525860864, Total=526106624, Free=525860864
Got drive 'F' - CDROM, vol=DN600ENU2, FileSys=CDFS
  AvailUser=0, Total=570886144, Free=0
Got drive 'G' - Removable
Got drive 'X' - Remote
Press any key to continue
```

System Software Information

The next section covers a few items of system software information which can often be useful — the names of the computer and logged-in user, system colors, and a whole set of metrics and system parameters.

Computer And User Names

In this section, we'll look at the functions available for manipulating the name of the computer and the user, and we'll add code to the **Systeminfo** class, so that we can make use of this functionality.

Manipulating The Computer Name

There are two functions that allow us to manipulate the computer name. First, **GetComputerName()** allows us to retrieve the name of the computer (that is, the name that the computer held at the time the computer was started):

```
BOOL GetComputerName(LPTSTR pName, LPDWORD pChars);
```

The second parameter is a pointer to a **DWORD**. It is used to specify the length of the name. On return, it contains the number of characters actually copied, minus the terminating null. The maximum length of a computer name is determined by the **MAX_COMPUTERNAME_LENGTH** system constant. If the function call fails, then the return value is **FALSE**.

Second, **SetComputerName()** allows us to change the name. Note that the change only comes into effect once the machine has been restarted:

```
BOOL SetComputerName(LPCTSTR pNewName);
```

Again, the return value is **FALSE** if the function call fails.

Getting The User's Name

The function `GetUserName()` returns the user name for the current thread:

```
BOOL GetUserName(LPTSTR pBuff, LPDWORD pSize);
```

On input, the second parameter specifies the size of the buffer. On output, it returns the number of characters retrieved.

The function usually retrieves the name of the logged-in user, but it is possible for a thread to impersonate another client, in which case the name of the client will be returned.

Extending The SystemInfo Class

If we want to get access to the computer and user name information, it would seem that the `SystemInfo` class is a good place to add it. To get these names, we simply need to add suitable buffers to the class as a data member, and inline functions to return them to the caller. Add the shaded lines to your `sysinfo.h` file:

```
class SystemInfo
{
    SYSTEM_INFO si;
    // system information block
    OSVERSIONINFO os;        // OS information block

    TCHAR sMachineName[MAX_COMPUTERNAME_LENGTH + 1];

    enum { USERNAME_LENGTH=256 };
    TCHAR sUserName[USERNAME_LENGTH];
    // ...
```

At this stage, we can also add a prototype for a function to set the computer name:

```
    DWORD majorVersion() { return os.dwMajorVersion; }
    DWORD minorVersion() { return os.dwMinorVersion; }
    // Machine name information
    LPCTSTR getName() { return sMachineName; }
    LPCTSTR getUserName() { return sUserName; }
    void setName(LPCTSTR name);
```

We can then call the relevant functions in the class constructor to fill in the buffers. Add this shaded code to `sysinfo.cpp`:

```
SystemInfo::SystemInfo()
{
    // Fill the information structures
    GetSystemInfo(&si);

    // GetVersionEx can return FALSE, so throw if it does
    os.dwOSVersionInfoSize = sizeof(OSVERSIONINFO);
    if (!GetVersionEx(&os))
        throw "SystemInfo: can't get OSVERSIONINFO";
```

```
    // Get the machine name
    DWORD dwSize = MAX_COMPUTERNAME_LENGTH + 1;
    if (!GetComputerName(sMachineName, &dwSize))
        throw "SystemInfo: can't get machine name";

    // Get the user name
    dwSize = USERNAME_LENGTH;
    if (!GetUserName(sUserName, &dwSize))
        throw "SystemInfo: can't get user name";
}
```

Setting the name merely requires a call to **SetComputerName()**, and throwing an error if the call fails:

```
void SystemInfo::setName(LPCTSTR name){
    if (!SetComputerName(name))
        throw "SystemInfo: can't set machine name";
}
```

System Color Information

Windows maintains a set of colors that are used for various on-screen elements, such as window backgrounds, text foregrounds and backgrounds, menu highlights and so on. Most of these can be set by the user, using the Control Panel. However, it's also possible to manipulate them programmatically.

With the **GetSysColor()** function, we can query the system color tables, and we can use the **SetSysColors()** functon to redefine the colors in the table.

Getting System Colors

The **GetSysColor()** function returns the color corresponding to an element specified by the parameter **nIndex**:

```
DWORD  GetSysColor(int  nIndex);
```

There are over 30 possible choices for the parameter. They're shown in the following table:

Element Name	Description
COLOR_3DDKSHADOW	Dark shadow color for 3D effects
COLOR_3DFACE	Face color for 3D effects
COLOR_3DHILIGHT	Highlight color for 3D effects (edges facing light source)
COLOR_3DLIGHT	Light color for 3D effects (edges facing light source)
COLOR_3DSHADOW	Shadow color for 3D effects (edges facing away from light)
COLOR_ACTIVEBORDER	Border for active window
COLOR_ACTIVECAPTION	Caption bar for active window
COLOR_APPWORKSPACE	Background for MDI frame window
COLOR_BACKGROUND	Windows desktop

Element Name	Description
COLOR_BTNFACE	Button face color
COLOR_BTNHILIGHT	Button highlight color
COLOR_BTNHIGHLIGHT	Same as COLOR_BTNHILIGHT
COLOR_BTNSHADOW	Button shadow color
COLOR_BTNTEXT	Button text color
COLOR_CAPTIONTEXT	Caption bar text color
COLOR_DESKTOP	Same as COLOR_BACKGROUND
COLOR_GRAYTEXT	Color of grayed text — may be set to 0 if the device driver doesn't support solid gray color
COLOR_HIGHLIGHT	Background of selected items (e.g. in a list or menu)
COLOR_HIGHLIGHTTEXT	Text color of selected items
COLOR_INACTIVEBORDER	Border of inactive window
COLOR_INACTIVECAPTION	Caption bar color for inactive window
COLOR_INACTIVECAPTIONTEXT	Text color for inactive window
COLOR_INFOBK	Tooltip background color
COLOR_INFOTEXT	Tooltip text color
COLOR_MENU	Menu background color
COLOR_MENUTEXT	Menu text color
COLOR_MSGBOX	Background color for message boxes and system dialogs
COLOR_MSGBOXTEXT	Text color for message boxes and system dialogs
COLOR_SCROLLBAR	Background color for scrollbars
COLOR_SHADOW	Color for automatic Windows shadows — cannot be set via the Control Panel
COLOR_WINDOW	Window background
COLOR_WINDOWFRAME	Window frame color
COLOR_WINDOWTEXT	Window text color

The color value is returned as a DWORD, which holds the red, green and blue components of the color. The usual Windows COLORREF type, which is used everywhere to manipulate RGB colors, is simply a typedef for a DWORD. Hence, you can use the return value from the GetSysColor() function anywhere you need a COLORREF.

Setting System Colors

The SetSysColors() function allows you to set one or more of these system color values:

```
BOOL SetSysColors(int nVals, CONST INT* pVals, CONST COLORREF* pColors);
```

To use this function, you must supply two arrays, in the second and third parameters. The second parameter holds the indices of the items that you want to set, and the third parameter holds the corresponding color values. The first parameter gives the size of both arrays. If the function fails (for instance, if one or both arrays are of the wrong length), it will return FALSE.

Constructing COLORREFS

Colors are defined as COLORREFs, which pack the red, green and blue values into a single number. The simplest way of constructing a COLORREF is using the RGB() macro, which is defined in **wingdi.h**:

```
#define RGB(r,g,b)
((COLORREF)(((BYTE)(r)|((WORD)((BYTE)(g))<<8))|(((DWORD)(BYTE)(b))<<16)))
```

The red, green and blue components can take values from 0 to 255.

Try It Out — Manipulating System Colors

Here's a sample program, **colors.cpp**, that demonstrates these functions in action. Try running it from a non-full screen DOS window with another application open in the background, and see how the colors change:

```cpp
// colors.cpp

#include <windows.h>

int main()
{
    // Get the current settings for the active and inactive caption bar colors
    COLORREF activeCol = GetSysColor(COLOR_ACTIVECAPTION);
    COLORREF inactiveCol = GetSysColor(COLOR_INACTIVECAPTION);

    // Declare arrays to hold the new values
    COLORREF cols[2];
    int uVals[2];

    // Set the active caption to yellow
    cols[0] = RGB(0,255,255);
    uVals[0] = COLOR_ACTIVECAPTION;

    // Set the inactive caption to green
    cols[1] = RGB(0,255,0);
    uVals[1] = COLOR_INACTIVECAPTION;

    // Change the colors
    SetSysColors(2, uVals, cols);

    // Wait so you can see what is going on
    Sleep(2000);

    // Set them back again
    cols[0] = activeCol;
    uVals[0] = COLOR_ACTIVECAPTION;
    cols[1] = inactiveCol;
    uVals[1] = COLOR_INACTIVECAPTION;
    SetSysColors(2, uVals, cols);

    return 0;
}
```

159

Metrics And Parameters

Two functions are available for retrieving a whole host of values relating to the system.

Getting Non-Graphical System Information

The first, `GetSystemMetrics()`, really belongs to the GDI graphics functions, but we'll consider it here because it also returns some useful non-graphical information:

```
int GetSystemMetrics(int nIndex);
```

The parameter is the index of the system metric whose value you want. There are over 75 possible metrics which can be retrieved using this function. The following table shows those which are non-GDI specific:

Index Value	Description
SM_CLEANBOOT	How was the machine started? May return 0 (normal boot), 1 (Fail-safe boot) or 2 (Fail-safe with network boot)
SM_DBCSENABLED	TRUE if the Double Byte Character Set version of **user.exe** is installed
SM_DEBUG	TRUE if the debug version of **user.exe** is installed
SM_KEYBOARDPREF	TRUE if the user relies on the keyboard rather than the mouse
SM_MOUSEPRESENT	TRUE if a mouse is present
SM_NETWORK	TRUE if the machine is connected to a network
SM_SECURE	TRUE if security is present
SM_SHOWSOUNDS	TRUE if the user wants applications to show visual events where otherwise only a sound would be used
SM_SLOWMACHINE	TRUE if the machine has a low-end processor

Getting And Setting System Parameters

The second function, `SystemParametersInfo()`, can be used to get and set a huge number of system parameters:

```
BOOL  SystemParametersInfo(
    UINT  uAction,      // the parameter to be get or set
    UINT  uParam,       // generic data item used by some parameters
    PVOID pParam,       // ditto
    UINT  uUpdate);     // user profile update flag
```

The first function parameter determines which system parameter the call is concerned with, and whether it is being retrieved or set. There are over 80 possible parameters. A representative selection of them is shown in the table below:

Value	Description
SPI_GETKEYBOARDDELAY	Gets the keyboard delay setting
SPI_GETMENUDROPALIGNMENT	Gets the menu alignment — whether menus drop down to the left or right
SPI_GETMOUSETRAILS	Are mouse trails active?
SPI_GETSCREENSAVEACTIVE	Is the screen saver enabled?
SPI_GETWINDOWSEXTENSION	Is the Windows Plus! pack installed?
SPI_GETWORKAREA	Get the desktop work area (the area not covered by the tray)
SPI_ICONVERTICALSPACING	Get the vertical spacing for icons
SPI_SETDESKPATTERN	Set the desktop pattern
SPI_SETDESKWALLPAPER	Set the desktop wallpaper
SPI_SETDOUBLECLICKTIME	Set the double-click delay
SPI_SETSCREENSAVEACTIVE	Enable or disable the screen saver

These system parameters may have associated data items, which are passed using the second and third function parameters. The precise nature of this data depends entirely on the system parameters, for example:

▶ SPI_ICONVERTICALSPACING uses the uParam value as the icon spacing in pixels

▶ SPI_SETSCREENSAVEACTIVE uses the uParam value to decide whether to enable or disable the screensaver

▶ SPI_SETDESKWALLPAPER uses the pParam value to point to a string representing the filename

Consult the online documentation for the full list of system parameters and the values they take.

The final parameter determines how the user profile in the registry will be updated. It can take the following values:

Value	Description
0	No update occurs
SPIF_SENDCHANGE	Broadcasts a WM_WININICHANGE message after the profile has been updated
SPIF_SENDWININICHANGE	Same as SPIF_SENDCHANGE
SPIF_UPDATEINIFILE	Writes the changes to the registry

Time Information

Win32 stores the system time as a Universal Coordinated Time (UTC) value. The UTC value is related to GMT. Because system times are stored as UTC, it is necessary for applications to call a function, in order to derive their appropriate local time.

Manipulating System Time

The system time is manipulated through calls to `GetSystemTime()` and `SetSystemTime()`:

```
void  GetSystemTime(LPSYSTEMTIME  lpTime);
BOOL  SetSystemTime(const  SYSTEMTIME*  lpTime);
```

Both calls use a **SYSTEMTIME** structure, which holds the information you would expect:

```
typedef struct _SYSTEMTIME {
    WORD wYear;
    WORD wMonth;
    WORD wDayOfWeek;
    WORD wDay;
    WORD wHour;
    WORD wMinute;
    WORD wSecond;
    WORD wMilliseconds;
} SYSTEMTIME;
```

Local Time Information

The `GetLocalTime()` function also returns the time in a **SYSTEMTIME** structure, as a local time which is corrected for any daylight saving which may be in operation. And since the local and system times are related, the `SetLocalTime()` function will also have the effect of setting the system time:

```
void  GetLocalTime(LPSYSTEMTIME  lpTime);
BOOL  SetLocalTime(const  SYSTEMTIME*  lpTime);
```

Converting between the system and local times involves knowing about the time zone which applies to the local time. This is set by the user from the Control Panel, and you can retrieve and modify the current settings using the `GetTimeZoneInformation()` and `SetTimeZoneInformation()` functions:

```
DWORD GetTimeZoneInformation(LPTIME_ZONE_INFORMATION  lptmz);
BOOL  SetTimeZoneInformation(const  TIME_ZONE_INFORMATION  *ptmz);
```

These functions contain information about the conversion factors between system and local time, as well as information on when daylight saving time starts and ends.

The return value from `SetTimeZoneInformation()` indicates whether the attempt to reset the time zone worked or not. The return value from `GetTimeZoneInformation()` tells you which time zone it found, and may be one of the following values:

Value	Description
`TIME_ZONE_ID_STANDARD`	The time zone is within the range for standard time
`TIME_ZONE_ID_DAYLIGHT`	The time zone is within the range for daylight saving time
`TIME_ZONE_ID_UNKNOWN`	Could not retrieve the time zone information

Both `SetTimeZoneInformation()` and `GetTimeZoneInformation()` functions make use of a `TIME_ZONE_INFORMATION` structure, as shown below:

```
typedef struct _TIME_ZONE_INFORMATION {
    LONG Bias;
    WCHAR StandardName[32];
    SYSTEMTIME StandardDate;
    LONG StandardBias;
    WCHAR DaylightName[32];
    SYSTEMTIME DaylightDate;
    LONG DaylightBias;
} TIME_ZONE_INFORMATION, *PTIME_ZONE_INFORMATION, *LPTIME_ZONE_INFORMATION;
```

The `StandardName` and `DaylightName` members give the descriptive names for the time zone — for example, 'British Summer Time' or 'CDT'. The `Bias` gives the difference (in minutes) between UTC and local time, and the `StandardBias` and `DaylightBias` members give the difference between system time and the standard and daylight local times. In most time zones, the `StandardBias` is zero, because the `Bias` member is used to calculate standard time.

The sum of the `Bias` and the `StandardBias` or `DaylightBias` gives the actual difference between system and local time. The two `SYSTEMTIME` members hold the dates when daylight saving time starts and finishes.

Try It Out — Manipulating Time Information

The following example program, **timemanip.cpp**, shows these time functions in use:

```
// timemanip.cpp

#include <windows.h>
#include <iostream>
#include <tchar.h>

using namespace std;

int main()
{
    SYSTEMTIME st;

    // Get system and local times
    GetSystemTime(&st);
    cout << "System time is " << st.wHour << ":" << st.wMinute
         << ":" << st.wSecond << endl;
```

```
    GetLocalTime(&st);
    cout << "Local time is " << st.wHour << ":" << st.wMinute
        << ":" << st.wSecond << endl;

    // Get timezone information
    TIME_ZONE_INFORMATION tmz;
    DWORD dwRet = GetTimeZoneInformation(&tmz);

    // Are we in daylight saving time?
    if (dwRet == TIME_ZONE_ID_UNKNOWN)
        cout << "Cannot get time zone information" << endl;
    else if (dwRet == TIME_ZONE_ID_STANDARD)
        cout << "We're in standard time" << endl;
    else if (dwRet == TIME_ZONE_ID_DAYLIGHT)
        cout << "We're in daylight saving time" << endl;

    // Look at time zone information
    TCHAR buff[255];

    // Convert name from wide characters
    char nm[80];
    WideCharToMultiByte(CP_ACP, 0, tmz.StandardName, -1, nm, 80, NULL, NULL);

    wsprintf(buff, "Standard name is %s, bias=%d", nm,
        tmz.Bias + tmz.StandardBias);
    cout << buff << endl;

    WideCharToMultiByte(CP_ACP, 0, tmz.DaylightName, -1, nm, 80, NULL, NULL);

    wsprintf(buff, "Daylight name is %s, bias=%d", nm,
        tmz.Bias + tmz.DaylightBias);
    cout << buff << endl;

    cout << "Daylight saving starts on " << tmz.DaylightDate.wDay << '/'
        << tmz.DaylightDate.wMonth << endl;
    cout << "Daylight saving ends on " << tmz.StandardDate.wDay << '/'
        << tmz.StandardDate.wMonth << endl;

    return 0;
}
```

Here is the output that I got when running this program:

> *Note that we have to convert the time zone names in order to print them. They are stored as an array of* WCHARs: *we need to convert them to a format that* cout *is happy to print. To do this we use the* WideCharToMultiByte() *function, which is discussed later in the chapter.*

Process Information

Now let's consider those functions which deal with the current process.

Retrieving Command Line Information

First of all, `GetCommandLine()` can be used to retrieve the command line which was used to start the program:

```
LPTSTR  GetCommandLine();
```

Also, the `GetStartupInfo()` function tells you how a process has been started up by its parent process. This function is covered in detail in Chapter 6.

Adding A Process Class

We'll find use for a class representing a process later on, but we can start building it now, and add a function to get the command line.

```cpp
// process.h

#ifndef PROCESS_H
#define PROCESS_H

class Process
{
public:
   Process();
   ~Process();

   LPCTSTR getCommandLine();
};

#endif
```

The `getCommandLine()` function is pretty simple:

```cpp
// process.cpp
#include "process.h"

LPCTSTR Process::getCommandLine()
{
   // Return a const pointer to the command line
   return static_cast<LPCTSTR>(GetCommandLine());
}
```

For safety's sake, we'll return the command line as a constant pointer.

> *One very useful extension to this class would be a function for parsing and returning command line arguments. Implementation of such a function is left as an exercise for the reader!*

Manipulating Environment Variables

The environment strings of the process can be manipulated using four functions, which are summarized in the following sections.

Retrieving Environment Strings

The function **GetEnvironmentStrings()** returns a pointer to the block of environment strings:

```
LPVOID GetEnvironmentStrings();
```

The return value points to a block of null-terminated strings, each of which is of the form *key=value*. The final string is followed by an extra null.

> *This data should be regarded as read-only, and no attempt should be made to modify the environment data using the pointer returned by GetEnvironmentStrings().*

Manipulating Environment Variables

In order to modify individual environment variables, the functions **GetEnvironmentVariable()** and **SetEnvironmentVariable()** are available.

Let's have a look at the **GetEnvironmentVariable()** function first:

```
DWORD GetEnvironmentVariable(LPCTSTR pName, LPTSTR pValue, DWORD dwSize);
```

The first parameter holds the name, and the second parameter is a pointer to a buffer, to hold the value. The third parameter gives the size of the buffer. The function returns 0 if the variable was not found. Otherwise it returns the number of characters written to the buffer. If the buffer is too small, then the return value represents the size of buffer needed.

The **SetEnvironmentVariable()** function is used to change the value of an environment variable or create a new one:

```
BOOL SetEnvironmentVariable(LPCTSTR pName, LPTSTR pValue);
```

The function returns **TRUE** if the function call succeeds, and **FALSE** if it fails.

Try It Out — Manipulating Environment Variables

The following example, **envvarmanip.cpp**, shows how to use these calls to create and read an environment variable.

All text following a **'/E'** *flag on the command line is taken to be the value of a new environment variable called* **'Test'**. *Note that for simplicity, this is an ASCII-only example.*

```cpp
// envvarmanip.cpp

#include <windows.h>
#include <iostream>

using namespace std;

int main()
{
   char szCmdLine[MAX_PATH + 20];

   // Get the command line and print it
   strcpy(szCmdLine, GetCommandLine());

   cout << "Command line was '" << szCmdLine << "'" << endl;

   // Look for the '/E' marker...
   LPTSTR pVar = strstr(szCmdLine, "/E");
   if (!pVar)
   {
      cout << "No environment variable on command line" << endl;
      exit(1);
   }

   // Step past the flag characters
   pVar += 2;

   // Create an environment variable called 'Test'
   char szName[32];
   char szVal[256];
   strcpy(szName, "Test");
   if (!SetEnvironmentVariable(szName, pVar))
   {
      cout << "Error setting environment variable" << endl;
      exit(1);
   }

   // Print the environment table
   LPTSTR pValue;
   LPTSTR pEnv = GetEnvironmentStrings();

   while (*pEnv)
   {
      // Find '=' separating key and value, and make it into a null.
      // pEnv now points to the key, and pValue to the value
      pValue = strstr(pEnv+1, "=");
```

```
        if (pValue)
        {
          *pValue = '\0';
           pValue++;
        }

        cout << pEnv << "  " << pValue << endl;

        // Jump over null
        pEnv += strlen(pEnv) + 1 + strlen(pValue) + 1;
    }

    // Get the environment variable and print it out
    GetEnvironmentVariable(szName, szVal, sizeof szVal);
    cout << "Value is " << szVal << endl;

    return 0;
}
```

The last few lines of output for this program is shown below:

More Environment Variable Manipulation

Our final environment function is `ExpandEnvironmentStrings()`, which is used to expand strings which include environment variable strings:

```
DWORD  ExpandEnvironmentStrings(LPCTSTR pSrc,  LPTSTR pDest,  DWORD nSize);
```

For example, the environment variable **windir** has the value **C:\WINNT** on my machine. This variable can be used in other strings by enclosing it in percent signs, like this:

```
%windir%\Profiles
```

The `ExpandEnvironmentStrings()` function can be used to expand this into

```
C:\WINNT\Profiles
```

The code that performs this transformation is as follows:

```
TCHAR szStr[255];
ExpandEnvironmentStrings("%windir%\\Profiles", szStr, sizeof szStr);
```

Adding Environment Functions

We can usefully create a class for manipulating environment variables, and especially to aid us in enumerating them. Here's the header file, **Env.h**:

```
// Env.h

#ifndef ENV_H
#define ENV_H

// Define a suitable size for the work buffer
#define ENV_BUFF_SIZE 256

class Env
{
    // work string used to return environment variables and strings.
    // you can't assume what this will hold from call to call.
    TCHAR sEnvValue[ENV_BUFF_SIZE];

    LPTSTR pEnv;     // Environment block pointer
    LPTSTR pCpy;     // Own copy of environment block
    int nVar;        // index used when enumerating

    long getTableSize();
    void initEnv();
    void freeEnv();

public:
    Env();
    ~Env();

    LPCTSTR getEnvVariable(LPCTSTR pName);
    bool setEnvVariable(LPCTSTR pName, LPCTSTR pValue);
    LPCTSTR expandEnvString(LPCTSTR pStr);
    bool enumEnvVars(LPCTSTR *ppName, LPCTSTR *ppValue);
    void reset();
};

#endif
```

We have direct wrapper functions for getting, setting and expanding environment variables, and an enumeration function to return us each one in turn.

> *Note that this version of the class isn't thread safe, and shouldn't be relied upon to work correctly if more than one thread within a process is accessing the same* Env *object. The following chapter discusses threads and the problems they can pose in more detail.*

The implementation starts with the constructor and destructor, which are simply wrappers for the **initEnv()** and **freeEnv()** functions:

```
// Env.cpp

#include "Env.h"
```

```
Env::Env()
{
   initEnv();
}

Env::~Env()
{
   freeEnv();
}
```

We do it this way because later we want to implement `reset()`, which needs to reinitialize the object, and this saves repeating code. The `initEnv()` function gets a pointer to the environment block, and then creates a local copy for use by the enumeration function:

```
void Env::initEnv()
{
   nVar = 0;
   pCpy = 0;
   pEnv = GetEnvironmentStrings();

   // Get the table size
   long size = getTableSize();

   // Make a copy
   pCpy = new TCHAR[size];
   memcpy(pCpy, pEnv, size);
}
```

The `freeEnv()` function deletes this memory, and frees the environment block pointer:

```
void Env::freeEnv()
{
   if (pCpy)
      delete[] pCpy;

   FreeEnvironmentStrings(pEnv);
}
```

The `getTableSize()` function finds the size of the environment block by looking for the two **NULL**s which signal the end:

```
long Env::getTableSize()
{
   long size = 0;
   LPTSTR pTemp = pEnv;
   for(;;)
   {
      if (*pTemp == _T('\0') && *(pTemp+1) == _T('\0'))
      {
         size += 2;
         break;
      }
      size++;
      pTemp++;
   }

   return size;
}
```

The wrapper functions to get, set and expand a variable are very simple:

```
LPCTSTR Env::getEnvVariable(LPCTSTR pName)
{
   if (!GetEnvironmentVariable(pName, sEnvValue, sizeof sEnvValue))
      throw "Env: cannot get environment variable";

   return sEnvValue;
}

bool Env::setEnvVariable(LPCTSTR pName, LPCTSTR pValue)
{
   if (!SetEnvironmentVariable(pName, pValue))
      return false;

   return true;
}

LPCTSTR Env::expandEnvString(LPCTSTR pStr)
{
   // expand the input string, and return it
   if (ExpandEnvironmentStrings(pStr, sEnvValue, sizeof sEnvValue) == 0)
      throw "Env: cannot expand environment string";

   return sEnvValue;
}
```

The `enumEnvVars()` function handles enumeration, returning one name/value pair each time it is called, until no more are left, when the function returns **FALSE**:

```
bool Env::enumEnvVars (LPCTSTR *pVName, LPCTSTR *pVVal)
{
   // enumerate the environment variables, and return false when done
   LPTSTR pVal;

   // pT points to the start of the next item in the block
   LPTSTR pT = pCpy+nVar;

   // find the next '='
   pVal = _tcsstr(pT+1, _T("="));
   if (pVal)
   {
      // replace it by a null and move on one character. pVal now points to
      // the start of the value
      *pVal = _T('\0');
      pVal++;
   }
   else
   {
      // no more equals were found, so we're finished
      pVName = pVVal = NULL;
      return false;
   }

   // move the position counter to point past this name/value pair
   nVar += _tcslen(pT) + 1 + _tcslen(pVal) + 1;
```

```
      // make up the return values
      *pVName = pT;    *pVVal = pVal;

      return true;
}
```

The function uses **nVar** as an index into the environment block, pointing at the start of the next variable to be retrieved. When the function is called, **pT** is used to point to the starting point in the block, and the functon searches for the next '='. If there isn't a '=' then we're finished, so the function returns **FALSE**. If there is a '=' then it is replaced by a **NULL**, and **pVal** moved to point to the next character. We then have **pT** pointing to the name string, and **pVal** to the value. The final actions are to update **nVar** to point to the next variable in the string, and to return the strings.

The **reset()** function lets you start enumeration over again. Since the enumeration process changes the environment string by replacing '=' symbols with nulls, we need to recreate the environment string by freeing up the old one and reinitializing the object:

```
void Env::reset()
{
   freeEnv();
   initEnv();
}
```

Try It Out — Using Environment Variables

Here's an example which shows the environment class in use:

```
// envtest.cpp

#include <windows.h>
#include <iostream>

using namespace std;

#include "Env.h"

int main()
{
   Env e;

   bool bOK;              // success flag
   LPCTSTR pN, pV;        // pointers to name and value strings

   // Enumerate the environment strings
   do
   {
      bOK = e.enumEnvVars(&pN, &pV);
      if (bOK)
         cout << pN << ": " << pV << endl;
   } while (bOK);
```

```
      // Set up a new environment variable and retrieve its value
      if (!e.setEnvVariable("fred", "hello"))
         cout << "setEnvVariable failed (" << GetLastError() << "'" << endl;
      else
         cout << "New variable 'fred' has value '" << e.getEnvVariable("fred")
              << "'" << endl;

      // Reset the Env variable, and enumerate the strings again
      e.reset();
      do
      {
         bOK = e.enumEnvVars(&pN, &pV);
         if (bOK)
            cout << pN << ": " << pV << endl;
      } while (bOK);

      return 0;
   }
```

Locale Information

Users of Windows 95 and NT will usually want to set up their machine to reflect the country and culture in which they are working. There are a number of settings that may need to be changed, such as the character set, keyboard layout, currency symbol, time zone information, and so on.

The collection of settings which define a particular nationality setup is called a **locale**. Locales play an important role in National Language Support (NLS) — this is the part of the Win32 API which deals with supporting language and nationality conventions. We'll be covering the NLS routines in this section (Locale Information) and the next section (String Manipulation).

To enable the user to select or edit locale information, there are various places within the Control Panel — for example, the Date / Time and Regional Settings applets.

In programs, locales are referred to by locale ID, or **LCID**. You have the option of creating a new locale at any time, by using the **MAKELCID** macro:

```
DWORD MAKELCID(WORD wLang, WORD wSortID);
```

The first parameter, **wLang**, is the language identifier, and the secon parameter, **wSortID**, is a sorting identifier. The documentation advises that **SORT_DEFAULT** should be used as the second parameter.

Language Identifiers

Language identifiers are created using the **MAKELANGID** macro:

```
WORD MAKELANGID(USHORT uPrimary, USHORT uSecondary);
```

There are two parameters to the macro. The first is a primary language identifier, such as **LANG_ARABIC** or **LANG_ENGLISH**. For certain languages, it is necessary to specify a secondary language identifier, in the second parameter. This is used to specify dialects — for example **SUBLANG_ENGLISH_US** or **SUBLANG_ENGLISH_UK**:

```
// Create a language ID for Jamaican English
WORD wl = MAKELANGID(LANG_ENGLISH, SUBLANG_ENGLISH_JAMAICA);

// Create a language ID for Brazilian Portugese
WORD wl = MAKELANGID(LANG_PORTUGESE, SUBLANG_PORTUGESE_BRAZILIAN);
```

There are three special combinations of language and sublanguage which have a particular meaning:

Language	Sublanguage	Meaning
LANG_NEUTRAL	SUBLANG_NEUTRAL	The locale is 'language neutral', and has no national language dependencies
LANG_NEUTRAL	SUBLANG_DEFAULT	The user's default language
LANG_NEUTRAL	SUBLANG_SYS_DEFAULT	The system default language

Although there are a large number of primary and secondary language identifiers detailed in the online help, we can create our own language IDs for any language which isn't covered by the standard list. This means that we can create a language ID for Welsh or Gaelic, with appropriate sublanguages, provided we use a value between **0x0200** and **0x03ff**. We'll see these macros being used in an example very shortly.

Standard Locales

Most of the time you don't need to create your own locale, as most software will run using the locale that the user has selected for their machine. There are two standard locales — the system default locale (**LOCALE_SYSTEM_DEFAULT**) and the user's current locale (**LOCALE_USER_DEFAULT**) — and you can use these predefined **LCID**s wherever a locale ID is requested.

You can test whether a locale ID is valid by using the **IsValidLocale()** function.

```
BOOL IsValidLocale(LCID lc, DWORD dwFlags);
```

The function tests the given locale ID is installed and supported (if the flag is **LCID_INSTALLED**) or supported (**LCID_SUPPORTED**).

Manipulating Locale Information

Now that we know what a locale is and how to create new ones, let's look at how to retrieve and manipulate locale information. As you might expect by now, we have a matching pair of functions to get and set locales, `GetLocaleInfo()` and `SetLocaleInfo()`:

```
int GetLocaleInfo(LCID loc, LCTYPE lct, LPTSTR lpBuff, int nSize);
int SetLocaleInfo(LCID loc, LCTYPE lct, LPCTSTR lpcBuff);
```

Both functions will return zero if an error occurs, and you can use `GetLastError()` to find out what went wrong.

The `LCID` parameter refers to the locale whose data we want to get or set. The `LCTYPE` parameter denotes which item of data is being retrieved from (or changed within) the locale. There are over 80 possible items associated with a locale. If you want the full list, you'll need to consult the online help (look under 'Locale Constants'). Some of the more common are shown in the table below:

Item Identifier	Meaning
LOCALE_ICOUNTRY	Country code, based on international phone codes
LOCALE_ILANGUAGE	The language identifier (as returned by MAKELANGID)
LOCALE_SCOUNTRY	The fully localized country name
LOCALE_SENGCOUNTRY	The English country name
LOCALE_SENGLANGUAGE	The English equivalent language name
LOCALE_SLANGUAGE	The fully localized language name
LOCALE_SDECIMAL	The decimal separator character
LOCALE_SLIST	The list item separator
LOCALE_STHOUSAND	The thousands separator
LOCALE_ICURRENCY	How the currency symbol is displayed (0=prefixed, 1=suffixed, 2=prefixed with separator, 3=suffixed with separator)
LOCALE_SCURRENCY	String used as local monetary symbol
LOCALE_INEGCURR	How negative currency amounts are displayed. Values can range from 0–15, and tell you (for instance) whether the minus sign comes before or after the currency symbol)
LOCALE_IDATE	Month/day/year ordering (0=month–day–year, 1=day–month–year, 2=year–month–day)
LOCALE_SABBREVDAYNAME1	Local abbreviation for 1st weekday
LOCALE_SLONGDATE	Long date format

The remaining parameters point to a buffer which either receives or contains the value for the locale item. Note that all items are passed as strings, even if they represent numeric values.

Try It Out — Manipulating Locale Information

The following example, `localemanip.cpp`, shows how to manipulate locale information:

```cpp
// localemanip.cpp

#include <windows.h>
#include <iostream>
#include <tchar.h>

using namespace std;

int main()
{
   TCHAR tCode[20];
   TCHAR tCountry[80];

   // Get and display some system locale info
   GetLocaleInfo(LOCALE_SYSTEM_DEFAULT, LOCALE_ICOUNTRY, tCode, 19);
   GetLocaleInfo(LOCALE_SYSTEM_DEFAULT, LOCALE_SCOUNTRY, tCountry, 79);

   cout << "(System) Country is " << tCountry << " (" << tCode << ")" << endl;

   // Do we support UK English?
   WORD wUKEng = MAKELANGID(LANG_ENGLISH, SUBLANG_ENGLISH_UK);
   LCID lcUKEng = MAKELCID(wUKEng, SORT_DEFAULT);
   if(IsValidLocale(lcUKEng, LCID_INSTALLED))
      cout << "UK English locale supported and installed" << endl;
   else
      cout << "UK English locale not installed" << endl;

   return 0;
}
```

Here is the output I got when I ran this on my machine:

The results you get when you run this example will depend on how your machine is set up — the UK English locale is present on my machine, but it might not be on yours. In that case you may wish to change the locale which the program looks for, to check for one which is present.

Finding What Locales Are Available

In order to enumerate all the locales which are supported by the system, we can use the `EnumSystemLocales()` function:

```cpp
BOOL EnumSystemLocales(LOCALE_ENUMPROC lpFunc, DWORD dwFlags);
```

As with most Win32 enumeration functions, the routine takes a pointer to a user-supplied callback function which returns a **BOOL** value and has the following prototype:

```
BOOL CALLBACK callbackFunc(
    LPTSTR pLocale);          // LCID of locale
```

The system calls this function once for each locale it supports. Passing it the **LCID** of the locale as a string parameter. The function the processes the locale, and returns **TRUE** if the enumeration is to continue. If the routine returns **FALSE**, the enumeration finishes.

Try It Out — Listing Locales

In this example, `localesearch.cpp`, the function **CALLBACK** always returns **TRUE** because we're simply listing all locales. In contrast, if we were looking for a *particular* locale then we'd write a function to return **FALSE** as soon as we'd found it, and set a global flag to tell the caller that the search was successful.

```cpp
// localesearch.cpp

#include <windows.h>
#include <iostream>

using namespace std;

// Define a buffer size
#define BUF_SIZE 255

BOOL CALLBACK EnumFunc(LPTSTR pLoc)
{
    LCID lc;
    char sCtry[BUF_SIZE+1];
    char sLang[BUF_SIZE+1];

    // Turn the string into an LCID
    sscanf((char*)pLoc, "%x", &lc);

    GetLocaleInfo(lc, LOCALE_SNATIVECTRYNAME, sCtry, BUF_SIZE);
    GetLocaleInfo(lc, LOCALE_SNATIVELANGNAME, sLang, BUF_SIZE);

    cout << "(" << lc << ") Country: " << sCtry << ", Language: " << sLang
        << endl;

    return TRUE;
}

int main()
{
    cout << "Installed Locales: " << endl << endl;
    EnumSystemLocales(static_cast<LOCALE_ENUMPROC>(EnumFunc), LCID_INSTALLED);

    cout << "Supported Locales: " << endl << endl;
    EnumSystemLocales(static_cast<LOCALE_ENUMPROC>(EnumFunc), LCID_SUPPORTED);

    return 0;
}
```

The flag parameter can take two values — `LCID_INSTALLED` and `LCID_SUPPORTED` — which enumerate the locales installed and supported by the system. These are then printed out as a long list, the last few dozen entries show below:

Getting The Default LCIDs

If you want to retrieve the actual `LCID`s corresponding to the defaults, you can use the `GetSystemDefaultLCID()` and `GetUserDefaultLCID()` functions.

Equivalent functionality is provided by the `ConvertDefaultLocale()` routine:

```
LCID  ConvertDefaultLocale(LCID ldef);
```

where `ldef` can take one of the following values:

- ▶ `LOCALE_SYSTEM_DEFAULT`
- ▶ `LOCALE_USER_DEFAULT`
- ▶ Zero (in this case, it returns the language-neutral default locale)
- ▶ Any language ID with a neutral sublanguage

Using Locales With Threads

OK, now we can find, create, interrogate and edit locales, how do we actually make a program use a given locale? Locales are associated with individual threads, so we can use the `SetThreadLocale()` and `GetThreadLocale()` functions to make a thread use a given locale, and find out which locale it is currently using. These function calls are very simple:

```
BOOL  SetThreadLocale(LCID lc);
LCID  GetThreadLocale();
```

The `SetThreadLocale()` function sets the thread to use a given locale ID. The function returns **FALSE** if an error occurs. This would happen, for example, if the locale ID is not supported or is otherwise invalid.

The `GetThreadLocale()` function returns the current locale of the calling thread.

Try it Out — Setting and Checking the Locale

We can modify the program **localemanip.cpp**, so that the primary thread uses the UK English locale:

```cpp
// localeset.cpp

#include <windows.h>
#include <iostream>
#include <tchar.h>

using namespace std;

int main()
{
   TCHAR tCode[20];
   TCHAR tCountry[80];

   // Get and display some system locale info
   GetLocaleInfo(LOCALE_SYSTEM_DEFAULT, LOCALE_ICOUNTRY, tCode, 19);
   GetLocaleInfo(LOCALE_SYSTEM_DEFAULT, LOCALE_SCOUNTRY, tCountry, 79);

   cout << "(System) Country is " << tCountry << " (" << tCode << ")" << endl;

   // Do we support UK English?
   WORD wUKEng = MAKELANGID(LANG_ENGLISH, SUBLANG_ENGLISH_UK);
   LCID lcUKEng = MAKELCID(wUKEng, SORT_DEFAULT);

   if(IsValidLocale(lcUKEng, LCID_INSTALLED))
   {
      cout << "UK English locale (" << hex << lcUKEng << dec
           << ") supported and installed" << endl;

      // OK, let's use the UK English locale
      BOOL bOK = SetThreadLocale(lcUKEng);
      if(!bOK)
         cout << "Error setting locale to UK English" << endl;
      else
      {
         LCID lc = GetThreadLocale();
         cout << "Thread locale is " << hex << lcUKEng << dec << endl;
      }
   }
   else
      cout << "UK English locale not installed" << endl;

   return 0;
}
```

179

Once we've established that the locale is supported, we use **SetThreadLocale()** to force the thread to use that locale. Then we call **GetThreadLocale()** to check what we have.

Here's the output that I got from my machine:

Your machine might give you something slightly different, depending on your local settings and support.

Locale-Related Conversion Routines

The locale information basically tells us how we need to format up various data items. We can get this information by using the **GetLocaleInfo()** function, with the appropriate flags — but there are a number of helper routines provided by the Win32 API which make life easier.

Here are four routines that help with converting the basic types affected by the locale — currency, dates, numbers and times. They all have fairly large argument lists, as you can see from their prototypes. The prototype of **GetCurrencyFormat()** is:

```
int GetCurrencyFormat(
    LCID  lc,                      // locale to use for conversion
    DWORD dwFlags,                 // conversion flags
    LPCTSTR lpVal,                 // the string to convert
    CONST CURRENCYFMT* lpFmt,      // pointer to a currency format
    LPTSTR lpOut,                  // converted string
    int cchCurr);                  // number of characters in returned
                                   // string
```

The remaining three routines are similar in structure:

```
int GetDateFormat(LCID lc, DWORD dwFlags, CONST SYSTEMTIME* pDate, LPCTSTR
                  lpFormat, LPTSTR lpOut, int nBuffSize);
int GetNumberFormat(LCID lc, DWORD dwFlags, LPCTSTR lpVal, CONST NUMBERFMT*
                  pFormat, LPTSTR pOut, int nBuffSize);
int GetTimeFormat(LCID lc, DWORD dwFlags, CONST SYSTEMTIME* pDate, LPCTSTR
                  lpFormat, LPTSTR lpOut, int nBuffSize);
```

They're fairly simple in operation. We just pass certain parameters to the function — a locale, an input string and a pointer to a format string (which may be **NULL**). If this pointer is non-**NULL**, then the format string is used to format up the value. If it is **NULL**, then the default format for the locale is used.

The second parameter, **dwFlags**, determines how the conversion will be done.

Function	Meaning of dwFlags Parameter
`GetCurrencyFormat()`	0 to use format overrides **LOCALE_NOUSEROVERRIDE** to use the locale default value
`GetDateFormat()`	**LOCALE_NOUSEROVERRIDE** to use the locale default value **DATE_LONGDATE** to use the long date format **DATE_SHORTDATE** to use the short date format **DATE_USE_ALT_CALENDAR** to use the alternate calendar (if one exists) to format up the string
`GetNumberFormat()`	As for currency
`GetTimeFormat()`	**LOCALE_NOUSEROVERRIDE** to use the locale default value **TIME_FORCE24HOURFORMAT** **TIME_NOMINUTESORSECONDS** **TIME_NOSECONDS** **TIME_NOTIMEMARKER**

Try It Out — Formatting the Locale

You can see how this works if we add code to the example **localeset.cpp** program, so that it formats up the current date, changes the locale, and then formats the date again:

```cpp
// localeformat.cpp

#include <windows.h>
#include <iostream>
#include <tchar.h>

using namespace std;

int main()
{
   TCHAR tCode[20];
   TCHAR tCountry[80];
   TCHAR szDateBuffer[255];

   // Get and display some system locale info
   GetLocaleInfo(LOCALE_SYSTEM_DEFAULT, LOCALE_ICOUNTRY, tCode, 19);
   GetLocaleInfo(LOCALE_SYSTEM_DEFAULT, LOCALE_SCOUNTRY, tCountry, 79);

   cout << "(System) Country is " << tCountry << " (" << tCode << ")" << endl;
   GetDateFormat(GetThreadLocale(),
       DATE_LONGDATE,
       NULL,
       NULL,
       szDateBuffer, 254);

   cout << "Date is " << szDateBuffer << endl;

   // Do we support UK English?
   WORD wUKEng = MAKELANGID(LANG_ENGLISH, SUBLANG_ENGLISH_UK);
   LCID lcUKEng = MAKELCID(wUKEng, SORT_DEFAULT);
```

```
if(IsValidLocale(lcUKEng, LCID_INSTALLED))
{
    cout << "UK English locale (" << hex << lcUKEng << dec
        << ") supported and installed" << endl;

    // OK, let's use the UK English locale
    BOOL bOK = SetThreadLocale(lcUKEng);
    if(!bOK)
        cout << "Error setting locale to UK English" << endl;
    else
    {
        LCID lc = GetThreadLocale();
        cout << "Thread locale is " << hex << lcUKEng << dec << endl;

        GetDateFormat(GetThreadLocale(),
            DATE_LONGDATE,
            NULL,
            NULL,
            szDateBuffer, 254);

        cout << "Date is " << szDateBuffer << endl;
    }
}
else
    cout << "UK English locale not installed" << endl;

return 0;
}
```

The output from this program will look something like this:

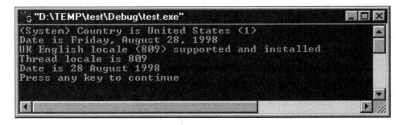

String Manipulation

Windows NT 4.0 has to support three operating environments — Win32, POSIX and MS-DOS —
and this brings with it a number of headaches in the area of string handling.

Part of this is due to the need to support old DOS applications, which use an old-fashioned
character set. In recent years, there has also been a growing need to make operating systems
and programs language-friendly, moving computers away from the Latin alphabet-centered view
which dominated DOS programs.

Character Sets

The Win32 API has to support three main types of character set:

▶ The ASCII sets — ANSI (the default for Win95) and OEM (the default for DOS)
▶ MBCS — the multi-byte character set
▶ Unicode — the default for NT

> *OEM stands for Original Equipment Manufacturer, which is another way of saying that this character set may vary from manufacturer to manufacturer.*

Let's briefly consider each of these in turn.

ASCII Character Sets

Both the ANSI and OEM 8-bit character sets are derivatives of the original ASCII (American Standard Code for Information Interchange) character set. ASCII is 7-bit code, which allows it to hold 127 characters — barely enough for the English alphabet, numbers and punctuation, plus a few special codes used to control output devices (control codes). Many of these control codes, such as form feed and vertical tab, are now all but obsolete, but are still included in the standard ASCII set.

The ANSI and OEM sets are 8-bit, which gives them the ability to store 256 characters. ANSI uses the space to add some national and mathematical symbols, while the OEM set adds IBM line-drawing symbols, and also defines symbols for special characters (control characters with numeric values less than 32).

Both have the same basic alphanumeric symbols (i.e. 'P' is 0x50 and space is 0x20), but the content and position of the special characters is different between the two.

MBCS

MBCS (Multi-Byte Character Set) is a standard C character set standard, which was developed by the American National Standards Institute (ANSI) in 1989. This character set allows characters to be represented by one or two bytes, a facility particularly important to countries such as China and Japan, which need to support very large (and sometimes multiple) character sets. An example of a multi-byte character set is the Japanese Industry Standard (JIS) character set, which supports several Japanese character sets including Kanji and Katakana/Hiragana.

The name MBCS is often used interchangeably with DBCS (Double Byte Character Set), but this isn't really accurate, as not all MBCS characters are two bytes. The single-byte characters in an MBCS character set usually map onto the normal ANSI single-byte set. Because strings may be made up of a mixture of single and double byte characters, processing an MBCS string is not as efficient as either ANSI or Unicode, which use purely single and double byte characters respectively.

> *In Visual C++ programs, you tend to use the preprocessor symbols **_MBCS** and **_UNICODE** to show which character set you're using. If you're using English characters and you use **_MBCS**, you'll end up with the single-byte MBCS characters which map onto the ANSI set. If you specify **_UNICODE**, you'll get double-byte Unicode characters.*

The intermixing of single and double byte characters is managed by defining 'lead bytes', which denote that the following byte is part of a double-byte character. These characters can be detected using the `IsDBCSLeadByte()`function, which is where the processing inefficiency shows up.

Unicode

Unicode is a multi-byte character set in which each character is composed of two bytes. Unicode is not a Microsoft invention, but has been developed by the Unicode Consortium, a body set up in 1989 by Xerox and Apple, and later joined by AT&T, IBM, Lotus, Microsoft, NeXT and Novell (visit `http://www.unicode.org` for more information). They published their first standard, Unicode 1.0, in 1990. At the same time, ISO had been working on a similar scheme, ISO 10646, which was a 32-bit system with room to handle 2 billion characters. In order to avoid confusion, the Unicode Consortium and ISO agreed to combine their standards, so that the Unicode 1.1 and ISO 10646 character sets are identical in their 16-bit ranges, but ISO 10646 retains the ability to store 32-bit characters.

The fact that all Unicode characters are two bytes gives a possibility of 65536 different characters. It makes character strings more efficient to handle, but at the expense of increased storage requirements. Unicode is used internally by Windows NT (and also by the Java programming language), but the increased storage requirements is one of the main reasons why it isn't heavily used in Windows 95.

> *As well as being the native character set for Windows NT, Unicode is used as the native Java character set, and is also used extensively in COM for passing character strings between COM (and OLE and ActiveX) components. If you want to use COM functionality with MBCS code, you'll soon get used to converting to and from Unicode.*

String Portability Types And Macros

When you start looking at the Win32 API, you will see a lot of character data types that you may not have met before, such as `LPTSTR` and `TCHAR`. These are special character macros designed to help write code which will work using either the ANSI or Unicode character sets.

The idea is that you write your code in terms of `TCHAR`s, and the preprocessor then converts those into references to ANSI or Unicode characters, depending on the preprocessor flags that are set. The possible preprocessor flags are

- `_UNICODE`, which causes Unicode to be used
- `_MBCS`, which causes the MultiByte Character Set to be used
- None, which causes single-byte ASCII to be used

There is also a range of generic string handling functions, which map onto variants that take the correct data types.

Portability Types

Here — slightly simplified — is the definition of TCHAR from winnt.h:

```
typedef wchar_t WCHAR;
...
#ifdef _UNICODE
typedef WCHAR TCHAR;
#else
typedef char TCHAR;
#endif
```

You can see from this that if the program is being compiled using Unicode, TCHAR ends up being mapped onto the C++ wide character type, wchar_t. If anything else is being used, TCHAR maps onto char.

So for maximum portability you should write your code in terms of TCHAR and its derived pointer types, LPTSTR (pointer to a TCHAR) and LPCTSTR (const pointer to a TCHAR).

Portable character constants are declared using the _T() macro. Instead of "abc", you would use _T("abc"). The preprocessor will expand the macro into the right sort of string or character constant.

Generic Functions

Many of the string handling functions you'll be familiar with, such as strcat() and strcpy(), are ASCII-only C Runtime Library functions. This means that we need new versions of these functions in order to work with Unicode and MBCS.

Microsoft have produced a set of generic string functions, and, once again, the preprocessor will map the generic function onto the right one for the character set in use.

As an example, the generic routine _tcscpy() maps onto the following routines:

Preprocessor Defines	Mapped Routine
None	strcpy(char*, const char*)
_UNICODE	wcscpy(wchar_t*, const wchar_t*)
_MBCS	_mbscpy(unsigned char*, const unsigned char*)

String Handling Functions

String data can come from any source, so we need to be able to convert freely between the three character sets.

Converting Between ANSI And OEM Sets

Conversions to and from the ANSI and OEM character sets uses four functions:

```
BOOL  CharToOem(LPCTSTR pSrc, LPTSTR pDest);
BOOL  CharToOemBuff(LPCTSTR pSrc, LPTSTR pDest, DWORD dwLength);
BOOL  OemToChar(LPCSTR pSrc, LPTSTR pDest);
BOOL  OemToCharBuff(LPCSTR pSrc, LPTSTR pDest);
```

The functions `CharToOem()` and `CharToOemBuff()` convert a string from the character set of the current locale to an OEM-defined character set. `CharToOem()` does the whole string, while `CharToOemBuff()` converts a specified number of characters. Any characters which don't exist in the OEM set are replaced by their nearest equivalent.

Note that all four of these functions always return **TRUE**

The `OemToChar()` functions translate the other way, once again choosing the best match for characters which don't exist in the ANSI character set. Data which originates from the DOS environment will need to be processed by one of these two functions before it can be used in the Windows environment.

Converting To And From Unicode

The `IsTextUnicode()` function can be used to determine whether text in a buffer is likely to be composed of Unicode characters. The prototype for this function is shown below:

```
DWORD  IsTextUnicode(CONST LPVOID pBuff, int nBuffSize, LPINT pFlags);
```

The `IsTextUnicode()` function takes a buffer of specified length, plus a pointer to an integer which specifies a set of flags. There are 18 possible flags, which determine the tests that will be used on the string. You can pass **NULL** in order to use them all. The return value from the function is 0 if the buffer does not pass all the tests, and non-zero if it does.

Note that this function only tells you whether a buffer is likely to contain a Unicode string

There is pair of functions that can be used to convert between Unicode and MBCS strings:

▶ `MultiByteToWideChar()` to convert from MBCS to Unicode
▶ `WideCharToMultiByte()` to convert from Unicode to MBCS

The first of these functions is shown below:

```
int  MultiByteToWideChar(
     UINT nCodePage,                // code page
     DWORD dwFlags,                 // translation flags
     LPCSTR lpMBCSBuff,             // pointer to input buffer
     int nMBCSBuffSize,             // input buffer length
     LPWSTR lpWideBuff,             // pointer to output buffer
     int nWideBuffSize);            // output buffer length
```

The operation of **MultiByteToWideChar()** is fairly simple. You pass it an input buffer, and the content is converted and stored in the output buffer. If you give a length of -1 for the input buffer, it is assumed to be null-terminated.

The return value tells you the number of characters copied, and will be zero if an error occurred.

The first argument specifies the code page to use for the translation to Unicode. Any valid code page can be used — it is very common to use the symbol **CP_ACP** to denote the default ANSI code page.

The translation flags are fairly esoteric. There are four altogether, but the only one of these you might need to use in day-to-day work is **MB_ERR_INVALID_CHARS**, which causes the function to abort and return zero if any invalid characters were found. If that happens, you can use **GetLastError()** and look for the **ERROR_NO_UNICODE_TRANSLATION** error. (We discussed how to use **GetLastError()** in the last chapter.)

The matching routine, **WideCharToMultiByte()**, is similar in operation, but takes a couple of extra parameters:

```
WideCharToMultiByte(
    UINT   nCodePage,         //  code  page
    DWORD  dwFlags,           //  translation  flags
    LPCWSTR lpWideBuff,       //  pointer  to  input  buffer
    int  nWideBuffSize,       //  input  buffer  length
    LPSTR  lpMBCSBuff,        //  pointer  to  output  buffer
    int  nMBCSBuffSize,       //  output  buffer  length
    LPCSTR  lpDefChar,        //  default  character
    LPBOOL  pbUsedDef);       //  was  default  character  used?
```

Because Unicode contains far more characters than MBCS can accommodate, it is possible that a Unicode string might contain characters for which no equivalent exists in MBCS. For this reason, we have the **lpDefChar** parameter, which is a pointer to a default character to be used if the translation of a particular character is not possible. If it is set to **NULL**, then the default character from the code page is used instead. If the default character translation is used, the **pbUsedDef** flag will be set. Once again, the flags are rather esoteric, and it is usual to use zero for this parameter.

Try It Out — Converting Strings

Here's an example program showing string conversion in action:

```
// stringconv.cpp

#include <windows.h>
#include <iostream>

using namespace std;

int main()
{
```

```
    // Here's a wide character string. Note how the 'L' denotes a wide string
    // constant
    WCHAR wideStr[] = L"A wide string";

    // The wcslen() function returns us the length of a wide string
    int nLen = wcslen(wideStr)+1;

    // Now the buffer to hold the converted characters
    char* pBuff = new char[nLen];

    // Convert the wide string
    if (WideCharToMultiByte(
        CP_ACP,                 // use default ANSI code page
        0,                      // no default character processing
        wideStr,                // string to convert
        -1,                     // assume null-termination
        pBuff,                  // buffer to take result
        nLen,                   // buffer size
        NULL, NULL) == 0)       // no default character processing
    {
        cout << "Conversion failed (" << GetLastError() << ")" << endl;
        return -1;
    }

    cout << "String is '" << pBuff << "'" << endl;

    return 0;
}
```

The output from the program is simply the following:

Other String Routines

We'll round off this discussion of strings by covering some of the miscellaneous string handling routines provided by the API.

`GetStringTypeEx()` gives you information about the characters in any single or multi-byte string.

```
BOOL  GetStringTypeEx(
    LCID  locale,           // locale ID
    DWORD dwInfoType,       // type of information wanted
    LPCTSTR pSrc,           // pointer to source string
    int  nChars,            // length of source string (-1 if null
                            // terminated)
    LPWORD  lpCharType);    // pointer to info array
```

The information type can take one of three values:

▶ **CT_CTYPE1** — to get character information

▶ **CT_CTYPE2** — to get bi-directional layout information

▶ **CT_CTYPE3** — to get text-processing information

The return value from the function is an array of WORDs, one for each character in the input string. Each of the 16 bits in a WORD denotes a particular flag, which is set by the function to denote the characteristics of the corresponding character.

We won't go into the full range of information that can be returned about characters here — this can be found in the online help. For the purposes of illustration, however, the table below shows the values that can be returned when character information (**CT_CTYPE1**) is requested:

Flag Value	Meaning
C1_ALPHA	Any linguistic character
C1_BLANK	Blank character
C1_CNTRL	Control character
C1_DIGIT	Digit
C1_LOWER	Lower-case character
C1_PUNCT	Punctuation character
C1_SPACE	Space character
C1_UPPER	Upper-case character
C1_XDIGIT	Hexadecimal digit

CT_CTYPE2 values tell you about the way the text has been laid out, and works for both European (left-to-right) and Arabic (right-to-left) text layouts. In addition to the **CT_CTYPE1** values, it will also return you such information as the text direction, and where numbers begin and end. The **CT_CTYPE3** level adds information about word-processing features, such as accents and symbols.

If you want to compare two character strings, the Win32 API provides the **CompareString()** function for this purpose. This function is rather more flexible than the old **strcmp()** method.

```
int CompareString(
    LCID locale,            // locale to use
    DWORD dwFlags,          // comparison flags
    LPCTSTR pString1,       // first string
    int nChars1,            // length of first string
    LPCTSTR pString2,       // second string
    int nChars2);           // length of second string
```

The flags comprising the second parameter control how the comparison is performed:

Flag Value	Meaning
`NORM_IGNORECASE`	Ignore case
`NORM_IGNOREKANATYPE`	Ignore distinction between Hiragana and Katakana characters
`NORM_IGNORENONSPACE`	Ignore non-spacing characters
`NORM_IGNORESYMBOLS`	Ignore symbols
`NORM_IGNOREWIDTH`	Ignore differences in character byte width
`NORM_STRINGSORT`	Treat punctuation as symbols

There are four possible return values for this function:

▶ 0 means an error has occurred

▶ 1 means string1 is less than string2

▶ 2 means string1 and string2 are equal within the specified length

▶ 3 means string1 is greater than string2

Try It Out — Getting String Information

We can extend the preceding program to get information about the type of characters stored in the string:

```
// stringinfo.cpp

#include <windows.h>
#include <iostream>

using namespace std;

int main()
{
    // Here's a wide character string. Note how the 'L' denotes a wide string
    // constant
    WCHAR wideStr[] = L"A wide string";

    // The wcslen() function returns us the length of a wide string
    int nLen = wcslen(wideStr)+1;

    // Now the buffer to hold the converted characters
    char* pBuff = new char[nLen];

    // Convert the wide string
    if (WideCharToMultiByte(
        CP_ACP,              // use default ANSI code page
        0,                   // no default character processing
        wideStr,             // string to convert
        -1,                  // assume null-termination
        pBuff,               // buffer to take result
        nLen,                // buffer size
        NULL, NULL) == 0)    // no default character processing
```

190

```
    {
       cout << "Conversion failed (" << GetLastError() << ")" << endl;
       return -1;
    }

    cout << "String is '" << pBuff << "'" << endl;

    // Allocate result buffer
    LPWORD pInfo = new WORD[nLen];

    // Get the type 1 information for the string
    if (!GetStringTypeEx(
       LOCALE_SYSTEM_DEFAULT,                // use default locale
       CT_CTYPE1,                            // get type 1 information
       static_cast<LPCTSTR>(pBuff),          // buffer to examine
       -1,                                   // assume it is null terminated
       pInfo))                               // array to hold results
    {
       cout << "GetStringTypeEx() failed (" << GetLastError() << ")" << endl;
       return -1;
    }

    // Print out the information - bits will be set in each WORD to show the
    // attributes of each character. We're not testing for every possible bit,
    // because we know that the sample string doesn't contain digits or punctuation

    for (int j=0; j<nLen; j++)
    {
       cout << pBuff[j] << ": ";

       if (pInfo[j] & C1_ALPHA) cout << "alpha ";
       if (pInfo[j] & C1_BLANK) cout << "blank ";
       if (pInfo[j] & C1_CNTRL) cout << "control ";
       if (pInfo[j] & C1_LOWER) cout << "lower ";
       if (pInfo[j] & C1_UPPER) cout << "upper ";

       cout << endl;
    }

    return 0;
}
```

When you run the program, you should get the following output. Notice how the terminating **NULL** shows up as a control character:

Logging-Off And Shutting Down

It is possible, when running under both Windows NT and Windows 95, to log the current user off, and even shutdown or reboot the machine. In this section, we're going to look at some of the functions provided by the Win32 API that enable you to to this programatically.

`ExitWindowsEx()` will close all open applications and log the user off. It can also optionally reboot or shutdown the machine. This function is often useful in applications such as installation programs, which need to restart the system as part of their normal functioning.

```
BOOL ExitWindowsEx(UINT  uOptions,  DWORD  dwRes);
```

The first parameter gives the type of action you require:

Value	Meaning
EWX_FORCE	Force processes to terminate
EWX_LOGOFF	Shut down applications for the current user and log them off
EWX_POWEROFF	Shut down processes and turn off the power. The system must support power-off, and the application must have **SE_SHUTDOWN_NAME** privilege
EWX_REBOOT	Shutdown and reboot the system. On NT, the application must have **SE_SHUTDOWN_NAME** privilege
EWX_SHUTDOWN	Shutdown to where it is safe to turn off the power. On NT, the application must have **SE_SHUTDOWN_NAME** privilege

The second parameter must currently be zero. The function returns **TRUE** if it works, and **FALSE** if it doesn't.

You may need to manipulate the privileges for the process in order to get the **SE_SHUTDOWN_NAME** privilege. Privileges and how to use them are discussed in Chapter 8, on security.

`ExitWindows()` is a macro which calls `ExitWindowsEx()` with the `EWX_LOGOFF` parameter, so that it closes down all applications and logs off the current user. Both parameters must be set to 0 in this call.

```
BOOL bOK = ExitWindows(0, 0);
```

Shutting Down With User Involvement

If you want to allow for user interaction when initiating a shutdown of the machine, you can do this using the `InitiateSystemShutdown()` function:

```
BOOL  InitiateSystemShutdown(
     LPTSTR  pMachine,       // machine  to  shutdown
     LPTSTR  pMessage,       // Message  to  display
     DWORD   dwTimeout,      // Time  to  display  dialog
     BOOL    bForce,         // Force  applications  with  unsaved  changes  to
                             // quit
     BOOL  bReboot);         // Reboot  flag
```

The function displays a message box asking the user whether or not they want to shut down. You can supply the message you wish to display as the second parameter, and the message box is displayed for a time specified by the third parameter, **dwTimeout** (in seconds). If this is zero, then the system shuts down immediately and does not display a message. The function returns **TRUE** if the shutdown request succeeds.

The last two parameters allow you to specify whether or not the machine should be rebooted, and whether applications with unsaved data should be forced to close.

If you want to shut down the local machine, you should pass zero for the machine name parameter, and obtain the **SE_SHUTDOWN_NAME** privilege. If you want to shut down a remote machine, you will need to have the **SE_SHUTDOWN_REMOTE_NAME** privilege.

Try It Out — Shutting Down

The following example shows this process in action. We haven't yet covered privileges and how to set them, but we're going to need to use them in this example. Included below is a listing for a function called **AdjustPrivilege()**, which we'll develop later in Chapter 8, so if you want to get to the bottom of how this function works and what it is doing, you should consult that chapter.

```cpp
// Shutdown.cpp

#include <windows.h>
#include <iostream>

using namespace std;

BOOL AdjustPrivilege(LPTSTR pPriv, BOOL bSet)
{
    HANDLE token;
    if(!OpenProcessToken(GetCurrentProcess(),
        TOKEN_ADJUST_PRIVILEGES | TOKEN_QUERY, &token))
    {
        cout << "Error in OpenProcessToken (" << GetLastError() << ")" << endl;
        return FALSE;
    }

    LUID lu;
    if(!LookupPrivilegeValue(0, pPriv, &lu))
    {
        cout << "Error in LookupPrivilegeValue (" << GetLastError() << ")" << endl;
        return FALSE;
    }

    TOKEN_PRIVILEGES tp;
    tp.PrivilegeCount = 1;
    tp.Privileges[0].Luid = lu;

    // Set or revoke privilege depending on flag
    tp.Privileges[0].Attributes = (bSet) ? SE_PRIVILEGE_ENABLED : 0;
```

```
    if(!AdjustTokenPrivileges(token, FALSE, &tp, 0, 0, 0))
    {
        cout << "Cannot adjust token privilege (" << GetLastError() << ")" << endl;
        return FALSE;
    }

    return TRUE;
}

int main()
{
    int retCode = 0;

    // Get the right privilege
    if (!AdjustPrivilege(SE_SHUTDOWN_NAME, TRUE))
    {
        cout << "Couldn't set shutdown privilege (" << GetLastError() << ")"
            << endl;
        return -1;
    }

    // Shutdown this machine, with a 30 second gap. Don't force apps
    // to quit or reboot
    if (InitiateSystemShutdown(0, "Shutdown started...", 30, FALSE, FALSE))
    {
        // We're going down...
        cout << "System shutting down" << endl;
    }
    else
    {
        // There was an error
        cout << "InitiateSystemShutdown failed, code " << GetLastError() << endl;
        retCode = -1;
    }

    AdjustPrivilege(SE_SHUTDOWN_NAME, FALSE);

    return retCode;
}
```

The example shown above uses the **AdjustPrivilege()** function to get the **SE_SHUTDOWN_NAME** privilege required for shutdown. If that succeeds, then **InitiateSystemShutdown()** is called to shut down the local machine, displaying the dialog box for 30 seconds. At the end of the countdown, running applications are shut down and the user logged off, leaving the machine displaying the "It is now safe to turn off your machine" message box.

If the shutdown didn't work, the error is displayed to the user and the privilege removed before shutting down.

Aborting Shutdown

It is possible to abort the shutdown process if you call **AbortSystemShutdown()** during the 'countdown' when the dialog is displayed:

```
BOOL AbortSystemShutdown(LPTSTR pMachine);
```

You still need the **SE_SHUTDOWN_NAME** privilege to use this call on your own machine, and the **SE_SHUTDOWN_REMOTE_NAME** privilege for a remote machine.

Try It Out — Aborting Shutdown

The code to abort a shutdown is almost identical to the previous example:

```cpp
// AbortShutdown.cpp

#include <windows.h>
#include <iostream>
using namespace std;

BOOL AdjustPrivilege(LPTSTR pPriv, BOOL bSet)
{
   // See code listing above
}

int main()
{
   int retCode = 0;

   // Get the right privilege
   if (!AdjustPrivilege(SE_SHUTDOWN_NAME, TRUE))
   {
      cout << "Couldn't set shutdown privilege (" << GetLastError() << ")"
           << endl;
      return -1;
   }

   // Abort the shutdown
   if (AbortSystemShutdown(0))
      cout << "System shutdown aborted" << endl;
   else
   {
      // There was an error
      cout << "AbortSystemShutdown failed, code " << GetLastError() << endl;
      retCode = -1;
   }

   AdjustPrivilege(SE_SHUTDOWN_NAME, FALSE);

   return retCode;
}
```

If you want to see how this works in practice, open two console windows and run the shutdown application from one of them, and then interrupt it by running the abort program from the other.

Summary

We've seen in this chapter that the Win32 API provides us with a wide range of functions which allow us to interact with the system and manipulate its resources.

System hardware information functions uses the **SYSTEM_INFO** structure to find out the system architecture, the number and type of the processor. The **OSVERSIONINFO** structure tells you the operating system name and version.

The disk information functions such as **GetDriveType()**, **GetVolumeInformation()** and **GetDiskFreeSpace()** let you work with logical drives, performing operations such as getting the number, type and drive letter for drives, finding free space and setting volume labels.

We've seen how we can get the computer and current user names from the system software information, and we've discussed how Win32 handles color information, before looking at the large number of system metrics and parameters that can be queried using **GetSystemMetrics()** and **SystemParametersInfo()**.

Windows NT stores time information as Universal Coordinated Time (UTC), and we saw how to manipulate both the time and timezone.

We can retrieve the command line with which a process was invoked, and manipulate its environment variables.

We've looked at locales, which are the way in which NT handles the difficult problem of internationalization by providing a way to describe culture or nationality-dependent information, such as alphabet, currency symbols and representation, number formatting and so on. We saw how they are referred to in programs by a locale ID (**LCID**), and how to find out whether a particular locale is supported.

String handling brings its own complications in Win32, because of the need to support more than one character set. ANSI, the Multi-Byte Character Set (MBCS) and Unicode are all supported under NT, with Unicode being used internally. Win32 provides a series of macros to make code portable between MBCS and ANSI, and conversion functions between the various character set types are also provided.

Finally **ExitWindowsEx()** and **InitiateSystemShutdown()** allow you to take control of system shutdown, logging off the current user, shutting down and even rebooting.

Threads and Processes

In this chapter we're going to look at one of the most powerful programming facilities offered by the Win32 — support for multi-threaded processes. Use of threads can add a lot of power and flexibility to your programs, but (as we will see) they can be tricky to control. By the time you've reached the end of this chapter you should have a good appreciation of how threads work, and how to use them in your programs.

Here's an outline of what we're going to cover:

- An introduction to threads and process, defining the terms and looking at what they can do and when they are useful

- The three sets of threading APIs available to C++ programmers under Win32, and the differences between them

- How threads work

- Thread creation and control

- Thread synchronization — the four objects (critical sections, mutexes, semaphores and events) and the wait functions (such as **WaitForSingleObject()** and **WaitForMultipleObjects()**)

- Problems with threads — deadlocks, race conditions and so on, and how to avoid them

- Creating processes using **CreateProcess()**

> *Everything in this chapter is applicable to both Win95 and Windows NT.*

Introducing Multitasking

Before we get onto threads, lets start with a brief discussion of **multitasking**. Multitasking is the ability for an operating system to run more than one program simultaneously. In fact, to be absolutely correct, this only happens on multi-processor systems. On single-processor systems the operating system simulates simultaneous operation by switching rapidly between running programs (known as **time slicing**). Provided this is done smoothly, it gives the illusion of programs operating together.

There are two forms of multitasking:

- Cooperative
- Pre-emptive

Cooperative Multitasking

Cooperative multitasking was used in 16-bit Windows and the Macintosh operating system up to System 7. As its name implies, this method relies upon programs cooperating with one another. A program has control of the processor until it decides to relinquish control, and there is nothing that the operating system can do to force it to pass control to another process.

In practice, cooperative multitasking uses the program's message loop to switch between tasks, making a program yield control to the system each time around the message loop, when it calls `GetMessage()` or `PeekMessage()`. This tends to work well for intensely message-based applications, such as Notepad, where the application is driven by mouse clicks, key presses and other actions which each generate a message. These messages tend not to result in a lot of processing — adding a character to a buffer, or copying some text — so the flow of messages through the message loop is smooth, which means that the multitasking is smooth too.

It isn't so hot for applications which do a lot of processing, because if the application dives off into a routine to do something which takes a few seconds, no other application is going to get a look in, and it can appear to the user that the whole system has frozen. In such cases, the programmer has to insert code into the processing routine to yield control at suitable intervals, so that the multitasking can continue to work smoothly.

Another drawback of cooperative multitasking is that the system can't use resources efficiently. If a program is waiting to read from disk, it would be more efficient if the system allowed another process to use the processor while the first one is blocked, waiting to read. You can see this in action by trying the old floppy-formatting test. Open a DOS window on a Windows 3.1 machine, start formatting a floppy, and try doing anything else... Then do the same thing on an NT machine, and compare their behavior.

Pre-emptive Multitasking

Pre-emptive multitasking is implemented by Windows NT and most other 'grown-up' operating systems such as Unix. In this case it is the operating system that decides which program is to be run at a given time, based upon factors such as the program's priority and whether it is blocked waiting to read or write.

To work well, pre-emptive multitasking needs a lot less programmer involvement than the old cooperative method, with the operating system working away in the background to make the system work efficiently, by balancing resources and processor allocation. We'll see later in the chapter how you can change the priority of a program in order to give it more time.

Multitasking in Windows NT

What happens if you want to run 16-bit Windows programs on Windows 95 or NT? NT runs them in a way which simulates the Win16 environment, so that by default 16-bit programs:

▶ All run together in a single address space

▶ Use cooperative multitasking with other 16-bit programs in that address space

This is done so that the programs will run in a typical 16-bit environment, just in case someone had written their code to depend on the way in which cooperative multitasking works.

It is also possible under NT to run 16-bit programs in their own address spaces, and in that case they'll all be run pre-emptively against one another.

What are Threads and Processes?

A **process** is the object which owns all the resources used by an application. A **thread** is a separate path of execution within a process. Threads share the process's virtual address space, code and global data, but execute independently of one another and have independent stacks. In the simplest case, a process has a single, main thread, known as the **primary thread**.

> *Note that NT schedules threads, not processes.*

The following diagrams illustrate two processes, one with a single thread:

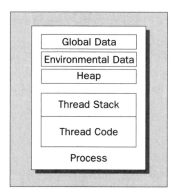

And one with three threads:

Note that they all have access to the process's global data, so that it is quite easy to share global data between threads. The figure above shows three different threads. If the same thread is launched several times, its code is only loaded once.

Where are threads useful? The simple answer is anywhere that we can define some sort of asynchronous task — one we can start up and which will then run on its own. Here are a few examples:

▶ Placing printing and saving into separate threads means that the user can continue interacting with the program while the background activity takes place in a separate thread

▶ For complex graphics programs, placing the screen redrawing code in a separate thread means that the user interface still remains responsive while redrawing is taking place

▶ Using threads can simplify the logic of server processes, where each new client can be handled by starting a new thread

▶ A suitable process can run one thread on each processor of a multi-processor system, so that there is genuine multitasking and the program will run faster

Threads vs Processes

One important difference between threads and processes is that it is much quicker and more efficient to switch between threads than it is between processes. To underline this difference, threads are sometimes called 'lightweight processes'. An NT application consisting of 500 processes is going to have a noticeable impact on system performance, whereas one using 500 threads will be much better behaved.

Context Switching

A thread's **context** consists of the data that describe the current state of the thread, including processor register contents, stack pointer and a pointer to the address space in which the thread runs. When the system switches between threads running within the same process, it has to save the context for one thread, and restore the context for the one that it now wants to execute. This is called a **context switch**, and is much quicker than switching between threads running in different processes, because that requires a lot more state information to be saved, such as the table of open handles and details of the address space.

NT vs Unix

NT is often compared with Unix, the other major multi-user, multitasking operating system. How do they compare in the area of threads and processes?

The major difference is that many flavors of Unix don't have threads or have only gained them recently, and where thread-like functionality is needed, Unix programmers tend to use the `fork()` system call to start another child process. This is possible because Unix processes are more lightweight than NT ones, so having a number of processes executing at once doesn't have quite the impact on system performance that it would under NT. Having said that, it is possible for a Win32 machine to be running 500 threads, while a Unix machine of the same specification may well have problems running 500 processes.

Another advantage of threads is that since they share the process global data, it is easy to pass data between threads belonging to the same process. Passing data between processes is harder, because it may need the complication of IPC (inter-process communication) calls, and there are also problems with sharing some data items between processes (such as handles to kernel objects, which are only meaningful within a single process).

> *You may come across mention of fibers, which were introduced into Win32 with NT version 4.0. A fiber is essentially a lightweight thread, which is scheduled manually by the application itself rather than by the system. Fibers run in the context of the thread which created them, and so the system will still schedule these threads. Fibers were introduced to ease the porting to NT of applications which had been designed to schedule their own threads, such as Win16 applications.*

Creating and Controlling Threads

We've seen what threads are and what they're used for. Now let's go on to see how we create and control threads within our programs.

Thread API Options

Rather confusingly for Win32 programmers, there are three separate APIs that can be used to create and control threads. Which one you choose depends partly on which toolset you're using, and partly on the level of control you require:

- At the bottom level, there's the Win32 API, which provides calls such as `CreateThread()`
- Next, there's the C runtime library calls, which are basically wrappers over the Win32 functions, with functions like `_beginthread()` and `_beginthreadex()`
- Lastly, there are higher-level calls provided by MFC, via its `CWinThread` class

As this book is concerned with programming at the Win32 API level, we'll be concentrating our attention on the first two of these, and we'll see a little later on which of these APIs we ought to be using and when.

*If you're using threads in an MFC application, you should always use **CWinThread** rather than any of the lower level calls, in order to make sure that your thread behaviour integrates properly with the rest of MFC.*

Creating Threads

Here's a simple program which doesn't use threads explicitly, with a main routine calling a single function. In fact, all programs consist of at least one thread, so this code is actually single-threaded:

```
#include <iostream>

using namespace std;

int square(int n);

int main()
{
    int result;

    result = square(5);

    cout << result << endl;

    return 0;
}

int square(int n)
{
    return n*n;
}
```

We all know how this works — the call to **square()** effectively 'blocks' the calling routine, which can't continue until **square()** returns, as shown below.

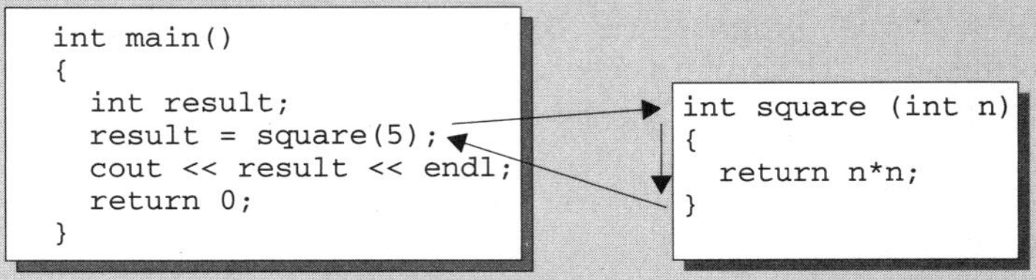

In non-threaded code, calling
square () blocks the calling routine

If we do the same sort of thing with multithreaded code, we end up with a program which looks like this:

```cpp
#include <windows.h>
#include <iostream>

using namespace std;

DWORD WINAPI threadFunc(LPVOID);

int main()
{
    HANDLE hThread = NULL;
    DWORD threadID = NULL;

    hThread = CreateThread(NULL, 0, threadFunc, 0, 0, &threadID);

    if (hThread == NULL)
    {
        cout << "Error creating thread" << endl;
        return -1;
    }

    cout << "Thread running" << endl;

    return 0;
}

DWORD WINAPI threadFunc(LPVOID p)
{
    // Do something...

    return 0;
}
```

In this very simple example, we're using the **CreateThread()** API call to create and run a thread. A thread has to have some code to execute, and we provide this by writing a **thread function**. This function can have any name you like, as long as it takes a single argument of type **LPVOID**, and returns a **DWORD**.

We'll see how **CreateThread()** works and what all the arguments mean in a minute. For now, just note that **CreateThread()** creates a thread for you and sets it running, executing the code in **threadFunc()**. It then returns immediately, so that the calling routine and **threadFunc()** are executing simultaneously. This is illustrated in the following diagram:

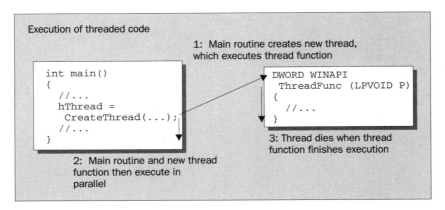

Execution of threaded code

1: Main routine creates new thread, which executes thread function

```
int main()
{
   //...
   hThread =
   CreateThread(...);
   //...
}
```

```
DWORD WINAPI
  ThreadFunc (LPVOID P)
{
   //...
}
```

3: Thread dies when thread function finishes execution

2: Main routine and new thread function then execute in parallel

And if we had three calls to **CreateThread()** in a row, we'd end up with four routines executing at once.

When the thread function has finished executing, either by returning from the thread function or calling **ExitThread()**, the thread expires and silently dies. It is important to realize that the created thread and the main routine are executing quite separately — once the thread has been started, it is on its own, and it doesn't need to have any further interaction with the function which created it.

If that is the case, you might be wondering at this point what the return value from the thread function represents, and how the creating function gets hold of it! The main routine can get the return code — we'll see how shortly — but the important thing to remember is that there doesn't need to be any further interaction once the thread has been started.

Note that if the main routine (the primary thread) dies before the thread functions have finished executing, then all threads will be forcibly terminated, and won't get a chance to clear up.

The CreateThread() Function

At this point, it will be useful to take a closer look at the **CreateThread()** function:

```
HANDLE hThread = CreateThread(
    LPSECURITY_ATTRIBUTES lpSec,      // security
    DWORD dwStack,                    // thread stack
    LPTHREAD_START_ROUTINE lpStart,   // address of thread function
    LPVOID lpParam,                   // pointer to parameters
    DWORD dwFlags,                    // thread creation flags
    LPDWORD lpThreadID);              // thread ID
```

This function takes a number of parameters, many of which we can often safely ignore. The first parameter is a pointer to a security attribute block, which can be used to govern who can access this thread. (We'll be covering the security system in Chapter 8) If you don't want to control access to your thread object, you can safely set this parameter to **NULL**, as we'll be doing in most of the examples presented here.

> On Win32 systems which don't support security, such as Windows 95, this
> parameter is ignored.

The second parameter gives the amount of stack space to be allocated for the thread. If you specify a value of zero, the stack size defaults to the same size as that of the primary thread, which should be quite adequate for most purposes. The stack will also grow, if necessary

The third and fourth parameters are the most essential, specifying the address of the thread function, and a pointer to any arguments that you might want to supply to it respectively. The arguments are passed via a single **void*** pointer, so you (rather than the compiler) are responsible for ensuring that the right data is passed through, and that it is cast back into the correct types at the far end.

As we've already mentioned, the thread function itself can be any function which has the prototype:

```
DWORD  WINAPI   SomeFunc(LPVOID   p);
```

The function returns a **DWORD**, which is used to provide some sort of status return, although what that value is and what it means, is up to you.

The fifth parameter allows you to supply flag values which will govern how the thread behaves when it is created. At the minute there's only one possible flag, **CREATE_SUSPENDED**, which will create the thread and immediately suspend it so that it doesn't start to run. We'll see later on why this is a useful thing to be able to do, when we talk about synchronization.

The last parameter is a pointer to the **thread ID**, which is related to the return value from **CreateThread()**, the **thread handle**. What are thread IDs and thread handles?

The thread ID is a unique global value, which any other thread or process can use to refer to your thread. Thread IDs are commonly used by tools such as schedulers and debuggers.

The thread handle is only valid within your process, and refers to the **kernel thread object** managing this thread. The value of the thread handle will be zero if the call to **CreateThread()** failed. Most of the thread API calls use the thread handle, and for security reasons, you can't get a thread's handle from its ID.

Kernel objects are managed by reference counting, with the system maintaining a count of who is accessing the thread object. This means that it isn't up to you to delete a thread object — you simply tell the system that you've finished with it. The system will finally delete a thread object when no-one is using it any more, that is, when its reference count has dropped to zero.

Terminating Threads

Since a thread actually exists as two objects — the user-mode thread object and the kernel thread object, the termination of the thread takes place in two parts.

When you've created a thread, you may be happy to let the thread execute and then finish, with no further involvement on your part. If that's the case, you can call **CloseHandle()** immediately after starting the thread:

```
// Create a thread
HANDLE hThread = CreateThread(...);
```

```
// ...and let it go its own way
BOOL bOK = CloseHandle(hThread);
```

`CloseHandle()` is how you tell the operating system that you have no further interest in the thread. Note that `CloseHandle()` doesn't stop the thread executing, it simply decrements the reference count of the kernel object by one (and it is quite possible that the thread function may have already finished when you call `CloseHandle()`).

If you have some interest in communicating further with the thread, you shouldn't call `CloseHandle()`, thus forcing the kernel object to hang around in memory.

If a process exits without calling `CloseHandle()`, the system will decrement the reference count of any kernel objects created by that process which are still open. It is still a good idea to call `CloseHandle()` yourself, though, because if you don't, your process could end up with a lot of superfluous kernel objects that should have been released.

The actual user-mode thread object dies when the thread function returns. What happens if you want to end a thread prematurely? In this case you use the `ExitThread()` function within the thread function you want to end, returning a `DWORD`:

```
VOID ExitThread(DWORD dwExitCode);
```

This function never returns. Instead, it exits the thread function and returns its argument as the thread's return value to the calling program. It is a little like the `exit()` function.

Try It Out — Simple Threads

Here's our simple multithreaded example again, expanded to make use of some of the functions we've just introduced:

```
// SimpleThreading.cpp

#include <windows.h>
#include <iostream>

using namespace std;

DWORD WINAPI threadFunc(LPVOID);

int main()
{
    HANDLE hThread = NULL;
    DWORD threadID = NULL;

    int i = 3;
    hThread = CreateThread(NULL, 0, threadFunc, reinterpret_cast<LPVOID>(i),
                           0, &threadID);

    if (hThread == NULL)
    {
        cout << "Error creating thread" << endl;
        return -1;
    }
```

```
        cout << "Thread running" << endl;

        // Tell the system we're finished with the thread
        CloseHandle(hThread);

        return 0;
    }

    DWORD WINAPI threadFunc(LPVOID p)
    {
        // If the value passed in is zero or positive, return it.
        // If it is negative, return 0... use ExitThread() to simulate a problem

        int n = reinterpret_cast<int>(p);
        if (n < 0)
            ExitThread(0);      // this call will never return

        return n;
    }
```

If you build and run this code, you should see the simple output:

Getting the Exit Status of a Thread

The next logical step is for the main routine to get the exit code from the thread function, which you can do using **GetExitCodeThread()**:

```
    BOOL GetExitCodeThread(HANDLE hThread, LPDWORD retCode);
```

Provided you've got a valid thread handle, this function will return you its exit status. If the thread is still running, then the system will return you the value **STILL_ACTIVE**. This means that you should never use this value (defined as **STATUS_PENDING**) as a thread return code.

Try It Out — Getting Thread Exit Status

We can now use this to check when the thread has finished executing, as shown in the code below:

```
// SimpleThreading2.cpp

#include <windows.h>
#include <iostream>

using namespace std;

DWORD WINAPI threadFunc(LPVOID);
```

```
int main()
{
    HANDLE hThread = NULL;
    DWORD threadID = NULL;

    int i = 3;
    hThread = CreateThread(NULL, 0, threadFunc, reinterpret_cast<LPVOID>(i),
                           0, &threadID);

    if (hThread == NULL)
    {
        cout << "Error creating thread" << endl;
        return -1;
    }

    cout << "Thread running" << endl;

    // Wait for the thread to exit
    // This is a very inefficient way to wait for a thread to exit!
    for(;;)
    {
        DWORD dwExit;
        GetExitCodeThread(hThread, &dwExit);
        if (dwExit == STILL_ACTIVE)
            cout << "Thread still running" << endl;
        else
        {
            cout << "Thread exit code was " << dwExit << endl;
            break;
        }
    }

    // Tell the system we're finished with the thread
    CloseHandle(hThread);

    return 0;
}

DWORD WINAPI threadFunc(LPVOID p)
{
    // If the value passed in is zero or positive, return it.
    // If it is negative, return 0... use ExitThread() to simulate a problem

    int n = reinterpret_cast<int>(p);

    // Add a delay to allow the main routine to loop a few times
    Sleep(200);

    if (n < 0)
        ExitThread(0);     // this call will never return

    return n;
}
```

We've added a 200ms delay to the thread function, so that the main routine gets a chance to loop round a few times before the thread finishes. If we didn't, the thread function would probably have finished before the loop was executed!

The main function sits in a loop until a value other than **STILL_ACTIVE** is returned from the thread. Sitting in a loop is a very inefficient way of finding when the thread has finished executing, and you wouldn't ever do it like this in practice. Later in this chapter we'll look at synchronization objects, which provide a better way to communicate with thread (and other) kernel objects.

The output from the program looks like this:

The Runtime Library Thread Functions

Now let's turn our attention to the second set of thread API calls — those provided by the C Runtime Library. These functions don't provide complete coverage — they're basically wrappers over the Win32 calls, and you'll sometimes need to use the Win32 calls as well.

If you're using Visual C++, you must ensure that you're linking with the multithreaded version of the library in order to use the C Runtime Library functions. You can check this by bringing up the Project | Settings dialog, and choosing the Code Generation category on the C/C++ tab. Make sure that Multithreaded or Debug Multithreaded is selected in the Use run-time library combo box.

The table below shows the Runtime Library functions, and their equivalent Win32 API calls.

Win32 API Function	Runtime Library Function
CreateThread()	_beginthread(), _beginthreadex()
CloseHandle()	
GetExitCodeThread()	
ExitThread()	_endthread(), _endthreadex()

Note that there's no runtime equivalent for the **CloseHandle()** and **GetExitCodeThread()** Win32 calls.

Runtime library functions whose names begin with an underscore, such as `_beginthread()`, are Microsoft extensions to the standard C Runtime library.

The _beginthread() and _beginthreadex() Functions

The C Runtime Library provides two functions for creating threads:

```
unsigned long _beginthread(void(__cdecl *start_addr)(void*),
                    unsigned stack_size, void *argList);

unsigned long _beginthreadex(void* security, unsigned stack_size,
                    void(__cdecl *start_addr)(void*), void *argList,
                    unsigned init_flag, unsigned *thAddr);
```

Why are there two functions? Well, the simple reason is that `_beginthread()` provides a very basic interface to `CreateThread()`, and doesn't allow access to the security or flag arguments, and doesn't allow the thread function to return an exit code. It was supposed to provide a really simple way of creating threads, but it turned out that the other arguments and the exit code were often wanted, so `_beginthreadex()` was added. More importantly, though, there's a show-stopper of a bug in `_beginthread()`, which has been fixed in `_beginthreadex()`, as we'll see.

One difference that you'll immediately notice between these functions and `CreateThread()` is the absence of Win32 data types. Instead of DWORDs and HANDLEs, we have standard C data types such as **unsigned**. This was done with the idea that these thread routines would then be portable to other operating systems. Unfortunately, their implementation means that we are still tied to Win32, because we need to call `CloseHandle()`, so the idea doesn't really work.

Try It Out — Creating Threads

Here's our simple thread example rewritten to use the C Runtime Library APIs:

To check that the correct runtime library is used, look at: Project | Settings..., on the C/C++ tab. With Category set to Code generation, the Use runtime library drop-down list should be set to Debug Multithreaded.

```cpp
// CRTThreading.cpp

#include <windows.h>
#include <process.h>
#include <iostream>

using namespace std;

unsigned __stdcall threadFunc(void* p);

int main()
{
    unsigned long th;
    unsigned ID;
```

```
         unsigned u = 3;
         th = _beginthreadex(NULL, 0, threadFunc, (void*)u, 0, &ID);

         if (th == 0)
         {
            cout << "_beginthreadex() failed " << endl;
            return -1;
         }
         cout << "Thread running";

         // Tell the system we're finished with the thread...
         // We still have to use the Win32 call
         if (th != NULL)
            CloseHandle(reinterpret_cast<HANDLE>(th));

         return 0;
      }

      unsigned __stdcall threadFunc(void* p)
      {
         // We can unpack the argument
         unsigned n = reinterpret_cast<unsigned>(p);

         // Do something useful here

         return 0;
      }
```

The program is very similar in structure to the Win32 version, the main difference being the argument and return types. Note that we still need to use the Win32 `CloseHandle()` call to tell the system that we're finished with the thread, and in order to use this we have to cast the thread ID returned by `_beginthreadex()` into a `HANDLE`.

Problems with _beginthread()

I mentioned earlier that there are real problems with `_beginthread()`, apart from not being able to access all the parameters, which are solved by using `_beginthreadex()`.

The problem arises from the fact that `_beginthread()` creates a thread and then immediately calls `CloseHandle()` on it, which `_beginthreadex()` doesn't do. I can only assume that this was done in order to try to hide the Win32 details, but it has an unfortunate consequence. The thread might have finished executing before the call to `_beginthread()` returns, in which case the handle returned will be invalid, and you'll have no way to get in contact with the thread object.

The simple way around this is to use `_beginthreadex()` in all cases, and leave `_beginthread()` well alone!

Terminating Threads

In order to terminate a thread which you've started with a C Runtime Library function, you use `_endthread()` (for threads started with `_beginthread()`) or `_endthreadex()` (for those started with `_beginthreadex()`).

```
void _endthread();
void _endthreadex(unsigned retval);
```

`_endthreadex()` takes an unsigned parameter which is used as the return value from the thread.

> *You don't often need to use _endthread() or _endthreadex(), because simply returning from the thread function will do the same tidying up for you.*

Using Handles

We need to use Win32 handles on two occasions when using the C Runtime Library thread functions. Firstly, `_endthreadex()` doesn't close the thread handle, and neither does `_beginthreadex()`, so if you've used either of these, you'll need to call `CloseHandle()` yourself. Secondly, you'll need to use `GetExitCodeThread()` if you want to retrieve the exit code returned from a call to `_endthreadex()`.

Try It Out — Extending the CRTThreading Example

Here's the simple thread example rewritten to use `_endthreadex()` and check the exit status of the thread:

```cpp
// CRTThreading2

#include <windows.h>
#include <process.h>
#include <iostream>

using namespace std;

unsigned __stdcall threadFunc(void* p);

int main()
{
    unsigned long th;
    unsigned ID;
    int i = 3;
    th = _beginthreadex(NULL, 0, threadFunc, (void*)i, 0, &ID);

    if (th == 0)
    {
        cout << "_beginthreadex() failed " << endl;
        return -1;
    }

    cout << "Thread running";

    // Wait for the thread to exit
    for(;;)
    {
        DWORD dwExit;
```

```
        GetExitCodeThread(reinterpret_cast<HANDLE>(th), &dwExit);
        if (dwExit == STILL_ACTIVE)
           cout << "Thread still running\n" << endl;
        else
        {
           cout << "Thread exit code was " << dwExit << endl;
           break;
        }
    }

    // Tell the system we're finished with the thread...
    // We still have to use the Win32 call
    CloseHandle((HANDLE)th);

    return 0;
}

unsigned __stdcall threadFunc(void* p)
{
    // If the value passed in is zero or positive, return it.
    // If it is negative, return 0... use ExitThread() to simulate a problem
    unsigned n = reinterpret_cast<unsigned>(p);

    Sleep(200);
    if (n < 0)
       _endthreadex(0);

    return n;
}
```

Which Thread API to Use?

Given that we have the choice of using either the Win32 API functions or the C Runtime Library, which of them should we use?

As well as handling the threads themselves, the C Runtime functions do some housekeeping needed by the library. This means that you should use the C Runtime Library functions and link with the multithreaded C runtime library if any thread in your program, other than the primary thread, is going to use functions from the Runtime Library — in other words:

- If you use floating point variables or functions
- If you use C's **malloc** and **free**, or C++'s **new** and **delete**
- If you call anything in **stdio.h** or **io.h**. Note that this doesn't include **wsprintf()**, which is a Win32 API function
- If you call any runtime functions which use a static buffer, such as **strtok()** or **rand()**

If your extra threads don't do any of the above, then you're probably safe to use the single-threading library and **CreateThread()**. In practice, though, you're probably going to end up using the C Runtime Library most of the time one way or another, so **_beginthreadex()** is the preferred way to create threads.

> *Remember — if you're using MFC, use the* CWinThread *class!*

Simple Thread Control

Before we leave basic thread creation and manipulation, let's consider some simple thread control mechanisms.

Sleeping

We've already seen one of these in our example program, when we used the **Sleep()** function to suspend the execution of the thread for a given number of milliseconds, effectively putting it to sleep.

```
void Sleep(DWORD ms);
```

A value of **0** will cause the thread to relinquish the remainder of its time slice, while a value of **INFINITE** will put it permanently to sleep.

It is common in some circles to use **Sleep()** to wait for some event to occur, similar to the way we did in our example:

```
for(;;)
{
    // Pause
    Sleep(200);

    // Wake up and see if we're ready…
    if (something_has_occurred)
    {
        // process it
        // and exit
        break;
    }
}
```

This sort of polling loop, called a 'busy wait', is not a very responsive mechanism, but you may have to use it in those cases where you have to go and poll some source to see when the event has occurred. Many events, especially those involving kernel objects such as threads, are able to signal that they've occurred, and in those cases there are much more responsive ways of waiting. We'll cover these later in the section on synchronization.

There is a second suspension function, **SleepEx()**, which is used with the extended I/O functions **ReadFileEx()** and **WriteFileEx()**, and allows you to put the thread to sleep until an I/O operation has occurred.

Suspend and Resume

It is possible for a thread to suspend and resume another thread, provided it has a handle to it. These calls have mainly been provided for use by tools such as debuggers, but they can be useful in other circumstances.

`SuspendThread()` stops the execution of the specified thread:

```
DWORD  SuspendThread(HANDLE  Thread);
```

A thread has a **suspend count**, which is incremented by calls to `SuspendThread()`, up to a maximum value of `MAXIMUM_SUSPEND_COUNT`. The return value from this function is the previous value of the suspend count, or `0xffffffff` if the call failed.

> *For* SuspendThread() *and* ResumeThread() *to work under NT, the handle must have* THREAD_SUSPEND_RESUME *access. Thread handles returned by* CreateThread() *have* THREAD_ALL_ACCESS *access set, which incorporates suspend/resume access.*

As you'd expect, `ResumeThread()` decrements the suspend count of a thread. When this count reaches zero, execution will resume.

```
DWORD  ResumeThread(HANDLE  hThread);
```

You need to be careful when using `SuspendThread()`. Don't let a thread suspend itself, because it then has no way of resuming by itself.

Problems with Threading

When you start using threads in earnest, you'll discover that there are numerous pitfalls awaiting you. We'll meet two of the most common here — **race conditions** and **deadlocks**, and then go on to discuss techniques which will help us to avoid them. Code which has been written to avoid the sort of problems we describe here is known as **thread safe**.

> *Many threading problems occur when you have a number of identical threads running at once, which may compete for resources and trip over one another. If you only have one or two threads which do different jobs, such as background printing or screen repainting, there may well be little interaction between them, and therefore less scope for unwanted interaction.*

Race Conditions

In a pre-emptively multitasked system, the operating system will switch between threads as it decides necessary. This means that the order of execution of multiple threads becomes unpredictable, as you don't know exactly when the operating system is going to decide to switch from one thread to another. Thus, if a context switch occurs during an operation such as incrementing a variable, or updating a database record, the shared data can be left in a corrupt state.

Suppose two threads are accessing the same global variable, which has an initial value of 4.

- Thread **A** reads the variable and gets **4**
- A context switch occurs

> Thread **B** read the variable and also gets **4**

> Thread **B** increments the variable and writes it back, so it is now set to **5**

> A context switch occurs

> Thread **A** decrements the variable and writes it back, setting it to **3**

The variable is now corrupt, because the process of incrementing and then decrementing a variable should leave it with the same value.

This is known as a **race condition**, because you don't know who is going to win the race to modify the data!

As an example, suppose you open a data file and retrieve a record for editing. You make your changes, but unknown to you, someone else has retrieved the same record and made their changes. Both of you then save the record back to the file... whose data gets stored? The one who wins the race!

Try It Out — A Race Condition

Here's a simple program demonstrating a race condition:

```cpp
// RaceCondition.cpp

#include <windows.h>
#include <iostream>

using namespace std;

// Prototype for the thread function
DWORD WINAPI writeData(LPVOID pv);

const int nThread = 5;

int main()
{
    HANDLE hThreads[nThread];
    DWORD threadId;
    int i;
    char* ps[] = {"one", "two", "three", "four", "five"};

    for (i=0; i<nThread; i++)
    {
        hThreads[i] = CreateThread(NULL,            // security attributes
                                   0,               // stack size
                                   writeData,       // thread function
                                   (LPVOID)ps[i],   // data to be passed
                                   0,               // creation flags
                                   &threadId );     // thread ID

        if (hThreads[i])
        {
            cout << "Thread " << i << "running" << endl;
            CloseHandle(hThreads[i]);
```

Chapter 6 - Threads and Processes

```
        }
    }

    // Hang around and wait for 1.5 seconds to let the threads complete.
    Sleep(1500);

    return 0;
}

// The thread function
DWORD WINAPI writeData(LPVOID pv)
{
    char* ps = reinterpret_cast<char*>(pv);

    for (int i=0; i<10; i++)
        cout << ps << endl;

    return 0;
}
```

Try compiling this as a console application and running it several times. You'll find that the output is different each time, and that the output from the threads is interleaved.

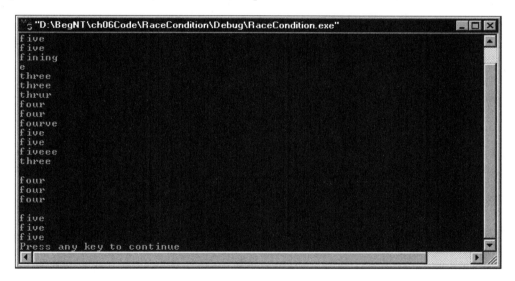

We create five threads, and immediately set them running. We thus have five simultaneously executing routines, all fighting to write their output to the screen at once. Because all the threads have the same priority, the operating system will switch between them in order to attempt to give them equal execution time, but we don't know which one will be executing at any one time. This is the race condition in action — it is a race as to which thread can write its data first.

As another example, suppose we have a program passing a variable to a thread, which increments it ten times in a loop and passes it back. If you have five threads running, then the final value should be 50 when in fact it probably won't be, because they'll all interfere with one another.

What we need is a way to ensure that the operating system can't switch threads while one of them is going round its output loop, and we can do this using **synchronization objects**.

Deadlocks

A **deadlock**, also called a 'deadly embrace', occurs when two or more threads manage to lock each other up, each one waiting for some resource that the other one is using.

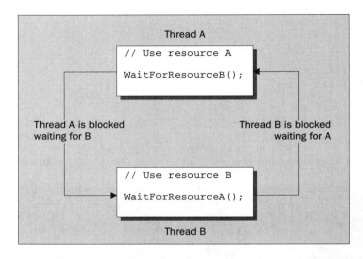

Thread **A** has resource **A**, thread **B** has resource **B**. **A** wants **B** and blocks till it gets it, while **B** wants **A** and also blocks. Result — a deadlock! This example only shows two threads in deadlock, but it is possible to get complicated deadlocks which involve many objects.

How to get round them? Avoiding problems such as deadlocks and race conditions can be quite hard, as some of the effects can be very subtle. In the end, part is due to design, and part is due to use of **thread synchronization**.

Thread Synchronization

Synchronization gives us the ability to control how threads interact, and how they use resources.

There are four software constructs which we can use to synchronize threads:

- **Critical sections**, which let you guard sections of code against being accessed by more than one thread at a time. These are the most basic constructs, and are by far the fastest.
- **Mutexes**, which enforce 'mutual exclusion'. They do the same job as critical sections, but can be shared between processes.
- **Semaphores** are like mutexes, but allow a user-specified number of threads to access the resource they're guarding.
- **Events** act as 'flags', and setting an event can be detected by other threads in the same or a different process.

There are several wait functions which work with them, such as:

- `WaitForSingleObject()`
- `WaitForMultipleObjects()`

The last three constructs (mutexes, semaphores and events) are examples of **kernel objects**.

Comparison of Synchronization Objects

Object	When To Use
Critical section	Use these when a section of code needs to be protected against access by more than one thread. They are the fastest of the synchronization objects.
Mutex	Use a mutex when you need to synchronize access to a resource between threads in different processes.
Semaphore	Semaphores have an associated count, so use them when you want to allow a number of threads access to a resource.
Event	Events are the most general of the synchronization objects, and are used as flags, to signal when an event has occurred.

Kernel Objects

There are various entities which are often used in system programming tasks, and which are used in similar ways. Rather than have a bunch of separate API functions to manipulate each of them, NT provides a common set of calls to manipulate these **kernel objects**.

The following entities are treated as kernel objects, and can be manipulated using handles:

- Threads
- Processes
- Semaphores, events and mutexes
- Files and file mappings
- Named pipes
- Console I/O

We've already met thread objects, and seen how we can manipulate them using their handles. In this section we'll be looking at the third group, the synchronization objects.

If you want to refer to a kernel object used in different threads within the same process, it is sufficient to know its handle. To refer to the same kernel object from a different process, however, we need to know its name.

Kernel Objects and Reference Counting

Kernel objects, as their name implies, are owned by the NT kernel, and it is the **Object Manager** in the kernel that manages their creation and deletion. The lifetime of an object is determined by a reference count which the kernel maintains, and when you've finished with a kernel object, you use an API call such as `CloseHandle()` to tell the kernel that you've finished, which allows it to manage the reference counting.

If you think about it, you can't be allowed to delete an object yourself, because it might be being used by another process. The NT kernel is the only thing which knows whether or not it is safe to remove the object.

Signalling of Objects

Objects can be **signalled** or **unsignalled**. Precisely what signalled or unsignalled means depends on the object we're talking about, as shown in the following table:

Object Type	Signalled When...
Thread	The thread terminates
Process	The process terminates
Timer	The timer reaches its due time
Mutex	It isn't owned by anyone
Event	Explicitly set
Semaphore	Its count is greater than zero

So, if we want to wait for a thread to finish then we want to be notified when the thread object becomes signalled, and we do this using the `WaitFor...()` functions.

Waiting for Objects

The `WaitForSingleObject()` API waits for a single object to enter the signalled state:

```
DWORD WaitForSingleObject(HANDLE hObj, DWORD dwTime);
```

The function takes a handle to a kernel object and a timeout period in milliseconds. If the object hasn't become signalled when the timeout period expires, the function returns. You can also specify the value `INFINITE`, in which case the function will wait until the object becomes signalled, without timing out.

If you set the timeout to zero, the function will check the status of the object and then return immediately. This is a useful way of testing the state of an object.

The return value will tell you what caused the function to return, and may be one of the following:

Return Value	Meaning
`WAIT_ABANDONED`	The object was a mutex, and its controlling thread exited without releasing it. See the section on mutexes.
`WAIT_OBJECT_0`	The object is signalled.
`WAIT_TIMEOUT`	The timeout period finished without the object becoming signalled.

Try It Out — Signalling You're Done

To show this in action, here's our earlier example rewritten to use `WaitForSingleObject()`:

```cpp
// KernelObjects.cpp

#include <windows.h>
#include <iostream>

using namespace std;

DWORD WINAPI threadFunc(LPVOID);

int main()
{
    HANDLE hThread= NULL;
    DWORD threadID = NULL;
    DWORD dwExit;

    int i = 3;
    hThread = CreateThread(NULL, 0, threadFunc, (LPVOID)i, 0, &threadID);

    if (hThread = NULL)
    {
        cout << "Error creating thread" << endl;
        return -1;
    }

    cout << "Thread running" << endl;

    // Wait for the thread to exit
    WaitForSingleObject(hThread, INFINITE);
    GetExitCodeThread(hThread, &dwExit);
    cout << "Thread exit code was " << dwExit << endl;

    // Tell the system we're finished with the thread
    CloseHandle(hThread);

    return 0;
}

DWORD WINAPI threadFunc(LPVOID p)
{
    // If the value passed in is zero or positive, return it.
    // If it is negative, return 0... use ExitThread() to simulate a problem

    int n = reinterpret_cast<int>(p);
```

```
      // Add a delay to allow the main routine to loop a few times
      Sleep(200);

   if (n < 0)
      ExitThread(0);      // this call will never return

   return n;
}
```

WaitForMultipleObjects() does the same for an array of objects. We'll see this in action as we look in detail at the synchronization objects.

If you build and run the above code, you should see output as follows:

Critical Sections

The **critical section** is the simplest and most basic of the synchronization mechanisms. They're also the fastest by far, and should be used in preference to the others if the design allows. A critical section is a piece of code which only one thread must be allowed to access at a time — in effect, it is defining a section of single-threaded code. This section of code could be operating on a single memory location, a data structure or a file — anything where simultaneous access by more than one thread could be disastrous.

Critical sections are not NT kernel objects, and can only be used between threads in the same process, because they exist in the address space of the process.

Because they aren't kernel objects, they are not identified by a handle, but instead by the address of a **CRITICAL_SECTION** structure in memory. This structure is defined in **winnt.h**, and applications don't access its members directly, but instead pass it round to the API functions which control the critical section.

Creating Critical Section Objects

Critical sections have to be initialized before they can be used, and cleaned up afterwards, using the **InitializeCriticalSection()** and **DeleteCriticalSection()** functions respectively.

```
   void InitializeCriticalSection(LPCRITICAL_SECTION lpSec);
   void DeleteCriticalSection(LPCRITICAL_SECTION lpSec);
```

Sections are then set up using the **EnterCriticalSection()** and **LeaveCriticalSection()** functions:

```
   void EnterCriticalSection(LPCRITICAL_SECTION lpSec);
   void LeaveCriticalSection(LPCRITICAL_SECTION lpSec);
```

Using Critical Sections

In order to use a critical section to protect some resource, we bracket the resource with a pair of `EnterCriticalSection()` and `LeaveCriticalSection()` calls, as shown below:

```
// Declare critical section variable
CRITICAL_SECTION cs;

// Initialize critical section structure
InitializeCriticalSection(&cs);

EnterCriticalSection(&cs);

// Code here can only be accessed by one thread at a time - this
// is the 'critical section'

LeaveCriticalSection(&cs);

// Tidy up critical section object
DeleteCriticalSection(&cs);
```

Note that all these calls simply take the address of the critical section object we declared. We don't have to do anything else with this object except pass its address around!

*If the critical section object is available, the current thread will gain ownership of the critical section object, and execution will continue. If the critical section is locked, the code will block until the critical section becomes available. If you don't want your code to block, you can use **TryEnterCriticalSection()** instead of **EnterCriticalSection()**:*

```
BOOL TryEnterCriticalSection(LPCRITICAL_SECTION lpSec);
```

*You'll need to have the preprocessor symbol **_WIN32_WINNT** set to **0x0400** or greater in order for **TryEnterCriticalSection()** to be available.*

This function will try to enter the section, but will return immediately with a zero value if the section is locked.

Try It Out — Using a Critical Section to Protect against Races

We'll modify the example we used to demonstrate the race condition, using a critical section to protect the thread function:

```
// CriticalSection.cpp

#include <windows.h>
#include <iostream>

using namespace std;

// Prototype for the thread function
DWORD WINAPI writeData(LPVOID pv);
```

```
CRITICAL_SECTION critSec;

const int nThread = 5;

int main()
{
    HANDLE hThreads[nThread];
    DWORD threadId;
    int i;
    char* ps[] = {"one", "two", "three", "four", "five"};


    InitializeCriticalSection(&critSec);

    for (i=0; i<nThread; i++)
    {
        hThreads[i] = CreateThread(NULL,            // security attributes
                                   0,               // stack size
                                   writeData,       // thread function
                                   (LPVOID)ps[i],   // data to be passed
                                   0,               // creation flags
                                   &threadId);      // thread ID

        if (hThreads[i])
            cout << "Thread " << i << "launched" << endl;
    }

    // Wait for the threads to complete.

    DWORD rc = WaitForMultipleObjects(nThread, hThreads, TRUE, INFINITE);

    for(i=0; i<nThread; i++)
        CloseHandle(hThreads[i]);

    DeleteCriticalSection(&critSec);

    return 0;
}

DWORD WINAPI writeData(LPVOID pv)
{
    __try
    {
        EnterCriticalSection(&critSec);

        char* ps = reinterpret_cast<char*>(pv);

        for (int i=0; i<10; i++)
            cout << ps << endl;

    }
    __finally
    {
        LeaveCriticalSection(&critSec);
    }
    return 0;
}
```

Build and run this program, and compare its output with the original version. This time, all the output from a thread occurs in a single block, because the use of the critical section prevents other threads from calling the thread function until the calling thread has finished with it.

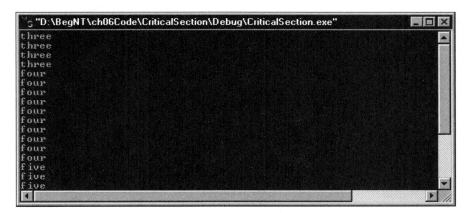

Note the use of structured exception handling in this example. Calls to enter a critical section must always be matched by a call to leave it. If this isn't the case, no other thread will be able to access this code. The use of the `__finally` block ensures that `LeaveCriticalSection()` will still be called, even if the code above throws an exception.

> *It is good practice not to lock any more code than is absolutely necessary, and not to leave it locked for any longer than you have to, because you may introduce unnecessary bottlenecks into your programs.*

The other change we've made is to use `WaitForMultipleObjects()` to wait for all the threads to finish, instead of sleeping.

```
DWORD WaitForMultipleObjects(DWORD nCount,       // number of objects to wait for
                             CONST HANDLE* lpHandles,  // pointer to
                                                       // object handles
                             BOOL bWaitAll,            // wait flag
                             DWORD dwTime);            // timeout
```

The first two parameters define an array of object handles, which can hold a maximum of **MAXIMUM_WAIT_OBJECTS** handles. Under NT, this is set to 64. The third one is set to **TRUE** if the function is to wait for all the objects to become signalled before returning, and **FALSE** if the function is to return when any one of them becomes signalled. If you choose the latter, the return value will tell you the handle of the object which became signalled. The final parameter is a timeout value, which works in the same way as it does in `WaitForSingleObject()`.

The return code takes similar values to the ones used in `WaitForSingleObject()`, but in the case of **WAIT_OBJECT** and **WAIT_ABANDONED**, the value returned is an index into the handle array, telling you which object the return refers to. The range of return values are thus from **WAIT_OBJECT_0** to (**WAIT_OBJECT_0 + nCount -1**), and from **WAIT_ABANDONED_0** to (**WAIT_ABANDONED_0 + nCount -1**).

In our example we're waiting for all the objects to become signalled, so the return value doesn't concern us.

227

Creating Synchronization Objects

We've seen that synchronization between threads can use several mechanisms which (with the exception of critical sections) are represented by kernel objects, and that we use a standard mechanism to wait for any of these objects to become signalled. This means that we should be able usefully to wrap these objects and mechanisms in C++ classes.

The SyncObj Base Class

All the Win32 synchronization objects share certain characteristics, such as the need to create them, wait for them to become signalled and unsignalled, and release them when we're finished. This means that it should be possible to define a base class for our synchronization object classes which holds common code. In our case, we'll call it **SyncObj**. Here is the class definition, **SyncObj.h**:

```
// SyncObj.h

#ifndef SYNCOBJ
#define SYNCOBJ

#include <windows.h>

class SyncObj
{
protected:
   HANDLE hObject;  // handle to the sync object
public:
   SyncObj::SyncObj();
   virtual ~SyncObj();

   // acquire will work with most classes which represent kernel
   // objects, but all classes must implement their own release function
   virtual bool acquire(DWORD dwTimeOut = INFINITE);
   virtual bool release() = 0;
};

#endif                 // SYNCOBJ
```

All kernel objects are referred to by a handle, so we'll include one as a data member. The class has two virtual functions, which are used to acquire the object, and release it when we've finished. Most synchronization objects can be acquired in the same way, through a call to **WaitForSingleObject()**, but they all need to be released in different ways (e.g. mutexes by a call to **ReleaseMutex()**). This means that we can supply a standard version of **acquire()** which can be overridden by derived classes if necessary, but we have to leave it to derived classes to supply their own version of **release()**. In order to ensure that they do, we'll make it a pure virtual function.

> *Since these classes are all related, and are pretty small, I've implemented them in a single pair of files called* **SyncObj.h** *and* **SyncObj.cpp***.*

The implementation code for **SyncObj** is very simple. The constructor and destructor initialize the handle, and close it, respectively:

```
// SyncObj.cpp

#include "SyncObj.h"

SyncObj::SyncObj()
{
   hObject = NULL;
}

SyncObj::~SyncObj()
{
   if (hObject != NULL)
   {
      ::CloseHandle(hObject);
      hObject = NULL;
   }
}
```

The basic **acquire()** function simply waits for the object, and returns **true** or **false** depending on whether the operation timed out or not:

```
bool SyncObj::acquire(DWORD dwTimeOut)
{
   if (WaitForSingleObject(hObject, dwTimeOut) == WAIT_OBJECT_0)
      return true;
   else
      return false;
}
```

The CritSec Class

The first synchronization object we'll add is a class defining a critical section object. It is structured slightly differently to the others we'll write, because a critical section isn't a kernel object, so we can't use the handle stored in the base class. Instead, we'll create our own private **CRITICAL_SECTION** object:

```
// CritSec.h

#include <windows.h>

#include "SyncObj.h"

class CritSec : public SyncObj
{
   CRITICAL_SECTION sec;
public:
   CritSec();
   ~CritSec();

   // Overridden base class functions
   virtual bool acquire(DWORD dwTimeOut = INFINITE);
   virtual bool release();

   // tryEnter is specific to critical sections
   bool tryEnter();
};
```

This is about as simple a class as we can get, but it will ensure that critical sections are created and deleted as required.

We'll provide a function to encapsulate the `TryEnterCriticalSection()` API call, in which we'll check the version of the `_WIN32_WINNT` flag, as this function was only introduced with Win95/NT4.

The constructor and destructor take care of initializing and deleting the critical section object:

```
// CritSec.cpp

#include "CritSec.h"

CritSec::CritSec()
{
   InitializeCriticalSection(&sec);
}

CritSec::~CritSec()
{
   DeleteCriticalSection(&sec);
}
```

Since critical sections don't use the kernel object locking mechanism, we need to provide both `acquire()` and `release()` functions:

```
bool CritSec::acquire(DWORD /*unused*/)
{
   EnterCriticalSection(&sec);
   return true;
}

bool CritSec::release()
{
   LeaveCriticalSection(&sec);
   return true;
}

bool CritSec::tryEnter()
{
   // Only use TryEnterCriticalSection() in the right places
#if (_WIN32_WINNT >= 0x0400)
   if (TryEnterCriticalSection(&sec))
      return true;
   else
#endif
   return false;
}
```

Try It Out — *Using a Critical Section object*

Here's the previous example program, rewritten to use a **CritSec** object:

```cpp
// CriticalSection2.cpp

#include <windows.h>
#include <iostream>

using namespace std;

#include "CritSec.h"

// Prototype for the thread function
DWORD WINAPI writeData(LPVOID pv);

CritSec cs;

const int nThread = 5;

int main()
{
    HANDLE hThreads[nThread];
    DWORD threadId;
    int i;
    char* ps[] = {"one", "two", "three", "four", "five"};

    for (i=0; i<nThread; i++)
    {
        hThreads[i] = CreateThread(NULL,          // security attributes
                                   0,             // stack size
                                   writeData,     // thread function
                                   (LPVOID)ps[i], // data to be passed
                                   0,             // creation flags
                                   &threadId );   // thread ID
        if (hThreads[i])
            cout << "Thread " << i << "launched" << endl;
    }

    // Wait for the threads to complete.

    DWORD rc = WaitForMultipleObjects(nThread, hThreads, TRUE, INFINITE);

    for(i=0; i<nThread; i++)
        CloseHandle(hThreads[i]);

    return 0;
}

DWORD WINAPI writeData(LPVOID pv)
{
    cs.acquire();

    char* ps = reinterpret_cast<char*>(pv);

    for (int i=0; i<10; i++)
        cout << ps << endl;
```

```
        cs.release();

    return 0;
}
```

You can see that there is now no need to initialize and delete the critical section structure, because that is done in the object's constructor and destructor. We simply acquire and release the **CritSec** object as required.

The Lock Class

Our **SyncObj** classes require us to do more coding than we need, because we need to call **release()** each time we finish with an object. We can get around this by creating a **Lock** class to operate on **SyncObj** objects.

Try It Out — Using SyncObj and Lock Objects

A **Lock** acquires a **SyncObj** when it is constructed, and releases it in its destructor. This means that we can simply declare a **Lock** object when we want to use a **SyncObj**, and don't have to worry about releasing the object when we're done. **Lock.h** is shown below:

```
// Lock.h

#include "SyncObj.h"

class Lock
{
    SyncObj* pObj;

public:
    Lock(SyncObj* po, DWORD dwTimeout=INFINITE);
    ~Lock();
};
```

Lock.cpp is as follows:

```
// Lock.cpp

#include "Lock.h"

Lock::Lock(SyncObj* po, DWORD dwTimeout)
{
    if (!po)
        throw "Lock: null pointer";

    pObj = po;
    pObj->acquire(dwTimeout);
}

Lock::~Lock()
{
    if (pObj)
        pObj->release();
}
```

This has one big advantage. In the previous example, we had to use structured exception handling and the **__finally** clause to ensure that the critical section was left, regardless of what happened in the code. When we encapsulate the acquire and release functionality in a class like this, we can use normal C++ exception handling, since we know that if we declare a **Lock** object inside a **__try** block, its destructor will get called.

The simplest way to use these objects just consists of creating a **SyncObj** when we need it, and then using a **Lock** to control it. Here's the **writeData()** function using a **Lock** object:

```
// CriticalSection3.cpp

#include <windows.h>
#include <iostream>

using namespace std;

#include "CritSec.h"
#include "Lock.h"

...

DWORD WINAPI writeData(LPVOID pv)
{
    // Lock the CritSec object, which results in entering the
    // section. It will automatically leave the section when the
    // Lock object destructs
    Lock l(&cs);

    char* ps = reinterpret_cast<char*>(pv);

    for(int i=0; i<10; i++)
        cout << ps << endl;

    return 0;
}
```

In the thread function we use a **Lock** object to acquire the critical section. Once the constructor has returned, we know we're safe to go and write. When the **Lock** goes out of scope, it automatically leaves the critical section.

Mutexes

Mutexes (**mut**ual **ex**clusion objects) provide a more sophisticated version of critical sections, but they sacrifice speed for increased flexibility.

There are several differences between a mutex and a critical section:

- ▶ It takes a lot longer (about 100 times longer) to lock a mutex than a critical section. This is because a mutex is kernel object, and so needs to involve the kernel in its operation.
- ▶ A critical section, on the other hand, is a data structure living in the process address space.
- ▶ Mutexes can be used between processes, while critical sections are restricted to threads within one process.

> You can specify a timeout when waiting for a mutex, which you can't for a critical section.

A mutex is signalled when no-one owns it, and is non-signalled when it is owned. If you find this confusing, it may help you to remember which state is which by remembering that the mutex *signals* its *availability*.

Creating Mutexes

Since mutexes can be shared between processes, we've now got two options — we can either create a new mutex, or open an existing one.

Let's first look at creating a mutex, using the **CreateMutex()** API function:

```
HANDLE  hMutex = CreateMutex(LPSECURITY_ATTRIBUTES  lpAtt, //  security
                                                           //  attributes
                             BOOL bInitialOwner,           //  initial  owner
                                                           //  flag
                             LPCTSTR  lpName);             //  mutex  name
```

The **bInitialOwner** argument determines whether this thread is going to be the owner of the mutex. 'Owning' a mutex doesn't mean what you might instinctively think — a mutex is 'owned' by whoever is currently executing the code guarded by the mutex, so the mutex owner will change over time. We'll see what this argument is used for when we look at how we use mutexes.

You need to specify a name if the mutex is to be used between processes. Remember to make your name unique — maybe by including some identifier such as the name of the process — in order to minimize the possibility of name clashes.

What if you want to open an existing mutex? In this case you call **CreateMutex()** with the name of an existing mutex, and you'll get back a handle to it. The only problem with this is that if you happen to misspell the name, **CreateMutex()** will silently create a new mutex for you.

For this reason there's also an **OpenMutex()** function,

```
HANDLE  hMutex  =  OpenMutex(DWORD  dwDesiredAccess,  //  Access  to  Mutex  object
                            BOOL  bInheritHandle,     //  Can  be  inherited  by
                                                      //  child  processes?
                            LPCSTR  lpName);          //  Mutex  name
```

which will open a mutex if it exists, but won't create a new one if it doesn't. You can thus use **CreateMutex()** when you're sure you want a new one, and **OpenMutex()** otherwise. It can also be useful if you have to access a mutex created by some other application, and want an error to be generated if the open fails.

Using Mutexes

Once we've created or opened a mutex, we can use it in a similar way to a critical section, by putting appropriate code around the resource we want to protect, like this:

```
// Create a mutex
HANDLE hMutex = CreateMutex(NULL, FALSE, "TestMutex");

// Wait for the mutex to become signalled
DWORD dwResult = WaitForSingleObject(hMutex, dwTimeout);

// Do whatever we need to do...

// Release the mutex for someone else to use
ReleaseMutex(hMutex);
```

We've seen the return codes from **WaitForSingleObject()** already. The result will be zero if the wait worked, and **WAIT_TIMEOUT** if the timeout expired before the mutex became signalled. If you're waiting on a mutex, there's a third possibility. If another thread owned the mutex but exited without releasing it, then **WAIT_ABANDONED_0** will be returned, and you'll get ownership of the mutex. Contrast this with the critical section, where it is possible that a section can remain locked if the current owner exits without releasing it.

Once the wait has returned, the mutex becomes non-signalled, meaning that we own it. We can then access the resource it is guarding, and when we're finished, we release the mutex by calling **ReleaseMutex()** on the mutex handle.

Releasing the mutex returns it to its signalled state, so that some other wait function will now unblock.

Try It Out — Mutex in Action

Here's the critical section example rewritten to use a mutex:

```
// UsingMutex.cpp

#include <windows.h>
#include <iostream>

using namespace std;

// Prototype for the thread function
DWORD WINAPI writeData(LPVOID pv);

HANDLE hMutex;

const int nThread = 5;

int main()
{
   HANDLE hThreads[nThread];
   DWORD threadId;
   int i;
   char* ps[] = {"one", "two", "three", "four", "five"};

   hMutex = CreateMutex(NULL, FALSE, "Test Mutex");
```

```
        for (i=0; i<nThread; i++)
        {
            hThreads[i] = CreateThread(NULL,          // security attributes
                                    0,                // stack size
                                    writeData,        // thread function
                                    (LPVOID)ps[i],    // data to be passed
                                    0,                // creation flags
                                    &threadId);       // thread ID
            if (hThreads[i])
                cout << "Thread " << i << "launched" << endl;
        }

        // Wait for the threads to complete.

        DWORD rc = WaitForMultipleObjects(nThread, hThreads, TRUE, INFINITE);

        for(i=0; i<nThread; i++)
            CloseHandle(hThreads[i]);

        CloseHandle(hMutex);
        return 0;
}

DWORD WINAPI writeData(LPVOID pv)
{
        __try
        {
            WaitForSingleObject(hMutex, INFINITE);

            char* ps = reinterpret_cast<char*>(pv);

            for (int i=0; i<10; i++)
                cout << ps << endl;

        }
        __finally
        {
            ReleaseMutex(hMutex);
        }
        return 0;
}
```

We create a mutex with no security attributes, which the primary thread doesn't own. It has a name, although it doesn't really need one since we aren't sharing it.
The thread function now waits for the mutex to become signalled, and when it gains ownership, it writes its output. When it has finished, it releases the mutex so another thread can have a turn.

When we no longer require the mutex, we can tell the kernel by calling **CloseHandle()**, just like we do for threads.

> *A thread might end up calling a* WaitFor...() *function more than once on a mutex. In this case, the mutex is only signalled when a matching number of* ReleaseMutex() *calls have been made.*

Using Multiple Mutexes

Mutexes can be very useful in helping to avoid deadlocks. Imagine that you have the following scenario: a data structure `SecData` includes a critical section, which is used to ensure the integrity of operations on its data, and functions are available which initialize and delete the section. We then have a function which needs to operate on two of these objects at once, so it makes sure that it locks both critical sections before proceeding:

```
// Declare two objects
void DoSomething(SecData* pOne, SecData* pTwo)
{
   EnterCriticalSection(pOne->critSec);
   EnterCriticalSection(pTwo->critSec);

   // Do operations on pOne and pTwo

   LeaveCriticalSection(pTwo->critSec);
   LeaveCriticalSection(pOne->critSec);
}
```

Supposing we now have two threads calling this routine, like this:

```
DoSomething(ObjA, ObjB);     // thread 1
DoSomething(ObjB, ObjA);     // thread 2
```

What happens if there's a context switch between them immediately after the first `EnterCriticalSection()` call? The first thread will have locked `ObjA`'s critical section and wants to lock `ObjB`, while the second one will have locked `ObjB` and wants `ObjA`. Result - deadlock!

Using mutexes along with `WaitForMultipleObjects()` can help solve this problem:

```
// Declare two objects
void DoSomething(SecData* pOne, SecData* pTwo)
{
   HANDLE hMutexes[2];
   hMutexes[0] = pOne->hMutex;
   hMutexes[1] = pTwo->hMutex;

   WaitForMultipleObjects(2, hMutexes, TRUE, INFINITE);

   // Do operations on pOne and pTwo

   ReleaseMutex(pTwo->hMutex);
   ReleaseMutex(pOne->hMutex);
}
```

This is much more satisfactory, because the wait function won't return until both mutexes are signalled, and there is no chance of deadlock occurring.

The Ownership Problem

Suppose we want to create a mutex and use it immediately, like this:

```
hMutex = CreateMutex(NULL, FALSE, "Test");
dwResult = WaitForSingleObject(hMutex, dwTimeout);
```

We have a problem because a potential race condition exists between the two lines of code. We may create the mutex, but before our **WaitForSingleObject()** gets a chance to execute, another thread could jump in and grab the mutex.

The way to avoid this is to use the **bInitialOwner** argument to **CreateMutex()**, which effectively creates the mutex in a non-signalled condition, so that no-one else can grab it from us. We can do what we want, and then release the mutex for someone else to use.

```
hMutex = CreateMutex(NULL, TRUE, "Test");   // mutex is owned
dwResult = WaitForSingleObject(hMutex, dwTimeout);
```

Atomic Operations

While we're on the subject of race conditions, let's mention three API calls which help avoid them.

Even a simple piece of code such as

```
i++;
```

may compile down to several machine instructions — like this on Intel processors:

```
mov ecx, dword ptr [i]        (retrieve the value of i)
add ecx, 1                    (increment it)
mov dword ptr [ps], edx       (store new value)
```

It is possible that even this apparently indivisible operation could be subject to a context switch while executing, and that, as a result, i could be incremented twice. We could guard against this by protecting the code using a critical section or mutex, but it is going to take a lot of work to protect every variable increment or decrement in this way.

Fortunately the Win32 API provides us with calls to perform such atomic operations safely, as shown in the following table:

Function	Purpose
`InterlockedIncrement()`	Increments a signed 32-bit integer
`InterlockedDecrement()`	Decrements a signed 32-bit integer
`InterlockedExchange()`	Atomically exchanges a pair of 32-bit variables
`InterlockedExchangeAdd()`	Increments a 32-bit variable by a specified amount (which may be negative if subtraction is required), returning the old value
`InterlockedCompareExchange()`	Increments a 32-bit variable by a specified amount if the variable is equal to a test value.(Supported by NT 4.0 and Win98 only.)

Their use is illustrated in the following code fragment:

```
LONG lVal = 10;
LONG lResult;

// Increment lVal by 1
lResult = InterlockedIncrement(&lVal);

// Decrement lVal by 1
lResult = InterlockedDecrement(&lVal);

// put 20 into lVal, and return old value
lResult = InterlockedExchange(&lVal, 20L);
```

A Mutex Class

The `Mutex` class represents a mutex object. It creates the mutex in its constructor, and uses the base class to store the handle. We also need to supply `acquire()`, which needs to check whether the mutex has been abandoned, and `release()`, which calls `ReleaseMutex()`:

```
// Mutex.h

#include "SyncObj.h"

class Mutex : public SyncObj
{
public:
    Mutex(LPCTSTR pName=NULL, BOOL bOwn=FALSE, LPSECURITY_ATTRIBUTES lps=NULL);

    virtual bool acquire(DWORD dwTimeOut);
    virtual bool release();
};
```

The constructor arguments mirror those required by `CreateMutex()`, and we use default arguments to provide sensible default values. Note that the order of arguments in the constructor is different to those in the `CreateMutex()` call, because it makes for more sensible handling of default arguments:

```
// Mutex.cpp

#include "Mutex.h"

Mutex::Mutex(LPCTSTR pName, BOOL bOwn, LPSECURITY_ATTRIBUTES lps)
{
   hObject = ::CreateMutex(lps, bOwn, pName);
   if (hObject == NULL)
      throw "Mutex: can't create kernel object";
}

bool Mutex::acquire(DWORD dwTimeOut)
{
   DWORD dwResult = WaitForSingleObject(hObject, dwTimeOut);
   if (dwResult == WAIT_OBJECT_0 || dwResult == WAIT_ABANDONED_0)
      return true;
   else
      return false;
}

bool Mutex::release()
{
   if (::ReleaseMutex(hObject))
      return true;
   else
      return false;
}
```

Monitor Objects

In the above example we're protecting access to standard output, but what if we're protecting access to a data item? In this case, we can often wrap the data item and the synchronization into a single class, hiding the details from the user. A structure which bundles data, the methods to handle it and synchronization is called a **monitor**. They were originally invented in the early 1970s for use in operating system programming, and are now quite easily implemented using C++.

Here's a very simple example of a monitor.

Try It Out — A Monitor Class

The `IntBuff` class manages an array of integers, and provides three member functions — one to set the array, one to print it out, and one to do both as a single operation. The main routine creates a global `IntBuff` variable, and then starts up five threads which want to use it. Here's the code.

First, we set up the relevant include files and namespaces, and declare the thread function:

```
// MonitorClass.cpp

#include <windows.h>
#include <iostream>
```

```
using namespace std;

#include "SyncObj.h"
#include "Mutex.h"
#include "Lock.h"

DWORD WINAPI threadFunc(LPVOID);
```

The monitor class itself uses a **Mutex** for protection. We don't give the mutex a name, since we're not working across processes in this example:

```
// Monitor class

class IntBuff
{
    // Mutex used for synchronisation
    Mutex mtx;

    int buff[30];
public:
    IntBuff();

    // fill the buffer with 10 values
    void set(int val);
    // print the values
    void print();
    // do both
    void both(int val);
};
```

Here are the member function definitions:

```
IntBuff::IntBuff()
{
    for(int i=0; i<30; i++)
        buff[i] = 0;
}

void IntBuff::set(int val)
{
    Lock l(&mtx);
    for(int i=0; i<30; i++)
        buff[i] = val;
}

void IntBuff::print()
{
    Lock l(&mtx);
    for(int i=0; i<30; i++)
        cout << buff[i] << ' ';
    cout << endl;
}

void IntBuff::both(int val)
{
    Lock l(&mtx);
    for(int i=0; i<30; i++)
        buff[i] = val;
```

```
    for(i=0; i<30; i++)
        cout << buff[i] << ' ';
    cout << endl;
}
```

Note how **Lock** objects are used to synchronize the operation of the member functions so that they will work correctly.

The main routine is similar to ones we've used before, creating a number of threads and starting them going. In this case, the value passed as an argument to the thread function will be the value set into the array:

```
// Create a global buffer object
IntBuff b;

int main()
{
    const int nThreads = 5;

    HANDLE hThreads[nThreads];
    DWORD threadID;

    for(int i=0; i<nThreads; i++)
    {
        hThreads[i] = CreateThread(NULL, 0, threadFunc, (LPVOID)i, 0, &threadID);
    }

    // Wait for all threads to finish
    WaitForMultipleObjects(nThreads, hThreads, TRUE, INFINITE);

    for(i=0; i<nThreads; i++)
        CloseHandle(hThreads[i]);

    return 0;
}

DWORD WINAPI threadFunc(LPVOID p)
{
    // set a value into the buffer object, then print it
    int n = reinterpret_cast<int>(p);

    b.set(n);
    b.print();

    return 0;
}
```

If you compile and run the project as it stands, you may well not get the output that you expect:

Why? Because there's the possibility of a context switch in between the **b.set()** and **b.print()** lines in the thread function. If you replace these lines with a call to

```
b.both(n);
```

you should see the correct output (shown below), as the entire set and print operation is now protected.

Semaphores

The concept of the semaphore was invented by Edsger Dijkstra in the 1960s, when he was researching into the new field of multithreaded computing. As such, they are a staple item in computer science courses.

A semaphore is like a mutex with a lock counter which has a maximum limit specified. So, whereas the resource guarded by a mutex can only be accessed by one thread at a time, code under the control of a semaphore can be accessed simultaneously by as many threads as its counter supports. Note that the counter counts the number of 'free places' left, so that when the counter reaches zero, all other threads waiting on the semaphore will be blocked until someone releases.

When are semaphores useful? Imagine a simulation of planes landing at an airport, where each plane is represented by a thread. The number of gates is less than the number of planes, so a semaphore can be used to control access to the gates — every time a plane leaves a gate one semaphore lock becomes free, so another plane can take its turn.

A mutex is essentially a semaphore with a maximum count of one, and is sometimes known as a **binary semaphore** for that reason.

> *In Win32 a semaphore with a count of one behaves differently to a mutex, in that the semaphore has no WAIT_ABANDONED return value.*

Semaphores are very useful for protecting a group of similar objects.

Creating Semaphores

We create a semaphore object using the **CreateSemaphore()** API function:

```
HANDLE CreateSemaphore(LPSECURITY_ATTRIBUTES lpSec, // security attribute block
                       LONG initCount,               // initial count
                       LONG maxCount,                // maximum count
                       LPCTSTR name);                // semaphore name
```

The function works in a very similar way to **CreateMutex()**, returning the handle of the new semaphore object. The first parameter enables you to set security attributes for the semaphore, and is only relevant under NT. The second parameter establishes the value that the semaphore's counter will have when it is created. It must lie between 0 and the maximum count.

The initial count parameter is provided for the same reason that the owner flag was provided for the mutex. By creating a semaphore with an initial count, the creating thread can give itself space to use the semaphore before other threads dive in and acquire all the locks.

Using Semaphores

Like the mutex, you use a semaphore by waiting on it. If the semaphore has more locks available, the wait will return immediately and you'll be able to use the resource. If the available lock count is zero, the wait function will block until a lock becomes available. Note that if a thread waits on a semaphore more than once, it will acquire a lock each time, so it is quite possible for a semaphore to have all its locks acquired by one thread.

When you've finished with the resource the semaphore is guarding, call **ReleaseSemaphore()**:

```
BOOL ReleaseSemaphore(HANDLE hSemaphore, LONG lCount, LPLONG pPrevVal);
```

The last two arguments are the amount by which the semaphore's counter should be incremented (usually one), and a pointer to a value in which the previous counter value will be stored, if it is of interest to you. If you're not interested, you can pass **NULL**. The provision of the increment value makes it easy for a thread to release a semaphore which it has acquired more than once.

Try It Out — Semaphores in Action

Here's an example showing how to use semaphores:

```cpp
// UsingSemaphores.cpp

#include <windows.h>
#include <cstdio>
#include <cstdlib>
#include <ctime>

DWORD WINAPI writeData(LPVOID);

const int nThread = 10;
```

```
int main()
{
    HANDLE hThreads[nThread];
    HANDLE hSem;   // local rather than global
    DWORD threadID;
    int i;

    srand(static_cast<unsigned>(time(NULL)));

    char* ps[] = {"one", "two", "three", "four", "five",
                  "six", "seven", "eight", "nine", "ten"};

    hSem = CreateSemaphore(NULL,        // no security
                           3,           // initial available lock count is 3
                           3,           // maximum is 3
                           "Sem1");     // semaphore name

    for(i=0; i<nThread; i++)
    {
        hThreads[i] = CreateThread(NULL, 0, writeData, (LPVOID)ps[i], 0, &threadID);

        if (hThreads[i])
            printf("Thread %d launched\n", i);
    }

    // Wait for all threads to finish
    WaitForMultipleObjects(nThread, hThreads, TRUE, INFINITE);

    for(i=0; i<nThread; i++)
        CloseHandle(hThreads[i]);

    return 0;
}

DWORD WINAPI writeData(LPVOID p)
{
    char* ps = reinterpret_cast<char*>(pv);

    HANDLE hSem = OpenSemaphore(SEMAPHORE_ALL_ACCESS, FALSE, "Sem1");
    printf("Thread %s waiting for semaphore %d\n", ps, hSem);

    WaitForSingleObject(hSem, INFINITE);

    // Sleep for a while...
    Sleep(rand() % 500);

    LONG lCount;
    ReleaseSemaphore(hSem, 1, &lCount);
    printf("Thread %s finished, semaphore count was %d\n", ps,lCount);

    CloseHandle(hSem);

    return 0;
}
```

The output is as follows:

```
"D:\BegNT\ch06Code\UsingSemaphores\Debug\UsingSemaphores.exe"          _ □ ✕
Thread one waiting for semaphore 124
Thread two waiting for semaphore 128
Thread three waiting for semaphore 132
Thread four waiting for semaphore 136
Thread five waiting for semaphore 140
Thread six waiting for semaphore 144
Thread 6 launched
Thread 7 launched
Thread 8 launched
Thread 9 launched
Thread seven waiting for semaphore 168
Thread eight waiting for semaphore 172
Thread nine waiting for semaphore 176
Thread ten waiting for semaphore 180
Thread one finished, semaphore count was 0
Thread two finished, semaphore count was 0
Thread four finished, semaphore count was 0
Thread three finished, semaphore count was 0
Thread seven finished, semaphore count was 0
Thread five finished, semaphore count was 0
Thread six finished, semaphore count was 0
Thread nine finished, semaphore count was 0
Thread ten finished, semaphore count was 1
Thread eight finished, semaphore count was 2
Press any key to continue_
```

The overall structure of the program is pretty similar to the previous mutex example, but there are a few differences.

The first thing to note is that I'm using C-style **printf()** output rather than C++ **iostream** output. This is simply because **printf()** makes it easier to read the output in this case. If we use **iostream**s, each line of output is printed by multiple function calls (for example, each of the operator << functions), so context switching can take place in the middle of a line of output, which makes it harder for us to see what is going on. The alternative would be to place each C++ output statement in a critical section.

The application creates a group of threads, each of which will want to use the thread function. It also creates a named semaphore with a lock count of three:

```
hSem = CreateSemaphore(NULL,      // no security
                       3,         // initial available lock count is 3
                       3,         // maximum is 3
                       "Sem1");   // semaphore name
```

Note that we're using a local semaphore handle in **main()**, rather than the global handle we used in the mutex example. This means that we need to name the semaphore, so that it can be opened in the thread function.

Each thread will immediately start executing the thread function, and the first thing it does is to open the semaphore, using **OpenSemaphore()**:

```
HANDLE hSem = OpenSemaphore(SEMAPHORE_ALL_ACCESS, FALSE, "Sem1");
```

The first parameter to **OpenSemaphore()** is the access flag, which says how you want to use the semaphore object. This flag can take one of the following values:

- **SEMAPHORE_ALL_ACCESS** specifies all possible access flags

- **SEMAPHORE_MODIFY_STATE** means you can use the semaphore handle in the **ReleaseSemaphore()** function to modify the semaphore's count

- **SYNCHRONIZE** is available under NT only, and allows the handle to be used in the wait functions.

When you're running on a system which supports security, the call will fail if the object's security descriptor doesn't permit the requested access.

> *This parameter will be ignored under Windows 95.*

The second parameter determines whether a process created by **CreateProcess()** can inherit the handle, and so also be able to use the semaphore. You'll usually leave this set to **FALSE**. The third parameter is the name of the semaphore you want to open, in our case **Sem1**.

If the call works, you'll get returned a handle to the semaphore. If it fails, you'll get **NULL** returned.

Once the semaphore has been opened, the thread waits on it by calling **WaitForSingleObject()**. We set up the semaphore with a lock count of three, so the first three threads which call **WaitForSingleObject()** will return immediately, each taking one of the locks. The fourth thread will block until a lock is freed.

Once a thread has obtained a lock, it goes to sleep for a random period before releasing the lock, to simulate the thread doing some work. After releasing one lock count, the thread closes the semaphore handle and exits.

A Semaphore Class

Like **Mutex**, the **Semaphore** class is fairly straightforward:

```
// Semaphore.h

#include "SyncObj.h"

class Semaphore : public SyncObj
{
public:
   Semaphore(LONG initCount, LONG maxCount, LPCTSTR pName=NULL,
           LPSECURITY_ATTRIBUTES lps=NULL);
   Semaphore(LPCTSTR lpName, DWORD dwDesiredAccess = SEMAPHORE_ALL_ACCESS,
           BOOL bInheritHandle = FALSE);
   bool release(LONG count, LPLONG pPrevCount);
   bool release(){return release(1,NULL);}

// bool open(LPCTSTR lpName, DWORD dwDesiredAccess = SEMAPHORE_ALL_ACCESS,
           BOOL bInheritHandle = FALSE);
};
```

The constructor takes the parameters needed for a call to **CreateSemaphore()**. Note that we can't supply default values for the initial and maximum count. When we release a semaphore we can choose how many locks to release, and whether we want the previous count returned to us. Since we often only want to release one lock (and aren't interested in the previous count), we'll provide these as default values.

```
// Semaphore.cpp

#include "Semaphore.h"

Semaphore::Semaphore(LONG initCount, LONG maxCount, LPCTSTR pName,
                     LPSECURITY_ATTRIBUTES lps)
{
   // Check the counts are valid
   if (initCount < 0 || maxCount <= 0 || initCount > maxCount)
      throw "Semaphore: invalid count parameter";

   // Create semaphore object
   hObject = ::CreateSemaphore(lps, initCount, maxCount, pName);
   if (hObject == NULL)
      throw "Semaphore: can't create kernel object";
}

Semaphore::Semaphore(LPCTSTR lpName, DWORD dwDesiredAccess, BOOL bInheritHandle)
{
   hObject = ::OpenSemaphore(dwDesiredAccess, bInheritHandle, lpName);
   if (hObject == NULL)
      throw "Semaphore: can't open kernel object";
}

bool Semaphore::release(LONG count, LPLONG pPrevCount)
{
   if (::ReleaseSemaphore(hObject, count, pPrevCount))
      return true;
   else
      return false;
}
```

Try It Out — Using The Semaphore Class

The **Semaphore** class in use looks something like this:

```
// UsingSemaphores2.cpp

#include <windows.h>
#include <cstdio>
#include <cstdlib>
#include <ctime>

#include "Semaphore.h"

DWORD WINAPI writeData(LPVOID);

const int nThread = 10;
```

```
int main()
{
    HANDLE hThreads[nThread];
    DWORD threadID;
    int i;

    srand(static_cast<unsigned>(time(NULL)));

    char* ps[] = {"one", "two", "three", "four", "five",
                  "six", "seven", "eight", "nine", "ten"};

    Semaphore Sem1(3, 3, "Sem1");

    for(i=0; i<nThread; i++)
    {
        hThreads[i] = CreateThread(NULL, 0, writeData, (LPVOID)ps[i], 0, &threadID);

        if (hThreads[i])
            printf("Thread %d launched\n", i);
    }

    // Wait for all threads to finish
    WaitForMultipleObjects(nThread, hThreads, TRUE, INFINITE);

    for(i=0; i<nThread; i++)
        CloseHandle(hThreads[i]);

    return 0;
}

DWORD WINAPI writeData(LPVOID p)
{
    char* ps = reinterpret_cast<char*>(pv);

    Semaphore Sem("Sem1");
    printf("Thread %s waiting for semaphore\n", ps);

    Sem.acquire();

    // Sleep for a while...
    Sleep(rand() % 500);

    LONG lCount;
    Sem.release(1, &lCount);

    printf("Thread %s finished, semaphore count was %d\n", ps, lCount);

    return 0;
}
```

Events

Events are the last of the synchronization objects we'll be considering, and they are rather different to the other three. Events are either signalled or non-signalled. When an event is signalled, wait functions will be satisfied (i.e. return immediately). When an event is non-signalled, the waiting function will be blocked.

Events are used in several situations:

▶ Since they can be named, they can be used in more than one process, and are useful for communicating between processes

▶ Because they are very simple, they can be used to build more complex synchronization mechanisms

▶ They are used in some of NT's advanced I/O operations

Creating Events

As you might have come to expect by now, event objects are created by a function called `CreateEvent()`:

```
HANDLE CreateEvent(LPSECURITY_ATTRIBUTES lpSec,   // security attribute block
                   BOOL bManualReset,             // manual reset flag
                   BOOL bInitState,               // initial state flag
                   LPCTSTR name);                 // semaphore name
```

There are two new arguments here — the reset and initial state flags. The reset flag determines how the event behaves when reset, and we'll look at what this does in a minute. The initial state flag says whether the event object will be created signalled or non-signalled. If you specify the name of an existing event it will be opened for you, and in that case the reset and state flag values are ignored.

When you've finished with the event object, you call `CloseHandle()` on its handle.

Manual and Automatic Events

Events can come in two flavours:

▶ **Automatic events** always set themselves back to non-signalled whenever they get signalled, so they act a little like a push-button — you push it, it makes contact, and then it springs back. This means that the stable state for an automatic event is non-signalled.

▶ **Manual reset events** are like a light switch — when you set them, they stay set until you reset them. The stable state for a manual reset event is in whatever state it finds itself. They are useful when doing asynchronous I/O (see Chapter 7).

Which sort of event object you create depends on the setting of the manual reset flag in the `CreateEvent()` function. If you set it to **TRUE** you'll get a manual reset event. If it is **FALSE**, you'll get an automatic event.

Using Events

Events are pretty simple to use. There are three API calls which can be used to manipulate an event:

▶ `SetEvent()`
▶ `ResetEvent()`
▶ `PulseEvent()`

How they behave depends on whether the event is manual or automatic:

Function	Automatic Events	Manual Events
SetEvent()	Sets the event to signalled and then back to non-signalled, waking up a single waiting thread	Sets the event to signalled, and leaves it there
ResetEvent()	No effect	Sets the event to non-signalled, and leaves it there
PulseEvent()	Has the same effect as SetEvent()	Sets the event to signalled and then back to non-signalled, waking up *all* waiting threads

PulseEvent() is provided so that you have an easy way to wake up a group of waiting threads. Note that if you call PulseEvent() or SetEvent() for an automatic event, and there's nothing waiting, then nothing will happen. It can be quite easy to lose wakeup requests in this way, that is, sending a wakeup call when no-one is listening for it.

Try It Out — An Event Example

As an example, let's write a trio of small applications which communicate using events:

- Wait1.exe creates an event called "Event1", and then waits for it to be set.
- Wait2.exe does the same for "Event2".
- Control.exe tries to open the two events, and if successful, immediately sets the first one. It then waits for two seconds before setting the second.

Here's the code, which should be pretty self-explanatory.

First, Wait1.cpp

```
// Wait1.cpp

#include <windows.h>
#include <iostream>
#include <tchar.h>

using namespace std;

int main()
{
   HANDLE hEvent1;

   // Create the event
   hEvent1 = CreateEvent(NULL, FALSE, FALSE, _T("Event1"));

   if (hEvent1 == NULL)
   {
      cout << "Error: " << GetLastError() << endl;
```

```
          return 0;
       }

    cout << "Waiting for event 1..." << endl;
    WaitForSingleObject(hEvent1, INFINITE);

    cout << "Event set!" << endl;

    // Close the event handle
    CloseHandle(hEvent1);

    return 0;
}
```

We create a named event object, and if the creation is successful, wait for it to be set. As you might suppose, `Wait2.cpp` is the same, but with all 1's changed to 2's.

`Control.cpp` is hardly any more complicated:

```
// Control.cpp

#include <windows.h>
#include <iostream>
#include <tchar.h>

using namespace std;

int main()
{
    HANDLE hEvent1, hEvent2;

    // Get the event handles...
    hEvent1 = OpenEvent(EVENT_ALL_ACCESS, FALSE, _T("Event1"));
    hEvent2 = OpenEvent(EVENT_ALL_ACCESS, FALSE, _T("Event2"));

    if (hEvent1 == NULL || hEvent2 == NULL)
    {
        cout << "Error: " << GetLastError() << endl;
        return 0;
    }

    cout << "Setting event 1..." << endl;
    SetEvent(hEvent1);

    Sleep(2000);

    cout << "Setting event 2..." << endl;
    SetEvent(hEvent2);

    CloseHandle(hEvent2);
    CloseHandle(hEvent1);

    return 0;
}
```

We open the two events to retrieve their handles. If that is successful, we immediately set the first one. After waiting two seconds, we set the second.

Build three console applications, and then open three console windows. Run `Wait1` and `Wait2` first, and you should see them block, waiting for the events to be set. When you run `Control`, you'll immediately see `Wait1` signal that the event has been set and then exit, followed two seconds later by `Wait2`.

Adding an Event Class

The `Event` class follows the pattern we've established in `Mutex` and `Semaphore`:

```cpp
// Event.h

#include "SyncObj.h"

class Event : public SyncObj
{
public:
   Event(LPCTSTR pName, BOOL bManual, BOOL bOwn=FALSE, LPSECURITY_ATTRIBUTES
lps=NULL);
   Event(LPCTSTR lpName, DWORD dwDesiredAccess = EVENT_ALL_ACCESS,
         BOOL bInheritHandle = FALSE);

   bool release();
   bool set();
};
```

The constructor takes the parameters needed for a call to `CreateEvent()`, including the initial ownership and manual reset flags.

```cpp
// Event.cpp

#include "Event.h"

Event::Event (LPCTSTR pName, BOOL bOwn, BOOL bManual, LPSECURITY_ATTRIBUTES lps)
{
   // Create the event object
   hObject = ::CreateEvent(lps, bManual, bOwn, pName);
   if (hObject == NULL)
      throw "Event: can't create kernel object";
}

Event::Event(LPCTSTR lpName, DWORD dwDesiredAccess, BOOL bInheritHandle)
{
   // Open the event object
   hObject = ::OpenEvent(dwDesiredAccess, bInheritHandle, lpName);
   if (hObject == NULL)
      throw "Event: can't open kernel object";

}

bool Event::release()
{
   // We don't have to release events
   return true;
}
```

```
bool Event::set()
{
   // Set the event
   if (::SetEvent(hObject))
      return true;
   else
      return false;
}
```

Try It Out — Using the Event Class

Change `Wait1.cpp` to:

```
// Wait1(EventClass).cpp

#include <windows.h>
#include <iostream>
#include <tchar.h>

#include "..\Event\Event.h"

using namespace std;

int main()
{
   try{
      Event Event1(_T("Event1"), FALSE);

      cout << "Waiting for event 1..." << endl;
      Event1.acquire();

      cout << "Event set!" << endl;
   }
   catch(const char* exception){cout << exception;}
   return 0;
}
```

The same applies to `Wait2.cpp`. The `Control.cpp` code now looks like:

```
// Control(EventClass).cpp

#include <windows.h>
#include <iostream>
#include <tchar.h>

#include "..\UsingEvents2\Event\Event.h"

using namespace std;

int main()
{
   try{
      // Get the event handles...
      Event Event1(_T("Event1"));
      Event Event2(_T("Event2"));
```

```
            cout << "Setting event 1..." << endl;

            Event1.set();

            Sleep(2000);

            cout << "Setting event 2..." << endl;

            Event2.set();
        }
    catch(const char* exception){cout << exception << endl;}
    return 0;
}
```

Creating Processes

A **process** is a running program and is the object which owns all the resources needed by that program, such as an address space, file handles and so on.

Creating a process means running a program, and there are a number of ways a user can do this, such as double-clicking an icon in Explorer, or executing a command line. Programs can also be run by using a run-time library function such as the **_spawn()** or **_exec()** families of functions, or by calling the underlying Win32 API function **CreateProcess()** directly. The run-time library functions do not offer the flexibility of **CreateProcess()**, but are useful when porting code from other environments, especially Unix, as the run-time library calls more closely match the Unix system calls.

> *The Win16 function* WinExec() *is considered obsolete but is still included for compatibility. It calls* CreateProcess().

Using CreateProcess()

CreateProcess() is a bit of a monster function, taking no fewer than 10 parameters, as shown in the following prototype:

```
fResult =   CreateProcess(
    LPCTSTR  lpProgName,                        // executable module name
    LPTSTR lpszCommandLine,                     // command line
    LPSECURITY_ATTRIBUTES lpProcessAtts,        // process security attributes
    LPSECURITY_ATTRIBUTES lpThreadAtts,         // thread security attributes
    BOOL bInheritHandles,                       // inheritance flag
    DWORD dwFlags,                              // creation flags
    LPVOID lpEnvironment,                       // pointer to new environment
                                                // block
    LPCTSTR lpCurrentDir,                       // current directory name
    LPSTARTUPINFO lpStartupInfo,                // pointer to STARTUP_INFO block
    LPPROCESS_INFORMATION lpProcessInfo);       // pointer to PROCESS_INFORMATION
                                                // block
```

Using it can also be rather daunting, as there are a lot of alternatives for some of the options. Let's look at these in order. The first two parameters are used together to specify the path to the program you want to execute and its command line, and there are several ways in which they can be used.

You can choose to use one, the other or both of the first two arguments:

▶ If both parameters are non-**NULL**, then the first is taken as the program name, and the second is the command line

▶ If the first parameter is **NULL**, then the first token of the command line is taken to be the process name, and used accordingly

▶ If the second parameter is **NULL**, then the **lpProgName** argument is taken to be the process name and command line

OK so far. Now, if you use the first parameter to specify the program name, you can specify a full path, but if you don't, the current drive and current directory are used to complete the path.

If you choose to use the second option, using the first token on the command line as the process name, different rules apply. If the name doesn't contain a path, Windows searches for the executable in the following sequence of places:

▶ The directory from which the application loaded

▶ The current directory of the parent process

▶ The Windows system directory (called SYSTEM32 under NT)

▶ Under Windows NT only, the 16-bit system directory (called SYSTEM)

▶ The Windows directory

▶ Directories in the path

> *If you're using* CreateProcess() *to start up a 16-bit process under NT, you should leave the first parameter as NULL, and use the command line to specify the full path to the executable.*

The next two parameters can be used to assign security attributes to the process itself, and to its primary thread. As usual, you don't have to specify these, and under Windows 95 they'll be ignored.

Parameter five determines whether the new process will inherit, and be able to use, handles which the parent has open. The topic of inheriting handles from the parent process is outside the scope of this book.

The sixth parameter is used to specify flags which control the creation of the process, and its priority. There are quite a few of these, summarized in the two tables below:

Creation Flag	Meaning
CREATE_DEFAULT_ERROR_MODE	Sets the default error mode for the new process, rather than inheriting from the parent. The error mode determines how process errors (such as GP faults and critical errors) are handled by the system
CREATE_NEW_CONSOLE	Creates a new console for this process, rather than inheriting one from its parent
CREATE_NEW_PROCESS_GROUP	Indicates that the process is to be the root of a new process group (see later)
CREATE_SEPARATE_WOW_VDM	For a 16-bit process, creates a new private virtual machine for the process. By default, all 16-bit applications run in a shared **VDM** (Virtual DOS Machine — allows DOS and Windows programs to run on NT). (Windows NT only)
CREATE_SHARED_WOW_VDM	For a 16-bit process, runs the process in the shared VDM. This may be needed if the **win.ini** file has the **DefaultSeparateVDM** flag set to **TRUE**. (Windows NT only)
CREATE_SUSPENDED	The primary thread of the new process is created in a suspended state, and will stay that way until woken by a call to **ResumeThread()**
CREATE_UNICODE_ENVIRONMENT	If set, the environment block uses Unicode. If not set, it uses ANSI characters
DEBUG_PROCESS	If this flag is set, the calling process is treated as a debugger, and will receive all debug events
DEBUG_ONLY_THIS_PROCESS	Specifies that the new process shouldn't be debugged using the same debugger as the parent process
DETACHED_PROCESS	Prevents the new process from accessing the console belonging to the parent process. Cannot be used in conjunction with the **CREATE_NEW_CONSOLE** flag

Priority Flag	Used For
REALTIME_PRIORITY_CLASS	Highest-priority tasks, preempting even system processes
HIGH_PRIORITY_CLASS	Time-critical applications which must be executed immediately, and which should not be preemptively interrupted
NORMAL_PRIORITY_CLASS	Normal process with no special needs
IDLE_PRIORITY_CLASS	Background process

We'll say more about priorities later in the chapter.

The last two parameters are pointers to information structures used in **CreateProcess()**. You pass in the **STARTUPINFO** block which contains information that controls the startup of the new process, and once the process has been started, the **PROCESS_INFORMATION** block returned to you will contain information about the new process and its primary thread.

> *The main difference between this and the Unix* `fork()` *call is that* `fork()` *creates a copy of the current process, whereas* `CreateProcess()` *creates a brand new one. This means that if something like a file handle is to be used in the child process, then it will have to be explicitly passed over, because the child won't inherit it (unless the fifth parameter is set to* `TRUE`), *as it would when forking a process under Unix.*

Console Groups

One of the flags to `CreateProcess()` creates a new **process group**. Although these are rather specialised in their applicability, we'll mention them in passing here for completeness. As its name implies, a process group is a group of processes, and you can use the `GenerateConsoleCtrlEvent()` function to send a signal, such as *Ctrl-C*, to a whole group of processes at once.

The STARTUPINFO Structure

This structure contains information which is used to control how the process behaves and appears on startup. As you can see from the listing below, it has quite a number of fields. Because of this, we don't usually create a structure from scratch, but instead retrieve the **STARTUPINFO** structure for the current process using `GetStartupInfo()`, and then modify the fields as necessary:

```
typedef struct _STARTUPINFO {
    DWORD     cb;                   // size of the structure, in bytes
    LPTSTR    lpReserved;           // reserved - set to NULL
    LPTSTR    lpDesktop;            // name of desktop and window station
    PTSTR     lpTitle;              // title for new console window
    DWORD     dwX;                  // offset of origin from top-left, in
                                    // pixels
    WORD      dwY;                  //
    WORD      dwXSize;              // window size, in pixels
    DWORD     dwYSize;              //
    DWORD     dwXCountChars;        // screen buffer width and height in
                                    // chars
    WORD      dwYCountChars;        // and rows
    DWORD     dwFillAttribute;      // initial text and background colours
    WORD      dwFlags;              // creation flags
    WORD      wShowWindow;          // how window is shown
    WORD      cbReserved2;          // must be zero
    LPBYTE    lpReserved2;          // must be NULL
    HANDLE    hStdInput;            // specify standard input handle
    HANDLE    hStdOutput;           // specify standard output handle
    HANDLE    hStdError;            // specify standard error handle
} STARTUPINFO, *LPSTARTUPINFO;
```

The fields shown below are applicable only to non-GUI applications, those which use a standard console window for text-mode output:

▶ The window title, `lpTitle`

▶ The screen buffer width and height in characters/rows, `dwXCountChars` and `dwYCountChars`

▶ The fill attribute, `dwFillAttribute`

These parameters will be ignored if passed when creating a GUI process.

The creation flags parameter `dwFlags` can take a number of values, as summarized in the table below:

Flag	Meaning
STARTF_USESHOWWINDOW	Use the value of the **wShowWindow** member to determine how the process window should be shown
STARTF_USEPOSITION	Use the **dwX** and **dwY** members to set the window position
STARTF_USESIZE	Use the **dwXSize** and **dwYSize** members to set the window size
STARTF_USECOUNTCHARS	Use the screen buffer width and height members to determine the size of the console window
STARTF_USEFILLATTRIBUTE	Use the **dwFillAttribute** member to set the console fill attributes
STARTF_FORCEONFEEDBACK	Display the feedback cursor for a few seconds after startup. This will be whatever cursor is used by the system to show that something is happening
STARTF_FORCEOFFFEEDBACK	Display the normal cursor on startup
STARTF_USESTDHANDLES	Causes the process handles to be set to the values specified in the **hStdInput, hStdOutput** and **hStdError** members of the structure

Using STARTUPINFO

Remember that you need to give the size of the structure as the first member, so you'll typically initialize a structure like this:

```
// Assume we're starting up a console (non-GUI) process

STARTUPINFO si;
memset(si, 0, sizeof si);
si.cb = sizeof si;

...

// Set the size in rows and columns
si.dwXCountChars = 80;
si.dwYCountChars = 24;

// Use blue text on a white background
si.dwFillAttribute = FOREGROUND_BLUE | BACKGROUND_RED | BACKGROUND_GREEN |
                                                        BACKGROUND_BLUE;

// Set the flags to take notice of the members we've set
si.dwFlags = STARTF_USEFILLATTRIBUTES | STARTF_USECOUNTCHARS;
```

The PROCESS_INFORMATION Structure

This structure is filled in by `CreateProcess()`, and contains information about the new process, in particular the handles to the kernel objects representing the process and its primary thread:

```
typedef  struct  _PROCESS_INFORMATION
{
     HANDLE  hProcess;        // process object handle
     HANDLE  hThread;         // primary thread object handle
     DWORD  dwProcessId;      // process ID
     DWORD  dwThreadId;       // primary thread ID
}  PROCESS_INFORMATION;
```

Remember that the handles are only valid within the context of the process which receives this information, and shouldn't be passed around.

It is also possible to get hold of the same information for the current process and thread:

```
DWORD  dwProcessID = GetCurrentProcessId();
DWORD  dwThreadID = GetCurrentThreadId();
HANDLE  hProcess = GetCurrentProcess();
HANDLE  hThread = GetCurrentThread();
```

> *Once again, the handles returned by these functions are only valid in the context of the current process or thread.*

Waiting for the New Process

Once a new process is created, both it and the creating process will be able to execute immediately. Often it is useful to wait until the new process has initialized and is idle, and waiting for its first input.

```
DWORD  WaitForInputIdle(HANDLE  hProcess,  DWORD  dwTimeout);
```

Note that you can specify a timeout, so that you don't sit waiting for ever for a process which might have crashed. Waiting for the new process to become idle was the normal behavior with older, non pre-emptive versions of Windows.

Terminating Processes

The `ExitProcess()` function terminates the calling process and all its threads, but doesn't automatically terminate child processes:

```
void  ExitProcess(UINT  exitCode);
```

The exit code returned is the exit code for the process.

`ExitProcess()` is the recommended way of terminating a process. This is because it cleans up properly, by performing the following steps:

- The process detaches from any DLLs it is using
- All the threads are terminated
- All object handles are closed
- The state of the process object and its thread objects become signalled
- The exit status of the process changes from **STILL_ACTIVE** to the specified exit code

As we'd expect by now, calling `ExitProcess()` may not cause the process object to disappear, because the handle may still have a reference count from somewhere else.

Try It Out — Starting Processes

The following example uses what we've just discussed to start a copy of Notepad running, and then wait until Notepad has exited:

```cpp
// Processes.cpp

#include <windows.h>
#include <iostream>

using namespace std;

int main()
{
    STARTUPINFO si;
    PROCESS_INFORMATION pi;
    BOOL bOK;

    // Rather than make up the entire startup info block, it
    // is easier to get the one for current process and use it,
    // modifying it if need be
    GetStartupInfo(&si);

    // Create child process
    bOK = CreateProcess(0, "notepad", 0, 0, FALSE, CREATE_NEW_CONSOLE,
                        NULL, NULL, &si, &pi);

    if (!bOK)
        cout << "Error: " << GetLastError() << endl;

    // Close our handles to the notepad process and thread
    CloseHandle(pi.hProcess);
    CloseHandle(pi.hThread);

    // Wait for child process to complete
    WaitForSingleObject(pi.hProcess, INFINITE);

    return 0;
}
```

Build this program, and then open a DOS session in a window and run it. You should see Notepad appear, and when you close Notepad the original program should exit.

Before we can create the new process, we need to fill in a **STARTUPINFO** block, and as we explained earlier, we use a call to **GetStartupInfo()** to retrieve the values for the current process. We could then modify these, although in this case we're happy to run with the values we're given.

Once we've got the startup information we can call **CreateProcess()**, specifying a command line which includes the program name. We start it running with a new console, because it makes no sense to have Notepad running attached to the console belonging to the DOS window.

Once the process has been created successfully and is running, we wait on the process handle. The process object becomes signalled when Notepad exits, and the parent process can then itself exit.

Process And Thread Priority

We've already mentioned the fact that processes and threads have priorities, which affect their 'importance', and which govern how much time they'll get to execute, and whether they can be pre-empted by another thread.

> *Remember that in Win32 it is threads, not processes, which are scheduled.*

The Windows NT Scheduler

A brief look at the Windows NT scheduling mechanism will help us to understand some of the issues involved in playing with thread priorities.

The scheduler maintains a series of queues, each holding threads of a particular priority, like this:

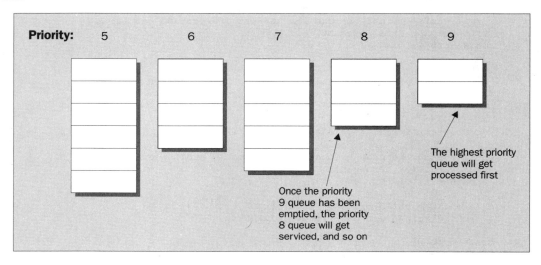

Priority: 5 6 7 8 9

Once the priority 9 queue has been emptied, the priority 8 queue will get serviced, and so on

The highest priority queue will get processed first

Windows lets a thread execute for a period of time, a time-slice (called a **quantum** in NT) of say 20 milliseconds, before moving on to the next one. The scheduler services all the threads in a given queue, giving each one its time slice in turn. If a thread is still ready for more time at the end of its slice, it is put at the back of the queue to wait for another go, and when the queue for a particular priority is empty, the scheduler moves to the next lowest priority queue.

If you are not certain of your use of priorities, don't play with them, because NT will adjust priorities dynamically for you. Don't increase your application's priority just to try to make it run better — if you do, overall system performance may well be worse. You can see how this may happen by looking at the diagram above — if a high priority thread sits in a loop processing, it may always be ready for more CPU time. In this case, the scheduler will put it back in the queue, with the net result that the queue for that priority never gets emptied. Lower priority threads will not get a chance to run, because they're getting locked out.

NT will actually give lower priority threads a few time slices, but they will be so few and far between that the user will not be happy with the way the system is running — it will for all useful purposes be locked up by the high priority thread.

Here's a rather extreme example of the sort of trouble you can cause... don't try this at home!

```
// Set the thread priority to maximum…
SetThreadPriority(GetCurrentThread(), THREAD_PRIORITY_TIME_CRITICAL);
// … and loop
while(someTest)
{
    // do processing
}
```

In this example, we get the handle to the current thread, and set that thread's priority to the absolute maximum. This value, **THREAD_PRIORITY_TIME_CRITICAL**, gives the thread a higher priority than just about anything else, including system processes. Going into a loop will lock up the system very effectively, as nothing else can get a look in, not even the Task Manager! If this loop doesn't exit for some reason, you've rendered the machine completely unusable.

Process Priorities

Every process starts off with a priority, which is determined by its **priority class**. There are four such classes:

▶ **IDLE_PRIORITY_CLASS** for low-priority, background and housekeeping jobs

▶ **NORMAL_PRIORITY_CLASS**, used for most applications

▶ **HIGH_PRIORITY_CLASS** for important applications which run briefly

▶ **REALTIME_PRIORITY_CLASS** for hardware related tasks of the absolute highest priority, such as applications which must talk to hardware devices in real time

Each of these classes has a **base priority**, which establishes the minimum priority the process will be given, as shown in the following table:

Priority Class	Base Priority
`IDLE_PRIORITY_CLASS`	4
`NORMAL_PRIORITY_CLASS`	7 (background) or 9 (foreground)
`HIGH_PRIORITY_CLASS`	13
`REALTIME_PRIORITY_CLASS`	24

The threads owned by a process can adjust their priority relative to this base value, by using one of the following thread priorities:

Thread Priority	Effect on Base Priority
`THREAD_PRIORITY_LOWEST`	-2
`THREAD_PRIORITY_BELOW_NORMAL`	-1
`THREAD_PRIORITY_NORMAL`	0
`THREAD_PRIORITY_ABOVE_NORMAL`	+1
`THREAD_PRIORITY_HIGHEST`	+2

There are also two addition values which set a thread's priority to an absolute value:

▶ `THREAD_PRIORITY_TIME_CRITICAL` gives the maximum possible priority, setting the thread priority to 31 if the process has `REALTIME_PRIORITY_CLASS`, and 15 otherwise

▶ `THREAD_PRIORITY_IDLE` gives the minimum possible priority, setting it to 16 if the process has `REALTIME_PRIORITY_CLASS`, and 1 otherwise

If you count up the possible combinations of process and thread priorities, you'll find that there are 22 possible priority values available to a thread.

Setting Process and Thread Priorities

You can change this base priority for a process or thread, by using the appropriate functions:

```
BOOL SetPriorityClass(HANDLE hProcess, DWORD dwPriorityClass);
BOOL SetThreadPriority(HANDLE hThread, int nPriority);
```

These functions take as parameters the handle of the thread or process, and the desired priority. They both return a boolean value which tells you whether the call succeeded. It could fail because you passed an invalid handle, or because you requested a priority outside the range allowed.

Dynamic Priority

We can specify the base priority for a process, but that is only half of the story. Windows itself may also increase or decrease the priority dynamically, for instance if a user clicks on a window to bring it to the front. Normal priority foreground threads will also have their priority set higher than normal priority background threads.

The scheduler does this in order to try to balance the load on the processor, and it usually makes a better job of it than you can manually!

> *The scheduler will not reduce the priority of a thread below the base priority set for the process.*

Threads and Data Storage

You may need to be rather careful when using global data with threads. Local variables, created on the stack, are no problem at all, because each thread has its own stack, and its own copy of all automatic variables.

Global data is another matter, because global data is owned by the process, and shared between threads. That is useful because it makes it quite easy to share data between threads, but it can also pose problems:

▶ You may need to synchronize access to global data to prevent corruption, using the mechanisms we've discussed

▶ Because there's only one copy of global data, there's no way to use this on a pre-thread basis, unless you use arrays and special housekeeping

The Win32 API provides a mechanism to help with this, called **Thread Local Storage**, or **TLS**, which lets us create global data items that maintain a different value for each thread using them.

Dynamic TLS

There are two flavours of Thread Local Storage — static and dynamic. Dynamic TLS is more flexible in that you can create and release storage as required, whereas static TLS is a lot easier to use.

Let's start by looking at dynamic TLS, which is implemented by four functions

▶ `TlsAlloc()`
▶ `TlsFree()`
▶ `TlsSetValue()`
▶ `TlsGetValue()`

This mechanism gives each thread belonging to a process its own copy of a 32-bit storage location. A process creates a TLS block by calling `TlsAlloc()`. This block is identified by an index, and contains one 32-bit value for each thread in existence.

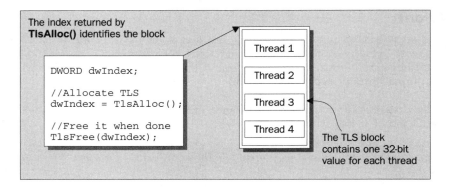

The diagram shows how to set up TLS blocks. A call to **TlsAlloc()** allocates a block of one or more 32-bit values, and returns an index. A process can set up as many blocks as it wishes, and each will get a unique index. Once a block has been finished with, a call to **TlsFree()** disposes of it.

A thread can use this block to store anything in its 32-bit value — a pointer, a long integer, whatever it wants. All it needs to know is the index of the block, and the operating system makes sure that the correct 32-bit value is used.

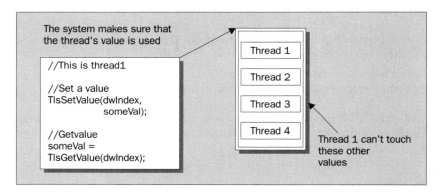

A call to **TlsSetValue()** will store a value, while one to **TlsGetValue()** (probably needing a cast to convert it back to the correct type) will retrieve a value.

Static TLS

Dynamic TLS is rather like using traditional global memory allocation. Static TLS, on the other hand, is more akin to declaring global variables in your code, rather than allocating space dynamically. Static TLS is rather easier to use, because there are no special API calls involved. If you use the special storage declarator

```
__declspec(thread)
```

when declaring global variables, the variable is created as a static TLS variable.

```
__declspec(thread) int nGlobal = 10;
```

All such variables are placed in a special memory segment called `.tls`, created in your process address space. There is one of these thread local storage segments for each thread, which is destroyed when the thread dies. The system ensures that each thread only has access to its own `.tls` area.

Try It Out — Thread Local Storage

Here's a simple code example which shows how you use TLS:

```cpp
// TLS.cpp

#include <windows.h>
#include <cstdio>

// TLS index, shared by all threads
DWORD dwIndex = 0;

DWORD WINAPI threadFunc(LPDWORD pData)
{
   // Create data to store, and store it away
   int* pi = new int;
   TlsSetValue(dwIndex, (LPVOID)pi);

   // Wait a little
   Sleep(500);

   // Retrieve the data
   printf("My pointer is %X \n", TlsGetValue(dwIndex));

return 0;
}

int main()
{
   HANDLE hTh[3];     // handles for three threads
   DWORD thrdID;      // thread ID (not used)

   // Allocate a TLS block
   dwIndex = TlsAlloc();
   if (dwIndex == 0xffffffff)
   {
      printf("TlsAlloc() call failed ( %d )\n", GetLastError());

      return -1;
   }

   // Create three threads
   for(int i=0; i<3; i++)
   {
     hTh[i] = CreateThread(NULL, 0, (LPTHREAD_START_ROUTINE)threadFunc, 0, 0,
                           &thrdID);
   }

   // Wait for them
   WaitForMultipleObjects(3, hTh, TRUE, 2000);
```

```
    // Close the handles
    for (i=0; i<3; i++)
        CloseHandle(hTh[i]);

    // Free the TLS block
    TlsFree(dwIndex);

    return 0;
}
```

The TLS index, **dwIndex**, is shared by all the threads in the program and so is declared as a global variable. The first thing the main routine does is to get a TLS block by calling **TlsAlloc()**, and checking the return value. Each thread can then use this index to store its data in the block, and the system will ensure that every thread gets a separate data value. We then kick off three threads, and wait for them to finish before freeing the TLS block.

The thread function creates some data to store in the TLS block — in this case a single integer. The address of the integer is then stored in the block by casting it to a void* and specifying the block index. After a short pause, the thread function retrieves the data from the block and prints out the address:

Conclusions

What we've seen in this chapter are some of the most computer science-like topics in the book. We've looked at the differences between threads and processes, seen how to create and destroy threads, and how to synchronize multiple threads which may be running together to do a job.

Much of what we've discussed is capable of giving real power to your applications, but there are quite a few subtleties that can become involved. Don't let the problems put you off experimenting with threading — just like the life-jacket drill on the plane, it is wise to know what *could* go wrong, even though the chances are it won't!

Files And Memory

In this chapter we will look at two topics which both relate to storing data — using files and using memory.

When you start looking around, you'll soon find that Win32 possesses a very rich set of functions for working with files and memory. There are dozens of routines, some of which are very commonly used, and others which seldom see the light of day. We'll look at most of them in this chapter, in more or less detail according to their usefulness, and you'll get a good idea of what Win32 can do for you.

To give you an idea, we'll be covering file and memory API functions related to:

- Creating/saving/deleting/moving files
- Changing file attributes
- Searching for files
- Notification of changes to files and directories
- Using memory mapped files
- Using the global and virtual memory API calls
- Working with memory using API calls

> *Most things in this chapter apply equally to Windows NT and Windows 95/98.*
> *Where there are differences, they've been flagged.*

In Chapter 1, we covered the basics of NT and its filing systems, so we'll just recap briefly here.

NT implements **installable file systems** by treating file system drivers as device drivers. This means that the file system isn't an integral part of the operating system, but is a 'plug-in' which can be removed, replaced or added to as required.

NT 4.0 supports three file systems as standard:

▶ FAT — the DOS File Allocation Table system
▶ NTFS — the NT File System
▶ CDFS — the CD file system used for CD drives

FAT is supported for backward compatibility with DOS and older versions of 16-bit Windows. It suffers from the limitations that everyone remembers well — the lack of security, lack of support for large volumes and so on. The FAT32 system has added some degree of support for long file names to this model.

NTFS, the NT File System is derived from the OS/2 HPFS system, and adds significant functionality over and above the old FAT model, the most notable being:

▶ Robustness
▶ Support for long filenames
▶ Security

See Chapter 1 for a more detailed discussion of NTFS and FAT.

> *Note that it isn't necessary to know any of the internal technical details of the file systems in order to write programs, beyond noting that some of the more advanced functionality, such as security, won't be supported if you're using a FAT disk.*

Using Files

Let's start by looking at using files under NT. Much of what we discuss here is applicable to both the FAT and NTFS file systems, but where there are differences, they'll be clearly pointed out.

File I/O

You may be wondering whether you should use NT's rich set of file related API functions or the higher level file-handling functionality found in languages and other libraries, such as C++'s file streams or MFC's **CFile** class. In simple cases these may be all you need, but they don't give access to all the functionality that Win32 provides, so sometimes it may be necessary to drop down to the Win32 level, especially if you want to deal with topics like **security, asynchronous I/O** or **change notification**.

Basic Operations

Let's start off by seeing how to create and open files, and how to do basic reading and writing.

Try It Out — Simple File Manipulation

Here's a simple example program which reads lines of text from the keyboard and saves them in a file:

```
// SimpleFileTest.cpp

#include <windows.h>
#include <iostream>

using namespace std;

int main(int argc, char* argv[])
{
   // Check we have an argument
   if (argc == 1)
   {
      cout << "Please give a filename!" << endl;
      return -1;
   }

   // Create a new file for writing, with no special attributes
   HANDLE hFile = CreateFile(argv[1],
                             GENERIC_WRITE,            // open for writing
                             0,                        // no sharing
                             NULL,                     // no security
                             CREATE_NEW,               // new file
                             FILE_ATTRIBUTE_NORMAL,    // no special attributes
                             NULL);                    // no template file

   // If there was a problem, tell the user
   if (hFile == INVALID_HANDLE_VALUE)
   {
      cout << "Error creating file, error code was " << hex
           << GetLastError() << dec << endl;
      return -1;
   }

   // Get the handle to standard input, so we can use ReadFile
   HANDLE hIn = GetStdHandle(STD_INPUT_HANDLE);

   char buff[250];
   DWORD nRead, nWritten;
   DWORD nTotal = 0;

   for(;;)
   {
      // Get a line if text from standard input
      BOOL bOK = ReadFile(hIn, buff, sizeof(buff), &nRead, NULL);
      if (!bOK)
      {
         cout << "Error from ReadFile, code was " << hex
              << GetLastError() << dec << endl;
         break;
      }
```

```
        // If a dot was the first character, exit
        if (buff[0] == '.')
            break;

        buff[nRead] = '\0';

        // Write the line to the file
        bOK = WriteFile(hFile, buff, strlen(buff), &nWritten, NULL);
        if (!bOK)
        {
            cout << "Error from WriteFile, code was " << hex
                << GetLastError() << dec << endl;
            break;
        }
        nTotal += nWritten;
    }

    // Print the amount we've written...
    cout << nTotal << " bytes written" << endl;

    CloseHandle(hFile);

    return 0;
}
```

The program starts by checking that a filename has been entered, and exits if this is not the case. We create a new file from the name passed in on the command line, using the **CreateFile()** API call, then get a handle for standard input. The use of **GetStdHandle()** for obtaining a handle for standard input is covered in Chapter 10, so for now we'll just note that it gets a handle which allows us to treat standard input as if it were a file. Lines of text are read from standard input (using **ReadFile()**) and copied to the output file (using **WriteFile()**), until a line starting with a '.' is entered. Note that we could just as easily use **cin** in C++ or **stdin** with C – we're just using **ReadFile()** because it helps to illustrate the Win32 file API calls.

Try building and executing the code, and entering some text into the console window. An example of the typical output from this program is shown below:

Let's take some time to look in more detail at the API calls we have used in this example. Firstly, Win32 uses the **CreateFile()** function to create or open files:

```
HANDLE CreateFile(
    LPCTSTR  name,                        //  name  of  file  to  create  or  open
    DWORD  dwAccess,                       //  desired  access
    DWORD  dwShare,                        //  how  the  file  should  be  shared
    LPSECURITY_ATTRIBUTES  lpSec,          //  security  attributes
    DWORD  dwCreate,                       //  creation  flags
    DWORD  dwAtts,                         //  attribute  flags
    HANDLE  hTemplate);                    //  template  file
```

There seems to be a lot of information to supply just to create a file, but this function isn't only used to create ordinary disk files. It can also be used to create or open many file-like things which all work in basically the same way, such as:

▶ Files

▶ Pipes

▶ Mailslots

▶ Communication resources

▶ Disk devices

▶ Consoles

▶ Directories

Obviously some of the arguments for the `CreateFile()` function apply more to some of the above object types than to others.

`CreateFile()` returns a handle if it is successful (and **INVALID_HANDLE_VALUE** if it isn't). This use of a single function to create or open all sorts of things and return a handle to them is an example of how NT likes to treat all resources as 'objects', which can, to a large extent, be treated in the same way.

Let's take a look at the values you can specify when creating or opening a file using `CreateFile()`. The first parameter is the name of the file you want to open or create.

The access mode specified by the second parameter says how you want to access the file, and can take three values:

▶ 0, meaning you want to query the attributes of the file without actually accessing it

▶ **GENERIC_READ** to read the file

▶ **GENERIC_WRITE** to get write access to the file

The share mode determines whether you want the file to be shareable by other processes. If we want to we can let other processes get access to the file while we have it open. There are four possible values:

▶ 0 if the file is not to be shared — our process has exclusive access, and other processes will fail if they try to open this file while we're using it

▶ **FILE_SHARE_READ** will share the file with other processes that want read access to the file

▶ **FILE_SHARE_WRITE** will share the file with other processes that want write access to the file

▶ **FILE_SHARE_DELETE** (*NT only*) will share the file with other processes that want delete access to the file

The fourth parameter specifies the security settings that you want applied to the file when it is created. If you don't want any special security settings, pass **NULL** for this parameter and you'll get the default, which is that you (as the creator) can do anything to the file. You should consult the next chapter if you want to know more about how to secure files.

Since Windows 95 and 98 have no security system, any value given for this parameter will be ignored when code is run on those operating systems.

The creation flags say what action to take when opening the file, and must be one of the following values:

▶ **CREATE_NEW** will create a new file — **CreateFile()** fails if the file already exists

▶ **CREATE_ALWAYS** will create a new file, overwriting the file if it already exists

▶ **OPEN_EXISTING** opens an existing file — function fails if the file doesn't exist

▶ **OPEN_ALWAYS** opens a file, creating it if it doesn't exist

▶ **TRUNCATE_EXISTING** opens a file and truncates its length to zero (in effect deleting what's in the file) — function fails if the file doesn't exist

The attributes parameter sets the file flags and attributes. There are a large number of possibilities from which to choose — the possible attribute values are listed below; note that they are a superset of the old DOS-style flags:

▶ **FILE_ATTRIBUTE_ARCHIVE** to set the archive bit, indicating that the file should be archived

▶ **FILE_ATTRIBUTE_COMPRESSED** to indicate that a file or directory is compressed

▶ **FILE_ATTRIBUTE_HIDDEN** to set the hidden attribute, so that the file doesn't appear in normal directory listings

▶ **FILE_ATTRIBUTE_NORMAL** to indicate that the file has no other attributes set — only valid when used alone

▶ **FILE_ATTRIBUTE_OFFLINE** indicates that the data in the file isn't immediately available, and is stored offline somewhere

▶ **FILE_ATTRIBUTE_READONLY** to indicate that the file is read-only

▶ **FILE_ATTRIBUTE_SYSTEM** to show that the file is part of (or belongs to) the operating system

▶ **FILE_ATTRIBUTE_TEMPORARY** to show that the file is a temporary file

The file flags take values from the following list:

- **FILE_FLAG_WRITE_THROUGH** instructs Windows to write through any intermediate caches, preventing the operating system from saving up writes and doing several at once.

- **FILE_FLAG_OVERLAPPED** specifies that you want to use asynchronous I/O (covered later in this chapter).

- **FILE_FLAG_NO_BUFFERING** opens a file with no intermediate buffering or caching. This can increase throughput when used with asynchronous I/O, but there are restrictions on how you use files without buffering (which are detailed in the online help).

- **FILE_FLAG_RANDOM_ACCESS** indicates that the file will be accessed randomly, by moving the file pointer. This can affect how the system caches data.

- **FILE_FLAG_SEQUENTIAL_SCAN** indicates that the file will be read sequentially from beginning to end. This can also affect how the system caches data.

- **FILE_FLAG_DELETE_ON_CLOSE** tells the system that the file should be deleted once all open handles to it have been closed. This is obviously useful for temporary files.

- **FILE_FLAG_BACKUP_SEMANTICS** (NT only) indicates that the file is opened as part of a backup operation. The operating system ensures that security checks are overridden, provided the calling process has the requisite privileges. You can also use this flag to obtain a handle to a directory, which can be passed to some Win32 functions in place of a file handle.

- **FILE_FLAG_POSIX_SEMANTICS** indicates that the file is to be accessed according to the Unix POSIX rules (which specify a portable subset of Unix), such as allowing filenames to differ only in case. Using this flag may result in files which can't be accessed under DOS or Windows.

- **FILE_FLAG_OPEN_REPARSE_POINT** inhibits the reparse behaviour of NTFS reparse points — it cannot be used with the **CREATE_ALWAYS** flag.

- **FILE_FLAG_OPEN_NO_RECALL** indicates that the file data is requested but should remain in remote storage. It is for use by remote storage handling systems or the Hierarchical Storage Management System.

Under NT, the final parameter for **CreateFile()** can be used to specify a handle to a template file, which is an existing (and open) file whose attributes are used in the creation of the new file. The handle must have at least **GENERIC_READ** access for this to work.

If you look back at the code example we saw earlier, you can see that once we've got the file handles, we can use **ReadFile()** and **WriteFile()** to perform I/O. Both these functions are similar to the C runtime library I/O functions, and are used to read and write streams of bytes.

```
BOOL  ReadFile(
      HANDLE  hFile,              // handle of file to be read
      LPVOID  pBuff,              // buffer to receive input
      DWORD  dwToRead,            // number of bytes to read
      LPDWORD  dwBytesRead,       // number of bytes actually read
      LPOVERLAPPED  pOver);       // used for overlapped I/O
```

The first two parameters passed to the `ReadFile()` function are a handle to a file from which it is to read and a pointer to a buffer which will receive the input. The third parameter gives the number of bytes to be read, which is often equal to the size of the buffer, and the fourth parameter returns the number of bytes which are actually read (if everything is performed successfully the third and fourth parameters should be the same). The final parameter is used when performing asynchronous (or overlapped) I/O — see later in the chapter for coverage of this topic.

The function will return `TRUE` if the read operation was successful. If the end of file is reached, the function will return `TRUE` and the number of bytes read will be zero, so you can test for end-of-file like this:

```
bOK = ReadFile(hFile, buff, sizeof(buff), &nRead, NULL) ;

// Check for end of file.
if (bOK && nRead == 0, )
{
    // we've reached the end of the file
}
```

The prototype for `WriteFile()` is very similar in form:

```
BOOL  WriteFile(
      HANDLE  hFile,              // handle of file to be read
      LPCVOID pBuff,              // buffer containing output
      DWORD   dwToWrite,          // number of bytes to write
      LPDWORD dwBytesWritten,     // number of bytes written
      LPOVERLAPPED pOver);        // used for overlapped I/O
```

In the initial example, we used `WriteFile()` like this:

```
bOK = WriteFile(hFile, buff, strlen(buff), &nWritten, NULL);
```

We passed the handle to the output file, the buffer and its size, and got back the number of bytes written. The final parameter was `NULL` because we aren't using asynchronous I/O.

Once you've finished I/O operations, the files are closed by closing their associated handles using `CloseHandle()`:

```
BOOL  CloseHandle(HANDLE  hFile);     // handle of file to be closed
```

This function is generally used to close handles for all the types of objects which can be opened with `CreateFile()`, and some others which you also access by handle, such as Events and Semaphores!

File Information

Win32 provides a number of functions to let you view (and occasionally manipulate) information about files. In this section, we'll be taking a look at some file API calls that allow us to access information about the size of files, times of creation and modification, and also file attributes.

As you might expect, `GetFileSize()` returns you the size of the file in bytes:

```
DWORD GetFileSize(
    HANDLE hFile,           // file handle
    LPDWORD lpSize);        // where to put high 32 bits of file size
```

If the file size can be expressed in less than 32 bits (as will be the case for all files on a FAT volume), then it is specified by the return value of this function. This mechanism is complicated by the fact that NTFS volumes can contain extremely large files, whose size is too big to fit in a `DWORD`.

If this is the case and the file size can't be expressed in the 32 bits of the return value, you need to pass a pointer to another `DWORD` where the high 32 bits will be stored (the second parameter), and the size will be returned to you in two parts. If you're sure you don't need (or don't want to bother with) the high `DWORD`, you can pass `NULL` for this parameter.

If there's an error, the function will return `0xffffffff` as its return value.

Here's the simple example program that we saw earlier, modified so that it reports the file size before it exits:

```
    cout << nTotal << " bytes written" << endl;

    DWORD dwLow, dwHigh;

    dwLow = GetFileSize(hFile, &dwHigh);
    cout << "Low 32 bits of size = " << dwLow << endl;
    cout << "High 32 bits of size = " << dwHigh << endl;

    CloseHandle(hFile);

    return 0;
}
```

Running it gives output like this:

The `GetFileTime()` function returns you three time values relevant to a file — the creation time, the last access time and the last write time.

```
BOOL  GetFileTime(
      HANDLE  hFile,
      LPFILETIME  creation,
      LPFILETIME  lastAccess,
      LPFILETIME  lastWrite);
```

If you don't want any of the time values, you can simply pass a **NULL** pointer for the corresponding argument.

> *Note that FAT file systems only support the last write time. NTFS supports all three values.*

The times returned by this function are supplied as **FILETIME**s, which are not the most friendly of things to deal with, since they are 64-bit quantities representing the number of 100 nanosecond intervals since January 1st 1601!

If all you want to do is to compare file times, then the **CompareFileTime()** function will help, but if you actually want to print the times, for example, you'll want to get them into a more friendly form. Luckily, the Win32 API provides a utility function, **FileTimeToSystemTime()**, to convert these times into something more manageable:

```
BOOL  FileTimeToSystemTime(
      CONST  FILETIME*  pFileTime,        //  file  time  to  convert
      LPSYSTEMTIME  pSysTime);            //  converted  value
```

The **SYSTEMTIME** structure and functions to manipulate it are described in Chapter 5. The structure itself looks like this:

```
typedef struct _SYSTEMTIME
{
   WORD wYear;             // year
   WORD wMonth;            // month (Jan=1)
   WORD wDayOfWeek;        // weekday (Sun=0)
   WORD wDay;              // day of month
   WORD wHour;             // hour
   WORD wMinute;           // minute
   WORD wSecond;           // second
   WORD wMilliseconds;     // milliseconds
} SYSTEMTIME;
```

GetFileType() returns you a value telling you what type the file is:

```
DWORD GetFileType(HANDLE hFile);              //  file  handle
```

As it happens, this function isn't very useful, since the return values are limited to:

- **FILE_TYPE_UNKNOWN** — the file type is unknown
- **FILE_TYPE_DISK** — it is a disk file
- **FILE_TYPE_CHAR** — it is a character file, typically meaning an LPT (printer) device or a console
- **FILE_TYPE_PIPE** — it is a named or anonymous pipe

280

We mentioned file attributes when discussing `CreateFile()`. The `GetFileAttributes()` function enables you to retrieve the attribute settings for a file:

```
DWORD GetFileAttributes(LPTSTR filename);              // file name
```

Note that the function takes a filename, not a handle. The resulting `DWORD` can be ANDed with the file attribute values, in order to see whether or not a given attribute is supported:

```
DWORD atts = GetFileAttributes("somefile.txt");
if (atts & FILE_ATTRIBUTE_NORMAL)
   cout << "File is normal" << endl;
```

The corresponding `SetFileAttributes()` function can be used to set the attributes for a file:

```
BOOL  SetFileAttributes(
      LPTSTR filename                  // file name
      DWORD dwNewAtts);                // new attributes
```

The `GetFileInformationByHandle()` gets a lot of these pieces of information at once:

```
BOOL GetFileInformationByHandle(
     HANDLE hFile,                            // file handle
     LPBY_HANDLE_FILE_INFORMATION pInfo);   // information block
```

The `BY_HANDLE_FILE_INFORMATION` structure returned from the function looks like this:

```
typedef struct _BY_HANDLE_FILE_INFORMATION
{
    DWORD    dwFileAttributes;       // attributes
    FILETIME ftCreationTime;         // creation time
    FILETIME ftLastAccessTime;       // last access
    FILETIME ftLastWriteTime;        // last write
    DWORD    dwVolumeSerialNumber;   // volume serial
    DWORD    nFileSizeHigh;          // high-order word of file size
    DWORD    nFileSizeLow;           // low-order word of file size
    DWORD    nNumberOfLinks;         // number of links to the file
    DWORD    nFileIndexHigh;         // high-order word of file index
    DWORD    nFileIndexLow;          // low-order word of file index
} BY_HANDLE_FILE_INFORMATION;
```

We've met most of the fields in this structure before. The volume serial gives the serial number of the volume on which the file resides. The number of links to the file will always be one for a FAT file, but can be more than one for an NTFS file, since NTFS supports file links.

> *A link is like a pointer — using NTFS, you can have an entry in a directory which looks like a file, but which refers to another file in another directory.*

The file index is a numeric value which uniquely identifies the file, and is constant from the time a file is opened until it is closed. You can use the volume serial and the file index to determine whether two file handles refer to the same file.

Finally, `GetFullPathName()` can be used to obtain the full path name for a file:

```
DWORD GetFullPathName(
    LPCTSTR filename,           // filename
    DWORD dwSize,               // size of path buffer
    LPTSTR buff,                // path buffer
    LPTSTR* pfile);             // pointer to file part
```

Given a filename, either in 8.3 (a filename of 8 characters with an extension of 3 characters) or long format, this function prefixes the current drive and directory to the filename to form a complete path. The final argument is a pointer to the file part of the path, and will be the long filename if there is one. Note that this function isn't guaranteed to return a valid path — it simply adds the current directory path and the filename, and returns the result.

Copying, Moving And Deleting Files

The Win32 API provides several functions which allow you to perform the common file operations in the same way you would from the command line. In this section, we'll take a look at some of the functions available for moving, copying and deleting files, and how we might go about using them.

Copying

The `CopyFile()` function takes source and destination filenames, plus a flag which determines whether or not an existing destination file will be overwritten:

```
BOOL CopyFile(
    LPTSTR src,                 // source file name
    LPTSTR dest,                // destination file name
    BOOL bFailIfExists);        // what to do if file exists
```

If `bFailIfExists` is set to `TRUE`, then no attempt will be made to overwrite existing files and the function will return `FALSE` if you try to.

Note that file attributes are copied to the new file, but security attributes aren't.

`CopyFile()` is fine for simple copying jobs, but there are times when you're copying a large file and you might want to monitor the copying process, or even cancel it. The `CopyFileEx()` function does the same job as `CopyFile()`, but gives you more interaction with the copying process:

```
BOOL CopyFileEx(
    LPCWSTR src,                    // source file name
    LPCWSTR dest,                   // destination file name
    LPPROGRESS_ROUTINE pProg,       // pointer to progress routine
    LPVOID pData,                   // argument for progress routine
    LPBOOL bCancelFlag,             // cancellation flag
    DWORD dwFlags);                 // copy flags
```

Note that CopyFileEx() is supported by NT 4.0 and above only.

The first two arguments are the same as for the `CopyFile()` function. The third and fourth arguments can be used to specify the address of, and an argument for a **progress routine** — a callback routine which is called whenever a portion of the file has been copied. If you don't want to use a progress routine, you should pass **NULL** for these arguments. You might, for example, use this function to display a progress bar, showing how much of the file has been copied. We'll look at the progress routine and how it is used shortly.

The fifth argument gives the address of a Boolean variable which can be used to cancel the copy operation. If this variable is set to **TRUE** during the copy operation (presumably by code running in another thread), it will cause the copy operation to be cancelled.

The final argument specifies how the file is to be copied:

- **COPY_FILE_FAIL_IF_EXISTS** will cause the operation to fail if the destination file already exists.

- **COPY_FILE_RESTARTABLE** makes the copy operation restartable. If the copying operation fails for some reason, calling `CopyFileEx()` with the same source and destination filenames will restart the copy operation from where it left off.

Let's take a moment to examine the progress routine and see how it is used. A function that is used as a progress routine must look like this, although you can call it anything you like:

```
DWORD WINAPI CopyProgressRoutine(
    LARGE_INTEGER totalFileSize,           // total file size in bytes
    LARGE_INTEGER totalBytesTransferred,   // number of bytes transferred
    LARGE_INTEGER streamSize,              // total size of stream in bytes
    LARGE_INTEGER streamBytesTransferred,  // bytes transferred for this stream
    DWORD dwStreamNumber,                  // the current stream
    DWORD dwCallbackReason,                // reason for the function being called
    HANDLE hSrc,                           // handle to source file
    HANDLE hDest,                          // handle to destination file
    LPVOID pData);                         // argument passed from CopyFileEx
```

Try It Out — Copying Files

Here's an example program showing how `CopyFileEx()` is used with a progress routine:

```cpp
// CopyFile.cpp

#define _WIN32_WINNT 0x0400
#include <windows.h>#include <stddef.h>#include <iostream>using namespace
std;DWORD WINAPI ProgRtn(LARGE_INTEGER tfs, LARGE_INTEGER tbytes,
                    LARGE_INTEGER ssize, LARGE_INTEGER sbytes,
                    DWORD dwSnum, DWORD dwReason, HANDLE hSrc,
                    HANDLE hDest, LPVOID pData)
{
  if (dwReason == CALLBACK_STREAM_SWITCH)
    cout << "* stream switched" << endl;
  else
    cout << "* chunk finished" << endl;
```

```
      return PROGRESS_CONTINUE;
   }

   int main()
   {
     char in[MAX_PATH+1], out[MAX_PATH+1];

     cout << "Source file: ";
     cin >> in;
     cout << "Destination: ";
     cin >> out;

     BOOL bOK = CopyFileEx(
         in,                             // input file
         out,                            // output file
         (LPPROGRESS_ROUTINE)ProgRtn,    // progress function
         NULL,                           // no arguments
         NULL,                           // no cancel flag
         COPY_FILE_FAIL_IF_EXISTS);

     if (bOK)
       cout << endl << "File copied" << endl;
     else
       cout << endl << "Copy failed" << endl;

     return 0;
   }
```

When run under NT 4.0, the program will copy one file to another, calling the progress routine during the copy. We start by defining our callback function, **ProgRtn**, which simply checks the reason and prints an appropriate string. We're simply printing the reason for the call every time the progress routine executes, but it would be easy to replace this with some other visual indication such as a row of dots, or (since you know the size of the file and how much has been copied) display the percentage completeness. Once we've done that, we use **CopyFileEx()** to do the copying, passing it the input and output file handles, the address of the progress routine, and telling it to fail if the file already exists. Typical output from this program is shown below:

The first two arguments are self explanatory, consisting of the total size in bytes of the file being copied, and the number of bytes which have been copied so far.

The second two give the total size and bytes transferred for the current stream, the number of which is given in the fifth argument. Every time a portion of the file is copied a stream is opened, so the stream number is incremented. This isn't the place to go into the inner workings of the NTFS file system, but the file system driver doesn't necessarily do I/O in a simple sequential manner. At any one time there may be several worker threads involved in an I/O operation, each performing part of the I/O process.

The reason argument can take one of two values:

▶ **CALLBACK_CHUNK_FINISHED**, meaning another part of the data file was copied

▶ **CALLBACK_STREAM_SWITCH**, meaning another stream has been created and is about to be copied — This is always the reason given when the callback is first invoked

The final three arguments are the handles to the source and destination files, and a pointer to the argument passed by **CopyFileEx()**.

The function should return one of the following values:

▶ **PROGRESS_CONTINUE** to continue the copy operation

▶ **PROGRESS_CANCEL** to cancel the operation and delete the destination

▶ **PROGRESS_STOP** to stop the operation, which can be restarted

▶ **PROGRESS_QUIET** to continue the copy, but stop calling the progress routine

Like **CopyFile()**, **CopyFileEx()** *doesn't copy security settings but does preserve file attributes.*

Deletion

DeleteFile() can be used to remove a file:

```
BOOL DeleteFile(LPTSTR pName);               // file to delete
```

Under NT, the function deletes the file immediately, provided no-one else has a handle open on it, in which case it will fail.

Note that under Windows 95, a file will be deleted even if it is open for I/O or is a memory-mapped file.

File Locking

When opening a file with **CreateFile()** we can use the third parameter to specify whether the file is to be shared:

```
HANDLE CreateFile(
    LPCTSTR name,                    // name of file to create or open
    DWORD dwAccess,                  // desired access
    DWORD dwShare,                   // how the file should be shared
```

```
        LPSECURITY_ATTRIBUTES lpSec,   // security attributes
        DWORD dwCreate,                // creation flags
        DWORD dwAtts,                  // attribute flags
        HANDLE hTemplate);             // template file
```

We can specify various levels of sharing, but these apply to the whole file, and sometimes this may be too coarse for our needs. We can get around this problem using the **LockFile()** and **UnlockFile()** functions, which enable us to set the sharing access for the file as a whole, but then allow applications to get exclusive access to ranges of bytes within a file.

It is thus possible to have more than one application writing safely to a file of records, because each can lock the record it needs to write, preventing any of the others from gaining access. These functions have obvious uses in applications such as databases.

You get exclusive access to a region in a file using **LockFile()**:

```
    BOOL  LockFile(
        HANDLE  hFile,                 // file handle to lock
        DWORD   dwOffsetLow,           // Low DWORD of offset
        DWORD   dwOffsetHigh,          // High DWORD of offset
        DWORD   dwRgnLow,              // Low DWORD of region size
        DWORD   dwRgnHigh);            // High DWORD of region size
```

The offset (in bytes) of the locked region from the start of the file is passed to the function as two **DWORD**s, as is the size of the area (**region**) you wish to lock, again in bytes. We need to specify high and low **DWORD**s for these parameters, because we may be dealing with very large files on NTFS volumes. For small files you would simply set the high **DWORD**s to zero. It is an error for one region to overlap another, but it isn't an error to specify a region which has a range beyond the end of the file.

The function returns **TRUE** if the lock request works, and **FALSE** otherwise.

> *Note that file locks aren't inherited by child processes.*

When you've locked a region, no other process can read or write to the region until you release the lock by calling **UnlockFile()**:

```
    BOOL  UnlockFile(
        HANDLE  hFile,                 // file handle to unlock
        DWORD   dwOffsetLow,           // Low DWORD of offset
        DWORD   dwOffsetHigh,          // High DWORD of offset
        DWORD   dwRgnLow,              // Low DWORD of region size
        DWORD   dwRgnHigh);            // High DWORD of region size
```

This function has exactly the same prototype as **LockFile()**, and the fact that you have to supply offset and size information implies that you can unlock parts of a region, and do not have to unlock the whole region at once.

The following code fragment illustrates how you might use `LockFile()`:

```
// Suppose we have a file of these structures:

struct T
{
   // data structure
};

...

// Open the file so that we (and everyone else) can write to it

HANDLE hFile = CreateFile(name, GENERIC_WRITE,
                          FILE_SHARE_WRITE,
                          0,OPEN_EXISTING,
                          0, 0);

...

// Lock record 10 in the file...
BOOL bOK = LockFile(hFile,
   sizeof(T) * 9, 0,      // Offset is nine records from the start
   sizeof(T), 0);         // Size is one record

if (bOK)
{
   // Lock was successful, so do what we need to do

   // Unlock region
   UnlockFile(hFile, sizeof(T) * 9, 0, sizeof(T), 0);
}
```

The `LockFileEx()` function does the same job as `LockFile()`, but (as is usual with the `...Ex()` functions) it adds some more functionality. Note that it is only available under NT, and not Windows 95:

```
BOOL  LockFileEx(
      HANDLE  hFile,           // file handle  to  lock
      DWORD   dwFlags,         // flags
      DWORD   dwReserved,      // reserved
      DWORD   dwRgnLow,        // Low DWORD  of region  size
      DWORD   dwRgnHigh,       // High DWORD  of region  size
      LPOVERLAPPED  pData);    // structure  containing offset  information
```

The file handle and region size are given as before. The second argument can be one or more of the following values:

▶ `LOCKFILE_FAIL_IMMEDIATELY` causes the function to return immediately if it can't get the lock. If not specified, it waits to acquire the lock.

▶ `LOCKFILE_EXCLUSIVE_LOCK` requests an exclusive lock, like the one you get from `LockFile()`. If you don't specify this, you'll get a shared lock (also known as a 'write lock'), which allows other processes to read the locked region.

The last parameter is an **OVERLAPPED** structure which contains information (including the offset) about the region to be locked:

```
typedef struct _OVERLAPPED
{
    DWORD Internal;         // reserved for operating system use
    DWORD InternalHigh;     // reserved for operating system use
    DWORD Offset;           // low DWORD of lock region offset
    DWORD OffsetHigh;       // high DWORD of lock region offset
    HANDLE hEvent;          // event to signal end of operation
} OVERLAPPED;
```

Only the third and fourth parameters are significant when this structure is used with **LockFileEx()**, and they are used to give the low and high DWORDs of the lock region offset.

Here's how we could modify the code fragment above to use **LockFileEx()**:

```
// Lock record 10 in the file...

OVERLAPPED ov;
ov.Offset = sizeof(T) * 9;
ov.OffstHigh = 0;
ov.hEvent = CreateEvent(0, TRUE, FALSE, 0);

BOOL bOK = LockFileEx(hFile,
    LOCKFILE_FAIL_IMMEDIATELY,   // fail immediately if can't lock
    0,                           // reserved
    sizeof(T), 0,                // size of region
    &ov);                        // offset info

if (bOK)
{
    // Lock was successful, so do what we need to do

    // Unlock region
    UnlockFile(hFile, sizeof(T) * 9, 0, sizeof(T), 0);
}
```

Random Access

The **SetFilePointer()** can be used to position the file pointer (that is, the position at which read or write operations will take place) within the file, in order to allow random access:

```
DWORD SetFilePointer(
    HANDLE hFile,       // file handle
    LONG lDistance,     // number of bytes to move file pointer
    PLONG pHigh,        // pointer to high-order word of distance
    DWORD dwMethod);    // how to move
```

The number of bytes given in the second parameter specifies how many bytes to move the file pointer — a positive value moves it forward in the file, while a negative value moves it backward. When operating on large files, the third parameter can be used to specify the high-order word for the number of bytes to move the pointer. If this is set to **NULL**, then the maximum file size is $2^{32}-1$ bytes, whereas if it is given the maximum size is $2^{64}-1$ bytes.

The final parameter specifies the starting point for the file pointer, and can be one of:

▶ **FILE_BEGIN**, meaning the start of the file

▶ **FILE_END**, meaning the end of the file

▶ **FILE_CURRENT**, meaning the current position

The return value is the low **DWORD** of the new pointer position; if the third parameter isn't **NULL**, the high **DWORD** is put into the variable pointed to by this pointer.

If you move the pointer by zero bytes, you can use this function to get the current file pointer.

> *Be careful using this function in multi-threaded applications, where setting the file pointer and reading, or writing, to the file must be protected by a synchronization mechanism such as a mutex.*

Using Temporary Files

It is often useful to be able to create temporary files, such as for holding intermediate results in calculations, and Win32 has two functions which help you to do this.

GetTempPath() retrieves the full path name of the Windows directory used to store temporary files:

```
DWORD  GetTempPath(
      DWORD  dwSize,          // size of buffer for path name
      LPTSTR  pathBuff);      // pointer to buffer
```

The return value is the number of characters copied to the buffer, not including the terminating **NULL**. If the buffer is too small, the value will tell you how big it needs to be. If the function fails, the return value will be zero.

The function looks for the value of the **TMP** environment variable, and if that isn't defined it looks for the **TEMP** variable. If neither can be found, the current directory is returned. Note that the function doesn't check whether the directory actually exists!

GetTempFileName() will give you a unique filename for a temporary file, and optionally creates the file itself:

```
UINT  GetTempFileName(
      LPCTSTR  pPath,         // path for new temp file
      LPCTSTR  pPrefix,       // prefix for temp file
      UINT  uVal,             // numeric value
      LPTSTR  filename);      // buffer for new filename
```

For the first two arguments, the function takes a path, possibly one returned by **GetTempPath()**, and a prefix string. The unsigned integer value passed as the third parameter can be non-zero, in which case the function creates the filename but not the file. If this is zero, then the function creates both the name and the file. The final parameter points to a buffer to hold the path to the new file, and it should be at least **MAX_PATH** characters in size.

289

The return value from this function specifies the unique numeric value used in the construction of the filename.

Try It Out — Tempory Files

Here's a short sample program showing how these functions can be used:

```cpp
// TempFile.cpp

#include <windows.h>
#include <iostream>
using namespace std;

int main()
{
   char tempPath[MAX_PATH + 1];

   DWORD dwRet = GetTempPath(MAX_PATH+1, tempPath);
   if (dwRet == 0)
   {
      cout << "Call to GetTempPath() failed (" << GetLastError() << ")" << endl;
      return -1;
   }

   cout << "Temp path is '" << tempPath << "'" << endl;

   char tempFile[MAX_PATH + 1];

   DWORD dwUnique = GetTempFileName(tempPath, "tmp", 0, tempFile);
   if (dwUnique == 0)
   {
      cout << "Call to GetTempFileName() failed (" << GetLastError() << ")"
         << endl;
      return -1;
   }

   cout << "Temp file is '" << tempFile << "'" << endl;

   return 0;
}
```

The program will produce output similar to the following:

```
D:\WINNT\System32\cmd.exe

D:\BegNT\TempFile\Debug>tempfile
Temp path is 'D:\TEMP\'
Temp file is 'D:\TEMP\tmp16.tmp'

D:\BegNT\TempFile\Debug>
```

Notice that the temp file name has the path and prefix which we specified, and the unique value **16**.

290

Directories

Several functions are provided to enable you to work with directories, and we're going to take a quick look at these in this section. Firstly, `CreateDirectory()` lets you create a new directory:

```
BOOL  CreateDirectory(
    LPCTSTR  dirName,              // pathname for new directory
    LPSECURITY_ATTRIBUTES  pSec);  // security settings
```

The directory name must specify the full pathname for the directory. If you don't wish to specify any security settings for the new directory, you can pass **NULL** for the second parameter. The function returns **TRUE** or **FALSE**, indicating whether or not the call was successful.

`CreateDirectoryEx()` is similar, except that in this case you can also provide a template directory whose attributes will be used when creating the new directory:

```
BOOL  CreateDirectoryEx(
    LPCTSTR  templateDir,          // pathname for template directory
    LPCTSTR  dirName,              // name for new directory
    LPSECURITY_ATTRIBUTES  pSec);  // security settings
```

Directories can be deleted using a `RemoveDirectory()`:

```
BOOL  RemoveDirectory(LPCTSTR  dirName)     // name of directory to remove
```

The directory must be empty before you can remove it.

Finding Files

The `SearchPath()` function will search either the system path or a given directory tree for a file:

```
DWORD  SearchPath(
    LPCTSTR  pPath,        // path to search
    LPCTSTR  pFile,        // file name
    LPCTSTR  pExt,         // file extension
    DWORD  dwSize,         // size of result buffer
    LPTSTR  pBuff,         // result buffer
    LPTSTR*  pFileName);   // pointer to file part of result path
```

The first parameter tells the function where to start looking for the file. You can either pass the name of a directory, or if the parameter is **NULL**, the function will search various system directories in the following order:

1 The directory from which the application loaded

2 The current directory

3 The 32-bit Windows system directory (**System32**)

4 The 16-bit Windows system directory (**System**)

291

5 The Windows directory

6 The directories listed in the **PATH** environment variable

> *The directories are slightly different when this function is used under Windows 9x, because there is only one system directory to be searched.*

The second and third parameters give the name and extension of the file to be found, and these must be specific — you cannot use wildcards with this function. Note that you can give the name all in one, including extension, as the second parameter and pass **NULL** for the third parameter if you wish. If you do pass a separate filename and extension, the extension string must start with a period.

The last three parameters are associated with the buffer which holds the pathname of the file when it has been found. You need to give the size of the buffer in bytes and a pointer to the buffer. On return, the final parameter will point to where the filename starts in the buffer.

The return value from the function tells you how many bytes were written to the buffer, and can be useful if the buffer you provided was too small.

> *The online help implies that this function should search the directory tree under the one you specify. It doesn't seem to do this, and only searches the actual directory you give.*

Try It Out — Finding Files

Shown below is an example program showing how the function can be used:

```
//FindFile.cpp

#include <windows.h>
#include <iostream>
using namespace std;

int main()
{
   char filename[MAX_PATH+1], dirname[MAX_PATH+1], buff[MAX_PATH+1];
   char ans, *pPath, *pFile;

   cout << "File to look for: ";
   cin >> filename;
   cout << "Search system path (Y or N): ";
   cin >> ans;

   if (ans == 'Y' || ans == 'y')
      pPath = NULL;
   else
   {
      cout << "Directory to search: ";
      cin >> dirname;
```

```
        pPath = dirname;
    }

    DWORD dwRet = SearchPath(pPath, filename, 0, MAX_PATH, buff, &pFile);

    if (dwRet == 0)
        cout << "File not found (" << GetLastError() << ")" << endl;
    else
        cout << "File found: " << buff << endl;

    return 0;
}
```

The program reads in the name of the file to be found and then the path to search if the system path is not requested. The filename and path are then passed to **SearchPath()**, which returns the length of the string copied to the buffer if the file was found, or zero if not. A message indicating the success or failure of the search is then displayed — the path to the named file is also displayed in the former case. Typical output from this program is shown below:

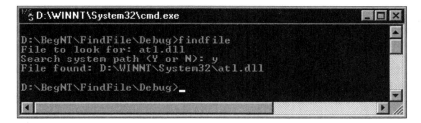

An alternative method of searching for files by name uses the **FindFirstFile()** and **FindNextFile()** functions. These can take wildcards in filenames, and so can be used to find all the files which match a given pattern. If you've ever used the **FindFirst()** and **FindNext()** functions in DOS, you'll find these familiar.

> *Note that these functions do not allow you to search for files based on attributes.*

FindFirstFile() is used to start a search:

```
HANDLE  FindFirstFile(
    LPCTSTR  pFileName,              //  file  to  find
    LPWIN32_FIND_DATA  pData);       //  pointer  to  find  information
```

The filename which you pass to the function can contain the wildcard characters **?** and *****, which have the usual meaning. You pass a pointer to a **WIN32_FIND_DATA** structure as the second parameter, and if a matching file is found it will be filled with information about the file. The structure looks like this:

```
typedef struct _WIN32_FIND_DATA
{
    DWORD dwFileAttributes;            // file attributes
    FILETIME ftCreationTime;           // creation time
    FILETIME ftLastAccessTime;         // last access time (NTFS only)
    FILETIME ftLastWriteTime;          // last write time  (NTFS only)
    DWORD nFileSizeHigh;               // high-order DWORD of file size in bytes
```

```
    DWORD nFileSizeLow;                 // low-order DWORD of file size in bytes
    DWORD dwReserved0;
    DWORD dwReserved1;
    TCHAR cFileName[MAX_PATH];          // null-terminated filename
    TCHAR cAlternateFileName[14];       // alternate name in 8.3 format
} WIN32_FIND_DATA;
```

Some of this information may look familiar, and it is the same as that returned by the `GetFileInformationByHandle()` function, which we saw earlier.

If the `FindFirstFile()` function executes successfully, you'll get passed a search handle, which can be used in subsequent find operations. If it fails, you'll get `INVALID_HANDLE_VALUE` returned.

> *Note that this handle isn't the same sort you get returned from* `CreateFile()`. *It is a search handle, and can only be used with the three* `Find...()` *functions.*

`FindNextFile()` is used to continue a search:

```
BOOL  FindNextFile(
      HANDLE hFind,                     // search handle
      LPWIN32_FIND_DATA pData);         // pointer to find information
```

The first argument is the search handle returned by `FindFirstFile()`, rather than the filename. You can reuse the same `WIN32_FIND_DATA` buffer you used with `FindFirstFile()`. If the function finds a file, it will return `TRUE` and if it fails it will return `FALSE`. `GetLastError()` will return `ERROR_NO_MORE_FILES` when no more can be found.

When you've finished a search, you can close the search handle with a call to `FindClose()`:

```
BOOL  FindClose(HANDLE  hFind);         // search handle
```

Once a search handle has been closed, it can't be used in any further `FindNextFile()` operations.

Moving/Renaming

The `MoveFile()` function renames (or moves... it amounts to the same thing) an existing file or directory. In the case of a directory, all children are also renamed:

```
BOOL  MoveFile(
      LPTSTR  src,                      // source file/directory name
      LPTSTR  dest);                    // destination file/directory name
```

If the destination already exists, the move will fail. The move operation is also atomic on NT, meaning that it will either fully complete or fail; you won't be left with a half-moved directory. Note also that `MoveFile()` will fail to move directories if the source and destination are on different volumes.

`MoveFileEx()` extends the functionality of `MoveFile()` by allowing you to specify flags to control how the move is to be done:

```
BOOL  MoveFileEx(
         LPTSTR  src,                    //  source  file/directory  name
         LPTSTR  dest,                   //  destination  file/directory  name
         DWORD  dwFlags);                //  flags
```

*MoveFileEx() **is only supported by Windows NT (version 3.1 or higher).***

The flags that you specify in the third parameter of `MoveFileEx()` can be any combination of:

▶ **MOVEFILE_COPY_ALLOWED**, which allows moving between volumes, by using the functionality of `CopyFile()` and `DeleteFile()` to move the file.

▶ **MOVEFILE_DELAY_UNTIL_REBOOT** does not actually move the file until the system is restarted. This provides a useful way to move system files which may be in use. This flag cannot be combined with the **MOVEFILE_COPY_ALLOWED** flag.

▶ **MOVEFILE_REPLACE_EXISTING** allows the move operation to overwrite existing files.

▶ **MOVEFILE_WRITE_THROUGH** only works on NT, and guarantees that the function won't return until the move operation has completed. It can be useful when used in conjunction with **MOVEFILE_COPY_ALLOWED** to ensure that a copy-and-delete operation has finished and all data has been flushed to disk. This flag has no effect if used in conjunction with **MOVEFILE_DELAY_UNTIL_REBOOT**.

Try It Out — Listing Files

The following example program lets you enter a wildcard file specification, and runs a find on the current directory, listing files and directories:

```cpp
// ListFiles.cpp

#include <windows.h>
#include <iostream>
using namespace std;

int main()
{
   char buff[MAX_PATH];

   cout << "Find: ";
   cin >> buff;

   WIN32_FIND_DATA data;
   HANDLE hSrch = FindFirstFile(buff, &data);
   if (hSrch == INVALID_HANDLE_VALUE)
   {
      cout << "FindFirstFile failed, error was " << hex
           << GetLastError() << dec << endl;
      return -1;
   }
```

```
      cout << data.cFileName;
      if (data.dwFileAttributes & FILE_ATTRIBUTE_DIRECTORY)
         cout << "(Dir) ";
      cout << endl;

      while (FindNextFile(hSrch, &data))
      {
         cout << data.cFileName;
         if (data.dwFileAttributes & FILE_ATTRIBUTE_DIRECTORY)
            cout << "(Dir) ";
         cout << endl;
      }

      FindClose(hSrch);
      return 0;
   }
```

We start by declaring a **WIN32_FIND_DATA** object to hold the results of the search, and then call **FindFirstFile()**. If it fails, it'll return an **INVALID_HANDLE_VALUE**   error, and we can use **GetLastError()** to tell us exactly what has gone wrong. We can then retrieve the attributes from the structure, and continue finding files until there are no more and the **FindNextFile()** returns **FALSE**.

Typical output from this program is shown below:

Detecting Changes To Directories And Files

Win32 incorporates some very useful API functions which will report changes to files and directories, so you can easily produce code which will notify you of any changes made to files or directories in a specified directory tree.

You can see this being used in several places, such as when Visual C++ tells you that a file has been modified outside the environment, and when Explorer updates its display if you create a file in some other application.

The notification mechanism uses three functions:

▶   **FindFirstChangeNotification()** to set up the first notification

▶   **FindNextChangeNotification()** to do subsequent ones

▶   **FindCloseChangeNotification()** to end

This works rather like the C Runtime Library **strtok()** function or DOS's **_findfirst()**/ **_findnext()** functions, in that the information is passed in the initial call, and subsequent simpler calls use the same string or directory.

FindFirstChangeNotification() provides something called a 'change handle', and like many other handles in NT, you can wait on them using one of the **Wait...()** functions. You use them by setting up a notification request using one of the **Find...()** functions, and then waiting on the handle. The **Wait...()** function will only return when a change of the required type has taken place.

Changes that can be detected in the directory or directory tree being watched include:

▶ **FILE_NOTIFY_CHANGE_FILE_NAME** notifies on any change to a filename. This includes creating and deleting files.

▶ **FILE_NOTIFY_CHANGE_DIR_NAME** notifies on any change to a directory name. This includes creating and deleting directories.

▶ **FILE_NOTIFY_CHANGE_ATTRIBUTES** notifies on any change to the attributes of any file.

▶ **FILE_NOTIFY_CHANGE_SIZE** notifies on any changes to file sizes.

▶ **FILE_NOTIFY_CHANGE_LAST_WRITE** notifies on any change in the last-write time of any file.

▶ **FILE_NOTIFY_CHANGE_SECURITY** notifies on any change to the security descriptors of any file or directory.

Try It Out — Notification

Here's a very simple example program which demonstrates how notification works in practice:

```
// Notification.cpp

#include <windows.h>
#include "iostream"

using namespace std;

int main()
{
   int retStat = 0;

   // Log changes in the \temp directory. You may need to change the path to
something
   // suitable for your machine
   HANDLE hChange = FindFirstChangeNotification(
      "d:\\temp",                 // notify of changes in the d:\temp directory
      FALSE,                      // only monitor \temp, not subdirectories
      FILE_NOTIFY_CHANGE_FILE_NAME); // monitor file modification, creation and
deletion

   if (hChange == INVALID_HANDLE_VALUE)
   {
```

```
        cout << "Error getting change handle (" << hex << GetLastError() << dec
            << endl;
        return -1;
    }

    // Wait for a change event to occur...
    WaitForSingleObject(hChange, INFINITE);
    cout << "Change notified" << endl;

    // Wait for three further changes, then exit
    for(int i=0;  i<3;  i++)
    {
        if (!FindNextChangeNotification(hChange))
        {
            cout << "Error from FindNextChangeNotification ("
                << hex << GetLastError() << dec << endl;
            retStat = -1;
            break;
        }

        WaitForSingleObject(hChange, INFINITE);
        cout << "Change notified" << endl;
    }

    // Tidy up
    FindCloseChangeNotification(hChange);

    return retStat;
}
```

In this code, I've chosen to monitor changes in the directory **d:\temp** only (you may need to amend the drive name), and not any subdirectories which it may contain. The program will notify me of four change events before exiting. Typical output from this code is shown here:

The first task is the get a change handle for the notifications, using **FindFirstChangeNotification()**:

```
HANDLE  FindFirstChangeNotification(
    LPCTSTR  path,              // path to watch
    BOOL  bSubDir,              // include subdirectories?
    DWORD  dwFilter);           // events to watch for
```

In the above example the path is set to **d:\temp**, the second parameter is set to **FALSE** since we don't want to watch subdirectories, and the filter is set to **FILE_NOTIFY_CHANGE_FILE_NAME**, which will notify us of changes to files, including renaming, creating and deleting them.

If the function works, we get a handle returned, and if it doesn't, the return value is
`INVALID_HANDLE_VALUE`.

Assuming that we have a valid handle, we can wait on it using `WaitForSingleObject()`,
which will only return when a notification has occurred. (Remember that we saw this function
in the last chapter.) At this point you find that Microsoft haven't taken this quite as far as they
might have done, because there's no mechanism for telling you what has changed. If you want
to know, you have to go and find out for yourself!

We then enter a loop which waits for three more notifications, using
`FindNextChangeNotification()`:

```
BOOL FindNextChangeNotification(HANDLE hChange);   // change handle to use
```

This function takes the change handle we already have, and uses it for the next change, so we
follow this by another call to `WaitForSingleObject()`.

When we've finished waiting for notifications, `FindCloseChangeNotification()` closes the
handle for us:

```
BOOL FindCloseChangeNotification(HANDLE hChange);   // change handle to close
```

Asynchronous I/O

Asynchronous I/O, also called **overlapped I/O**, allows you to start an I/O operation, pass it over
to NT for processing, and then carry on doing other things until it finishes.

> *Asynchronous file I/O is only supported by NT — it doesn't work for files in
> Windows 9x, although the other object types (such as mutexes and events) are
> supported.*

Asynchronous I/O not only works for files, but for any file-like object, such as files, pipes and
mailslots. It can create the impression of multithreading, without you having to start more than
one thread, and lets threads in a process manipulate the same file object simultaneously.

> *Note that since we're using concepts which touch on threads and synchronization, you
> might want to go back and read the last chapter (on threads), if you haven't done so already!*

So, how do we go about using this mechanism?

1 Create or open a file using `CreateFile()`, making sure that you specify the
`FILE_FLAG_OVERLAPPED` flag.

2 Create an event object, which will be used to tell us when the I/O has been completed.

3 Create and initialize an `OVERLAPPED` structure, passing it the handle to the event object
you created. Make sure this is a manual reset event.

4 Use `ReadFile()` or `WriteFile()` to do the I/O. The function will return immediately.

5 If the I/O operation hasn't completed, continue processing.

6 Check the status of the event or use `GetOverlappedResult()` to find out when it has completed. If `GetOverlappedResult()` returns `ERROR_IO_PENDING`, then it hasn't finished yet.

If you open a file using the `FILE_FLAG_OVERLAPPED` flag, you *must* use overlapped reading and writing. You can't mix synchronous and asynchronous I/O on the same file handle.

We've already met the `OVERLAPPED` structure, and seen that it contains file pointer information:

```
typedef struct _OVERLAPPED
{
    DWORD Internal;          // reserved for operating system use
    DWORD InternalHigh;      // reserved for operating system use
    DWORD Offset;            // low DWORD of offset
    DWORD OffsetHigh;        // high DWORD of offset
    HANDLE hEvent;           // event to signal end of operation
} OVERLAPPED;
```

The reason for using this structure is because we may have more than one thread accessing a file at a time, so there is no concept of a single file pointer for a file being accessed by asynchronous I/O. Instead, each thread uses its `OVERLAPPED` structure to keep track of where it is in the file.

The `Offset` and `OffsetHigh` members are used to keep track of the file pointer during overlapped operations, and it is important to remember that *you* are responsible for updating the position after read and write operations. `ReadFile()` and `WriteFile()` will use the information in the `OVERLAPPED` structure, but they won't update the offset.

> *Note that if you use multiple overlapped I/O requests, there's no guarantee of the order of execution.*

When you call `ReadFile()` or `WriteFile()`, one of three things may happen:

> If the amount of data requested is small or it is readily available (e.g. held in cache), then the operation will complete during the time it takes to make the call. In this case, the I/O function will return `TRUE`, and you can use the data immediately.

> The function may need time to get the data. In this case it will return `FALSE`, and if you check the error code with `GetLastError()`, it will be `ERROR_IO_PENDING`.

> The third possibility is that the function may encounter a real error.

You can now continue to do other things in your code, while occasionally checking whether the I/O operation has completed. You can find out how the I/O operation is proceeding using `GetOverlappedResult()`:

```
BOOL GetOverlappedResult(
    HANDLE hFile,              // file handle
    LPOVERLAPPED pOvr,         // OVERLAPPED structure
    LPDWORD pdwBytes,          // number of bytes transferred
    BOOL bWait);               // whether to wait or not
```

You pass the function the handle of the file you're working on, and a pointer to the **OVERLAPPED** structure associated with this file. You also pass a logical value which determines whether the function will wait for the operation to complete. If this flag is **FALSE**, the function will return immediately.

If the overlapped operation succeeded, the function will return **TRUE**. If it failed, it will return **FALSE** and you can use **GetLastError()** to find out why. If **GetLastError()** returns **ERROR_IO_PENDING**, the operation hasn't finished yet.

Try It Out — Asynchronous I/O

The following example program demonstrates how you could use asynchronous I/O to read data from a file:

```cpp
// Async.cpp

#include <windows.h>#include <iostream>using namespace std;#define BLOCK_SIZE
500int main(){   char name[MAX_PATH+1];   cout << "File: ";   cin >> name;

    HANDLE hFile = CreateFile(name, GENERIC_READ, 0, 0,
        OPEN_EXISTING, FILE_FLAG_OVERLAPPED, 0);

    if (hFile == INVALID_HANDLE_VALUE)
    {
        cout << "Error opening file" << endl;
        return -1;
    }

    DWORD dwRead;
    char buff[BLOCK_SIZE];
    OVERLAPPED ov;
    HANDLE hEvt = CreateEvent(0, TRUE, FALSE, 0);

    // Set the initial position and the event into the OVERLAPPED structure
ov.Offset = 0;   ov.OffsetHigh = 0;   ov.hEvent = hEvt;   BOOL bOK =
ReadFile(hFile, buff, BLOCK_SIZE, &dwRead, &ov);
    if (!bOK)
    {
        if (GetLastError() == ERROR_IO_PENDING)
        {
            // Loop till operation completes
            BOOL bDone;
            DWORD dwCount;
            do
            {
                bDone = GetOverlappedResult(
                    hFile,              // file handle
                    &ov,                // overlapped structure
```

301

```
                    &dwCount,              // bytes transferred
                    FALSE);                // don't wait

            // Could do something useful at this point...
            cout << '.';
        } while (!bDone);
    }
    else
        cout << "Unknown error (" << GetLastError() << ")" << endl;
}

cout << "operation complete" << endl;

// Update file pointer
ov.Offset += dwRead;

CloseHandle(hFile);
CloseHandle(hEvt);

return 0;
}
```

We open a file using `CreateFile()`, specifying that we're going to use asynchronous I/O. We then set up an **OVERLAPPED** structure, and the event object which will be used to signal completion. We place the event object handle into the **OVERLAPPED** structure, and initialise the offset so that we start reading from the start of the file.

We're then ready to read from the file, passing the **OVERLAPPED** structure to `ReadFile()` to show that it is to do asynchronous I/O. In this simple example, we then sit in a loop examining the return from `GetOverlappedResult()` until the operation finishes.

Typical output from this program is shown below:

As an alternative to using `GetOverlappedResult()`, you can wait directly on the event handle you put into the **OVERLAPPED** structure, like this:

```
    if (GetLastError() == ERROR_IO_PENDING)   {        // Loop till event signalled
BOOL bRet;

    do
    {
        cout << "Waiting..." << endl;
        // Check event
        bRet = WaitForSingleObject(hEvt, 0);
    } while (bRet == WAIT_TIMEOUT);
}
```

This approach may be more useful if you're waiting for several overlapped I/O requests to finish, because you can use `WaitForMultipleObjects()` (covered in Chapter 6) to wait for them all, whereas `GetOverlappedResult()` will only let you wait for one at a time.

Completion Routines

Completion routines, also called **Asynchronous Procedure Calls** (APCs), give you another way to perform asynchronous I/O. In the example above, we saw how we could find out whether or not the I/O operation had finished by either calling `GetOverlappedResult()` or waiting on an event object.

This tends to be less than convenient if you need to manage a number of overlapped I/O requests, many of which will need different processing when the requests complete. Another good reason for using completion routines is that you're also limited to waiting for 64 objects when using `WaitForMultipleObjects()`, and this may not be enough for high-throughput server applications.

APCs give you a way of defining a routine which is called when the I/O operation completes, so you can specify what is to happen when the operation completes, fire off the request, and then forget about it.

In order to use a completion routine, you use the `ReadFileEx()` and `WriteFileEx()` functions in conjunction with some special synchronization routines.

`ReadFileEx()` looks like this:

```
BOOL  ReadFileEx(
    HANDLE  hFile,                              //  file  handle
    LPVOID  pBuff,                              //  data  buffer
    DWORD  dwBytes,                             //  number  of  bytes  to  read
    LPOVERLAPPED  pOvr,                         //  offset  information
    LPOVERLAPPED_COMPLETION_ROUTINE  pRtn);  //  completion  routine
```

As well as a pointer to a buffer for the results and an indication of how many bytes to read, we pass an **OVERLAPPED** structure containing the offset information for the read, and a pointer to a completion routine.

All completion routines have a prototype of the form:

```
VOID WINAPI CompletionRoutine(
    DWORD dwCode,                 // status code
    DWORD dwBytesTransferred,     // number of bytes transferred
    LPOVERLAPPED pOvr);           // offset information
```

When it gets called, the status code will indicate whether the operation completed successfully — it can be zero (for successful completion) or **ERROR_HANDLE_EOF** if a read operation went past the end of the file. The second parameter tells you how many bytes got transferred, and the third parameter is a pointer to the **OVERLAPPED** structure associated with the I/O request.

Note that the completion routine won't necessarily get called as soon as the I/O request finishes. The thread which made the I/O request has to indicate that it is in a safe state before Windows will execute the completion routines, and this only happens when it is in an **alertable wait** state.

A thread enters an alertable wait state when it uses one of the following synchronization functions with the alertable flag set to **TRUE**:

▶ `MsgWaitForMultipleObjectsEx()`

▶ `SignalObjectAndWait()`

▶ `SleepEx()`

▶ `WaitForSingleObjectEx()`

▶ `WaitForMultipleObjectsEx()`

If the thread isn't in an alertable state, then any APCs will be queued up, and will execute when it next enters an alertable wait. This means that your application won't be interrupted in the middle of a calculation, but may mean that you need to take special action when you want to process completion routines.

Try It Out — Using Completion Routines

Here's our previous example above, modified to use a completion routine:

```cpp
// ComplRout.cpp

#include <windows.h>#include <iostream>
using namespace std;
#define BLOCK_SIZE 50000
VOID WINAPI completionRoutine(DWORD dwCode, DWORD dwBytes, LPOVERLAPPED pOvr)
{
   if (dwCode == 0)
      cout << "completionRoutine: " << dwBytes << " read" << endl;
   else
      cout << "Error passed to completionRoutine (" << dwCode << ")" << endl;
}

int main()
{
   char name[MAX_PATH+1];

   cout << "File: ";
   cin >> name;

   HANDLE hFile = CreateFile(name, GENERIC_READ, 0, 0,
      OPEN_EXISTING, FILE_FLAG_OVERLAPPED, 0);

   if (hFile == INVALID_HANDLE_VALUE)
   {
      cout << "Error opening file" << endl;
      return -1;
   }

   char buff[BLOCK_SIZE];
   OVERLAPPED ov;
   HANDLE hEvt = CreateEvent(0, TRUE, FALSE, 0);
```

```
    ov.Offset = 0;
    ov.OffsetHigh = 0;
    ov.hEvent = hEvt;

    BOOL bOK = ReadFileEx(hFile, buff, BLOCK_SIZE, &ov,
        (LPOVERLAPPED_COMPLETION_ROUTINE)completionRoutine);
    if (!bOK)
    {
        cout << "Error from ReadFileEx (" << GetLastError() << ")" << endl;
    }

    cout << "Calling Sleep()..." << endl;
    Sleep(2000);
    // Wait for operation to complete...
    cout << "Calling SleepEx()..." << endl;
    SleepEx(INFINITE, TRUE);

    cout << "operation complete" << endl;

    CloseHandle(hFile);

    return 0;
}
```

The completion routine simply prints out the number of bytes which were transferred, or the error code if it was not zero. We open the file as before, and this time use `ReadFileEx()`, specifying the address of the completion routine. Once `ReadFileEx()` has returned, we sleep for two seconds using the normal `Sleep()` function, and then wait using `SleepEx()`. You'll find that nothing happens during the first sleep, because this isn't an alertable wait. As soon as we call `SleepEx()` with the second parameter set to **TRUE**, the completion routine is executed.

`SleepEx()` is a special version of `Sleep()` which will sleep until either the timeout period has expired or an I/O completion routine is called.

If you try building and running this code, you should see output similar to that shown below:

We will now look at an aspect of file handling that involves the other main theme of this chapter — NT's use of memory.

Memory Mapped Files And Shared Memory

Windows NT does not allow two or more processes to share data in memory. Instead it incorporates a feature known as Memory Mapped Files to achieve the same effect.

Background Information

Before we start to look at the actual API calls, it's interesting to learn a little background, because memory mapped files are a very important part of the Windows NT system. Every time you execute a program you are using memory mapped files. When you ask NT to execute a program, rather than start by loading the program into memory and then executing it, NT reserves some memory for the process, then maps the executable file into that address space and starts to execute it. The underlying NT architecture automatically takes care of ensuring that the data from the file is loaded into memory as required, loading new parts of the file (called sections) as the threads of execution require them.

Memory pages that have been used for executable code are always loaded as read-only, because executing code cannot be changed while in memory . The system keeps track of all pages that are in use for executing code. If the system runs short of memory, it knows that it can discard these pages from memory without saving them to the paging file, since if they are ever required in memory again, they can be re-read from the original EXE or DLL disk file.

Memory Mapped File API

Now we know how important memory mapped files are, let's take a look at the API calls. Because memory mapped files are useful even in single processes that need random access to data in files, we will start by learning how to allow a single process to map a file into its memory space. Multiple processes sharing data in this way are covered in Chapter 11.

Normally, applications read and write files using the **CreateFile()**, **ReadFile()**, **WriteFile()** and other associated APIs (as described earlier). This is fine, and quite efficient, where long sequences of bytes are being read and written. Where the application needs to read and write a few bytes scattered throughout the file, not only do the standard APIs become less efficient, they also get rather messy to code, requiring the file pointer to be moved round the file before each read or write. It would be neater if we could simply use a pointer to access the bytes that we require, as though the file was in memory. In fact, if it's a small file, we could allocate some memory and simply read the whole file in, do all our work on the file, and then save it again when we've finished. This is a reasonable solution for small files, but for files that are many megabytes (or gigabytes) in size, it's not very sensible or practical to use precious memory in this profligate fashion.

With memory mapped files, not only does NT manage the moving of pages of memory to and from disk for us, it also ensures that when we have finished, the data is written back to disk. For the simple case of needing random read access to a large file, mapping the file into memory is an excellent solution. It also works well for read and write access, but is not so well suited for use where the size of the file is not fixed. For dynamically growing files, the traditional methods of file access are probably best. In Chapter 11 we will see how multiple processes can map the same file simultaneously and share data.

To get a file mapped into memory there are several stages:

▶ Get a handle to the open file

▶ Create a **file mapping object** (an internal structure used to maintain a copy of the file's contents, known as the **file view**)

▶ Map a view of the file into our address space

Once we have finished, we unmap the file view, close the mapping object, and close the file handle. NT automatically saves any changed data not yet written to disk. There is an extra call to allow us to flush data that we have changed to disk, without closing the file. This is not normally needed except for long-running servers, since it is almost always more efficient to allow NT to manage the buffering of disk writes and physical memory usage.

The `CreateFile()` function (which we discussed earlier in this chapter) is needed first, to get a handle on the file we want to map:

The next function API that we need is `CreateFileMapping()`. This creates a file mapping object from an existing file handle.

```
HANDLE CreateFileMapping(
    HANDLE hFile,                            // handle to file to map
    LPSECURITY_ATTRIBUTES lpFileMappingAttributes, // optional security
                                             // attributes
    DWORD flProtect,                         // protection for mapping object
    DWORD dwMaximumSizeHigh,                 // high-order 32 bits of object size
    DWORD dwMaximumSizeLow,                  // low-order 32 bits of object size
    LPCTSTR lpName);                         // name of file-mapping object
```

The first parameter, `hFile`, is the file handle that we obtain from `CreateFile()`. `lpFileMappingAttributes` is a pointer to a security structure. This must be **NULL** for Windows 95, which is also an acceptable value for NT. The parameter `flProtect` tells NT how to manage the memory pages that map your file, and can take one of the following values:

▶ **PAGE_READONLY** — used if it is a read-only file being mapped

▶ **PAGE_READWRITE** — used for read/write access

▶ **PAGE_WRITECOPY** — make a copy if written to.

The parameters `dwMaximumSizeHigh` and `dwMaximumSizeLow` are the high and low bits of the file size — we saw how this works earlier, in the *File Information* section. If you want to map the whole file without knowing its size, then setting both high and low bits to zero tells Windows to use the size of the file you are mapping.

The final parameter, `lpName`, gives the name of the mapping object. It must not contain a backslash (\) character. If you pass **NULL**, then the mapping object will be unnamed, which is fine for a single process, but when we come to use memory mapped files shared between different processes, we will have to name the mapping objects. Just as for synchronization objects like mutexes and semaphores, there is no way for a different process to refer to the same mapping object if they aren't named.

If the call is successful a file mapping object handle is returned; if it fails **NULL** is returned.

> *If we were trying to map an existing object, then the file handle returned should be the handle of that object, and a call to* GetLastError() *returns* ERROR_ALREADY_EXISTS. *If we have created a new object, then* GetLastError() *will return 0.*

There are a few things to note about this API:

- If you pass a handle **(HANDLE)0xFFFFFFFF** instead of the result of **CreateFile()**, then NT will create a mapping object to map an unnamed file that does not exist in the filesystem (this is useful if you want no one else to access the file), but you must specify its size

- You should not use normal file operations, such as **ReadFile()** and **WriteFile()**, on file handles that have been associated with mapping objects

- If you tell **CreateFileMapping()** to map a region larger than the file you are mapping, the file will automatically grow

The final step we need to take to map a file into memory is to call **MapViewOfFile()**, which makes the file appear in our address space.

```
LPVOID MapViewOfFile(
    HANDLE hFileMappingObject,      // file-mapping object to map into
                                    // address space
    DWORD  dwDesiredAccess,         // access mode
    DWORD  dwFileOffsetHigh,        // high-order 32 bits of file offset
    DWORD  dwFileOffsetLow,         // low-order 32 bits of file offset
    DWORD  dwNumberOfBytesToMap);   // number of bytes to map
```

hFileMappingObject is the handle to the map object created earlier. **dwDesiredAccess** is a set of flags giving the access mode. Possible values are:

- **FILE_MAP_WRITE**, which, curiously, allows both read and write
- **FILE_MAP_READ** for read only
- **FILE_MAP_ALL_ACCESS**, which is the same as **FILE_MAP_WRITE**
- **FILE_MAP_COPY**, for copy on write access

> *The last of these values can only be used in Windows 95 if you pass* **PAGE_WRITECOPY** *to* CreateFileMapping().

The final three parameters give the start address (in two of the parameters) and the number of bytes to map. Normally, all three can be set to zero to map the entire file.

On success, a pointer to the memory location where the file mapping starts is returned, and on error, **NULL** is returned.

Once we've completed these steps, we should have a pointer that allows us to access a file as though it is a block of memory.

> *It is important to be very careful about the access rights that you request. You must be consistent about asking for read only, write only, or read and write access. If you mix them up, then at best, some function calls may fail, and at worst, your program will fail in unexpected ways!*

Before we look at a real example, there are three other calls that we need to know about. Fortunately they are nice and simple.

The function `UnmapViewOfFile()` releases a mapping:

```
BOOL  UnmapViewOfFile(LPCVOID  lpBaseAddress);      // address where mapped
                                                    // view begins
```

You pass `lpBaseAddress` as the pointer that was returned from `MapViewOfFile()`, and the return value is non-zero if the call succeeded. In addition, Windows arranges to write any changed data back to disk, though the call will return before the data has actually been written.

The function `FlushViewOfFile()` requests NT to write any changed data in the mapping back to disk.

```
BOOL  FlushViewOfFile(
      LPCVOID  lpBaseAddress,          // start address of byte range to flush
      DWORD  dwNumberOfBytesToFlush);  // number of bytes in range
```

`lpBaseAddress` is a pointer to the first address to flush to disk, and is normally the return from `MapViewOfFile()`. The second parameter, `dwNumberOfBytesToFlush`, gives the size of the area to flush. If this is zero, then the entire mapped region is flushed.

On success a non-zero value is returned.

> *Note that NT will optimize its use of memory and cache changes in memory, rather than writing them to disk immediately. This results in vastly improved performance, which will be lost if you call this function frequently. NT will always write the changes back to disk when you unmap the region or close the mapping object, so there is rarely a reason for calls to FlushViewOfFile().*

Our final function in the group is `CloseHandle()`, which is used to close both file handles and mapping object handles.

```
BOOL  CloseHandle(HANDLE  hObject);    // handle to object to close
```

The `hObject` parameter is the handle to be closed. You should close the mapping handle before the file handle, thus:

```
CloseHandle(hFileMappingHandle);
CloseHandle(hFileHandle);
```

The return value is nonzero on success.

Since you need to use quite a few functions in the correct order, here is a short piece of pseudo code just to summarize the main functions we have met so far, and the order in which we need to use them.

To create a mapping:

```
// Get handle to the file
FileHandle = CreateFile(filename, access, …)
if (FileHandle == INVALID_HANDLE_VALUE) then failure….

// Create mapping object
MappingObjectHandle = CreateFileMapping(FileHandle, NULL,  access mode, ….)
if  (MappingObject == NULL) then failure…

// Map file into address space
lpFileInMemoryPointer = MapViewOfFile(MappingObjectHandle, access mode, …)
if (lpFileInMemoryPointer == NULL) then failure…
```

Notice that `CreateFile()` and `CreateFileMapping()` both return handles, but the test for success is different for each function.

Then to tidy up and close down:

```
UnmapViewOfFile(lpFileInMemoryPointer)
CloseHandle(MappingObjectHandle)
CloseHandle(FileHandle)
```

There, that wasn't so hard was it?

Try It Out — A Single Process Memory Mapped File

Let's start by creating a text file called `catdog.txt`, that contains the text `"The cat sat on the mat"`. We will now write a program that flips the text in that file between `"cat"` and `"dog"` each time it's run. To keep it simple we will make it a console application, with only limited error handling.

```cpp
// SharedMemory.cpp

#include <windows.h>
#include <iostream>
#include <string.h>

using namespace std;

#define TESTFILENAME "catdog.txt"

HANDLE hFile = NULL, hMemoryMapping = NULL;
LPVOID  lpvMappedFile = NULL;
LPSTR lpChar = NULL;

int main()
{

    hFile = CreateFile(TESTFILENAME,
                       GENERIC_READ | GENERIC_WRITE,
                       0,
                       NULL,
```

```
                        OPEN_EXISTING,
                        FILE_ATTRIBUTE_NORMAL,
                        NULL);

    if (hFile == INVALID_HANDLE_VALUE)
    {
       LPVOID lpMsgBuf;
       FormatMessage(FORMAT_MESSAGE_ALLOCATE_BUFFER | FORMAT_MESSAGE_FROM_SYSTEM,
                     NULL,
                     GetLastError(),
                     MAKELANGID(LANG_NEUTRAL, SUBLANG_DEFAULT),
                     (LPTSTR) &lpMsgBuf,
                     0,
                     NULL);

       cout << "CreateFile failed: " << reinterpret_cast<char*>(lpMsgBuf) << endl;
       LocalFree(lpMsgBuf);
       return(1);
    }
```

The first thing we need to do is get a file handle to our `catdog.txt` file, opening the file with both read and write permissions. Note that this will fail (because we used `OPEN_EXISTING`) if the file is not found. This stops us accidentally creating a new file if we get the name wrong.

Now we have a handle to the file, we can create a mapping object.

```
    hMemoryMapping = CreateFileMapping(hFile, NULL, PAGE_READWRITE, 0, 0, 0);

    if (hMemoryMapping == NULL)
    {
       LPVOID lpMsgBuf;
       FormatMessage(FORMAT_MESSAGE_ALLOCATE_BUFFER | FORMAT_MESSAGE_FROM_SYSTEM,
                     NULL,
                     GetLastError(),
                     MAKELANGID(LANG_NEUTRAL,
                     SUBLANG_DEFAULT),
                     (LPTSTR) &lpMsgBuf,
                     0,
                     NULL );

       cout << "CreateFileMapping failed: " << reinterpret_cast<char*>(lpMsgBuf)
            << endl;
       LocalFree(lpMsgBuf);
       return(1);
    }
```

Notice that we again create the object with read and write permissions, and request that it maps the whole file, because we did not specify a start address nor a size.

Finally we get to map the file into our address space:

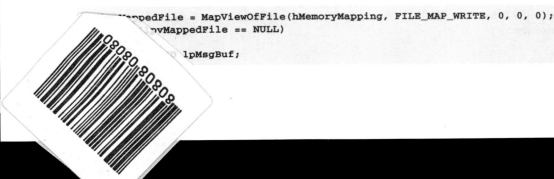

```
    ͫappedFile = MapViewOfFile(hMemoryMapping, FILE_MAP_WRITE, 0, 0, 0);
        ͫvMappedFile == NULL)

            lpMsgBuf;
```

```
FormatMessage(FORMAT_MESSAGE_ALLOCATE_BUFFER | FORMAT_MESSAGE_FROM_SYSTEM,
              NULL,
              GetLastError(),
              MAKELANGID(LANG_NEUTRAL, SUBLANG_DEFAULT),
              (LPTSTR) &lpMsgBuf,
              0,
              NULL );

cout << "MapViewOfFile failed: " << reinterpret_cast<char*>(lpMsgBuf)
     << endl;
LocalFree(lpMsgBuf);
return(1);
}
```

Again, we ask for read and write permissions. **FILE_MAP_WRITE**, unlike previous function flags, includes read permission. We request that the whole file be mapped into memory.

Now let's flip the text between cat and dog:

```
lpChar = strstr((LPSTR)lpvMappedFile, "cat");
if (lpChar != NULL)
    strncpy(lpChar, "dog", 3);
else
{
    lpChar = strstr((LPSTR)lpvMappedFile, "dog");
    if (lpChar != NULL)
        strncpy(lpChar, "cat", 3);
}
```

Notice how we treat the file exactly as though it was memory. For simplicity, we assume ASCII 8 bit characters.

Last, but not least, we tidy up and exit:

```
UnmapViewOfFile(lpvMappedFile);
    CloseHandle(hMemoryMapping);
    CloseHandle(hFile);

    cout << "Finished." << endl;
    return 0;
}
```

Here, we unmap the view, then close the mapping object, and finally close the file. Windows automatically arranges that the changed memory pages will be written back to disk, although this may actually happen after the program has ended.

If you try building and running this code, you should find that it switches the words round in your **catdog.tx**t file as expected.

We've now covered just about all the file-handling functions in the Win32 API, and I think you'll agree that they're pretty far reaching. Now we've exhausted files, let's go on to see how Win32 lets you use memory.

Memory

For the rest of this chapter we're going to be looking at handling memory in Win32 applications. You may wish to refer to the introduction to memory management concepts in Chapter 1.

When we look at how we can allocate memory in Windows programs, we find that there are three levels at which we can do it:

- ▶ The language level, by using **new** in C++ or **malloc** in C
- ▶ The Win32 memory allocation functions such as **GlobalAlloc()**
- ▶ The Win32 virtual memory functions such as **VirtualAlloc()**

Each of these is higher level — less system-specific and more portable — than the one below, and in general you should use the highest-level one that you can, as it will simplify coding, may take care of language-specific issues and will make your code more portable to other systems.

Let's start with a brief introduction to the whole topic. When you dynamically allocate memory, you get it by default from the 'heap' given to your process when it starts. This heap is the pool of memory available for allocation. As we'll see later, you can create 'sub-heaps' and allocate from them, which is useful in certain circumstances. In 16-bit Windows we had the concept of 'local' and 'global' heaps, but this distinction has disappeared in Win32, so we just have the concept of a single heap which is used for all allocation.

As we saw in Chapter 1, Win32 uses a system of virtual memory organised into pages. The top two layers of memory management work at a level well above this, but it is possible to work directly with the virtual memory system when you need direct control over the allocation, and use, of memory.

The Global Functions

Win32 gives you a collection of functions (named **Global...()**) to handle memory allocation. These include:

Function	Description
GlobalAlloc()	Allocates a block of memory
GlobalRealloc()	Reallocates a block, growing or shrinking it as needed, and copies the data
GlobalFree()	Frees a block of memory
GlobalFlags()	Gets flags describing the attributes of a block
GlobalSize()	Gets the size of a memory block
GlobalMemoryStatus()	Gets the status of a memory block

Back in the days of 16-bit Windows every `Global...()` function had a matching `Local...()` version, so we have `LocalAlloc()`, `LocalFree()` and so on. The need for this arose because of the Intel segmented architecture used by Win16, but now that we have 32-bit flat addressing there is no need for two sets of memory handling functions. You'll still find `LocalAlloc()` and the other routines in the API, but in Win32, they are the same as the `Global...()` functions and you can use whichever function names you prefer.

Memory Block Types

Windows works with three types of memory block:

- Fixed
- Moveable
- Discardable

Fixed

Fixed blocks are the ones you'll use most of the time in Win32, and correspond to what you get when you use `malloc` or `new`. You are given a pointer to a block of memory which isn't going to move, so you can use the pointer with impunity. There's no theoretical limit to the number or size of fixed blocks that you can create, although in practice, of course, you'll be limited by avaliable RAM and swap file space.

Moveable

Moveable blocks are now only used for special applications, and are required by certain API functions, such as those dealing with the clipboard and multimedia. You don't need to use moveable blocks unless an API call requires it.

When you create a moveable block, you're given a handle which represents the block. Since you don't know where it might be at any given time, you need to lock the handle before you can use the block. This returns a valid pointer to the current location of the block, and Windows will not move the block again until you unlock it.

Discardable

Discardable blocks can be truncated to zero length if Windows needs space. You'll lose the information in the block when this happens, so they are normally used when the information they contain can readily be regenerated, such as being re-read from disk.

> Note that you are restricted to 65535 moveable and discardable memory blocks per process.

16 And 32-Bit Windows

16-bit Windows discouraged the use of fixed blocks, because they could not be moved by the operating system, and so could lead to fragmentation of available memory. This meant that most 16-bit programs used moveable or discardable blocks, and were forever locking and unlocking handles to get pointers to memory.

32-bit Windows handles memory allocation at a lower level using hardware support, and it can even move 'fixed' blocks around while preserving their addresses. This means that there is now much less need to use moveable blocks, with all the attendant locking and unlocking of handles. Some programmers, perhaps out of force of habit, still allocate moveable blocks and lock them, but there is normally no need to do this, and you'll do just as well to stick to fixed blocks.

Creating And Releasing Blocks

The basic routines for allocating and deallocating memory are `GlobalAlloc()` and `GlobalFree()`, which perform the same function as **malloc** and **free**, or **new** and **delete**.

```
HGLOBAL  GlobalAlloc(
    UINT  flags,              // memory attributes
    DWORD dwBytes);           // number of bytes to allocate
```

As well as the number of bytes we need, we can specify attributes for the memory block using combinations of the flags listed below:

Flag	Meaning
`GMEM_FIXED`	Allocates memory which cannot be moved
`GMEM_MOVEABLE`	Allocates moveable memory
`GPTR`	Combines `GMEM_FIXED` and `GMEM_ZEROINIT`
`GHND`	Combines `GMEM_MOVEABLE` and `GMEM_ZEROINIT`
`GMEM_DDESHARE`	Indicates that memory is to be used with Windows Dynamic Data Exchange (DDE), which is an old method of exchanging data between Windows applications — generally meaningless in Win32
`GMEM_DISCARDABLE`	Allocates discardable memory — cannot be specified in conjunction with `GMEM_FIXED`
`GMEM_LOWER`	Obsolete
`GMEM_NOCOMPACT`	Obsolete
`GMEM_NODISCARD`	Obsolete
`GMEM_NOT_BANKED`	Obsolete
`GMEM_NOTIFY`	Obsolete
`GMEM_SHARE`	Same as `GMEM_DDESHARE`
`GMEM_ZEROINIT`	Initializes memory block to zero

> *Those marked as obsolete are retained only for compatibility with existing Win16 code, but have no meaning in Win32.*

The most common flag to use when allocating memory is **GPTR**, which returns you a pointer to a fixed block of zero-initialized memory. Note that because Win32 does its memory manipulation at a lower level than Win16, the actual location of this block may change, although the pointer you use will always be valid. When you specify **GPTR**, you can use `GlobalAlloc()` in the same way as you would use **malloc** in C:

```
MyStruct* pm = static_cast<MyStruct*>(GlobalAlloc(GPTR, sizeof(MyStruct)));
```

GPTR automatically zeroes the memory out for you, which is going to take time for large blocks. If you're going to use the memory immediately, you can save time by avoiding the zeroing out process — specify **GMEM_FIXED** instead, and initialize the memory yourself.

Once you've finished with a block, you release it using **GlobalFree()**:

```
HGLOBAL GlobalFree(HGLOBAL hMem);          // handle of block
```

If the operation works, the return value will be zero; if it fails, you'll get the memory block handle returned to you again.

The following code fragment illustrates how we could allocate and use a fixed block:

```
int* pInt;

// Allocate memory
pInt = static_cast<int*>(GlobalAlloc(GPTR, 1000*sizeof(int)));

if (pInt == NULL)
{
    // Allocation failed
}

for(int i=0; i<1000; i++)
   pInt[i] = i*2;

// Free memory
GlobalFree(pInt);
```

If we wanted to use a moveable block, we'd have to lock the handle before using it, which necessitates calls to **GlobalLock()** and **GlobalUnlock()**:

```
LPVOID GlobalLock(HGLOBAL hMem);          // handle of block to lock
```

If the function succeeds, it returns us a pointer to the first byte of the block, which is valid until the block is unlocked. If the function fails, a **NULL** pointer will be returned.

Note that each call to **GlobalLock()** increments the object's lock count for non-fixed blocks. For every call to **GlobalLock()**, a corresponding call to **GlobalUnlock()** will be needed before the object is once again unlocked. If you call **GlobalLock()** on a fixed block, the lock count is always zero, and the pointer you get back is the same as the one you got from **GlobalAlloc()**.

GlobalUnlock() is very similar to **GlobalLock()**:

```
BOOL GlobalUnlock(HGLOBAL hMem);          // handle of block to lock
```

Microsoft has chosen a rather strange way to return a value from this function. If the object is still locked after this call, the return value will be non-zero. If it is zero the function has 'failed', and you then use **GetLastError()** to see what has happened. If **GetLastError()** returns **NO_ERROR**, then the object is unlocked, and the function actually worked.

Shown below is the code snippet we saw earlier, rewritten to use a moveable block:

```
HGLOBAL hg;
int* pInt;

// Allocate the memory
hg = GlobalAlloc(GHND, 1000*sizeof(int));

if (hg == NULL)
{
   // Allocation failed
}

// Lock the handle
pInt = static_cast<int*>(GlobalLock(hg));

if (pInt == NULL)
{
   // Lock failed
}

for(int i=0; i<1000; i++)
   pInt[i] = i*2;

// Unlock block
BOOL bOK = GlobalUnlock(hg);

if (!bOK && GetLastError() != NO_ERROR)
{
   // Unlock failed
}

// Free block
GlobalFree(hg);
```

Finding Out About Blocks

The `GlobalFlags()` function can be used to get information about a block:

```
UINT GlobalFlags(HGLOBAL hMem);          // handle of block
```

The high-order byte of the low-order word of the result contains the allocation flags for the block. The value can be zero, or a combination of the following values:

▶ **GMEM_DDESHARE**, showing that the block is marked for use by Dynamic Data Exchange (DDE)

▶ **GMEM_DISCARDABLE**, showing that the memory block can be discarded

▶ **GMEM_DISCARDED**, showing the block has been discarded

The low-order byte of the low-order word of the result contains the lock count for the block, and will always be zero for fixed blocks. You can get at the lock count using the **GMEM_LOCKCOUNT** mask:

```
UINT uCount = GlobalFlags(hg) & GMEM_LOCKCOUNT;
```

`GlobalSize()` will tell you the size of a block in bytes, or return zero in the case of an error:

```
DWORD GlobalSize(HGLOBAL hMem);            // memory block handle
```

There are two things to note about this function. Firstly, allocated blocks may be larger than the amount you asked for, and secondly, you should check whether a discardable block has in fact been discarded before making this call. Because discarded blocks have a size of zero, you can't tell whether a zero return means an error or a discarded block.

It is possible to check that a memory pointer is valid before trying to use it, by using one of four functions:

▶ `IsBadCodePtr()` to check a function pointer

▶ `IsBadReadPtr()` to check a pointer for read access

▶ `IsBadStringPtr()` to check a string pointer

▶ `IsBadWritePtr()` to check a pointer for write access

`IsBadCodePtr()` takes the address of a function, and returns **FALSE** if the memory is accessible:

```
BOOL IsBadCodePtr(FARPROC pFunc);          // address of function to check
```

`IsBadReadPtr()` and `IsBadWritePtr()` take an address and a byte count, and return **FALSE** if the range of memory is accessible:

```
BOOL IsBadReadPtr(
     CONST BYTE* pAddr,           // address to check
     UINT uBytes);               // number of bytes to check

BOOL IsBadWritePtr(
     CONST BYTE* pAddr,           // address to check
     UINT uBytes);               // number of bytes to check
```

`IsBadStringPtr()` takes a string pointer and a number of bytes, and checks that the string is accessible for read access up to the end of the string or the number of bytes, whichever comes first:

```
BOOL IsBadStringPtr(
     LPCTSTR pAddr,               // address to check
     UINT uBytes);               // number of bytes to check
```

Manipulating Blocks Of Memory

In this section, we'll be looking at some the functions provided by the Win32 API that allow you to manipulate blocks of memory, in particular:

▶ `GlobalReAlloc()`

▶ `ZeroMemory()`

▶ `FillMemory()`

- `CopyMemory()`
- `MoveMemory()`

Firstly, `GlobalReAlloc()` lets you alter the size and/or the attributes of an existing memory block.

```
HGLOBAL GlobalReAlloc(
    HGLOBAL hMem,              // handle of block to reallocate
    DWORD dwBytes,            // size of block
    UINT flags);             // attributes of block
```

This function returns you a handle to the reallocated block, which may or may not be the same as the one you passed in as the first parameter, but which will contain your data.

The second parameter gives the new size of the block. If you shrink a block, it will be truncated but the rest of its content will be untouched. The flags specify how to reallocate the object. If the `GMEM_MODIFY` flag is used, then only the attributes are modified and the size parameter is ignored. This flag can be combined with either or both of the following flags:

- `GMEM_DISCARDABLE`, which allocates discardable memory if the object is already moveable, or if the `GMEM_MOVEABLE` flag is also specified
- `GMEM_MOVEABLE`, which changes a fixed block to a moveable one

If `GMEM_MODIFY` is not used, the flags parameter controls how the reallocation is done, and the value can be a combination of the following flags:

- `GMEM_MOVEABLE` can have several results, depending on the current type of the block. See below for a discussion
- `GMEM_NOCOMPACT` prevents memory from being compacted or discarded to satisfy the request
- `GMEM_ZEROINIT` causes any additional memory to be initialized to zero

Exactly what `GMEM_MOVEABLE` flag does depends on the current state of the object and the value for the new size. This is shown in the following table:

New Size	Existing Type	Effect
0	Moveable or discardable	Discards block if lock count is zero, otherwise function fails
0	Fixed	Function fails
Non-zero	Any type	Resizes block without changing attributes

Note that when a block is resized there may be insufficient room to keep it at the same address, so a different handle may be returned.

Let's look at a few examples to see how this can be used. If `hMem` is a handle to a fixed memory block of less than 2000 bytes in size, the following line will resize it to 2000 bytes and zero the additional memory:

```
hMem2 = GlobalReAlloc(hMem, 2000, GMEM_MOVEABLE | GMEM_ZEROINIT);
```

The effect of the **GMEM_MOVEABLE** flag here is to make the block temporarily moveable, so that it can be moved if necessary.

The following line will change the fixed block to a moveable one:

```
hMem2 = GlobalReAlloc(hMem, 2000, GMEM_MODIFY | GMEM_MOVEABLE);
```

We'll finish off this section by briefly considering four utility functions, which provide analogous functionality to the C Runtime Library functions **memset()** and **memcpy()**. Firstly, you can zero out all or part of a block of memory using **ZeroMemory()**:

```
VOID  ZeroMemory(
    PVOID  pDest,       // address to start filling
    DWORD  dwLen);      // number of bytes to fill
```

FillMemory() does the same thing, but allows you to specify the byte used for the fill:

```
VOID  FillMemory(
    PVOID  pDest,       // address to start filling
    DWORD  dwLen,       // number of bytes to fill
    BYTE   bFill);      // fill byte
```

CopyMemory() lets you copy a block of memory from one location to another:

```
VOID  CopyMemory(
    PVOID  pDest,       // address of destination
    CONST  VOID* pSrc,  // address for source
    DWORD  dwLen);      // number of bytes to copy
```

The result of the operation is undefined if the blocks overlap. If that is the case, you need to use **MoveMemory()**:

```
VOID  MoveMemory(
    PVOID  pDest,       // address of destination
    CONST  VOID* pSrc,  // address for source
    DWORD  dwLen);      // number of bytes to move
```

Private Heaps

When you use the `Global...()` functions you are allocating memory blocks from the default pool of memory (also called the 'default heap' or 'free store') belonging to the process. Win32 does a good job of managing this default heap, but there are times when you have to think carefully about how your application is using memory, and when using the default heap can seriously degrade performance.

Let's consider an example. We talked in Chapter 1 about how memory is managed, and how the virtual memory mechanism divides memory up into 4KB pages which are swapped in and out of physical memory as required. If an application tries to access data on a page which is currently swapped out, a page fault is generated and the operating system steps in to reload the page before the application can continue.

In your application, you may have complex data structures which hold lists of arrays and other such dynamically allocated items. If you create these as needed, you may well end up with the objects being created far apart in memory, so that each address is on a different page. If that is the case, simply traversing a list from one end to the other may result in a page fault being generated as each item in the list is accessed. This is going to have quite an impact on performance, and in the worst case can result in 'thrashing', where the system spends all its time swapping pages in and out, and very little time doing anything useful.

In order to circumvent problems like this, it is possible to create one or more heaps that are private to the process which created them, and whose size (and contiguous storage) are guaranteed. You can then allocate blocks of memory from a private heap in the same way that you allocate them from the global heap, but have a lot more control over which pages are used.

Creating And Deleting Heaps

You use `HeapCreate()` to create a private heap, which returns you a handle for use in subsequent heap operations:

```
HANDLE  HeapCreate(
    DWORD  dwFlags,          // creation flags
    DWORD  dwInitSize,       // initial size in bytes
    DWORD  dwLimit);         // maximum size in bytes
```

For this function, you specify the initial and maximum sizes of the heap and Win32 allocates a range of memory addresses equal to the maximum size, then commits the amount actually specified in the initial size parameter. When you use more than the initial size, page faults are generated, which cause the system to commit more actual memory. Being able to set the initial size in this way is helpful when you need to allocate a certain amount of contiguous storage for a process.

If you don't know the maximum size of the heap you're going to need, you can specify 0 for the maximum size, in which case the size of the heap will be limited only by the available memory.

The flag parameter can be zero, or one or both of the following:

▶ `HEAP_GENERATE_EXCEPTIONS`, which causes all allocation failures to cause an exception rather than returning `NULL`

▶ `HEAP_NO_SERIALIZE`, which does not serialize thread access to the heap

The first flag will cause an exception to be raised if any calls to `HeapAlloc()` fail. Note that this is a Win32 structured exception here, not a C++ language exception (we discussed structured exception handling in Chapter 4).

The `HEAP_NO_SERIALIZE` flag governs how threads access the heap. By default, access to the heap by multiple threads is protected by synchronization mechanisms, which make for safer access, but at the expense of extra work. If you know that the heap is only going to be used by one thread, or if you've provided your own mechanism for protecting access to the heap, you can turn off the checking by specifying `HEAP_NO_SERIALIZE`.

When you're finished with a heap you can remove it using `HeapDestroy()`:

```
BOOL HeapDestroy(HANDLE hHeap);                    // handle to heap
```

You can find the handles to all the private heaps belonging to a process by calling `GetProcessHeaps()`:

```
DWORD GetProcessHeaps(
     UINT  uCount,                    //  buffer  size
     LPHANDLE  pHandles);             //  buffer  to  receive  handles
```

The function takes an array of handles and the array size, and fills the array with the handles of all the heaps belonging to the process. The return value tells you how many handles have been stored in the array, with a value of zero indicating an error. This implies that there's always one heap present, which is in fact the case.

Using Heaps

Once you've created a heap, you can allocate blocks from it using `HeapAlloc()`, in the same way as you would use `GlobalAlloc()`:

```
LPVOID HeapAlloc(
     HANDLE  hHeap,                   //  handle  to  heap
     DWORD  dwFlags,                  //  creation  flags
     DWORD  dwSize);                  //  amount  to  allocate  in  bytes
```

The function allocates a block of storage from the heap, whose handle is specified by the first parameter. The flags may be zero, or a combination of the following:

▶ **HEAP_GENERATE_EXCEPTIONS**, which causes an allocation failure to cause an exception rather than returning **NULL**. You don't need to specify this if you specified it when the heap was created.

▶ **HEAP_NO_SERIALIZE**, which does not serialize thread access to the heap. Again, you don't need to specify this if you specified it when the heap was created.

▶ **HEAP_ZERO_MEMORY**, which zeroes out the memory.

Once you have the pointer to the block of memory, you can cast it to the required type and use it just as you would a pointer returned by `GlobalAlloc()`.

As you might expect, `HeapFree()` is used to free a block allocated from a heap:

```
BOOL  HeapFree(
     HANDLE  hHeap,                   //  handle  to  heap
     DWORD  dwFlags,                  //  operation  flags
     LPVOID  pAddr);                  //  pointer  to  block
```

The only flag permitted here is **HEAP_NO_SERIALIZE**, and once again you don't need to specify it if it has already been set when the heap was created.

The Virtual...() Functions

At the lowest level of Win32's memory management functions come those that work directly with virtual memory. We'll mention them here, although most of the normal things you want to do in an application program can usually be handled using either language-specific constructs or the `Global...()` functions.

One time when you may want to work with memory at this level is when you *might* need a large contiguous area of memory, but won't be sure until run-time. These calls let you reserve a range of memory addresses for future use, and you can then allocate memory to use those addresses, in the sure knowledge that they won't be allocated to anyone else.

Let's start with `VirtualAlloc()` which allows you to reserve or commit an area of memory within the address space of the calling process. You can use the function to perform the following operations:

- Reserve a region of free pages
- Commit some or all of the pages reserved by a previous call to `VirtualAlloc()`
- Reserve and commit a region of pages in one go

A **reserved** page is one which cannot be used by other memory allocation functions, but which has no physical storage associated with it, and so is not accessible. Before a reserved page can be used it must be **committed**, when storage is allocated for the page and access protection applied. The system only initializes and loads a committed page at the first read or write operation. It is not an error to try to commit a page which is already committed — the request will work, but will do nothing.

This means that you can use the function to reserve a block of pages within the process's virtual address space, an operation which doesn't consume any physical storage but which guarantees that a certain range of virtual memory will be available as required. Then, as pages are actually needed, they can be committed, and it is only at this point that they'll take up any physical memory.

Creating And Destroying Pages

Here's what the function looks like:

```
LPVOID VirtualAlloc(
    LPVOID pAddress,        // address of start of region
    DWORD  dwSize,          // size of region in bytes
    DWORD  dwAllocType,     // type of allocation
    DWORD  dwProtect);      // access protection
```

The first two parameters are just what you'd expect — the address at which you want allocation to start and the size of the region you want to allocate. If you aren't concerned where the region is allocated, you can pass `NULL` for the first parameter, and the system will place it for you.

If successful, the function returns the starting address of the allocated region, which might not be the same as the address you specified. This is because when reserving pages the address is rounded down to the nearest 64KB boundary, and when committing it is rounded down to the nearest page boundary.

The size you give determines how many pages are reserved or committed. Note that even if only a single byte falls in a new page, that entire page must be included in the allocation.

The third parameter in the call to `VirtualAlloc()` specifies the type of the allocation, and can be any combination of the following flags:

- ► **MEM_COMMIT**, which allocates physical storage in memory or the paging file for the range of pages specified
- ► **MEM_RESERVE**, which reserves a range of the process's virtual address space, without allocating any actual storage. Reserved pages can't be used with any other allocation function until they have been released
- ► **MEM_TOP_DOWN**, which allocates memory at the highest possible address

The final parameter specifies the access protection given to the page, and can be any one of the following flags:

- ► **PAGE_READONLY**, which allows only read access to the pages
- ► **PAGE_READWRITE**, which allows read and write access
- ► **PAGE_EXECUTE**, which allows execute access only (any attempt to read or write will cause an access violation)
- ► **PAGE_EXECUTE_READ**, which allows execute and read access
- ► **PAGE_EXECUTE_READWRITE**, which allows execute, read and write access
- ► **PAGE_NOACCESS**, which disables all access to the page (any attempt to access the page results in a General Protection Fault)

Note that some of these access types may not be supported on all Win32 platforms.

Two modifiers can be applied to all access protection flags apart from **PAGE_NOACCESS**:

- ► **PAGE_GUARD**, which turns the pages in the region into guard pages (see below)
- ► **PAGE_NOCACHE**, which does not permit caching of the pages in the region

Any attempt to read or write a page marked as a guard page will cause the operating system to throw a **STATUS_GUARD_PAGE** exception, and they thus act as an access alarm. They are often used to place guards around data structures, so that it is possible to detect any attempt to write outside the boundaries of the structure.

Note that once a guard page has been 'triggered', the system removes the **PAGE_GUARD** status, and the page reverts to its underlying access protection type.

Once you've finished with a block of memory, you can release it using `VirtualFree()`:

```
BOOL VirtualFree(
    LPVOID pAddress,        // address of region to free
    DWORD dwSize,           // size of region to free
    DWORD dwType);          // type of free operation
```

As with `VirtualAlloc()` you can use this function to do more than one thing. You can:

▶ Decommit a region of committed pages

▶ Release a region of reserved pages

▶ Decommit and release a region of committed pages

The first two parameters specify the address of the block and the size of the region you want to free. If you're decommitting memory, the size will determine how many pages are decommitted. If you're releasing memory, the size must be zero or the function will fail.

The third parameter determines what happens, and must be one of:

▶ `MEM_DECOMMIT` to decommit pages

▶ `MEM_RELEASE` to release pages

If you're going to release a region of pages, they must all be in the same state (committed or reserved) and you must release the entire region at once. If some of the pages are committed and some reserved, you must first decommit the committed pages with a call to `VirtualFree()`, and then call it again to release the range. If the pages aren't compatible with the operation you're trying to perform on them, the free operation will fail and no pages will be freed.

We should also note the `VirtualAllocEx()` function, which is identical to `VirtualAlloc()`, except that it has an extra parameter which allows you to specify the handle of another process in which to allocate memory. There's also a matching `VirtualFreeEx()` function, and you need to have `PROCESS_VM_OPERATION` access to the process if you want to use these functions.

Other Virtual Memory Functions

You can set or change the protection of pages using `VirtualProtect()`:

```
BOOL  VirtualProtect(
    LPVOID  pAddress,          // address of  region
    DWORD   dwSize,            // size  of  region
    DWORD   dwProt,            // new  protection  to  apply
    PDWORD  pdwOldProt);       // old  protection  returned
```

You can pass any of the access protection flags used with `VirtualAlloc()`. If you pass `NULL` for the last parameter, the previous protection won't be returned.

`VirtualLock()` can be used to lock a page or range of pages in memory so that subsequent access doesn't generate a page fault:

```
BOOL  VirtualLock(
    LPVOID  pAddress,          // address of  region  to  lock
    DWORD   dwSize);           // size  of  region  in  bytes
```

All pages in a region must be committed before they can be locked, and you can't lock pages which have the `PAGE_NOACCESS` flag set. The number of pages that a process can lock is limited to 30 by default. This low value reflects the fact that locking pages in memory can have a severe impact on system performance, and you should never lock pages unless it is strictly necessary.

Once you've finished with these pages, you should call **VirtualUnlock()** to remove the lock:

```
BOOL VirtualUnlock(
    LPVOID  pAddress,             // address of region to lock
    DWORD   dwSize);              // size of region in bytes
```

Note that unlike **GlobalLock()** there is no lock count associated with virtual pages, so it isn't necessary to call **VirtualUnlock()** more than once.

> *Locking virtual pages isn't implemented on Windows 95/98, so* **VirtualLock()** *is implemented as a stub function which always returns* **TRUE**.

VirtualQuery() returns information about a range of pages:

```
DWORD VirtualQuery(
    LPCVOID pAddress,                       // address of region
    PMEMORY_BASIC_INFORMATION pBuff,        // address of information buffer
    DWORD dwLength);                        // size of buffer
```

The **MEMORY_BASIC_INFORMATION** structure gives you a variety of information about a block of memory:

```
typedef struct _MEMORY_BASIC_INFORMATION
{
    PVOID BaseAddress;          // base address of region
    PVOID AllocationBase;       // allocation base address
    DWORD AllocationProtect;    // initial access protection
    DWORD RegionSize;           // size, in bytes, of region
    DWORD State;                // committed, reserved, free
    DWORD Protect;              // current access protection
    DWORD Type;                 // type of pages
} MEMORY_BASIC_INFORMATION;
```

The **BaseAddress** member tells you the base address of the range of pages within which the address that you passed to **VirtualQuery()** falls. **AllocationBase** is the base address of the original range of pages allocated by **VirtualAlloc()**. The access protection applied when the region was originally allocated (such as **PAGE_READONLY**, **PAGE_READWRITE** and so on) is given by **AllocationProtect**, while **Protect** specifies the current access flag for the region. **RegionSize** tells you the size of the region, beginning at the base, within which all pages have the same attributes. The state of the pages in the region is given by **State**, which can take one of the following values:

- **MEM_COMMIT**, denotes committed pages for which physical memory has been allocated
- **MEM_FREE**, denotes free pages available for allocation
- **MEM_RESERVE**, denotes reserved pages — virtual memory reserved but no physical memory allocated

Finally, **Type** tells you whether the pages in the region are private (**MEM_PRIVATE**), are mapped onto the view of a section (**MEM_MAPPED**) or mapped onto the view of an image section (**MEM_IMAGE**).

The return value from the function tells you how many bytes were returned in the buffer.

VirtualQueryEx() does the same thing as **VirtualQuery()**, but also allows you to query memory blocks in another process.

Try It Out — *Using Virtual Memory*

The following sample program shows how to allocate, and query, virtual memory using the functions we've described:

```
// VirtualMemory.cpp

#include <windows.h>#include <iostream>using namespace std;

void printMemInfo(MEMORY_BASIC_INFORMATION& mbi)
{
    // Size
    cout << "Region size = " << mbi.RegionSize << endl;

    // Allocation protection
    cout << "Allocation Protection: ";
    if (mbi.AllocationProtect & PAGE_READONLY) cout << "Read-only ";
    if (mbi.AllocationProtect & PAGE_READWRITE) cout << "Read-write ";
    if (mbi.AllocationProtect & PAGE_EXECUTE) cout << "Execute-only ";
    if (mbi.AllocationProtect & PAGE_EXECUTE_READ) cout << "Execute-read ";
    if (mbi.AllocationProtect & PAGE_EXECUTE_READWRITE) cout
        << "Execute-read-write ";
    if (mbi.AllocationProtect & PAGE_NOACCESS) cout << "No access ";
    cout << endl;

    // Protection
    cout << "Protection: ";
    if (mbi.Protect & PAGE_READONLY) cout << "Read-only ";
    if (mbi.Protect & PAGE_READWRITE) cout << "Read-write ";
    if (mbi.Protect & PAGE_EXECUTE) cout << "Execute-only ";
    if (mbi.Protect & PAGE_EXECUTE_READ) cout << "Execute-read ";
    if (mbi.Protect & PAGE_EXECUTE_READWRITE) cout << "Execute-read-write ";
    if (mbi.Protect & PAGE_NOACCESS) cout << "No access ";
    cout << endl;

    // State
    cout << "State: ";
    if (mbi.State & MEM_COMMIT) cout << "Committed ";
    if (mbi.State & MEM_RESERVE) cout << "Reserved ";
    if (mbi.State & MEM_FREE) cout << "Free ";
    cout << endl;
```

```
      // Type
      cout << "Type: ";
      if (mbi.Type & MEM_PRIVATE) cout << "Private ";
      if (mbi.Type & MEM_MAPPED) cout << "Mapped ";
      if (mbi.Type & MEM_IMAGE) cout << "Image ";
      cout << endl;
  }
```

The first step is to provide a function to write out the interesting parts of a
MEMORY_BASIC_INFORMATION structure. This function takes one of these structures and starts
by simply finding the size of the region in question. The various flags that are set for the
AllocationProtect member are found by taking logical combinations of these flags with
AllocationProtect, and the results are output to the screen. This is then repeated for the
Protect, **State** and **Type** members of the structure.

Now let's look at the main body of the code:

```
  int main()
  {
    int* pInt, *pInt2;

    // Reserve a block of memory
    pInt = static_cast<int*>(  VirtualAlloc(0,          // let the system find the
                                                        // address
                              20000 * sizeof(int),      // grab a lot of bytes
                              MEM_RESERVE,              // only reserve it here
                              PAGE_READWRITE))           // read-write access

    if (!pInt)
    {      cout << "Error reserving pages (" << GetLastError() << ")" << endl;
        return -1;
    }    // See what we've got
                    MEMORY_BASIC_INFORMATION mbi;
                    DWORD dwSize = VirtualQuery(pInt, &mbi, sizeof(mbi));
                    cout << "Query reserved block:" << endl;

    printMemInfo(mbi);

    // Now commit a page
    pInt2 = static_cast<int*>(  VirtualAlloc(pInt,      // let the system find the
                                                        // address
                              500 * sizeof(int),        // grab a page
                              MEM_COMMIT,               // commit the memory
                              PAGE_READWRITE));          // read-write access

    if (!pInt2)
    {      cout << "Error committing pages (" << GetLastError() << ")" << endl;
        return -1;
    }    dwSize = VirtualQuery(pInt2, &mbi, sizeof(mbi));
                    cout << endl << "Query committed block:" << endl;

    printMemInfo(mbi);

    // Decommit the committed pages
    if (!VirtualFree(pInt2, 500 * sizeof(int), MEM_DECOMMIT))
       cout << "Freeing committed pages failed (" << GetLastError() << ")" << endl;
    else
```

```
        cout << "Pages decommitted" << endl;

    // Release all pages
    if (!VirtualFree(pInt, 0, MEM_RELEASE))
        cout << "Freeing reserved pages failed (" << GetLastError() << ")" << endl;
    else
        cout << "Pages released" << endl;

    return 0;
}
```

If you try building and running this code, you should see output something like this:

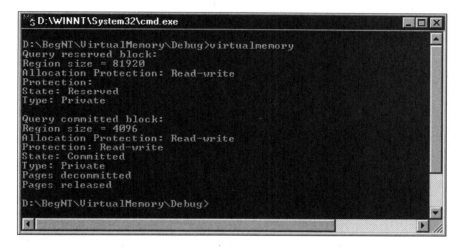

Let's see what's going on here. The main routine begins by reserving a block of memory:

```
// Reserve a block of memory
pInt = static_cast<int*>(   VirtualAlloc(0,          // let the system find the
                                                     // address
                            20000 * sizeof(int),     // grab a lot of bytes
                            MEM_RESERVE,             // only reserve it here
                            PAGE_READWRITE));        // read-write access
```

In our call to **VirtualAlloc()**, we reserve enough space for 20000 integers, giving it read-write access, and we let the system allocate the address. Once we've done this, we query the block for it's attributes using **VirtualQuery()**, and then output the information from the resulting **MEMORY_BASIC_INFORMATION** structure using our **printMemInfo()** function.

Notice that the region size of the reserved block is bigger than the 80000 bytes we asked for, because it is rounded up to the next whole page. The allocation protection shows what we asked for when we called **VirtualAlloc()**, but there is no protection yet because this memory hasn't been committed. The state of the block is reserved, and it is private to our process.

Next, we commit a page from the range we've reserved:

```
// Now commit a page
   pInt2 = static_cast<int*>( VirtualAlloc(pInt,       // let the system find the
                                                       // address
                               500 * sizeof(int),      // grab a page
                               MEM_COMMIT,             // commit the memory
                               PAGE_READWRITE));       // read-write access
```

Again, we query the block and print out the information.

The information tells us that we have a block of 4096 bytes, which is committed. Again, this figure is rounded up to the nearest page. We can also see that the protection has been set to read-write.

The final stage in the process is to decommit and release the pages, which we have to do in two stages because not all of the original allocation is in the same state.

Summary

In this chapter we've looked at the use of storage in Win32, and we started off by looking at files.

We've seen how to use **CreateFile()** to open or create files, and seen that it can also be used for other objects, besides files, as well. The basic operations are **ReadFile()** and **WriteFile()**, which let us read and write at the byte level, and the 'Ex' versions have the important ability to use asynchronous I/O, where we let NT go away and do the operation for us, whilst we get on with other tasks. Win32 also provides a plethora of other file manipulation functions, including the ability to be notified of changes to files and directories.

The second part of the chapter was concerned with using memory, and we saw how there are three ways to use memory under NT — using language-specific features, such as '**new**' or '**malloc**', using the higher-level Win32 methods, such as **GlobalAlloc()**, and working directly with virtual memory using the **Virtual...()** functions. We pointed out that you should use the highest level approach possible, and that you'll fairly seldom need to use virtual memory directly.

Windows NT Security

In this chapter, we come to one of the most complex, and the most misunderstood topics in the whole of Windows NT — the **Security System**.

Security in NT is administered by the Security subsystem, which you talk to using a group of about 100 API functions. With a rich (and for 'rich' read 'extremely complicated') set of new concepts to get to grips with, the learning curve can be fairly steep — and this is quite apart from all the new acronyms you will have to learn along the way! The purpose of this chapter, therefore, is to introduce you to this complex system, and give you a starting point from which you'll be able to use NT Security in your own applications.

When do you want or need to use NT security? If you want to restrict or control access to parts of the NT system, then you'll need to use the security API. The following list shows a selection of tasks which involve security:

- Changing access permissions on files and directories from within programs
- Setting access to registry entries so that only certain users or groups can modify (or even read) the entries
- Creating system objects, such as threads or mutexes, which only certain users can access
- Creating a named pipe for talking to a process which only those with administrator privilege can use

By the end of this chapter you should know enough to start performing tasks such as those we've just listed. In the next few pages we will have covered:

- What the NT Security system is and how it functions
- The concepts underlying the NT Security mechanism, such as access tokens, SIDs, security descriptors, DACLs and ACEs
- How to retrieve, set and modify security information for an object
- How to work with access tokens
- How to work with privileges

> *At present only Windows NT implements security, so nothing in this chapter applies to Windows 95 or 98*

Introduction to Security

One of the principal design criteria for NT was that it should be *secure*. Putting it simply, this means that access to system resources must be controlled, such that no-one can access anything they are not supposed to. Resources include files and directories, named pipes, synchronization objects such as mutexes, and even registry entries.

The US Department of Defense (DoD) has a series of guidelines which can be used to evaluate the level of security provided by a computer system. Various levels are defined, and Windows NT implements level C2 (as does modern Unix). Without going into undue detail, this level of security involves:

▶ A **security policy** — objects must be protected from unauthorized access, and owners of objects can control who accesses them. When allocated, objects must not contain any data which the user is unauthorized to see.

▶ **Accountability** — users must identify themselves before they can use the system. If required, the system must be able to maintain an audit trail identifying all accesses to objects.

▶ **Assurance** — the security mechanism must be protected from tampering by users.

▶ **Life-Cycle Assurance** — the security mechanism must be tested to ensure correct operation, and guard against obvious flaws such as people being able to access part or all of the system without logging in.

Windows NT implements the requirements of level C2 using:

▶ Secure logins with username and password — NT traps the *Ctrl-Alt-Del* key combination, and no other process can trap this interrupt.

▶ Discriminating access control — all resources are owned, and the owner can control who accesses it.

▶ Auditing — security events can be logged whenever someone tries to create, delete or even access a resource.

▶ Protecting memory from being read by other processes — NT initializes memory by filling it with zeroes, so a process cannot read what a previous user of the memory might have left there. It is also not possible for one process to read memory belonging to another process.

▶ The security mechanism runs as a protected NT subsystem, free from user interference.

Contrast this with the situation we have in Windows 9x (and even Windows 3.x), where logging in is optional, and where the only security you have is the flimsy DOS file permissions. With these operating systems, anyone who can get to your machine can do anything with it.

Note that the only way to guarantee security, even under NT is to physically lock the machine away. It is still possible to boot an NT machine using a DOS boot disk, and read files even if they're on an NTFS partition.

Level C2 security uses **discretionary access control**, meaning that the owner of an object can grant access to a user, regardless of security classification. For example, the owner of a 'highly secret' object can allow access to someone with only a 'secret' clearance level. Future versions of NT may move to stronger forms of security, such as 'mandatory access control', which would prevent an object's owner giving access to anyone with a lower clearance level.

On most of the occasions that you interact with the NT security system, you will be concerned with access control, that is, allowing or denying access to files, directories and other resources. It is this aspect of the NT security system that we'll be focussing on in this chapter.

Note that if you are not concerned with security in a particular application, then you can usually ignore it, and the defaults provided will be sensible.

NT Security Concepts

There is a large number of new concepts and new jargon associated with NT security, as well as over 100 API functions. Obviously, we can't cover all these functions in one chapter, but we'll be taking a look at some of the most useful ones. By the time you've finished this chapter, you'll be an expert in talking about security concepts in TLAs and ETLAs (three letter acronyms and extended three letter acronyms).

Because of all this complexity, we don't want to plunge straight into the morass of structures and API calls. Instead, we'll start by discussing security concepts in general terms, before then going on to see how we deal with the security system in several practical programming examples.

Access Tokens And SIDs

The first new concepts we need to explain are **access tokens** and **security identifiers (SIDs)**.

Information about all the user accounts in a domain is stored in a database called the **Security Access Monitor (SAM)**. In Windows NT, a **domain** is a collection of computers networked together, which can share resources and have centralized security. If an NT machine isn't connected to a network, then it becomes a domain on its own, and is responsible for its own security. For a system of networked NT machines, one server is designated as the *Primary Domain Controller*, which is responsible for managing the security of the domain, and which holds the SAM database for the domain.

When you log on to an NT system, pressing *Ctrl-Alt-Del* starts the **Local Security Access (LSA)** process, which validates your user ID and password against data in the SAM. The same thing happens when a user logs in from another machine, within the domain.

If the login is successful, your user process is assigned a **Security Access Token (SAT)**, which is often just called an **access token**. This contains all the security information that the system has about your user ID, and all the processes that you create get a copy of this access token, so they inherit your identity and security rights.

One of the fundamental requirements of level C2 security is that every process is tagged with its owner's security information, so that every action can be controlled and audited. In NT, this requirement is fulfilled by attaching an access token to each process.

Many different kinds of objects in the system have a **security descriptor** attached to them, which describes who can access them, and what they can and cannot do. We'll meet security descriptors in more detail later, but for now think of them as locks and access tokens as keys. An object can only be 'unlocked', if an access token 'key' matches its security descriptor 'lock'. (We'll discuss what we mean by 'object' later in the chapter.)

> *Permission to access an object is granted or refused on the basis of matching the access token of the client process against the security descriptor of the object it wishes to access.*

SIDs

An important part of both the access token and security descriptor is the **security identifier**, universally abbreviated to **SID**.

A SID is simply a unique numeric ID which identifies you, the user, to NT. Each user, and group of users, has a unique SID. A typical SID might look like this:

```
S-1-5-123-456
```

The `S-1-5` shows that this SID was created by NT, `123` is the ID of an NT domain, and `456` is the unique ID of the individual user.

Encoding the domain into the SID means that SIDs are unique across domains, and it also means that creating a new account for a user on a new domain entails creating a new SID, which will consequently need to have all its rights set up. This means that, by default, a user moving from one domain to another will tend to lose the rights they had on the old domain.

There are lots of functions in the API for checking and manipulating SIDs, such as `IsValidSid()`, `LookupAccountName()`, and `InitializeSid()`. We'll meet many of the more common ones later in the chapter.

Access Tokens

An access token is a data structure containing information on who you are, what user groups you belong to, and what rights you have been given by the administrator who created your account. The information on you and your groups is given in the form of SIDs, so an access token looks like this:

Structure of an Access Token

Note that you do not directly access the access token structure, but can manipulate it using security API calls, so that you can, for example, add or remove rights or group memberships.

Privileges

As well as lists of SIDs, an access token also contains a list of the **privileges** which have been granted to the user. These might include abilities such as:

▶ Performing backups

▶ Changing process priorities

▶ Shutting down the system

You need to be very careful with privileges, because they can be used to override the security mechanism which we're about to describe. Why would you want to do this? Let's take an example. Consider the case of writing a program to back up all the files on a disk. Many of these files may have security settings to say who can read or write to them, but a backup program needs to be able to ignore them, otherwise it will only be able to back up those files for which it has read access. Privileges provide a way to grant selected users special rights to perform system tasks.

Security Descriptors

Many of the objects in an NT system can have access control applied to them using a **security descriptor**, which says who can do what to the object. These are called **securable objects**.

The following list shows the NT securable object types:

- Files and directories, but only those on NTFS volumes — FAT volumes do not support NT security
- Processes and threads
- Mutexes, semaphores and events
- Registry entries
- Named pipes on a machine and over a network
- Anonymous pipes on a single machine
- Mailslots on a single machine
- Console screen buffers
- Services
- File mappings
- Private objects

We've already come across numerous API calls in other chapters where we could have specified a security descriptor via an **LPSECURITY_DESCRIPTOR** pointer. NT objects, such as those in the list above, always have an associated security descriptor, so if you pass a security descriptor structure on object creation, this will determine who is allowed to access the object.

As an example, consider the **CreateFile()** API function, which we'll meet in some detail later in the chapter:

```
HANDLE CreateFile(
    LPCTSTR pFileName,              // filename
    DWORD dwAccess,                // access mode
    DWORD dwShare,                 // share mode
    LPSECURITY_ATTRIBUTES pSec,    // security attributes
    DWORD dwCreate,                // how to create
    DWORD dwFlags,                 // file attribute flags
    HANDLE hTemplate               // template file
);
```

When we create a file using this function we can, if we wish, pass a pointer to a **SECURITY_ATTRIBUTES** structure as the fourth parameter. If it is non-**NULL**, then the information in the structure will be used to set the security attributes for the object. If you pass **NULL**, then the system will create a default security descriptor which allows you (and anyone belonging to the same group) to access the object. This is a sensible default, and means that you shouldn't run into difficulties if you don't require security.

A security descriptor has four main components, as shown in the following diagram:

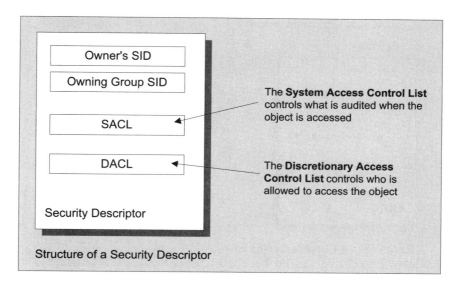

Structure of a Security Descriptor

The first field identifies the owner of the object. As you might expect, the owner can do just about anything with the object. The second field is there mainly to support NT's POSIX subsystem, and can be safely ignored by Win32 programmers.

The heart of the security descriptor lies in the two lists, the **System Access Control List** (usually known as the **SACL**) and the **Discretionary Access Control List** (known as the **DACL**).

The DACL

The Discretionary Access Control List (hereinafter referred to as the DACL) is the structure you'll have most to do with, as it is this which controls who can and cannot access an object.

A DACL is simply a list made up of entries called **access control entries**, more commonly known as **ACEs**. Each ACE is used to allow or deny a set of access rights to a particular SID. For example, one ACE might give user 'Joe Smith' write access, whilst another might deny write access to group 'Everyone'.

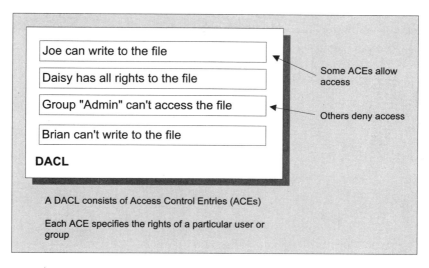

A DACL consists of Access Control Entries (ACEs)

Each ACE specifies the rights of a particular user or group

The structure of an ACE is illustrated below:

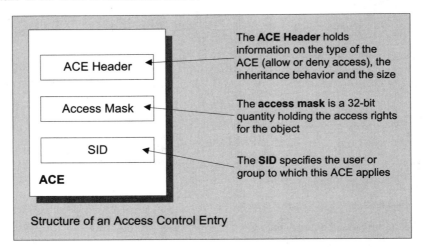

Structure of an Access Control Entry

We can see from this diagram that an ACE entry consists of three parts:

▶ The ACE header, which denotes the type of ACE (i.e. allow or deny access) and inheritance properties (e.g. whether rights for a directory are passed on to files created in that directory)

▶ The access mask, saying what can or cannot be done to the object

▶ The SID, specifying to whom this ACE applies

Access Rights

The access rights form part of the ACEs that we have just seen, and they specify what kinds of things can be done to the object, for example, whether or not it can be modified or deleted. Access rights come in three flavors:

▶ Standard — this applies to all types of objects on the system

▶ Specific — applies to particular object types

▶ Generic — pre-defined combinations of standard and specific rights

They are held in a 32-bit access mask, as shown in the diagram below:

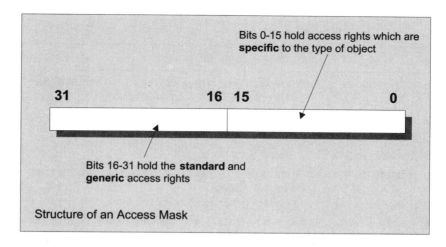

Structure of an Access Mask

Bits 16 to 31 of the access mask contain the standard and generic rights, as follows:

Bit Position	Flag	Meaning
16	DELETE	Allows or denies deletion of the object, depending on the type of the ACE
17	READ_CONTROL	Allows the client to obtain some control information from the object, the DACL and the security descriptor
18	WRITE_DAC	Allows the client to modify the DACL in any way it likes
19	WRITE_OWNER	Allows the client to change the owner of the object
20	SYNCHRONIZE	Allows the object handle to be used with synchronization functions such as `WaitForSingleObject()`
21	(unused)	
22	(unused)	
23	(unused)	
24	ACCESS_SYSTEM_SECURITY	Can modify audit and alarm control for the object
25	MAXIMUM_ALLOWED	Not really an access bit – it affects how NT scans the DACL
26	(reserved)	
27	(reserved)	
28	GENERIC_ALL	All generic permissions
29	GENERIC_EXECUTE	Generic execute permission
30	GENERIC_WRITE	Generic write permission
31	GENERIC_READ	Generic read permission

Various combinations of standard permissions are also provided:

Permission	Corresponds To:
STANDARD_RIGHTS_ALL	DELETE | READ_CONTROL | WRITE_DAC | WRITE_OWNER | SYNCHRONIZE
STANDARD_RIGHTS_EXECUTE	READ_CONTROL
STANDARD_RIGHTS_READ	READ_CONTROL
STANDARD_RIGHTS_WRITE	READ_CONTROL
STANDARD_RIGHTS_REQUIRED	DELETE | READ_CONTROL | WRITE_DAC | WRITE_OWNER

Bit positions 0 to 15 hold access bits whose meaning is specific to the type of object so that, for instance, bit 0 means **FILE_READ_DATA** for a file object, **FILE_LIST_DIRECTORY** for a directory object, and **THREAD_TERMINATE** for a thread object. Appendix A lists the access bits which apply to the various NT object types.

Using The DACL

When a process wants to use an object, the type of access it requires will be held in a set of 'desired access bits'. The system walks through the ACE entries in the object's DACL, from the first to the last. For an 'access allowed' ACE, it checks the SID in the ACE against the SIDs in the client's access token, and if there is a match, it clears those bits which the SID and the desired access have in common. The effect will be that the desired access should be zero once all the ACEs have been processed. If it isn't, then some access hasn't been granted, and the request fails. (I told you you'd become an expert in talking acronyms!)

For an 'access denied' ACE, the system checks whether any bits in the desired access match those in the ACE, and if they do, it will immediately refuse access.

The process is outlined in the following pseudo-code:

```
for all ACEs
{
   if it is an 'allow' ACE
      if the SID is in the access token
      {
          remove the bits in the ACE mask from desiredAccess
          if desiredAccess is zero
             return "OK"
          else
             continue with next ACE
      }
   else if it is a 'deny' ACE
      if the SID is in the access token
      {
          if (desiredAccess & ACEMask) is not zero
          return "access denied"
      }
}
```

```
   if desiredAccess is zero
      return "OK"
else
      return "access denied"
```

There are several important points we should note here.

The first is that the order of the ACEs in the DACL is significant. If a 'deny' ACE is processed, it will deny access to the object, regardless of whether an 'allow' ACE might grant permission further down. The reverse is also true, because once access has been allowed, the relevant bits are set to zero in the desired access mask, so access cannot later be denied. This means that it is very important to get the ACEs in the right order. When you change the permissions on an object using the NT Explorer (using the security tab on the properties dialog), the 'deny' ACEs are always placed before the 'allow' ones, but you have to be careful to order them properly yourself if you're manipulating a DACL from within code.

The second point to note is that access is denied unless it is specifically granted in the DACL. If anything is left in the desired access after all the ACEs have been read, it will be taken that not all access has been granted, and so access will be denied.

> *Remember, though, that this mechanism can be overridden if the user has the appropriate privileges. Even if the DACL shows that a user shouldn't have read access to a file, they will still be able to if they have backup privilege, because that allows reading of all files regardless of their security settings. For that reason, privileges should only be given out to those who really need them.*

As a final point, note that there is a big difference between an object having an empty DACL, and one having no DACL at all. An object with no DACL has no security settings, and so all accesses to the object are granted. An object with an empty DACL, i.e. one with no ACEs in its list, has no permissions set, and so all accesses are denied. You can add an empty DACL to an object by simply giving "No Access" permission to the "Everyone" group, in which case only the object's creator can access it.

MAXIMUM_ALLOWED Access

If you look back at the table of standard and generic rights for an access mask, you'll see that the entry for bit 25 is called **MAXIMUM_ALLOWED**. We said that this affects the way in which NT scans the DACL. This bit can only be set in a desired access mask (not in an ACE), and it asks NT to grant the maximum access that the client is allowed for an object, according to the access rights as set up in the DACL. This can be very useful when you don't want, or need, to be too precise, and simply want to use the object with the rights you already have.

If this is set, then NT processes the DACL differently. It walks the list of ACEs, adding in the bits for each 'allow' ACE and taking off the bits for each 'deny' ACE, such that you end up with the maximum access allowed. In this particular case, the order of the ACEs in the list doesn't matter.

Note that if any bits apart from **MAXIMUM_ALLOWED** are set in the desired access mask, then NT will assume that that bit is required, and the request will fail if that bit doesn't end up being set by the scan through the DACL.

The SACL

The System Access Control List (SACL) is similar to the DACL, in that it too consists of a list of ACEs. In this case, the ACEs specify what audit events should be logged for the object. For example, if the SACL contains an ACE that has the SID for user 'Joe Smith' and read permission, then an audit entry will be made each time that Joe Smith reads the file.

The Two Sorts Of Security Descriptor

Just to complicate matters, security descriptors come in two flavors — absolute and self-relative. This distinction refers to the way the descriptor stores its information, and can usually be ignored, unless you're trying to modify a security descriptor, when you may well need to convert between the two forms.

We've seen how a security descriptor contains four pieces of information:

- The owner's SID
- The group SID
- The SACL
- The DACL

When you create a new security descriptor, you get an absolute one. An **absolute security descriptor** holds pointers to the various bits of information, which live in their own areas of memory:

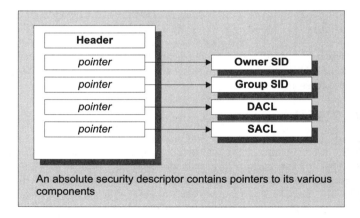

An absolute security descriptor contains pointers to its various components

On the other hand, a **self-relative security descriptor** contains all the information in a single block of memory, such that pointers to each of the parts of the descriptor refer to other locations within the same block of memory:

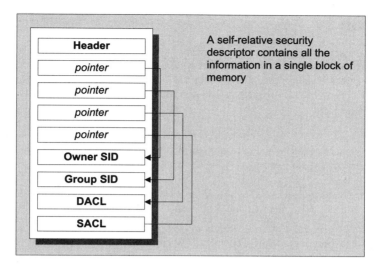

When you want to attach a security descriptor to an object, either by creating a new one or modifying an old one, you need to pass it an absolute descriptor. The problem is that when you request a security descriptor from NT, it gives you back a self-relative one, which has no room for you to add extra ACEs to the SACL or DACL. In this case, you'll need to convert from the self-relative form to the absolute form, so that you can then modify it, and we'll see just how we can do that later on in this chapter.

Private Objects

As well as NT's built-in securable objects, it is possible for you to create your own object types that use the security system. You may wish to protect records in a database, for example, or to protect access to specialized hardware, or something else not covered by the standard object types.

These **private objects** use security descriptors to control access, but as they're not known to NT, you're responsible for handling all the security yourself, checking each access to see whether it should be allowed or not. Private object security is handled by four API functions:

- ▶ `CreatePrivateObjectSecurity()`
- ▶ `DestroyPrivateObjectSecurity()`
- ▶ `GetPrivateObjectSecurity()`
- ▶ `SetPrivateObjectSecurity()`

We won't be mentioning private objects any more in this chapter, but it is useful to know that the facility exists.

Impersonation

The access token, carried by each process uniquely identifies the process and its access rights. Many applications, especially in client-server systems, carry out operations on behalf of a client, so they need to operate using the client's security settings rather than their own. Impersonation allows them to do this, by temporarily allowing them to assume the security settings in the client's access token.

There obviously needs to be some control over this process, so each access token has an attribute called the **impersonation level** which governs how far impersonation may go. This attribute can take one of the following values:

▶ `SecurityImpersonation`, where a server can get security information about the client, and can impersonate it on a local system

▶ `SecurityIdentification`, which allows a server to get security information (such as the SID and privileges) but doesn't allow impersonation

▶ `SecurityAnonymous`, which doesn't allow the server to get any information, and obviously doesn't allow impersonation either

Note that it is not possible for a server to impersonate a client on a remote system.

Impersonation can be applied in various situations, such as at the server end of a named pipe or a DDE conversation (using `ImpersonateNamedPipeClient()` and `DdeImpersonateClient()` respectively), and with RPC calls (using `RpcImpersonateClient()`).

Once again, we won't go any further into this topic.

Programming The Security System

Now that we've been through a brief an overview of how the security system works, it's time to get on with programming. We'll see the data structures that we discussed in the first part and show examples of how to use them. There are over 100 Win32 API functions which deal with security, and rather than just list them all, we'll introduce them in the context of the programming examples in the rest of the chapter.

In fact, we're not even going to *try* to cover them all. What we'll do is to look at how to use the most commonly used security routines to perform some useful tasks. In the process we'll discover many of the major data structures and API functions, and you will get a feel for how they're used.

For quick reference, the API functions we'll be covering in this section are:

▶ `AddAccessAllowedAce()`

▶ `AddAccessDeniedAce()`

▶ `AddAce()`

- ▶ AddAuditAccessAce()
- ▶ AdjustTokenPrivileges()
- ▶ GetAce()
- ▶ GetAclInformation()
- ▶ GetFileSecurity()
- ▶ GetKernelObjectSecurity()
- ▶ GetLengthSid()
- ▶ GetSecurityDescriptorDacl()
- ▶ GetSecurityDescriptorGroup()
- ▶ GetSecurityDescriptorOwner()
- ▶ GetTokenInformation()
- ▶ InitializeAcl()
- ▶ InitializeSecurityDescriptor()
- ▶ LookupAccountName()
- ▶ LookupAccountSid()
- ▶ LookupPrivilegeDisplayName()
- ▶ LookupPrivilegeName()
- ▶ LookupPrivilegeValue()
- ▶ OpenProcessToken()
- ▶ PrivilegeCheck()
- ▶ SetKernelObjectSecurity()
- ▶ SetSecurityDescriptorDacl()

Using Security Descriptors

We'll start off by showing how to perform basic operations on security descriptors, that is how to retrieve, create and modify them. We'll provide simple examples working with file objects, as it's easier to understand what is going on with this type of object.

> *Note that the file examples will only work with files which are stored on an NTFS partition, because the FAT filing system doesn't support NT security. If you want to experiment with this code and have a FAT system, you may need to create yourself a small new NTFS partition using the Disk Administrator.*

Try It Out — Retrieving Security Descriptors

The first example we'll look at is a program that retrieves a security descriptor from a file. We'll pass the file name to the program, and it will print out information about the the owner, the group and the DACL. We'll use the Win32 API function GetKernelObjectSecurity(), so that we can easily modify the code for other kernel objects, such as pipes, processes and registry entries.

The code for the main program is shown below:

```
// GetFileSecurityInfo.cpp

#include <iostream>
#include <windows.h>

using namespace std;

bool DoOwner(SECURITY_DESCRIPTOR* pSec);
bool DoGroup(SECURITY_DESCRIPTOR* pSec);
bool DoDACL(SECURITY_DESCRIPTOR* pSec);

int main(int argc, char* argv[])
{
   // make sure we were given a filename
   if (argc == 1)
   {
      cout << "Need a filename" << endl;
      return -1;
   }

   // Open the file
   HANDLE hHand = CreateFile(argv[1],      // filename
      GENERIC_READ,                        // get read access
      0,                                   // no sharing
      NULL,                                // no security
      OPEN_EXISTING,                       // open mode
      FILE_ATTRIBUTE_NORMAL,
      NULL);

   if (hHand == INVALID_HANDLE_VALUE)
   {
      cout << "Failed to open file ("
           << hex << GetLastError() << dec << ")" << endl;
      return -1;
   }

   // Next step is to get the security info for the object. First, find out how
   // big the data is going to be, by calling GetKernelObjectSecurity(). Note
   // that we're expecting an 'insufficient buffer size' error when the function
   // is called in this way, so don't fail on it.

   DWORD dwSize = 0;

   BOOL bOK = GetKernelObjectSecurity(hHand,
                 OWNER_SECURITY_INFORMATION |
                 GROUP_SECURITY_INFORMATION |
                 DACL_SECURITY_INFORMATION,
                 NULL, 0, &dwSize);
```

```
   DWORD dwLastErr;
   if (!bOK)
      dwLastErr = GetLastError();

   if (!bOK && dwLastErr != ERROR_INSUFFICIENT_BUFFER)
   {
      cout << "Failed to get security info size ("
           << hex << dwLastErr << dec << ")" << endl;
      return -1;
   }

   // Allocate memory
   SECURITY_DESCRIPTOR* pSec = NULL;
   pSec = static_cast<SECURITY_DESCRIPTOR*>(GlobalAlloc(GPTR, dwSize));
   if (!pSec)
   {
      cout << "Failed to get memory for security info ("
           << hex << GetLastError() << dec << ")" << endl;
      return -1;
   }

   // Now call GetKernelObjectSecurity() again to retrieve the info
   if (!GetKernelObjectSecurity(hHand,
               OWNER_SECURITY_INFORMATION |
               GROUP_SECURITY_INFORMATION |
               DACL_SECURITY_INFORMATION,
      pSec, dwSize, &dwSize))
   {
      cout << "Failed to get security info ("
           << hex << GetLastError() << dec << ")" << endl;
      return -1;
   }

   // Now close the file handle, because we have what we need
   CloseHandle(hHand);

   // Process owner information
   if (!DoOwner(pSec))
      return -1;

   // Process group information
   if (!DoGroup(pSec))
      return -1;

   // Process DACL info
   if (!DoDACL(pSec))
      return -1;

   // Free global memory
   if (GlobalFree(pSec))
   {
      cout << "Failed to free memory ("
           << hex << GetLastError() << dec << ")" << endl;
      return -1;
   }

   return 0;
}
```

Let's take this code step by step so that we can understand what's happening. Along the way, we'll introduce the API functions and data structures as we use them.

Opening The File

We start by getting the filename from the command line — this will be the second element of the **argv[]** array. (If **argc** is set to 1 then we know that the user has not entered a filename, so we output a suitable message and exit the program.) We then open the file using the Win32 API function call, **CreateFile()**, which we met in the last chapter. By passing **GENERIC_READ** as the second argument, we gain read access to the file, which we need so that we can access the security descriptor. If this call is successful, we'll have a handle to an open file.

Retrieving The Security Descriptor

Once we have the handle, we can use **GetKernelObjectSecurity()** to retrieve the security information for the file object:

```
BOOL GetKernelObjectSecurity(
     HANDLE hObj,                      // handle to object
     SECURITY_INFORMATION sec,         // information to retrieve
     PSECURITY_DESCRIPTOR pSD,         // security descriptor to receive data
     DWORD dwSize,                     // size of security descriptor
     LPDWORD dwReqSize);               // amount of space required
```

We can use this call to get security information for any kernel object. We pass a handle to the object, plus a **SECURITY_INFORMATION** item that specifies the information in which we are interested. A **SECURITY_INFORMATION** item is a **DWORD**, which can contain one or more of the following flags:

- OWNER_SECURITY_INFORMATION
- GROUP_SECURITY_INFORMATION
- DACL_SECURITY_INFORMATION
- SACL_SECURITY_INFORMATION

We're not interested in the SACL, so we'll just OR together the first three values when we make the call:

```
BOOL bOK = GetKernelObjectSecurity(hHand,
                OWNER_SECURITY_INFORMATION |
                GROUP_SECURITY_INFORMATION |
                DACL_SECURITY_INFORMATION,
                NULL, 0, &dwSize);
```

The security descriptor is passed back through the pointer that we provide as the third argument in the call, and you might be wondering why we've passed **NULL** for this argument. Well, there is a minor complication here. What we get passed back from the function is a self-relative security descriptor, whose size will depend on the number of ACEs in the DACL. This means that we cannot say how big the security descriptor is going to be when we make the call.

The solution to this problem is to call the function twice — the first time with **NULL** passed for the security descriptor and zero for the size. No information will be retrieved, but the final parameter (**dwSize**) will return the size of the information we're interested in. You need to be aware that calling the function like this will result in a spurious "The data area passed to a system call is too small" error (**ERROR_INSUFFICIENT_BUFFER** or **0x7a**), which can safely be ignored.

We can then allocate a block of memory of the correct size, and pass this in a second call to **GetKernelObjectSecurity()**. When we call the function this time, we pass in a pointer to a security descriptor, **pSec**, as the third parameter:

```
// Allocate memory
SECURITY_DESCRIPTOR* pSec = NULL;
pSec = static_cast<SECURITY_DESCRIPTOR*>(GlobalAlloc(GPTR, dwSize));
if (!pSec)
{
   cout << "Failed to get memory for security info ("
        << hex << GetLastError() << dec << ")" << endl;
   return -1;
}

// Now call GetKernelObjectSecurity() again to retrieve the info
if (!GetKernelObjectSecurity(hHand,
             OWNER_SECURITY_INFORMATION |
             GROUP_SECURITY_INFORMATION |
             DACL_SECURITY_INFORMATION,
             pSec, dwSize, &dwSize))
{
   cout << "Failed to get security info ("
        << hex << GetLastError() << dec << ")" << endl;
   return -1;
}
```

When the call to **GetKernelObjectSecurity()** returns, we can query our pointer to the **SECURITY_DESCRIPTOR** structure for information about the owner, the group and the DACL.

What does a **SECURITY_DESCRIPTOR** structure look like? Officially it is undocumented, because you're only supposed to access it via the API functions provided for the purpose. If you look in **<winnt.h>**, you'll see that it looks like this:

```
typedef struct _SECURITY_DESCRIPTOR {
  BYTE   Revision;                        // revision number
  BYTE   Sbz1;
  SECURITY_DESCRIPTOR_CONTROL Control;
  PSID Owner;                             // pointer to owner SID
  PSID Group;                             // pointer to group SID
  PACL Sacl;                              // pointer to SACL
  PACL Dacl;                              // pointer to DACL
  } SECURITY_DESCRIPTOR, *PISECURITY_DESCRIPTOR;
```

> *Win32 calls these 'opaque data types', meaning that you shouldn't need to know their internal structure, but should only access them using API functions. Doing this obviously helps maintain compatibility with future releases of NT, and you shouldn't use the internals of these data types unless you have very good reason.*

Extracting Owner Information

The first task is to extract and print out the owner of the object, which is done by the
`DoOwner()` function:

```
bool DoOwner(SECURITY_DESCRIPTOR* pSec)
{
    PSID ps;
    BOOL bDef;

    // Get the owner information
    if (!GetSecurityDescriptorOwner(pSec, &ps, &bDef))
    {
        cout << "Failed to get owner info ("
             << hex << GetLastError() << dec << ")" << endl;
        return false;
    }

    if (!ps)
    {
        // Null means no owner
        cout << "Descriptor has no owner ("
             << hex << GetLastError() << dec << ")" << endl;
    }
    else
    {
        // Get owner info from the SID
        DWORD dwOwnerSize = 0;
        DWORD dwDomainSize = 0;
        SID_NAME_USE stype;

        // Find the size of the buffers we need
        BOOL bOK = LookupAccountSid(NULL,      // this machine
                        ps,                 // SID to look up
                        0,                  // buffer
                        &dwOwnerSize,       // size of owner string
                        0,                  // no buffer
                        &dwDomainSize,      // size of domain string
                        &stype);            // SID type (user, group, domain etc)

        DWORD dwLastErr;
        if (!bOK)
            dwLastErr = GetLastError();

        if (!bOK && dwLastErr != ERROR_INSUFFICIENT_BUFFER)
        {
            cout << "Failed to get SID buffer sizes ("
                 << hex << GetLastError() << dec << ")" << endl;
            return false;
        }

        // Allocate buffers
        dwOwnerSize += 1;
        LPTSTR owner = new TCHAR[dwOwnerSize];
        dwDomainSize += 1;
        LPTSTR domain = new TCHAR[dwDomainSize];
```

```
           if (!LookupAccountSid(NULL,        // this machine
                             ps,              // SID to look up
                             owner,           // string to hold owner
                             &dwOwnerSize,    // size of owner string
                             domain,          // string to hold domain
                             &dwDomainSize,   // size of domain string
                             &stype))         // SID type (user, group, domain etc)
         {
            cout << "Failed to lookup owner SID ("
                 << hex << GetLastError() << dec << ")" << endl;
            return false;
         }

         // Print the owner info
         cout << "Descriptor owner is '" << owner
              << "' from '" << domain << "'" << endl;
      }

      return true;
   }
```

All the NT security data consist of a series of nested structures, and the API provides calls to let you 'drill down' through the layers. Here, we're using a call to the `GetSecurityDescriptorOwner()` function to retrieve the owner SID from a security descriptor. As you might expect, there are matching `Set...()` functions, which we'll meet in due course.

```
   BOOL GetSecurityDescriptorOwner(
       PSECURITY_DESCRIPTOR pSD,     // security descriptor to read
       PSID* psid,                   // address of pointer to a SID
       LPBOOL pbDefault);            // default owner flag
```

This function takes as arguments a pointer to a security descriptor, a pointer to a SID, to hold the return data, and a flag, which says whether this owner was set as the result of some sort of default creation mechanism.

The `SID` structure is another Win32 opaque data type, so we won't consider its internal details any further.

If the SID pointer comes back `NULL`, then the object has no owner. If it isn't `NULL`, then we can retrieve the owner account name and domain using the `LookupAccountSid()` function:

```
   BOOL LookupAccountSid(
       LPCTSTR pSystem,          // system name  (NULL = local  machine)
       PSID sid,                 // address SID to look up
       LPTSTR name,              // string to hold owner name
       LPDWORD pSize1,           // size of owner string
       LPTSTR domain,            // string to hold domain name
       LPDWORD pSize2,           // size of domain name
       PSID_NAME_USE pUse);      // SID type
```

This function can be used to look up a SID on local and remote machines. We're only interested in the local machine here, so we pass `NULL` for the first parameter. The function returns strings for the owner's name and domain, and a `SID_NAME_USE` value which says what this SID represents, such as a user, a domain or a group.

We call the function twice. The first time is to find the size of the buffers we'll need, and as before, we expect the function to fail with an **ERROR_INSUFFICIENT_BUFFER** error. Once we've allocated the buffers, we can call the function a second time to retrieve the information.

If this second call works, we can print out the name and group information that we have retrieved.

Extracting The Group Information

The second function retrieves the group information, and is almost identical. In fact, in a real-life program you could cut down the amount of code considerably:

```
bool DoGroup(SECURITY_DESCRIPTOR* pSec)
{
    PSID ps;
    BOOL bDef;

    // Get the group information
    if (!GetSecurityDescriptorGroup(pSec, &ps, &bDef))
    {
        cout << "Failed to get group info ("
            << hex << GetLastError() << dec << ")" << endl;
        return false;
    }

    if (!ps)
    {
        // Null means no group
        cout << "Descriptor has no group info" << endl;
    }
    else
    {
        // Get group info from the SID
        DWORD dwGroupSize = 0;
        DWORD dwDomainSize = 0;
        SID_NAME_USE stype;

        // Find the size of the buffers we need
        BOOL bOK = LookupAccountSid(NULL,        // this machine
                    ps,                 // SID to look up
                    0,                  // buffer
                    &dwGroupSize,       // size of group string
                    0,                  // no buffer
                    &dwDomainSize,      // size of domain string
                    &stype);            // SID type (user, group, domain etc)

        DWORD dwLastErr;
        if (!bOK)
            dwLastErr = GetLastError();

        if (!bOK && dwLastError != ERROR_INSUFFICIENT_BUFFER)
        {
            cout << "Failed to get SID buffer sizes ("
                << hex << GetLastError() << dec << ")" << endl;
            return false;
        }
```

```
                // Allocate buffers
                dwGroupSize += 1;
                LPTSTR group = new TCHAR[dwGroupSize];
                dwDomainSize += 1;
                LPTSTR domain = new TCHAR[dwDomainSize];

                if (!LookupAccountSid(NULL,        // this machine
                                ps,                // SID to look up
                                group,             // string to hold group
                                &dwGroupSize,      // size of group string
                                domain,            // string to hold domain
                                &dwDomainSize,     // size of domain string
                                &stype))           // SID type (user, group, domain etc)
                {
                    cout << "Failed to lookup group SID ("
                            << hex << GetLastError() << dec << ")" << endl;
                    return false;
                }

                // Print the group info
                cout << "Descriptor group is '" << group
                        << "' from '" << domain << "'" << endl;
            }

        return true;
    }
```

You can see from the code that the only difference between the two functions is that here we are calling the API function, `GetSecurityDescriptorGroup()`, instead of `GetSecurityDescriptorOwner()`.

Extracting Information From The DACL

The third function is rather more complex, as we need to walk the list of ACE entries in the DACL, and print information about each one:

```
bool DoDACL(SECURITY_DESCRIPTOR* pSec)
{
    PACL pac;
    BOOL bDef, bDacl;

    // Get the owner information
    if (!GetSecurityDescriptorDacl(pSec, &bDacl, &pac, &bDef))
    {
        cout << "Failed to get DACL info ("
                << hex << GetLastError() << dec << ")" << endl;
        return false;
    }

    if (!bDacl)
    {
        // FALSE means unrestricted access, because there is no DACL
        cout << "Descriptor has unrestricted access" << endl;
    }
    else
    {
```

```
            if (bDef)
               cout << "Descriptor has default DACL"
                    << endl;  // TRUE means it is default
            else
               cout << "Descriptor has non-default DACL" << endl;

            ACL_SIZE_INFORMATION acSize;
            ACCESS_ALLOWED_ACE* pAce;

            // Get information about the ACL
            if (!GetAclInformation(pac,           // pointer to DACL
                        &acSize,                  // ACL size info block
                        sizeof(ACL_SIZE_INFORMATION),
                        AclSizeInformation))      // class of information wanted
            {
               cout << "Failed to get ACL information ("
                    << hex << GetLastError() << dec << ")" << endl;
               return false;
            }

            // Print the ACL information
            for (int i=0; i<acSize.AceCount; i++)
            {
               // Get ACE info
               if (!GetAce(pac, i, reinterpret_cast<LPVOID*>(&pAce)))
               {
                  cout << "Failed to get ACE information ("
                       << hex << GetLastError() << dec << ")" << endl;
                  return false;
               }

               // Get the name from the SID in the ACE
               DWORD dwNameSize = 0;
               DWORD dwDomainSize = 0;
               SID_NAME_USE stype;

               // Get buffer sizes
               BOOL bOK = LookupAccountSid(NULL,       // this machine
                              &pAce->SidStart,  // SID to look up
                              0,                // string to hold name
                              &dwNameSize,      // size of name string
                              0,                // string to hold domain
                              &dwDomainSize,    // size of domain string
                              &stype);          // SID type (user, group, domain etc)

               DWORD dwLastErr;
               if (!bOK)
                  dwLastErr = GetLastError();

               if (!bOK && dwLastErr != ERROR_INSUFFICIENT_BUFFER)
               {
                  cout << "Failed to get SID buffer sizes ("
                       << hex << GetLastError() << dec << ")" << endl;
                  return false;
               }
```

```
            // Allocate buffers
            dwNameSize += 1;
            LPTSTR name = new TCHAR[dwNameSize];
            dwDomainSize += 1;
            LPTSTR domain = new TCHAR[dwDomainSize];

            if (!LookupAccountSid(NULL,        // this machine
                          &pAce->SidStart,     // SID to look up
                          name,                // string to hold name
                          &dwNameSize,         // size of name string
                          domain,              // string to hold domain
                          &dwDomainSize,       // size of domain string
                          &stype))             // SID type (user, group, domain etc)
            {
                strcpy(name, "(unknown)");
                strcpy(domain, " ");
            }

            // Print out the ACE information
            cout << "ACE [" << i << "]: type=";
            if (pAce->Header.AceType == ACCESS_ALLOWED_ACE_TYPE)
                cout << "allow";
            else if (pAce->Header.AceType == ACCESS_DENIED_ACE_TYPE)
                cout << "deny";
            else if (pAce->Header.AceType == SYSTEM_AUDIT_ACE_TYPE)
                cout << "audit";
            else
                cout << "unknown";

            cout << ", Mask=" << hex << pAce->Mask << dec;
            cout << ", owner=" << name << ", domain=" << domain << endl;
        }
    }

    return true;
}
```

The first step is to call `GetSecurityDescriptorDacl()`, which should get us the DACL information from the security descriptor, in much the same way that we got the owner and group information:

```
BOOL GetSecurityDescriptorDacl(
    PSECURITY_DESCRIPTOR pSD,       // security descriptor to read
    LPBOOL pPresent,                // address of 'present' flag
    PACL *pAcl,                     // address of pointer to ACL
    LPBOOL pDefault);               // address of 'default' flag
```

This function retrieves the DACL from the security descriptor, if one is present, and sets the `pPresent` flag to `TRUE`. If there is no DACL, the `pPresent` flag is set to `FALSE`, so if this is the case, then we simply print this fact and then exit. The `pDefault` flag tells us whether the DACL was supplied by some sort of default mechanism (`TRUE`) or provided by a user (`FALSE`).

If the file has a DACL, we use this last flag to print whether or not it is a default one. The next task is to use `GetAclInformation()` to return us information about the ACL:

```
BOOL GetAclInformation(
    PACL  pAcl,                       // pointer to an ACL
    LPVOID pInfo,                     // pointer to ACL info
    DWORD dwSize,                     // size of info
    ACL_INFORMATION_CLASS cls);       // type of info wanted
```

This function will work for both discretionary ACLs (DACLs) and system ACLs (SACLs). **pAcl** points to the ACL about which we want information, **pInfo** points to the buffer which holds the information when the function returns, and **dwSize** tells you the size of the buffer. Precisely what information is returned depends on the value given for the final parameter, which can be either **AclRevisionInformation** to get information about the revision number of the ACL, or **AclSizeInformation** to get the size of the ACL. The revision number is updated when Microsoft change the structure of ACLs, and is seldom needed by ordinary programmers.

In this example, we're asking for size information, so on return the pointer points to an **ACL_SIZE_INFORMATION** structure which looks like this:

```
typedef struct _ACL_SIZE_INFORMATION {
    DWORD   AceCount;        // number of ACEs in ACL
    DWORD   AclBytesInUse;   // bytes being used in ACL
    DWORD   AclBytesFree;    // bytes free in ACL
} ACL_SIZE_INFORMATION;
```

We can then use the count information (**AceCount**) to step though all the ACEs in the ACL. **GetAce()** returns us a pointer to one of the ACEs in an ACL:

```
BOOL  GetAce(
    PACL  pAcl,             // pointer to ACL
    DWORD dwIndex,          // index of ACE to retrieve
    LPVOID* pAce);          // pointer to ACE structure
```

dwIndex is the zero-based index to an ACE, and the ACE information is returned as a pointer to the ACE information, **pAce**.

What the ACE contains depends on what sort of ACE it is, but all of them consist of a header followed by type-dependent data. The **ACE_HEADER** structure contains a type specifier to tell you what sort of data follows, a set of flags and a size:

```
typedef struct _ACE_HEADER
{
    BYTE AceType;      // type specifier
    BYTE AceFlags;     // flags
    WORD AceSize;      // size
} ACE_HEADER;
```

The type may be one of:

- **ACCESS_ALLOWED_ACE_TYPE**, to allow access

- **ACCESS_DENIED_ACE_TYPE**, to deny access

- **SYSTEM_AUDIT_ACE_TYPE**, to cause audit entries to be written. Note that this type of ACE is used in the SACL, whereas the other two are used in the DACL

There is a fourth type, **SYSTEM_ALARM_ACE_TYPE**, but it isn't supported in the current release of NT (version 4.0).

The flags control the behavior of the ACE, such as whether it is inherited by other objects, and when messages are generated for audit ACEs. For more details on these flags, see the online help

At present, the structure of all types of ACE is identical, and looks like this:

```
typedef struct _ACCESS_ALLOWED_ACE
{
    ACE_HEADER Header;        // header information
    ACCESS_MASK Mask;         // access mask
    DWORD SidStart;           // start of SID
} ACCESS_ALLOWED_ACE;
```

We can therefore use the pointer that we're given to access the header, the mask and the start of the SID. In the example program we use the header information to print out the ACE type and the corresponding mask, and we use **LookupAccountSid()** to get the account name and domain from the **SidStart** member.

Program Output

Building and running the program on a randomly-selected file gives output like this:

We wrote the example program above to be general, in that the handle returned from **CreateFile()** is a kernel object just like any other, and so we can use **GetKernelObjectSecurity()** to access the security descriptor. This means that it is now possible for us to modify the code to report on other kinds of objects apart from files. Very shortly, we'll show how simple it is to report on a process rather than a file.

Before we do that, however, let's just note that there's a special function called **GetFileSecurity()**, which works in exactly the same way as the one we have used above, **GetKernelObjectSecurity()**, except that it takes a filename instead of a handle. This could be used to simplify the code in our example, by cutting step of using **CreateFile()** to get the file handle.

Try It Out — Modifying The Program For Other Kernel Objects

In order to report on a process, we need to get a process handle in place of the file handle, and we can simply modify the code to read the numeric value of a process handle instead of a file name, like this:

```cpp
// GetProcessSecurityInfo.cpp

#include <iostream>
#include <windows.h>

using namespace std;

bool DoOwner(SECURITY_DESCRIPTOR* pSec);
bool DoGroup(SECURITY_DESCRIPTOR* pSec);
bool DoDACL(SECURITY_DESCRIPTOR* pSec);

int main(int argc, char* argv[])
{
    // Use process handle instead
    // make sure we were given a process ID
    if (argc == 1)
    {
        cout << "Need a process ID" << endl;
        return -1;
    }

    DWORD dwProc = atoi(argv[1]);
    cout << "Process ID: 0x" << hex << dwProc << dec << endl;

    HANDLE hHand = OpenProcess(READ_CONTROL, FALSE, dwProc);
    if (hHand == NULL)
    {
        cout << "Failed to open process" << endl;
        return -1;
    }

    // Next step is to get the security info for the object. First, find out how
    // big the data is going to be, by calling GetKernelObjectSecurity(). Note
    // that we're expecting an 'insufficient buffer size' error when the function
    // is called in this way, so don't fail on it.
    .
    .
    .
```

Here, we have simply changed the code to read a **process ID** (PID) from the command line and convert it to a number, using **atoi()**. We then use **OpenProcess()** (rather than **CreateFile()**) to obtain a handle to the process, specifying **READ_CONTROL** in order that we can read the security descriptor. After this, the code is exactly the same.

An easy way to get a PID is to start the NT Task Manager and select the Processes tab:

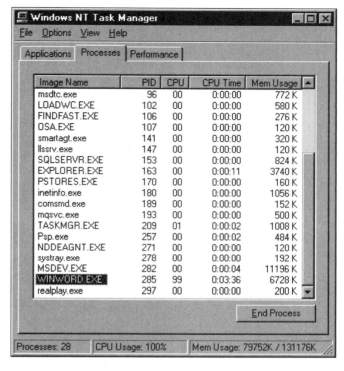

The second column contains all the process IDs. Choosing one arbitrarily, such as **Winword.exe** (PID 285 on my machine) gives this output:

The second column contains all the process IDs. Choosing one arbitrarily, such as `Winword.exe` (PID 285 on my machine) gives this output:

Creating Security Descriptors

Now we've seen how to look at the security descriptor belonging to a file or process, let's move on to the next logical step, which is discovering how to create a security descriptor and add it to an object. You will need to do this if you want to create an object with controlled access, such as a directory that can only be read by certain users, or a program that can only be executed by administrators.

Once again we'll use a file as the example, but remember that the same sort of mechanism applies to other types of kernel objects.

When you create a file using the `CreateFile()`function, the fourth parameter can be used to set the security attributes for the file:

```
HANDLE CreateFile(
  LPCTSTR pFileName,
  DWORD dwAccess,
  DWORD dwShare,
  LPSECURITY_ATTRIBUTES pSec,    // security attributes for file
  DWORD dwCreation,
  DWORD dwFlags,
  HANDLE hTemplate);
```

You'll frequently set this to **NULL**, which means that the file will have default security settings, so that it can be accessed by the creator and other members of the same group. If you want to have security settings other than default, however, you can create a **SECURITY_ATTRIBUTES** structure and pass it to `CreateFile()`.

The **SECURITY_ATTRIBUTES** structure looks like this:

```
typedef struct _SECURITY_ATTRIBUTES
{
  DWORD  nLength;
  LPVOID lpSecurityDescriptor;
  BOOL   bInheritHandle;
} SECURITY_ATTRIBUTES;
```

It comprises three members:

▶ A length, which is set to `sizeof(SECURITY_ATTRIBUTES)`.

▶ A pointer to a security descriptor — if this is **NULL**, then the file will inherit the default security descriptor of the process calling the function. (We already know that the security descriptor is an opaque data type, which we don't manipulate ourselves.)

▶ A flag which determines whether this structure will be inherited by child processes.

So, in order to set the security attributes for a file, we need to perform these steps:

▶ Verify the user name, and get its SID

▶ Create a security descriptor and an ACL

▶ Initialize the DACL

▶ Add the appropriate ACEs to the DACL

▶ Create a **SECURITY_ATTRIBUTES** structure

▶ Add the security descriptor to the **SECURITY_ATTRIBUTES**

▶ Use the security descriptor in the call to **CreateFile()**

Try It Out — Setting The Security Attributes

It seems pretty long-winded, but it isn't too bad when you break it down step by step. Here's a sample program which does all that:

```cpp
// CreateSecurityDescriptor.cpp

#include <windows.h>
#include <iostream>
#include <string>

using namespace std;

int main(int argc, char* argv[])
{
    // Get the arguments - user, filename and mode
    string user, fileName, mode;
    cout << "User: ";
    cin >> user;
    cout << "Filename: ";
    cin >> fileName;
    cout << "Access (R,W or A): ";
    cin >> mode;

    // Check the access before going further
    DWORD dwAccess;
    if (mode == "R" || mode == "r")
        dwAccess = GENERIC_READ;
    else if (mode == "W" || mode == "w")
        dwAccess = GENERIC_WRITE;
    else if (mode == "A" || mode == "a")
        dwAccess = GENERIC_ALL;
    else
    {
        cout << "Unknown access mode - must be R, W or A!" << endl;
        return -1;
    }

    // Get details for the user
    const int BUFF_CHARS = 100;

    BYTE sidBuff[BUFF_CHARS];
    DWORD dwSidSize = BUFF_CHARS;
    PSID pSid = static_cast<PSID>(&sidBuff);
    TCHAR domain[BUFF_CHARS];
    DWORD dwDomSize = BUFF_CHARS
    SID_NAME_USE sidUse;

    if (!LookupAccountName(0, user.c_str(), pSid, &dwSidSize, domain,
          &dwDomSize, &sidUse))
    {
        cout << "Error from LookupAccountName ("
            << hex << GetLastError() << dec << ")" << endl;
        return -1;
    }
```

```
    // Initialize the SD
    SECURITY_DESCRIPTOR desc;
    if (!InitializeSecurityDescriptor(&desc, SECURITY_DESCRIPTOR_REVISION))
    {
        cout << "Error from InitializeSecurityDescriptor ("
            << hex << GetLastError() << dec << ")" << endl;
        return -1;
    }

    // Initialize the ACL so it can hold one 'allow' ACE
    DWORD dwSize = sizeof(ACL) + sizeof(ACCESS_ALLOWED_ACE) +
                   GetLengthSid(pSid) - sizeof(DWORD);

    BYTE* aclBuff = static_cast<BYTE*>(GlobalAlloc(GPTR, dwSize));
    PACL pAcl = reinterpret_cast<PACL>(aclBuff);

    if (!InitializeAcl(pAcl, dwSize, ACL_REVISION))
    {
        cout << "Error from InitializeAcl ("
            << hex << GetLastError() << dec << ")" << endl;
        return -1;
    }

    // Create and add the ACE
    if (!AddAccessAllowedAce(pAcl, ACL_REVISION, dwAccess, pSid))
    {
        cout << "Error from AddAccessAllowedAce ("
            << hex << GetLastError() << dec << ")" << endl;
        return -1;
    }

    // Set the ACL into the SD
    if (!SetSecurityDescriptorDacl(&desc, TRUE, pAcl, FALSE))
    {
        cout << "Error from SetSecurityDescriptorDacl ("
            << hex << GetLastError() << dec << ")" << endl;
        return -1;
    }

    // Set up the SA
    SECURITY_ATTRIBUTES satt;
    satt.nLength = sizeof(SECURITY_ATTRIBUTES);
    satt.bInheritHandle = FALSE;
    satt.lpSecurityDescriptor = &desc;

    // Create the file
    HANDLE hFile = CreateFile(fileName.c_str(),GENERIC_WRITE, 0,
        &satt,
        CREATE_NEW, FILE_ATTRIBUTE_NORMAL, 0);
    if (hFile == NULL)
    {
        cout << "Error from CreateFile (" << hex << GetLastError() << dec << ")"
            << endl;
        return -1;
    }

    CloseHandle(hFile);

    return 0;
}
```

We start by asking the user to specify a user name, the name of a file to create, and the access which they'd like to give it. For simplicity, they are given three choices, corresponding to the the generic access flags:

▶ **GENERIC_READ** (R)

▶ **GENERIC_WRITE** (W)

▶ **GENERIC_ALL** (A)

If you look back at the list of steps for setting the security attributes, then you'll see that the first task is to get the SID for the user name. We can do this using the **LookupAccountName()**, which is the opposite of the **LookupAccountSid()** function that we've already used. It takes virtually identical parameters, but this time you give it a name and retrieves the corresponding SID:

```
BOOL  LookupAccountName(
    LPCTSTR  pSystem,              // system name (NULL = local machine)
    LPCTSTR  name,                 // name to look up
    PSID  sid,                     // address of SID buffer
    LPDWORD  pdwSize,              // size of SID buffer
    LPTSTR  domain,                // string to hold domain name
    LPDWORD  pdwSize2,            // number of characters in domain name
    PSID_NAME_USE  pUse);         // SID type
```

Note that the second to last parameter holds the number of characters in the string, and not the number of bytes. Although the latter will work with an ANSI string, we need the number of characters if using Unicode.

Assuming we get the SID we want, we can then go on to initialize the security descriptor, using a call to **InitializeSecurityDescriptor()**:

```
BOOL InitializeSecurityDescriptor(
    PSECURITY_DESCRIPTOR pSec,        // buffer to initialize
    DWORD  dwRev);                     // revision level
```

You pass it the address of the buffer to initialize, and a revision level value. At present the only valid value for this parameter is **SECURITY_DESCRIPTOR_REVISION**.

The next task is to initialize the ACL, and it is here that we meet a slight complication. An ACL is a list of ACE entries, so its size is going to depend on the number of entries it contains. Calculating this size isn't completely straightforward, but you do have two possible solutions. The first, and less satisfactory, way is to pick an arbitrary size, large enough to store what you need. The second way is to calculate it properly, using the following formula:

```
// Note: this is pseudo-code!
nBytes = sizeof(ACL) +
         nEntries * (sizeof(ACE) - sizeof(DWORD)) +
         nEntries * sizeof(SID)
```

We can see from this that the size of the ACL is equal to the size of the ACL structure itself, plus the size of however many ACEs and SIDs you want to store. We only want one entry in this example, so we calculate it as:

```
DWORD dwSize = sizeof(ACL) + sizeof(ACCESS_ALLOWED_ACE) +
               GetLengthSid(pSid) - sizeof(DWORD);
```

We cannot deal with the SID data structure directly, so we use the **GetLengthSid()** function in our calculation to return the size of the SID. Setting the size of the ACL in this way has obvious consequences if we want to add more entries later, and we'll tackle this question in the next section.

Once we've got the size of the ACL, we can call **InitializeAcl()** to do the work:

```
BOOL  InitializeAcl(
    PACL  pAcl,            // pointer to ACL
    DWORD dwSize,          // size of ACL
    DWORD dwRev);          // ACL revision
```

The first two parameters give a pointer to the ACL and the size we need it to be, and the third gives the ACL revision number. This must be set to the value **ACL_REVISION**, which is the current revision of the ACL structure.

An initialized ACL can have different kinds of ACEs added to it using one of the appropriate functions — **AddAccessAllowedAce()** and **AddAccessDeniedAce()** which add ACEs to the DACL, and **AddAuditAccessAce()**, which adds an ACE to the SACL. Here's the one we're using, which, as you'd expect, adds an 'allow' ACE to the ACL:

```
BOOL  AddAccessAllowedAce(
    PACL  pAcl,            // add to this ACL
    DWORD dwRev,           // ACL revision level
    DWORD dwAccess,        // access mask
    PSID  pSid);           // pointer to SID
```

All the parameters here should be pretty obvious — first is the ACL to which we're adding the ACE, along with its revision level (which has to be **ACL_REVISION**). This is followed by the mask specifying the access rights we want to set. Remember that we set **dwAccess** at the beginning of the program, according to the user's choice. The final parameter is the SID to which this ACE applies.

So, we've now got an initialized security descriptor, plus an ACL containing one ACE. We need to attach the ACL to the security descriptor, and that's the job of **SetSecurityDescriptorDacl()**:

```
BOOL  SetSecurityDescriptorDacl(
    PSECURITY_DESCRIPTOR  pSec,   // descriptor to modify
    BOOL  bGotDacl,               // DACL present flag
    PACL  pAcl,                   // ACL to attach
    BOOL  bDef);                  // default flag
```

We attach an ACL to a security descriptor by calling this function. The first of the two flags we pass says whether or not we're intending the ACL argument to be attached as the DACL. If it is false, then the last two arguments will be ignored. The second flag says whether this DACL has come from some default mechanism. In our case, we are supplying the DACL, so the first flag is **TRUE** (use the ACL) and the second is **FALSE** (it isn't default).

We're nearly there — we have a complete security descriptor, which we now need to plug into a security attribute structure for use with `CreateFile()`. We've already seen what this structure looks like, and it is very simple to set the `lpSecurityDescriptor` member of the structure to point to the security descriptor we've just created:

```
SECURITY_ATTRIBUTES satt;
satt.nLength = sizeof(SECURITY_ATTRIBUTES);
satt.bInheritHandle = FALSE;
satt.lpSecurityDescriptor = &desc;
```

The final step is to call `CreateFile()` using our security attribute structure to specify the security attributes of the new file. If you build and run the program, you can create a new file and then examine its security via the Properties entry on the Explorer context menu.

I ran the program specifying 'Guest' as the user, **'test.txt'** as the filename, and **GENERIC_ALL** access. Looking at the properties in NT Explorer, I see the following permissions for the file I created:

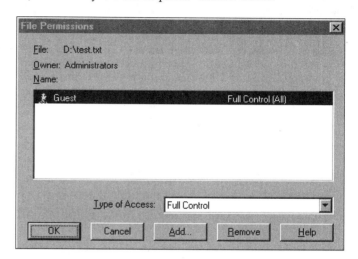

The owner is Administrator, because that is what I was logged in as when I ran the program. As expected, the only access is available to Guest, who has full access. You cannot modify or delete this file unless you're logged in as Guest.

Modifying Security Descriptors

In this chapter so far, we have learned how to read and create security descriptors, so the final task is to find out how to modify existing descriptors, specifically for adding or deleting ACEs. Simply editing an existing entry isn't too difficult, but it isn't so easy if we want to add new entries.

We've seen already the difficulty that we face here. When we retrieve a security descriptor we are given a self-relative descriptor, which has no room for new entries in the DACL or SACL. If we want to add more, we have to get around this problem by creating a new *absolute* security descriptor, and then copy the entries over from the old one to the new one, before we can add any new entries.

The example program in this section adds a new ACE to allow a named user to access a file. Here are the steps we'll need to follow in order to add entries to a descriptor:

▶ Get the existing descriptor as a self-relative security descriptor

▶ Create a new absolute security descriptor and initialize it

▶ Allocate memory for new DACL and initialize it

▶ Copy ACEs from existing DACL to new one

▶ Replace existing security descriptor with new one

Try It Out — Modifying The Security Descriptor

Many of the steps in this process involve things we've already done, so what we'll do is modify an earlier piece of code, the **main()** function of **GetFileSecurityInfo.cpp**, and make additions and alterations where necessary. Here is the first part of the program code, with the new additions and modifications highlighted:

```cpp
// ModifySecurityDescriptor.cpp

#include <windows.h>
#include <iostream>

using namespace std;

int main(int argc, char* argv[])
{
   // make sure we were given a filename
   if (argc == 1)
   {
      cout << "Need a filename" << endl;
      return -1;
   }

   // Open the file
   HANDLE hHand = CreateFile(argv[1],       // filename
      READ_CONTROL | WRITE_DAC,             // enabling read and write access
      0,                                     // no sharing
      NULL,                                  // no security
      OPEN_EXISTING,                         // open mode
      FILE_ATTRIBUTE_NORMAL,
      NULL);

   if (hHand == INVALID_HANDLE_VALUE)
   {
      cout << "Failed to open file" << endl;
      return -1;
   }

   // Get the SID for the user we want to add

   // Get details for the user
   BYTE sidBuff[100];
   PSID pSid = static_cast<PSID>(&sidBuff);
   TCHAR domain[80];
```

```
        SID_NAME_USE sidUse;
        DWORD dwSidSize = sizeof(sidBuff);
        DWORD dwDomSize = sizeof(domain);

        // When running the code yourself, replace 'julian' with a suitable userid
        // existing on your machine
        if (!LookupAccountName(0, "julian", pSid, &dwSidSize, domain,
            &dwDomSize, &sidUse))
        {
            cout << "Error from LookupAccountName ("
                << hex << GetLastError() << dec << ")" << endl;
            return -1;
        }
```

The first part of this code should now be familiar. We start by simply opening a file and getting
its handle. Note the change to the second parameter of **CreateFile()** to allow read/write
access to the new file. The **WRITE_DAC** parameter means that we'll be able to write our new
security descriptor to the file.

In order to give a new user access to the file, we'll have to make up a new ACE and add it to
the DACL. Making up a new ACE requires us to know the SID of the user, so the next step is
to find the SID. We do this using **LookupAccountName()**, which takes a user ID and returns
us its SID.

The second new piece of code is inserted after this section:

```
    // Now call GetKernelObjectSecurity() again to retrieve the info
    if (!GetKernelObjectSecurity(hHand,
                OWNER_SECURITY_INFORMATION |
                GROUP_SECURITY_INFORMATION |
                DACL_SECURITY_INFORMATION,
        pSec, dwSize, &dwSize))
    {
        cout << "Failed to get security info ("
            << hex << GetLastError() << dec << ")" << endl;
        return -1;
    }
```

```
    // Create a new SD and initialize it
    SECURITY_DESCRIPTOR newSD;

    if (!InitializeSecurityDescriptor(&newSD, SECURITY_DESCRIPTOR_REVISION))
    {
        cout << "Failed to initialize new SD" << hex << GetLastError() << endl;
        return -1;
    }

    PACL pac;
    BOOL bDef, bDacl;

    // Get information about the existing DACL and find its current size.
    if (!GetSecurityDescriptorDacl(pSec, &bDacl, &pac, &bDef))
    {
        cout << "Failed to get DACL info" << endl;
        return -1;
    }
```

```
         DWORD dwUsed = 0;
         ACL_SIZE_INFORMATION acSize;

         if (bDacl)
         {

            // Get information about the ACL
            if (!GetAclInformation(pac,        // pointer to DACL
                     &acSize,                  // ACL size info block
                     sizeof(ACL_SIZE_INFORMATION),
                     AclSizeInformation))      // class of information wanted
            {
               cout << "Failed to get ACL information" << hex << GetLastError() << endl;
               return -1;
            }

            dwUsed = acSize.AclBytesInUse;
         }

         // Calculate the new size. This is the existing size plus room for one SID
         DWORD newSize = dwUsed + sizeof(ACCESS_ALLOWED_ACE) +
                         GetLengthSid(pSid) - sizeof(DWORD);

         // Allocate memory and initialize the ACL
         BYTE* aclBuff = static_cast<BYTE*>(GlobalAlloc(GPTR, newSize));
         PACL pAcl = reinterpret_cast<PACL>(aclBuff);

         if (!InitializeAcl(pAcl, newSize, ACL_REVISION))
         {
            cout << "Error from InitializeAcl ("
                 << hex << GetLastError() << dec << ")" << endl;
            return -1;
         }

         // Copy any existing entries to the new DACL

         if (bDacl)
         {
            ACCESS_ALLOWED_ACE* pAce;
            for (int i=0; i<acSize.AceCount; i++)
            {
               if (!GetAce(pac, i, reinterpret_cast<LPVOID*>(&pAce)))
               {
                  cout << "Failed to get ACE information" << endl;
                  return false;
               }
               if (!AddAce(pAcl, ACL_REVISION, MAXDWORD, pAce, pAce->Header.AceSize))
               {
                  cout << "Failed to copy ACE" << endl;
                  return false;
               }
            }
         }

         // Add new ACE entry

         if (!AddAccessAllowedAce(pAcl, ACL_REVISION, GENERIC_ALL, pSid))
         {
            cout << "Error from AddAccessAllowedAce ("
```

```
                    << hex << GetLastError() << dec << ")" << endl;
        return -1;
    }


    // Set the ACL into the security descriptor
    if (!SetSecurityDescriptorDacl(&newSD, TRUE, pAcl, FALSE))
    {
        cout << "Error from SetSecurityDescriptorDacl ("
            << hex << GetLastError() << dec << ")" << endl;
        return -1;
    }


    // Replace the security descriptor in the object

    if (!SetKernelObjectSecurity(hHand, DACL_SECURITY_INFORMATION, &newSD))
    {
        cout << "Error from SetKernelObjectSecurity ("
            << hex << GetLastError() << dec << ")" << endl;
        return -1;
    }


    // Tidy up

    // Free global memory
    if (GlobalFree(pSec))
    {
        cout << "Failed to free memory for security info" << endl;
        return -1;
    }

    // Close the file handle
    CloseHandle(hHand);

    return 0;
}
```

Once we have the SID, we then need to get the existing security information for the file we have opened so that we can modify it, and this is done using `GetKernelObjectSecurity()` as we did in the earlier example. The security information will be returned to us as a self-relative security descriptor, which we cannot modify, so the next step is to create a new absolute security descriptor, into which we'll copy the existing information. We create a new **SECURITY_DESCRIPTOR** object, and initialize it with a call to `InitializeSecurityDescriptor()`.

In order to allocate the memory for the DACL, we need to find the size of the DACL in the old security descriptor. We first obtain a pointer to the DACL by calling the function `GetSecurityDescriptorDacl()`. If there is a DACL present in the security descriptor, we can then use this pointer in a call to `GetAclInformation()` in order to retrieve the structure containing the DACL size information (`acSize`).

The **AclBytesInUse** member of the `acSize` structure tells us the number of bytes actually used by the DACL to store the ACEs. If the old security descriptor does not contain a DACL, then we simply set the existing size to zero. We can then add the amount needed for one ACE onto the size to give us the total amount of memory we require. Once we have this, we use `GlobalAlloc()` to grab the amount of memory we need, which is then initialized by a call to `InitializeAcl()`.

Now we are in a position to copy over any existing ACEs from the old DACL to the new one, which we do using calls to `GetAce()` and `AddAce()`. In this example we're going to add the new ACE onto the end of the list, so once we have copied over all the existing ACEs, we add our new one using a call to `AddAccessAllowedAce()`. If order was important, however, we could insert an ACE somewhere in the middle of the list. The call to `SetSecurityDescriptorDacl()` puts the new DACL into our new (absolute) security descriptor.

The final step is to replace the security descriptor in the file object, via a call to `SetKernelObjectSecurity()`:

```
BOOL  SetKernelObjectSecurity(
    HANDLE  hObj,                      //  handle  to  object
    SECURITY_INFORMATION  si,          //  type  of  information  to  set
    PSECURITY_DESCRIPTOR  pSec);       //  pointer  to  security  descriptor
```

As with `GetKernelObjectSecurity()`, the second parameter says what type of security information we're setting, and it takes the same values. In this case we're only replacing the DACL, so we use the `DACL_SECURITY_INFORMATION` flag.

Try building and running this program — you can create a file in Notepad to use to test it out. Use Explorer to verify that the permissions have been set as you expect:

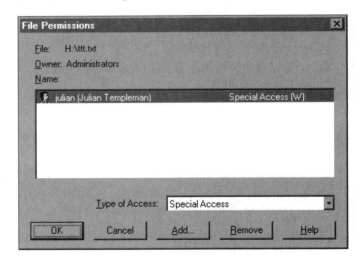

Using Access Tokens

A major part of using the security system involves security descriptors, but there are also occasions when it is useful to be able to work with access tokens.

As we saw back at the start of the chapter, a security descriptor is a 'lock' which protects objects against unauthorised access. The access token is the 'key' which will allow access to objects only if the permissions it contains match those in the object's security descriptor. Anyone who logs onto the system is given an access token, which is copied to all processes started during the log-in session. As a result, every process has the same security settings as the user who initiated it, and as such can only do what the original user allowed it to do.

An access token contains three pieces of information:

- The SID of the originating user
- The SIDs of the groups the user belongs to
- Any special permissions that have been granted to the user

Although you probably won't have as much to do with access tokens as you will with security descriptors, there are some tasks which you may well need to perform on them, such as:

- Finding out the SID of the user who originated a process
- Finding out what groups they belong to
- Finding out what privileges they hold
- Enabling or revoking privileges for a process

We'll see how to do all those things in this section.

All the things we are able to retrieve from an access token are listed in the members of the **TOKEN_INFORMATION_CLASS** enumerated type:

```
typedef enum _TOKEN_INFORMATION_CLASS
{
    TokenUser = 1,
    TokenGroups,
    TokenPrivileges,
    TokenOwner,
    TokenPrimaryGroup,
    TokenDefaultDacl,
    TokenSource,
    TokenType,
    TokenImpersonationLevel,
    TokenStatistics
} TOKEN_INFORMATION_CLASS;
```

In this section, we'll be dealing with three of these:

- **TokenUser** — the user associated with this token
- **TokenGroups** — the list of groups associated with the token
- **TokenOwner** — the default SID that will be applied to new objects

The following section will deal with another:

- **TokenPrivileges**, which represents the privileges associated with this token (and hence the process)

Try It Out — Getting Information From An Access Token

Let's see how access tokens work by writing a little program in which we will dump information from a process's access token. As we go through the code, you'll see that the process is very similar to the one we used when dumping the security descriptor earlier in the chapter.

Here's the main function for the program:

```
// AccessTokens.cpp

#include <windows.h>
#include <iostream>

using namespace std;

bool DoOwner(HANDLE hToken);
bool DoUser(HANDLE hToken);
bool DoGroups(HANDLE hToken);

int main(int argc, char* argv[])
{
    // Make sure we were given a process ID
    if (argc == 1)
    {
        cout << "Need a process ID" << endl;
        return -1;
    }

    DWORD dwProc = atoi(argv[1]);
    cout << "Process ID: 0x" << hex << dwProc << dec << endl;

    HANDLE hHand = OpenProcess(PROCESS_QUERY_INFORMATION, FALSE, dwProc);
    if (hHand == NULL)
    {
        cout << "Failed to open process" << endl;
        return -1;
    }

    // Get the access token for the process
    HANDLE hToken;
    if (!OpenProcessToken(hHand, TOKEN_QUERY, &hToken))
    {
        cout << "Failed to get access token ("
            << hex << GetLastError() << dec << ")" << endl;
        CloseHandle(hHand);
        return -1;
    }

    // Close process handle, because we have what we want
    CloseHandle(hHand);

    // Print owner data
    if (!DoOwner(hToken))
        return -1;
```

```
      // Print user data
   if (!DoUser(hToken))
      return -1;

      // Print group data
   if (!DoGroups(hToken))
      return -1;

      // Close access token handle
   CloseHandle(hToken);

   return 0;
}
```

Much of this is similar to the code examples we have already seen, so there is little to comment on here. We start by getting a process ID from the command line and using `OpenProcess()` to get a handle for the process specified by the user. We can then pass this handle to the function, `OpenProcessToken()`, which gives us a pointer to the access token for the process:

```
BOOL  OpenProcessToken(
      HANDLE  hProcess,             //  process  handle
      DWORD   dwAccess,             //  desired  access
      PHANDLE pToken);              //  pointer  to  token  handle
```

Given a handle to a process, the function returns us a pointer to the process's access token, provided we have the access to do what we want. The desired access is compared with the token's DACL to determine whether access is allowed or not. The following access rights are defined for tokens:

Value	Meaning
TOKEN_ADJUST_DEFAULT	Change the default ACL, primary group or owner
TOKEN_ADJUST_GROUPS	Change the groups associated with a token
TOKEN_ADJUST_PRIVILEGES	Change the privileges associated with a token
TOKEN_ALL_ACCESS	Combines **STANDARD_RIGHTS_REQUIRED** access and all the individual rights for a token
TOKEN_ASSIGN_PRIMARY	Attach a primary token to a process (also needs **SE_CREATE_TOKEN_NAME** privilege)
TOKEN_DUPLICATE	Duplicate a token
TOKEN_EXECUTE	Combines **STANDARD_RIGHTS_EXECUTE** access and **TOKEN_IMPERSONATE**
TOKEN_IMPERSONATE	Attach an impersonation access token to a process
TOKEN_QUERY	Query the contents of a token
TOKEN_QUERY_SOURCE	Query the source of a token
TOKEN_READ	Combines **STANDARD_RIGHTS_READ** access and **TOKEN_QUERY**
TOKEN_WRITE	Combines **STANDARD_RIGHTS_WRITE** access and the three **TOKEN_ADJUST** privileges

Since all we want to do is get at the contents of the token, we call the `OpenProcessToken()` function with the value `TOKEN_QUERY`. Once we have the pointer to the token, we can then use it to retrieve the token contents via three functions:

- `DoOwner()`
- `DoUser()`
- `DoGroups()`

Extracting Owner Information

The `DoOwner()` function gets information about the owner of the token:

```cpp
bool DoOwner(HANDLE hToken)
{
   // Get the token information
   DWORD dwSize;

   // Call function once to get the size, and ignore spurious error
   BOOL bOK = GetTokenInformation(hToken, TokenOwner, NULL, 0, &dwSize);
   if (!bOK && GetLastError() != ERROR_INSUFFICIENT_BUFFER)
   {
      cout << "Failed to get token info size("
           << hex << GetLastError() << dec << ")" << endl;
      CloseHandle(hToken);
      return false;
   }

   // Allocate the memory
   TOKEN_OWNER* pData = static_cast<TOKEN_OWNER*>(GlobalAlloc(GPTR, dwSize));
   if (!pData)
   {
      cout << "Failed to get token info memory ("
           << hex << GetLastError() << dec << ")" << endl;
      CloseHandle(hToken);
      return false;
   }

   // Get the information
   if (!GetTokenInformation(hToken, TokenOwner, static_cast<VOID*>(pData),
       dwSize, &dwSize))
   {
      cout << "Failed to get token info ("
           << hex << GetLastError() << dec << ")" << endl;
     CloseHandle(hToken);
     return false;
   }

   // Get owner info from the SID
   TCHAR owner[80], domain[80];
   DWORD dwOwnerSize = 80;
   DWORD dwDomainSize = 80;
   SID_NAME_USE stype;
```

```
        if (!LookupAccountSid(NULL,         // this machine
                      pData->Owner,         // SID to look up
                      owner,                // string to hold owner
                      &dwOwnerSize,         // size of owner string
                      domain,               // string to hold domain
                      &dwDomainSize,        // size of domain string
                      &stype))              // SID type (user, group, domain etc)
        {
           cout << "Failed to lookup user SID" << endl;
           return false;
        }

        // Print the owner info
        cout << "Token owner is '" << owner << "' from '" << domain << "'" << endl;

        // Free memory
        GlobalFree(pData);
        return true;
    }
```

The API function `GetTokenInformation()` gets various items of information from within a token.

```
BOOL  GetTokenInformation(
      HANDLE  hToken,                     // handle of access token
      TOKEN_INFORMATION_CLASS  ti,        // type of information to retrieve
      LPVOID  pInfo,                      // address of retrieved information
      DWORD  dwSize,                      // size of buffer for information
      PDWORD  pdwLength                   // required buffer size
);
```

The first argument is the handle to the access token we want to interrogate, and the second says what we want to retrieve. We can use one of the ten possible values:

- `TokenUser`, to find out about the user associated with this token
- `TokenGroups`, to find out about the groups associated with this token
- `TokenPrivileges`, to find out about the set of privileges for this token
- `TokenOwner`, to find out about the token's owner
- `TokenPrimaryGroup`, to find the primary group SID for a token
- `TokenDefaultDacl`, to retrieve the default DACL for this token
- `TokenSource`, to find the source of the access token, such as Session Manager, LAN Manager or RPC Server
- `TokenType`, to find out whether this token is being used in impersonation
- `TokenImpersonationLevel`, to find out about current impersonation settings
- `TokenStatistics`, to retrieve statistics about the token

Each of these items will return its information in a different type of structure, so that TokenUser returns a **TOKEN_USER** structure, TokenStatistics a **TOKEN_STATISTICS** structure and so on. When we use the function, we need to create a structure of the appropriate type before calling.

We need to use it in the same way we did **GetKernelObjectSecurity()**, by calling it a first time to see how much space we need, allocating the necessary space, and then calling it a second time to get the information.

In this first function, we specify **TokenOwner**, which fills in a **TOKEN_OWNER** structure giving us the SID which owns this token:

```
typedef struct _TOKEN_OWNER
{
    PSID Owner;
} TOKEN_OWNER;
```

Remember that the 'owner' SID is the one which will become the owner of any objects created by this process. Once we've got this SID, we can use **LookupAccountSid()** as we've done before, to find the user and domain names associated with the SID.

Extracting the User Information

The **DoUser()** function gets us information on the SID who is currently using the token:

```
bool DoUser(HANDLE hToken)
{
    // Get the token information
    DWORD dwSize;

    // Call function once to get the size, and ignore spurious error
    BOOL bOK = GetTokenInformation(hToken, TokenUser, NULL, 0, &dwSize);
    if (!bOK && GetLastError() != ERROR_INSUFFICIENT_BUFFER)
    {
        cout << "Failed to get token info size("
            << hex << GetLastError() << dec << ")" << endl;
        CloseHandle(hToken);
        return false;
    }

    // Allocate the memory
    TOKEN_USER* pData = static_cast<TOKEN_USER*>(GlobalAlloc(GPTR, dwSize));
    if (!pData)
    {
        cout << "Failed to get token info memory ("
            << hex << GetLastError() << dec << ")" << endl;
        CloseHandle(hToken);
        return false;
    }

    // Get the information
    if (!GetTokenInformation(hToken, TokenUser, static_cast<VOID*>(pData),
        dwSize, &dwSize))
    {
        cout << "Failed to get token info ("
            << hex << GetLastError() << dec << ")" << endl;
        CloseHandle(hToken);
        return false;
    }
```

```
                // Get owner info from the SID
                TCHAR user[80], domain[80];
                DWORD dwUserSize = 80;
                DWORD dwDomainSize = 80;
                SID_NAME_USE stype;

                if (!LookupAccountSid(NULL,        // this machine
                             pData->User.Sid,   // SID to look up
                             user,              // string to hold user
                             &dwUserSize,       // size of user string
                             domain,            // string to hold domain
                             &dwDomainSize,     // size of domain string
                             &stype))           // SID type (user, group, domain etc)
                {
                   cout << "Failed to lookup user SID" << endl;
                   return false;
                }

                // Print the owner info
                cout << "Token user is '" << user << "' from '" << domain << "'" << endl;

                // Free memory
                GlobalFree(pData);
                return true;
            }
```

This time we specify `TokenUser` as the type of information we want, and we get a `TOKEN_USER` structure filled in for us:

```
typedef struct _TOKEN_USER
{
   SID_AND_ATTRIBUTES User;
} TOKEN_USER;
```

This is, in turn, a wrapper for a `SID_AND_ATTRIBUTES` structure:

```
typedef struct _SID_AND_ATTRIBUTES
{
   PSID Sid;
   DWORD Attributes;
} SID_AND_ATTRIBUTES ;
```

We can use this structure to retrieve the user's SID, and then call the function, `LookupAccountSid()` to get the name and domain. Note that there aren't any attributes associated with a user at present, so we just use the SID.

Extracting Group Information

The final function, `DoGroups()`, gets information about the groups represented by this token:

```
bool DoGroups(HANDLE hToken)
{
   // Get the token information
   DWORD dwSize;
```

```cpp
// Call function once to get the size, and ignore spurious error
BOOL bOK = GetTokenInformation(hToken, TokenGroups, NULL, 0, &dwSize);
if (!bOK && GetLastError() != ERROR_INSUFFICIENT_BUFFER)
{
   cout << "Failed to get token info size("
       << hex << GetLastError() << dec << ")" << endl;
   CloseHandle(hToken);
   return false;
}

// Allocate the memory
TOKEN_GROUPS* pData = static_cast<TOKEN_GROUPS*>(GlobalAlloc(GPTR, dwSize));
if (!pData)
{
   cout << "Failed to get token info memory ("
       << hex << GetLastError() << dec << ")" << endl;
   CloseHandle(hToken);
   return false;
}

// Get the information
if (!GetTokenInformation(hToken, TokenGroups, static_cast<VOID*>(pData),
     dwSize, &dwSize))
{
   cout << "Failed to get token info ("
       << hex << GetLastError() << dec << ")" << endl;
   CloseHandle(hToken);
   return false;
}

// Get the information for each group
for (int i=0; i< pData->GroupCount; i++)
{
   // Get group info from the SID
   TCHAR group[80], domain[80];
   DWORD dwGroupSize = 80;
   DWORD dwDomainSize = 80;
   SID_NAME_USE stype;

   if (!LookupAccountSid(NULL,            // this machine
                pData->Groups[i].Sid, // SID to look up
                group,                 // string to hold group
                &dwGroupSize,          // size of group string
                domain,                // string to hold domain
                &dwDomainSize,         // size of domain string
                &stype))               // SID type (user, group, domain etc)
   {
      // If we can't get the group name, use a default
      strcpy(group, "???");
   }

   // Print the group info
   cout << "Group '" << group << "' from '" << domain << "', attributes 0x"
       << hex << pData->Groups[i].Attributes << dec << endl;
}
```

```
    // Free memory
    GlobalFree(pData);

    return true;
}
```

In this third function, we specify `TokenGroups` in the call to `GetTokenInformation()`, which fills in a `TOKEN_GROUPS` structure:

```
typedef struct _TOKEN_GROUPS
{
    DWORD GroupCount;
    SID_AND_ATTRIBUTES Groups[ANYSIZE_ARRAY];
} TOKEN_GROUPS;
```

The structure contains a group count, and an array of SIDs and attributes for the groups.

Unlike the user, groups can have the following attributes:

▶ **SE_GROUP_MANDATORY** — this group cannot be disabled

▶ **SE_GROUP_ENABLED_BY_DEFAULT** — this group is enabled by default

▶ **SE_GROUP_ENABLED** — this group is currently enabled

▶ **SE_GROUP_OWNER** — the user is the owner of the group, or the SID can be assigned as the owner

▶ **SE_GROUP_LOGON_ID** — the group is a logon identifier

We use the count to step through the list of groups, retrieving and printing the SID for each group.

As before, you can get a process ID from the Task Manager. Running the program on a suitable process (in this case it was Explorer) gives this output:

Using Privileges

NT security includes privileges, which operate over and above the access rights that users and objects have, and which are granted to users by the system administrator. We're now used to the idea that NT objects hold their security information in security descriptors, but there are two particular categories of security information which cannot be held there.

The first category comprises those operations which do not relate to objects, and so cannot be held in object security descriptors. This category includes things like the ability to set the system time and shut the machine down.

The second category comprises operations which apply to all objects, such as the ability to backup files. It would be inefficient to store this information with every file, so instead it is stored in the access tokens of those users who have the privilege. This implies that privileges can override existing security settings in security descriptors, since someone with backup privilege can make backup copies of files to which they have no access. For this reason, privileges should be used sparingly.

The table below shows the possible privilege settings, along with their meanings and their 'display names', which are strings used to refer to them in system calls. Some are rather esoteric, and we're not going to try to explain all of them.

Privilege	Display Name	Meaning
SE_ASSIGNPRIMARYTOKEN_NAME	SeAssignPrimaryTokenPrivilege	Can assign a process's primary token
SE_AUDIT_NAME	SeAuditPrivilege	Can create audit entries in the log
SE_BACKUP_NAME	SeBackupPrivilege	Can do backups
SE_CHANGE_NOTIFY_NAME	SeChangeNotifyPrivilege	Can receive file and directory change notifications (all user get this by default)
SE_CREATE_PAGEFILE_NAME	SeCreatePagefilePrivilege	Can create a pagefile
SE_CREATE_PERMANENT_NAME	SeCreatePermanentPrivilege	Can create a permanent object
SE_CREATE_TOKEN_NAME	SeCreateTokenPrivilege	Can create a primary token
SE_DEBUG_NAME	SeDebugPrivilege	Can debug processes
SE_INC_BASE_PRIORITY_NAME	SeIncreaseBasePriorityPrivilege	Can change process priority
SE_INCREASE_QUOTA_NAME	SeIncreaseQuotaPrivilege	Can change process quotas
SE_LOAD_DRIVER_NAME	SeLoadDriverPrivilege	Can load and unload device drivers

Privilege	Display Name	Meaning
SE_LOCK_MEMORY_NAME	SeLockMemoryPrivilege	Can lock memory pages
SE_PROF_SINGLE_PROCESS_NAME	SeProfileSingleProcessPrivilege	Can get profiling data for a process
SE_REMOTE_SHUTDOWN_NAME	SeRemoteShutdownPrivilege	Can shutdown a remote machine
SE_RESTORE_NAME	SeRestorePrivilege	Can restore data
SE_SECURITY_NAME	SeSecurityPrivilege	Can view security logs etc.
SE_SHUTDOWN_NAME	SeShutdownPrivilege	Can shutdown the local machine
SE_SYSTEM_ENVIRONMENT_NAME	SeSystemEnvironmentPrivilege	Can modify system configurations
SE_SYSTEM_PROFILE_NAME	SeSystemProfilePrivilege	Can profile the entire system
SE_SYSTEMTIME_NAME	SeSystemtimePrivilege	Can change the system time
SE_TAKE_OWNERSHIP_NAME	SeTakeOwnershipPrivilege	Can take ownership of an object
SE_TCB_NAME	SeTcbPrivilege	Makes user part of the 'trusted computer base'
SE_UNSOLICITED_INPUT_NAME	SeUnsolicitedInputPrivilege	Can read unsolicited input from a terminal

Try It Out — Enumerating Privileges

Let's find out more about access privileges by extending the previous example. We'll add a `DoPrivileges()` function, which will list the privileges associated with an access token, in much the same way as we found the user and group information:

```
bool DoPrivileges(HANDLE hToken)
{
    // Get the token information
    DWORD dwSize;

    // Call function once to get the size, and ignore spurious error
    BOOL bOK = GetTokenInformation(hToken, TokenPrivileges, NULL, 0, &dwSize);
    if (!bOK && GetLastError() != 0x7a)
    {
        cout << "Failed to get token info size("
            << hex << GetLastError() << dec << ")" << endl;
        CloseHandle(hToken);
        return false;
    }
```

```
   // Allocate the memory
   TOKEN_PRIVILEGES* pData = static_cast<TOKEN_PRIVILEGES*>(GlobalAlloc(GPTR,
dwSize));
   if (!pData)
   {
      cout << "Failed to get token info memory ("
          << hex << GetLastError() << dec << ")" << endl;
      CloseHandle(hToken);
      return false;
   }

   // Get the information
   if (!GetTokenInformation(hToken, TokenPrivileges, static_cast<VOID*>(pData),
       dwSize, &dwSize))
   {
      cout << "Failed to get token info ("
          << hex << GetLastError() << dec << ")" << endl;
      CloseHandle(hToken);
      return false;
   }

   // Get the information for each privilege
   for (int i=0; i< pData->PrivilegeCount; i++)
   {
      // Get owner info from the SID
      TCHAR name[80], displayName[80];
      DWORD dwNameSize = 80;
      DWORD dwDisplayNameSize = 80;

      if (!LookupPrivilegeName(NULL,                     // this machine
                  &(pData->Privileges[i].Luid), // privilege ID to look up
                  name,                          // string to hold name
                  &dwNameSize))                  // size of name string
      {
         cout << "Failed to lookup privilege name" << endl;
         return false;
      }

      DWORD langID;
      if (!LookupPrivilegeDisplayName(NULL,    // this machine
                  name,                        // privilege name to look up
                  displayName,                 // string to hold name
                  &dwDisplayNameSize,          // size of name string
                  &langID))                    // language ID
      {
         cout << "Failed to lookup display name" << endl;
         return false;
      }

      // Print the privileges info
      cout << "Privilege '" << name << "' (" << displayName << "), attributes 0x"
          << hex << pData->Privileges[i].Attributes << dec << endl;
   }

   // Free memory
   GlobalFree(pData);

   return true;
}
```

As with the previous functions, we call `GetTokenInformation()` twice, this time passing a `TOKEN_PRIVILEGES` structure over to be filled in:

```
typedef struct _TOKEN_PRIVILEGES
{
    DWORD PrivilegeCount;
    LUID_AND_ATTRIBUTES Privileges[ANYSIZE_ARRAY];
} TOKEN_PRIVILEGES;
```

This structure is similar to the one we used when accessing the groups associated with a token, but this structure contains a `LUID_AND_ATTRIBUTES` entry rather than a `SID_AND_ATTRIBUTES` entry.

A LUID is a large (64-bit) integer which identifies a particular privilege. It is only guaranteed to be unique on the system on which it was generated, and even then, it is only unique until the system is restarted.

> *Anyone who knows anything about COM might find a bell ringing at this point, and you'd be right — a LUID is a Locally Unique ID and is the complement to a GUID.*

The attributes defined for privileges are:

- `SE_PRIVILEGE_ENABLED_BY_DEFAULT`
- `SE_PRIVILEGE_ENABLED`
- `SE_PRIVILEGE_USED_FOR_ACCESS`

The last one of these means that this privilege is used to access an object or service, and can be used to point out the significant privileges in a set which may contain other, irrelevant ones.

The LUID does not mean much to us on its own, but we can use them to find the name of the privilege which is identified by that value, using `LookupPrivilegeName()`:

```
BOOL  LookupPrivilegeName(
      LPCTSTR  pSystem,         // system on which to find name
      PLUID    pLuid,           // LUID to look up
      LPTSTR   pName,           // string to hold name
      LPDWORD  pSize);          // size of name buffer
```

If the system name is `NULL`, then the local machine is assumed. We pass a LUID, and the address and size of a buffer which will hold the result. The size parameter holds the number of characters written, or the size of the buffer which is needed, if the one given is too small.

If you know the name, you can retrieve the LUID using the `LookupPrivilegeValue()` function:

```
BOOL  LookupPrivilegeValue(
      LPCTSTR  pSystem,         // system on which to find name
      LPCTSTR  pName,           // name to look up
      PLUID    pLuid);          // LUID corresponding to name
```

As well as a name, a privilege has a more user-friendly 'display name', which can be retrieved using `LookupPrivilegeDisplayName()`:

```
BOOL  LookupPrivilegeDisplayName(
    LPCTSTR  pSystem,       //  system  on  which  to  find  name
    LPCTSTR  pName,         //  name  to  look  up
    LPTSTR   pDisplay,      //  string  to  hold  display  name
    LPDWORD  pSize,         //  size  of  display  name  buffer
    LPDWORD  pLang);        //  language  ID  for  display  name
```

Given a privilege name, the function returns the display name, together with a language ID which identifies which language the display name is in.

The final task in our `DoPrivileges()` function is to print out the name, display name and attributes information for the various privileges.

Running The Code

If you want to run this code, you'll need to extend the code in `main()` from the previous example, **AccessTokens.cpp**, to call the `DoPrivileges()` function:

```
// Print owner data
if (!DoOwner(hToken))
    return -1;

// Print user data
if (!DoUser(hToken))
    return -1;

// Print group data
if (!DoGroups(hToken))
    return -1;

// Print privilege data
if (!DoPrivileges(hToken))
    return -1;

// Close access token handle
CloseHandle(hToken);

    return 0;
}
```

Obviously, you'll also need to declare the function at the start of your code too:

```
bool DoOwner(HANDLE hToken);
bool DoUser(HANDLE hToken);
bool DoGroups(HANDLE hToken);
bool DoPrivileges(HANDLE hToken);
```

Running the program gives the following output:

```
"C:\TEMP\test\Debug\test.exe" 265
Process ID: 0x109
Token owner is 'adriany' from 'WROX_UK'
Token user is 'adriany' from 'WROX_UK'
Group 'Domain Users' from 'WROX_UK', attributes 0x7
Group 'Everyone' from '', attributes 0x7
Group 'Users' from 'BUILTIN', attributes 0x7
Group '???' from 'BUILTIN', attributes 0xc0000007
Group 'LOCAL' from '', attributes 0x7
Group 'INTERACTIVE' from 'NT AUTHORITY', attributes 0x7
Group 'Authenticated Users' from 'NT AUTHORITY', attributes 0x7
Privilege 'SeChangeNotifyPrivilege' (Bypass traverse checking), attributes 0x3
Privilege 'SeShutdownPrivilege' (Shut down the system), attributes 0x0
Press any key to continue_
```

Checking Privileges

If you're a server process, how do you check whether a given client has the right privileges to access you? If you can get hold of the client's access token, you can use the `PrivilegeCheck()` function to do it:

```
BOOL  PrivilegeCheck(
    HANDLE  hToken,            //  token  to  be  checked
    PPRIVILEGE_SET  pSet,      //  set  of  privileges
    LPBOOL  bResult);          //  result  of  check
```

You pass the function an access token and a set of privileges presented as a `PRIVILEGE_SET` structure:

```
typedef struct _PRIVILEGE_SET
{
    DWORD PrivilegeCount;
    DWORD Control;
    LUID_AND_ATTRIBUTES Privilege[ANYSIZE_ARRAY];
} PRIVILEGE_SET;
```

The structure contains a count of the number of privileges included in the set, a control `DWORD`, and a set of `LUID_AND_ATTRIBUTES` values. The `PrivilegeCheck()` function checks the privileges in the access token against the set provided in the above structure, and returns `TRUE` or `FALSE` depending on whether or not they match.

The `Control` flag is used when a `PRIVILEGE_SET` is used to control how the privileges are matched. It currently only has one value defined. If it is set to `PRIVILEGE_SET_ALL_NECESSARY`, then all the privileges in the set must be held in the client's access token if the check is to pass. If it isn't specified, then the presence of any of the privileges in the set is sufficient.

387

Setting And Revoking Privileges

We can use a process's access token to modify the privileges held by the process, using the `AdjustTokenPrivileges()` function. Since this is something we quite often want to do, it is useful to provide a utility function which handles it for us:

```
BOOL AdjustPrivilege(LPTSTR pPriv, BOOL bSet){    HANDLE token;
if(!OpenProcessToken(GetCurrentProcess(),       TOKEN_ADJUST_PRIVILEGES |
TOKEN_QUERY, &token))
    {
        cout << "Error in SetPrivilege (" << GetLastError() << ")" << endl;
        return FALSE;
    }

    LUID lu;
    if(!LookupPrivilegeValue(0, pPriv, &lu))
    {
        cout << "Error in LookupPrivilegeValue (" << GetLastError() << ")" << endl;
        return FALSE;
    }

    TOKEN_PRIVILEGES tp;
    tp.PrivilegeCount = 1;
    tp.Privileges[0].Luid = lu;

    // Set or revoke privilege depending on flag
    tp.Privileges[0].Attributes = (bSet) ? SE_PRIVILEGE_ENABLED : 0;

    if(!AdjustTokenPrivileges(token, FALSE, &tp, 0, 0, 0))
    {
        cout << "Cannot adjust token privilege (" << GetLastError() << ")" << endl;
        return FALSE;
    }

    return TRUE;
}
```

You might remember that we needed this function in a couple of examples back in Chapters 3 and 5.

The parameters of the `AdjustPrivilege()` function shown above are a privilege name and a Boolean flag, which indicates whether the privilege is to be set (**TRUE**) or revoked (**FALSE**). We assume that the function is to operate on the current process, although it would be easy to modify it to work on a supplied process handle.

The access token for the current process is obtained with **TOKEN_QUERY** and **TOKEN_ADJUST_PRIVILEGES** rights, which will enable us to modify the privileges. We then find the LUID for the named privilege using `LookupPrivilegeValue()`. Once we have that, we build a **TOKEN_PRIVILEGES** structure holding the LUID and the appropriate attribute, which will be **SE_PRIVILEGE_ENABLED** if we're enabling the privilege and 0 otherwise.

The new privilege is set into the token using **AdjustTokenPrivileges()**:

```
BOOL AdjustTokenPrivileges(
    HANDLE hToken,                  // access token
    BOOL bDisableAll,               // quick way to disable all privileges
    PTOKEN_PRIVILEGES pNew,         // pointer to new privilege info
    DWORD dwSize,                   // size of old info buffer
    PTOKEN_PRIVILEGES pOld,         // old info buffer
    PDWORD pOldSize);               // actual size of old info returned
```

We specify a token handle and a pointer to a new **TOKEN_PRIVILEGES** structure. If you are interested, you can pass a pointer to another **TOKEN_PRIVILEGES** structure which will be used to return you the previous privilege settings. The **bDisableAll** flag is provided as a quick way to disable all privileges.

In the chapter on System Information we saw the function being used like this:

```
int main()
{
  // Get the right privilege
  if (!AdjustPrivilege(SE_SHUTDOWN_NAME, TRUE))
  {
    cout << "Couldn't set shutdown privilege (" << GetLastError() << ")" << endl;
    exit(1);
  }

  // Shutdown this machine, with a 30 second gap. Don't force apps
  // to quit or reboot
  if (InitiateSystemShutdown(0, "Shutdown started...", 30, FALSE, FALSE))
  {
    // We're going down...
    cout << "System shutting down" << endl;
  }
  else
  {
    // There was an error
    cout << "InitiateSystemShutdown failed, code " << GetLastError() << endl;
    exit(1);
  }

  AdjustPrivilege(SE_SHUTDOWN_NAME, FALSE);

  return 0;
}
```

Summary

This chapter has really only touched on the basics of using the NT security system which I'm sure you'll agree by now is rather complex, and rich in new concepts and jargon.

To summarize what we have learnt, users and groups have SIDs which identify them to the system. When you log on you're given an access token which describes your SID, those of the groups to which you belong, and your privileges. This access token is inherited by every process which you start. Most NT objects are 'securable', meaning that they have a security descriptor which governs who can access them. When a process tries to access an object, its access token is checked against the object's security descriptor, and if the desired access matches the rights and privileges that the process has in the objects security descriptor, access is granted.

Windows NT Services

We are now going to investigate an extremely useful type of application provided for us by Windows NT — the **NT Service**.

In this chapter we'll see:

- What NT services are, and what they are used for
- How services work
- How to create services
- How to install and remove services
- What the NT Event Logging service is
- How to use the Event Logging service

Though a subset of the service Win32 API operates under Windows 95/98, its capacity to run service applications is very limited. Therefore this chapter applies primarily to Windows NT.

What Is A Service?

Rather confusingly, the term 'service' is used to denote two different things in Windows NT. The term 'NT Services' refers to special types of *NT processes*, but it is also used to refer to *kernel-mode device drivers*. Both these types of service are loaded and controlled by an NT system application called the **Service Control Manager** (commonly abbreviated to **SCM**).

*You may have come across the term 'Service Control Manager' before — in the context of DCOM. Although the name is the same, the two concepts are not — DCOM's SCM does a completely different job from NT's. Needless to say, we're talking **exclusively** about the NT SCM.*

We will only concern ourselves with the first type of service — the NT processes — which is the one most commonly encountered by NT programmers. In a nutshell, this type of service is a Win32 process that is run by NT itself — as opposed to being executed by a user. Thus, it can run unattended, and is very similar in concept to a Unix *daemon*.

Just about any process that needs to be implemented as a background process, running independently of the logged-in user, is a good candidate for a service. Examples of such processes include:

- Virus checking software
- RPC servers
- Automatic backup programs
- Fax software
- Email systems

NT's Use Of Services

NT itself uses services extensively. When you install a basic NT system there are over a dozen services available and if you install other optional system components, such as those used in networking, then you'll get other additional service.

One service of note is the **Event Log** service, which is used to log system events — such as drivers that didn't load, or processes that couldn't start for some reason. The event log can be viewed using the Event Viewer application, which you'll find in the Administrative Tools program group (choose Start|Programs|Administrative Tools|Event Viewer). We'll be looking at this service in more detail later on.

A Windows NT installation will come with a range of services installed as standard. Precisely what you have on your machine will depend on the installation options. My NT Workstation machine has 19 services installed, including:

- Event Log, for logging system messages to a central place
- Net Logon, for handling network logins
- Plug and Play, for supporting PnP devices
- Spooler, for print spooling
- Scheduler, for scheduling automatic execution of tasks
- Telephony Service, for providing external telephone services
- UPS, for handling an Uninterruptible Power Supply, if you have one fitted

You can get access to the services that are running on your machine, via the Services Control Panel application, as shown below:

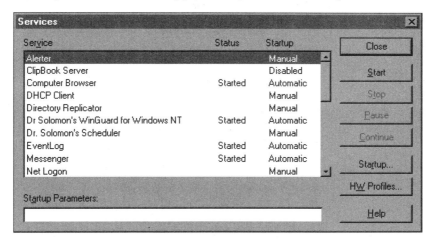

When you start up the Control Panel application, you'll see a dialog like this:

The Services dialog shows you a list of the services that are currently installed. In addition, the dialog displays the status of each service, and whether it is started automatically (on boot-up) or manually (on demand).

The buttons down the right hand side of the dialog allow you to control the services using the four standard commands:

▶ Start will start a dormant service, causing it to reinitialize itself

▶ Stop will terminate a running service

▶ Pause will tell the service to pause, but won't terminate it

▶ Continue will tell a paused service to resume execution

A service can be in one of seven states, as shown below:

State	Meaning
`SERVICE_STOPPED`	The service has stopped
`SERVICE_START_PENDING`	The service is in the process of starting
`SERVICE_RUNNING`	The service is running
`SERVICE_PAUSED_PENDING`	The service is in the process of pausing
`SERVICE_PAUSED`	The service is paused
`SERVICE_CONTINUE_PENDING`	The service is in the process of restarting
`SERVICE_STOP_PENDING`	The service is in the process of stopping

We'll use these states when we write a service later on. Most of the interaction between a service and the SCM (or a program using the service control API) consists of the controlling program telling the service when to change state, and the service notifying the controlling program when it changes state.

Services are controlled by the Service Control Manager (SCM), which maintains a list of installed services in the Registry, under the `HKEY_LOCAL_MACHINE\System\CurrentControlSet\Services` key. Each service has an entry under this key:

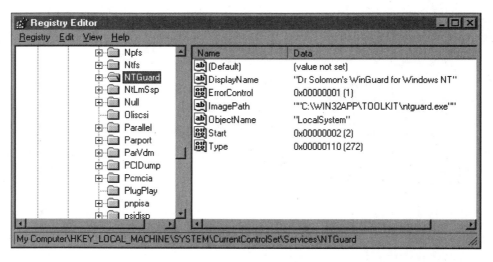

Be very careful if you ever edit the Services key by hand, because it also contains information on hardware devices. If you modify something wrongly in here, your machine may no longer boot!

Each service subkey contains information that controls the operation of that service. The example below shows subkeys and values for the Dr. Solomon's NTGuard service in the registry:

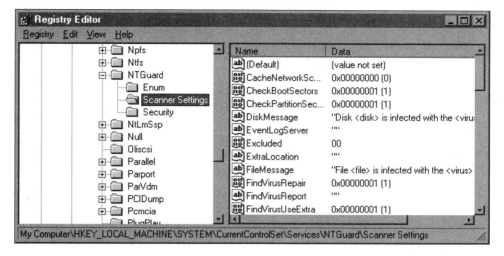

These entries will be created when the service is installed, and while it is possible to install a service by directly writing information to the registry, this isn't to be encouraged. There are service controller API calls available for this purpose, and you should use them because you could be stuck if Microsoft decide to change the way services are registered in a future release of NT.

Advantages Of Services

Services have four properties that make them especially useful:

▶ There are some processes which need to run regardless of who is logged on, and even if no-one is logged on at all. An NT service can be started when the system boots up, and will remain running in the background until the system shuts down or it is stopped manually.

▶ An NT log-in ID gives a user certain privileges that govern exactly what the user can and cannot access on the system. Therefore, each NT service can be given the additional privileges needed to complete its tasks, and can also be used to perform tasks on behalf of less privileged users.

▶ There is a common set of API commands that can be used to start, stop and pause a service. Any service can be controlled either by using the standard Services Control Panel, or by calling these API functions from other applications.

▶ Since this API is implemented in the form of an RPC server, you can control services on other machines, if you have the right privilege level.

Services and GUIs

Most services run as background tasks. Such services do not require any sort of user interface. However, it is possible to create services which present a GUI to the logged-in user.

Non-GUI services can be written as standard console applications, which contain a **main()** function, and that is what we'll be doing for the most part in this chapter. We'll also explain how a service can show a message-box to the logged-in user — this is a simple example of a service interacting with the user. If you want to interact with a service through any sort of complex GUI, then it's often best to write a separate front-end program that communicates with a background service — using a mechanism such as a named pipe.

Creating A Service

You can create services which have user interfaces. However, as we mentioned above, most services run as system processes (and start before any users are logged in) — and therefore take the form of console programs.

Services And The SCM

The structure of a service is built around its interaction with the SCM. The service is controlled by the SCM, and therefore the service code must have hooks that the SCM can call in order to exercise control. We'll get to those shortly. First, consider the diagram below, which shows an executable that contains a single service, and summarizes its interaction with the Service Control Manager (SCM):

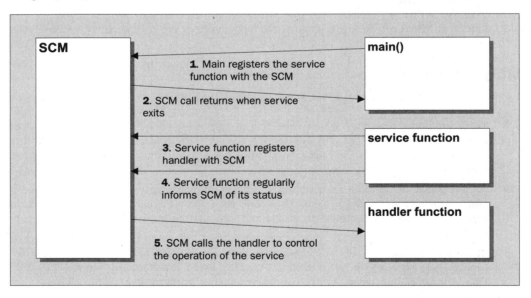

As we've said, services are implemented in executable files, and a single executable can hold one or more services. On startup, the **main()** routine interacts with the SCM, registering the service by passing the addresses of the functions that implement the services. The SCM then uses these addresses to create threads in which the service code runs.

*For simplicity, the example code and discussions in this chapter have only one service per executable. However, if you want to run more than one service at once, you may want to think about implementing them all in a single executable, because the creation of a single process with **one thread per service** is more efficient than creating **one process per service**.*

Now lets look at the process in more detail. When the service executable starts up, it calls `StartServiceCtrlDispatcher()` from its **main()** routine. This call does two things — it tells the SCM that it has started, and passes the addresses of the entry points to the service functions. These service functions are where the actual work of the service is done. Note that `StartServiceCtrlDispatcher()` doesn't return until all the service threads have finished executing. So when this call returns, the executable can terminate.

`StartServiceCtrlDispatcher()` starts a new thread for each service, using the addresses it has been passed as the addresses for the thread functions.

As soon as it starts executing, the service function calls `RegisterServiceCtrlHandler()`, passing the address of a callback function. This is used by the SCM to pass commands (such as stop, pause or continue) to the service. `RegisterServiceCtrlHandler()` returns a handle, which is used in the callback function to tell the SCM that the command has been processed.

From this description, we can see that a service will consist of three main parts:

- A main routine, that calls `StartServiceCtrlDispatcher()`
- A thread function, that calls `RegisterServiceCtrlHandler()` and does the work of the service
- A callback function, that handles commands from the SCM

An Outline Of A Simple Service

Now that we've seen how a service is structured, here is the outline of a very simple service, showing all the essential parts. First, we code a few global variables that are needed by the service code:

```
#include <windows.h>
#include <tchar.h>

SERVICE_STATUS_HANDLE hSrv;
DWORD dwCurrState;
LPCTSTR srvName = _T("ServiceName");
```

The `SERVICE_STATUS_HANDLE` is the handle passed back when the service function registers itself with the SCM, and is used to reply to SCM commands. The current state of the thread is stored in `dwCurrState`, and the name of the service is defined in `srvName`.

The Main Routine

Next we come to the executable's main routine, which is usually pretty simple. There will only be one of these, regardless of how many services the executable contains:

```
// Main function for service executable
int main()
{
   // Build the table of services in this exe
   SERVICE_TABLE_ENTRY stbl[] = {
      {srvName, reinterpret_cast<LPSERVICE_MAIN_FUNCTION>(ServiceMainFn)},
      {NULL, NULL}
   };

   // Call the SCM
   StartServiceCtrlDispatcher(stbl);

   return 0;
}
```

The main function interacts with the SCM, passing an array of **SERVICE_TABLE_ENTRY** structures — one for each service that the executable supports. Each table entry consists of the service's name and the address of its main function, and it is terminated by a **NULL** entry. Once the SCM has been called — through **StartServiceCtrlDispatcher()** — this routine will block until the call completes, when it can then exit.

> *Note that, after the main routine starts, it has only 30 seconds in which to call*
> ***StartServiceCtrlDispatcher()*** *— otherwise the SCM will assume that*
> *something is wrong, and will terminate the process. This means that you shouldn't try to*
> *do too much initialization processing before calling*
> ***StartServiceCtrlDispatcher()***, *just in case you run out of time!*

The Service Main Function

Now for the service's main function. Each service supported by the executable has to have a function of this form, which is started in a separate thread by the SCM:

```
void ServiceMainFn(DWORD dwArgc, LPTSTR* lpszArgv)
{
   // Register our handler routine with the SCM
   hSrv = RegisterServiceCtrlHandler(srvName,
                     reinterpret_cast<LPHANDLER_FUNCTION>(ServiceHandlerFn);
   if (hSrv == 0)
      return;

   // Tell the SCM we're starting
   TellSCM(SERVICE_START_PENDING, 0, 1);

   // Do any initialization that may be needed...

   // Tell the SCM we're ready to go
   TellSCM(SERVICE_RUNNING, 0, 0);
```

```
        // Do what we need to do...

        // And exit when we're done
   }
```

The function can be passed arguments just like a normal main routine. These can come either from the Services Control Panel application, or by using the `StartService()` API call.

First, the function must register the service's callback handler — using the `RegisterServiceCtrlHandler()` function — and store away the handle for future use. If the value returned by `RegisterServiceCtrlHandler()` is zero, then registration hasn't worked, so we should exit.

It is important for a service to keep the SCM informed of what it's doing at all times — at the very least, so that the SCM can regularly update the display in the Control Panel application. When we're initializing, we tell SCM that the start is pending, and when we've finished initializing, we tell it that we've started. Note that we don't have to tell the SCM when we've finished — this is implicit when we exit from the thread function.

Notifying the SCM is done using the `SetServiceStatus()` API call. We could call the `SetServiceStatus()` function directly, every time we want to notify the SCM. However, we can simplify calls to `SetServiceStatus()` by writing a wrapper function. There's further justification for setting up the wrapper function, namely, that a lot of the setting up to call `SetServiceStatus()` is the same each time. In the thread function above, we've employed a wrapper function called `TellSCM()`. We'll see what this looks like in a minute, but first we'll look at the `SetServiceStatus()` function.

Using SetServiceStatus()

Using `SetServiceStatus()` involves setting up a `SERVICE_STATUS` structure and passing it as an argument. This is what the `SERVICE_STATUS` structure looks like:

```
typedef struct _SERVICE_STATUS {
    DWORD   dwServiceType;                  // service type
    DWORD   dwCurrentState;                 // its current state
    DWORD   dwControlsAccepted;             // what commands it will accept
    DWORD   dwWin32ExitCode;                // Win32 exit code
    DWORD   dwServiceSpecificExitCode;      // Service exit code
    DWORD   dwCheckPoint;                   // checkpoint counter
    DWORD   dwWaitHint;                     // wait interval
} SERVICE_STATUS, *LPSERVICE_STATUS;
```

The `dwServiceType` field says what sort of service this is. This parameter can take several values, including:

Service Type	Description
`SERVICE_DRIVER`	If the service is an NT device driver
`SERVICE_WIN32_OWN_PROCESS`	If the service isn't a driver and there is one service in the process
`SERVICE_WIN32_SHARE_PROCESS`	If the service isn't a driver and there is more than one process in the executable

Service Type	Description
SERVICE_INTERACTIVE_PROCESS	The service is allowed to access the Windows desktop and therefore is visible to the user
SERVICE_TYPE_ALL	If you aren't interested in differentiating between service types

As we've already mentioned, non-driver services may have their own process, or may share a process. Unless you have a specific reason to have more than one service sharing a process, you'll normally use the SERVICE_WIN32_OWN_PROCESS type.

The dwCurrentState field tells the SCM what state the service is in, and can take one of the values we tabulated earlier:

- SERVICE_STOPPED
- SERVICE_START_PENDING
- SERVICE_STOP_PENDING
- SERVICE_RUNNING
- SERVICE_CONTINUE_PENDING
- SERVICE_PAUSE_PENDING
- SERVICE_PAUSED

Most of these are self-explanatory. The 'pending' states are used when the service is in transition between one state and another, as shown in the diagram below. When you're using 'pending' states, you should call the SCM often, incrementing the dwCheckPoint field every time you do so. By changing the value of the checkpoint, SCM can tell that the service is making progress in changing state.

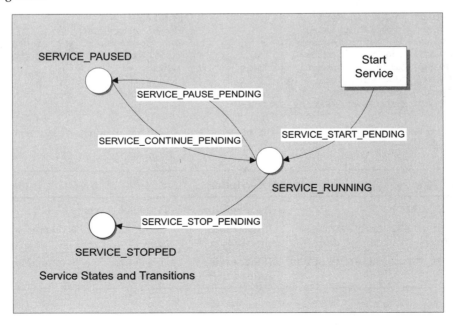

Service States and Transitions

The `dwControlsAccepted` field tells the SCM which of its notifications the service will accept. This can take any of the following values:

- `SERVICE_ACCEPT_STOP`
- `SERVICE_ACCEPT_PAUSE_CONTINUE`
- `SERVICE_ACCEPT_SHUTDOWN`

The `dwWin32ExitCode` and `dwServiceSpecificExitCode` fields set the exit codes for this service. The first is used to specify a Win32 error code, which is returned when the service encounters an error on starting or stopping. It should be set to `NO_ERROR` for normal termination, and while it is running. If you want the service to return an error other than a Win32 error code, you should set `dwWin32ExitCode` to `ERROR_SERVICE_SPECIFIC_ERROR`, and then set the error code in the `dwServiceSpecificExitCode` parameter.

The `dwCheckPoint` field specifies a value that the service increments occasionally when performing a lengthy operation. The SCM can check that this value is changing, and uses this as a way of verifying that the service is still alive.

Finally, `dwWaitHint` gives the SCM an idea of how long it should wait (in milliseconds) before looking for another `SetServiceStatus()` call. If this timeout period elapses without another call, the SCM may assume that the service has died.

Using A Wrapper Function To Implement SetServiceStatus()

Creating and filling out one of these structures every time we need to talk to the SCM is unnecessary work, especially since a lot of the fields don't change between calls. For that reason, I've provided a function, `TellSCM()`, which does most of the work for you. In writing this function I've assumed that only the state, exit code and checkpoint values will change:

```
BOOL TellSCM(DWORD dwState, DWORD dwExitCode, DWORD dwProgress)
{
   // Declare a SERVICE_STATUS structure, and fill it in
   SERVICE_STATUS srvStatus;

   // We're a service running in our own process
   srvStatus.dwServiceType  = SERVICE_WIN32_OWN_PROCESS;

   // Set the state of the service from the argument, and save it away
   // for future use
   srvStatus.dwCurrentState = dwCurrState = dwState;

   // Which commands will we accept from the SCM? All the common ones...
   srvStatus.dwControlsAccepted = SERVICE_ACCEPT_STOP |
                    SERVICE_ACCEPT_PAUSE_CONTINUE |
                    SERVICE_ACCEPT_SHUTDOWN;

   // Set the Win32 exit code for the service
   srvStatus.dwWin32ExitCode = dwExitCode;

   // Set the service-specific exit code
   srvStatus.dwServiceSpecificExitCode = 0;

   // Set the checkpoint value
   srvStatus.dwCheckPoint = dwProgress;
```

```
     // 3 second timeout for waits
     srvStatus.dwWaitHint = 3000;

     // pass the structure to the SCM
     return SetServiceStatus(hSrv, &srvStatus);
  }
```

The `TellSCM()` function takes three parameters. The first is a value showing the current state of the service, and can be one of the values we saw earlier. The second is the exit code that this service wants to use when it exits, and the third is the checkpoint value, for use in pending states. Note that we assume that this function is called each time the state of the service changes, so we use calls to this function to save the current state.

The Handler Function

The third function we need to provide is the notification callback function, which will be called when the state of the service needs changing. These commands may originate from the SCM itself, or from applications (such as the Control Panel **Services** application) which use the service controller API functions.

The function takes a single argument, which is the ID of the command being passed in:

```
   void ServiceHandlerFn(DWORD dwCommand)
   {
     // Switch on the command that has arrived
     switch(dwCommand)
     {
     // Sent to tell us to stop what we're doing
     case SERVICE_CONTROL_STOP:
        // Tell the SCM we're stopping
        TellSCM(SERVICE_STOP_PENDING, 0, 1);

        // Do whatever is needed to stop...

        // And tell the SCM we're stopped
        TellSCM(SERVICE_STOPPED, 0, 0);
        break;

     // Sent to tell us to pause what we're doing, but don't finish completely
     case SERVICE_CONTROL_PAUSE:
        // Tell the SCM we're pausing
        TellSCM(SERVICE_PAUSE_PENDING, 0, 1);

        // Do whatever is needed to pause...

        // And tell the SCM we're paused
        TellSCM(SERVICE_PAUSED, 0, 0);
        break;

     // Sent to tell us to continue from a pause
     case SERVICE_CONTROL_CONTINUE:
        // Tell the SCM we're going to continue
        TellSCM(SERVICE_CONTINUE_PENDING, 0, 1);

        // Do whatever is needed to restart...
```

```
      // And tell the SCM we're going again
      TellSCM(SERVICE_RUNNING, 0, 0);
      break;

   // Sent to ask us to tell the SCM what state we're in
   case SERVICE_CONTROL_INTERROGATE:
      TellSCM(dwCurrState, 0, 0);
      break;

   // Sent when the system is shutting down. According to the documentation, you
   // have about 20 seconds to perform essential shutdown operations
   case SERVICE_CONTROL_SHUTDOWN:
      // Do whatever we need to do before shutdown...
      break;
   }
}
```

As you can see, the entire function simply consists of a **switch** statement, that acts on the incoming command ID. Note that the function uses lots of **TellSCM()** calls, to let the SCM know what we're doing as we do it. This may seem over-fussy, but your service will work a lot better if you keep the SCM well informed of what you are doing.

Try It Out — Building A Simple Service

We've seen how a service is put together, so let's use that to build a simple service in practice. The service we will build is about the simplest possible — it will simply signal its existence by beeping at intervals of a few seconds.

We need an ordinary Win32 application (not a Windows GUI one), so if you're using Visual C++ start by creating a Win32 console application called "Beep1". Add a C++ source file to the project, and add the following code:

```cpp
// Beep1.cpp

#include <windows.h>
#include <tchar.h>

SERVICE_STATUS_HANDLE hSrv;
DWORD dwCurrState;

// The service name
LPTSTR srvName = _T("Beep1");

// Flag to tell us when to stop
bool bStopFlag = false;

// Flag to control whether to beep or not
bool bBeepFlag = true;

// Function prototypes
void ServiceMainFn(DWORD dwArgc, LPTSTR* lpszArgv);
BOOL TellSCM(DWORD dwState, DWORD dwExitCode, DWORD dwProgress);
void ServiceHandlerFn(DWORD dwCommand);
```

Next, add the main routine for the service executable, whose job is to call the SCM immediately the service starts:

```cpp
// Main function for service executable
int main()
{
   // Build the table of services in this exe
   SERVICE_TABLE_ENTRY stbl[] = {
      {srvName, reinterpret_cast<LPSERVICE_MAIN_FUNCTION>(ServiceMainFn)},
      {NULL, NULL}
   };

   // Call the SCM
   StartServiceCtrlDispatcher(stbl);

   return 0;
}
```

Now we need to add the main function for the one service in this executable. We provided a skeleton before, so we now need to fill in the code to perform the processing the service will undertake:

```cpp
void ServiceMainFn(DWORD dwArgc, LPTSTR* lpszArgv)
{
   // Register our handler routine with the SCM
   hSrv = RegisterServiceCtrlHandler(srvName,
                       reinterpret_cast<LPHANDLER_FUNCTION>(ServiceHandlerFn));
   if (hSrv == 0)
      return;

   // Tell the SCM we're starting
   TellSCM(SERVICE_START_PENDING, 0, 1);

   // There's no initialization in this case, so move straight on to run

   // Tell the SCM we're ready to go
   TellSCM(SERVICE_RUNNING, 0, 0);

   // Here's where the work of the service is done... loop, beeping every two
seconds if
   // required, until the stop flag gets set.
   for(;;)
   {
      if (bStopFlag)
         break;

      if (bBeepFlag)
         Beep(500, 500);

      Sleep(2000);
   }
}
```

Once we've started the service, we enter an endless loop, which is only broken when the stop flag is set. Note that the service only beeps if the **bBeepFlag** Boolean is set, which effectively lets us pause and resume the operation of the service. Setting these flags is the job of the handler function, which we'll present shortly. Before that, add the `TellSCM()` utility function to simplify SCM notifications:

```
BOOL TellSCM(DWORD dwState, DWORD dwExitCode, DWORD dwProgress)
{
   // Declare a SERVICE_STATUS structure, and fill it in
   SERVICE_STATUS srvStatus;

   // We're a service running in our own process
   srvStatus.dwServiceType  = SERVICE_WIN32_OWN_PROCESS;

   // Set the state of the service from the argument, and save it away
   // for future use
   srvStatus.dwCurrentState = dwCurrState = dwState;

   // Which commands will we accept from the SCM? All the common ones...
   srvStatus.dwControlsAccepted = SERVICE_ACCEPT_STOP |
                   SERVICE_ACCEPT_PAUSE_CONTINUE |
                   SERVICE_ACCEPT_SHUTDOWN;

   // Set the Win32 exit code for the service
   srvStatus.dwWin32ExitCode = dwExitCode;

   // Set the service-specific exit code
   srvStatus.dwServiceSpecificExitCode = 0;

   // Set the checkpoint value
   srvStatus.dwCheckPoint = dwProgress;

   // 3 second timeout for waits
   srvStatus.dwWaitHint = 3000;

   // pass the structure to the SCM
   return SetServiceStatus(hSrv, &srvStatus);
}
```

The final part of the service is the handler function, which handles commands from the SCM:

```
void ServiceHandlerFn(DWORD dwCommand)
{
   // Switch on the command that has arrived
   switch(dwCommand)
   {
   // Sent to tell us to stop what we're doing
   case SERVICE_CONTROL_STOP:
      // Tell the SCM we're stopping
      TellSCM(SERVICE_STOP_PENDING, 0, 1);

      // Set the stop flag to exit the loop
      bStopFlag = true;

      // And tell the SCM we've stopped
      TellSCM(SERVICE_STOPPED, 0, 0);
      break;

   // Sent to tell us to pause what we're doing, but don't finish completely
   case SERVICE_CONTROL_PAUSE:
```

```
               // Tell the SCM we're pausing
               TellSCM(SERVICE_PAUSE_PENDING, 0, 1);

               // Set the beep flag to false to tell it to stop beeping
               bBeepFlag = false;

               // And tell the SCM we've paused
               TellSCM(SERVICE_PAUSED, 0, 0);
               break;

         // Sent to tell us to continue from a pause
         case SERVICE_CONTROL_CONTINUE:
               // Tell the SCM we're going to continue
               TellSCM(SERVICE_CONTINUE_PENDING, 0, 1);

               // Set the beep flag to true to tell it to resume beeping
               bBeepFlag = true;

               // And tell the SCM we're going again
               TellSCM(SERVICE_RUNNING, 0, 0);
               break;

         // Sent to ask us to tell the SCM what state we're in
         case SERVICE_CONTROL_INTERROGATE:
               TellSCM(dwCurrState, 0, 0);
               break;

         // Sent when the system is shutting down. According to the documentation, you
         // have about 20 seconds to perform essential shutdown operations
         case SERVICE_CONTROL_SHUTDOWN:
               // Do whatever we need to do before shutdown...
               break;
      }
   }
```

We need to use global variables to communicate between the various routines which make up the service. This isn't an ideal solution, and we'll see in a later section how threads give us a much neater implementation.

At this stage you can compile and build the service, but you can't run it. Installing and removing services are quite complex tasks, for which there are no standard tools, so you need to write installation and removal code yourself.

Installing And Removing Services

In the introduction, we explained how the Service Control Manager (SCM) maintains a list of installed services in the Registry, under the
HKEY_LOCAL_MACHINE\System\CurrentControlSet\Services key, and how each service has entries under its own subkey. When we want to install or remove a service, we need to modify those entries in the registry. We could do this by hand, but it is better to use the API functions provided — as we mentioned — thus protecting us from any changes in the registry layout in future versions of NT.

Services, like DLLs, often live in the NT System32 directory, but can be placed anywhere you wish.

Installing a Service

There are two functions which are used to register a service:

▶ `OpenSCManager()` — connects you to the SCM

▶ `CreateService()` — installs the service

Note that, in order to connect to the SCM, you must be logged in as Administrator.

Connecting To The SCM

Let's take a closer look at `OpenSCManager()`:

```
SC_HANDLE  OpenSCManager(
    LPCTSTR  lpMachine,         // machine name
    LPCTSTR  lpDatabase,        // database name
    DWORD  dwAccess);           // access required
```

The machine name parameter, `lpMachine`, gives the name of the machine whose SCM we want to use. If it is `NULL`, or points to an empty string, then the local machine is assumed.

The database parameter, `lpDatabase`, denotes the SCM database which we want to access, and should be set to `SERVICES_ACTIVE_DATABASE` (or `NULL`, in which case `SERVICES_ACTIVE_DATABASE` is assumed). It is possible to maintain different databases of service configuration data, but we will invariably use the default active database.

With the final parameter `dwAccess`, we can specify the access to the database that we need, which then governs which API functions we can call. Although there are several possible values for this parameter, the two most useful are as follows:

Value	Meaning
SC_MANAGER_CREATE_SERVICE	Enables us to use the `CreateService()` function to create a new service and add it to the database
SC_MANAGER_ENUMERATE_SERVICE	Enables us to use `EnumServicesStatus()` to list the services in the database

If the call succeeds, the return value is a handle to an SCM database, which you need to use in future calls. If the call failed, the value returned will be zero and you can use `GetLastError()` to find out more information.

Installing The Service

The function `CreateService()` is used to actually create the service, and enter its details into the database:

```
SC_HANDLE CreateService(
    SC_HANDLE  hSCM,            // handle to service control manager database
    LPCTSTR  lpSrvName,         // name of service to create
    LPCTSTR  lpDspName,         // name by which service will be known to
                                // the user
    DWORD  dwAccess,            // type of access to service
    DWORD  dwSrvType,           // type of service
    DWORD  dwStartType,         // when to start service
    DWORD  dwErrorControl,      // severity if service fails to start
    LPCTSTR  lpBinPathName,     // name of executable file
    LPCTSTR  lpLoadOrderGrp,    // name of load ordering group
    LPDWORD  lpdwTagId,         // pointer to variable to get tag identifier
    LPCTSTR  lpDepends,         // array of dependency names
    LPCTSTR  lpSrvStartName,    // account name of service
    LPCTSTR  lpPassword);       // password for service account
```

This function has a lot of parameters. Luckily, many of them will take default values a lot of the time. Let's have a look at these parameters in a little more detail.

The first parameter `hSCM` is the handle that was returned from our call to `OpenSCManager()`. Next is `lpSrvName`, which is the name of the service. This can be up to 256 characters, and is usually just the name of the `.exe` file (without the extension).

The next parameter is `lpDspName`, the display name, which is also a string of up to 256 characters. This parameter identifies the service to user-oriented tools, such as the Control Panel application.

The `dwAccess` parameter identifies the access rights, that govern what the service will be allowed to do. There are a number of settings possible here, which are detailed in the online help. If you're not interested in limiting the access your service has, you can specify `SERVICE_ALL_ACCESS` for this parameter.

The service type parameter, `dwSrvType`, can take one of five values, which are similar to those used in the `SetServiceStatus()` function:

Value	Meaning
`SERVICE_WIN32_OWN_PROCESS`	Denotes that the service has its own process
`SERVICE_WIN32_SHARE_PROCESS`	Denotes that it shares a process (usually because there is more than one service supported by the `.exe` file)
`SERVICE_KERNEL_DRIVER`	Denotes that the service is a kernel-mode device driver
`SERVICE_FILE_SYSTEM_DRIVER`	Denotes a file-system driver
`SERVICE_INTERACTIVE_PROCESS`	Denotes that the service will interact with the desktop (and is only valid along with the `SERVICE_WIN32_OWN_PROCESS` or `SERVICE_WIN32_SHARE_PROCESS` flags)

The `dwStartType` parameter indicates when the service should be started. There are several possible values, the first two of which are only valid for drivers:

Value	Meaning
SERVICE_BOOT_START	The driver will be loaded at boot up
SERVICE_SYSTEM_START	The driver will be loaded at system start

The other three apply to non-driver services, and are fairly self-explanatory:

Value	Meaning
SERVICE_AUTO_START	Causs the SCM to start the service automatically at system startup
SERVICE_DEMAND_START	Starts the service when the `StartService()` function is called (which will often be from the Services Control Panel application)
SERVICE_DISABLED	Specifies that a service cannot be started

Try It Out — Installing A Service

Here is an example of a service installation program, showing how these functions can be used to install the sample service we just wrote.

```cpp
// SrvInstall.cpp

#include <windows.h>
#include <iostream>
#include <tchar.h>
using namespace std;

int main()
{
   // Prepare to install a service
   SC_HANDLE hSCM = OpenSCManager(NULL, NULL, SC_MANAGER_CREATE_SERVICE);
   if (hSCM == NULL)
   {
      cout << "OpenSCManager failed!" << endl;
      return -1;
   }
   else
      cout << "OpenSCManager OK" << endl;


   // Services usually live in the NT System32 directory, so get the path
   TCHAR winDir[MAX_PATH+1];
   GetSystemDirectory(winDir, MAX_PATH+1);
```

```
    // Make up the full path to the service file, which for our test service is
    // "Beep1"
    // (Note that _stprintf() comes from tchar.h, and will resolve to sprintf() or
    // swprintf() depending on whether it is compiled as ANSI or Unicode)
    TCHAR srvPath[MAX_PATH+1];
    _stprintf (srvPath, _T("%s\\%s.exe"), winDir, _T("Beep1"));

    // Create the service "Beep1", and give it the display name "Test Beeper 1"
    SC_HANDLE hService = CreateService(hSCM,
                    _T("Beep1"),
                    _T("Test Beeper 1"),
                    SERVICE_ALL_ACCESS,
                    SERVICE_WIN32_OWN_PROCESS,
                    SERVICE_DEMAND_START,
                    SERVICE_ERROR_IGNORE,
                    srvPath,
                    NULL, NULL, NULL, NULL, NULL);

    if (hService == NULL)
    {
        cout << "CreateService failed (" << GetLastError() << ")" << endl;
        CloseServiceHandle(hSCM);
        return -1;
    }
    else
        cout << "CreateService succeeded" << endl;

    // Tidy up and return
    CloseServiceHandle(hService);
    CloseServiceHandle(hSCM);

    return 0;
}
```

The important part of the code is the call to **CreateService()**, where we specify all the details of our new service. The parameters set up the service as follows:

- The second parameter gives the name of the service
- The third gives the long name by which it will be displayed in the Control Panel Services application
- The fourth parameter, **SERVICE_ALL_ACCESS**, says that we want to have all possible access to the service
- Parameter five says that the service is the only one in the process
- Parameter six says that the service can be started on demand, as opposed to one which starts automatically
- The seventh parameter tells the system that if there's an error starting this service, it should log the error and continue
- Parameter eight is the full path to the executable containing the service

Before you run this program, make sure you build the service and copy the executable to the NT System32 directory, because that's where the install program will look for it.

Once the install program has run, open the Services Control Panel application and check that the service appears in the list. Note that it is listed under the display name, rather than the service name:

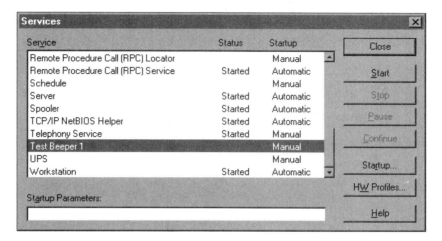

The service is currently stopped, and as we specified in the call to `CreateService()`, it needs to be started manually. Pressing the Start button causes the SCM to try to start the service. You should start hearing beeps, and the display will change:

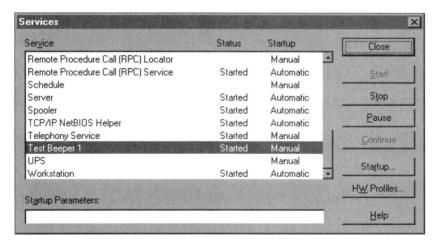

Notice that the service status is now 'started', and we have the choice of stopping or pausing it. If you press Pause, the beeping will stop, and the display will change. When you're satisifed that all is working correctly, use the Stop button to terminate the service.

Removing a Service

Removing a service uses the same sort of code, but calls **DeleteService()** to do the removal. Note that you cannot remove a running service, so we will need to stop the service first. This is a useful little example that shows how to use some of the Service Control API functions. We'll focus on the functions **OpenService()**, **ControlService()** and **DeleteService()**.

Accessing An Existing Service

OpenService() gives you access to the SCM database entry for an existing service:

```
SC_HANDLE OpenService(
     SC_HANDLE hSCM,          // handle to service control manager database
     LPCTSTR lpSrvName,       // pointer to name of service to open
     DWORD dwAccess);         // desired access
```

The parameters are very similar to those for **CreateService()**. For the access parameter, **dwAccess**, there are a number of flags that can be specified, as shown in the following table:

Flag	Meaning
DELETE	Enables us to call **DeleteService()**
READ_CONTROL	Allows us to use **QueryServiceObjectSecurity()** to read the security settings of the service
WRITE_DAC | WRITE_OWNER	Allows us to call **SetServiceObjectSecurity()**, to modify the security settings of the service
STANDARD_RIGHTS_REQUIRED	Combines the three above
SERVICE_CHANGE_CONFIG	Allows us to call **ChangeServiceConfig()**, to change the service configuration
SERVICE_ENUMERATE_DEPENDENTS	Allows us to call **EnumDependentServices()**, to enumerate all services dependent on this one
SERVICE_INTERROGATE	Allows us to call **ControlService()** to get the service to report its status
SERVICE_PAUSE_CONTINUE	Allows us to call **ControlService()** to pause or resume the service
SERVICE_QUERY_CONFIG	Allows us to call **QueryServiceConfig()** to get the service configuration
SERVICE_QUERY_STATUS	Allows us to call **QueryServiceConfig()** to get the service status from the SCM
SERVICE_START	Allows us to call **StartService()** to start the service
SERVICE_STOP	Allows us to call **ControlService()** to stop the service
SERVICE_USER_DEFINED_CONTROL	Allows us to call **ControlService()** to specify a user-defined control code
SERVICE_ALL_ACCESS	Combines all the above

For simplicity, we'll use **SERVICE_ALL_ACCESS** for the access flag in the example below, as we did on service creation. However, we could simply specify **DELETE** to get delete access.

Passing Control Codes To A Service

ControlService() sends a control code to a service, and receives the latest service status:

```
SC_HANDLE ControlService(
    SC_HANDLE hSCM,              // handle to service control manager
                                 // database
    DWORD dwControl,             // control code
    LPSERVICE_STATUS pStat);     // service status return
```

The following codes can be used for the **dwControl** parameter:

Code	Meaning
SERVICE_CONTROL_PAUSE	Tell the service to pause. The service handle must have been opened with **SERVICE_PAUSE_CONTINUE** access.
SERVICE_CONTROL_CONTINUE	Tell the service to continue. The service handle must have been opened with **SERVICE_PAUSE_CONTINUE** access.
SERVICE_CONTROL_STOP	Tell the service to stop. The service handle must have been opened with **SERVICE_STOP** access.
SERVICE_CONTROL_INTERROGATE	Tell the service to immediately update its status and report to the SCM. The service handle must have been opened with **SERVICE_INTERROGATE** access.
SERVICE_CONTROL_SHUTDOWN	**ControlService()** fails if this value is used!
Values 128 to 255	Specifies a user-defined control code. The service does whatever has been defined for this control code. The service handle must have been opened with **SERVICE_USER_DEFINED_CONTROL** access.

We'll use **SERVICE_CONTROL_STOP** to stop our service before deleting it. Note that you can specify a user-defined control code in the range 128–255. What the service does in response to this code is entirely defined by the service itself.

Marking The Service For Deletion

DeleteService() marks the service for deletion, but won't actually remove the service from the database until all handles have been closed by the **CloseServiceHandle()** function, and the service has stopped running.

```
SC_HANDLE DeleteService(
    SC_HANDLE hServ);            // handle to service
```

Try It Out — Removing a Service

Here's a program which will remove our test service:

```cpp
// SrvRemove.cpp

#include <windows.h>
#include <iostream>
#include <tchar.h>
using namespace std;

int main()
{
    SC_HANDLE hSrv;
    SC_HANDLE hSCM;
    SERVICE_STATUS ss;

    // The name of the service to be removed
    LPTSTR srvName = _T("Beep1");

    hSCM = OpenSCManager(0, 0, SC_MANAGER_ALL_ACCESS);
    if (!hSCM)
    {
        cout << "Failed to open the SCM: exiting" << endl;
        return -1;
    }
    else
        cout << "Opened SCM" << endl;

    hSrv = OpenService(hSCM, srvName, SERVICE_ALL_ACCESS);
    if (!hSrv)
    {
        // Failed to open the service, close the SCM before returning
        cout << "Failed to open the service: exiting" << endl;
        CloseServiceHandle(hSCM);
        return -1;
    }
    else
        cout << "Opened service" << endl;

    // See what state the service is in...

    if (!QueryServiceStatus(hSrv, &ss))
        cout << "QueryServiceStatus failed (" << GetLastError() << ")" << endl;
    else
    {
        // If it isn't stopped, try stopping it
        if (ss.dwCurrentState != SERVICE_STOPPED)
        {
            cout << "Stopping service...";
            if (!ControlService(hSrv, SERVICE_CONTROL_STOP, &ss))
                cout << "ControlService failed" << endl;
            else
                Sleep(1000);    // give the service time to stop
        }
```

```
                    // Check it is stopped now...
                    if (!QueryServiceStatus(hSrv, &ss))
                        cout << "QueryServiceStatus failed (" << GetLastError() << ")" << endl;
                    else
                    {
                        if (ss.dwCurrentState == SERVICE_STOPPED)
                        {
                            cout << "Service stopped" << endl;
                            // Now we can remove it
                            if (DeleteService(hSrv))
                                cout << "Service removed" << endl;
                            else
                                cout << "Failed to remove service" << endl;
                        }
                        else
                            cout << "Error: Couldn't stop service" << endl;
                    }
                }

                // Close the service handle
                CloseServiceHandle(hSrv);

                // Close the SCM before returning
                CloseServiceHandle(hSCM);

                return 0;
            }
```

We start by opening a link to the SCM database, and then use **OpenService()** to get a handle to the service we want to delete. If that doesn't work, we close the SCM and exit.

We then check the status of the service, and if it isn't **SERVICE_STOPPED**, we use **ControlService()** to attempt to stop it. After calling **ControlService()** we pause to let the service shut itself down, which we know this particular service is going to be able to do very quickly. In more general purpose code you'd want to set up a loop, checking the service status until it has stopped, or until a timeout period has expired.

We then check the service status again, and if it has stopped we can call **DeleteService()** to remove it from the SCM. Note that the Service Control Panel application doesn't update its display dynamically, so you'll need to close and reopen it in order to confirm that the service has been removed.

More Advanced Services

Now that we've seen how to create a simple service and install it, let's round off our discussion by looking at two more advanced topics — how to use threads to make services easier to write and control, and how to display dialog boxes from a service.

Services And Threads

If you look at the skeleton we've just presented, it may occur to you that the actual processing for the service could usefully be packaged up as a thread. In particular, the SCM may require the service to pause and resume processing, and it is easy to suspend and resume threads without needing to supply special housekeeping code. All we need to do is to create a thread in the main service function `ServiceMainFn()`, and start it running. We can then use a synchronization object to wait until the thread has ended. The thread handler function can then pause and resume processing by simply calling `PauseThread()` and `ResumeThread()`. Packaging up the code as a thread function also has another advantage for us — it will make it easier to write a service C++ class, as we'll go on to do shortly.

Using A Thread

In order to use a thread, we'll need to add two global variables — one to represent the thread handle, and one to represent the synchronization object that we're going to wait on:

```
#include <windows.h>
#include <tchar.h>

SERVICE_STATUS_HANDLE hSrv;
DWORD dwCurrState;
LPTSTR srvName = _T("Beep1");
HANDLE hThread = NULL;
HANDLE hEvent = NULL;
```

In the `ServiceMainFn()` routine, we create and start the thread:

```
void ServiceMainFn(DWORD dwArgc, LPTSTR* lpszArgv)
{
    // Thread ID
    DWORD tid;

    // Register our handler routine with the SCM
    hSrv = RegisterServiceCtrlHandler(srvName,
                        reinterpret_cast<LPHANDLER_FUNCTION>(ServiceHandlerFn));
    if (hSrv == 0)
        return;

    // Tell the SCM we're starting
    TellSCM(SERVICE_START_PENDING, 0, 1);

    // Do any initialization that may be needed...

    TellSCM(SERVICE_START_PENDING, 0, 2);

    // Create the Event on which we'll wait
    hEvent = CreateEvent(NULL, FALSE, FALSE, NULL);
    if (hEvent == 0)
        return;

    TellSCM(SERVICE_START_PENDING, 0, 3);

    // Create the thread and set it going
    hThread = CreateThread(
        0,          // default security descriptor
```

418

```
   0,          // default stack size
   reinterpret_cast<LPTHREAD_START_ROUTINE>(ServiceThreadFunc),
               // thread function
   NULL,       // pointer to parameters
   0,          // creation flags - 0 means run immediately
   &tid);      // thread ID

if (hThread == 0)
{
   CloseHandle(hEvent);
   return;
}

   // Tell the SCM we're ready to go
   TellSCM(SERVICE_RUNNING, 0, 0);

   // Wait for the event to be signalled, which tells us that we need
   // to finish
   WaitForSingleObject(hEvent, INFINITE);

   // Tidy up
   CloseHandle(hThread);
   CloseHandle(hEvent);
}
```

The function now creates an event object, then creates and starts a thread which will execute a function called **ServiceThreadFunc()**. As is usual for a thread function, this function has the following prototype:

```
DWORD ServiceThreadFunc(LPDWORD pParam);
```

LPTHREAD_START_ROUTINE is a **typedef** of a function pointer to this type of function. Parameter information can be passed in via the **pParam** argument. See Chapter 6 for more information on setting up and using threads.

Here's a very simple thread function, which simply beeps every two seconds:

```
DWORD ServiceThreadFunc(LPDWORD pParam)
{
   // This is the function that is executed in order to do the job of the service
   for(;;)
   {
      Beep(500, 500);
      Sleep(2000);
   }

   return 0;
}
```

Once we've started the thread and the service is running, we need to be able to control its operation – to stop, pause and resume it. In the previous example we used a pair of global variables to do this, but there is a more elegant method. We'll use two constructs to control the operation of the service:

> The event synchronization object, which will be signalled when the service is told to stop

> Thread suspending and resuming API calls to control the operation of the thread function

We create the event object before starting the thread, and then call **WaitForSingleObject()**, which will block until the event becomes signalled. This will occur when it is time to exit, that is in response to a **SERVICE_CONTROL_STOP** command being sent to the handler function:

```
case SERVICE_CONTROL_STOP:
    // Tell the SCM we're stopping
    TellSCM(SERVICE_STOP_PENDING, 0, 1);

    // Set the event to say we've stopped
    SetEvent(hEvent);

    // And tell the SCM we've stopped
    TellSCM(SERVICE_STOPPED, 0, 0);
    break;
```

In the previous example pausing and continuing the service was done by setting a global flag. Now that the work of the service is done by a thread, we can suspend and resume the thread in order to control the service:

```
// Pause what we're doing, but don't finish completely
case SERVICE_CONTROL_PAUSE:
    // Tell the SCM we're pausing
    TellSCM(SERVICE_PAUSE_PENDING, 0, 1);

    // Pause the worker thread
    SuspendThread(hThread);

    // And tell the SCM we're paused
    TellSCM(SERVICE_PAUSED, 0, 0);
    break;

// Continue from a pause
case SERVICE_CONTROL_CONTINUE:
    // Tell the SCM we're going to continue
    TellSCM(SERVICE_CONTINUE_PENDING, 0, 1);

    // Restart the thread
    ResumeThread(hThread);

    // And tell the SCM we're going again
    TellSCM(SERVICE_RUNNING, 0, 0);
    break;
```

Some services may need to tidy up when they're paused, so simply suspending and resuming may be too coarse a level of control. In this case you wouldn't use **SuspendThread()** *and* **ResumeThread()**, *but could instead implement additional events which would be set when the service is paused and resumed, and which the thread would check in the thread function.*

Displaying A Dialog To The User

Services usually run invisibly in the background. However, if something unusual happens then you may want to alert the user. It is rare for a service to have a GUI, and if you need some sort of GUI input you'd usually have a separate process which talks to the service. However, it's quite simple to arrange for a service to display a dialog box.

The main change that we need to perform, is to turn your program into a Windows GUI program (rather than a console program). All this involves is changing the code to use **WinMain()** rather than **main()** as the program entry point. This means that we'll have to compile your code differently, building it as a 'Win32 application' rather than a console application.

In order to display a message box, we use the normal Win32 **MessageBox()** function, but we need to set two special styles:

> **MB_DEFAULT_DESKTOP_ONLY**, which will display the message box only if the current desktop is the user's default desktop

> **MB_SETFOREGROUND**, which brings the message box to the front

You can see this in action in the fourth parameter of the **MessageBox()** function call, in the code below. We could also use **MB_SERVICE_NOTIFICATION**, which will display the message box on the active desktop, even if there are no users logged in. In this case, the **hWnd** parameter to the **MessageBox()** call must be **NULL**.

> *If you're going to run this service on NT 3.x, you'll need to check the version and use the **MB_SERVICE_NOTIFICATION_NT3X** style instead.*

As a very simple example, let's modify the beeper service so that it sleeps for a few seconds and then displays a message box before it exits. We need to change the **main()** routine so that it is called **WinMain()**:

```
int WINAPI WinMain(HINSTANCE hInst, HINSTANCE hPrev, LPSTR lpCmd, int nCmdShow)
{
    // Build the table of services in this exe
    SERVICE_TABLE_ENTRY stbl[] = {
        {srvName, (LPSERVICE_MAIN_FUNCTION)ServiceMainFn},
        {NULL, NULL}
    };

    // Call the SCM
    StartServiceCtrlDispatcher(stbl);

    return 0;
}
```

We also need to modify the thread function so that it waits and then displays the dialog:

```
DWORD ServiceThreadFunc(LPDWORD pParam)
{
    // This is the function that is executed in order to do the job of the service
```

```
    // Wait a bit...
    Sleep(4000);

    // And display a message box before exiting
    MessageBox(NULL, "Done beeping!", "Test Service",
        MB_DEFAULT_DESKTOP_ONLY | MB_SETFOREGROUND | MB_OK);

    return 0;
}
```

Build and install the service, and when you run it from the Control Panel **Service** application, you should see the dialog appear after a few seconds pause.

A Service Class

Let's encapsulate what we've developed into a simple class that can handle a service. When we've finished developing this class, it will enable us to:

▶ Initialize and run a service

▶ Install a service

▶ Delete a service

Because we've already explained the service architecture in some detail, we'll present the class fairly briefly, without repeating the details.

Class Design

It would be ideal if we could instantiate more than one **Service** object at one time, in case we need to handle several services. However, we hit an immediate problem. We need to pass the addresses of the service main and handler routines to the SCM, and this means that the **ServiceMainFn()** and the **ServiceHandlerFn()** routines need to be static members of the class.

> *We can't pass the addresses of non-static C++ member functions to Windows API functions because of the way they pass the* **this** *pointer as an implicit first argument.*

We now have one main function and one handler, and hence one thread, for this class — because they are static members. Consequently, we can only have *one* service object running. (Multiple instances of the same service don't make any more sense than multiple instances of the same window or I/O port.)

In C++ terminology this makes the class a singleton, limited to a single instance. In order to enforce this, we use the well-known method of making the constructor protected, and then providing a static member function which creates a single object. Subsequent calls to the create function will simply return a pointer to the existing object, and in this way we ensure that there is never more than one **Service** object in existence at a time. As a further safeguard, we make the copy constructor private so that service objects cannot be copied.

Service Class Definition

Here's the definition of the **Service** class:

```cpp
// Service.h

#include <windows.h>
#include <tchar.h>

class Service
{
   SERVICE_STATUS_HANDLE hSrv;
   DWORD dwCurrState;
   LPTSTR srvName;
   HANDLE hThread;
   HANDLE hEvent;
   LPTHREAD_START_ROUTINE pThreadFn;

   static Service* pInstance;

   static BOOL TellSCM(DWORD dwState, DWORD dwExitCode, DWORD dwProgress);

   // Private copy constructor to prohibit copying
   Service(const Service& s) {}

protected:
   // Only create a service object via the create function
   Service(LPTSTR pName, LPTHREAD_START_ROUTINE pThreadFunc, LPVOID pParams);

public:
   // Create the static service object
   static Service* Create(LPTSTR pName, LPTHREAD_START_ROUTINE pThreadFunc,
                          LPVOID pParams = 0);
   // Return a pointer to the static instance
   static const Service* Instance();

// Virtual destructor
   virtual ~Service();

   // Callbacks for SCM
   static void CALLBACK SCMHandler(DWORD dwCommand);
   static void CALLBACK ServiceMainFn(DWORD dwArgc, LPTSTR* lpszArgv);

   // Non-static functions
   BOOL Run();

   // Static installation and deletion functions
   static bool Install(LPCTSTR pName, LPCTSTR pDisplayName);
   static bool Delete(LPCTSTR pName);

   // Overridables to hook into service code
   virtual void OnServiceStart();
   virtual void OnServiceStopping();
   virtual void OnServiceStopped();
   virtual void OnServicePausing();
   virtual void OnServicePaused();
   virtual void OnServiceResuming();
   virtual void OnServiceResumed();
};
```

We'll meet the data members as we go along, and won't explain most of them at this point, except to point out the static member **pInstance** that holds a pointer to the single instance of the class.

The **ServiceMainFn()** and **SCMHandler()** functions provide the service's main function and SCM handler, and are virtually identical to those we've already developed. The **Run()** function calls **StartServiceCtrlDispatcher()** to start the service up.

We also provide a set of virtual functions that enable us to hook into the service when it is being started, stopped, paused or resumed.

Service Object Creation

Now for the implementation of the class. In the following sections we'll give the full set of code for the member functions of the **Service** class. When we come to test the class shortly, this code will need to be contained in a new file, called **Service.cpp**. The first few lines of the file should contain the following header information:

```
// Service.cpp

#include "Service.h"
#include <iostream>
using namespace std;
```

Now to the meat and drink of the class. The first task is to initialize the static member:

```
Service* Service::pInstance = 0;
```

The protected constructor simply sets the data members to appropriate values:

```
Service::Service(LPTSTR pName, LPTHREAD_START_ROUTINE pThreadFunc, LPVOID pParams)
{
   hSrv = NULL;
   dwCurrState = SERVICE_STOPPED;
   srvName = pName;
   hThread = NULL;
   hEvent = NULL;
   pThreadFn = pThreadFunc;
}
```

There are three arguments to the constructor: the service name, the pointer to the thread function, and any parameters which may be needed by the thread function. Our object has the following data members:

- ▶ **hSrv**, which is a **SERVICE_STATUS_HANDLE**, that will hold the service status handle we get back from the SCM
- ▶ **dwCurrState**, which is an indication of its current state
- ▶ **srvName**, the name of the service
- ▶ A thread handle **hThread**
- ▶ An event handle **hEvent** for signaling when the thread has finished
- ▶ A pointer to the thread function **pThreadFn** which is going to do the work of the service

This constructor will be called by the static **Create()** function, which is responsible for ensuring that there is only one instance of the **Service** class in existence at a time:

```
Service* Service::Create(LPTSTR pName, LPTHREAD_START_ROUTINE pThreadFunc, LPVOID
pParams)
{
    if (pInstance == 0)
        pInstance = new Service(pName, pThreadFunc, pParams);

    return pInstance;
}
```

If the static instance pointer is zero, then a new **Service** object is created. Otherwise the existing pointer is returned.

We'll also add an accessor function, which simply returns the instance pointer:

```
inline const Service* Service::Instance()
{
    return pInstance;
}
```

The class destructor needs to delete the static instance and set the pointer to zero again:

```
Service::~Service()
{
    if (pInstance)
    {
        delete pInstance;
        pInstance == NULL;
    }
}
```

Initializing And Running The Service

The **Run()** member function registers the service with the SCM and starts it going:

```
BOOL Service::Run()
{
    // Build the table of services in this executable
    SERVICE_TABLE_ENTRY stbl[] = {
        {srvName, reinterpret_cast<LPSERVICE_MAIN_FUNCTION>(ServiceMainFn)},
        {NULL, NULL}
    };

    // Call the SCM
    return StartServiceCtrlDispatcher(stbl);
}
```

The call to **StartServiceCtrlDispatcher()** won't return until the service has finished executing.

The **ServiceMainFn()** is virtually the same as the one we developed earlier in the chapter:

```
void CALLBACK Service::ServiceMainFn(DWORD dwArgc, LPTSTR* lpszArgv)
{
   if (pInstance == NULL)
      return;

   // Thread ID
   DWORD tid;

   // Register our handler routine with the SCM
   SERVICE_STATUS_HANDLE hService = RegisterServiceCtrlHandler(pInstance->srvName,
                           reinterpret_cast<LPHANDLER_FUNCTION>(SCMHandler));
   if (hService == 0)
      return;
   else
      pInstance->hSrv = hService;

   // Tell the SCM we're starting
   TellSCM(SERVICE_START_PENDING, 0, 1);

   // Do any initialization that may be needed...
   pInstance->OnServiceStart();

   TellSCM(SERVICE_START_PENDING, 0, 2);

   // Create the Event on which we'll wait
   HANDLE hEv = CreateEvent(NULL, FALSE, FALSE, NULL);
   if (hEv == 0)
      return;
   else
      pInstance->hEvent = hEv;

   TellSCM(SERVICE_START_PENDING, 0, 3);

   // Create the thread and set it going
   HANDLE hT = CreateThread(
       0,          // default security descriptor
       0,          // default stack size
       pInstance->pThreadFn,  // thread function
       NULL,       // pointer to parameters
       0,          // creation flags - 0 means run immediately
       &tid);      // thread ID

   if (hT == 0)
   {
      CloseHandle(pInstance->hEvent);
      pInstance->hEvent = NULL;
      return;
   }
   else
      pInstance->hThread = hT;

   // Tell the SCM we're ready to go
   TellSCM(SERVICE_RUNNING, 0, 0);

   // Wait for the event to be signalled, which tells us that we need
   // to finish
   WaitForSingleObject(pInstance->hEvent, INFINITE);
```

```
      // Tidy up
   CloseHandle(pInstance->hThread);
   CloseHandle(pInstance->hEvent);
}
```

There are a couple of differences here. Firstly, we've provided a 'hook' in the form of a virtual member function called `OnServiceStart()`, which normally does nothing:

```
void Service::OnServiceStart()
{
}
```

If you need to perform initialization, you can derive a class from `Service` and override this function.

Secondly, since this is a static function, the routine must reference the data members of the static instance. We create the various things we need — the `SERVICE_STATUS_HANDLE` and the event and the thread handles — and save them away in the static instance for later use.

`TellSCM()` is also virtually identical to the version we gave earlier in the chapter — we've made the same modifications to the data member references:

```
BOOL Service::TellSCM(DWORD dwState, DWORD dwExitCode, DWORD dwProgress)
{
    // Declare a SERVICE_STATUS structure, and fill it in
    SERVICE_STATUS srvStatus;

    // We're a service running in our own process
    srvStatus.dwServiceType  = SERVICE_WIN32_OWN_PROCESS;

    // Set the state of the service from the argument, and save it away
    // for future use
    srvStatus.dwCurrentState = pInstance->dwCurrState = dwState;

    // Which commands will we accept from the SCM? All the common ones...
    srvStatus.dwControlsAccepted = SERVICE_ACCEPT_STOP |
                                   SERVICE_ACCEPT_PAUSE_CONTINUE |
                                   SERVICE_ACCEPT_SHUTDOWN;

    // Set the Win32 exit code for the service
    srvStatus.dwWin32ExitCode = dwExitCode;

    // Set the service-specific exit code
    srvStatus.dwServiceSpecificExitCode = 0;

    // Set the checkpoint value
    srvStatus.dwCheckPoint = dwProgress;

    // 3 second timeout for waits
    srvStatus.dwWaitHint = 3000;

    // pass the structure to the SCM
    return SetServiceStatus(pInstance->hSrv, &srvStatus);
}
```

We finally come to the handler function. Again, this is much the same as the version we developed earlier in the chapter — except that this new version references the static instance:

```cpp
void CALLBACK Service::SCMHandler(DWORD dwCommand)
{
   // Switch on the command that has arrived
   switch(dwCommand)
   {
   // Stop what we're doing
   case SERVICE_CONTROL_STOP:
      // Tell the SCM we're stopping
      TellSCM(SERVICE_STOP_PENDING, 0, 1);

      // Call the overridable 'stopping' function
      pInstance->OnServiceStopping();

      // Set the Event to say we've stopped
      SetEvent(pInstance->hEvent);

      // Call the overridable 'stopped' function
      pInstance->OnServiceStopped();

      // And tell the SCM we're stopped
      TellSCM(SERVICE_STOPPED, 0, 0);
      break;

   // Pause what we're doing, but don't finish completely
   case SERVICE_CONTROL_PAUSE:
      // Tell the SCM we're pausing
      TellSCM(SERVICE_PAUSE_PENDING, 0, 1);

      // Call the 'pausing' function
      pInstance->OnServicePausing();

      // Pause the worker thread
      SuspendThread(pInstance->hThread);

      // Call the 'paused' function
      pInstance->OnServicePaused();

      // And tell the SCM we're paused
      TellSCM(SERVICE_PAUSED, 0, 0);
      break;

   // Continue from a pause
   case SERVICE_CONTROL_CONTINUE:
      // Tell the SCM we're going to continue
      TellSCM(SERVICE_CONTINUE_PENDING, 0, 1);

      // Call the 'resuming' function
      pInstance->OnServiceResuming();

      // Restart the thread
      ResumeThread(pInstance->hThread);

      // Call the 'resumed' function
      pInstance->OnServiceResumed();
```

```
        // And tell the SCM we're going again
        TellSCM(SERVICE_RUNNING, 0, 0);
        break;

    // Tell the SCM what state we're in
    case SERVICE_CONTROL_INTERROGATE:
        TellSCM(pInstance->dwCurrState, 0, 0);
        break;

    // Shutdown altogether
    case SERVICE_CONTROL_SHUTDOWN:
        // Do whatever we need to do before shutdown...
        break;
    }
}
```

Notice that we've included hooks here, via calls to the six `OnService...()` functions. By overriding these, the user can insert their own processing.

Overridable Functions

The hook functions are provided so that you can add your own processing steps when the service stops, pauses or resumes:

```
void Service::OnServiceStopping()
{
}

void Service::OnServiceStopped()
{
}

void Service::OnServicePausing()
{
}

void Service::OnServicePaused()
{
}

void Service::OnServiceResuming()
{
}

void Service::OnServiceResumed()
{
}
```

To use these functions, you need to derive a class from the `Service` class, and override them.

Installing A Service

The code for installing a service is exactly the same as before. We've lifted the code out of the previous example, and made it a static member of the **Service** class:

```
bool Service::Install(LPCTSTR pName, LPCTSTR pDisplayName)
{
   // Prepare to install a service
   SC_HANDLE hSCM = OpenSCManager(NULL, NULL, SC_MANAGER_CREATE_SERVICE);
   if (hSCM == NULL)
   {
      cout << "OpenSCManager failed!" << endl;
      return false;
   }
   else
      cout << "OpenSCManager OK" << endl;


   // Services usually live in the NT System32 directory, so get the path
   TCHAR winDir[MAX_PATH+1];
   GetSystemDirectory(winDir, MAX_PATH+1);

   // Make up the full path to the service file
   // (Note that _stprintf() comes from tchar.h, and will resolve to sprintf() or
   // swprintf() depending on whether it is compiled as ANSI or Unicode)
   TCHAR srvPath[MAX_PATH+1];
   _stprintf (srvPath, _T("%s\\%s.exe"), winDir, pName);

   // Create the service "Beep1", and give it the display name "Test Beeper 1"
   SC_HANDLE hService = CreateService(hSCM,
               pName,
               pDisplayName,
               SERVICE_ALL_ACCESS,
               SERVICE_WIN32_OWN_PROCESS,
               SERVICE_DEMAND_START,
               SERVICE_ERROR_IGNORE,
               srvPath,
               NULL, NULL, NULL, NULL, NULL);

   if (hService == NULL)
   {
      cout << "CreateService failed (" << GetLastError() << ")" << endl;
      CloseServiceHandle(hSCM);
      return false;
   }
   else
      cout << "CreateService succeeded" << endl;

   // Tidy up and return
   CloseServiceHandle(hService);
   CloseServiceHandle(hSCM);

   return true;
}
```

Remember that this is a static function, so you need to call it like this:

```
bool bOK = Service::Install("myService", "Test service");
```

Removing A Service

Again, the code for deleting a service is virtually identical to the code we've already developed:

```
bool Service::Delete(LPCTSTR pName)
{
    SC_HANDLE hSrv;
    SC_HANDLE hSCM;
    SERVICE_STATUS ss;

    hSCM = OpenSCManager(0, 0, SC_MANAGER_ALL_ACCESS);
    if (!hSCM)
    {
        cout << "Failed to open the SCM - exiting" << endl;
        return false;
    }

    hSrv = OpenService(hSCM, pName, SERVICE_ALL_ACCESS);

    if (!hSrv)
    {
        // Failed to open the service - close the SCM before returning
        cout << "Failed to open the service - exiting" << endl;
        CloseServiceHandle(hSCM);
        return false;
    }

// See what state the service is in...

    if (!QueryServiceStatus(hSrv, &ss))
        cout << "QueryServiceStatus failed (" << GetLastError() << ")" << endl;
    else
    {
        // If it isn't stopped, try stopping it
        if (ss.dwCurrentState != SERVICE_STOPPED)
        {
            cout << "Stopping service...";
            if (!ControlService(hSrv, SERVICE_CONTROL_STOP, &ss))
                cout << "ControlService failed" << endl;
            else
                Sleep(1000);   // give the service time to stop
        }

        // Check it is stopped now...
        if (!QueryServiceStatus(hSrv, &ss))
            cout << "QueryServiceStatus failed (" << GetLastError() << ")" << endl;
        else
        {
            if (ss.dwCurrentState == SERVICE_STOPPED)
            {
                cout << "Service stopped" << endl;
                // Now we can remove it
```

```
                if (DeleteService(hSrv))
                    cout << "Service removed" << endl;
                else
                    cout << "Failed to remove service" << endl;
            }
            else
                cout << "Error: Couldn't stop service" << endl;
        }
    }

    // Close the service handle
    CloseServiceHandle(hSrv);

    // Close the SCM before returning
    CloseServiceHandle(hSCM);

    return true;
}
```

Try It Out — Testing The Class

We can test the class using the same example as before — a service which beeps every few seconds. We can use the functionality built into the **Service** class to produce one executable which can be used to install, run and remove a service:

```cpp
// testservice.cpp

#include <windows.h>
#include <iostream>
#include "Service.h"
using namespace std;

DWORD ServiceThreadFunc(LPDWORD pParam)
{
    // This is the function that is executed in order to do the job of the service
    for(;;)
    {
        Beep(500, 500);
        Sleep(2000);
    }

    return 0;
}

// Example program - we can run this in three ways:
//   1) with '-r', which starts the service going
//   2) with '-i' which installs it
//   3) with '-d' which deletes it

int main(int argc, char* argv[])
{
    if (argc < 2)
    {
        cout << "Usage: " << endl;
        cout << "  testservice -r     runs the service" << endl;
        cout << "  testservice -i     instals the service" << endl;
```

```
            cout << "  testservice -d     removes the service" << endl;
    }
    else
    {
        if (!strcmp(argv[1], "-r"))
        {
            // Create the service and run it
            Service* pS = Service::Create("Beep1",
                    (LPTHREAD_START_ROUTINE)ServiceThreadFunc, NULL);
            // Set it running
            bool bOK = pS->Run();

            // When this returns, the service has finished executing
        }
        else if (!strcmp(argv[1], "-i"))
        {
            // Install
            cout << "Installing service..." << endl;
            if (Service::Install("Beep1", "Test Beeper 1"))
                cout << "Service installed OK" << endl;
            else
                cout << "Error installing service (" << GetLastError() << ")" << endl;
        }
        else if (!strcmp(argv[1], "-d"))
        {
            // Remove
            cout << "Removing service..." << endl;
            if (Service::Delete("Beep1"))
                cout << "Service removed OK" << endl;
            else
                cout << "Error removing service (" << GetLastError() << ")" << endl;
        }
        else
        {
            cout << "Unknown option - " << argv[1] << endl;
        }
    }

    return 0;
}
```

The main routine can be called in three ways:

▶ If called with the '-r' flag, it will run the service
▶ If called with the '-i' flag, it will install the service
▶ If called with the '-d' flag, it will remove the service

Event Logging

The NT **Event Logging** service provides a mechanism whereby all sorts of applications, including drivers, services and the operating system itself, can log information to a central location. It's an excellent example of a service, and is also useful to software developers. Hence it is a good candidate for study in this chapter.

Once a message has been logged, it can be viewed by interested parties (e.g. systems administrators and software developers) who browse the central location using the Event Viewer tool, `eventvwr.exe`.

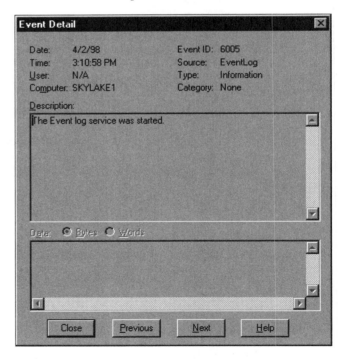

Date	Time	Source	Category	Event	User	Computer
4/3/98	10:47:00 AM	NETLOGON	None	5719	N/A	SKYLAKE1
4/3/98	10:31:57 AM	NETLOGON	None	5719	N/A	SKYLAKE1
4/3/98	10:16:57 AM	NETLOGON	None	5719	N/A	SKYLAKE1
4/3/98	10:01:58 AM	NETLOGON	None	5719	N/A	SKYLAKE1
4/3/98	9:46:59 AM	NETLOGON	None	5719	N/A	SKYLAKE1
4/3/98	9:31:39 AM	NETLOGON	None	5719	N/A	SKYLAKE1
4/3/98	9:31:28 AM	Srv	None	2012	N/A	SKYLAKE1
4/3/98	9:31:28 AM	Srv	None	2012	N/A	SKYLAKE1
4/3/98	9:31:28 AM	Srv	None	2012	N/A	SKYLAKE1
4/3/98	9:31:04 AM	EventLog	None	6005	N/A	SKYLAKE1
4/3/98	9:31:28 AM	Srv	None	2012	N/A	SKYLAKE1

The viewer allows us to browse the event database, enabling us to view various categories of event, such as system, application or security. We can also search for events, and filter the information displayed in the list. By double-clicking on an entry in the list, we are presented with a dialog that displays the details of the event, as in the picture below:

At the top of the dialog, you can see various items of information about the event. These are followed by an edit control containing the message text, and a second control which displays any raw data bytes which may have been sent when the message was logged.

When developing programs and distributing them to clients, the Event Log can be an invaluable tool. We can use it to record the stages of program execution, as well as occurrences such as assertion failures. In addition, we can use it when a client runs software, to provide a record of program behavior and failures. If there's a serious failure at a client site, and the causes of failure are documented in the Event Log, then it's relatively easy to remedy the problem. It is possible for the client to use the Viewer to examine the log, and it is even possible to access it from a remote machine.

The Win32 API includes a number of routines that enable us to write information to the Event Log, and to access its contents from within a program. Unfortunately, this API is rather complex and not well documented. It is, however, usually possible to get by with just a handful of functions for writing to the Log. There are routines for manipulating the Event Log, but their use is not usually necessary — the Event Viewer allows us to do just about all that is required.

What Is An Event?

An event is simply a message which is written to the Event Log. There are three sorts of events which we can log:

▶ **ⓘ Informational events** log the fact that an activity has occurred, such as a driver loading, or a program starting up

▶ **⊙ Warning events** are used for recoverable errors, such as low disk-space warnings

▶ **⬡ Error events** are used for non-recoverable errors, such as inability to start a service

If required, these three event types can be further subdivided into **categories**, which are defined by the application. Althought this is done by some Microsoft services (such as Exchange and SQL Server), few other services seem to use it.

How Does Event Logging Work?

So how do we add an entry to the Event Log? Unfortunately, it's not as simple as calling a function and passing a text string. Microsoft have gone to town on the event handling mechanism, and the result is a rather complex procedure.

In order to use event logging from an application, you need to perform the following steps:

▶ Create a Windows resource, which contains the pre-defined messages for the events you're going to use

▶ Add this resource to a DLL or **.exe** file

▶ Add some application-specific information to the registry when you install your program

▶ Use the event log API functions at run-time to write events to the log

*Note that this topic mentions **resources**, which are not normally used in console applications, but are used in Win32 GUI programs. We won't cover resources in great detail here, and if you need more information, you should consult a book on Windows GUI programming.*

In the following sections, we'll look at each of these steps in turn.

Messages And The Message Compiler

As we've already mentioned, the information that is sent to the Event Log isn't quite as simple as a string of text. If you know anything about Windows programming, then you may already know that Event Log messages are **resources**, and can be used rather like menus and dialogs. Hence, it's possible for an application to create custom messages on the fly — in the same way that we can create dialogs or menus at run time in a Windows program. Normally, we know what our message strings are going to be, and therefore we can build a message table to hold your predefined messages, as described here.

Information about each message — its message ID, its severity, its language and the actual message text — is prepared in a script file which is turned into a binary Windows resource. You can then add the message resource to the executable which is going to use it, or you can create a resource-only DLL. The latter option is useful if you want a set of messages which can be shared by several applications.

Microsoft has introduced a special resource type, called a **MESSAGETABLE**, to hold these event messages. At run time, the client code loads a message resource from the executable, and uses it as an argument to one of the event log API functions.

The process for creating the executable is outlined below:

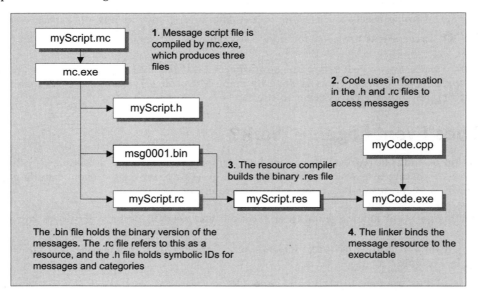

The first step is to prepare the message script, and save it as a **.mc** file. This script file is then processed by the message compiler **mc.exe**, yielding several output files. There may be one or more binary message files (with **.bin** extensions), plus a **.rc** resource file containing **MESSAGETABLE** statements, and a header file containing message definitions. The **.rc** resource file can then be compiled by the resource compiler **rc.exe** to produce a binary **.res** file.

> *Unfortunately, the message compiler isn't very well documented. However, you will find a help file (**mc.hlp**) which provides a certain amount of information.*

The final step is to build a DLL which contains the resources. This resource-only DLL must obviously be distributed with your application, and may possibly be shared between applications.

Creating The Message Script File

The message script file can be produced using any text editor, and consists of two portions — a **header** and a **set of message descriptions**.

The Header

The header is used to define values which are used in the messages, and has the following form:

```
MessageIdTypedef=[type]
SeverityNames=(name=number[:name])
FacilityNames=(name=number[:name])
LanguageNames=(name=number:filename)
```

Let's briefly describe the elements of the header. The first line determines what sort of values are used to hold message IDs, and is a standard Windows data type, such as a **DWORD**.

SeverityNames allows you to list up to four severity codes which are used to describe messages. If you miss this out, the following default set of values is used:

Name	Value
Success	0x00
Informational	0x01
Warning	0x02
Error	0x03

If you want to define your own then you will need to give them a name, a 2-bit code, and an optional symbolic name for use in the header file that **mc.exe** will generate.

FacilityNames allows you to define your own facility codes, which say where a message originated. Suppose you have an application composed of an executable plus several DLLs and device drivers, you may want to define facility codes that tell you which part of the system a particular message come from. If you omit this line, you can use the two default values: Application (0xfff) and System (0x0ff). Note that if you define your own facility codes, the first 256 values are reserved for system use.

Finally, **LanguageNames** defines the language in which messages are written. More than one value can be set, thus making it possible for a message DLL to contain several versions of the same message in different languages. In the discussion and examples which follow, we're assuming the default language, which is English.

Let's look at an example header. If we decide to use the default facility and language values, then our header might look like this:

```
MessageIdTypedef=DWORD
SeverityNames=(Success=0x00:SEVERITY_SUCCESS
            Informational=0x01:SEVERITY_INFORMATIONAL
            Warning=0x2:SEVERITY_WARNING
            Error=0x3:SEVERITY_ERROR)
```

In this example, the `SeverityNames` field has been used to provide symbolic names for the four default severity levels.

The Messages

The header section is followed by one or more messages. Each message takes the following form:

```
MessageId=[number | +number]
Severity=severity_name
Facility=facility_name
SymbolicName=name
Language=language_name
text of message
.
```

Let's take a quick look at the components of a message.

Each message must start with a `MessageId` line. The default is to use the value of the previous message number, incremented by 1. Alternatively, you can either give a specific message number, or use the '+n' format to give an increment that will be applied to the previous message number.

The `Severity`, `Facility` and `Language` lines either take standard values, or accept values that were defined in the header. The `SymbolicName` line allows you to specify a symbolic name that will be included in the header file, and can be used to reference this message in your code.

These lines are followed by one or more lines of message text. Note that the whole message is ended by a single period, on a line of its own.

> *In order to present the message in more than one language, simply type each language/text pair at the end of the message entry. The actual text retrieved for this message at run time will depend on the language setting for the logged-in user.*

Here's what a couple of message entries might look like:

```
MessageId=0x1
Severity=Warning
Facility=Application
SymbolicName=MSG_NO_CONFIG_INFO
Language=English
The configuration file, %1, could not be found.
Using default values.
.
```

```
MessageId=0x2
Severity=Informational
Facility=Application
SymbolicName=MSG_SAVE_CONFIG
Language=English
Wrote new configuration file %1.
.
```

The message text can contain whitespace and blank lines, as well as the **printf**-style formatting characters shown in the following table:

Format	Meaning
%0	Finish message text line without adding a newline
%%	Insert a '**%**' character
%	If at the end of a line, generates a hard line break
%r	Generates a carriage return without a trailing newline
%b	Puts a space character in the formatted text
%.	Generates a single period character (in case you need one to start a line)
%!	Generates a single exclamation point, which will be useful if you want to generate one straight after an insertion
%n[!fmt!]	Specifies a string insertion, where the value of *n* can range from 1 to 99, optionally followed by a **printf**-style format specifier between two exclamation marks

The string insertion format code will put a placeholder into a message. The appropriate item will be placed there when the resource is used at run time with the **FormatMessage()** API function. You can see this being used in the examples above.

As we've noted in the table, a string insertion can be followed by a format specifier (between exclamation marks), which defines the format for the text. The specifier takes the form of a **printf** format specifier, without the leading '**%**'. For example, **%6!6.2f!** would insert **6** using **%6.2f** format. The default is **!s!**, to format the insertion as a string.

Try It Out — Compiling The Message File

We compile a message file by running the message compiler **mc.exe** from the command line. This tool is installed with Visual C++, and can be found in the **Microsoft Visual Studio\vc98\bin** directory.

The first step is to save the header and messages above into a single script file, called **myScript.mc**. Here's a sample message source file containing two messages:

```
// myScript.mc

// header
MessageIdTypedef=DWORD
SeverityNames=(Success=0x00:SEVERITY_SUCCESS
               Informational=0x01:SEVERITY_INFORMATIONAL
```

```
                    Warning=0x2:SEVERITY_WARNING
                    Error=0x3:SEVERITY_ERROR)

// messages
MessageId=0x1
Severity=Warning
Facility=Application
SymbolicName=MSG_NO_CONFIG_INFO
Language=English
The configuration file, %1, could not be found.
Using default values.
.


MessageId=0x2
Severity=Informational
Facility=Application
SymbolicName=MSG_SAVE_CONFIG
Language=English
Wrote new configuration file %1.
.
```

The lines beginning with a semicolon are comments. Note that they'll be passed onto the header file as-is, with just the semicolon removed, so you need to include C++ comment markers in order to make them valid C++.

Now, open up a DOS session and go to the directory in which the file **myScript.mc** is saved. Type the following command at the prompt to run the compiler:

```
mc myScript.mc
```

The files produced will include three which we're going to use:

▶ The header file **myScript.h**
▶ The resource file **myScript.rc**
▶ The binary message file **MSG00001.bin**

The header file contains definition information which will give you access to the messages from within your code. The binary message file contains the message information in binary, and the resource file contains information which will enable the linker to attach the binary data to the resource DLL.

Here's the **myScript.h** that I got when I compiled **myScript.mc** using **mc.exe**:

```
//
//  Values are 32 bit values layed out as follows:
//
//   3 3 2 2 2 2 2 2 2 2 2 2 1 1 1 1 1 1 1 1 1 1
//   1 0 9 8 7 6 5 4 3 2 1 0 9 8 7 6 5 4 3 2 1 0 9 8 7 6 5 4 3 2 1 0
//  +---+-+-+-----------------------+-------------------------------+
//  |Sev|C|R|     Facility          |               Code            |
//  +---+-+-+-----------------------+-------------------------------+
//
```

```
//   where
//
//        Sev - is the severity code
//
//             00 - Success
//             01 - Informational
//             10 - Warning
//             11 - Error
//
//        C - is the Customer code flag
//
//        R - is a reserved bit
//
//        Facility - is the facility code
//
//        Code - is the facility's status code
//
//
// Define the facility codes
//


//
// Define the severity codes
//
#define SEVERITY_WARNING                 0x2
#define SEVERITY_SUCCESS                 0x0
#define SEVERITY_INFORMATIONAL           0x1
#define SEVERITY_ERROR                   0x3


//
// MessageId: MSG_NO_CONFIG_INFO
//
// MessageText:
//
//   The configuration file, %1, could not be found.
//   Using default values.
//
#define MSG_NO_CONFIG_INFO              ((DWORD)0x80000001L)

//
// MessageId: MSG_SAVE_CONFIG
//
// MessageText:
//
//   Wrote new configuration file %1.
//
#define MSG_SAVE_CONFIG                 ((DWORD)0x40000002L)
```

There are quite a few comments in this file, and if you read the first few lines you should recognize the form of the error code as being identical to the system error codes described in Chapter 4. The file contains the symbolic constants for the messages and the severity codes we defined in the header section of the file **myScript.mc**.

Here's the **myScript.rc** file that I got from the compilation — as you can see, it's much smaller:

```
LANGUAGE 0x9,0x1
1 11 MSG00001.bin
```

The purpose of this file is to provide information on where the binary message text can be found, and on the language associated with the file. Here, the messages are stored in file `MSG00001.bin`, and the language is English.

Try It Out — Viewing the Resource File

Now, we'll create a simple console application which, when run, will write some messages to the Event Log. In Visual C++, create a new console mode program called **Log**.

Move the **myScript.mc** file, plus the three files that were generated by `mc.exe`, into this directory, and add **myScript.rc** to the project files (you can do this from the File View tab: right-click on Log Files, select Add Files to Project, and then select myScript.rc). When you do this, you'll find that the browser window suddenly gains a ResourceView tab. Selecting this tab will show you the message resource:

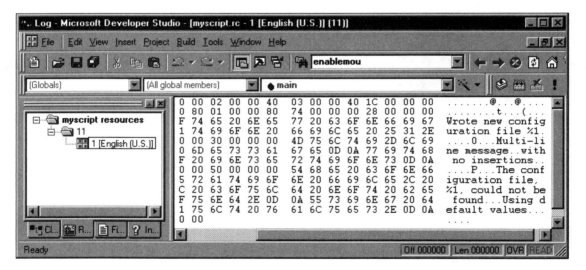

The resource is displayed as binary, but you can still see the message text to the right of the screen. That's all we can do for now — there are a couple of other things we need to attend to before we can actually create an executable and write to the Event Log.

Registry Modifications

The registry holds information about all the executable files which hold message resources to be used by the Event Log. This includes both resource-only message DLLs and executables which contain message resources. If a message file isn't correctly registered, then we won't be allowed to use it to write to the Event Log.

The registry holds event log information under the
`HKEY_LOCAL_MACHINE\SYSTEM\CurrentControlSet\Services\EventLog` key, which has
three subkeys. Each of these subkeys represents a separate event log file in
`\winnt\system32\config`. These files are listed in the third column:

Subkey	Description	Represents Log File
`Application`	Holds Event Log information for applications	`appevent.evt`
`Security`	For security system event information	`secevent.evt`
`System`	For system information	`sysevent.evt`

We're only interested in the first of these subkeys.

When an application wants to record data in the Event Log, it will create a unique subkey
under `Application`. the name of this unique subkey is usually based on the name of the
application. Several subkeys can then be added under this key, two of which are mandatory:

Subkey	Type	Description
`EventMessageFile`	`REG_EXPAND_SZ`	Gives the complete path to the message DLL or EXE
`TypesSupported`	`REG_DWORD`	A bit-mask which says which event types this application supports, a typical value being `EVENTLOG_ERROR_TYPE` | `EVENTLOG_WARNING_TYPE` | `EVENTLOG_INFORMATIONAL_TYPE`

If your message file supports categories, you can add two other subkeys:

Subkey	Type	Description
`CategoryMessageFile`	`REG_EXPAND_SZ`	Gives the path to the file containing the category definitions
`CategoryCount`	`REG_DWORD`	Gives the number of categories

Here is what a typical entry looks like in RegEdit:

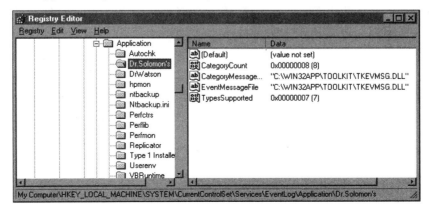

Unfortunately, there is no system tool that will add subkeys to the Event Log on your behalf. You have to add them manually or write code to do it for you. As you would expect, you have to be an Administrator in order to be able to do this.

Try It Out — Registering An Application

This means that before we can write and run a program which uses the Event Log we need to have a registration mechanism. This sample stand-alone program shows how you can register an application:

```cpp
// evtreg.cpp

#include <windows.h>
#include <iostream>
#include <tchar.h>
using namespace std;

int main(int argc, char* argv[])
{
    TCHAR rk[255], rkval[255], msgfile[255];
    DWORD numCats;

    // Get the registry key value
    cout << "Registry key: " << endl;
    cin >> rkval;
    // Get the message file path
    cout << "Message file: " << endl;
    cin >> msgfile;
    // Get the number of categories
    cout << "Number of categories: " << endl;
    cin >> numCats;

    // Make up the full registry key path
    _tcscpy(rk, "SYSTEM\\CurrentControlSet\\Services\\EventLog\\Application\\");
    _tcscat(rk, rkval);

    HKEY hKey;
    DWORD disp;

    // Create the key
    LONG ret = RegCreateKeyEx(HKEY_LOCAL_MACHINE, rk, 0, NULL,
        REG_OPTION_NON_VOLATILE, KEY_SET_VALUE, NULL, &hKey, &disp);
    if (ret != ERROR_SUCCESS)
    {
        cout << "Key creation failed" << endl;
        return -1;
    }

    if (disp == REG_OPENED_EXISTING_KEY)
        cout << "Key already exists - updating it" << endl;
```

```
      // Create the message file value
      ret = RegSetValueEx(hKey, "EventMessageFile", 0,
         REG_EXPAND_SZ, reinterpret_cast<LPBYTE>(msgfile), _tcslen(msgfile)+1);
      if (ret != ERROR_SUCCESS)
         cout << "Couldn't add EventMessageFile value" << endl;

      DWORD types = EVENTLOG_INFORMATION_TYPE |
         EVENTLOG_WARNING_TYPE | EVENTLOG_ERROR_TYPE;

      // Create the types value
      ret = RegSetValueEx(hKey, "TypesSupported", 0,
         REG_DWORD, reinterpret_cast<LPBYTE>(&types), sizeof types);
      if (ret != ERROR_SUCCESS)
         cout << "Couldn't add TypesSupported value" << endl;

      // Add category info, if any categories are aupported
      if (numCats)
      {
         ret = RegSetValueEx(hKey, "CategoryCount", 0,
                           REG_DWORD, reinterpret_cast<LPBYTE>(&numCats),
                           sizeof numCats);
         if (ret != ERROR_SUCCESS)
            cout << "Couldn't add CategoryCount value" << endl;

         ret = RegSetValueEx(hKey, "CategoryMessageFile", 0,
                           REG_EXPAND_SZ, reinterpret_cast<LPBYTE>(msgfile),
                           _tcslen(msgfile)+1);
         if (ret != ERROR_SUCCESS)
            cout << "Couldn't add CategoryMessageFile value" << endl;
   }

   RegCloseKey(hKey);
   cout << rkval << " entered in registry successfully" << endl;

   return 0;
}
```

The program prompts the user for three items — the key under which this information is going to be entered in the registry, the path to the executable containing the messages, and the number of message categories (if any) implemented in the file. In order to register the event logging application we're in the process of constructing, we can run the program with the following parameters:

```
Registry key = LogTest
Message file = D:Temp\Log\Debug\Log.exe
Categories = 0
```

These values tell us that the entries will be created under the **HKEY_LOCAL_MACHINE\System\CurrentControlSet\Services\EventLog\Application\LogTest** key, that the source for Event Log messages is **D:Temp\Log\Debug\Log.exe**, and that it doesn't support categories. Naturally, when you run the program you'll replace the message file string by the full path to your executable.

If you use RegEdit, you can verify that the entries have been correctly created:

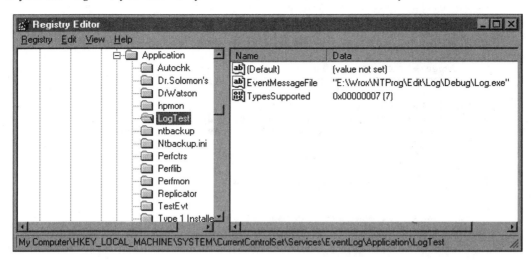

Logging Events At Runtime

Once you've got this far, actually logging an event is quite simple, and only uses three API calls. Let's have a look at each of them, before we see them in action.

The first is **RegisterEventSource()**, which is used to tell the Event Log service that we wish to log events, and must be called before any logging occurs:

```
HANDLE RegisterEventSource(
    LPCTSTR  lpServer,              // server where source is located
    LPCTSTR  lpSource);            // source name
```

The first parameter, **lpServer**, specifies the Universal Naming Code (UNC) name of the server on which the logging source resides. If it is **NULL**, the local machine is used. The second parameter, **lpSource**, is the **source name**, a string which must match one of the entries in the registry under the **HKEY_LOCAL_MACHINE\SYSTEM\CurrentControlSet\Services\EventLog\Application** key. This will be the name under which you registered the logging application, so we'll need to use "LogTest", since that is the name under which we registered our application.

If the function executes without error, it returns a handle, which must be used when reporting events.

Once we've finished logging the function **DeregisterEventSource()** informs the Event Log and closes the handle:

```
BOOL DeregisterEventSource(HANDLE hSrc);
```

ReportEvent() is what we use to log the event. It can take quite a number of parameters:

```
BOOL  ReportEvent(
      HANDLE  hLog,            //  handle  to  event  log
      WORD  wType,             //  what  sort  of  event  this  is
      WORD  wCategory,         //  ID  of  event  category
      DWORD  dwEventID,        //  ID  of  message  to  log  for  this  event
      PSID  pSid,              //  SID  for  current  user
      WORD  wNumStrings,       //  number  of  strings
      DWORD  dwSize,           //  amount  of  raw  data
      LPCTSTR*  pStrings,      //  pointer  to  strings
      LPVOID  pRawData);       //  pointer  to  raw  data
```

Starting from the top, we first need the handle we got from `RegisterEventSource()`. This is followed by a parameter denoting the type of the event, which can be one of

▶ `EVENTLOG_INFORMATION_TYPE`, for an information message

▶ `EVENTLOG_WARNING_TYPE`, for a warning message

▶ `EVENTLOG_ERROR_TYPE`, for an error message

▶ `EVENTLOG_AUDIT_SUCCESS`, indicating a Success Audit event

▶ `EVENTLOG_AUDIT_FAILURE`, indicating a Failure Audit event

The third parameter is used to specify the event category, if you've implemented categories in the message file, and the fourth is the symbolic name of the message from the message file. You'll get these symbolic names from the header file generated by `mc.exe`.

These are followed by the SID for the current user, which can be passed as `NULL` if it isn't relevant. The SID (Security ID) is a value which uniquely identifies the current user, and it may be useful to report this in some circumstances. You can find out more about SIDs and how to use them in Chapter 8.

The last four parameters represent the size of (and pointers to) two items — a list of strings, and some raw data. If you're using messages with text insertions, then the list of strings gives the values which will be inserted at appropriate places in the message. The raw data pointer allows you to write binary data into the Log, should this be useful.

Try It Out — Writing to the Event Log

Let's now add the code to our logging project so that it can write to the Event Log. Create a new C++ source file and add it to the project:

```cpp
// logwrite.cpp

#include <windows.h>
#include <tchar.h>
#include <iostream>

using namespace std;

// Include the message header file generated by mc.exe
#include "myScript.h"
```

```
int main()
{
   int nRet = 0;

   HANDLE hLog = RegisterEventSource(NULL, "LogTest");
   if (hLog == NULL)
   {
      cout << "Can't get log handle (" << GetLastError() << ")" << endl;
      return -1;
   }

   cout << "Logging message..." << endl;

   LPCTSTR pStr = _T("config.01");

   BOOL bRet = ReportEvent(
      hLog,                          // handle to event log
      EVENTLOG_INFORMATION_TYPE,     // message type
      0,                             // no category
      MSG_SAVE_CONFIG,               // message ID
      NULL,                          // no SID
      1,                             // number of strings
      0,                             // no raw data
      &pStr,                         // one substitution string
      NULL                           // no raw data
   );

   if (!bRet)
   {
      cout << "Failed to write log message (" << GetLastError() << ")" << endl;
      nRet = -1;
   }
   else
      cout << "Message successfully logged" << endl;

   DeregisterEventSource(hLog);

   return nRet;
}
```

At the start of the program, we include the header file **myScript.h**, generated earlier by
mc.exe, to give us access to the symbolic ID of the messages.

We use **RegisterEventSource()** to get a handle to the Event Log, and we indicate that we
want to use an event source called **LogTest**. Since this program contains the message resource,
we need to have registered this program as **LogTest** before this will work.

> *If the messages were in a separate DLL, we would need to have registered that DLL.*

Once we have a handle, we can use **ReportEvent()** to write to the log. We write one
information message with the **MSG_SAVE_CONFIG** ID, which takes a single text substitution, like
this:

```
Wrote new configuration file %1
```

We set up a string that will be substituted into the message, passed into the function as the eighth argument.

Build the program and run it a few times, then start the Event Log. Make sure that you select the Application view from the Log menu, and you should see something like this:

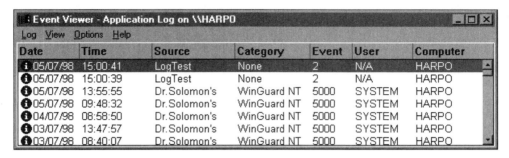

The first few entries have been written by our application. The icon shows that they are information messages, and the source shows that they've come from our program. Double-clicking on one of the entries will show you the details of the event:

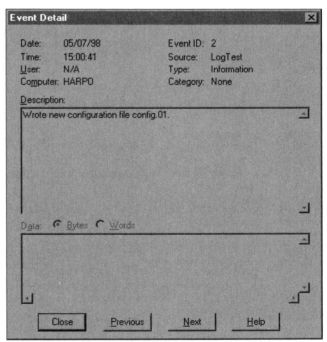

You can see that the message has had the string config.01 substituted at the appropriate place.

A Simple Event Log Class

We can usefully encapsulate event logging in a simple class **EventLog** which will have the following functions:

▶ **AddSource()**, which creates a new source in the registry.

▶ **LogMsg()**, which registers, logs a message and deregisters again. This function can use text insertions if necessary, but doesn't allow logging raw data.

This represents the most basic set of functions which we need to use the Event Log. If you need more, you can add them!

Here is the simple class definition:

```
class EventLog
{
public:
   bool AddSource(LPCTSTR key, LPTSTR msgpath, DWORD numCats);
   bool LogMsg(LPTSTR src, WORD type, WORD cat, DWORD id,
               WORD numStr=0, LPCTSTR* pStr=NULL);
};
```

AddSource() will create a new source under the Application key in the registry:

```
bool EventLog::AddSource(LPTSTR key, LPTSTR msgpath, DWORD numCats)
{
   TCHAR kk[MAX_PATH];
   LONG lErr = ERROR_SUCCESS;

   // Make up the full registry key path
   _tcscpy(kk, "SYSTEM\\CurrentControlSet\\Services\\EventLog\\Application\\");
   _tcscat(kk, key);

   HKEY hKey;
   DWORD disp;

   // Create the key
   LONG ret = RegCreateKeyEx(HKEY_LOCAL_MACHINE, kk, 0, NULL,
      REG_OPTION_NON_VOLATILE, KEY_SET_VALUE, NULL, &hKey, &disp);
   if (ret != ERROR_SUCCESS)
      lErr = ret;

   // Create the message file value
   ret = RegSetValueEx(hKey, "EventMessageFile", 0,
      REG_EXPAND_SZ, (LPBYTE)msgpath, _tcslen(msgpath)+1);
   if (ret != ERROR_SUCCESS)
      lErr = ret;

   DWORD types = EVENTLOG_INFORMATION_TYPE |
      EVENTLOG_WARNING_TYPE | EVENTLOG_ERROR_TYPE;

   // Create the types value
   ret = RegSetValueEx(hKey, "TypesSupported", 0,
      REG_DWORD, (LPBYTE)&types, sizeof types);
```

```
      if (ret != ERROR_SUCCESS)
         lErr = ret;

      // Add category info, if any categories are aupported
      if (numCats)
      {
         ret = RegSetValueEx(hKey, "CategoryCount", 0,
            REG_DWORD, (LPBYTE)&numCats, sizeof numCats);
         if (ret != ERROR_SUCCESS)
            lErr = ret;

         ret = RegSetValueEx(hKey, "CategoryMessageFile", 0,
            REG_EXPAND_SZ, (LPBYTE)msgpath, _tcslen(msgpath)+1);
         if (ret != ERROR_SUCCESS)
            lErr = ret;
      }

      RegCloseKey(hKey);

      return lErr == ERROR_SUCCESS;
}
```

The code is nearly identical to that of the previous example program. We pass in the name for the source, the path to the file containing the message resource, and the number of categories.

`LogMsg()` is once again very similar to the code we used in the previous example:

```
bool EventLog::LogMsg(LPTSTR src, WORD type, WORD cat, DWORD id,
                      WORD numStr, LPCTSTR* pStr)
{
   HANDLE hLog = RegisterEventSource(NULL, src);
   if (hLog == NULL)
      return false;

   BOOL bRet = ReportEvent(
      hLog,                     // handle to event log
      type,                     // message type
      cat,                      // no category
      id,                       // message ID
      NULL,                     // no SID
      numStr,                   // number of strings
      0,                        // no raw data
      pStr,                     // array of substitution strings
      NULL);                       // no raw data

   if (!bRet)
      return false;

   DeregisterEventSource(hLog);

   return true;
}
```

451

Try It Out — Using the Event Logging Class

Now we will write a test program to use the event logging class. Create a new console application, and copy into the project directory the three files we originally created by running `mc.exe`: `myscript.rc`, `myscript.h` and `msg00001.bin`.

Add `myscript.rc` to the project files, and ensure that your project gains a resource view. Next, create a C++ source file and add the appropriate header information:

```cpp
// EventLog.cpp

#include <windows.h>
#include <iostream>
#include <tchar.h>
using namespace std;

#include "myScript.h"
```

Now type into it the definition and implementation of the EventLog class as shown above, and finally add a main routine which will test out the class:

```cpp
int main(int argc, char* argv[])
{
    EventLog e;

    // Add some new source information to the registry. It will be added under key
    // "NewSource", and will point to a specified executable you choose

    if (!e.AddSource("NewSource", "c:\\temp\\bill.exe", 0))
        cout << "Add source failed" << endl;
    else
        cout << "Source added" << endl;

    // Log a message to the Event Log using the "LogTest" source
    LPCTSTR pStr = _T("config.01");

    if (!e.LogMsg("LogTest", EVENTLOG_INFORMATION_TYPE, 0, MSG_SAVE_CONFIG, 1,
&pStr))
        cout << "Log message failed" << endl;
    else
        cout << "Message logged" << endl;

    return 0;
}
```

When you've built and run the program, verify that the correct entries have been made to both the registry and the Event Log.

Summary

Services are the NT equivalent of Unix daemon processes, and provide a way to run programs in the background regardless of who is logged in. Services are created as executables, and more than one can be packaged into a single executable if desired. They usually run in the background, but it possible to modify them so that they can display a message box to the user.

Services are managed by the NT Service Control Manager (SCM), which has the ability to start, stop, pause and resume services. Users can interact with the SCM using the Service Control Panel application, and it is also possible to interact with the SCM from within a program, by using the Service Control API functions.

All services must provide the same functionality, in order to support their interaction with the SCM. They need to register a handler with the SCM, which is called when the service needs to be stopped, paused or resumed, and it is up to the service to inform the SCM of *all* changes in status.

It is convenient to encapsulate the work the service is to perform in a worker thread. When this is done, it is then possible to provide a skeleton service which will suffice for the majority of applications.

Using Consoles

In this chapter we're going to look at something which appears to be a fairly well-kept secret—the **Win32 Console API**. We'll be looking at some of the most useful functions, and the use of these API calls will be illustrated in several practical coded examples.

Along the way we'll see how to:

▶ Allocate and free consoles

▶ Control output to the screen, including changing the position of the cursor and attributes of the text

▶ Scroll down the screen

▶ Handle control signals and mouse events

▶ Switching between screen buffers

Toward the end of the chapter, we'll create a console class that wraps up some of these API calls and simplifies their use.

What Is A Console?

We all know that the main emphasis in Windows programming is on creating applications with a graphical user interface, complete with menus, dialogs, toolbars and all the other paraphernalia we've come to know and love.

Sometimes, though, it is useful to let applications run in a text-mode window, like the one you get when you click on the Command Prompt icon. You may be porting a command-line program from another OS, such as DOS or Unix, where a GUI is perhaps not desirable or necessary, or you may just want to output text from a GUI application; in either case, Win32 makes it possible to write text-mode windows applications which can be quite sophisticated.

These text mode windows are called **console windows**, and the Win32 API contains a collection of functions to help you create and use them in both Windows NT and Win95.

In fact, the Win32 Console API includes all the runtime library's command line I/O functionality. You can get output to a window simply by including **<iostream>** and writing to **cout**, like this:

```
// Simple_Application.cpp

#include <iostream>
#include <tchar.h>
using namespace std;

int main()
{
   cout << _T("hello world") << endl;
   return 0;
}
```

> *Note that we're including* **tchar.h** *and using the* **_T()** *macro in order to make our strings portable between ANSI and Unicode. This header also includes the portable versions of the string manipulation functions, and you'll need to ensure that* **tchar.h** *is included in order to run the code in this chapter.*

If you execute this program by clicking on the executable in Explorer, you'll see that a console window is opened to display the output and immediately closed again once the program has finished. If you run it from the Command Prompt window, you'll see your output appear in that window (which remains open).

What's happening here is that all programs started from the Command Prompt share the same console window, so that you can see what is already on the screen. If you start your program from somewhere else, such as Explorer, then there isn't a console to share, so the program has its own console created for it.

That may be all you need for the simplest programs, but if you need more control over your output, then the rest of the Console API is there to help.

The Console API

The **Console API** provides a rich set of functions to enable you to write text-mode programs, giving you support for:

- Full-screen operation, including splitting the screen into blocks which can be independently scrolled
- Color and mouse support
- Character attribute support
- Line- or character-oriented input modes

Putting these together makes it feasible to write sophisticated programs, such as terminal emulators, but be warned that the coding can get quite long-winded at times — just like writing Win32 GUI applications, in fact!

Try It Out — A Simple Console Application

As an introduction to the Console API, let's rewrite our simple example, but this time we'll use the Console API to write the string. Here's the code:

```cpp
// Simple_Console_Application.cpp
#include <windows.h>
#include <tchar.h>
#include <iostream>

using namespace std;

int main()
{
    DWORD n;                          // number of characters output
    LPTSTR buff = _T("hello world\n");

    BOOL bOK = WriteFile(GetStdHandle(STD_OUTPUT_HANDLE),
                         buff,
                         _tcslen(buff)*sizeof(TCHAR),
                         &n,
                         NULL);
    if (!bOK)
        cout << _T("Error from WriteFile()") << endl;
    return 0;
}
```

We're now using the `WriteFile()` function to write a buffer to the screen, and in order to use this, we need to include the `windows.h` header. We'll meet the `WriteFile()` function in more detail later; for now, just note that we write to a file handle, and the function `GetStdHandle()` is used to get a handle corresponding to one of the standard streams. We also pass the buffer and its size, and get back the number of bytes written.

Note that since `WriteFile()` takes the number of bytes to write as an argument, and not the number of characters, we have to account for the fact that we might the using 16-bit characters by calculating the number of bytes in the string.

Allocating and Freeing Consoles

As we saw earlier, a program run from the command line will use the console which is already provided by the Command Prompt. More generally, if a process is started by a parent process which has a console, the child process will tend to inherit the parent's console, and won't need to create one of its own. If you start a console program off by itself (or if it can't inherit a console from its parent) then the system will recognise that it needs a console, and create one for it.

Some programs, such as GUI programs, won't have a console created by default. In these cases you'd use the `AllocConsole()` function to create a new console and attach it to the process:

```cpp
BOOL  AllocConsole();
```

If the console is correctly allocated, the function returns **TRUE**. The complementary call, **FreeConsole()**, is used to detach a process from its console:

```
BOOL FreeConsole();
```

Once again, the function returns **TRUE** if the call worked. Note that the lack of any sort of handle as argument or return type means that a process is limited to a single console.

> *Note that a process can only be associated with one console at a time. If the process already has a console, then a call to* AllocConsole() *will fail.*

Try It Out — An Application Using Its Own Console

Although it isn't strictly necessary, we could modify the simple example so that it runs using its own console, like this:

```cpp
// OwnConsole.cpp

#include <windows.h>
#include <iostream>
#include <tchar.h>

using namespace std;

int main()
{
    DWORD n;    // number of characters output
    LPTSTR buff = _T("hello world\n");

    // Write a string to the original console...
    cout << "This is the original console..." << endl;

    // Free the console
    if (!FreeConsole())
    {
        cout << "Error returned from FreeConsole()";
        return -1;
    }

    // Pause so you can see the effect
    Sleep(2000);

    // Grab a new console and write to it. If there's a problem, then we may not
    // have a console to write to, so use a message box to report the error
    if (!AllocConsole())
    {
        MessageBox(NULL, "Error returned from AllocConsole()", "Error", MB_OK);
        return -1;
    }

    WriteFile(GetStdHandle(STD_OUTPUT_HANDLE),
            buff, _tcslen(buff)*sizeof(TCHAR),
            &n, NULL);
```

```
// Pause so you can see the effect
   Sleep(2000);

   return 0;
}
```

If you build this program and run it from the command line, you'll see that the output no longer appears in the command line window. Instead, a new console window briefly appears and then disappears, showing that the process has indeed got its own console.

You can use **AllocConsole()** to create a console for a GUI program too, which can be very useful when you want to display debugging or trace information. All you need to do is to create a console, and then use either **cout** or **WriteFile()** to write to it.

Console Handles

All processes, even GUI ones, have a notion of standard input, output and error handles, which represent the standard places where input can be obtained, and where program output and error output will be written. These handles are what C programmers call **stdin**, **stdout** and **stderr**, and which C++ users access with the **cin**, **cout** and **cerr** objects.

We can get the standard handles using the **GetStdHandle()** function:

```
HANDLE  GetStdHandle(DWORD  dwWhich);
```

The argument to the function determines which handle will be returned, and can be one of:

▶ **STD_INPUT_HANDLE** for standard input

▶ **STD_OUTPUT_HANDLE** for standard output

▶ **STD_ERROR_HANDLE** for standard error

The following code will retrieve all three standard handles:

```
HANDLE stdin = GetStdHandle(STD_INPUT_HANDLE);
HANDLE stdout = GetStdHandle(STD_OUTPUT_HANDLE);
HANDLE stderr = GetStdHandle(STD_ERROR_HANDLE);
```

Since these are standard handles, we can use them either from ordinary C or C++ I/O, or using the **ReadFile()** and **WriteFile()** API functions.

Setting The Console Mode

Once we have a console, we can find and alter some of its properties using **GetConsoleMode()** and **SetConsoleMode()**, which work with a **DWORD** value containing the **mode bits**.

```
BOOL  GetConsoleMode(HANDLE  hConsole,  LPDWORD  mode);

BOOL  SetConsoleMode(HANDLE  hConsole,  DWORD  mode);
```

The console knows about five possible settings:

- **ENABLE_LINE_INPUT**, where input is only returned when the enter key is pressed
- **ENABLE_ECHO_INPUT**, where characters are echoed to **stdout**
- **ENABLE_PROCESSED_INPUT**, where control characters (*Ctrl+C*, backspace, linefeed and newline) are handled by the console
- **ENABLE_WINDOW_INPUT**, where window size changes are reported
- **ENABLE_MOUSE_INPUT**, where mouse events are reported

The last two use a callback mechanism, which we'll look at later in the chapter.

Try It Out — Setting The Console Mode

We can use **GetConsoleMode()** to see how the mode bits are set for the console in our simple application:

```
// SettingConsoleMode.cpp

#include <windows.h>
#include <iostream>
#include <tchar.h>

using namespace std;

int main()
{
    DWORD n;    // number of characters output
    LPTSTR buff = _T("hello world\n");

    // AllocConsole() and FreeConsole() calls removed, so we're using
    // the console we've inherited from the Command Prompt

    HANDLE hOut = GetStdHandle(STD_OUTPUT_HANDLE);
    DWORD mode;
    BOOL bOK = GetConsoleMode(hOut, &mode);
    if (!bOK)
    {
        cout << "Error getting console mode" << endl;
        return -1;
    }

    cout << "console mode is " << mode << endl;

    cout << "mode bits set are:" << endl;
    if (mode & ENABLE_LINE_INPUT) cout << "line input" << endl;
    if (mode & ENABLE_ECHO_INPUT) cout << "echo input" << endl;
    if (mode & ENABLE_PROCESSED_INPUT) cout << "processed input" << endl;
    if (mode & ENABLE_WINDOW_INPUT) cout << "window input" << endl;
    if (mode & ENABLE_MOUSE_INPUT) cout << "mouse input" << endl;
```

```
    cout << endl;

    WriteFile(hOut, buff, _tcslen(buff)*sizeof(char), &n, NULL);

    return 0;
}
```

Note how the `GetStdHandle()` call is now a statement in its own right, as we want to use the handle in two separate calls. Running this program should give you output similar to that shown below:

As we'd expect with the Command Prompt, we're using **cooked mode**, where input is line-oriented (meaning that input is read a line at a time when the user presses the enter key) and the console handles control characters for us.

We'll learn more about console modes when we investigate **raw mode** in the *Cursor Control* section.

Simple Console Input

Before we take a look at input, we need to explain the two input modes — **raw** and **cooked**. These names originated in the Unix world, and are also used in the Win32 API.

In cooked mode you get the same sort of I/O as when you use the `printf()` and `scanf()` functions, or the `cout` and `cin` streams. This mode is best for programs which want input one line at a time, because the Console API handles backspaces and breaks for you, and input is echoed to the screen (i.e. printed on the screen) as it is typed.

In raw mode, you get each character as it is typed, and there is no echoing to the screen or automatic handling of editing keys. Raw mode also gives you access to character attributes, such as colour, and lets you handle mouse input. This makes raw mode the obvious choice for full-screen or mouse-driven applications, such as a spreadsheet or word-processor. It is also possible to use asynchronous (overlapped) I/O to retrieve input when in raw mode, which enables you to do other processing while waiting for a character to be typed. (You may remember that asynchronous I/O was discussed in Chapter 7.)

We'll start discussing raw mode in the next section. For now, lets look at a simple example of doing console I/O using the API functions `ReadFile()` and `WriteFile()`.

Try It Out — Console Input/Output

This simple application will read lines and echo them to the screen, until a line beginning with a period is entered.

```cpp
// ConsoleIO.cpp

#include <windows.h>
#include <iostream>
#include <string>

using namespace std;

int main()
{
    // Get standard handles, which must be valid
    HANDLE hIn  = GetStdHandle(STD_INPUT_HANDLE);
    HANDLE hOut = GetStdHandle(STD_OUTPUT_HANDLE);
    if (hIn == INVALID_HANDLE_VALUE || hOut == INVALID_HANDLE_VALUE)
    {
        cout << "Error getting standard handles" << endl;
        return 0;
    }

    BYTE buff[250];
    DWORD dwRead = 0;
    DWORD dwWritten = 0;

    for (;;)
    {
        ReadFile(hIn, buff, sizeof(buff)-1, &dwRead, NULL);
        if (buff[0] == '.')
            break;

        buff[dwRead] = '\0';

        WriteFile(hOut, buff, dwRead, &dwWritten, NULL);
    }

    return 0;
}
```

We start by getting the handles for standard input and output, and checking that they're valid. If they aren't, then something is wrong, so we return. The **ReadFile()** and **WriteFile()** functions are used to get buffers of data from standard input, and write them to standard output. Since we're working in cooked mode, you should see the characters echoed as you type them — you can also correct errors by using backspace. When you press enter the program repeats the line by calling **WriteFile()**.

> *Note that in this case we don't include **tchar.h**. This is because **ReadFile()** and **WriteFile()** work directly in bytes, and not characters. Because we're reading bytes and then writing them again without processing them inbetween, Unicode/ANSI issues don't arise.*

Cursor Control

Now we've seen how to do line-oriented I/O, let's move on to see how we can do full-screen I/O, moving the cursor around and writing characters at arbitrary points on the screen.

The first thing that we'll need to do is to switch the console to raw mode, like this:

```
DWORD mode, newMode;

// Get the current mode
BOOL bOK = GetConsoleMode(hOut, &mode);
// Handle error if FALSE returned

// Remove cooked mode attributes
newMode = mode & ~(ENABLE_LINE_INPUT | ENABLE_ECHO_INPUT);

// Reset the mode
bOK = SetConsoleMode(hOut, newMode);
// Handle error if FALSE returned
```

Screen Buffer Information

In order to be able to write characters to the screen, we need to:

▶ Know the size of the screen

▶ Be able to change the position of the cursor

We can get this information using the `GetConsoleScreenBufferInfo()` function:

```
BOOL  GetConsoleScreenBufferInfo(
    HANDLE  hConsole,                        // handle to a console
    PCONSOLE_SCREEN_BUFFER_INFO  info);      // buffer to contain information
```

Each console has an associated screen buffer, which holds the characters being displayed by the console. We can retrieve data from the screen buffer that will tell us about attributes such as the size of the console buffer, how much is currently being displayed, and the current cursor position. This data is held in a structure like this:

```
typedef struct _CONSOLE_SCREEN_BUFFER_INFO {
   COORD dwSize;                    // console size
   COORD dwCursorPosition;          // cursor position
   WORD wAttributes;                // colour attributes
   SMALL_RECT srWindow;             // area being displayed
   COORD dwMaximumWindowSize;       // maximum size
} CONSOLE_SCREEN_BUFFER_INFO;
```

If you only want the maximum window size, the following function will return it:

```
COORD  GetLargestConsoleWindowSize(HANDLE  hConsole);
```

The `COORD` structure that is returned gives the height and width of the window:

```
typedef struct _COORD
{
    SHORT X;
    SHORT Y;
} COORD;
```

This structure corresponds to the `dwMaximumWindowSize` member of the `CONSOLE_SCREEN_BUFFER_INFO` structure. Note that coordinates are zero-based, so that (0,0) represents the top-left cell.

Unfortunately, there isn't a `SetConsoleScreenBufferInfo()` function for modifying the screen buffer information. Instead, you need to use one or more of the following three functions:

```
BOOL SetConsoleCursorPosition(HANDLE hConsole, COORD dwPos);

BOOL SetConsoleScreenBufferSize(HANDLE hConsole, COORD dwSize);

BOOL SetConsoleWindowInfo(HANDLE hConsole, BOOL bAbs, CONST SMALL_RECT* pWnd);
```

As you might expect, these set the cursor position, the size of the screen buffer, and the current size and position of the screen buffer's window. The `bAbs` parameter determines whether the coordinates passed in `pWnd` are absolute or offsets to the current coordinate values.

Try It Out — Cursor Positioning

Shown below is the full code for an example which demonstrates how we can use the calls just discussed above. It accepts characters typed by the user, and echoes each one to the screen at a randomly chosen position, continuing until a *q* is entered:

```
// CursorPositioning.cpp

#include <windows.h>
#include <iostream>
#include <string>
#include <ctime>
#include <cstdlib>

using namespace std;

int main()
{
    srand(static_cast<unsigned>(time(NULL)));

    // Get standard handles, which must be valid
    HANDLE hIn  = GetStdHandle(STD_INPUT_HANDLE);
    HANDLE hOut = GetStdHandle(STD_OUTPUT_HANDLE);
    if (hIn == INVALID_HANDLE_VALUE || hOut == INVALID_HANDLE_VALUE)
    {
        cout << "Error getting standard handles" << endl;
        return -1;
    }
```

```
    // Get our own console
    if (!FreeConsole())
    {
       cout << "Error returned from FreeConsole()";
       return -1;
    }

    if (!AllocConsole())
    {
       MessageBox (NULL, "Error returned from AllocConsole()", "Error", MB_OK);
       return -1;
    }

    // Set it into raw mode
    DWORD mode, newMode;

    // Get the current mode
    if (!GetConsoleMode(hOut, &mode))
    {
       cout << "Error returned from GetConsoleMode()";
       return -1;
    }

    // Remove cooked mode attributes
    newMode = mode & ~(ENABLE_LINE_INPUT | ENABLE_ECHO_INPUT);

    // Reset the mode
    if (!SetConsoleMode(hIn, newMode))
    {
       cout << "Error returned from SetConsoleMode()";
       return -1;
    }

    // Get the screen buffer info
    CONSOLE_SCREEN_BUFFER_INFO info;
    GetConsoleScreenBufferInfo(hOut, &info);

    char buff = 'x';

    while (buff != 'q')
    {
       DWORD nRead;
       ReadFile(hIn, &buff, 1, &nRead, NULL);

       SHORT xSize = info.dwSize.X;
       SHORT ySize = info.dwSize.Y;

       info.dwCursorPosition.X = rand() % xSize;
       info.dwCursorPosition.Y = rand() % ySize;
       SetConsoleCursorPosition(hOut, info.dwCursorPosition);

       DWORD nWritten = 0;
       WriteFile(hOut, &buff, 1, &nWritten, NULL);
    }

    return 0;
}
```

We start by getting the handles to the standard input and output streams, and checking that they're valid handles. Next, we detach from the console we've inherited from the parent process and create our own, once again checking that the operation worked. The effect of this will be seen when you run the program (from Explorer or Visual Studio, rather than a Command prompt); an initial console will open, and then be replaced by the second one, which is created by the call to **AllocConsole()**.

The next step is to switch to raw mode, by getting the console mode flags, turning off the line input and echo bits and resetting the mode. Getting the console screen buffer information tells us how big the console screen is, which we need to know for calculating the output position.

We can then enter a loop, getting a character at a time, and calculating a random position based on the console screen size. Setting the cursor position before a call to **WriteFile()** will ensure that the character appears where we want it.

If you try out this example, you should see an output something like the one shown below:

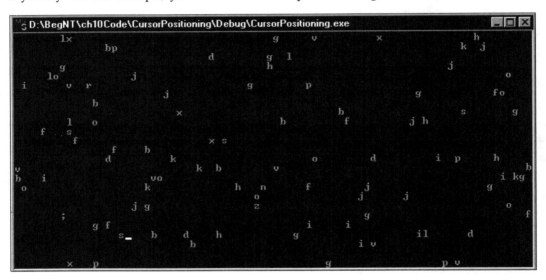

Modifying The Cursor

It is also possible to get information about the cursor, using **GetConsoleCursorInfo()**:

```
BOOL GetConsoleCursorInfo(HANDLE hConsole, PCONSOLE_CURSOR_INFO pi);
```

The **CONSOLE_CURSOR_INFO** structure contains information about the size and visibility of the cursor:

```
typedef struct _CONSOLE_CURSOR_INFO
{
    DWORD dwSize;           // cursor size
    BOOL bVisible;          // is cursor visible
} CONSOLE_CURSOR_INFO, *PCONSOLE_CURSOR_INFO;
```

The `dwSize` member gives the percentage of a character cell which is filled by the cursor; it can take values in the range 1 to 100 — a value of 1 means that the cursor is a thin line at the bottom of the cell, while 100 means that the cursor completely fills the cell. You can change the cursor or make it invisible by setting `bVisible` to `FALSE`, and passing one of these structures to `SetConsoleCursorInfo()`.

Using The WriteConsoleOutput() Functions

The previous example used the `ReadFile()` and `WriteFile()` functions together with explicit cursor positioning. This allowed us to write text to a point on the screen, but it didn't give us any control over the text attributes, such as the foreground and background colours. The Console API provides another way to output text which does allow control over text attributes, using the `WriteConsoleOutput...()` group of functions:

▶ `WriteConsoleOutputCharacter()`

▶ `WriteConsoleOutputAttribute()`

▶ `WriteConsoleOutput()`

The first two of these functions write the text and attributes to the screen separately, while the third writes both text and attributes in one go.

WriteConsoleOutputCharacter()

This function lets you write a block of text to a particular position on the screen:

```
BOOL  WriteConsoleOutputCharacter(
    HANDLE  hConsoleOutput      // handle  to  a  console  screen  buffer
    LPCTSTR lpBuffer,           // pointer  to  buffer  with  data  to  write
    DWORD   dwLength,           // number  of  characters  in  source  buffer
    COORD   dwCoord,            // cell  to  start  writing
    LPDWORD &dwChars);          // number  of  characters  written
```

Writing starts at the cell you specify, and will wrap onto succeeding rows as required. If the write would exceed the number of rows left in the buffer, the buffer is filled and the `dwChars` argument will tell you how many characters were actually written. Neither the current cursor position nor the attributes of cells are changed by this function.

We can easily modify the previous example to use this function. Here's the loop rewritten so that it prints out the string 'aardvarks' until you type a *q*:

```
while (buff != 'q')
    {
        DWORD nRead;
        ReadFile(hIn, &buff, 1, &nRead, NULL);

        SHORT xSize = info.dwSize.X;
        SHORT ySize = info.dwSize.Y;

        COORD c;
        c.X = rand() % xSize;
        c.Y = rand() % ySize;
```

```
                    // Write a string at random positions
                    DWORD nCellsWritten;
                    WriteConsoleOutputCharacter (hOut, "aardvarks", 9, c, &nCellsWritten);
    }
```

You'll see that most of the code is the same, but that we now set the position of the cursor implicitly in the call to `WriteConsoleOutputCharacter()`, rather than explicitly via a call to `SetConsoleCursorPosition()`. We've also declared and used a local `COORD` variable to hold the initial position, to save typing `info.dwCursorPosition` too many times!

The screenshot below shows typical output from the program. Note how the text wraps around to the following line where necessary:

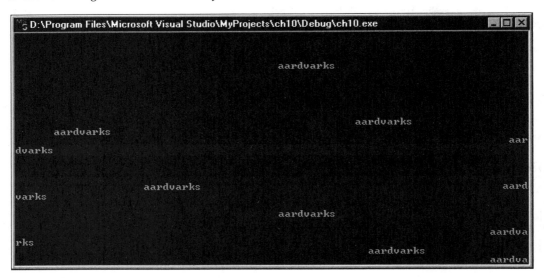

WriteConsoleOutputAttribute()

The `WriteConsoleOutputAttribute()` function is almost identical to `WriteConsoleOutputCharacter()`, the only difference being that the attributes of the cells are being changed, rather than their text:

```
    BOOL   WriteConsoleOutputAttribute(
           HANDLE  hConsoleOutput,        // handle to a console screen buffer
           CONST  WORD*  lpAtts,          // pointer to attribute data
           DWORD  dwLength,               // number of characters in source
                                          // buffer
           COORD  dwCoord,                // cell to start writing
           LPDWORD  &dwChars);            // number of attributes written
```

The function works in the same way as `WriteConsoleOutputCharacter()`, with the number of attributes actually written to the screen being returned in `dwChars`.

Attributes can be set by using a combination of the following set of values:

- **BACKGROUND_BLUE**
- **BACKGROUND_RED**
- **BACKGROUND_GREEN**
- **BACKGROUND_INTENSITY**
- **FOREGROUND_BLUE**
- **FOREGROUND_RED**
- **FOREGROUND_GREEN**
- **FOREGROUND_INTENSITY**

As you can see, color control is fairly limited in its sophistication. You can make up colors for the text foreground and background by specifying red, green and blue components, and the 'intensity' setting allows you to select the plain or bright version of a colour. For example, the following combination would give you bright green text on a white background:

```
FOREGROUND_GREEN | FOREGROUND_INTENSITY |
    BACKGROUND_RED | BACKGROUND_GREEN | BACKGROUND_BLUE
```

This function can be illustrated by extending the previous example so that as well as writing a string to the screen at a random location, it also changes the attributes of a random block of text.

```
while (buff != 'q')
{
   DWORD nRead;
   ReadFile(hIn, &buff, 1, &nRead, NULL);

   SHORT xSize = info.dwSize.X;
   SHORT ySize = info.dwSize.Y;

   COORD c;
   c.X = rand() % xSize;
   c.Y = rand() % ySize;

   // Write string at random positions
   DWORD nCellsWritten;
   WriteConsoleOutputCharacter(hOut, "aardvarks", 9, c, &nCellsWritten);

   c.X = rand() % xSize;
   c.Y = rand() % ySize;

   // Write attributes at random positions
   WORD wAttributes[9];
   for(int i=0; i<9; i++)
   wAttributes[i] = FOREGROUND_GREEN | FOREGROUND_INTENSITY | BACKGROUND_RED |
                       BACKGROUND_GREEN | BACKGROUND_BLUE;
   WriteConsoleOutputAttribute(hOut, wAttributes, 9, c, &nCellsWritten);
}
```

469

The only thing you have to remember when changing attributes in this way is that you can't just supply a single value, and have it applied to a range of cells. You need to pass a pointer to an array of attribute values, one for each cell you want to change. This makes it easy to provide fancy formatting to text, but makes it less easy to change a range of cells to a single set of attributes. There is, however, a way around this, which we'll look at shortly.

Once again, running the program will give a display similar to this:

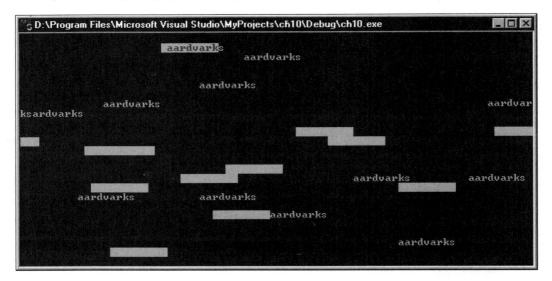

Although it isn't apparent from the grayscale picture, where a call to `WriteConsoleOutputAttribute()` has changed the attributes of a block of cells, the foreground and background colors of existing text have changed! This shows that this call can be very useful if you need to change the attributes of text already present on the screen, without needing to rewrite the text itself.

Filling Attributes And Characters

When you want to set a range of cells to the same character or set of attributes, it isn't very efficient having to fill in an array with a number of identical values. The Console API provides two functions, `FillConsoleOutputCharacter()` and `FillConsoleOutputAttribute()`, which allow you to fill a range of cells with a single character or set of attributes. They work the same way as their `WriteConsoleOutput...()` counterparts, but only take a single value for the character or attribute. Here's the prototype for `FillConsoleOutputAttribute()` to give you the idea:

```
BOOL  FillConsoleOutputAttribute(
    HANDLE  hConsoleOutput,         //  handle  to  a  console  screen  buffer
    WORD  Attribute,                //  attribute  data
    DWORD  dwSize,                  //  number  of  characters  in  source
                                    //  buffer
    COORD  dwCoord,                 //  cell  to  start  writing
    LPDWORD  &dwChars);             //  number  of  cells  written
```

WriteConsoleOutput()

If you want to set the text and the attributes at once, you can use `WriteConsoleOutput()`, but it works in a slightly different way from the other two calls:

```
BOOL  WriteConsoleOutput(
      HANDLE  hConsoleOutput,          //  handle  to  a  console  screen  buffer
      CONST  CHAR_INFO  *lpBuffer,     //  pointer  to  buffer  with  data  to  write
      COORD  dwBufferSize,             //  column-row  size  of  source  buffer
      COORD  dwBufferCoord,            //  upper-left  cell  to  write  from
      PSMALL_RECT  lpWriteRegion);     //  pointer  to  rectangle  to  write  to
```

There are two major differences between this call and the previous two:

> It copies a block of text from a buffer of **CHAR_INFO** items (we will discuss this structure shortly), each of which contains both a character and its formatting

> It copies the text to a specified rectangle in the console buffer, rather than as a series of lines

You specify a rectangle on the screen to which you want to write, using the `lpWriteRegion` parameter. A rectangular region of the same size is mapped onto the source buffer at the point **dwBufferCoord**, and the size of the source buffer is given by **dwBufferSize**. Characters and attributes are copied from the source buffer to the console, with the output being clipped to the size of the screen buffer. If the destination rectangle is larger than the source, cells for which no source data exists will be left unchanged.

Note that this function has no effect on the current cursor position.

The CHAR_INFO And SMALL_RECT Structures

Each cell in the buffer passed to `WriteConsoleOutput()` contains both a character and the attributes which determine the cell's appearance. The **CHAR_INFO** structure is used to encapsulate both these items, and will work for both ASCII and Unicode characters:

```
typedef struct _CHAR_INFO
{
   union
   { /* Unicode or ANSI character */
      WCHAR UnicodeChar;
      CHAR AsciiChar;
   } Char;
   WORD Attributes;              // text and background colors
} CHAR_INFO, *PCHAR_INFO;
```

You'll need to store the character in the appropriate member of the union, depending on whether you're using Unicode or ANSI. You can decide which member to use by means of a simple **#ifdef _UNICODE** test.

The rectangle on the screen, into which we want to copy the buffer, is specified by a **SMALL_RECT** structure, which looks like this:

```
typedef struct _SMALL_RECT {
   SHORT Left;
   SHORT Top;
   SHORT Right;
   SHORT Bottom;
} SMALL_RECT;
```

It shouldn't be necessary to explain how you use this particular structure!

For Example...

Let's modify our simple example yet again, this time writing out a three-by-three block of asterisks at a random position, every time a key is pressed. Here's the requisite part of the code:

```
char buff = 'x';
```

```
// set up the source block
CHAR_INFO ci[9];
for (int i=0; i<9; i++)
{
   ci[i].Char.AsciiChar = '*';
   ci[i].Attributes =
         BACKGROUND_GREEN | BACKGROUND_BLUE | BACKGROUND_INTENSITY;
}
```

```
while (buff != 'q')
{
   DWORD nRead;
   ReadFile(hIn, &buff, 1, &nRead, NULL);

   SHORT xSize = info.dwSize.X;
   SHORT ySize = info.dwSize.Y;

   COORD c;
   c.X = rand() % xSize;
   c.Y = rand() % ySize;
```

```
   // Character buffer size and origin
   COORD bufSize, origin;
   bufSize.X = bufSize.Y = 3;
   origin.X = origin.Y = 0;

   // Screen rect to write to
   SMALL_RECT sr;
   sr.Left = c.X;
   sr.Top = c.Y;
   sr.Right = c.X + 2;
   sr.Bottom = c.Y + 2;

   WriteConsoleOutput(hOut, ci, bufSize, origin, &sr);
```
```
}
```

The first task is to set up the block of text to be copied to the screen. Since we're copying to a three-by-three region of cells, we set up a nine-element array of **CHAR_INFO** structures, each of which specifies an asterisk as the character, with black text on a bright cyan background.

Within the loop, we need to set up the position and size information. Two **COORD** structures hold the size of the source buffer in rows and columns, and the position in the buffer from which copying will take place. A **SMALL_RECT** structure holds the rectangle on the screen into which we want to copy the buffer.

Running the program gives a display like this:

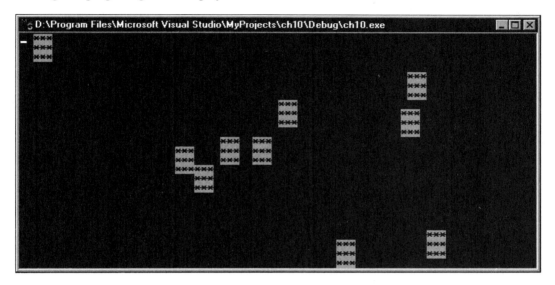

Scrolling The Screen

We can now put text anywhere on the screen, but for many text-handling applications we'll want to scroll the screen as well. The Console API is very flexible in the way it allows you to scroll areas of the screen, using the **ScrollConsoleScreenBuffer()** function:

```
BOOL  ScrollConsoleScreenBuffer(
      HANDLE  hConsoleOutput,            // handle to a screen buffer
      CONST  SMALL_RECT*  lpScrollRect,  // rectangle to scroll
      CONST  SMALL_RECT*  lpClipRect,    // optional clipping rectangle
      COORD  dwDest,                     // new origin for rectangle
      CONST  CHAR_INFO*  lpFill);        // how to fill blank lines
```

When calling **ScrollConsoleScreenBuffer()**, you specify a rectangular region of the screen, **lpScrollRect**, and move its origin to a new position, specified by **dwDest**. Any blank lines which are exposed as a result of the move will be filled with the character and attributes specified in **lpFill**. You can also, if you wish, supply a clipping rectangle; if supplied, only changes which fall within that rectangle are shown.

Since you can specify which rectangles on the screen are to be scrolled, it is possible to use this function to achieve sophisticated multi-windowing effects, like the sort of thing you'd see on a VT100 terminal emulator.

Try It Out — Scrolling The Screen

This example program reads characters one at a time in raw mode until a # is entered, and echoes them to the screen, handling newlines and scrolling the screen when it reaches the bottom:

```cpp
// ScrollingScreen.cpp

#include <windows.h>
#include <iostream>
#include <string>
#include <ctime>

using namespace std;

int main()
{
   srand(static_cast<unsigned>(time (NULL)));

   // Get standard handles, which must be valid
   HANDLE hIn  = GetStdHandle(STD_INPUT_HANDLE);
   HANDLE hOut = GetStdHandle(STD_OUTPUT_HANDLE);
   if (hIn == INVALID_HANDLE_VALUE || hOut == INVALID_HANDLE_VALUE)
   {
      cout << "Error getting standard handles" << endl;
      return 0;
   }

   // Get our own console
   if (!FreeConsole())
   {
      cout << "Error returned from FreeConsole()";
      return 0;
   }

   if (!AllocConsole())
   {
      cout << "Error returned from AllocConsole()";
      return 0;
   }

   // Set it into raw mode
   DWORD mode, newMode;

   // Get the current mode
   if (!GetConsoleMode(hOut, &mode))
   {
      cout << "Error returned from GetConsoleMode()";
      return 0;
   }

   // Remove cooked mode attributes
   newMode = mode & ~(ENABLE_LINE_INPUT | ENABLE_ECHO_INPUT);

   // Reset the mode
   if (!SetConsoleMode(hIn, newMode))
```

```
    {
        cout << "Error returned from SetConsoleMode()";
        return 0;
    }

    // Get the screen buffer info
    CONSOLE_SCREEN_BUFFER_INFO info;
    GetConsoleScreenBufferInfo(hOut, &info);

    char buff = 'x';

    // Read characters till we get an escape character
    while (buff != '#')
    {
        DWORD nRead, nWritten;
        ReadFile(hIn, &buff, 1, &nRead, NULL);

        // If we got a '\r' handle the new line, else put
        // the character out
        if (buff == '\r')
        {
            info.dwCursorPosition.X = 0;
            // If we're on the last line, scroll
            if (info.dwCursorPosition.Y == info.dwSize.Y - 1)
            {
                // Scroll the screen... first define the area to scroll
                SMALL_RECT sr;
                sr.Top = sr.Left = 0;
                sr.Bottom = info.dwSize.Y - 1;
                sr.Right = info.dwSize.X - 1;

                // Now the destination of the scrolled rectangle. Moving the
                // buffer to (0,-1) effectively loses the first line off the
                // top of the screen.
                COORD c;
                c.X = 0;
                c.Y = -1;

                // How do we want the blank line filled? With blanks, using
                // whatever attributes are currently set
                CHAR_INFO ci;
                ci.Attributes = info.wAttributes;
                ci.Char.AsciiChar = ' ';

                // Scroll the screen
                ScrollConsoleScreenBuffer(hOut, &sr, 0, c, &ci);
            }
            else
                info.dwCursorPosition.Y += 1;

            // Set the new cursor position
            SetConsoleCursorPosition(hOut, info.dwCursorPosition);
        }
        else
            WriteFile(hOut, &buff, 1, &nWritten, NULL);
    }

    return 0;
}
```

Let's take a look at what we're doing in more detail. The main loop reads a character and sees if it is a '\r' (i.e. whether you have pressed *enter*); if it isn't, the character is output at the current cursor position using **WriteFile()**, and another character is read.

> *Note that in a console application you'll get '\r' for end-of-line in raw mode, and '\n' in cooked mode.*

If the character was a '\r', we move the cursor back to the start of the line. We then need to check whether we're on the last line of the buffer; if we aren't, we can increment the **Y** position of the cursor, and we're done. If we are on the last line, we need to scroll the buffer to give a new blank line.

In order to do this, we need to set up some data structures. The first is a **SMALL_RECT** defining the area we want to scroll, and in this case we set it to include the entire screen. The second is the new position for the scrolled area; we want to move the entire screen up by one line, so we do this by specifying the new position as (0,-1), thus moving the top line off the top of the screen. Specifying coordinates which are outside the bounds of the screen buffer is quite legal, and the scrolling function will simply clip anything which doesn't fit on the screen.

The final thing we need to specify is how we want to fill blank lines. Scrolling a region may well result in some blank lines appearing, so we pass the function a **CHAR_INFO** structure telling it how these lines should be filled. We'll just fill them with blanks, using whatever attributes are currently set for the buffer. After you've set these up, scrolling the screen simply involves a call to **ScrollConsoleScreenBuffer()**.

Handling Backspace

As a final embellishment, lets extend the example so that it correctly handles the backspace key. This turns out to be pretty simple to do — when we recognise a backspace, all we have to do is move the cursor one position backwards, output a space, and then move the cursor back again so that it is over the cell containing the space. For simplicity, we won't let the user backspace past the beginning of the line; we could add the ability to do this, but it would require us to store information about the length of lines, thus complicating matters considerably.

Here's the main loop with the backspace handling code added:

```
while (buff != '#')
    {
        DWORD nRead, nWritten;
        ReadFile(hIn, &buff, 1, &nRead, NULL);

        // If we got a '\r' handle the new line, else put
        // the character out
        if (buff == '\r')
        {
            info.dwCursorPosition.X = 0;
            // If we're on the last line, scroll
            if (info.dwCursorPosition.Y == info.dwSize.Y - 1)
            {
                // Scroll the screen... first define the area to scroll
                SMALL_RECT sr;
                sr.Top = sr.Left = 0;
                sr.Bottom = info.dwSize.Y - 1;
                sr.Right = info.dwSize.X - 1;
```

```
                    // Now the destination of the scrolled rectangle. Moving the
                    // buffer to (0,-1) effectively loses the first line off the
                    // top of the screen.
                    COORD c;
                    c.X = 0;
                    c.Y = -1;

                    // How do we want the blank line filled? With blanks, using
                    // whatever attributes are currently set
                    CHAR_INFO ci;
                    ci.Attributes = info.wAttributes;
                    ci.Char.AsciiChar = ' ';

                    // Scroll the screen
                    ScrollConsoleScreenBuffer(hOut, &sr, 0, c, &ci);
                }
                else
                    info.dwCursorPosition.Y += 1;

                    // Set the new cursor position
                    SetConsoleCursorPosition(hOut, info.dwCursorPosition);
            }
            else if (buff == '\b')
            {
                // handle backspace... only move back to beginning of the line
                GetConsoleScreenBufferInfo(hOut, &info);
                if (info.dwCursorPosition.X > 0)
                info.dwCursorPosition.X -= 1;

                // Set the new cursor position
                SetConsoleCursorPosition(hOut, info.dwCursorPosition);

                // Write a space to blank out previous character
                buff = ' ';
                WriteFile(hOut, &buff, 1, &nWritten, NULL);

                // Reset the cursor position to the cell containing the blank
                SetConsoleCursorPosition(hOut, info.dwCursorPosition);
            }
            else
                WriteFile(hOut, &buff, 1, &nWritten, NULL);
        }
```

Reading The Screen

The `WriteConsoleOutput()` functions have a corresponding set of three functions:

- ► `ReadConsoleOutput()`
- ► `ReadConsoleOutputCharacter()`
- ► `ReadConsoleOutputAttribute()`

We know what writing output does, but you could be forgiven for wondering what reading the console output gets you. The answer is that these allow you to read text and attributes from the screen, in the same way that the `WriteConsoleOutput()` functions let you set them. `ReadConsoleOutputCharacter()` reads a number of characters, `ReadConsoleOutputAttribute()` reads attributes, and `ReadConsoleOutput()` reads both at once.

To show you how similar the `WriteConsoleOutput...()` and `ReadConsoleOutput...()` functions are, here's the prototype for `ReadConsoleOutputCharacter()`:

```
BOOL  ReadConsoleOutputCharacter(
      HANDLE  hConsoleOutput,    // handle to a console screen buffer
      LPTSTR  lpBuffer,          // pointer to buffer to receive data
      DWORD   dwNumber,          // number of cells to read
      COORD   dwCoord,           // cell to start reading
      LPDWORD &dwChars);         // number of characters read
```

It is almost identical to `WriteConsoleOutputCharacter()`, except that the buffer pointer is not constant.

Once you've worked out how to use `WriteConsoleOutputCharacter()`, you should have no trouble reading the screen using these functions. You'll be able to set up a process which lets the user fill in a form, and then reads the data from the screen when they're finished.

Control Handlers

Every console process can handle **control signals** from the operating system and user. If you've used Unix, you'll be familiar with the idea of signals and installing signal handlers — console applications allow you to work in a very similar way.

Control signals are generated under the following circumstances:

▶ The user pressing *Ctrl-C* or *Ctrl-Break* — generates the **CTRL_C_EVENT** or **CTRL_BREAK_EVENT** signals, respectively

▶ The user closing the console, logging off or shutting down the system, which generates **CTRL_CLOSE_EVENT**, **CTRL_LOGOFF_EVENT** and **CTRL_SHUTDOWN_EVENT** respectively

A console process has a handler function, which by default simply calls `ExitProcess()` to terminate the process. It is possible to add other handler functions using the `SetConsoleCtrlHandler()` API call:

```
BOOL  SetConsoleCtrlHandler(
      PHANDLER_ROUTINE ph,       // address of handler routine
      BOOL bAdd);                // whether to add or remove handler
```

When a signal comes into the process, its handlers are called in order, with the most recently registered being called first. If a handler processes the signal, it returns **TRUE**, otherwise it returns **FALSE**. If no handler returns **TRUE**, the default handler will be called and the process will terminate.

The handler function needs to have the following prototype:

```
BOOL Handler(DWORD dwEvent);
```

It is fairly straightforward, and the only complication arises from the different ways in which you can handle *Ctrl-C* signals.

The function can be used in two ways:

▶ If the address of a handler function is given in the first parameter, it is added or removed from the handler list, depending on the value of the second argument.

▶ If the first parameter is **NULL**, then the second parameter controls whether *Ctrl-C* is ignored or not. A value of **TRUE** will cause the process to ignore *Ctrl-C* signals, while **FALSE** will resume processing. This behaviour will be inherited by child processes.

> *Note that Ctrl-Break signals are always processed, and can't be controlled in the same way as Ctrl-C*

You can also use **SetConsoleMode()** to turn off the **ENABLE_PROCESSED_INPUT** flag, which will result in *Ctrl-C* signals being reported as keyboard input instead of as signals.

Try It Out — Adding A Handler

As an example, here's how to add a handler to our *Console Cursor Positioning* program. We'll simply handle *Ctrl-C* and *Ctrl-Break* signals, and will beep when each is handled. We'll also take no further action for *Ctrl-C*, but let *Ctrl-Break* through so that the default handler can terminate the program.

The handler function itself looks like this:

```
BOOL EventFunc(DWORD dwEvent)
{
    switch(dwEvent)
    {
        case CTRL_C_EVENT:
        // For Ctrl-C, beep and don't allow process to exit
        MessageBeep(MB_OK);
        return TRUE;

        case CTRL_BREAK_EVENT:
        // For Ctrl-Break, beep and allow default handler to exit
        MessageBeep(MB_OK);
        return FALSE;
    }

    return FALSE;
}
```

We only handle the **CTRL_C_EVENT** and **CTRL_BREAK_EVENT** signals, and beep each time. For the **CTRL_C_EVENT**, signal we return **TRUE**, showing that we've completely handled the signal. For all others we return **FALSE**, so that the default handler gets a chance to process them.

The only other thing we need to do is to add the code to install the handler:

```
// Reset the mode
if (!SetConsoleMode(hIn, newMode))
{
    cout << "Error returned from SetConsoleMode()";
    return 0;
}
```

```
// Add handler
if (!SetConsoleCtrlHandler((PHANDLER_ROUTINE)EventFunc, TRUE))
{
    cout << "Error returned from SetConsoleCtrlHandler()";
    return 0;
}
```

```
// Get the screen buffer info
CONSOLE_SCREEN_BUFFER_INFO info;
GetConsoleScreenBufferInfo(hOut, &info);
```

Low-Level Structured Input

The Console API has both high-level and low-level ways of performing I/O. The high-level ways use **ReadFile()** and **WriteFile()**, and as we've seen, they handle a lot of the mundane tasks for you, such as automatically positioning the cursor.

We've also seen how to do low-level output handling:

- Positioning the cursor where we want
- Setting screen attributes using the **WriteConsoleOutput()** functions
- Reading the screen using the **ReadConsoleOutput()** functions

As you might expect, there is a matching set of functions for getting low-level control over input operations.

Events

Low-level input is based on the notion of events — as things happen, event records are added to the input stream for the console, and get processed in turn. There are three sorts of events we may want to deal with:

- Keyboard events
- Mouse events
- Window resize events

Functions such as **ReadFile()** access this stream, selectively processing the keyboard events.

We can use Win32 functions like **WaitForSingleObject()** to wait for console input to become available. To do this, use the console handle as the parameter of the wait function:

```
WaitForSingleObject(hInput, 0);
```

The console input buffer handle becomes signalled when the buffer is not empty. See Chapter 6 for more details on this function and how to use it.

The INPUT_EVENT Structure

Just as Windows has the **MSG** structure for representing Windows messages, console input events are represented by **INPUT_EVENT** structures, which look like this:

```
typedef struct _INPUT_RECORD
{
   WORD EventType;
   union
   {
      KEY_EVENT_RECORD KeyEvent;
      MOUSE_EVENT_RECORD MouseEvent;
      WINDOW_BUFFER_SIZE_RECORD WindowBufferSizeEvent;
      MENU_EVENT_RECORD MenuEvent;
      FOCUS_EVENT_RECORD FocusEvent;
   } Event;
} INPUT_RECORD;
```

An event input record consists of a discriminator, **EventType**, which says what sort of event is held in the record. It can take one of five values

- **KEY_EVENT**
- **MOUSE_EVENT**
- **WINDOW_BUFFER_SIZE_EVENT**
- **MENU_EVENT**
- **FOCUS_EVENT**

Depending on the type, the **Event** union will hold one of a number of other types:

- A **KEY_EVENT_RECORD** holding data about a key press
- A **MOUSE_EVENT_RECORD** holding information about mouse movements and button presses
- A **WINDOW_BUFFER_SIZE_RECORD** giving the new size of the screen buffer, when the window size changes

There are two other event types, **MENU_EVENT_RECORD** and **FOCUS_EVENT_RECORD**, which are used internally by the console system, and should be ignored by programs utilising consoles.

Key Events

As you might expect, a **KEY_EVENT_RECORD** contains information about the state of the keyboard when a key was pressed:

```
typedef struct _KEY_EVENT_RECORD
{
   BOOL bKeyDown;              // TRUE = key press, FALSE = key release
   WORD wRepeatCount;          // repeat count
   WORD wVirtualKeyCode;       // device-independent virtual key code
   WORD wVirtualScanCode;      // device-dependent virtual scan code
   union
   {
      WCHAR UnicodeChar;
      CHAR AsciiChar;
   } uChar;                    // Unicode or ASCII character
   DWORD dwControlKeyState;    // state of control keys
} KEY_EVENT_RECORD;
```

Most of the time when processing key events, you'll want to use the **uChar** union, together with the state of the control keys. Remember that you'll need to used the Unicode or ANSI members of the union, depending on how you're building the application. The **dwControlKeyState** member will take its value from a combination of the following values:

▶ CAPSLOCK_ON

▶ ENHANCED_KEY

▶ LEFT_ALT_PRESSED

▶ LEFT_CTRL_PRESSED

▶ NUMLOCK_ON

▶ RIGHT_ALT_PRESSED

▶ RIGHT_CTRL_PRESSED

▶ SCROLLLOCK_ON

▶ SHIFT_PRESSED

The nesting of structures and unions means that actually getting to the character generated by a keyboard event takes quite a lot of code:

```
INPUT_RECORD inp;
CHAR c;
...
// Save the character away on the key up event
if (inp.EventType == KEY_EVENT && !inp.Event.KeyEvent.bKeyDown)
   c = inp.Event.KeyEvent.uChar.AsciiChar;
```

Mouse Events

The `MOUSE_EVENT_RECORD` structure looks like this:

```
typedef struct _MOUSE_EVENT_RECORD
{
    COORD dwMousePosition;          // position of mouse in cell coordinates
    DWORD dwButtonState;            // mouse button information
    DWORD dwControlKeyState;        // state of control keys
    DWORD dwEventFlags;             // type of mouse event
} MOUSE_EVENT_RECORD;
```

The position is reported in cell coordinates. The bits in the `dwButtonState` member tell you which button, or buttons, were being used when the event was being generated. A bit is set to 1 if the button was used, and the key is as follows:

> The least significant bit represents the leftmost button

> The next bit represents the rightmost button

> Remaining bits then correspond to remaining buttons, from left to right

The control key state will be formed from the same range of possible values as for key events. The `dwEventFlags` member can have one of two values — `MOUSE_MOVED` for a change in mouse position, and `DOUBLE_CLICK` for the second click of a double click. Note that before you get a double click event, you'll have already had a single click event, as is the case with Windows messages.

Window Size Events

The `WINDOW_BUFFER_SIZE_RECORD` structure is very simple, with a single member:

```
typedef struct _WINDOW_BUFFER_SIZE_RECORD
{
    COORD dwSize;
} WINDOW_BUFFER_SIZE_RECORD;
```

The `dwSize` member gives the new size of the screen buffer.

ReadConsoleInput() And PeekConsoleInput()

We can get at the console's input event buffer using `ReadConsoleInput()`:

```
BOOL  ReadConsoleInput(
    HANDLE hConsole,              //  console  handle
    PINPUT_RECORD lpBuff,        //  address  of  buffer  for  events
    DWORD nLength,               //  number  of  event  records  to  read
    LPDWORD pdwEvents);          //  number  of  records  read
```

This function allows us to read a number of events from the buffer, each of which will be stored in the array of `INPUT_RECORD` structures which we provide. If there aren't enough records in the buffer to satisfy the request, the number actually read will be returned in the final parameter. Note that the function will not return until at least one record has been read. We'll see how this function can be used later on, when we write a class to handle console operations.

Reading an event is destructive, in that it 'consumes' the event, removing it from the buffer. Sometimes we want to look and see what is waiting in the buffer without removing events, and that's what `PeekConsoleInput()` lets us do. It has exactly the same form as `ReadConsoleInput()`:

```
BOOL PeekConsoleInput(
    HANDLE hConsole,           //  console  handle
    PINPUT_RECORD lpBuff,      //  address  of  buffer  for  events
    DWORD nLength,             //  number  of  event  records  to  read
    LPDWORD pdwEvents);        //  number  of  records  read
```

We'll see an example which uses `ReadConsoleInput()` when we look at handling mouse input in the *Mouse Support* section.

WriteConsoleInput()

Should you ever want to do so, you can place events into a console's event buffer manually, using `WriteConsoleInput()`:

```
BOOL WriteConsoleInput(
    HANDLE hConsole,              //  console  handle
    CONST INPUT_RECORD* lpBuff,  //  address  of  buffer  holding  events
    DWORD nLength,               //  number  of  event  records  to  write
    LPDWORD pdwEvents);          //  number  of  records  written
```

Events will be placed into the event buffer after any pending items, and the buffer will be expanded to cope with the new events, if necessary.

Why might you ever want to do this? Well, you could, for instance, have program which will expand input text, recognising abbreviations and expanding them by placing key events into the queue.

Other Input Functions

The `GetNumberOfConsoleInputEvents()` function can tell you the number of events in the console's input buffer.

```
BOOL GetNumberOfConsoleInputEvents(
    HANDLE hConsole,     //  console  handle
    LPDWORD pdwNum);     //  buffer  to  store  number  of  events
```

Incidentally this function was once a worthy contender for the 'Longest API Name' prize. However, with the advent of COM, it has been comprehensively beaten by `CoMarshalInterThreadInterfaceInStream()`, *which weighs in at a massive 37 characters!*

The `FlushConsoleInputBuffer()` function can be used to clear out the input buffer:

```
BOOL FlushConsoleInputBuffer(HANDLE hConsole);     //  console  handle
```

Mouse Support

Console windows can handle mouse input (as you'd guess from the provision of a **MOUSE_EVENT_RECORD** data type). They have mouse input enabled by default, because the **ENABLE_MOUSE_INPUT** console mode flag is set, but you do have to make sure that you're getting input in the right way.

As you probably realize, in order to use the mouse, you need to use **ReadConsoleInput()** instead of **ReadFile()**, because the latter only handles keystrokes. We've seen that **ReadConsoleInput()** recognizes other kinds of input events as well, and passes back an **INPUT_RECORD** structure which contains data about a keyboard event, a mouse event or a window resize event.

Note that using **ReadConsoleInput()** also sets the input mode to raw mode. This is because you don't want echoing when handling mouse input, and also you want to get events immediately, and not have them buffered. This means that the current **SetConsoleMode()** cooked or raw settings are disregarded.

Try It Out — Mouse Event Handling

This program will print a string wherever the mouse is double-clicked, until an escape character is entered. It illustrates the use of **ReadConsoleInput()** as well as mouse event handling.

Here's the program code. The lines which implement the event handling are highlighted:

```cpp
// MouseEventHandler.cpp

#include <windows.h>
#include <iostream>
#include <string>

using namespace std;

int main()
{
    // Get standard handles, which must be valid
    HANDLE hIn  = GetStdHandle(STD_INPUT_HANDLE);
    HANDLE hOut = GetStdHandle(STD_OUTPUT_HANDLE);
    if (hIn == INVALID_HANDLE_VALUE || hOut == INVALID_HANDLE_VALUE)
    {
        cout << "Error getting standard handles" << endl;
        return -1;
    }

    // Get our own console
    if (!FreeConsole())
    {
        cout << "Error returned from FreeConsole()";
        return 0;
    }
```

```
        if (!AllocConsole())
        {
            cout << "Error returned from AllocConsole()";
            return 0;
        }

        // Set it into raw mode
        DWORD mode, newMode;

        // Get the current mode
        if (!GetConsoleMode(hOut, &mode))
        {
            cout << "Error returned from GetConsoleMode()";
            return 0;
        }

        // Remove cooked mode attributes
        newMode = mode & ~(ENABLE_LINE_INPUT | ENABLE_ECHO_INPUT);
        // Ensure we can get mouse input
        newMode |= ENABLE_MOUSE_INPUT;

        // Reset the mode
        if (!SetConsoleMode(hIn, newMode))
        {
            cout << "Error returned from SetConsoleMode()";
            return 0;
        }

        while (1)
        {
            INPUT_RECORD rec;
            DWORD nRead;
            ReadConsoleInput(hIn, &rec, 1, &nRead);

            COORD c;

            if (rec.EventType == KEY_EVENT)
            {
                // Finish if an escape character was entered
                if (rec.Event.KeyEvent.uChar.AsciiChar == '\033')
                break;
            }
            else if (rec.EventType == MOUSE_EVENT)
            {
                // Move the cursor to the position given in the event
                if (rec.Event.MouseEvent.dwEventFlags & DOUBLE_CLICK)
                {
                    c.X = rec.Event.MouseEvent.dwMousePosition.X;
                    c.Y = rec.Event.MouseEvent.dwMousePosition.Y;
                    SetConsoleCursorPosition(hOut, rec.Event.MouseEvent.dwMousePosition);

                    // And write the string here
                    DWORD nCellsWritten;
                    WriteConsoleOutputCharacter(hOut, "aardvarks", 9, c, &nCellsWritten);
                }
            }
        }
```

```
        return 0;
    }
```

The first thing to do is to ensure that we've enabled mouse input, by setting the **ENABLE_MOUSE_INPUT** flag. We don't strictly need to set the console to raw mode, since the call to **ReadConsoleInput()** will do it for us, but I've left it in.

The loop reads one event from the buffer, and takes action depending· on its type. If it is a key event, it ignores all characters except for *escape* (which exits the loop). For mouse events, the event flag **DWORD** is checked to look for double-click events. When one is found a string is output to the screen at the coordinates held in the event structure.

Screen Buffers

Each console comes with one screen buffer, but it is possible to create extra buffers and switch between them. This ability is obviously very useful if you are writing something like a text editor which can open multiple files, or a multi-session terminal emulator.

New buffers are created with the **CreateConsoleScreenBuffer()** API:

```
HANDLE  CreateConsoleScreenBuffer(
    DWORD  dwAccess,                      // access  flag
    DWORD  dwMode,                        // share  mode
    LPSECURITY_ATTRIBUTES  lpSec,         // security  attributes
    DWORD  dwFlags,                       // creation  flags
    LPVOID  lpData);                      // reserved
```

The access flag can be one or both of **GENERIC_READ** and **GENERIC_WRITE**, depending on the sort of access you require. The second parameter determines whether the buffer can have other open operations applied to it. It can take one or both of the values **FILE_SHARE_READ** and **FILE_SHARE_WRITE**, or be set to zero to indicate no sharing.

The **lpSec** parameter specifies a Windows NT security descriptor, which controls whether this console handle will be inherited by child processes. If **NULL** is passed for this parameter, the handle won't be inherited.

The fourth parameter, **dwFlags**, says what kind of console to create. At present, it can only take one value, **CONSOLE_TEXTMODE_BUFFER**. The final parameter is reserved, and should be passed as zero.

The function returns a handle to a new buffer, which can be used in any of the console functions we've discussed so far. The new buffer has the same size as the existing buffer, but this can be changed using **SetConsoleScreenBufferSize()**:

```
BOOL  SetConsoleScreenBufferSize(
    HANDLE  hConsole,                     // console  handle
    COORD  cSize);                        // new  size
```

The size that you specify can't be less than the minimum size for a screen buffer, which you can find by using the **SM_CXMIN** and **SM_CYMIN** values returned from the **GetSystemMetrics()** function, which we met back in Chapter 5.

Screen buffers are treated as system objects, just like threads and mutexes, so when you no longer require the buffer, you can get rid of it using `CloseHandle()`. This function is described in more detail in Chapter 6.

A process can read and write any buffer, but only one is displayed on the screen at a time. This one is referred to as the **active buffer**, and will be the default screen buffer created when the console process started, unless you change it.

You can make a buffer active using the `SetConsoleActiveScreenBuffer()` API:

```
BOOL SetConsoleActiveScreenBuffer(HANDLE hConsole);        // console  screen
                                                          // buffer  handle
```

As soon as this function is called, the new buffer will appear.

Try It Out — Screen Buffer

Here's a simple example using screen buffers. Using the *Console Cursor Positioning* example as a basis, we output a string to the screen every time a key is pressed, exiting when *q* is entered. In this case, we allocate a new buffer, and if *s* is pressed we toggle between the original output buffer and the new one:

```cpp
// ScreenBufferToggle.cpp

#include <windows.h>
#include <iostream>
#include <string>

using namespace std;

int main()
{
    // Get standard handles, which must be valid
    HANDLE hIn  = GetStdHandle(STD_INPUT_HANDLE);
    HANDLE hOut = GetStdHandle(STD_OUTPUT_HANDLE);
    if (hIn == INVALID_HANDLE_VALUE || hOut == INVALID_HANDLE_VALUE)
    {
        cout << "Error getting standard handles" << endl;
        return -1;
    }

    // Create a new buffer for reading and writing
    HANDLE hNew = CreateConsoleScreenBuffer(GENERIC_READ | GENERIC_WRITE,
                                    0, 0, CONSOLE_TEXTMODE_BUFFER, 0);
    if (hNew == INVALID_HANDLE_VALUE)
    {
        cout << "Invalid handle returned from CreateConsoleScreenBuffer()" << endl;
        return -1;
    }

    HANDLE hActive = hOut;

    // Set it into raw mode
    DWORD mode, newMode;
```

```
   // Get the current mode
   if (!GetConsoleMode(hOut, &mode))
   {
      cout << "Error returned from GetConsoleMode()";
      return -1;
   }

   // Remove cooked mode attributes
   newMode = mode & ~(ENABLE_LINE_INPUT | ENABLE_ECHO_INPUT);

   // Reset the mode
   if (!SetConsoleMode(hIn, newMode))
   {
      cout << "Error returned from SetConsoleMode()";
      return -1;
   }

   // Get the screen buffer info
   CONSOLE_SCREEN_BUFFER_INFO info;
   GetConsoleScreenBufferInfo(hOut, &info);

   char buff = 'x';

   LPCTSTR s1 = "one";
   LPCTSTR s2 = "two";
   LPCTSTR s = s1;

   // Write strings till a 'q' is input. If an 's' is input, switch the buffers
   while (buff != 'q')
   {
      DWORD nRead;
      if (!ReadFile(hIn, &buff, 1, &nRead, NULL))
      {
         cout << "Error returned from ReadFile()";
         return -1;
      }

      if (buff == 's')
      {
         if (hActive == hOut)
         {
            hActive = hNew;
            s = s2;
         }
         else
         {
            hActive = hOut;
            s = s1;
         }

         if (!SetConsoleActiveScreenBuffer(hActive))
         {
            cout << "Error returned from SetConsoleActiveScreenBuffer()";
            return -1;
         }
      }

      SHORT xSize = info.dwSize.X;
      SHORT ySize = info.dwSize.Y;
```

```
        COORD c;
        c.X = rand() % xSize;
        c.Y = rand() % ySize;

        // Write string at random positions
        DWORD nCellsWritten;
        if (!WriteConsoleOutputCharacter(hActive, s, 3, c, &nCellsWritten))
        {
            cout << "Error returned from WriteConsoleOutputCharacter()";
            return -1;
        }
    }

    return 0;
}
```

The new buffer is created by a call to `CreateConsoleScreenBuffer()`, and the handle saved. In the reading loop, the input of an *s* causes the active buffer handle to be toggled between the default and new buffers, and the text string changed accordingly. Output is then written to the active buffer.

A Console Class

As you doubtless appreciate by now, the Console API allows you to write sophisticated text-mode applications, but there's a lot of housekeeping work to be done in order to make them functional. We'll now develop a console class, which will make it much simpler to create and manage consoles.

The Class Definition

This class is fairly thin, in the sense that it doesn't hold a lot of state — unlike (say) the `Service` class that we developed in the last chapter. Its main purpose is to provide wrapper functions which will simplify and unify calls to the Console API functions.

Here's the class definition:

```
// Console.h

#include <tchar.h>

using namespace std;

#include <memory.h>

const WORD NORMAL_TEXT = FOREGROUND_RED | FOREGROUND_GREEN | FOREGROUND_BLUE;

class Console
{
    HANDLE hIn, hOut;                   // stdin and stdout handles
    HANDLE hActive;                     // the active buffer
    DWORD mode;                         // console mode
    CONSOLE_SCREEN_BUFFER_INFO info;    // screen buffer info
```

```
    SHORT xsize, ysize;              // screen buffer width and height
    SHORT xpos, ypos;               // current position

    INPUT_RECORD lastRec;           // last record
public:
    Console();
    void UpdateScreenBufferInfo();
    bool NewConsole();

    // Console modes
    bool SetMode(DWORD m);
    bool SetRawMode();
    DWORD GetMode() const { return mode; }
    bool SetCursorPosition(SHORT x, SHORT y);
    void EnableMouseInput();

    // Reading input
    DWORD Read(LPTSTR buff, DWORD size);
    DWORD ReadAt(LPTSTR s, DWORD dwNum, SHORT x, SHORT y);
    DWORD ReadAttributesAt(LPWORD wAtts, DWORD dwNum, SHORT x, SHORT y);

    // Low-level input - event handling
    WORD GetEvent();
    COORD GetMousePos();
    long GetMouseKeys();
    long GetMouseEventType ();
    bool IsMouseEvent();
    bool IsMouseMove();
    bool IsMouseDoubleClick();
    bool IsKeyEvent();
    bool IsBufferSizeEvent();

    // Screen output
    void ClearScreen();
    DWORD Write(LPCTSTR s);
    DWORD Write(TCHAR c, int count=1);
    DWORD WriteAt(LPCTSTR s, SHORT x, SHORT y,
            WORD att=FOREGROUND_RED|FOREGROUND_GREEN|FOREGROUND_BLUE);
    DWORD WriteAttributesAt(WORD wAtts, DWORD dwNum, SHORT x, SHORT y);
    DWORD WriteLine(LPCTSTR s);
    void WriteRectAt(LPCTSTR s, SHORT rows, SHORT cols, SHORT x, SHORT y,
                WORD att=FOREGROUND_RED|FOREGROUND_GREEN|FOREGROUND_BLUE);

    // Screen buffer functions
    HANDLE CreateBuffer();
    HANDLE SetActiveBuffer(HANDLE h);
    HANDLE ResetActiveBuffer();
    HANDLE GetActiveBuffer();

    // Miscellaneous
    SHORT Width() { return xsize; }
    SHORT Height() { return ysize; }
};
```

The class maintains handles for the standard input and output buffers, plus one for the active buffer, which is used when more than one screen buffer has been created. It also holds variables for the:

▶ Current console mode

▶ Console screen buffer information settings

▶ Current screen size

▶ Current cursor position

▶ Last input event record

Constructor and Utility Functions

The class constructor initializes many of the data items. The code for this is shown here:

```
Console::Console()
{
    hIn  = GetStdHandle(STD_INPUT_HANDLE);
    hOut = GetStdHandle(STD_OUTPUT_HANDLE);
    if (hIn == INVALID_HANDLE_VALUE || hOut == INVALID_HANDLE_VALUE)
        throw "Error getting standard handles";

    // The default active buffer is stdout
    hActive = hOut;

    // Get the mode and screen buffer info settings
    GetConsoleMode(hOut, &mode);
    GetConsoleScreenBufferInfo(hOut, &info);

    xsize = info.dwSize.X;     // screen width and height
    ysize = info.dwSize.Y;

    // Default initial cursor position is (0,0)
    xpos = ypos = 0;
}
```

We check to see that the handles for standard input and output are valid, and throw an exception if they aren't.

The **NewConsole()** function performs a **FreeConsole()**/**AllocConsole()** pair of operations:

```
bool Console::NewConsole()
{
    if (!FreeConsole())
        return false;

    if (!AllocConsole())
        return false;

    return true;
}
```

492

The simple functions, **Width()** and **Height()**, which return the dimensions of the screen in character cells, are implemented as inline functions in the header file.

```
SHORT Width() { return xsize; }
SHORT Height() { return ysize; }
```

Screen Mode And Buffer Info Functions

The class saves the current screen mode, and provides simplified functions for manipulating it. It also provides methods for updating the screen buffer and setting the position of the cursor.

SetMode() sets the mode and saves the value:

```
bool Console::SetMode(DWORD m)
{
   mode = m;

   if (!SetConsoleMode(hIn, mode))
      return false;

   return true;
}
```

GetMode() returns the current value of the mode member, and is implemented as a simple inline function in the header file that we saw earlier:

```
DWORD GetMode() const { return mode; }
```

The method **SetRawMode()** alters the mode flags to enable raw mode I/O:

```
bool Console::SetRawMode()
{
   mode = mode & ~(ENABLE_LINE_INPUT | ENABLE_ECHO_INPUT);

   // Reset the mode
   if (!SetConsoleMode(hIn, mode))
      return false;

   return true;
}
```

And **EnableMouseInput()** does the same to enable mouse input:

```
void Console::EnableMouseInput()
{
   mode |= ENABLE_MOUSE_INPUT;
}
```

Although we update the screen buffer information when we change anything significant, we provide a function so that the user can cause it to be updated:

```
void Console::UpdateScreenBufferInfo()
{
    GetConsoleScreenBufferInfo(hOut, &info);
    xsize = info.dwSize.X;
    ysize = info.dwSize.Y;
}
```

The cursor position can be explicitly set using `SetCursorPosition()`:

```
bool Console::SetCursorPosition(SHORT x, SHORT y)
{
    COORD c;
    xpos = c.X = x;
    ypos = c.Y = y;

    return SetConsoleCursorPosition(hActive, c)!=0;
}
```

Note that we also save the position in the **xpos** and **ypos** data members.

Writing

We have seen in this chapter that there are quite a few ways in which we can write characters and attributes to the screen. This class implements a number of useful writing-related functions — you may well be able to think of others. The ones we're implementing here are:

- **ClearScreen()** which clears the screen buffer
- Two versions of the **Write()** function, one of which writes a string, and the other of which repeats a single character a number of times — this function continues writing from where the previous operation left off
- **WriteAt()** which writes a string at a position on the screen, with or without attributes
- **WriteAttributesAt()** which sets the attributes for a range of cells
- **WriteLine()** which writes a line up to and including the first newline character — this function scrolls the screen if necessary
- **WriteRectAt()** which writes a rectangular block of text, with attributes, to the screen at a given position

Let's see how these functions are implemented. **ClearScreen()** sets the cursor position to (0,0), and then writes blanks over the whole screen:

```
void Console::ClearScreen()
{
    // Clear the buffer
    SetCursorPosition(0,0);
    // Make sure we know how big the buffer is
    UpdateScreenBufferInfo();

    // Write spaces over the whole lot
    Write(' ', xsize * ysize);
}
```

This function makes use of one of the variants of **Write()**, which writes a single character to the screen a number of times:

```
DWORD Console::Write(TCHAR c, int count)
{
    DWORD dwWritten = 0;

    if (count == 0)
        return 0;

    // Allocate the new buffer and zero it. Remember that we need to check the
    // size of a character, in case we're using Unicode
    LPTSTR buff = new TCHAR[count+1];
    memset(buff, c, count * sizeof(TCHAR));
    buff[count] = _T('\0');

    WriteFile(hActive, buff, count, &dwWritten, NULL);

    return dwWritten;
}
```

The other **Write()** function does the same operation on a string:

```
DWORD Console::Write(LPCTSTR s)
{
    DWORD dwWritten = 0;

    DWORD dwLen = _tcslen(s);
    if (dwLen == 0)
        return 0;

    WriteFile(hActive, s, dwLen, &dwWritten, NULL);
    return dwWritten;
}
```

Both the above functions use the inbuilt cursor position maintained by **WriteFile()**, and will continue writing where the previous write operation left off. If you need to alter the cursor position, you'll need to use **SetCursorPosition()**.

To write text at a particular position, you can use **WriteAt()**:

```
DWORD Console::WriteAt(LPCTSTR s, SHORT x, SHORT y, WORD wAtt)
{
    // Write a string at a position, and return number of characters written.
    DWORD dwCellsWritten = 0;
    DWORD dwLen;
    COORD c;

    dwLen = _tcslen(s);
    if (dwLen == 0)
        return 0;

    c.X = x;
    c.Y = y;
```

```
      // Write string
      WriteConsoleOutputCharacter(hActive, s, dwLen, c, &dwCellsWritten);

      // If the attributes are anything other than normal text, output them too
      if (wAtt != NORMAL_TEXT)
         WriteAttributesAt(wAtt, dwLen, x, y);

      return dwCellsWritten;
   }
```

This function writes a string at a given position. If an attribute value is passed which isn't **NORMAL_TEXT** (i.e. white text on a black background), then the characters are drawn with those attributes.

Writing attributes separately from characters is done using **WriteAttributesAt()**:

```
DWORD Console::WriteAttributesAt(WORD wAtt, DWORD dwNum, SHORT x, SHORT y)
{
   // Write an attribute to a range of cells, starting at a given position
   DWORD dwCellsWritten = 0;
   COORD c;

   if (dwNum == 0)
      return 0;

   c.X = x;
   c.Y = y;

   FillConsoleOutputAttribute(hActive, wAtt, dwNum, c, &dwCellsWritten);

   return dwCellsWritten;
}
```

This function fills a range of cells with a given attribute value. There isn't a function which allows an array of different attribute values to be applied to a range of cells, but you could easily add one.

We often want to write text in lines, which means we need to add the idea of a 'newline', and we also need to scroll the buffer up when it gets full. **WriteLine()** provides this functionality, building on the scrolling code we've already produced:

```
DWORD Console::WriteLine(LPCTSTR s)
{
   // Write the text, starting at beginning of current line
   xpos = 0;
   DWORD dwWritten = WriteAt(s, xpos, ypos);

   // If we're on the last line, scroll
   if (ypos == info.dwSize.Y - 1)
   {
      // Scroll the screen... first define the area to scroll
      SMALL_RECT sr;
      sr.Top = sr.Left = 0;
      sr.Bottom = info.dwSize.Y - 1;
      sr.Right = info.dwSize.X - 1;
```

496

```
            // Now the destination of the scrolled rectangle. Moving the
            // buffer to (0,-1) effectively loses the first line off the
            // top of the screen.
            COORD c;
            c.X = 0;
            c.Y = -1;

            // How do we want the blank line filled? With blanks, using
            // whatever attributes are currently set
            CHAR_INFO ci;
            ci.Attributes = info.wAttributes;
#ifdef UNICODE
            ci.WChar = _T(' ');
#else
            ci.Char.AsciiChar = _T(' ');
#endif

            // Scroll the screen
            ScrollConsoleScreenBuffer(hOut, &sr, 0, c, &ci);
    }
    else
        ypos += 1;

    // Set the new cursor position
    SetCursorPosition(xpos, ypos);

    return dwWritten;
}
```

The last output function, `WriteRectAt()`, allows us to write rectangular blocks of text and
attributes to the screen:

```
void Console::WriteRectAt(LPCTSTR s, SHORT rows, SHORT cols, SHORT x, SHORT y,
                          WORD att)
{
    // Write a block of characters to the screen at a given position.
    // s is the input buffer, with a given number of rows and columns. It is
    // written at (x,y), and has the attributes 'att'. One set of attributes
    // applies to the whole block, and defaults to white text on black.

    // Set up the source block
    CHAR_INFO *pci = new CHAR_INFO[rows*cols];
    for (int i=0; i<(rows*cols); i++)
    {
#ifdef UNICODE
        pci[i].Char.WChar = s[i];
#else
        pci[i].Char.AsciiChar = s[i];
#endif
        pci[i].Attributes = att;
    }

    COORD c;
    c.X = x;
    c.Y = y;
```

497

```
    // Character buffer size and origin
    COORD bufSize, origin;
    bufSize.X = cols;
    bufSize.Y = rows;
    origin.X = origin.Y = 0;

    // Screen rect to write to
    SMALL_RECT sr;
    sr.Left = c.X;
    sr.Top = c.Y;
    sr.Right = c.X + cols - 1;
    sr.Bottom = c.Y + rows - 1;

    WriteConsoleOutput(hActive, pci, bufSize, origin, &sr);
}
```

Once again, we're building on code we've already produced. We take an input string together with the dimensions of the rectangle it is to fill, and build a **CHAR_INFO** array from the data.

Reading

The member functions for reading from the screen are rather simpler:

- **Read()** reads a specified number of characters from standard input
- **ReadAt()** reads the screen at a specified position
- **ReadAttributesAt()** reads the attributes at a specified position

Read() is a simple wrapper for a call to **ReadFile()**:

```
DWORD Console::Read(LPTSTR buff, DWORD size)
{
    DWORD dwRead = 0;
    if (!ReadFile(hIn, buff, size, &dwRead, NULL))
        return (DWORD)0;
    else
        return dwRead;
}
```

ReadAt() reads the characters from a number of cells using
ReadConsoleOutputCharacter():

```
DWORD Console::ReadAt(LPTSTR s, DWORD dwNum, SHORT x, SHORT y)
{
    // Write a string at a position, and return number of characters written.
    // Doesn't do attributes at all
    DWORD dwCellsRead = 0;
    COORD c;

    c.X = x;
    c.Y = y;

    // Read string
    if (!ReadConsoleOutputCharacter(hActive, s, dwNum, c, &dwCellsRead))
```

```
            return 0;
        else
            return dwCellsRead;
    }
```

ReadAttributesAt() does the same thing, but reads the attributes instead of the characters themselves:

```
DWORD Console::ReadAttributesAt(LPWORD wAtts, DWORD dwNum, SHORT x, SHORT y)
{
    DWORD dwCellsRead;
    COORD c;

    c.X = x;
    c.Y = y;

    // Read attributes
    ReadConsoleOutputAttribute(hActive, wAtts, dwNum, c, &dwCellsRead);

    return dwCellsRead;
}
```

Event And Mouse Handling

We are mainly concerned with handling events in order to get mouse input, so we implement the following event-related functions:

- **GetEvent()**, which waits to read an event, saves it and returns its type
- **IsMouseEvent()**, **IsKeyEvent()** and **IsBufferSizeEvent()**, which let you query the type of the last event
- **GetMousePos()** which returns the position from a mouse event
- **GetMouseKeys()** which returns the control key flag for a mouse event
- **GetMouseEventType()** which tells you if it was a double-click or move event
- **IsMouseMove()** returns **true** if it was a move event
- **IsMouseDoubleClick()** returns **true** if it was a double-click event

We know that we can use the low-level input functions to read input events of various types, and we need to use this if we're going to be able to handle mouse input. The first function, **GetEvent()**, waits for an event to occur:

```
WORD Console::GetEvent()
{
    // Read a record, and return its type
    DWORD nRead;
    ReadConsoleInput(hIn, &lastRec, 1, &nRead);
    return lastRec.EventType;
}
```

The event is stored in the **lastRec** member, and the type of the event is returned. The function won't return until an event record has been read.

Three small functions let you check the type of the last event, without having to remember the symbolic IDs for each one:

```
inline bool Console::IsMouseEvent()
{
   return lastRec.EventType == MOUSE_EVENT;
}

inline bool Console::IsKeyEvent()
{
   return lastRec.EventType == KEY_EVENT;
}

inline bool Console::IsBufferSizeEvent()
{
   return lastRec.EventType == WINDOW_BUFFER_SIZE_EVENT;
}
```

All the other event-related functions are to do with mouse input handling, although it would be simple to add similar functions for keyboard events. If the last event was a mouse event, **GetMousePos()** returns you the position as a **COORD** structure:

```
COORD Console::GetMousePos()
{
   COORD c;

   if (lastRec.EventType == MOUSE_EVENT)
   {
      c.X = lastRec.Event.MouseEvent.dwMousePosition.X;
      c.Y = lastRec.Event.MouseEvent.dwMousePosition.Y;
   }
   else
      c.X = c.Y = -1;

   return c;
}
```

If it wasn't a mouse event, you get position (-1,-1) returned.

GetMouseKeys() and **GetMouseEventType()** return the state of the control keys reported by the event, and also whether the event was a mouse move or a double-click:

```
long Console::GetMouseKeys()
{
   long lFlags;

   if (lastRec.EventType == MOUSE_EVENT)
   {
      lFlags = static_cast<long>(lastRec.Event.MouseEvent.dwControlKeyState);
   }
   else
      lFlags = -1;

   return lFlags;
}
```

```
long Console::GetMouseEventType()
{
   long lType;

   if (lastRec.EventType == MOUSE_EVENT)
   {
      lType = static_cast<long>(lastRec.Event.MouseEvent.dwEventFlags);
   }
   else
      lType = -1;

   return lType;
}
```

The `IsMouseMove()` and `IsMouseDoubleClick()` functions provide simple ways to tell what sort of mouse event we're processing:

```
bool Console::IsMouseMove()
{
   if (lastRec.EventType == MOUSE_EVENT)
   {
      return lastRec.Event.MouseEvent.dwEventFlags == MOUSE_MOVED;
   }
   else
      return false;
}

bool Console::IsMouseDoubleClick()
{
   if (lastRec.EventType == MOUSE_EVENT)
   {
      return lastRec.Event.MouseEvent.dwEventFlags == DOUBLE_CLICK;
   }
   else
      return false;
}
```

It would be simple to add analogous functions for the state of the various control keys.

Screen Buffer Functions

Four functions let us work with screen buffers:

- `CreateBuffer()` creates a new screen buffer
- `SetActiveBuffer()` sets the active buffer for output
- `ResetActiveBuffer()` sets the output buffer back to standard output
- `GetActiveBuffer()` returns the handle of the current output buffer

`CreateBuffer()` is a very thin wrapper for `CreateConsoleScreenBuffer()`:

```
HANDLE Console::CreateBuffer()
{
   return CreateConsoleScreenBuffer(GENERIC_READ | GENERIC_WRITE,
                          0, 0, CONSOLE_TEXTMODE_BUFFER, 0);
}
```

The other three functions are also trivial in their implementation:

```
HANDLE Console::SetActiveBuffer(HANDLE h)
{
    // Switch the active console buffer, and return previous value.
    HANDLE t = hActive;
    hActive = h;
    SetConsoleActiveScreenBuffer(hActive);
    return t;
}

HANDLE Console::ResetActiveBuffer()
{
    // Switch the active console buffer to hOut, and return previous value.
    HANDLE t = hActive;
    hActive = hOut;
    SetConsoleActiveScreenBuffer(hActive);
    return t;
}

HANDLE Console::GetActiveBuffer()
{
    return hActive;
}
```

Try It Out — Using the Console Class

To round off the chapter, and show how using the console class can make programming easier, here's the buffer-swapping example rewritten to use the console class:

```
// ScreenBufferToggle2.cpp

#include <windows.h>
#include <iostream>
#include <string>
#include "Console.h"

using namespace std;

int main()
{
    Console c;
    c.SetRawMode();

    HANDLE hOld = c.GetActiveBuffer();
    HANDLE hNew = c.CreateBuffer();
```

```
        HANDLE hActive = hOld;

        char buff = 'x';
        LPCTSTR s1 = "one";
        LPCTSTR s2 = "two";
        LPCTSTR s = s1;

        while (buff != 'q')
        {
           DWORD dwRead = c.Read(&buff, 1);
           if (dwRead == 0)
           {
              cout << "Error returned from Read()";
              return -1;
           }

           if (buff == 's')
           {
              s = (hActive == hNew) ? s1 : s2;
              hActive = (hActive == hNew) ? hOld : hNew;
              c.SetActiveBuffer(hActive);
           }

           SHORT x = rand() % c.Width();
           SHORT y = rand() % c.Height();

           c.WriteAt(s, x, y);
        }
        return 0;
     }
```

Notice how the details of manipulating the console, such as using the mode flags, are now completely hidden from us. If you build this example, you should find that it works in exactly the same way as the previous code.

Summary

We've seen in this chapter how to use the Console API to write text-mode applications, which can employ full cursor positioning and mouse handling, as well as being able to read the screen for full form-handling capability.

Consoles are not limited simply to porting existing character-based applications — in fact, it may be difficult to port straight to the Console API, since the way it works is unlike many other text handling systems. It is, however, extremely valuable in letting you create original text-mode applications, or adding a console to a GUI application which needs line-based I/O.

IPC and Networking

In this chapter we will explore how to use the facilities that Windows NT provides for interprocess communication (IPC).

> *Much of what is covered in this chapter applies to both Windows 95 as well as NT. Where significant differences occur, these will be pointed out in boxes like this one.*

In Chapter 6 we discussed how an application can be divided into a number of separately executing threads. Within a multi-threaded application it is a relatively simple matter to share data, such as common global variables, between threads.

In some cases it is advantageous to divide an application into separately executing processes, with one or more programs cooperating to achieve the desired result. For example, a database application might be split into a data-entry program with a separate query or reporting function. In this way, it becomes possible to extend the application in a number of ways, running multiple data-entry tasks with a single 'back end', or using a dedicated database server across a network.

During the course of this chapter, we will develop and refine a fairly simple application, starting with a self-contained executable and ending with a multi-user, network-distributed system. We will look at various ways to manage data, and pass it between executing programs.

> *The networking examples need to be run on a networked workstation with TCP/IP networking installed. They have been tested on a local area network, but should work on computers with a dial-up connection.*

Windows NT (and Windows 95, and even Windows 3.1) provides a number of APIs for interprocess communication. Some of these are limited to use between computers running Windows, such as **Mailslots**, but others, such as **sockets**, can be used to communicate with other systems, notably Unix-based machines and computers across the Internet. Along the way, we will point out those methods that are portable, and those that can only be used for Windows.

There is not enough room in a single chapter to cover all of these topics in great depth. We hope to give you a taste of what is available, so that you will be able to build on this starting point. We'll introduce:

▶ Sockets

▶ Named pipes

▶ Remote procedure calls

▶ Memory maps

▶ Mailslots

▶ WinINET

Topics we won't cover, but which you may find you need eventually include:

▶ Asynchronous extensions

▶ Windows networking (WNET)

▶ COM/DCOM

▶ CORBA

▶ Messaging (for example, MSMQ)

The Currency Application

Our simple application is a currency converter. If you have an amount of one currency, say US dollars, and you need to know how many UK pounds sterling that would buy, then this is the application for you. Over the course of this chapter we will develop this from a very simple single machine application through various different multi-process and networked versions as we demonstrate the different forms of interprocess communication available.

Try It Out — Simple Currency Converter

The first version of the program is a single process console application, just to keep things nice and simple. The core of the program is the function `ConvertCurrency()` which, together with two helper functions, defines the interface to our application, prototyped in `Currency.h`:

```
// Currency.h

// Return the number of currencies recognized
short NumberOfCurrencies(void);

// Return the name of the currency
const char* CurrencyName(short CurrencyNum);

// Convert an amount from one to another
double ConvertCurrency(double Amount, short From, short To);
```

We define an integer index for the different currencies that we can convert between. The index is **short** to minimize network traffic, which also has the benefit of ensuring that there is no confusion about the size of an **int**. The main functionality is provided by **ConvertCurrency()**, which takes an **Amount** in the source currency (**From**), and returns the equivalent amount (as a **double**) in the desired currency (specified by **To**).

The helper functions will assist us later, when we divide the application into client and server — the client will be able to present the user with a list of currencies and give their descriptive names.

This first version of our application reads its exchange rate data from a file. For simplicity's sake, we'll assume that this file is in the same current working directory as the application. The file, **Rates.ini**, has a simple format: one line per currency. Each currency is defined in relation to an arbitrary base currency. Here is a sample:

```
1.0   Dollars
1.5   Zingies
23.4 Wibblies
0.2   Yarbots
```

> In order to concentrate on the IPC aspects of this application, we have not used the
> Windows 3.1 INI file structure or API functions.

Here we see that the base currency is equivalent to Dollars, there being 1.5 Zingies to the Dollar at the moment. Of course, as exchange rates fluctuate, this file will need to be updated.

Despite its restrictions, this sample application should serve our purpose. We hope that by keeping the application straightforward, we can concentrate on demonstrating the IPC techniques.

Even though this first version is a single program, we are going to separate the user interface from the conversion functions. This will allow us to preserve as much code as possible when we move to a distributed client/server arrangement.

The conversion and support functions are implemented in **ServerUtils.cpp**, with an additional interface file **ServerUtils.h**:

```
// ServerUtils.h

#include <iostream>
// Utility functions used by the server

// Read the rates file
void ReadRates(const char* File);
void ReadRates(std::istream& is);
```

The implementation is as follows:

```
// ServerUtils.cpp

#include <fstream>
#include "Currency.h"
#include "ServerUtils.h"
```

```
using namespace std;

static const short MaxNumCurrencies = 10;
static const int MaxNameLength = 20;

static char CurrencyNames[MaxNumCurrencies][MaxNameLength];
static double RateWrtBase[MaxNumCurrencies];
static short NumCurrencies = 0;

short NumberOfCurrencies(void)
{
   return NumCurrencies;
}

const char* CurrencyName(short CurrencyNum)
{
   return CurrencyNames[CurrencyNum];
}

double ConvertCurrency(double Amount, short From, short To)
{
   double Converter = RateWrtBase[To] / RateWrtBase[From];
   return Amount * Converter;
}

void ReadRates(const char* File)
{
   ifstream f(File);
   if (!f)
      return;
   ReadRates(f);
}

void ReadRates(istream& is)
{
   NumCurrencies = 0;

   short i;
   for (i = 0; i < MaxNumCurrencies; ++i)
      if (!(is >> RateWrtBase[i] >> CurrencyNames[i]))
         break;

   NumCurrencies = i;
}
```

The exchange rates are stored in an array, **RateWrtBase**, and the conversion function, **ConvertCurrency()**, simply applies the multiplication factors to convert the currency values. In the real world we would have to take care here about arithmetic overflows and rounding errors. In fact, currency conversion can be quite complex including rules regarding precision. For our purposes however, the simple 'multiply by exchange rate' approach works well enough.

The main program simply takes care of initializing the exchange rate data (by calling a function, **ReadRates()**), parsing command line arguments and calling the conversion function. The code for this is shown below:

```cpp
// Simple.cpp

#include <iostream>
#include <cstdlib>
#include "Currency.h"
#include "ServerUtils.h"

using namespace std;

int main (int argc, char* argv[])
{
   ReadRates("rates.ini");
   short NumCurrencies = NumberOfCurrencies();

   if (NumCurrencies == 0)
   {
      cerr << "Could not read rates details file\n" ;
      return 1;
   }

   if (argc != 4)
   {
      cerr << "Usage\n\t" << argv[0] <<
                  " amount from to\n\twhere from & to can take the values:\n";
      for (short i = 0; i < NumCurrencies; ++i)
         cerr << "\t\t" << i << '\t' << CurrencyName(i) << endl;
      return 1;
   }

   double Amount = atof(argv[1]);
   short From = static_cast<short>(atoi(argv[2]));
   short To = static_cast<short>(atoi(argv[3]));

   if (From < 0 || From >= NumCurrencies || To < 0 || To >= NumCurrencies)
   {
      cerr << "Illegal currency specification\n";
      return 1;
   }

   double Converted = ConvertCurrency(Amount, From, To);

   cout << Amount << ' ' << CurrencyName(From) << " is "
        << Converted << ' ' << CurrencyName(To) << endl;

   return 0;
}
```

When we run the application we see this:

```
MS
 S Command Prompt                                      _ □ ×
C:\BegNT\Ch11\Simple>simple
Usage
        simple amount from to
        where from & to can take the values:
                0               Sterling
                1               Zingies
                2               Wibblies
                3               Yarbots

C:\BegNT\Ch11\Simple>simple 10 0 1
10 Sterling is 15 Zingies

C:\BegNT\Ch11\Simple>
```

The Update Problem

Let us imagine that our currency converter is a huge success. It is installed on many computers within our organization and it is used on a daily basis.

Currency exchange rates change. Often. Our application uses a fixed table for the exchange rates for the currencies it converts. Every time the exchange rates change we need to distribute a new **Rates.ini** to all of our users, which is clearly an administrative nightmare. There are many ways that we can address this problem, some of which have intriguing possibilities.

A Client and Server

So far, our program runs as a single program — that is, one program for each user of the application. We can picture this as a single composite application:

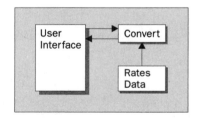

If we separate the user interface from the conversion process, then we can modify the conversion process more easily. The advantage here is that the client can remain the same, even if the conversion server changes. Our application would then look like this:

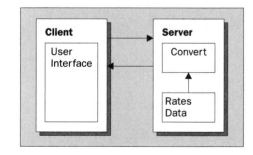

In this configuration, the ideal arrangement is to have a single server program running on a network handling requests from many clients, although for simplicity the diagram only shows a single client. By having a single server, only one update is needed as exchange rates change, and the (possibly many) clients can all remain unaltered.

One of the strong points of NT is that this client-server communication can be implemented in a number of different ways, and we'll use the next few sections of this chapter to explore them.

Network Transports

To understand how network applications work under Windows NT, it is useful to know a little about the network itself. Unfortunately, one chapter provides insufficient space to cover the whole range of networking options available to Windows NT programmers, but we will spend a moment or two looking at how network communication is achieved on a local area network (such as Ethernet) or via a dial-up connection.

To communicate effectively (or, indeed, at all) two computers connected to a network need to agree about how they're going to exchange data, and the format the data is going to take. This is called a **protocol**. There are many different possible protocols, but to gain widespread usefulness, they need to be standardized. In the early days of personal computer networking, there were many proprietary protocols in use, which were developed and maintained by manufacturers such as IBM, Microsoft and Novell. Even where the underlying network technology was the same, such as Ethernet, machines of different types could not communicate easily. These proprietary protocols, such as Microsoft's NETBIOS, Novell's IPX/SPX, and a few other less common ones, persist to this day, although different operating systems now often support each other's protocols.

Internet Protocols

Through the development of the Internet, a suite of protocols has become an established standard. Chief among these is IP (for Internet Protocol). It forms the basis for nearly all Internet communication today. IP is well suited to reliable local area networks such as Ethernet and to less reliable point-to-point links, such as modem dial-up links into the Internet. The specifications are publicly available, and are widely supported by computer manufacturers and operating systems; for example, it is the principal networking technology in UNIX.

IP-based networks support two distinct types of communication:

- ▶ **UDP** — the Unacknowledged Datagram Protocol — a connectionless single shot protocol
- ▶ **TCP** — the Transmission Control Protocol — a connection-based protocol for delivering a stream of data

With UDP, one computer sends single, unconnected packets of data to another. It may or may not arrive correctly, but the sender has no way of knowing, unless the receiver explicitly sends something back. This kind of service is quick and cheap in terms of resources, because there is no error correction or retransmission to worry about, and so it is useful for providing information that can be lost without causing problems. For example, a server might send out periodic status reports to a monitoring station. One or two going astray will not affect the operation of the system, as the monitor may only raise an alarm when several consecutive expected reports have gone missing. In some ways UDP is a bit like sending a letter via the postal service, usually letters arrive in the order you post them, but occasionally they arrive out of order, or may sometimes not arrive at all.

> *Data loss on networks is an unfortunate fact of life. Many things can cause packets to be dropped by a network, such as congestion, errors on the cable, failure of other network components and so on.*

Using a TCP connection rather than UDP can help eliminate problems caused by data loss. TCP maintains a logical connection between communicating computers for the duration of some transaction, rather like a telephone call. Each packet sent has a serial number so that the sender knows that the information was received, and missing ones can be identified and resent. This type of connection is used when it is important that all the data gets delivered, or if not, at least we get to know that it didn't. File transfers, HTTP web sessions, interactive login sessions and electronic mail all use TCP connections when running on IP networks.

It is common to use the general term **TCP/IP** to refer to IP network services, including UDP, and we will stick to that usage here.

Windows and TCP/IP

Microsoft first produced a TCP/IP protocol add-on for Windows some time ago (for Windows 3.x), and included it with Windows 95 and NT. TCP/IP is very widely used, since it is the principal protocol for the Internet, and is also very popular on corporate networks, due to its excellent scalability, and the wide range of networking components that support it.

Because TCP/IP is now so widely used, we will not consider in detail any other protocols in this chapter.

A Network Client

Before we can write a client program for our currency converter that will connect to a server across a network, we need to know a few things about the server. Specifically we need to know:

▶ How to address any packets we send

▶ What protocol the server is using

▶ How to connect to the currency service (via sockets, remote procedure calls, and so on, of which more anon)

IP Addressing

Each computer on an IP network has a unique address. The IP address is a 32-bit value often written as a 'dotted quad', four decimal byte values separated by periods. For systems directly connected to the Internet, these addresses must be allocated by a regional body . Very often an Internet Service Provider (ISP) will have a block of addresses and will allocate one of these to each subscriber, or for dial-up links an address may be allocated each time the dial-up link is made.

For example, on a small local network you might have the following machines, listed here with their IP addresses.

```
192.168.1.1    zeus
192.168.1.2    hermes
192.168.1.3    barney
192.168.1.4    dewey
192.168.1.5    nomad
```

Each packet transmitted on an IP network contains a source and destination IP address. For packets sent to machines on the same network, this information is sufficient. To send information to computers on other networks, over the Internet for example, the packet is sent first to a **gateway** machine, which in turn sends the packet to the next machine in a chain of links stretching across the Internet. This is known as **routing**. The gateway used on any network as the first choice destination for packets intended for machines on remote networks is the 'default gateway'.

> *A detailed explanation of how network routes are configured (and how to troubleshoot them) is beyond the scope of this book. We refer you to* TCP/IP Network Administration, *ISBN 0-937175-82-X, published by O'Reilly & Associates.*

IP Services and Port Numbers

We are almost ready to write our first client. If we know the server's IP address we can send data to it. However, that is not quite the end of the story. A server may provide a number of different functions. It may act as an electronic mail host, a World Wide Web proxy, and a multitude of other things, as well as our currency converter. A **port number** identifies each of these services.

A port number is a 16-bit integral value. Some of these (those below 1024) are reserved for so-called 'well-known' services. Higher ones can be used by communicating computers to identify a specific, on-going conversation.

Every connection made on an IP network specifies source and destination port numbers as well as IP addresses. This means that we can have more than one conversation between clients and servers.

One way of thinking about port numbers is to consider a large office building with a telephone switchboard. Suppose we wish to speak to a support engineer within the office building. All incoming calls to the office are made to a single number, say 555-1000. This is equivalent to the IP address of a server. The support engineer is on extension 123, which we can dial direct or be put through to by the receptionist. This is equivalent to the port number.

Windows Sockets

The **socket** interface was introduced in the Berkeley versions of the UNIX operating system. It provides a uniform way of using network services, supports a range of network transports and also has a local operating mode (so that sockets can connect processes on the same machine).

The Windows Sockets API (universally known as **Winsock**) was developed to provide a sockets interface on Windows networks. Due to the nature of the Windows 3.x operating system, some features could not be made to work very well, which led to a number of incompatibilities with UNIX sockets.

Today, however, it is possible on Windows 9x and NT to write sockets programs that are almost identical to their UNIX counterparts. This portability can pay real dividends for the professional programmer. Being able to move clients and/or servers from one operating system environment to another can be very attractive.

A socket-based client can be very simple — as it need only carry out the following basic steps:

▶ Call **socket()** to create a socket of the required type, specifying a server IP address and port number

▶ Call **connect()** to establish a connection to the server

▶ Call **send()** and **recv()** (or variants on them) to send and receive arbitrary binary data

▶ Close the socket when done

Network byte ordering

One thing we must be aware of when writing network applications is that different types of processor architectures may use different representations for common data types.

Let's consider the humble integer as an example. Even with such a simple data type two problems can arise:

▶ Size

▶ Byte ordering

For example, **int** types are commonly 32-bit values on modern machines, and we may well soon see computers that use 64-bit integers as standard. Current 64-bit machines, such as those based on the Alpha chipset can handle 64-bit quantities already, but for compatibility the **int** type is still usually 32-bits in length.

If we send an integer value from one machine to another on the network, we must make sure that the receiver is able to deal with what we send, whether it is four or eight bytes.

Byte ordering can also be a problem. A 32-bit value is generally stored as four consecutive bytes. When writing 32-bits, some processors store these values with the least significant byte in the first location (called **little endian** storage) and others store the most significant byte in the first location (**big endian**). If we use a network application to transmit these multibyte values, then we must be sure that the sender and receiver agree on the ordering of the bytes. Current Intel processors are little endian.

A value of **0x12345678** will be stored as the bytes **0x12 0x34 0x56 0x78** on a big endian machine. The same value on a little endian machine would be stored as **0x78 0x56 0x34 0x12**. So if we transfer the value without any translation from the big endian machine to the little endian machine, we will end up with the value **0x12345678** becoming **0x78563412**.

Of course, if we are restricted to sending data between machines which use the same storage scheme, then we would not have any trouble, but that is an unwise assumption. In any case, there is a simple solution.

The Winsock API defines a network byte ordering so that there is a standard for the order in which multibyte values are sent over the network. There are a number of functions that can be used to translate 16-bit and 32-bit values into the network byte order, and back again to the host byte order. On machines where the host byte order is the same as the network byte order, these are null operations. However, even in this case, it is strongly recommended that you still call the routines in order to maintain portability between systems.

The functions for manipulating multi-byte values are defined in the **winsock.h** header file, and summarized in the following table:

Byte Order Function	Description
`u_short PASCAL FAR htons(u_short)`	host to network (short)
`u_short PASCAL FAR ntohs(u_short)`	network to host (short)
`u_long PASCAL FAR htonl(u_long)`	host to network (long)
`u_long PASCAL FAR ntohl(u_long)`	network to host (long)

Two other functions are available to map strings containing 'dotted quad' IP addresses to network byte ordered 32-bit values and back again.

```
char FAR* PASCAL FAR inet_ntoa(struct in_addr)
unsigned long PASCAL FAR inet_addr(const char FAR*)
```

The function **inet_ntoa()** takes a network byte ordered IP address (32-bit value) and returns a pointer to a static string containing the address as a dotted quad. (We will meet the **in_addr** structure shortly.) In contrast, **inet_addr()** returns a 32-bit network byte ordered IP address from a dotted quad string. Note that, unlike much of the Windows API, the socket library does not support Unicode, and all strings contain simple 8-bit characters only.

Network transparency issues also affect other types of data. Floating point values cannot generally be passed from one computer to another without being converted to a common form first. One such form would be strings of ASCII characters, so the value 1.23 would be sent as "1.23" and interpreted by the receiver. Other forms, such as IEEE standards for floating point values are beyond the scope of this book.

Using Sockets

Sockets provide bidirectional communication across a network. A server creates a socket and listens for connections, while a client creates a socket connecting it to the server. Once the connection is accepted by the server, communication can take place — the server will have created a new socket just for this connection. Any data written to a socket by one party can be read by the other, and vice versa. The server may also continue to listen for new connections at the same time as dealing with existing client connections.

515

The Winsock API

Each Winsock application must explicitly start up and shut down the Winsock API. This is done with calls to **WSAStartup()** before making any socket API calls and calling **WSACleanup()** before exiting. These prototypes are defined in **winsock.h**.

```
int WSAStartup (WORD wVersionRequired, LPWSADATA lpWSAData);
int WSACleanup (void);
```

The parameters to **WSAStartup()** are an indication of the Winsock API version that we need. The options currently available are 1.0, 1.1 and 2.0. We will be using version 1.1 since that supports all we require, letting us run on systems with version 1.1 or greater. The parameter value can be created with **MAKEWORD**:

```
wVersionRequired = MAKEWORD(1,1);
```

WSAStartup() will return a non-zero value if Winsock cannot be started.

Creating Sockets

We create a socket (an object of type **SOCKET**) by calling the function **socket()**.

```
SOCKET PASCAL FAR socket(int af, int type, int protocol);
```

The **af** parameter specifies the address format. We need to consider one format, that for IP addresses, **AF_INET** (**PF_INET** is a synonym). The **type** parameter specifies how the socket is to behave, and for IP sockets can take one of the following values:

- **SOCK_DGRAM** — datagram sockets, unacknowledged, unsequenced
- **SOCK_STREAM** — connection-oriented, acknowledged, reliable

The **protocol** parameter specifies which communication protocol should be used. It is best to leave this at **0**, indicating the default for the specified behaviour. For IP sockets this is TCP for **SOCK_STREAM** and UDP for **SOCK_DGRAM**.

> *Although it is possible to use sockets for both UDP connections and TCP connections, all our examples in this chapter will use TCP so that the communication is reliable.*

The returned value from **socket()** is a descriptor used for accessing the newly created socket for reading and writing as well as closing. A value of **INVALID_SOCKET** is returned if the call fails, and a specific error code can be obtained by calling **WSAGetLastError()**.

Connecting

We establish a socket connection by calling **connect()**:

```
int PASCAL FAR connect(SOCKET s, const struct sockaddr FAR* name, int
namelen);
```

The **sockaddr** structure is used to specify the remote end of the desired socket connection — its 'name'. For IP sockets, this is characterized by an IP address and port number. Such an address is specified using a **sockaddr_in** structure that has to be cast to the required **sockaddr** pointer. The **sockaddr_in** has the following interesting members:

- **sin_family** — address family (set to **AF_INET**)
- **sin_addr.s_addr** — set to the IP address (use **inet_addr**)
- **sin_port** — Port number (remember to use **htons**)

The **namelen** parameter should be set to the size of the **sockaddr** structure used, in this case, the size of our **sockaddr_in** structure.

The call to **connect()** will return a zero value in the case of a successful connection being made, otherwise it returns **SOCKET_ERROR**. Again, calling **WSAGetLastError()** will retrieve a more specific error code.

Transferring Data

Sending and receiving data using a socket is very similar to low-level file operations. For sockets we use **send()** and **recv()**:

```
int PASCAL FAR send(SOCKET s, const char FAR* buf, int len, int flags);
int PASCAL FAR recv(SOCKET s, char FAR* buf, int len, int flags);
```

Data is read from a socket by a call to **recv()**. Data up to a maximum of **len** bytes is read into the buffer pointed to by **buf**. The number of bytes received is returned if there has been no error, and a value of zero indicates that the socket has been closed by the remote end. If an error occurs, a value of **SOCKET_ERROR** is returned.

Data is written to a socket by a call to **send()** in much the same way. The return value is the number of bytes written to the socket (which may be less than **len**). The call will not return until data is sent, but this does not mean that the data has necessarily been delivered to the remote end —it may still be in transit.

The **flags** parameter controls how data is received. It is usually set to zero, but can be set to **MSG_PEEK** for a call to **recv()**, in which case the data is read into **buf**, but not removed from the input queue. It will be re-read with the next call to **recv()**. Other flag values are outside the scope of this book — but they're listed in the MSDN library.

Closing Sockets

A socket is closed by calling **closesocket()**:

```
int PASCAL FAR closesocket(SOCKET s);
```

The return value is usually **0**, unless an error (**SOCKET_ERROR**) has occurred. The action of **closesocket()** will vary according to the way the socket is being used. It is possible that data has been queued in the socket and not yet transmitted. We can arrange for the call to **closesocket()** to wait until all data has been sent, or to close the socket immediately. This is achieved by setting socket options **SO_LINGER** or **SO_DONTLINGER** via the function **setsockopt()**. However, a detailed explanation of the use of socket options is beyond the scope of this chapter — check out the MSDN documentation for more information.

Try It Out — A Socket-based Client Application

We are now ready to create our first network client for the currency conversion application. Later, we'll see how the server is implemented, but for now let's assume that it is already running on a machine whose IP address is 192.168.1.1 and providing the currency service on port 1234.

Up to now, we've been talking about using TCP/IP and packets. However, raw TCP packets are too unstructured for our purposes, so we need to impose our own currency conversion protocol on top of TCP, just as FTP and SMTP protocols exist for their particular applications.

We will send requests to the server and it will send data back to us. First of all we need to define the high-level programming structures that define the structure of the data that will be our message formats. This is done in `CurrencyConv.h`, which we will be using throughout the rest of the chapter.

```
// CurrencyConv.h

// The messages to pass back and forth

// No data to pass in NumberOfCurrenciesRequest, hence no struct

struct NumberOfCurrenciesResult
{
    short num; // The number of currencies
};

struct CurrencyNameRequest
{
    short num; // A currency number
};

struct CurrencyNameResult
{
    char name[20]; // The name of a currency
};

struct ConvertCurrencyRequest
{
    double amount;   // The amount to convert
    short  from;   // the currency number to convert from
    short  to;     // The  currency number to convert to
};

struct ConvertCurrencyResult
{
    double amount;   // The result of the conversion
};

// Constants instead of just an enum since sizeof enum is not guaranteed to be 1
byte
const unsigned char MSG_NUMBER_OF_CURRENCIES = 1;
const unsigned char MSG_CURRENCY_NAME        = 2;
const unsigned char MSG_CONVERT_CURRENCY     = 3;
const unsigned char MSG_TERMINATE            = 4;      // Special one to terminate
                                                       // the process
```

```
struct MessageRequest
{
    unsigned char type;
    union
    {
        // Nothing for NumberOfCurrencies
        CurrencyNameRequest    currencyName;
        ConvertCurrencyRequest convertCurrency;
    };
};

struct MessageResult
{
    unsigned char type;
    union
    {
        NumberOfCurrenciesResult numberOfCurrencies;
        CurrencyNameResult       currencyName;
        ConvertCurrencyResult    convertCurrency;
    };
};
```

We use a fixed length message containing one of three request types:

▶ The number of currencies
▶ The currency name
▶ A conversion

We expect to receive a response of the same type containing the answer to our query. For administration purposes, we also include a message to terminate the server, although a normal user should not expect to have access to this facility!

Note that we are sending and receiving floating point values in our messages. Since no data translation is performed by the socket interface, we can only be sure that the values will arrive correctly if the sender and receiver use the same internal representation for the type **double**. For transferrence of data between Win32 machines using Intel processors, this will be OK. When we communicate between dissimilar machines, however, we may run into trouble. One way to solve this problem would be to convert our values to strings (perhaps with **sprintf()**) prior to sending them, and then convert them back (with **sscanf()**) on receipt. Later on, we'll meet a more general way of solving the problem of differing internal representations when we discuss remote procedure calls (RPC).

The client program is shown below. It uses a utility function, **SendAndReceive()**, to send a request and receive a response from the server, checking that the message types match. Remember the three conversion functions defined in **Currency.h** we saw earlier in the chapter — **NumberOfCurrencies()**, **CurrencyName()** and **ConvertCurrency()**.The client portions of these functions bundle their arguments into the **CurrencyConv** message formats, send a request and hand back the answer from the server's reply. The **main()** routine looks very similar to the single application version. To keep the code as small as possible, we have limited the error checking to gross errors and we exit the application when they occur.

> *Remember to link with wsock32.lib or ws2_32.lib when building these applications to ensure that the Winsock APIs are available. You can do this by adding the library name to the Object/library modules list under the Project | Settings | Link tab.*
>
> *Under NT, two versions of Winsock are available: Winsock 1.1, using header* winsock.h *and library* wsock32.lib; *and Winsock 2.0, using* winsock2.h *and* ws2_32.lib. *Winsock 2 contains many extensions to the earlier library, but either will suffice for the examples here.*

The Windows sockets system is initialized by a function, `InitialiseSockets()`, declared in `SocketUtils.h` and closed down by a call to `WSACleanup()`.

```cpp
// Client.cpp

#include <windows.h>
#include <winsock.h> // or <winsock2.h>
#include <iostream>
#include <cstdlib>
#include "CurrencyConv.h"
#include "Currency.h"
#include "SocketUtils.h"

using namespace std;

SOCKET Sock;
MessageRequest req;
MessageResult  res;

void SendAndReceive()
{
   if (send (Sock, reinterpret_cast<char*>(&req), sizeof (req), 0) ==
             SOCKET_ERROR)
   {
      cerr << "Error writing socket\n";
      exit(1);
   }
   if (recv(Sock, reinterpret_cast<char*>(&res), sizeof (res), 0) == SOCKET_ERROR)
   {
      cerr << "Error reading socket\n";
      exit (1);
   }

   if (res.type != req.type)
   {
      cerr << "Unexpected message returned\n";
      exit (1);
   }
}

short NumberOfCurrencies()
{
   req.type = MSG_NUMBER_OF_CURRENCIES;
   SendAndReceive();
   return res.numberOfCurrencies.num;
}
```

```
// Return the name of the currency
const char* CurrencyName(short CurrencyNum)
{
   req.type = MSG_CURRENCY_NAME;
   req.currencyName.num = CurrencyNum;
   SendAndReceive ();
   return res.currencyName.name;
}

// Convert an amount from one to another
double ConvertCurrency(double Amount, short From, short To)
{
   req.type = MSG_CONVERT_CURRENCY;
   req.convertCurrency.amount = Amount;
   req.convertCurrency.from   = From;
   req.convertCurrency.to     = To;
   SendAndReceive ();
   return res.convertCurrency.amount;
}

int main(int argc, char* argv[])
{
   if (argc < 2)
   {
      cerr << "At least the server IP address must be given\n";
      return 1;
   }

   // Call a utility function to start the Winsock DLL and check the version
   InitialiseSockets ();

   Sock = socket (PF_INET, SOCK_STREAM, 0);
   if (Sock == INVALID_SOCKET)
   {
      cerr << "Could not create socket\n";
      return 1;
   }

   // Declare and initialize the socket address information
   struct sockaddr_in Address;
   Address.sin_family = AF_INET;
   Address.sin_addr.s_addr = inet_addr (argv[1]);
   Address.sin_port = htons (1234);

   if (connect (Sock, reinterpret_cast<sockaddr*>(&Address), sizeof (Address))
             == -1)
   {
      cerr << "Could not connect\n";
      return 1;
   }

   short NumCurrencies = NumberOfCurrencies ();

   if (argc != 5)
   {
      cerr << "Usage\n\t" << argv [0] << " hostip amount from to\n";
      for (short i = 0; i < NumCurrencies; ++i)
         cerr << "\t\t" << i << '\t' << CurrencyName (i) << endl;
```

```
            return 1;
      }

      double Amount = atof (argv[2]);
      short From = static_cast<short>(atoi (argv[3]));
      short To = static_cast<short>(atoi(argv[4]));

      if (From < 0 || From >= NumCurrencies || To < 0 || To >= NumCurrencies)
      {
         cerr << "Illegal currency specification\n";
         return 1;
      }

      double Converted = ConvertCurrency (Amount, From, To);

      cout << Amount << ' ' << CurrencyName (From) << " is ";
      cout << Converted << ' ' << CurrencyName (To) << endl;

      closesocket(Sock);

      WSACleanup();

      return 0;
}
```

The initialization of the Windows sockets requires a call to `WSAStartup()`. The only complication is that we have to indicate which version of the Windows Sockets API we want to use.

> *Note that in a real-life example, you would need to be more cautious with error handling code, and ensure that the application cleaned up after itself and shut down the Winsock API before exiting. However, in order to simplify the code in these demonstration examples, the error handling has been kept to a minimum.*

To keep the code tidy we extract the initialization of the Windows sockets layer to separate source and header files.

```
// SocketUtils.h

void InitialiseSockets();
```

```
// SocketUtils.cpp

#include <winsock.h>
#include <iostream>
#include "SocketUtils.h"

using namespace std;

void InitialiseSockets()
{
   WORD version = MAKEWORD( 1, 1 );
   WSADATA wsa;
   if( WSAStartup( version, &wsa ) != 0 )
   {
```

```
         cerr << "Error starting sockets\n";
         exit( 1 );
     }
}
```

We'll be able to try out this client program shortly, once we have the server up and running. Let's take a look at that now.

Winsock APIs for servers

Before we can implement our server, we must introduce a few more function calls that are used for handling incoming connections, possibly many at once.

A sockets-based server creates a socket used for listening for new connections. This socket is created in the usual way, using **socket()**, but is then set up as a 'listen socket' by calls to **bind()** and **listen()**.

```
int PASCAL FAR bind(SOCKET s, const struct sockaddr FAR* name, int
namelen);
```

The **bind()** function gives a name to a listen socket. Its parameters are the same as those for **connect()**, except that the address we specify is that of the client from which we wish to accept connections. In fact, since we want to accept connections from more than one client, indeed any client, we can use the special address **INADDR_ANY** in the **sin_addr.s_addr** field of our **sockaddr_in** structure, like this:

```
struct sockaddr_in Address;
Address.sin_family = AF_INET;
Address.sin_addr.s_addr = INADDR_ANY;
Address.sin_port = htons(1234);
bind(ServerSock, reinterpret_cast<sockaddr*>(&Address), sizeof(Address));
```

The call to **bind()** will fail and return **SOCKET_ERROR** if the socket has already been bound or if the requested port number is already in use. A successful call to **bind()** returns zero.

The **listen()** function readies the socket for incoming connections:

```
int PASCAL FAR listen(SOCKET s, int backlog);
```

To take our telephone analogy a little further, it is the call to **listen()** that makes it possible for the phone to ring and for the receptionist to answer calls coming into our building.

The **backlog** parameter specifies the length of an internal queue, used to buffer incoming connections. Should more that one client try to connect to a server at roughly the same time, the server may take a short while to answer the first of them, during which time the others are held in this queue. Typically, **backlog** is set to 5. If you request too large a **backlog** (greater than **SOMAXCONN**, defined in **winsock.h**) Windows will silently set the **backlog** to a 'reasonable' number, but there is no way of knowing what the actual number is. When the queue limit is reached, a client will receive a **WSAECONNREFUSED** error from its call to **connect()**, but otherwise clients are unaware of being held in a queue.

The server accepts connections using the **accept()** function.

```
SOCKET PASCAL FAR accept(SOCKET s, struct sockaddr FAR* addr);
```

The socket passed to **accept()** is the one set up to be the listening socket, and the one returned is a new socket that can be used for communicating with the newly connected client. If an error occurs, the value **INVALID_SOCKET** is returned, and, as before, a specific error code can be retrieved by calling **WSAGetLastError()**. The output parameter **addr** specifies the address of the connecting client.

Try It Out — A Sockets-based Server

The server for a sockets-based implementation is not too difficult to write. It needs to create a socket to listen for clients trying to connect, and each client connection will result in a new socket for the server to use to pass responses to the clients' requests. Because we need to handle many clients at the same time, we start a new thread to deal with each client. (Threads are discussed in more detail in Chapter 6.)

Remember to link the server applications with multithreading libraries, by selecting the appropriate library on the Project | Settings | C/C++ tab, under the code generation category, otherwise the compiler will complain about not being able to find **_beginthread()**.

We can keep the **ServerUtils.h** and **ServerUtils.cpp** the same for the sockets server as they deal with reading the rates data from a file and the basic conversion functions.

In the interests of simplicity with have ignored synchronization issues that might arise if the currency table is updated whilst the server is running.

Here is the server main program:

```
// Server.cpp

#include <windows.h>
#include <winsock.h>
#include <iostream>
#include <string>
#include <process.h>
#include "Currency.h"
#include "ServerUtils.h"
#include "CurrencyConv.h"
#include "SocketUtils.h"

using namespace std;

void SockProcess(void* s)
{
    SOCKET Sock = reinterpret_cast<SOCKET>(s);

    // Run the server forever
    for (;;)
    {
        MessageRequest req;
        MessageResult  res;
```

```
          // Wait for reqests...
          while (recv (Sock, reinterpret_cast<char*>(&req), sizeof( req ), 0) !=
                       SOCKET_ERROR)
        {
           res.type = req.type;

           // Depending on the type of request invoke the appropriate fundtion
           switch (req.type)
           {
           case MSG_NUMBER_OF_CURRENCIES:
              res.numberOfCurrencies.num = NumberOfCurrencies ();
              break;

           case MSG_CURRENCY_NAME:
              strcpy (res.currencyName.name, CurrencyName (req.currencyName.num));
              break;

           case MSG_CONVERT_CURRENCY:
              res.convertCurrency.amount = ConvertCurrency
                                            (req.convertCurrency.amount,
                                            req.convertCurrency.from,
                                            req.convertCurrency.to);

              break;

           default:
              if (req.type != MSG_TERMINATE)
                 cerr << "Illegal message\n";
              closesocket (Sock);
              return;
        } // end switch

        if (send (Sock, reinterpret_cast<char*>(&res), sizeof( res ), 0)
                       == SOCKET_ERROR)
        {
          cerr << "Error writing socket\n";
          exit (1);
        }
      } // end while receiving socket requests
    } // end forever loop
  }
```

`SockProcess()` is the routine that actually receives and processes the messages.

In `main()`, we see pretty much the same code as before:

```
int main (int argc, char* argv[])
{
   ReadRates ("rates.ini");
   if (NumberOfCurrencies () == 0)
   {
      cerr << "Could not read rates details file\n";
      return 1;
   }
```

We then create our socket, and set up the address information.

```
InitialiseSockets();

SOCKET ServerSock = socket (PF_INET, SOCK_STREAM, 0);
if (ServerSock == INVALID_SOCKET)
{
   cerr << "Could not create socket\n";
   return 1;
}

struct sockaddr_in Address;
Address.sin_family = AF_INET;
Address.sin_addr.s_addr = INADDR_ANY;
Address.sin_port = htons (1234);
```

Here, we bind the socket to the address. Which address, you may ask. Well, **INADDR_ANY** is a special, not fully-qualified address. It looks like a broadcast address in fact (or a subnet mask if you like), but it says we will *only* accept connections from *anyone*!

```
bind (ServerSock, reinterpret_cast<sockaddr*>(&Address), sizeof (Address));
```

The program listens for connections. When it gets one, it accepts it and starts a thread to process the data.

```
listen (ServerSock, 3);
for (;;)
{
   int AddressSize = sizeof (Address);
   SOCKET ClientSock = accept (ServerSock,
            reinterpret_cast<sockaddr*>(&Address), &AddressSize);
   _beginthread (SockProcess, 0, reinterpret_cast<void*>(ClientSock));
}
```

This simple example can never actually exit the **for** loop, but for completeness here is the tidy up code that should be executed on normal completion of the program.

```
closesocket (ServerSock);

WSACleanup ();

return 0;
}
```

You are now ready to build the server code and set the server running. Try running the client code now, and you should see an output something like this:

C:\BegNT\Ch11\Socket>client
At least the server IP address must be given

C:\BegNT\Ch11\Socket>client 127.0.0.1 20 3 1
20 Yarbots is 150 Zingies

C:\BegNT\Ch11\Socket>_

If you are running a single computer, you can still experiment with some of the TCP/IP networked examples, by using the local 'loopback' IP address 127.0.0.1 (which always refers to the local machine) and run both the server and the client on the same machine.

Winsock Information Services

As humans we much prefer to label the things around us with names. It is much easier for us to remember the name of our network server (**zeus**) than a cryptic IP address. In our use of Windows networking, we are familiar with using names and having the details hidden.

In our network programming, we would also like to be able to use computers' names. This would isolate our programs from any network re-organization that might take place. It would be ideal if, when the IP address of the server changes, our applications remain unaltered.

Domain Name Service

Networks that support IP protocols generally also provide a mechanism for translating from machine names to IP addresses. This is **DNS**, the **Domain Name Service**. In fact, DNS is a global service, providing for the translation of any Internet address. This is achieved by hierarchy of servers, each resolving network names for a wider and wider area (domains). The root name servers are possibly the most important computers on the Internet.

On the local network, the DNS can be supplemented with a text file that a computer will use to speed up name resolution. This file, called **HOSTS**, is found in the Windows system area:

▶ `%SystemRoot%\System32\drivers\etc\HOSTS` (Windows NT)

▶ `C:\WINDOWS\HOSTS`   (Windows 95)

The format of the hosts file has a line for each server which gives it's IP address. Additional names (nicknames) can be given for each computer listed in the **HOSTS** file. You can see and example below.

As we mentioned before, the special address, `127.0.0.1`, refers to the computer the file resides on, commonly also given the nickname `localhost`. With the TCP/IP protocol installed, but no network adapter or dial-up link present, it is still possible to program network applications. One computer can act as client and server, using the `localhost` address to make connections to itself.

Here is an example hosts file:

```
# Copyright (c) 1993-1995 Microsoft Corp.
#
# This is a sample HOSTS file used by Microsoft TCP/IP for Windows NT.
#
# This file contains the mappings of IP addresses to host names. Each
# entry should be kept on an individual line. The IP address should
# be placed in the first column followed by the corresponding host name.
# The IP address and the host name should be separated by at least one
# space.
#
```

```
# Additionally, comments (such as these) may be inserted on individual
# lines or following the machine name denoted by a '#' symbol.
#
# For example:
#
#     102.54.94.97      rhino.acme.com          # source server
#      38.25.63.10      x.acme.com              # x client host

127.0.0.1        localhost
192.168.1.1      zeus          zeus.domain.net
```

Where a computer (or host) name is given complete with it's internet domain it is known as a **fully qualified domain name (FQDN)**, it is the system's full name and, like the IP address, is unique in the network.

The Windows Sockets API provides some routines for mapping IP addresses to and from host computer names.

As we saw earlier, TCP/IP connections also use a port number, in addition to an address, which allows connections to an address to use a specific port number in order to access a specific 'service'. For example, the FTP service is usually run on port 21, and the SMTP service for mail transport is usually run on port 25. A file called **SERVICES** that defines these 'well known' port numbers is usually available in the same location as the **HOSTS** file we met earlier. Its format is very similar. Here is an excerpt from Windows NT:

```
# Copyright (c) 1993-1995 Microsoft Corp.
#
# This file contains port numbers for well-known services as defined by
# RFC 1060 (Assigned Numbers).
#
# Format:
#
# <service name>  <port number>/<protocol>  [aliases...]   [#<comment>]
#

daytime           13/tcp
daytime           13/udp
ftp-data          20/tcp
ftp               21/tcp
telnet            23/tcp
smtp              25/tcp      mail
bootp             67/udp                     # boot program server
```

Here you can see that to make a connection to send electronic mail using the SMTP service, we would need to make a TCP connection to port 25.

As with host computer names, the Windows Sockets API provides some routines for performing the mapping of service names to port number and protocol.

Mapping Routines

The Winsock APIs for mapping host names, addresses and services are defined in **winsock.h**. They are:

```
struct hostent FAR* PASCAL FAR gethostbyname(const char FAR* name);
struct hostent FAR* PASCAL FAR gethostbyaddr(const char FAR* addr, int
len, int type);
struct servent FAR* getservbyname(const char FAR* name, const char FAR*
proto);
```

The **hostent** structure contains the following members:

▶ char FAR* h_name — the official name of the host

▶ char FAR* FAR* h_aliases — a null-terminated list of nicknames

▶ short h_addrtype — type of address

▶ short h_length — length in bytes of the address

▶ char FAR* FAR* h_addr_list — a null-terminated list of addresses

For our purposes the address type (**h_addrtype**) will always be **PF_INET**. This specifies that we are using the 'Internet protocol family'. Since IP addresses are 32-bit values, the length (**h_length**) will always be four.

> *Note that the pointer returned by these functions refers to space allocated by the Winsock implementation. You must not attempt to modify or free any of the members of the returned structure. Furthermore, there is only one such structure per thread in any application. Any information you need to keep must be copied out before any further Winsock API calls are made.*

If we want to use the server's name instead of an IP address in our client example, we could add a call to the database routine **gethostbyname()** to provide it.

```
char* host = argv[1];
struct hostent* hostinfo;
hostinfo = gethostbyname(host);

if (!hostinfo) //something went wrong, cannot get address
{
   cerr << "Could not read host\n";
   return 1;
}
```

We now have a list of addresses for the server. We will just use the first of these in place of the explicit IP address:

```
Address.sin_addr.s_addr = *(reinterpret_cast<u_long*>(*(hostinfo->h_addr_list)));
```

Similarly, if we had an entry in the **SERVICES** database for our currency server, we could use the **getservbyname()** call, which retrieves service names and protocols. This would allow us to look up the port number rather than using an explicit constant (1234 in our currency converter example).

Non-blocking Sockets

Up until now, we have used blocking function calls for all of the sockets-based applications, client and server. This means that none of the functions we have used return until their work is done (or at least started in the case of **send()**). The client waits until the call to **connect()** completes, and the server spends most of its time in a call to **accept()**, waiting for clients to connect to it. We have used multiple threads in the server to handle client communications, and all of these threads spend most of their time waiting for a call to **recv()** to complete.

If we want our applications to have more control over the way they execute, we have a couple of choices. We can use the **select()** function to wait on a number of sockets at the same time, and if there is activity, to deal with it without blocking. In this way, the clients can be notified when a response is available from the server instead of blocking client execution. Similarly, the server could be implemented in a single thread, and could be notified when there has been any activity on its listening socket or any of the client sockets.

The **select()** call is part of the standard sockets interface and is portable to other systems, such as UNIX. We will not discuss it further here.

There is another way to create asynchronous behavior under Windows, called **asynchronous extensions**. This applies specifically to Windows programs with a message loop.

Microsoft Windows-specific Socket Extensions

Classic Windows applications generally do not block, except in their message loop(s), if we ignore thread and file I/O functions. We can avoid blocking by making use of a set of Winsock extensions that perform the same tasks as the sockets functions we have already met, but which, instead of blocking, send a message to a specified window when they complete. In this way the application can continue to run.

This topic will not be discussed further here since in this book we are concentrating on console applications. The interested reader is referred to *Network Programming in NT*, by Alok Sinha, (ISBN 0-201-59056-5, Addison-Wesley).

Named Pipes

We will now take a very brief look at another, Windows-specific, communication mechanism that shares quite a lot of the functionality of sockets, **named pipes**. In fact, a great deal of our currency application will remain the same if we convert to named pipes, so **ServerUtils** will completely unchanged.

A named pipe is a shared network resource. It has a name that has the same form as a network share, for example,

```
\\SERVER\PIPE\ANAME
```

Both the client and the server must agree on the name of the pipe. The client can use the usual Win32 **ReadFile()** and **WriteFile()** functions to read and write the pipe, but the server must use specific functions for creating the pipe in the first instance, and must run on Windows NT, not Windows 95.

The main advantage of using named pipes is that they are network-transport independent, although they do rely on Microsoft Networking to provide the sharing.

Named pipes can be used in one of two modes, byte or message mode. We will use message mode for our application. In this mode, data is read and written in a transactional style, typically a request message followed by a response message in the opposite direction. With byte mode, arbitrary data is written and read. In fact, in byte mode we can use any file access mechanism on the pipe, including **stdio** and **iostream**, as well as Win32 file reading and writing functions.

Try It Out — A Named Pipe Client

The named pipe client is actually quite simple, and is based on the file read and write functions.

Since the client only uses functions we have met before, we can write it straight away. Here is a modified currency client application using named pipes instead of sockets. The named pipe sections are highlighted.

```cpp
// PipeClient.cpp

#include <windows.h>
#include <iostream >
#include <cstdlib>
#include "CurrencyConv.h"
#include "Currency.h"

using namespace std;

HANDLE pipe;
MessageRequest req;
MessageResult res;

void SendAndReceive()
{
    DWORD bytes;
    if (!WriteFile (pipe, reinterpret_cast<char*>(&req), sizeof (req), &bytes,
                        NULL))
    {
        cerr << "Error writing pipe\n";
        exit (1);
    }
    if (!ReadFile (pipe, reinterpret_cast<char*>(&res), sizeof (res), &bytes,
                        NULL))
    {
        cerr << "Error reading pipe\n";
        exit (1);
    }

    if (res.type != req.type)
    {
        cerr << "Unexpected message returned\n";
        exit (1);
    }
}
```

```
short NumberOfCurrencies()
{
   req.type = MSG_NUMBER_OF_CURRENCIES;
   SendAndReceive ();
   return res.numberOfCurrencies.num;
}

// Return the name of the currency
const char* CurrencyName (short CurrencyNum)
{
   req.type = MSG_CURRENCY_NAME;
   req.currencyName.num = CurrencyNum;
   SendAndReceive ();
   return res.currencyName.name;
}

// Convert an amount from one to another
double ConvertCurrency (double Amount, short From, short To)
{
   req.type = MSG_CONVERT_CURRENCY;
   req.convertCurrency.amount = Amount;
   req.convertCurrency.from   = From;
   req.convertCurrency.to     = To;
   SendAndReceive ();
   return res.convertCurrency.amount;
}

int main (int argc, char* argv[])
{
   if (argc < 2)
   {
      cerr << "At least the pipe name must be given\n";
      return 1;
   }

   pipe = CreateFile(argv[1], GENERIC_READ | GENERIC_WRITE, 0, NULL,
                     OPEN_EXISTING,
                     FILE_ATTRIBUTE_NORMAL, NULL);
   if (pipe == INVALID_HANDLE_VALUE)
   {
      cerr << "Error opening pipe\n";
      return 1;
   }

   // Set the pipe into message mode.
   DWORD mode = PIPE_READMODE_MESSAGE | PIPE_WAIT;
   if (!SetNamedPipeHandleState (pipe, &mode, NULL, NULL))
   {
      cerr << "Error setting pipe into message mode\n";
      return 1;
   }

   short NumCurrencies = NumberOfCurrencies ();

   if (argc != 5)
   {
      cerr << "Usage\n\t" << argv[0] << "pipename amount from to\n";
```

```
        for (short i = 0; i < NumCurrencies; ++i)
            cerr << "\t\t" << i << '\t' << CurrencyName (i) << endl;

        return 1;
    }

    double Amount = atof (argv[2]);
    short From = static_cast<short>(atoi (argv[3]));
    short To = static_cast<short>(atoi (argv[4]));

    if (From < 0 || From >= NumCurrencies || To < 0 || To >= NumCurrencies)
    {
        cerr << "Illegal currency specification\n";
        return 1;
    }

    double Converted = ConvertCurrency (Amount, From, To);

    cout << Amount << ' ' << CurrencyName (From) << " is ";
    cout << Converted << ' ' << CurrencyName (To) << endl;

    CloseHandle (pipe);

    return 0;
}
```

Apart from the fact that we have to explicitly set the pipe to message mode, as far as the client is concerned, the named pipe acts like a file that can be read and written. In this case, we are reading and writing from statically allocated messages since we know there can only be one outstanding response to one request.

We'll see this client in action shortly, once we've written the code for our named pipe server.

Named Pipes Server functions

The server for named pipes is only slightly more complex.

Creating Pipes

A named pipe is created using `CreateNamedPipe()`:

```
HANDLE CreateNamedPipe(
    LPCTSTR lpName,                // pointer to pipe name
    DWORD dwOpenMode,              // pipe open mode
    DWORD dwPipeMode,             // pipe-specific modes
    DWORD nMaxInstances,          // maximum number of instances
    DWORD nOutBufferSize,         // output buffer size, in bytes
    DWORD nInBufferSize,          // input buffer size, in bytes
    DWORD nDefaultTimeOut,        // time-out time, in milliseconds
    LPSECURITY_ATTRIBUTES lpSecurityAttributes); // pointer to sec.
                                                  // attributes structure
```

The pipe name (`lpName` parameter) must uniquely identify the pipe and must be of the form

```
\\.\PIPE\PIPENAME
```

The pipe name is not case sensitive, and may not contain further backslashes.

A server is able to create more than one instance of a named pipe, enabling it to communicate with a number of clients at one time. The operating mode of all instances of the pipe must be the same. This operating mode is given by the **dwOpenMode** parameter and can be one of the following:

> ▶ **PIPE_ACCESS_DUPLEX** — bi-directional communications allowed
> ▶ **PIPE_ACCESS_INBOUND** — client to server transfer only
> ▶ **PIPE_ACCESS_OUTBOUND** — server to client transfer only

Additionally, the **dwOpenMode** parameter may contain flags to modify the operating mode on a per-instance basis. These flags are:

> ▶ **FILE_FLAG_WRITE_THROUGH** — writes do not return until complete
> ▶ **FILE_FLAG_OVERLAPPED** — allow simultaneous reads and writes

The method of writing to the named pipe is given by **dwPipeMode** and is either **PIPE_TYPE_BYTE** or **PIPE_TYPE_MESSAGE**. As you might expect, data from byte type pipes is written as a stream of bytes, while message type pipes are written as streams of messages. All instances of a pipe must use the same write mode.

The method of reading from a pipe can be different for each instance of a named pipe. The **dwPipeMode** parameter can include flags to indicate the desired read type. These are **PIPE_READMODE_BYTE** and **PIPE_READMODE_MESSAGE**. The default is for pipes to be read in byte mode (even for message type pipes).

Specifying the flag **PIPE_WAIT** or **PIPE_NOWAIT** in the parameter **dwPipeMode** can alter the behaviour of the pipe with regard to blocking (the default). With **PIPE_WAIT**, reads will wait until there is data to read, and writes will block until data is written. With the **PIPE_NOWAIT** flag, **ReadFile()** and **WriteFile()** will always return immediately.

The parameter **nMaxInstances** specifies the maximum number of instances of this pipe that can be created. This can be **PIPE_UNLIMITED_INSTANCES** to indicate that there should be no limit.

The parameters **nOutBufferSize** and **nInBufferSize** specify the size, in bytes (4k to 64k is a sensible range), of the buffers that should be allocated for data in transit within the pipe.

You can specify a timeout, in milliseconds, with the **nDefaultTimeout** parameter. This is then used for calls to **WaitNamedPipe()** that use **NMP_USE_DEFAULT_WAIT** as a timeout. Each instance of the pipe must use the same default.

Finally, the **lpSecurityAttributes** structure is used to set access controls for the pipe and may be safely set to **NULL**.

The return value will either be a valid handle to the new pipe, or **INVALID_HANDLE_VALUE**.

Connecting Pipes

To connect a named pipe to a client we call `ConnectNamedPipe()`:

```
BOOL ConnectNamedPipe(HANDLE pipe, LPOVERLAPPED lpOverlapped);
```

In this function, we use a handle to a pipe obtained from `CreateNamedPipe()`. The `lpOverlapped` structure is used when the pipe is operating in `FILE_FLAG_OVERLAPPED` mode. We won't discuss asynchronous I/O any further here — see Chapter 7 for more details. The parameter may safely be set to `NULL` for normal named pipe applications.

The call to `ConnectNamedPipe()` usually does not return until a client has opened the pipe. This is similar to the call to `accept()` in the sockets version that we saw earlier. If the pipe is operating in non-blocking mode, the call will return zero immediately. This provides a way of monitoring a pipe for client connections as in this case `GetLastError()` will return a range of errors indicating the pipe state:

- `ERROR_PIPE_LISTENING` — there is no client
- `ERROR_PIPE_CONNECTED` — there is already a client connected
- `ERROR_NO_DATA` — the client has disconnected, but the server has yet to close the pipe

Setting the State of a Pipe

The read mode and the blocking state of a named pipe can be changed with a call to `SetNamedPipeHandleState()`:

```
BOOL SetNamedPipeHandleState(
    HANDLE  hNamedPipe,             // handle of named pipe
    LPDWORD lpMode,                 // address of new pipe mode
    LPDWORD lpMaxCollectionCount,   // address of max. bytes before remote
                                    // transmission
    LPDWORD lpCollectDataTimeout);  // address of max. time before remote
                                    // transmission
```

The `lpMode` parameter is a pointer to a 32-bit variable used to set the flags for read and write. It uses the same values as the `dwPipeMode` parameter of `CreateNamedPipe()` discussed above.

The transmission characteristics of the named pipe can be altered by setting values for a maximum amount of data required (`lpMaxCollectionCount`) and/or length of time to wait for data in milliseconds before transmission starts (`lpCollectionDataTimeout`). This can improve network performance by sending fewer, larger data bursts. These pointer values can safely be set to `NULL`.

There is a corresponding function, `GetNamedPipeHandleState()` that retrieves information about a named pipe — you can find its definition in the MSDN library.

Closing Pipes

A named pipe is closed by calling `DisconnectNamedPipe()`:

```
BOOL DisconnectNamedPipe(HANDLE pipe);
```

As usual a zero return result indicates an error, and you can get the error code using `GetLastError()`.

Try It Out — A Named Pipe Server

Here is our server application modified to use named pipes. It creates a number of pipes (in this case five) to service client connections.

```cpp
// PipeServer.cpp

#include <windows.h>
#include <iostream>
#include <cstring>
#include <process.h>
#include "Currency.h"
#include "ServerUtils.h"
#include "CurrencyConv.h"

using namespace std;
const int NUM_PIPES = 5;

void PipeProcess (void* p)
{
    HANDLE Pipe = static_cast<HANDLE>(p);
    for (;;)
    {
        // Attempt to connect to the named pipe
        if (!ConnectNamedPipe (Pipe, NULL))
        {
            cerr << "Error connecting to pipe\n";
            return;
        }

        MessageRequest req;
        MessageResult  res;
        DWORD bytes;

        // read from the pipe
        while (ReadFile (Pipe, reinterpret_cast<char*>(&req), sizeof (req), &bytes,
                    NULL))
        {
            res.type = req.type;

            // determine the request time and act accordingly
            switch (req.type)
            {
                case MSG_NUMBER_OF_CURRENCIES:
                    res.numberOfCurrencies.num = NumberOfCurrencies();
                    break;
                case MSG_CURRENCY_NAME:
                    strcpy (res.currencyName.name, CurrencyName
                                (req.currencyName.num));
                    break;
                case MSG_CONVERT_CURRENCY:
                    res.convertCurrency.amount = ConvertCurrency
                                (req.convertCurrency.amount,
```

```
                                                        req.convertCurrency.from,
                                                          req.convertCurrency.to);
                break;
              default:
                  if (req.type != MSG_TERMINATE)
                      cerr << "Illegal message\n";
                  DisconnectNamedPipe (Pipe);
                  CloseHandle (Pipe);
                  return;
          } // end switch

          WriteFile (Pipe, reinterpret_cast<char*>(&res), sizeof (res), &bytes,
                      NULL);
      } // end while getting requests

      // Now we have send a response we can disconnect the pipe
      DisconnectNamedPipe (Pipe);
  } // end forever loop
}

int main (int argc, char* argv[])
{
  if (argc != 2)
  {
    cerr << "Usage\n\t" << argv[0] << " pipename\n";
    return 1;
  }

  ReadRates ("rates.ini");
  if (NumberOfCurrencies() == 0)
  {
    cerr << "Could not read rates details file\n";
    return 1;
  }

  int i;
  for (i = 0; i < NUM_PIPES; ++i)
  {
    HANDLE p = CreateNamedPipe (argv[1],
                                PIPE_ACCESS_DUPLEX,
                                PIPE_TYPE_MESSAGE | PIPE_READMODE_MESSAGE |
                                PIPE_WAIT,
                                NUM_PIPES,
                                sizeof (MessageResult),
                                sizeof (MessageRequest),
                                60 * 1000,
                                NULL );
    if (p == INVALID_HANDLE_VALUE)
    {
      cerr << "Error creating pipe\n";
      return 1;
    }

    _beginthread (PipeProcess, 0, reinterpret_cast<void*>(p));
  }

  // Wait for a key (newline) to be hit
  cin.get();
```

```
    // This code is a lot like the client - get a connection to the
    // "other end" of the pipe and send a close message
    for (i = 0; i < NUM_PIPES; ++i)
    {
        HANDLE pipe = CreateFile (argv[1], GENERIC_READ | GENERIC_WRITE,
                                  0, NULL, OPEN_EXISTING, FILE_ATTRIBUTE_NORMAL,
                                  NULL);
        if (pipe == INVALID_HANDLE_VALUE)
        {
            cerr << "Error opening pipe\n";
            return 1;
        }

        // Only sending a single byte - no need to change the mode to message
        unsigned char term = MSG_TERMINATE;
        DWORD bytes;
        WriteFile (pipe, reinterpret_cast<char*>(&term), 1, &bytes, NULL);
        CloseHandle (pipe);
        Sleep (100);
    }

    return 0;
}
```

Now try building and running the code. Remember that you'll need to change the Code Generation setting under the C++ tab of Project | Settings to Multithreaded. To test the code over two machines, you'll need to have the **PipeServer** executable (together with **RATES.INI**) on the server machine, *server_name*, and set this running using the syntax:

```
PipeServer \\.\pipe\pipe_name
```

On the client machine, you should then use the syntax:

```
PipeClient \\server_name\pipe\pipe_name amount to from
```

> Note that, for simplicity, we have set the security parameter to **NULL** in the call to **CreateNamedPipe()**. This means that in order to run the example, you will need to be logged on to both client and server machines as the same user. See Chapter 8 for more information on security.

You now should be able to see the same output as the earlier example. As we have seen, named pipes are simpler than sockets, but less flexible and restricted to Windows NT platforms. This concludes our discussion of named pipes.

RPC – Remote Procedure Calls

All the networking we have looked at so far has been the transfer of data between systems. Sometimes we want to go further than just data transfer, and ask the remote system to do some work for us. The most common and probably best-known type of request for remote processing is the database server. The client program could an application or a simple SQL front end, such as WISQL (the front end program for Sybase and MS SQL servers). This passes all data requests to the database engine, which then carries out the data processing and returns the result to the client. Where large database engines are run on dedicated machines, the request and response pass over a network. Another example is a search engine on the Web, where you fill in a question page on your local machine and the remote machine does the searching for you, before returning the links to pages found.

This is fine for some processing tasks, but not for more general applications. We wouldn't want to ask our database server to update the system time for example. UNIX systems commonly have a set of commands called the 'r' commands, including `rcp` (remote copy) and `rsh` (remote shell), which allow remote users with the appropriate permissions to execute user level commands on remote machines. NT servers have the ability to remotely manage client machines. These are all good examples of the ability of programs on one machine to get a remote machine to do work for us.

Different systems have their own ways of programming this functionality. Java has a particularly elegant way, called RMI — Remote Method Invocation — which is well explained in the Wrox book, *Beginning Java*. For the C and C++ languages, the most common method is the **Remote Procedure Call**, or **RPC**. There are more sophisticated multitier, cross language solutions, such as Microsoft's DCOM, and the multitier, cross-language, multivendor and cross-platform solution CORBA, from the Object Management Group. However DCOM and CORBA are beyond the scope of this book, so we will content ourselves with Remote Procedure Calls. The fact that DCOM is built on RPC makes that decision even easier — nothing you learn here will be wasted if you start playing with such higher-level distributed object / component-based mechanisms.

> *For more general information on CORBA, consult either the Object Management Group's highly informative web pages at* **http://www.omg.org**, *or one of several CORBA and distributed object books by Robert Orfali, Dan Harkey, and Jeri Edwards, published by Wiley.*
>
> *And for more information on COM, look at* **http://www.microsoft.com/com**, *Professional DCOM, ISBN 1 Richard Grimes and Essential COM, Don Box.*

Basic Principles

The basic idea behind RPC is very simple — we want to make a procedure call on one machine, but we want the actual processing to happen on a different machine. Conventionally, the machine making the request is referred to as the client and the one servicing the request as the server.

In order to implement a remote procedure call, there are a few practical difficulties that must be overcome:

- The client must locate the server and verify that it is available.
- The client and server must agree that the procedure to be invoked is available on the server, and that the specification on both machines is compatible. (Notice the compatible, rather than identical. We will see later that versioning allows the server to implement backward-compatible procedures).

> The arguments for the remote procedure must be converted into an architecturally neutral format and transferred across the network to the server.

> Once the remote procedure has completed, any results must be transferred back to the client. They also need to be converted to and from an architecturally neutral format.

> The system must cater for the inherent unreliability of the connecting network.

> It must also cope with the smaller, but still possible, problem of either the client or server failing during the procedure call.

> Last, but not least, the server needs a security mechanism to ensure that the client is permitted to execute the procedure on the server.

This sounds like hard work, but fortunately, apart from the initial code needed to set up the client and server programs, the actual work of calling and implementing the remote procedure is surprisingly easy, as we shall see shortly.

As you can see from the above list, RPCs seek to resolve some of the issues that we met earlier with sockets, such as network data transparency and reliability, without giving you, the application programmer, significantly more work.

We can illustrate the execution thread of an RPC call like this:

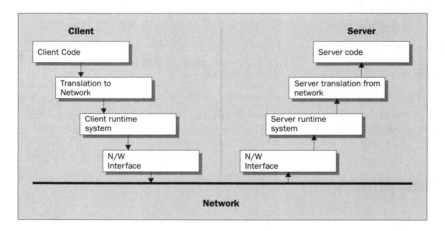

When the server code completes, the results come back along the same path, in reverse.

Many network protocols can be used by RPC, including NetBEUI, SPX, IPX and others. Of course, both client and server must choose a common protocol. A client using RPC over NetBEUI cannot talk to a server providing RPC over TCP/IP, though a server can support multiple protocols simultaneously. The most common protocol used to support RPC, and the one that we'll use here, is TCP/IP.

RPC Definitions

There are actually two similar but incompatible versions of RPC. One was originally proposed by Sun Microsystems, and is defined in RFC 1831, which can be found at `http://rs.internic.net/rs-internic.html`, or one of the many RFC repositories on the Internet. This is commonly referred to as the SUN Open Network Computing (ONC) implementation of RPC. The other version was defined by The Open Group, (`http://www.opengroup.org`) as part of their **Distributed Computing Environment** (**DCE**) specification. More about the full DCE specification can be found at `http://www.camb.opengroup.org/tech/dce`.

The DCE version of RPC is fairly common, particularly on UNIX machines, not least since a public domain implementation is available (look for the file `PD-DCE-RPC.tar.Z` in a DCE sub-directory on any Internet archive). Fans of Linux might like to checkout the (ongoing at the time of writing) port to Linux — information can be found at `http://www.members.aa.net/~mtp`.

Microsoft choose to work from the DCE version of the RPC specification, and their version is usually quoted as 'interworking' with UNIX and other DCE implementations. Microsoft state: "Microsoft's implementation of RPC is compatible with the OSF standard with the exception of some minor differences. Client or server applications written using Microsoft RPC will interoperate with any DCE RPC client or server whose run-time libraries run over a supported protocol".

Now we know a bit of background to RPC, and the problems it must solve, let's look at some implementation details of Microsoft's RPC.

RPC on Win32 Systems

RPC is available on both Windows 95 and NT, and can either act as a server or client, though Windows 95 only supports TCP as a transport.

Let's start by looking at the steps we need to go through to develop an RPC application, then we will update our currency conversion application to use RPC across a network.

The Interface Definition

The first thing we need to do is define an **interface** between our client and server programs, which will specify:

- The functions available on the server
- How to call them

A problem here is uniqueness. We know that we want to implement several functions, one of which is `char* CurrencyName(short Currency)`. Suppose at a later date our server needs to support many RPC services, and our currency converter program expands well beyond this initial design. As we add new interfaces we would have to check that no other RPC interface on the server had this prototype. Indeed, if our server application ran on many different machines, none of them would be able to have a different RPC service with the same prototype.

The Universally Unique Identifier

Providing a unique RPC interface is not an insurmountable problem, but it is clear that simply using the function prototype is not going to scale well across even a corporate network, let alone the Internet. What is needed is an extra *unique* piece of information, and for RPC, this is the **Universally Unique Identifier** or **UUID**, a 128-bit value which can be used to uniquely identify an RPC service. UUIDs are normally shown as a string of hex digits, such as **2fac1234-31f8-11b4-a222-08002b34c003**.

If you're using Visual C++, you can generate a UUID using the command **uuidgen**, which is usually to be found in **DevStudio\VC\bin** (or **Common\Tools** in Visual C++ 6.0) or on the **Tools** menu. You should get a string in a similar format to the above example. Your machine's network card is a key part of creating the UUID, so if your machine is standalone your UUID's uniqueness will be compromised if used on a different machine. In which case you'll get a warning. Try the command several times and you will see the UUID changing.

The IDL file

Now we have a unique identifier string, what we do with it?

We need to store it in a definition file, written using **IDL**, or **Interface Definition Language**, which is a way of specifying an RPC service in a language-independent manner, giving it a UUID and showing which functions it implements. The file also gives information on how the function arguments are to be handled, and allows an IDL compiler to generate various bits of C code for us, which can save us a lot of work.

IDL files usually have the extension **.idl**. Let's re-run the **uuidgen** command, but this time we'll store the output in a file called **currency.idl**.

```
uuidgen /i /ocurrency.idl
```

If you look at **currency.idl**, you should see something like:

```
[
uuid(75227400-ED6F-11D1-8CC9-0060979788FD),
version(1.0)
]
interface INTERFACENAME
{

}
```

The IDL file has two parts:

- The header (in **square** brackets), specifying the UUID and a version number
- The body (the section after the **interface** keyword), where the C style definitions of the remote functions go

Let's update this file with the rest of the information we need to make our currency converter run remotely:

```
[
    uuid( 75227400-ED6F-11D1-8CC9-0060979788FD ),
    version( 1.0 ), // Optional
    pointer_default(unique)
]

interface ICurrency
{
    double ConvertCurrency( [in] double Amount, [in] short From, [in] short To );
    short   NumberOfCurrencies( void );
    [string] char* CurrencyName( [in] short Currency );
};
```

We have added a line to the header section:

```
    pointer_default(unique)
```

This defines the default type of all pointers passed across the interface as 'unique' type pointers. We will return to the meaning of this shortly.

In the body we have followed convention and given the name `ICurrency` to the whole interface specification; and we have added 'C' style definitions for the remote procedure calls we will use. Note that this is not exactly the same as the C definition. We also add usage specifiers; in this case `[in]` to the passed parameters, since they are all values passed 'in' to the procedure. We could also have specified `[out]`, or `[in,out]` to define exactly how parameters need to be passed and returned from the procedure.

Notice that the version number is in two parts, a major version, `1`, and a minor version, `0`. The use of major and minor version numbers lets us handle updates to the interface definition in a flexible way.

Suppose we have a server and a large number of clients, distributed and running. If we change the server interface in an incompatible way, then we need to prevent older clients, which are incompatible with the new interface, from using the updated server until we have a chance to update all the clients. To do this, we increment the major version number in the IDL file. Once the server has been built and installed using the new version number, clients built with a different major version number will refuse to connect to the old service. We then know that we can send out new clients, safe in the knowledge that any older client will refuse to use the service until they have been updated.

However, sometimes we might want to update the server in a way that is still compatible with older clients, and allow older clients to connect to the service in the interim, before they are updated. To do this we increment the minor number. Clients built with a lower minor version number, but the same major version number, can still connect and use the service.

Type Definitions.

One of the problems with the definition of the C programming language is that machines are allowed to interpret the 'C' types as the most efficient natural machine types on any given machine. Whilst this makes the C code execute efficiently, it's not so good if the client of an RPC interface passes an integer that is 64 bits wide, but the server was expecting an integer to be 32 bits wide. For this reason RPC defines a set of base types that can be passed, and these are summarized in the table below:

Type	Notes
`hyper`	A 64-bit signed integer.
`long`	A 32-bit signed integer.
`short`	A 16-bit signed integer.
`small`	An 8-bit signed integer.
`unsigned hyper`	A 64-bit unsigned integer.
`unsigned long`	A 32-bit unsigned integer.
`unsigned short`	A 16-bit unsigned integer.
`unsigned small`	An 8-bit unsigned integer.
`char`	An 8-bit unsigned character.
`unsigned char`	An 8-bit unsigned character (same as `char`).
`boolean`	**TRUE** or **FALSE**, though Microsoft extensions permit **1** (`true`) and **0** (`false`).
`byte`	8 bits of data, passed between client and server with no conversion.
`void`	Usually used to indicate that a procedure takes no parameters.
`Float`	A 32-bit floating point number
`Double`	A 64-bit floating point number
`error_status_t`	A Microsoft extension used for error indication.
`wchar_t`	A Microsoft extension for internationalization of character sets, actually the same as an `unsigned short`.
`handle_t`	Used for primitive handle types that are not transmitted on the network.

There is one 'gotcha' in handling characters and strings (character arrays): in C++, a `char` is distinct from an `unsigned char` and a `signed char`, whereas in IDL, the first two are synonymous. This means that code using RPC generally has to cast between `char` and `unsigned char` with monotonous regularity.

In addition to these base types, it is also possible to pass arrays, in the form `[in] unsigned short sMyArray[10]`. Strings are handled in a similar fashion — for example, `[in, string] char szName[]`. You can also pass variable sized arrays.

We can pass structures to RPC functions, providing they are composed only of the allowed base types listed above. Unions are also possible, but only with special handling, which is beyond the scope of this book, but you can find further information in Sinha's *Network Programming in Windows NT*.

Pointers need a special mention. When the remote procedure is called, it executes on a different machine from that which did the calling. So, if the client were to pass to the server a pointer to a memory location, it would be of no use to the server, since it points to an object in the client's memory, not in the server's memory. Thanks to some automatic memory management, pointers *can* be used in RPC, but they need careful handling, and there is some requirement on the user to specify exactly how the pointers are being used.

Pointers for RPC are split into three types:

- Reference pointers, which point to a fixed location, have no aliases (no other pointer points to the same location), and will never be **NULL**

- Unique pointers, which are similar to reference pointers, except they may be **NULL**

- Full pointers, where not only may they be **NULL**, but also other pointers might point to the same location.

More generally defined pointer types introduce more overhead into the RPC call, so 'full pointers' impose a larger overhead than 'unique pointers', which in turn impose a larger overhead than 'reference pointers'.

If necessary, each pointer can have its RPC type individually defined. However, it is convenient to put a **pointer_default** specification in the header section of the IDL file, and ensure that any pointers that will be used conform to the rule associated with the chosen pointer type. For example, in the example we've just seen, we defined the default pointer to be the unique type.

There is one other thing we might sometimes want to do in the **IDL** file, and that is to define the connection point for the RPC service. To do this we can add an **endpoint** declaration into the header section of the **IDL** file, as shown below:

```
endpoint("ncacn_ip_tcp:[1234]")
```

This says that the RPC service will be using TCP/IP on port 1234. We will discuss endpoints in more detail later, in the section on RPC clients. Note that the endpoint can also be defined at runtime in the server's code.

To complete our RPC specification there is one more definition file we need, the ACF file.

The ACF file

The IDL file discussed above is concerned mainly with the data being transported between client and server. The **ACF (Application Configuration File)** defines some of the environment of the RPC server. For our application, we require little of this, but we do need to specify something about 'binding handles'.

> *A full explanation of binding handles is outside the scope of this book, but again, a good place to look for more information is* Network Programming in Windows NT.

In broad terms, we can either look after the handles ourselves, passing them to each RPC invocation, or we can let the RPC system supply them implicitly, a bit like the **this** pointer in C++ member functions. The latter is normally sufficient, and is what we chose for our **acf** file, **Currency.acf**:

```
[
    implicit_handle(handle_t hICurrency)
]
interface ICurrency
{}
```

Although, as in this case, the IDL and ACF files are kept separate, it is possible to combine them into one when using the Microsoft IDL compiler (MIDL).

Generating code

So far, all we have done is create definitions. Now it's time to use these definitions to create some code, and also complete two stub code procedures we must write ourselves.

> *A stub is an in-process object, the representative of the client on the serve's process, or vice versa.*

The Microsoft IDL compiler

Now that we have our IDL and ACF files, we can take the first step in building our application. We need to use the definitions in the files to create some code to which we can link. To do this, we use the **midl** command, which takes the IDL and ACF files and creates some C files ready for compiling and linking. We can either do this from the command line, or, more usually, by adding the IDL file to our project and specifying a custom build command, like this:

```
midl /acf currency.acf currency.idl
```

This creates three new files, which we should specify as output files in the custom build section. For us, these are **currency.h**, **currency_s.c** and **currency_c.c**. (Notice in this case, we're generating the **currency.h** header file, instead of using a manually written one as in all the previous examples.)

We will need to include the header file in our other source files and we'll need to compile and link the two C files with our source files. The **_s.c** file is compiled and linked with the server side, the **_c.c** file with the client side.

Memory Stubs

The RPC interface is doing quite a lot of work for us, in terms of managing pointers and re-arranging parameters into a machine-independent form. To do this, it often needs access to memory. To provide some control over how the application does this, the internal RPC code always uses a pair of functions that you must supply to manage memory. The first function is for allocating memory,

```
void __RPC_FAR* __RPC_API midl_user_allocate(size_t len)
```

and the second is for releasing it again:

```
void __RPC_API midl_user_free(void __RPC_FAR* ptr)
```

Since we are writing a C++ program for this example, we use the C++ idiom of **new** and **delete**. Shown below is a source file, **RPCUtils.cpp**, which we must create to implement these two functions. Note that you have to write just these two functions for RPC to use internally. There is no need to write functions to allocate other types as far as RPC is concerned.

```
// RPCUtils.cpp

#include "Currency.h"

void __RPC_FAR* __RPC_API midl_user_allocate(size_t len)
{
    return new char[ len ];
}

void __RPC_API midl_user_free(void __RPC_FAR* p)
{
    delete [] reinterpret_cast<char*>(p);
}
```

If you are writing a C program, then you would use some equivalent C memory management routines such as **malloc** and **free**.

This utilities file will need to be compiled and linked with both our server and client side code sections.

Before we move on and look at the actual client and server code, let's just re-cap with a quick summary of all the different elements that need to go together to make a server and client RPC program. Only the shaded sections in the following diagram need to be written by the programmer — the rest are generated by the RPC tools.

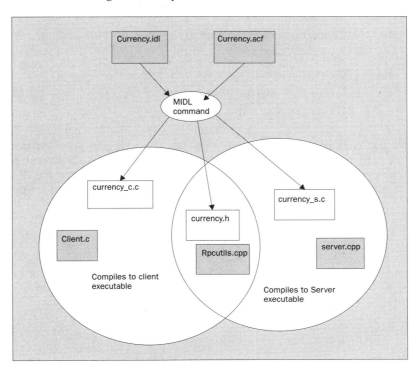

The Client

Starting from our defined interface, we can write some code that will allow the client and server to initialize the RPC interface, and locate each other so they are ready for the RPC calls to take place.

Initializing the Client Side

We will start with the client side, since that is the simpler. The principal API call we need is `RpcBindingFromStringBinding()` which allows the client to locate the server:

```
RPC_STATUS RPC_ENTRY RpcBindingFromStringBinding(
    unsigned char* StringBinding,  // points to a string representation of
                                   // a binding
    RPC_BINDING_HANDLE* Binding);  // returns a pointer to the handle
```

The intricacy here is in the first parameter, the string binding. This needs to specify an endpoint to which the client is trying to connect, that is, both a protocol and a protocol-specific address.

In the general case, a string is built using the `RpcStringBindingCompose()` function. However, for this book we are concentrating on TCP/IP, and we can easily build a TCP/IP address binding ourselves.

The first part of the string is always a protocol. The principal ones are shown in the table below:

String	Description
ncacn_ip_tcp	Connection-oriented TCP/IP
ncacn_nb_nb	Connection-oriented NetBEUI
ncacn_nb_tcp	NetBIOS over TCP/IP
ncadg_ip_udp	Connectionless IP (using the UDP protocol)
ncacn_np	Connection-oriented named pipes
ncalrpc	Local procedure call — good for testing!

Since we are using TCP/IP, we'll use `ncacn_tcp_ip`. The next part we need to specify is an address. For TCP/IP, the most explicit address is a dotted quad IP address and port number. The protocol is separated from the address by a colon, and the port from the IP address by enclosing it in square brackets. Thus we end up with a string binding that looks like this:

```
ncacn_ip_tcp:192.168.1.1[2265]
```

In our simple client, we get this from a command line argument.

The other parameter for `RpcBindingFromStringBinding()` is a binding handle, and is defined for us in the code generated by the `midl` command. We simply need to pass a reference to it. In our case it is called `hICurrency`.

When our client is finished, we need to release the binding again. To do this, we use the `RpcBindingFree()` function, which takes as a parameter a reference to the same handle we passed to the binding call.

Try It Out — Calling from the Client Side

After all this effort, we are finally in a position to write some code to use the RPC interface. It may seem like we have done a lot of work for not much gain, but we are about to see that all the preparation makes the actual use of the RPC procedures very simple indeed.

We can call the procedure directly as though it were local — there are no functions to compose and decompose messages, or send them to the server:

```
NumCurrencies = NumberOfCurrencies()
```

However, there is one other thing we ought to take care of — error handling. Because the procedure is executing remotely over a network, we do need to take account of potential errors. This is straightforward, and uses a method modeled on standard C++ **try**/**catch** blocks.

We wrap the call in a **RpcTryExcept** block, handle errors in an **RpcExcept** block and mark the end of the RPC section with an **RpcEndExcept**, like this:

```
RpcTryExcept
{
   NumCurrencies = NumberOfCurrencies();
}
RpcExcept( 1 ) // Any non-zero constant will trap *all* exceptions
{
   cerr << "There was an RPC error - " << RpcExceptionCode() << " to be
                  exact\n";
   return 1;
}
RpcEndExcept;
```

And that's all there is to it, at least for the client side.

Here is the full client code:

```
// RPCClient.cpp

#include <iostream>
#include <cstdlib>
#include "Currency.h"

using namespace std;

int main (int argc, char* argv[])
{
   if (argc < 2)
   {
      cerr << "Need at least a binding\n";
      return 1;
   }
```

```
      // Get an RPC binding
      RPC_STATUS status = RpcBindingFromStringBinding (reinterpret_cast<unsigned
                                                       char*>(argv[1]),
                                                       &hICurrency);

   if (status != 0)
   {
      cerr << "RpcBindingFromStringBinding failed\n";
      return 1;
   }

   short NumCurrencies;

   // Wrap the RPC call in some error handling (omitted around other
   // RPC calls for brevity)
   RpcTryExcept
   {
      NumCurrencies = NumberOfCurrencies ();
   }
   RpcExcept (1) // Any non-zero constant will trap *all* exceptions
   {
      cerr << "There was an RPC error - " << RpcExceptionCode () << " to be
                     exact\n";
      return 1;
   }
   RpcEndExcept;

   if (NumCurrencies == 0)
   {
      cerr << "Could not read rates details file\n" ;
      return 1;
   }

   if (argc != 5)
   {
      cerr << "Usage\n\t" << argv[0]
           << " binding amount from to\n\twhere from & to can take the
                     values:\n";
      for (short i = 0; i < NumCurrencies; ++i)
      {
         char* Name = reinterpret_cast<char*>(CurrencyName (i));
         cerr << "\t\t" << i << '\t' << Name << endl;
         delete [] Name;
      }
   }
   else
   {
      double Amount = atof (argv[2]);
      short From = static_cast<short>(atoi (argv[3]));
      short To = static_cast<short>(atoi (argv[4]));
      if (From < 0 || From >= NumCurrencies || To < 0 || To >= NumCurrencies)
      {
         cerr << "Illegal currency specification\n";
         return 1;
      }

      double Converted = ConvertCurrency (Amount, From, To);
```

```
        char* FromName = reinterpret_cast<char*>(CurrencyName (From));
        char* ToName   = reinterpret_cast<char*>(CurrencyName (To));
        cout << Amount << ' ' << FromName << " is "
             << Converted << ' ' << ToName << endl;
        delete [] FromName;
        delete [] ToName;
    }

    RpcBindingFree (&hICurrency);

    return 0;
}
```

The Server

The server is a little more complex than the client, because it needs to register itself as available for client RPC calls.

The first thing the server needs to do is to specify which protocol is it using. How this is done depends on whether the endpoint was specified in the IDL file, or whether we are going to define it at runtime. The former scenario is a little simpler, but let's look at the latter first.

Specifying the Endpoint at Runtime

There are several steps the server needs to carry out in this case. First, we need to call the following functions for the setup:

- `RpcServerUseProtseq()`
- `RpcServerRegisterIf()`
- `RpcServerInqBindings()`
- `RpcEpRegister()`

Then we ask for the representation of the binding that the client will need:

- `RpcBindingToStringBinding()`

Next, we start the server listening for requests:

- `RpcServerListen()`

Finally, we must tidy up when we have finished:

- `RpcMgmtStopServerListening()`
- `RpcServerUnregisterIf()`

Let's take a look at these functions and what they do in a little more detail. First the server needs to specify which protocol is going to be used, which it does with the `RpcServerUseProtseq()` function:

```
RPC_STATUS RPC_ENTRY RpcServerUseProtseq(
    unsigned char* ProtSeq,
    unsigned int MaxCalls,
    void* SecurityDescriptor);
```

The **ProtSeq** parameter is the protocol string we saw in the client, except that this time we specify only the protocol, not an address. For our simple server example shown below, we just pass this on the command line.

The **MaxCalls** parameter determines how many concurrent procedure calls we want to accept.

The **SecurityDescriptor** parameter is for NT only, and points to a security descriptor. This should be set to **NULL** for Windows 9x, and **NULL** is an acceptable default for NT as well.

If a server needs to accept requests via many different protocols, then it must call **RpcServerUseProtseq()** many times, once for each protocol it wishes to use.

Having defined the protocol sequence it will use, the server must now register the interface. It does this by calling **RpcServerRegisterIf()**.

```
RPC_STATUS RPC_ENTRY RpcServerRegisterIf(
    RPC_IF_HANDLE IfSpec,      // a MIDL generated data structure
    UUID* MgrTypeUuid,         // points to a type UUID
    RPC_MGR_EPV* MgrEpv);      // manager routines entry point
```

In the simplest case, you just pass the interface handle data structure generated by the **midl** command for the first parameter, which can be found in the **currency.h** file. For the other two parameters, you can simply pass **NULL**. In our example, the handle is called **ICurrency_v1_0_s_ifspec**.

The next step is to recover the binding handles that the RPC interface has allocated us. We do this with the **RpcServerInqBindings()** function:

```
RPC_STATUS RPC_ENTRY RpcServerInqBindings(RPC_BINDING_VECTOR** BindingVector);
```

Next, we need to register the server address, with the **RpcEpRegister()** function. Like **RpcServerRegisterIf()**, we can simply pass an interface handle data structure, plus the binding interface vector we just recovered.

```
RPC_STATUS RPC_ENTRY RpcEpRegister(
    RPC_IF_HANDLE IfSpec,                  // The interface to register
    RPC_BINDING_VECTOR* BindingVector,     // the vector of binding handles
    UUID_VECTOR* UuidVector,               // the vector of object UUIDs
    unsigned char* Annotation);            // comment string
```

We need some way of finding out what that endpoint is, so we can use it in the client. We can do this with the **RpcBindingToStringBinding()** function:

```
RPC_STATUS RPC_ENTRY RpcBindingToStringBinding(
    RPC_BINDING_HANDLE Binding,         // Binding handle to convert
    unsigned char** StringBinding);     // the string representation
```

In the general case, there could be multiple endpoints, so this call could be made in a loop, like this:

```
RPC_BINDING_VECTOR* bv;
RpcServerInqBindings (&bv);

...

for( unsigned long i = 0; i < bv->Count; ++i )
{
    char* s;
    RpcBindingToStringBinding( bv->BindingH[ i ], reinterpret_cast<unsigned
                                char**>(&s) );
    cerr << "Endpoint " << s << endl;
}
```

In order to allow the server to receive RPC calls, we use the `RpcServerListen()` function:

```
RPC_STATUS RPC_ENTRY RpcServerListen(
    unsigned int MinimumCallThreads,    // Minimum number of call threads
    unsigned int MaxCalls,              // Suggest limit of concurrent
                                        // calls
    unsigned int DontWait);             // Do we wait for calls to
                                        // complete flag
```

The first two parameters to this function simply specify the minimum and maximum number of concurrent call threads, and final one specifies when the funtion returns. If 0 is passed in for this parameter means that the server will listen until it closes down.

In our case, we pass **MinmumCallThreads** 1, for at least a single call thread, **MaxCalls** 5, to allow five concurrent client calls, and **DontWait FALSE**, to request that the RPC server listens until it is closed down.

The call of the currency conversion procedure is hidden away, and happens for us automatically, thanks to the RPC stub code generated from the IDL file calling our conversion functions directly.

Should the server exit for any reason, we need to release the RPC resources. We do this with a pair of calls:

```
RpcMgmtStopServerListening(NULL);
RpcServerUnregisterIf(NULL, NULL, FALSE);
```

These functions are defined as:

```
RPC_STATUS RPC_ENTRY RpcMgmtStopServerListening(RPC_BINDING_HANDLE Binding);
RPC_STATUS RPC_ENTRY RpcServerUnregisterIf(
    RPC_IF_HANDLE IfSpec,                   // interface to unregister
    UUID* MgrTypeUuid,                      // the UUID type
    unsigned int WaitForCallsToComplete);   // indicator flag
```

Using **NULL** for the binding handle and interface specification stops all of our listen operations.

Now, let's see how this works in practice.

Shown below is the full code listing for the server:

```cpp
//RPCServer.cpp

#include <iostream>
#include "Currency.h"
#include "ServerUtils.h"

using namespace std;

int main (int argc, char* argv[])
{
   if (argc != 2)
   {
      cerr << "Usage:\n\t" << argv[0]
           << " protocol\n\twhere the protocol could be "
           << "ncacn_np, ncacn_ip_tcp, ncalrpc, ...\n";
      return 1;
   }

   ReadRates ("rates.ini");
   if (NumberOfCurrencies () == 0)
   {
      cerr << "Could not read rates details file\n";
      return 1;
   }

   RPC_STATUS status = RpcServerUseProtseq (reinterpret_cast<unsigned
                                            char*>(argv[1]),
                                            1, NULL);
   if (status != 0)
   {
      cerr << "RpcServerUseProtseq failed\n";
      return 1;
   }

   status = RpcServerRegisterIf (ICurrency_v1_0_s_ifspec, NULL, NULL);
   if (status != 0)
   {
      cerr << "RpcServerRegisterIf failed\n";
      return 1;
   }

   RPC_BINDING_VECTOR* bv;
   status = RpcServerInqBindings (&bv);
   if (status != 0)
   {
      cerr << "RpcServerInqBindings failed\n";
      return 1;
   }

   status = RpcEpRegister (&ICurrency_v1_0_s_ifspec, bv, NULL, NULL);
   if (status != 0)
   {
```

```
            cerr << "RpcEpRegister failed\n";
            return 1;
    }

    for (unsigned long i = 0; i < bv->Count; ++i)
    {
        char* s;
        RpcBindingToStringBinding (bv->BindingH[i], reinterpret_cast<unsigned
                                    char**>(&s));
        cerr << "Endpoint " << s << endl;
    }

    status = RpcServerListen (1,     // Minimum number of threads
                                     5,     // Maximum number of clients
                                     0);    // Blocking call
    if (status != 0)
    {
        cerr << "RpcServerListen failed\n";
        return 1;
    }

    // In this incarnation, these won't actually be invoked I'm afraid
    RpcMgmtStopServerListening (NULL);
    RpcServerUnregisterIf (NULL, NULL, FALSE);

    return 0;
}
```

> *You must link with rpcrt4.lib when building these applications to ensure that the RPC APIs are available.*

Try building the code and running it. You'll need to specify `ncacn_ip_tcp` as an argument for the server — this is passed as an argument to `RpcServerUseProtseq()` and tells the server that we want to use TCP/IP as our protocol. The server should then output the endpoint, which will take the form:

```
ncacn_ip_tcp:ip_address[port_number]
```

This is what you need to specify as an argument when you run the client, in order to make the RPC connection. Then add the currencies you wish to convert between.

Specifying the Endpoint in IDL

If we want to force the server to use a particular binding, the sequence is slightly easier. Add an **endpoint** specification to the IDL file. The example here specifies that the protocol is TCP/IP, and the port to use is 1234.

```
endpoint ("ncacn_ip_tcp:[1234]")
```

Then, for our server, we first need to call the following setup routines:

```
RpcServerUseAllProtseqsIf()
    RpcServerRegisterIf()
```

Then we start the server listening for requests:

```
RpcServerListen()
```

Finally we tidy up when we have finished:

```
RpcMgmtStopServerListening()
RpcServerUnregisterIf()
```

*The code for this version of the project, **RPCWellKnown**, is available in the source code that accompanies this book, which you can download from the Wrox web site.*

Notice this time we do not need the binding vectors, since we specified the endpoint explicitly in the **idl** file. But of course we must be sure that the server machine isn't already using port 1234 for something else!

RPC Summary

RPC is a big topic, and in this chapter, we don't have the room to cover all the options and possibilities. Although setting up RPC involves quite a lot of initial work, once the basics are in place, it becomes very easy to extend the interface with additional procedure calls.

The version of RPC we have seen here is actually the foundation on which COM and DCOM is built. To make it easier to build these applications Microsoft has provided the Active Template Library, which makes life easier for most COM programmers.

Two final methods conclude our currency conversion applications. The first, **memory mapped files**, could be useful where the updater is running on the same machine as the server and the amount of data is reasonably large. We've seen this technique in Chapter 7, but we can now apply it to our client/server example.

The second, **mailslots** could be used where the updater is remote and providing many regular updates for fast changing environments.

Memory Mapped Files and Shared Memory

Let's quickly recap the ideas behind memory mapped files. Since all processes running on a machine can see disk files (providing the process has appropriate permissions), it is possible for two or more processes to communicate by simultaneously accessing a file. Of course some careful synchronization is needed to turn this into a reliable way for processes to communicate. Another problem with simple file sharing is that it is very inefficient, but using a feature of Windows NT called **memory mapped files**, we can devise a solution that is much more efficient than simple file sharing.

It would be nice if there was a simple way of simply arranging for two or more processes to share data in memory, without using a file at all. Unlike Unix, NT does not have such a feature, because all processes are isolated in their own address spaces, but as we saw in Chapter 7, memory mapped files allow us to achieve much the same effect. Programmers who have used Unix may know of the Unix **mmap()** system call, which allows Unix processes to map files into their address space. Windows NT has a similar system, but with a rather more complex API. In both cases, the contents of a file appear to be a local array.

We have seen the basic principles of memory mapped files, so let's look at how our application can share data using them to give us shared memory.

Try It Out — A Shared Memory Application

To do this, we need to map an unnamed file in the server memory space, which it will use for its currency rates, and then allow another process to attach to it, so that the second program can write new rates directly into the server process memory space.

First, we declare a structure to hold the currency information, so that we can reference the whole set of data easily in one lump of shared memory. This will be used both by the server program and the updater program that changes the information.

```
// ServerUtils.h

struct CurrencyDetails
{
    unsigned char CurrencyNames[MaxNumCurrencies][MaxNameLength];
    double RateWrtBase[MaxNumCurrencies];
    short NumCurrencies;
};

void MapCurrencyDetails (HANDLE map);

...
```

We can re-implement **ServerUtils.cpp** to make use of this new structure:

```
#include <fstream>
#include <cstring>
#include "Currency.h"
#include "ServerUtils.h"

using namespace std;

CurrencyDetails* Currencies = NULL;

short NumberOfCurrencies (void)
{
    if (!Currencies)
        return 0;
    return Currencies->NumCurrencies;
}

unsigned char* CurrencyName (short CurrencyNum)
{
    if (!Currencies)
        return NULL;
```

```
      char* NameSrc = reinterpret_cast<char*>(Currencies
                                      ->CurrencyNames[CurrencyNum]);
      char* NameDst = reinterpret_cast<char*>(midl_user_allocate (strlen (NameSrc)
                                      + 1));
      strcpy (NameDst, NameSrc);
      return reinterpret_cast<unsigned char*>(NameDst);
}

double ConvertCurrency (double Amount, short From, short To)
{
   if (!Currencies)
      return 0.0;
   double Converter = Currencies->RateWrtBase[To] / Currencies->RateWrtBase[From];
   return Amount * Converter;
}

void ReadRates (const char* File)
{
   ifstream f(File);
   if (!f)
      return;
   ReadRates(f);
}

void ReadRates (istream& is)
{
   if (!Currencies)
      return;

   Currencies->NumCurrencies = 0;

   short i;
   for (i = 0; i < MaxNumCurrencies; ++i)
      if (!(is >> Currencies->RateWrtBase[i] >> Currencies->CurrencyNames[i]))
         break;

   Currencies->NumCurrencies = i;
}

void MapCurrencyDetails (HANDLE map)
{
   Currencies = static_cast<CurrencyDetails*>(MapViewOfFile (map,
                                      FILE_MAP_ALL_ACCESS,
                                      0, 0, 0));

   if (!Currencies)
   {
      cerr << "Map view failed\n";
      return;
   }
}
```

The memory-mapped area must be created by one of the programs which is going to use it. We choose to let the server do the deal.

```
HANDLE map = CreateFileMapping (reinterpret_cast<HANDLE>(0xFFFFFFFF),
                                          NULL,
                                          PAGE_READWRITE,
                                          0,
                                          sizeof (CurrencyDetails),
                                          "CurrencyObject");

if (!map)
{
   cerr << "Could not create file mapping\n";
   return 1;
}


MapCurrencyDetails (map);
```

Notice the 'magic number' file handle. We give the file mapping a name, **CurrencyObject**, so the updater program can refer to it. Since the mapping does not refer to a file, we also need to give it a size — the size of the **CurrencyDetails** structure we wish to share between the two programs.

We need to map the view into the server's address space, casting to a pointer of the correct type, and this we do in the **MapCurrencyDetails()** function:

```
Currencies = static_cast<CurrencyDetails*>(MapViewOfFile (map,
                                        FILE_MAP_ALL_ACCESS, 0, 0, 0));
```

For the server, that's it.

The updater program is very similar:

```
#include <windows.h>
#include <iostream>
#include "ServerUtils.h"

using namespace std;

int main (int argc, char* argv[])
{
   HANDLE map = OpenFileMapping (FILE_MAP_ALL_ACCESS, FALSE, "CurrencyObject");
   if (!map)
   {
      cerr << "Could not map memory\n";
      return 1;
   }

   CurrencyDetails* Currencies = static_cast<CurrencyDetails*>(MapViewOfFile (map,
                                        FILE_MAP_ALL_ACCESS, 0, 0, 0));
   if (!Currencies)
   {
      cerr << "Map view failed\n";
      return 1;
   }
```

```
        if( Currencies->NumCurrencies > 1 )
            --(Currencies->NumCurrencies);

        return 0;
    }
```

Since the server has created the mapping, we only need to open the mapping here with `OpenFileMapping()`, then map the view into the updater memory space.

Now both programs have a pointer called **Currencies**, that points to a shared memory area, so updates written by one will be seen by the other. To see this, set a breakpoint in **Updater.cpp**, and look at the **CurrencyDetails** structure once it has been set.

Memory Mapped File Restrictions

There is one very important restriction on sharing data using memory mapped files — don't do it across a network! If you share a file across a network, then map it into two or more processes, on different machines, NT does not ensure that all the processes see a consistent view of the file. If one process changes data in the file, there is an indeterminate interval before other processes will see the change. For this reason you should never memory map writable networked files.

Mailslots

Up to now all the interprocess communication we have looked at has either been two-way, reliable, or both. Often this is just the kind of communication you need — reliable two-way exchanges of data. However, sometimes you can make do with one-way communication, without guaranteed delivery.

The two-way reliability of TCP/IP sockets does not come without a price — the overhead imposed on the underlying network to make the communications reliable. If we have an application to send information to a large number of clients, but can live with the risk that some clients may not always receive every message, it can be useful to minimize the overhead we place on the underlying network.

A typical example of such a need might be the need to distribute 'ticker tape' type news headlines to many client machines on a local network. It's not terribly important that all clients get all messages all the time, but it may be important that we don't swamp the network with the low grade traffic, at the expense of more important data such as applications and file sharing.

Windows NT (and Windows 9x) provides an API for just such a requirement, the **Mailslot API**. This is a set of functions that can be used to implement one-way communication, with non-guaranteed delivery. Like many of the interprocess techniques we have seen, Win32 mailslots does not rely on any particular underlying network protocol. The exact impact of sending a large number of mailslot messages to a number of clients will depend not only on the capabilities of the network that it is used on, but also how efficiently the underlying network protocols implement one way 'unreliable' transport. On our preferred protocol, TCP/IP, the UDP protocol provides almost exactly what the high-level APIs need, so we can reasonably expect the implementation to use the network efficiently, although we have no control of how Windows actually implements the Mailslot.

Mailslot addressing

Mailslot addressing takes one of four forms, depending on how messages are to be addressed. These are summarized in the table below:

Address	Meaning
`\\.\MAILSLOT\MAILSLOTNAME`	Local addressing to a specific mailslot name
`\\COMPUTERNAME\MAILSLOT\MAILSLOTNAME`	Directed to a specific mailslot name on a specific machine
`\\DOMAINNAME\MAILSLOT\MAILSLOTNAME`	Directed to a specific mailslot name on all machines in a given domain
`\\*\MAILSLOT\MAILSLOTNAME`	Directed to a specific mailslot name on all computers in the systems primary domain

It is important to remember one additional detail — if the machines in a domain are spread across a local area network, the network may be configured to prevent broadcast packets spreading far beyond the local segment. This is usually good network configuration, minimizing and dividing the load on the network. However, it does have a side effect in that trying to broadcast a mailslot to a large number of machines may not succeed, because messages may not be forwarded by the underlying network to every possible machine in the domain.

Don't expect your network administrator to re-configure his network to take account of your mailslot program! You can probably work round any problems by sending mailslots to specifically named machines, which will avoid the broadcast problem on the underlying network.

Mailslot Paradigm

The mailslot API is based on the idea of files, a little like the named pipe implementation we met earlier in the chapter.

There are two processes that take part in a mailslot communication:

▶ The sender of the message — the client
▶ The receiver of the message — the server

The mailslot is created by the server, and can then be written to by the client. However the client has no way of knowing if the message has been delivered, if it has been read, or in the case of broadcast mailslots, even how many machines the message was sent to. The server can read messages as they arrive, but once a message is read, it is automatically deleted from the incoming mailslot, so it can never be read again.

Mailslots have a maximum allowable message size. On a local machine, they can be up to 64k, but if sent via NetBEUI, then they must be less than 400 bytes. The server program that creates the mailslot can, however, force an even lower limit to the message size if it chooses.

Although there is no limit specified on the number of messages in a mailslot, there is no guaranteed delivery, so we can never be sure that excess messages will not be discarded at some point.

561

Mailslot API Functions

There are three procedures specific to mailslots, with all the other work being done by standard file handling APIs. Mailslots have handles, just like files, and are even read and written to using the standard file handling procedures.

Let's look at the server side first. Remember the server is the program that owns the mailslot, and receives messages in it.

The first thing it needs to do is to create a mailslot. This is achieved with the `CreateMailslot()` function:

```
HANDLE CreateMailslot(
    LPCTSTR  lpName,                 // pointer to string for mailslot name
    DWORD  nMaxMessageSize,          // maximum message size
    DWORD  lReadTimeout,             // milliseconds before read time-out
    LPSECURITY_ATTRIBUTES lpSecurityAttributes);  // pointer to security
                                                   // structure
```

The name is a pointer to the mailslot name that is required. It must always be of the general form *machine*\MAILSLOT*mailslotname*. We can also specify the maximum size of messages we are prepared to receive, any timeout values, and a security attributes structure, for NT only. As before, the security attribute parameter can be a **NULL**.

The `lReadTimeout` parameter controls how long a read of the mailshot will take. If the value is zero, then any read of the mailshot will return immediately, whether or not a message is available. A value of **MAILSLOT_WAIT_FOREVER** will cause a read to hang until a message is received.

On success, a handle is returned, and on failure **INVALID_HANDLE** is returned.

The next procedure is `GetMailslotInfo()`, which allows the server to 'peek' inside the mailslot pseudo-file:

```
BOOL GetMailslotInfo(
    HANDLE  hMailslot,               // mailslot handle
    LPDWORD  lpMaxMessageSize,       // address of maximum message size
    LPDWORD  lpNextSize,             // address of size of next message
    LPDWORD  lpMessageCount,         // address of number of messages
    LPDWORD  lpReadTimeout);         // address of read time-out
```

The meaning of these parameters is summarized below:

▶ `hMailslot` is the handle to an existing mailslot.

▶ `lpMaxMessageSize` points to a location where the function will place the maximum message size. This might be larger than that specified in `CreateMailslot()`.

▶ `lpNextSize` points to a location where the function will fill in the size of the message waiting to be read. If no message is waiting the value will be **MAILSLOT_NO_MESSAGE**.

▶ `lpMessageCount` points to a location where the number of message waiting to be read will be placed.

▶ `lpReadTimeout` points to a location that will take the timeout value.

Any of these parameters, except the handle, can be **NULL** if the information is not required.

If the function fails, zero is returned and **GetLastError()** gives more information if required.

The final mailslot procedure is **SetMailslotInfo()** and allows the timeout value to be changed. As with **CreateMailslot()**, the **0** and **MAILSLOT_WAIT_FOREVER** magic numbers are allowed.

```
BOOL  SetMailslotInfo(
      HANDLE  hMailslot,        //  mailslot  handle
      DWORD  lReadTimeout);     //  read  time-out
```

On failure **FALSE** is returned.

You will notice there is no delete mailslot procedure. This is because mailslots are automatically deleted as soon as there are no handles that refer to them. For the sake of clarity, though, it is still a good idea to call **CloseHandle()** on the mailslot handle before your program exits.

Since the reading and writing of mailslots is done with the standard file APIs we have already used, we are now ready to use mailslots.

Try It Out — A Mailslot Application

You will recall from earlier in the chapter that we wanted to be able to update the conversion rates in our server program remotely, without restarting the server. Mailslots will let us do this. In practice, this is probably not a good choice of method, because there is no guaranteed delivery of mailslot messages. Getting the currency rates wrong could prove very expensive if an update is missed, although we could use a client to check them.

However, mailslots might be ideal for keeping a large number of client machines that continuously show updating approximate conversion rates — providing, of course, the real rate is checked before any money changes hands!

So, for the purposes of illustration, here is our server program updated to allow its rates to be set by mailslots. Since most of this code has been seen before, we only present the main points here. The full example can be downloaded from the Wrox web site.

In the server we declare a mailslot name and message size. Note the horrendous back-slash quoting we need!

```
const char* MailslotName = "\\\\.\\mailslot\\updater";
const int MAX_MESSAGE_SIZE = 4000;
```

We can then create the mailslot, making it wait forever if no messages are received:

```
HANDLE Slot = CreateMailslot (MailslotName, MAX_MESSAGE_SIZE,
                              MAILSLOT_WAIT_FOREVER, NULL);
if (Slot == INVALID_HANDLE_VALUE)
{
   MessageBox (NULL, Name, "Could not create mailslot", 0);
   return 1;
}
```

Our mailslot example is based on our earlier RPC example, and we need to ensure that mailslot updates run independent of both the RPC calls. To do this we start the mailslot processing in its own thread:

```
_beginthread(MailslotProcess, 0, (void*)Slot);
```

Note that there is a concurrency problem here; in a real application we would have to implement a critical section to ensure that the mailslot update never overlapped with a RPC currency conversion, as described in Chapter 6, since the end result might be a bad conversion.

The actual mailslot process is very simple — whenever a mailslot message arrives, it is read just as though the mailslot was a file. Since we requested **WAIT_FOR_EVER** when we created the mailslot, the **ReadFile()** will block until a message is received.

```
void MailslotProcess(void* s)
{
   HANDLE Slot = reinterpret_cast<HANDLE>(s);

   for (;;)
   {
      char Buff [MAX_MESSAGE_SIZE];
      DWORD Len;

      if ( !ReadFile (Slot, Buff, MAX_MESSAGE_SIZE, &Len, NULL))
      {
         MessageBox (NULL, "Error reading mailslot", Name, 0);
         return;
      }

      istrstream s (Buff, Len);
      ReadRates (s);
   }
}
```

The final thing we need to do is delete the mailsot as the program ends. Closing the handle to the mailslot does this:

```
CloseHandle (Slot);
```

That's all the changes we need to the server.

The updater is almost as simple:

```
#include <windows.h>
#include <iostream>

using namespace std;

static char NewRates[] = "1.0 Dollars\n2.4 Wibblies\n3.9 Dibblies";

int main (int argc, char* argv[])
{
   if (argc != 2)
```

```
    {
       cerr << "Usage:\n\t" << argv[0] << " mailslot\n";
       return 1;
    }

    // Create the mailslot file
    HANDLE Slot = CreateFile (argv[1], GENERIC_WRITE, FILE_SHARE_READ, NULL,
                              OPEN_EXISTING, FILE_ATTRIBUTE_NORMAL,
                              NULL);
    if (Slot == INVALID_HANDLE_VALUE)
    {
       cerr << "Unable to open mailslot\n";
       return 1;
    }

    DWORD BytesWritten;
    if (!WriteFile (Slot, NewRates, sizeof (NewRates), &BytesWritten, NULL))
    {
       cerr << "Failed to write to mailslot\n";
       return 1;
    }

    // tidy up the mailslot handle
    CloseHandle (Slot);

    return 0;
}
```

We pass in a mailslot name, in the format given earlier, and then program the update as though we were writing to an existing file.

And that's all there is to mailslots.

WinInet

Another approach to transferring data across networks, is to use Microsoft's internet access library, **WinInet**. Although this is not strictly part of the Win32 API, it is an interesting extension to the networking mechanisms discussed in this chapter.

Protocols such as FTP and HTTP are built on top of TCP/IP, and traditionally clients and servers for systems using these protocols have been written directly at the sockets level. The WinInet library encapsulates much of the detail in handling uniform resource locators (URLs), FTP, HTTP and Gopher transactions — on dial-up networked machines, you don't even have to worry about managing your modem as the library will take care of dialling as necessary.

Our currency conversion application could be written as clients interrogating an Internet or intranet server to get rate information. In fact, the 'server' could be a page on one of the many already available financial information sites. The client could download the rates page and extract the desired information. However, because this is a chapter on communications, we're just going to briefly show the access methods and leave the HTML parsing up to you!

The steps in performing an Internet transaction are:

▶ Initialise WinInet — `InternetOpen()`

▶ Open a URL — `InternetOpenUrl()`

▶ Loop, polling for data and reading it — `InternetQueryDataAvailable()` and `InternetReadFile()`

▶ Finally, closing everything down — `InternetCloseHandle()`

Full details can be found in the WinInet SDK documentation.

The sample program below, which grabs a page off the Internet and stores it in a local file, illustrates all of these functions. The scope of the WinInet library is much too great to cover here, but further information can be found on Microsoft's MSDN site (`http://msdn.microsoft.com/developer`).

Here is the example code for fetching a page from the Web:

```cpp
// GetWebPage.cpp

#include <windows.h>
#include <wininet.h>
#include <iostream>
#include <fstream>

using namespace std;

int main (int argc, char* argv[] )
{
    if (argc != 3)
    {
        cerr << "Usage:\n\t" << argv[0] << " url filename\n";
        return 1;
    }

    char* Url      = argv[1];
    char* Filename = argv[2];

    ofstream File (Filename);
    if (!File)
    {
        cerr << "Cannot write to " << Filename << endl;
        return 1;
    }

    HINTERNET Inet = InternetOpen ("GetWebPage",   // Name of the requesting agent
                            INTERNET_OPEN_TYPE_PRECONFIG,   // use default
                                                            // config
                            NULL,              // no proxy setting
                            NULL,              // no proxy bypass
                            0);                // no special options
    if (!Inet)
    {
        cerr << "Could not start WinInet\n";
        return 1;
    }
```

```
      // Get a handle to the connection
      HINTERNET Connection = InternetOpenUrl (Inet,        // handle from InternetOPen
                                              Url,         // The URL to open
                                              NULL,        // Any headers for the server
                                              0,           // Size of additional headers
                                              0,           // no special flags
                                              0);          // no context for callback
                                                           // functions

   if (!Connection)
   {
      cerr << "Could not connect to server\n";
      return 1;
   }

   DWORD BytesDownloaded;
   do
   {
      DWORD Size;

      // Check how much data is available to read
      if (!InternetQueryDataAvailable (Connection,&Size,0,0))
      {
         cerr << "Failure in getting length information\n";
         return 1;
      }

      if (Size == 0)
         break;

      char* Data = new char [Size];

      // Read the data back from the network
      if (!InternetReadFile (Connection, static_cast<void*>(Data), Size,
         &BytesDownloaded))
      {
         cerr << "Read failure\n";
         return 1;
      }

      File.write (Data, Size);

      delete [] Data;
   } while (BytesDownloaded != 0);

   // Close down gracefully
   InternetCloseHandle (Connection);
   InternetCloseHandle (Inet);

   return 0;
}
```

Note that in order to build this code, you'll need to add `wininet.lib` to the list of libraries you link to in Project | Settings.

This example gives you a flavor of how the WinInet APIs can give you basic access to information on a network, without needing to resort to lower-level programming.

Conclusion

In this chapter we have taken a whirlwind tour of many of the different ways NT and Windows 95 programs can communicate:

- Sockets
- Named Pipes
- RPC
- Shared memory
- Mailslots
- WinInet

We saw that sockets are the method of choice for general IPC programming, and also offer the best compatibility with other systems. Named pipes are easier to use — but restricted to Windows operating systems. Mailslots are a special solution to the problem of broadcasting data, but only when guaranteed delivery isn't required. Finally we looked briefly at WinInet, which offers a simple way of interacting with the Internet.

Remote procedure calls go much further than the others — they not only transfer data between machines, but also transfer a thread of execution between machines. Although there is some overhead in defining RPC functions, once defined they are actually quite easy to use.

You should now be well equipped to create distributed applications as easily as standard programs.

Windows NT Access Rights

The following tables show the Windows NT access rights for various NT object types.

The following table shows the standard access rights:

Access Specifier	Value	Description
DELETE	0x00010000	Ability to delete an object
READ_CONTROL	0x00020000	Read the security descriptor, excluding the SACL
WRITE_DAC	0x00040000	Modify the DACL
WRITE_OWNER	0x00080000	Modify the owner in the security descriptor
SYNCHRONIZE	0x00100000	Use synchronization with this object

Combinations of these rights are provided as follows:

Access Specifier	Combines
STANDARD_RIGHTS_ALL	DELETE | READ_CONTROL | WRITE_DAC | WRITE_OWNER | SYNCHRONIZE
STANDARD_RIGHTS_EXECUTE	READ_CONTROL
STANDARD_RIGHTS_READ	READ_CONTROL
STANDARD_RIGHTS_WRITE	READ_CONTROL
STANDARD_RIGHTS_REQUIRED	DELETE | READ_CONTROL | WRITE_DAC | WRITE_OWNER

The following table shows the generic access types:

Access Specifier	Value	Description
GENERIC_ALL	0x10000000	Full access
GENERIC_EXECUTE	0x20000000	Execute access
GENERIC_WRITE	0x40000000	Write access
GENERIC_READ	0x80000000	Read access

The following table shows the access rights for file objects:

Access Specifier	Value	Description
FILE_READ_DATA	0x0001	Read data from the file
FILE_WRITE_DATA	0x0002	Write data to the file
FILE_APPEND_DATA	0x0004	Append data to the file
FILE_READ_EA	0x0008	Read extended attributes of a file
FILE_WRITE_EA	0x0010	Write extended attributes of a file
FILE_EXECUTE	0x0020	Execute a file
FILE_READ_ATTRIBUTES	0x0080	Read attributes of a file
FILE_WRITE_ATTRIBUTES	0x0100	Write attributes of a file

Combinations of file rights are provided as follows:

Access Specifier	Combines
FILE_GENERIC_READ	STANDARD_RIGHTS_READ | FILE_READ_DATA | FILE_READ_ATTRIBUTES | FILE_READ_EA | SYNCHRONIZE
FILE_GENERIC_WRITE	STANDARD_RIGHTS_WRITE | FILE_WRITE_DATA | FILE_WRITE_ATTRIBUTES | FILE_WRITE_EA | FILE_APPEND_DATA | SYNCHRONIZE
FILE_GENERIC_EXECUTE	STANDARD_RIGHTS_EXEUTE | FILE_READ_ATTRIBUTES | FILE_EXECUTE | SYNCHRONIZE

The following table shows the access rights for directory objects:

Access Specifier	Value	Description
FILE_LIST_DIRECTORY	0x0001	List the directory
FILE_ADD_FILE	0x0002	Add a file to the directory
FILE_ADD_SUBDIRECTORY	0x0004	Add a subdirectory
FILE_READ_EA	0x0008	Read extended attributes of a directory
FILE_WRITE_EA	0x0010	Write extended attributes of a directory
FILE_TRAVERSE	0x0020	Traverse a directory
FILE_READ_ATTRIBUTES	0x0080	Read directory attributes
FILE_WRITE_ATTRIBUTES	0x0100	Write directory attributes

The following table shows the access rights for process objects:

Access Specifier	Value	Description
PROCESS_TERMINATE	0x0001	Terminate a process
PROCESS_CREATE_THREAD	0x0002	Create threads
PROCESS_VM_OPERATION	0x0008	Perform operations in process memory space
PROCESS_VM_READ	0x0010	Read from process memory space
PROCESS_VM_WRITE	0x0020	Write to process memory space
PROCESS_DUP_HANDLE	0x0040	Duplicate handles
PROCESS_CREATE_PROCESS	0x0080	Create another process
PROCESS_SET_QUOTA	0x0100	Set resources available to process
PROCESS_SET_INFORMATION	0x0200	Set information about a process
PROCESS_QUERY_INFORMATION	0x0400	Query process information

The following table shows the access rights for thread objects:

Access Specifier	Value	Description
THREAD_TERMINATE	0x0001	Terminate a thread
THREAD_SUSPEND_RESUME	0x0002	Suspend and resume threads
THREAD_GET_CONTEXT	0x0008	Retrieve thread context information
THREAD_SET_CONTEXT	0x0010	Set thread context information
THREAD_SET_INFORMATION	0x0020	Set thread information (e.g. priority)
THREAD_QUERY_INFORMATION	0x0040	Query thread information
THREAD_SET_THREAD_TOKEN	0x0080	Modify thread access token

Access Specifier	Value	Description
THREAD_IMPERSONATE	0x0100	Use thread security information
THREAD_DIRECT_IMPERSONATION	0x0200	Server thread can impersonate client

The following table shows the access rights for registry keys:

Access Specifier	Value	Description
KEY_QUERY_VALUE	0x0001	Retrieve information in a registry key
KEY_SET_VALUE	0x0002	Write information to a registry key
KEY_CREATE_SUB_KEY	0x0004	Create a new subkey
KEY_ENUMERATE_SUB_KEYS	0x0008	Enumerate subkeys of a key
KEY_NOTIFY	0x0010	Get change notifications for a key
KEY_CREATE_LINK	0x0020	Create a link to a registry key

The following table shows the access rights for services:

Access Specifier	Value	Description
SERVICE_QUERY_CONFIG	0x0001	Can call ServiceQueryConfig() function
SERVICE_CHANGE_CONFIG	0x0002	Can call ServiceChangeConfig() function
SERVICE_QUERY_STATUS	0x0004	Query the status of a service
SERVICE_ENUMERATE_DEPENDENTS	0x0008	Can call EnumDependentServices() function
SERVICE_START	0x0010	Start a service
SERVICE_STOP	0x0020	Stop a service
SERVICE_PAUSE_CONTINUE	0x0040	Pause and continue a service
SERVICE_INTERROGATE	0x0080	Get service status information
SERVICE_USER_DEFINED_CONTROL	0x0100	Can use ControlService() function

The following table shows the access rights for access tokens:

Access Specifier	Value	Description
TOKEN_ASSIGN_PRIMARY	0x0001	Attach a primary token to a process
TOKEN_DUPLICATE	0x0002	Duplicate a token
TOKEN_IMPERSONATE	0x0004	Attach an impersonation token to a process
TOKEN_QUERY	0x0008	Retrieve information from a token
TOKEN_QUERY_SOURCE	0x0010	Query the source of an access token
TOKEN_ADJUST_PRIVILEGES	0x0020	Adjust the privileges in a token
TOKEN_ADJUST_GROUPS	0x0040	Adjust the groups in a token
TOKEN_ADJUST_DEFAULT	0x0080	Adjust default information in a token

Symbols

A

B

backspace key
 handling 476
Beep()
 audible signals 128
big endian
 storage 514
binary semaphore
 see mutexes
**BY_HANDLE_FILE_INFORMATION
structure 281**
 fields 281
byte ordering 514
 Winsock 515

C

C Runtime Library 185
 advantages 215
 threads 203, 211, 212
C++
 mangled names
  #pragma provides alias 49
  exporting 48
  linker definition file provides alias 49
  linker definition files 45
  providing alias 49
  without alias 52
 throw statement
  and SEH 121
C++ exception handling
 and SEH 105, 125
 compared to SEH 112
C++ exception mechanism
 compared to SEH 34
C2 security 334
 discretionary access control 335
CD file system
 see CDFS
CDFS 31, 272
CHAR_INFO structure 471, 473, 476
character sets
 ASCII 183
 MBCS 183
 Unicode 183, 184
CharToOem()
 string conversion functions 186
CharToOemBuff()

string conversion functions 186
checkHiveName() 72, 82
cleaning out registry
 CleanReg 68
 RegClean.exe program 68
 RegMaid 68
 uninstall routine 68
CleanReg
 cleaning out registry 68
ClearScreen() 494
client and server 510
**CloseHandle()
207, 208, 213, 278, 309**
color
 GetSysColor() 157
 SetSysColors() 157, 158
color information 157
COLORREFs 159
COM
 and registry 64
 compared to DLLs 39
CompareFileTime() 280
CompareString() 189
completion routines 303, 305
computer names 155
ConnectNamedPipe() 535
console class 490, 502
 definition 490
console process 478
 handlers 478
**CONSOLE_CURSOR_INFO
structure 466**
consoles 12
 _T() macro 456
 allocating 457
 cursors 463
  modifying 466
 freeing 457
 GUIs 457
 handles 459
 introduction 455
 mouse 485
 reading 498
 screen buffers 463, 487, 501
 scrolling the screen 473
 summary 503
 windows 455
 writing 494
CONTEXT structure 117
context switching 203
 deadlock 237

 prevented by mutexes 237
control codes
 NT services 415
control objects
 microkernel objects 15
ControlService() 415, 417
ConvertCurrency() 506
ConvertDefaultLocale()
 locale 178
cooked mode 461
CopyFile() 282
 does not copy security settings 285
CopyFileEx() 282, 283
 does not copy security settings 285
CopyMemory() 320
CORBA 539
CreateBuffer()
 and CreateConsoleScreenBuffer()
 502
**CreateConsoleScreenBuffer()
487, 490**
 and CreateBuffer() 502
CreateDirectory()
 directory 291
CreateDirectoryEx()
 directory 291
CreateEvent() 250
**CreateFile()
109, 274, 275, 285, 302, 307, 338, 350, 359, 362**
 and security attribute 367
 and security descriptors 367
 and SECURITY_ATTRIBUTES
 structure 362
CreateFileMapping() 307
createKeyAbs() 77, 82
 and createKeyRel() 85
createKeyRel() 77, 78
 and createKeyAbs() 85
 and RegCreateKeyEx() 78
 and upOneLevel() 85
CreateMailslot() 562
CreateMutex() 234, 238, 239
CreateNamedPipe() 533
CreatePrivateObjectSecurity() 345
CreateProcess() 255, 258, 260
CreateSemaphore() 244, 248
CreateService() 410, 412, 413
CreateThread() 203, 205, 206
creating
 DLLs 42
critical sections 220

Register Beginning Windows NT Programming and sign up for a free subscription to The Developer's Journal.

A bi-monthly magazine for software developers, The Wrox Press Developer's Journal features in-depth articles, news and help for everyone in the software development industry. Each issue includes extracts from our latest titles and is crammed full of practical insights into coding techniques, tricks, and research.

Fill in and return the card below to receive a free subscription to the Wrox Press Developer's Journal.

WROX PRESS INC.

Wrox writes books for you. Any suggestions, or
ideas about how you want information given in
your ideal book will be studied by our team.
Your comments are always valued at Wrox.

Free phone in USA 800-USE-WROX
Fax (312) 397 8990

UK Tel. (0121) 706 6826   Fax   (0121) 706 2967

Computer Book Publishers

NB. If you post the bounce back card below in the UK, please send it to:
Wrox Press Ltd. 30 Lincoln Road, Birmingham, B27 6PA